THE ORIGINS OF THE 'SECOND' TEMPLE

BibleWorld

Series Editor: Philip R. Davies, University of Sheffield

BibleWorld shares the fruits of modern (and postmodern) biblical scholarship not only among practitioners and students, but also with anyone interested in what academic study of the Bible means in the twenty-first century. It explores our ever-increasing knowledge and understanding of the social world that produced the biblical texts, but also analyses aspects of the bible's role in the history of our civilization and the many perspectives – not just religious and theological, but also cultural, political and aesthetic – which drive modern biblical scholarship.

Recent and forthcoming books in the series:

Sodomy: A History of a Christian Biblical Myth
Michael Carden

Yours Faithfully
Virtual Letters from the Bible
Edited by Philip R. Davis

Israel's History and the History of Israel
Mario Liverani

The Apostle Paul and His Letters
Edwin D. Freed

An Introduction to the Bible (Revised edition)
John Rogerson

The Morality of Paul's Converts
Edwin D. Freed

The Mythic Mind
Essays on Cosmology and Religion in Ugaritic and Old Testament Literature
N. Wyatt

THE ORIGINS OF THE 'SECOND' TEMPLE

PERSIAN IMPERIAL POLICY AND THE REBUILDING OF JERUSALEM

DIANA EDELMAN

LONDON   OAKVILLE

Published by

Equinox Publishing Ltd

UK: Unit 6, The Village, 101 Amies St., London SW11 2JW

US: 28 Main Street, Oakville, CT 06779

www.equinoxpub.com

First published 2005 by Equinox Publishing Ltd.

British Library Cataloguing-in-Publication Data
A catalogue record for this book is available from the British Library.

Library of Congress Cataloging-in-Publication Data
Edelman, Diana Vikander, 1954-
  The origins of the 'Second' Temple : Persian imperial policy and the rebuilding of Jerusalem / Diana Edelman.-- 1st ed.
      p. cm. -- (BibleWorld)
  Includes bibliographical references and index.
  ISBN 1-84553-016-0 -- ISBN 1-84553-017-9 (pbk.)
 1. Temple of Jerusalem (Jerusalem)--History. 2. Jerusalem--History--To 1500. 3. Bible. O.T. Ezra I-VI--History of Biblical events. 4. Bible. O.T. Nehemiah--Chronology. 5. Bible. O.T. Haggai--Chronology. 6. Bible. O.T. Zechariah--Chronology. 7. Yehud (Persian province) 8. Artaxerxes I, King of Persia, d. 425 or 4 B.C.--Relations with Jews. I. Title. II. Bible world (London, England)
  DS109.3.E34 2005
  221.9'5--dc22
                              2004023176

ISBN 1-84553-016-0   (hardback)
        1-84553-017-9   (paperback)

Typeset by CA Typesetting, www.sheffieldtypesetting.com
Printed and bound in Great Britain by Antony Rowe, Chippenham, Wiltshire

To my parents, Arthur and June Vikander,
whose gift of a top-quality education has
enriched my life in so many ways
and given me the tools to pursue my interests and dreams

CONTENTS

PREFACE

This volume is not intended to be an exhaustive study of the various issues involved in determining when and why the Persian-era temple was rebuilt; it is more a programmatic investigation. It was researched and written in two years, from August 2002–September 2004, and
during the first year, I was teaching undergraduates, carrying out a number of administrative
duties, and advising postgraduate students. During the second year, I had a one-semester
sabbatical leave from the Department of Biblical Studies at the University of Sheffield and a
Research Grant from the Arts and Humanities Research Board that relieved me of teaching and
administrative duties during the second semester as well. My only academic responsibilities
during the entire second year involved advising my MPhil and PhD research students, which,
nevertheless, involved hours of reading chapters and rough drafts. As a result, I did not have
the luxury of being able to devote my full attention and energies to researching and producing
this volume, which I think is the case for almost everyone after they complete their doctoral
research.

I have tried to obtain as much relevant secondary literature as possible but have not been able
to trace the historical discussion of each topic thoroughly. Since the inter-library loan system in
the UK is costly to a Department's research budget, I also had to be selective in the end about
which articles and books would be likely to be the most useful for my project. Thus, any
oversights are just that and not deliberate attempts to avoid having to interact with or respond
to a particular article or book. I cover a wide range of topics in this volume and could have spent
many additional years filling out footnotes, but I think such work would not have changed my
arguments substantially. I welcome others to pursue more in-depth analyses of any of the issues
in the future and will modify my positions in light of their findings, when appropriate.

I am deeply indebted to the Arts and Humanities Research Board, which awarded me a
Research Fellowship that allowed me to continue my writing during the second semester of the
2003–2004 academic year. Without this grant, I would not have been able to complete the
project in such a timely manner, while ideas were fresh and coherent in my mind and I had few
distractions. I also want to thank my colleagues in the Department of Biblical Studies, Keith
Whitelam, Cheryl Exum, Loveday Alexander, Barry Matlock, and Jorunn Økland, who took
over my teaching duties in the first semester of the 2003–2004 academic year and my administrative duties for the year. They all had heavy schedules before having to do this work and
their assumption of the additional workload was greatly appreciated. I owe many thanks as well
to the two departmental secretaries, Mrs Alison Bygrave and Mrs Gill Fogg, who took care of
numerous concerns and mini-crises on my behalf while I was away from the UK.

During September–December, 2003, I was graciously granted visiting scholar status at
MacQuarie University and the University of Sydney, where I was able to write Chapters 2 and 3

using their library facilities. Their assistance, especially with interlibrary loan orders, was most welcome. I wish to thank Yairah and Rami Amit for their hospitality in early June, 2004. Yairah arranged for me to have access to the Department of Archaeology Library at the University of Tel Aviv, where I worked quite productively with the helpful assistance of Naamah Scheftelowitz, the head librarian. The remainder of June I spent at the Ecole Biblique et Archaéologique Française de Jerusalem, using their excellent library facilities. I am grateful to the Dominican brothers for allowing me to stay in the hostel and use the library. I completed Chapters 4 and 5 while in Jerusalem. I also owe thanks to Stephanie and Christopher Dalley, whose generous hospitality in April and again in August, 2004 gave me the luxury of using the Oxford Library in two uninterrupted stretches of time, in which I was able to sort out a lot of footnote details.

I received valuable comments on drafts of various chapters of this book from a number of colleagues and thank them for their time and efforts: Hans Barstadt, Joe Blenkinsopp, and Philip Davies. I owe special thanks to Joe Blenkinsopp and Graeme Auld, who wrote in support of my AHRB grant application and must have done a superior job. My daughter Evelyn and son Will read through the manuscript for me and generated the list of terms for the glossary; I know this was a labor of love for both of them. Evelyn's primary field of study was evolutionary biology, though she also took a number of courses in religion, while Will's was political science and sociology, and I thank them both very much.

In spite of the complexity of the subject matter, I have tried to make this volume user-friendly for advanced undergraduates, graduates, and interested non-specialists who have some background in the subject matter. To this end, I have transliterated the foreign language words to reflect their pronunciation rather than using the standard conventions of transliteration, except in instances where a spelling is so well known that it would have been confusing to readers to alter it. I have tried to explain grammatical issues in ways that can be grasped by those who do not know the grammar and syntax of biblical Hebrew. I have included a glossary, I have explained the meaning of terms more fully than I would have otherwise for colleagues, and I have included surveys and background materials that I would not ordinarily have deemed necessary. I have also cited English translations of books, where available, to allow these readers to follow up on points more easily.

List of Illustrations and Maps

INTRODUCTION

Challenging the status quo is always a thankless endeavor that draws fire from all sides, but scholarship is not meant to play by the rules of a popularity contest. When so little data exists about the early Achaemenid period (c. 538–424 BCE) in general and about specific events that took place in Yehud under this political regime, it is necessary to reassess our working hypotheses from time to time to see if they still offer the most logical explanations of the facts at hand. While our interpretation of past events seeks to create a chain of logical cause and effect between events, it is not necessarily the case that such events were interrelated at the time they transpired. In hindsight we link them, whether rightly or wrongly, to fit neatly into an interpretive framework that we find meaningful. The less data available, the more rival hypotheses can be advanced to create interrelationships. However, this being the case, the existence of a comfortable status quo for a period that has little raw data with which to work should raise eyebrows.

A number of plausible recreations of the events surrounding the rebuilding of the temple in Jerusalem during the early Achaemenid empire (c. 538–424 BCE) should exist and vie for primacy of place, yet they do not. Instead, we find the biblical account of this process accepted at face value as a reliable historical record, with only a few harmonizations and modifications proposed from time to time. It is time to reconsider the tacit acceptance of the accuracy of the biblical depiction and dating of these events, to determine what is likely to be fact and likely to be literary and ideological embellishment within the biblical portrayal of Haggai–Zechariah 8 and Ezra 1–6, and to situate the process of rebuilding the temple within the framework of contemporary historical inquiry.

The Topic of Inquiry

Why was the temple in Jerusalem rebuilt in the Persian period and when? The Bible provides conflicting answers to each of these questions, giving modern historians the opportunity to examine both questions afresh and propose an answer that is grounded on currently available archaeological and textual testimony within the framework of early twenty-first century discourse.

Different reasons why the temple was rebuilt are provided in various biblical texts. All agree that the rebuilding was the result of divine initiative, but they point to different levels of human involvement. In Haggai, for example, Yahweh's displeasure over the people's failure to rebuild his house after they had built themselves nicely panelled houses, coupled with his desire to have a house in which he could take pleasure, where he could appear in his glory, led him to send a drought on the land (Hag. 1.4-11). When Haggai pointed this out to the people, they duly repented. Then, under divine inspiration and the leadership of Zerubbabel, the local governor, and Yeshua, the high priest, they set to work and built a new temple. Here divine jealousy led to human punishment, human repentance, divine forgiveness, and the divine inspiration of human agents, who then took direct responsibility for the work of temple-rebuilding.

According to the book of Ezra, on the other hand, Yahweh charged Cyrus, king of Persia, with building his temple in Jerusalem (Ezra 1.2). Cyrus dutifully issued a decree ordering the rebuilding in the first year of his reign and sent back a group of repatriates under the leadership of Sheshbazzar to undertake the physical work. Although work was halted by 'adversaries' shortly after the foundation was laid, it was eventually resumed again when Haggai and Zechariah inspired Zerubbabel and Yeshua (Ezra 5.1-2), in the name of the God of Israel, to begin construction anew. After a divine decree issued by Darius, the elders of the Jews completed the project (Ezra 6.14-15).

Comparing the two we see, on the one hand, divine initiative motivated by jealousy in Haggai and on the other, divine initiative in Ezra with no underlying motivation specified. Such a theological explanation for why the temple was rebuilt was acceptable to the ancient mindset but is not an acceptable explanation by modern-day standards of cause and effect. Divine intervention is no longer considered a feasible reason for why events happen on earth.

We also see different human agents who carry out the divine plan; in Ezra, the Persian king is ultimately responsible on the human level for rebuilding the temple. Work begins under a decree of Cyrus and when it is stopped, it is only completed some sixty-five years later after a royal decree issued by Darius. In Haggai, on the other hand, the people work together with Zerubbabel and Yeshua during the reign of Darius to rebuild the temple from its foundation upwards; there is no mention of any royal Persian decree or sponsorship. Yet according to the larger narrative, none of these people would have acted without divine mandate or divine inspiration. The temple-rebuilding did not occur to them and was not their idea.

The Bible also provides conflicting testimony about the date of the temple's rebuilding. The book of Ezra has a twenty-three-year process, which began in the first year of the reign of Cyrus, 538 BCE (Ezra 3.1) and was only completed in the sixth year of Darius, 515 BCE (Ezra 6.15). The books of Haggai and Zechariah, on the other hand, date the beginning of the rebuilding to the second year of Darius in 520 BCE (Hag. 1.12-15). The final date of completion and rededication is not given, but Zech. 7.1 implies that the temple had become functional either in 518 or in 517 BCE. If one thinks that the delegation in 7.2-3 was sent in response to learning about the completion of the temple, the earlier date would be indicated; if it were sent in anticipation of the imminent completion of the temple, before the next annual fast commemorating its destruction, then the latter date would be possible.

Genealogical information in Nehemiah and Chronicles, on the other hand, appears to indicate that Zerubbabel, governor under Darius I (522–486 BCE) and Nehemiah, a subsequent 'governor' or appointed official under King Artaxerxes I (465–407 BCE), were at most one generation apart in age and possibly, contemporaries. Details relating to members of seven generations, beginning with the repatriates under Zerubbabel and Yeshua and ending with the generation in place when Alexander conquered the Persian empire in 332 BCE, show that the two men either succeeded one another in office, or that they were contemporaries. In the latter instance, Nehemiah would have been a special envoy overseeing building works in Jerusalem during the governorship of Zerubbabel. Nehemiah's mission and governorship are said to have begun in year 20 of Artaxerxes, 445 BCE (Neh. 2.1) and to have lasted for twelve years until 433 BCE (Neh. 5.14). If Zerubbabel were his immediate predecessor, then he and the repatriates under his supervision would have begun to rebuild the temple sometime before the twentieth year of Artaxerxes, c. 444 BCE. It could have been completed before Nehemiah's arrival or after he took over as governor; no information about the year of its beginning or completion is given.

The range of dates for the temple's rebuilding presented in the biblical books spans some sixty-five to one hundred and and six years. A beginning can be set as early as 538 BCE under Cyrus I, at a middle date of 520 BCE under Darius I, or as late as sometime between 464–445 BCE, under Artaxerxes I. A completion date can be set as early as 518 BCE under Darius I, a middle date sometime in the reign of Darius I, or a date before the end of Nehemiah's governorship in 432 BCE, under Artaxerxes I.

Although the range of dates provides a modern historian with a good starting point to assess *when* the temple was rededicated, none of the biblical accounts provides a logical reason for *why* the temple was rebuilt. Within the context of the opening years of the twenty-first century, we should not be satisfied with an answer about why the temple was rebuilt that does not demonstrate what benefit such a rebuilding would have had to the Persian king who authorized the work or endorsed the project. A modern historian needs to understand the temple rebuilding within the wider context of Persian policy in Yehud during the reign of a specific king, in relation to economic, military, and commercial needs within the larger empire.

A Brief Survey of Past Hypotheses

A representative survey of reconstructions by biblical scholars of when and why the temple was rebuilt shows that few of them have been bothered by the lack of an adequate rationale for the project. There has been a tendency to favor the account in Ezra over that in Haggai and Zechariah and to accept the main outline of whichever account is preferred. The accounts are not mutually exclusive, however; Haggai and Zechariah provide an insider's view that attempts to motivate the people to undertake the heavy labor by appealing to divine anger rather than to imperial decree. An appeal to higher divine authority, the source of agricultural and animal fertility necessary for the people's survival, would have been more persuasive than an appeal to the mandate of the ruling human king, who would have been perceived as a foreign oppressor demanding the performance of corvée labor to complete public work projects (Smith 1908: 210-11). The failure of either prophet to mention the existence of an imperial decree is not proof that none had existed.

Suggested dates in Ezra or Haggai and Zechariah for the rebuilding process are generally accepted at face value. George Smith's comment made almost a century ago remains the prevailing attitude even today: 'That the temple was built by Zerubbabel and Jeshua in the beginning of the reign of Darius I may be considered as one of the unquestionable data of our period' (1908: 193). Even the minority position that argues for a dating to the reign of Darius II Nothus (423–404 BCE) rather than Darius I Hystaspis (521–485 BCE) assumes the accuracy of the biblical account but credits a younger namesake with the rebuilding process

(Havet 1889: 799; DeQueker 1993: 68). Claims of divine initiative are transferred into more plausible human terms, though not always ones that have logical rationales.

The date indications in the genealogical material of the books of Nehemiah and Chronicles have not been tapped because there has not been a perceived need to do so. There has been a widespread assumption that Haggai and Zechariah 1–8 were written and edited into their current form soon after the events they describe and so are reliable as historical witnesses to what transpired (so, e.g., Rudolph 1976: 22-23, 62-63; Smith 1984: 149, 169; Meyers and Meyers 1987: xlv; Tollington 1993: 19-23). It is widely thought that the author of Ezra 1–6 was able to access official correspondence from the time of Cyrus and Darius I concerning the temple's rebuilding and so has produced a generally reliable account of the events that transpired (so, e.g., Meyer 1896: 41-46; Bickerman 1946; Myers 1965: xlix-l; de Vaux 1972; Clines 1984: 8-9). Some scholars have rejected the author's claim that the foundation was initially laid during the reign of Cyrus because it conflicts with the claims in Haggai and Zechariah 1–8 that the foundation was laid by Zerubbabel under Darius I. Nevertheless, they have tended to accept the genuineness of Cyrus' reported edict, probably because of the account in Ezra 6.1-5, which claims that Darius had ordered a search to be made for it in response to Tattenai's report to him about the building project and that it had been found in Ecbatana (so, e.g., Thomson 1932: 103-104; Herrmann 1975: 300-301; Williamson 1985: 80-81; Meyers and Meyers 1987: xxxi, xxxiv; Wolff 1988: 41, 44; Bedford 2001: 152-57).

Martin Noth has argued that Cyrus' decree mandating the rebuilding of the temple was an act of reparation that should be set within the broad context of a Persian desire to preserve or restore ancient local religious traditions. He uses the Cyrus cylinder, which orders the repatriation of gods and peoples whom the last Neo-Babylonian king, Nabonidus, had exiled. In his opinion, after witnessing Cyrus' restoration of ancient religions and peoples in Mesopotamia, some deported Jews in Babylonia drew the attention of the Persian court to the fact that a Neo-Babylonian ruler had destroyed a sanctuary in Jerusalem. They received permission and public funds for the project. Two motivations are attributed to Cyrus: (1) to gain the favor of the people by establishing a different religious policy to that practised by the last Neo-Babylonian ruler, who had suppressed a number of cults in his empire; and (2) to demonstrate his role as successor to the former kings of Judah by assuming care for the former royal sanctuary. Although the edict did not provide for repatriation, a small number of Jews may have returned to Yehud under Cyrus. The temple foundation was relaid by the main group of people not exiled, who had remained in the land and who had continued to worship in the holy place after the destruction of the temple. Work then ceased because of a drought and the personal worries and concerns of the populace. It resumed again, however, under Darius I, at the instigation of the prophecies of Haggai and Zechariah, during the local governorship of Zerubbabel. The temple was completed in 515 BCE (1960: 306-15).

Jacob Myers accepts the account of Ezra 1–6 as historically reliable, reflecting a twenty-three-year rebuilding process for the temple that began under Cyrus but was only completed under Darius. In an attempt to explain the motivations of both kings, he suggests that Darius and Cyrus were benevolently inclined toward the religions of their subject peoples within the empire. He cites Darius' reversal of the policy of his father, Cambyses, in Egypt by restoring a number of temples his father had destroyed and giving them a royal endowment. Additional evidence he finds relevant is Darius' command to the local Egyptian satrap to appoint administrative heads for the various temples. He adds that the concern of the Persian kings for the various temples and gods of subject groups was probably due to 'political reasons', which he fails to explicate. He also thinks, however, that some of the kings who were Zoroastrians may have been intrigued by the Jewish concept of Yahweh, making them favorably disposed toward his cult; again, he provides no additional elaboration (1965: xxix).

Peter Ackroyd has proposed that Cyrus' permission for the temple rebuilding had three motivations. The first was a desire to resettle an exiled god. He does not develop this point any further. The second was a desire to win local favor for Persian rule as the successor to the royal line in Jerusalem by sponsoring the former royal shrine. The third was a concern for political security in the border region of the as-yet unconquered Egypt. He gives no further clarification. After a half-hearted start under Cyrus, Zerubbabel's arrival during the reign of Cambyses as Persian forces moved into Egypt led to the dedication of the altar and a genuine beginning. A brief interruption in the building process took place during an official inquiry under Darius but the work was completed in 515 BCE after imperial authorization was given (1968: 140-52).

Joel Weinberg has proposed that two factors motivated Cyrus to issue a decree allowing Jews living outside of Judah to return to their ancestral homeland and rebuild the temple: (1) a desire to leave the existing neo-Babylonian administrative system intact, under which the region of Judah was formally part of the province of Samaria, and (2) a desire to make Palestine a secure staging point for his planned conquest of Egypt. The temple was intended to provide a gathering place and point of solidarity for the returning Jews, who could not stand up to the existing Palestinian population without support from the central power. Darius' subsequent decree did not change either motivation, but facilitated the completion of the building work. Once the temple was functional, a citizen-temple community was established that was unique amongst all such alleged units within the Persian empire in that the temple owned no lands itself, had no economy, and had no tax-exempt status. It was not until the reign of Artaxerxes I, who appointed Nehemiah to become the leader of the citizen-temple community in 458/457 BCE, that this entity was granted tax-exempt status, self-governance and other privileges, signaling the official establishment and recognition of the citizen-temple community as an autonomous local administrative unit. Soon afterwards, Artaxerxes established Yehud as an independent province, but because the co-existence of, and differentiation between, two powers in a small territory was not possible in the long term, there was a gradual unification of both administrations (1992: 28-9, 103, 106, 111-12, 117-18, 123; originals written in the 1970s).

Siegfried Herrmann dates the initial permission to rebuild the temple to Cyrus but its eventual building under Darius. Cyrus' edict reflects the Persian concern to foster local traditions and cults. Herrmann proposes that some Jewish exiles may have obtained an audience before Cyrus soon after he captured Babylon and may have drawn the king's attention to this relatively small and insignificant temple in a small corner of the empire. But three considerations are seen to point to the probability that the first repatriation only took place under Cambyses in connection with his military campaign to conquer Egypt in 525 BCE. These include the failure for the edict to mention the return of exiles, the failure of Haggai or Zechariah to mention recent returnees, and the failure of the temple to be built until the reign of Darius. The Persians may have wanted to secure and consolidate the situation in Palestine and more petitions from Jews to be allowed to return home may have found a ready hearing. The timing of the temple's rebuilding in the second year of Darius is tied to the upheavals at this monarch's accession and a local desire to restore Jerusalem as a political and spiritual centre in accordance with pre-exilic tradition. Zerubbabel was not the leader of the returning group under Cambyses but a locally-born Davidic descendant whom the Persians appointed as an official (1975: 300-305).

Elias Bickerman ties the temple-building effort to the widespread revolts at the beginning of the reign of Darius I in 522 BCE, which preoccupied him to such a degree that Zerubbabel felt he could initiate the rebuilding of the temple without repercussions. Recognizing the problem with the dates in Haggai and Zechariah, which would set the rebuilding efforts after the revolts, he re-dates Haggai 2 to October-December, 521 BCE, to correspond with the last known revolt in Babylonia. Zechariah 1.7 is similarly re-dated to 26 February, 520 BCE and announces the return of imperial peace (1981: 23-28).

John Hayes thinks that Cyrus' edict concerning the return of the gods of Sumer and Akkad to their home sanctuaries reflected a more general attitude toward other regions and cults. Nabonidus, the last Neo-Babylonian king, had removed a number of gods from their homes in the regions of Sumer and Akkad to Babylon and allegedly had exiled some of their worshippers from their homes as well. Cyrus' edict permitted the return of both gods and people to their homes, reversing the policy of his predecessor. As a sensitive region along the road to Egypt, the need to assure Judah's loyalty to Persian authority might have led Cyrus to apply this policy there as well. Hayes acknowledges, however, that according to the two edicts Cyrus purportedly issued to Jewish exiles (Ezra 1.2-4; 6.3-5), the repatriation was specifically for reconstruction work on the temple and not a full-fledged grant of exilic repatriation. Four possible Persian motivations are suggested: (1) the policy was judged to be in the best interests of the Persian cause; (2) the permission may have been a reward for the pro-Persian sentiments of many Jewish exiles (the author of Isaiah 40–55, known as second Isaiah, exemplifies this positive stance); (3) by supporting the temple, Cyrus was claiming to be a successor to the Davidic royal line since the temple had been a royal shrine under royal patronage; and (4) political realities on the south-western borders of his empire could have made such a gesture expedient. An inevitable attack against Egypt would have been aided by a pro-Persian Judean community. Returnees were initially few under Cyrus, but were reinforced after Cambyses moved into Palestine en route to Egypt in 526–525 BCE. The revolts that took place at Darius' succession may have encouraged a larger migration back to Yehud. The rebuilding of the temple began under Cyrus but was not completed until the sixth year of Darius, 515 BCE (Miller and Hayes 1986: 440-60).

Carol and Eric Meyers have placed the temple's rebuilding in the broader framework of a Persian imperial policy committed to building and resettlement as part of a policy of restoring conquered subjects when politically feasible. This was driven by the further desire to install loyal colonies in critical geopolitical areas. Cyrus sent back a group of repatriates under the leadership of Sheshbazzar, who had permission to rebuild the temple, but due to political difficulties with neighbors and Sheshbazzar's relative lack of power as the first Persian governor of Yehud, this group was unable to restore the temple. In addition, a lack of tax revenues would have hampered the building process. Darius' reorganization of the provinces after his suppression of widespread rebellions at his accession to the throne resulted in Yehud's formation as an independent province, to be headed by loyal, local leadership who were to use indigenous administrative structures. Darius wanted to reinforce loyalty among his subject peoples by encouraging the ongoing use of traditional political and social organizations in the various regions within his empire but kept ultimate control through his overarching satrapal administration run primarily by Persians. To this end, he sent a second group of repatriates to Yehud under Zerubbabel and Yeshua, who were vested with more authority, and they were able to complete the rebuilding project. The temple provided a physical setting and legitimization for the indigenous priestly leaders who, working in cooperation with the Persian-appointed governor, were to handle local affairs. It served as the administrative center of Judah, whose officials oversaw political, economic and judicial matters (1987: xxxi-xl; 37-38; 390).

Gösta Ahlström has proposed that Cyrus authorized the rebuilding of the temple as a way to control Yehud and as a money-making venture. Like other temples throughout the empire, it would have been under the jurisdiction of the crown and, thus, a source of revenue. Its presence would have been a visible expression that the inhabitants were a distinctive ethnic group united by their common worship of Yahweh. At the same time, it would have allowed the region to be governed according to the laws of the empire and to become part of its economic system. The permission to build was an official acknowledgement of Judah as a *medinah* or province. Opposition between locals and the returnees to the land from Mesopotamia seriously hampered rebuilding efforts but the temple was completed under Darius I in 515 BCE (1993: 841-48).

Jon Berquist suggests that Darius ordered the building of the temple in Jerusalem as a means of supplying food for his imminent overland campaign against Egypt, which began in 519 BCE. To this end, he sent Zerubbabel with a group of repatriates back to Yehud to produce food surpluses that could be used by the soldiers en route. The group arrived in October of 520 BCE. The intention behind authorizing the immediate rebuilding of the temple was to have it serve many functions simultaneously: imperial government, financial administration, the renewed worship of the people's deity, and food production. As the chief location of new social resources, it would attract the types of political, economic, and religious power and influence that were able to transform society (1995: 57-63).

Peter Bedford has rejected the historical reliability of Ezra 1.1–4.5 and, on the basis of the books of Haggai, Zechariah and Ezra 5–6, argues that the rebuilding of the temple was a local initiative, but one undertaken with the permission of the imperial authorities. In the eyes of the Persian authorities, it would have been a minor local shrine and would have played no immediate role in the administration of the province. Although the permission to rebuild was given initially by Cyrus, no work was undertaken until Zerubbabel arrived during the reign of Darius I. As a member of the royal Davidic line, he was seen by the local community, as well as the repatriates who arrived with him, as a legitimate temple-builder, so that both groups banded together to rebuild under his guidance. They were motivated by the hope that it would be the first step toward the re-establishment of an independent kingdom of Judah once again. The temple was completed in 515 BCE (2001: 301-310).

For Bedford, the temple represented to the local Judeans the end of the divine wrath that had destroyed the nation of Judah, exiled segments of the Judahite population, and led to the divine abandonment of Jerusalem. It re-established them as a single people living in their homeland once again. By combining the ensconced population that had never been exiled with those who had recently been repatriated, the inhabitants of the province became one people under the direction of its national god, who once more was enthroned as the sovereign, divine king. He finds no evidence of tension between the non-*golah* and *golah* groups at the time the temple was rebuilt; no ideas of social division or separatism are evident in the three key texts examined (2001: 303-304, 306).

The foregoing survey highlights a general acceptance of the historical reliability of Ezra 1–6, with slight modifications here and there, as a scholarly trend until the 1990s (although W.H. Kosters [1895], C.C. Torrey [1896] and G. Hölscher [1923: 495] were notable early exceptions). It also demonstrates how scholars have tended to repeat the arguments of their predecessors without re-assessing each issue independently. It has only been within the last fifteen years that skepticism has set in about how close the author of Ezra lived to the events reported and how reliable his source material was, especially the three sets of official correspondence found 'quoted' in these chapters. It has been assumed that the content of post-exilic books would have been reliable since the authors lived close to the times they described and in an age when literacy was more widespread and access to sources would have been easy. As will be demonstrated in Chapters 2 and 3, however, these assumptions have been ill-founded and have hampered the progress of a critical historical investigation into the reasons for, and date of, the rebuilding of the temple.

When the events in Haggai, Zechariah and Ezra surrounding the temple-building are set beside those in Nehemiah about the resettlement of Jerusalem, a picture emerges in which the temple was erected in an otherwise ruined city in 515 BCE, under Darius I. It remained an isolated kind of pilgrimage site for Jews from the local region as well as from the diaspora for seventy years, until c. 445 BCE, when Artaxerxes I decided to establish Jerusalem as a fortified site that housed a Persian garrison.

In Nehemiah the claim is made that only in the reign of Artaxerxes I (464–424 BCE), as a result of an imperial commission, was Nehemiah sent from Susa with army officers and cavalry to Jerusalem to rebuild the city that lay waste (Neh. 2.5-8) and make it a *birah*, a fortified citadel that included a Persian fortress (for the meaning of this term, see Lemaire and Lozachmeur 1987; Will 1987). He is credited with repairing the walls, using locally conscripted labour gangs (Nehemiah 3–7) (Demsky 1983), and with moving one tenth of the provincial population into the city (Neh. 11.1-2) once the walls were completed. Prior to that, there had been no houses (Neh. 7.4), even though the account of the wall repair mentions a number of residences already in existence inside the walls (Neh. 3.10, 20, 23, 24, 28-29). These chapters in the book of Nehemiah claim that the resettlement of Jerusalem only took place during the governorship of Nehemiah, which began in the twentieth year of Artaxerxes, 444 BCE.

It would seem much more logical for the temple to have been re-established at the same time that Jerusalem was rebuilt as a *birah*. It would have been part of the larger building project that established a temple to Yahweh, the local god, for the newly resettled population and local conscripts posted to the garrison to use to honor him. If the dates in Nehemiah are to be trusted, however, this would have taken place during the reign of Artaxerxes I (464–424 BCE), not during the reign of Darius I (521–485 BCE). As a result, we would have to dismiss the dates found in the books of Haggai and Zechariah as later, unreliable additions. It would also mean that the repatriates led by Zerubbabel and Yeshua would have first arrived under Artaxerxes I to carry out the work and then settle in the province. Finally, it would imply that Nehemiah and Zerubbabel were contemporaries rather than being some sixty-five years apart, as the biblical dates currently suggest. In this case, Nehemiah may well have succeeded Zerubbabel as governor or worked beside him as a special imperial envoy. Since Nehemiah arrived in Jerusalem with army officers and cavalry, it is logical to assume that the fortress had been recently completed and was being staffed.

While these implications may seem radical, they are supported by the genealogical material found in the books of Nehemiah and 1 Chronicles, as will be detailed in the next chapter. In addition, they are chronologically consistent with the claim in 2 Macc. 1.18–2.15 that Nehemiah built the temple and altar, which Josephus repeats (*Ant.* 10.165). Furthermore, the statement in 1 Esd. 5.40, that during the enrollment of those who arrived in Yehud with Zerubbabel, Nehemiah, his excellency, *hattishrata*, banned certain men from sharing in the holy things until a high priest wearing Urim and Thummim appeared, also suggests that the two men were contemporaries. Some have considered Nehemiah's name to be a gloss here, however, since the parallel passage in Ezra 2.63 contains only the title *hattishrata*, 'excellency', and so is a reference to Zerubbabel, mentioned in previous verses. Yet, using the principle of retaining the more difficult reading as genuine and taking into consideration the strong emphasis on Ezra at the expense of Nehemiah that typifies 1 Esdras, it is possible to argue for the authenticity of this reference, especially since it would have been easy for the author to specify Zerubbabel instead, as the passage in Ezra implies.

An Outline of Chapters

In this monograph, I will argue that new answers need to be given about when and why the temple was rebuilt. Zerubbabel, as an agent of Artaxerxes I, rebuilt the temple in Jerusalem probably sometime during the 440s BCE. It was rebuilt as part of a larger Persian policy that established a network of *birot*, guard stations, inns, and caravanserai along the major road systems of the empire, to facilitate trade, imperial communication, and military mobility. The decision by Artaxerxes I to augment the population in the sparsely inhabited Judean hill-country and shephelah (western foothills) would have been part of a larger plan to supply a labor force and tax base to support a series of new relay stations being built in Yehud while simultaneously increasing food production along the route to Egypt. The decision to rebuild Jerusalem as the new provincial seat, replacing the long-serving Mizpah, would have been the result of strategic considerations. Jerusalem lay at a major north–south and east–west crossroads, whereas Mizpah only commanded a position along the main north–south route in the central highlands. It also had a perennial water source on-site, unlike Mizpah.

A number of issues will be addressed in order to argue the above answers. In Chapter 1, I will use genealogical information in the books of Nehemiah and 1 Chronicles to reconstruct key figures in six generations of the repatriated *golah* community, beginning with the generation before that of Zerubbabel and Yeshua and ending with the generation in place when Alexander conquered Darius III (335–330 BCE) and ended Persian rule. This material will then be used to argue that Zerubbabel and Nehemiah were roughly contemporaries, with overlapping or consecutive terms of office.

In Chapter 2, I will discuss the secondary, unreliable nature of the dates under Darius I in the literary unit consisting of Haggai–Zechariah 8, suggesting they were derived from a loose application of Jeremiah's prophecy that the land of Judah would lay desolate for seventy years (Jer. 25.11-12) The chapter will include a survey of dating formulae used from the Iron Age through the Hellenistic period as well as a consideration of the possible influence of the Babylonian almanac and menological systems on the choice of propitious days within a given month and specific propitious months for activities associated with temple-building or temple repair. I also will discuss how Haggai and Zechariah 1–8 each were formulated as temple-building accounts, and how their secondary combination and interlacing through the addition of the dates created a new temple-building account that differed from both originals in its details and implications.

In Chapter 3, I will review the historical inconsistencies in Ezra 1–6 as well as the sources that most likely were used to construct the narrative. I hope to convince my readers that the author of this narrative drew all of his material from existing biblical tradition relating to the Solomonic temple in 2 Chronicles, the vision of the restored temple in Ezekiel 40–48, and various prophetic statements in 2 Isaiah, Jeremiah, and Haggai–Zechariah 8 concerning the restoration of the temple and Jerusalem after its destruction in 586 BCE. The author had no other documents or sources dealing with the rebuilding process at his disposal; none of the six purported letters and edicts written by Cyrus, Darius, or Artaxerxes I are authentic. My goal will be to highlight the unreliability of this account and the need to develop an alternative, historical recreation of the reasons and date for the rebuilding of the temple.

In Chapter 4, I will examine the likely boundaries of Yehud under Artaxerxes I. I will argue that none of the three lists of settlements in the book of Nehemiah that have been used as sources to define the provincial limits (3; 7.6-69 and 11.25-35) reflects the actual territory of Yehud under Artaxerxes. Even so, I will argue that the Negev region was included in the province of Yehud at this time because it is unlikely that the king would have authorized the resettlement of groups from Mesopotamia in Yehud had the southern boundary only been at Bet-Zur, as it came to be c. 400 BCE. This territory is very compact and already had a sizeable population concentrated in the northern areas; an influx of settlers would not have been needed. In my estimation, the southern portion of Yehud was made into the separate province of Idumea c. 400 BCE, after the loss of Egypt from the Persian control. With the frontier of the empire now in the Negev, it was deemed wise to fortify the Beersheva Valley more heavily and to establish a separate provincial administration to deal with the logistics of supplying these outposts.

In Chapter 5 I will deal with the thorny issue of settlement patterns and administrative facilities that existed in Yehud during the Persian period and what they might be able to contribute toward our understanding of the underlying motivations of the Persian court for its policy of sending people of Judahite descent back to Yehud. It is difficult to identify which sites might have been occupied in the fifth century BCE and impossible to know which would have been built or inhabited during the reign of Artaxerxes I. Nevertheless, the location of such sites and their relative sizes can provide insight into Persian policy within the province.

Finally, in Chapter 6, I will examine the events prior to and during the reign of Artaxerxes I (464–424 BCE) that would have influenced the establishment of Jerusalem as a *birah* and new regional capital over a recently resettled and expanded Yehud, with outlying forts, relay stations, and a network of farmsteads and unwalled, small hamlets. I will suggest what policy Artaxerxes I decided to implement for the redevelopment of Yehud, and why. My proposed recreation will also serve as a summary and conclusion to my research.

Two appendices provide English translations of two major Persian documents: (1) the Behistun inscription of Darius I and (2) the Cyrus Cylinder. They are included to allow readers to assess the arguments I make concerning various points they contain by reading the texts in question immediately. They are followed by a glossary containing definitions of more technical terms associated with the geography and socio-political organization of Persian Yehud, as well as less familiar terms used in literary analysis and foreign words that are best not translated into English since they do not have an immediate equivalent. Finally, there is an index of authors cited, of biblical and classical references, and of subjects before the bibliography.

This volume is intended to demonstrate the historical enterprise in an extended case study. For this reason, readers are taken through the full process whereby sources are critically evaluated for the contribution they might make to the topic under investigation. My primary intention is to have readers understand that little in the area under investigation is 'black' or 'white'; what one person considers to be a clear 'fact' another may well consider to be unreliable 'fiction'. History involves interpretation at every step of the way, so that what I ultimately identify as reliable data can be contested by others who do not share my analytical and analogous deductions. I am presenting what I consider to be the most cogent history of the building of the second temple, but it is only one of many possible histories of this event that can be recreated from the same, limited set of available sources.

For the sake of general readers and students, I have placed more detailed arguments and discussions of collateral issues in indented paragraphs in smaller type. You can skip over these sections without losing the main thread or becoming bogged down in small details that I feel corroborate the larger argument or have some bearing on the larger issue. So feel free to decide how many of these sections you want to tackle on a first reading. As you get deeper into the subject area, you might want to return to them. I am walking you through a number of complex issues and arguments that you need to be aware of so that you can fully appreciate the task of a historian and be able to decide at each step of the way if you agree or disagree with my assessment of the sources. Undoubtedly, you will feel overwhelmed at some points; please persevere or at least skim the material that is not very interesting at the moment. I have summarized my conclusions at the end of each subsection and again at the end of each chapter, so they can serve as beacons in the fog that hopefully will steer you back to the main track should you get lost or lose interest. I have tried to keep footnotes to a minimum so they are not distracting and have placed them as endnotes for the same reason.

As a historian, I am viewing certain books within the Bible as potential sources of information for understanding the culture and world-view of Yehud during the Persian period, especially during the reign of Artaxerxes I. While recognizing that the Bible is a document of faith for today's Judeo-Christian communities, I am approaching the set of books contained within it as literature written by scribes belonging to the elite of society, who used the standard literary conventions of their day to convey their intended messages to their audiences. They presumed a world-view that differs greatly from those in vogue in the western world today. The subject matter of their narratives was religious in that they wrote about the relationship of the nations of Israel and Judah to the deity Yahweh over time. However, my approach, which is typical of biblical studies conducted in secular universities and colleges, recognizes that these books are human compositions. They have undergone editing over time to adjust them to changing understandings of the divine and changing historical and cultural circumstances. As such, the accuracy of the depiction of past events that they portray is open to scrutiny and needs to be established rather than automatically presumed. These books are not written using our modern standards of critical, historical investigation, so if we want to determine what information contained within them might be reliable in its detail, we have to subject the books to critical examination.

The following conventions are used. When citing biblical references, if I refer to an entire book, I will use its name. If I cite a full chapter within a book, I will write out the name of the book in full and then give the chapter number: Nehemiah 7. If I cite one or more verses in a book, then I will abbreviate the name of the book, give the chapter, and after a full stop, give the relevant verse(s): Neh. 7.5-24. I refer to the Hebrew and early Jewish god by the scholarly reconstruction of his likely name, Yahweh. In Hebrew manuscripts, the name is always written with the four consonants YHWH and no vowels, so it is uncertain how the name was pronounced. The Jewish prohibition against taking the name of God in vain was followed from early times. The custom never to pronounce the name but to substitute titles like 'Lord' or 'The Name' instead continues in Orthodox and Conservative Jewish tradition. I have transliterated other Hebrew words in such a way as to try to reflect their pronunciation for those who do not know the ancient or modern language.

You can find a list of abbreviations for the biblical books cited at the beginning of the citation index. Other standard abbreviations include: (1) v. for verse and vv. for verses; (2) ch. for chapter and chs. for chapters; and (3) c. for *circa*, meaning 'approximately' or 'about'; (4) BCE for 'before the Common Era' (the religiously neutral equivalent of BC, 'before Christ') and CE for 'Common Era' (the neutral equivalent of AD, 'anno Domini' i.e. 'in the year of our Lord'); and (5) § for section and §§ for sections.

Chapter 1

WHEN GENERATIONS REALLY COUNT: DATING ZERUBBABEL AND NEHEMIAH
USING GENEALOGICAL INFORMATION IN THE BOOK OF NEHEMIAH

Introduction

The genealogical material in Nehemiah and 1 Chronicles 1–9 closes the gap considerably between the missions of Zerubbabel and of Nehemiah as portrayed in the book of Ezra. Rather than being in power some sixty-five years apart, according to this material, the two were at most a generation apart in age. Nehemiah either succeeded Zerubbabel as governor in Yehud, or he worked as a special envoy during Zerubbabel's governorship. Partial information about six generations is provided, beginning with the three generations who returned from exile to Yehud with Zerubbabel until or through the reign of Darius III (335–330 BCE) and the end of Persian rule (Neh. 12.22). But we need first to confirm the chronological end-point of the list.

While it is the case that the wording in Neh. 12.22 does not explicitly state that Yaddua was high priest through the reign of Darius III, it seems to imply that this was the situation, and the Jewish historian Josephus (c. 37–96 BCE) places Yaddua in office at the time of Alexander's conquest of the Levant (332 BCE), which ended the rule of Darius III (*Ant.* 10.8.7). The reference in v. 22 to 'Darius the Persian' is vague, leaving open the possibility that it was intended to refer to Darius II (424–404 BCE) rather than Darius III (335–330 BCE). This is the common view, based largely on the assumption that the first Darius had come to be mistakenly known in Jewish tradition as Darius 'the Mede' (Dan. 5.31 [6.1 Hebrew]; Daniel 6) so that the second Darius would have been distinguished from him by applying the contrasting geographical epithet, 'the Persian' (so, e.g., Wilson 1915: 193; Rudolph 1949: 193). However, as J.C. Vanderkam has pointed out, Josephus places Yohanan, Yaddua's predecessor, still in office under Darius II's successor, Artaxerxes II (405/404–359/358 BCE) (*Ant.* 11.7.1) so Yaddua could not have been in office under Darius II (2000: 196).

> The suggestion by H.G.M. Williamson that the reference to the priests registered under Darius the Persian in v. 22b is a later scribal gloss intended to refer to an event that had taken place much earlier in the reign of Darius I does not clarify matters (1985: 364-64). Instead of linking the statement to what precedes in v. 22a, he is linking it to what follows. He proposes that it is intended to show that the priests had been recorded from the beginning of the temple, under Darius I, just as the Levites continued to be for generations. He could be correct that the phrase has been added secondarily; the reference to a registration by a king is slightly uncharacteristic; usually, such registrations are listed under the name of the high priest in office at the time. However, the statement seems to be either confirming or qualifying what precedes it rather than what follows, and the author or a later editor could equally have used it to clarify the latest king under whom the final

high priest named in the first half of the verse had served. Williamson wants to remove Yaddua as a secondary addition to the first half of the list, which is not necessary (1985: 361).

In light of the above considerations, two explanations of the information in Neh. 12.22 can be given. In the first, the registration of the priests that lasted until the reign of 'Darius the Persian' is intended to cover the same period of time as the registration of the heads of the fathers' houses of the Levites under the high priests Eliashiv, Yoiada, Yohanan and Yaddua. In this case, 'Darius the Persian' would refer to Darius III, under whom Yaddua would have served as high priest. He was in office in 332 BCE when Alexander ended the Persian empire, making Greece the new world ruler. In the second, the period during which the heads of the priestly houses were registered does not coincide with that in which the heads of the Levitical houses were recorded. Instead, for some reason, the priestly houses were only registered until the time of 'Darius the Persian' or Darius II and not until the end of the Persian era under Darius III (so, e.g., Vanderkam 2000: 190). In this case, the verse gives no indication of when Yaddua had served as high priest.

The first option makes more sense since it squares with the known historical data. Yaddua had been high priest under Darius III, and it would have been odd not to have recorded the heads of the priestly houses at the same time as the heads of the Levitical houses. This is particularly the case since the priests were classed as 'Levites' or administrative personnel, though afforded more status than those who did not officiate in the cult. While every priest was also considered a Levite, not every Levite was a priest. Since the priesthood was a specialized branch of the Levitical corps, any registration of Levitical leaders should have automatically included a listing of the heads of priestly houses at the time as well. Thus, it makes the most sense to assume that the registration of the priests lasted the same length of time as that of the Levites in general. As a corollary, it is logical to conclude that the final registration under Yaddua had been done during the reign of Darius III, prior to the demise of the Persian empire.

Genealogies had many uses in the ancient world beyond the familiar ones today of maintaining a family tree as proof of social privilege or inherited title and lands, or of tracing one's ancestry out of curiosity about one's roots. The former would have been important in ancient Yehud for purposes of taxation on land, army and corvée conscription, proving eligibility to a profession that was passed on from father to son like the priesthood, establishing marriage eligibility between families and defining status, rank, office, social rights and obligations. The idiom of kinship was also used in ancient genealogies to express various social, political and religious relationships even though there was no blood bond between the elements being presented as fathers, sons and brothers. In these cases, the genealogies would be setting up a hierarchy that expressed political relationships between nations, or status relationships within a given group, or economic, geographical, or cultic position (Wilson 1977; Johnson 1969).

In the book of Nehemiah, genealogies seem to function in a variety of ways. The reported enrollment of the people of the province in Nehemiah 7 creates an artificial, one-generation genealogy that defines who was considered a member of Israel. Constituents are listed either by their clan or by place of residence and a further distinction is made between the lay segment of the society and those associated with the temple (priests, Levites, Solomon's servants and temple servants). The list of those who lived in Jerusalem in Nehemiah 11 serves a similar function for the provincial seat in vv. 1-24, but then goes on to create a second, geographical genealogy for the province in vv. 25-32. The priestly genealogy given in Neh. 12.10-11, on the other hand, is based on blood ties and functions to legitimate the line of the high priesthood that passed from father to son. Finally, we should note the custom of identifying an individual by his or her father's name (patronymic) (i.e. Malkiyah the son of Rekav), creating a two-generation genealogy. In this way, one's place in society was determined by the status of one's immediate family in the community and the reputation that had been earned by one's father.

The framework for the generations I will present is built from the list of high priests found in Neh. 12.1-26, who officiated from the repatriation under Zerubbabel until the end of the Persian empire under Darius III. Since this office was traditionally hereditary, the list should present a reliable detailing of successive generations that can serve as a skeleton that can be fleshed out by placing named individuals who are associated with the various high priests into their corresponding generational contexts.

At any given time, there is a three-generational span of people interacting: the elders, aged fifty and up, who are ending their political and public careers, their children, the middle-aged, perhaps ages twenty-five to forty-nine, who are entering and then peaking in their careers, and the grandchildren, aged birth to twenty-four, who are learning the ways of the world and being groomed to follow in the footsteps of the two older generations.[1] These figures reflect the life spans of the well-to-do who did not engage regularly in physical labor and who had an adequate diet. Commoners, on the other hand, were thought only to have lived on average into their fifties (Roth 1987: 747). The individuals named in the genealogies in Nehemiah were all in privileged positions, serving as priests, Levites, scribes, and influential heads of local families. As a result, they are likely to have lived longer than their lower-status contemporaries. The age boundaries for each generation can be adjusted, however, without negating the underlying insight that three generations tended to be alive simultaneously at any given time.

Bearing in mind the three-generation span alive at any time, the reader might object that it is difficult to know how to situate an individual age-wise, and this is certainly the case in a number of instances. For this reason, only individuals about whom there are enough textual details supplied that allow them to be assigned to a particular generation with a reasonable degree of confidence will be discussed.

There is no simple way to wade through the mass of data that is about to be discussed. This may account in part for why this analysis has never been tackled before, to my knowledge. Genealogies are famous for bringing a certain glaze to the reader's or listener's eyes, often prompting them to 'tune out' and let their mind wander to thoughts about things of more personal interest or simply to skip over these 'dull bits' to the place where the story line resumes. There is a huge 'payload' at the end for those who persevere, however.

In order to try to assist you, I have taken the following measures. First, I have placed a chart at the beginning of each of the six generational sections that gives the names of the individuals I think belong to that generation and the relevant biblical passages that provide information about them. In the case of generations 3, 4, and 5, I supply a second chart detailing contemporaries who were not members of the Jewish community in Yehud but who had relationships with it, nonetheless.

Then, I systematically work down each chart, discussing what is known about each individual, why they have been assigned to this particular generation, what extra-biblical evidence might exist for him or her, and how it might help provide a firm dating peg for that particular individual and, by extension, the others assigned to the same generation. I am well aware that your heads will begin to ache after a while as you wade through this material and you will experience a sense of being overwhelmed by 'too much data' whose significance is not immediately clear. Please do not despair.

After this initial run-through generation by generation, I will address the chronological implications of the various observations made in the preceding discussions of individuals in the seven generations. Here I will specifically have as a goal the determination of the generation to which Nehemiah is to be assigned and the relative dates that can be associated with various generations from extra-biblical correlations. As will become clear, the book of Nehemiah portrays Nehemiah to have had personal dealings with members of generations 2, 3, 4, and 5. This is possible, since during a person's lifetime, he or she will have contact with four generations, even though only three would have been alive at a given time. I will then propose the assignment of Nehemiah to generation 3 since it is most consistent with the bulk of the data.

Two major complications arise during the course of this already complex analysis. The first is the likelihood that in generation 5, two sons of Yehoiada, Yohanan and Yonatan, served successively as high priest. Nehemiah is portrayed to have had dealings with a son of Yehoiada, whom he 'chased away' because he had married a daughter of Sinuballit the Harranite (Neh. 13.28). Thus, it is possible that the person in question was the older son, whom Nehemiah deposed in favor of the next eldest. However, this is not certain, especially since the majority of Nehemiah's contacts are otherwise with members of generations 2 and 3, and this incident is part of the final summary of reforms Nehemiah allegedly undertook when he returned to Yehud at some point after building the walls. The historicity of 13.15-30 is uncertain, as is the intended time frame of the entire chapter in relation to the earlier narrative.[2] This section has Nehemiah initiate the same reforms in year 32 of Artaxerxes that Ezra allegedly has already undertaken in year 7. In addition, the circumstances of the reported return to Jerusalem in year 32 are vague, suggesting this section might be secondary. The possibility of an additional high priest in the lineage after Nehemiah is important in terms of the overall chronology in which only two high priests would have spanned the seventy-year time period from 410–335 BCE. Unfortunately, as a member of the same generation as his brother, his addition does not change the situation dramatically.

The second complication involves Sanballat the Horonite, who served as governor of Samerina during this period and probably belonged to generation 3. Josephus has transposed the account of the marriage of his daughter to a fifth-generation son of the high priest Yehoiada (Neh. 13.28) into a marriage to the brother of the sixth-generation high priest. As a result, he has opened the door to the needless multiplication of Sanballats. Assuming the principle of papponymy or the naming of grandsons after grandfathers became the vogue in the Persian period, F.M. Cross Jr has 'discovered' the existence of three separate individuals named Sanballat, all of whom served as governors of Samerina (1974: 20-22). The idea of a second historical Sanballat is widely encountered, especially in the publications of his many students. However, the available textual and artifactual evidence from Nehemiah, the Elephantine papyri, the Wadi ed-Daliyeh papyri and Samarian coins can be explained by the existence of a single Sanballat. There is no need to create fictitious namesakes to fill in the many holes in our knowledge about the Persian period.

Before beginning, I think it would be helpful to provide background information on bullae and on two collections of papyri, one from Elephantine and the other from the Wadi ed-Daliyeh, for those not familiar with either topic. All three will be cited as sources of evidence in the ensuing discussion.

Bullae are small lumps of clay used to fasten closed papyrus or leather scrolls. The personal seals of the witnesses and parties to the transactions recorded on the documents are pressed into pinched pieces of soft clay, which then leave visible imprints of the seals' designs. Since papyrus and leather are made of perishable materials that tend to rot away unless preserved inside covered jars or in arid conditions, bullae are often the only telltale remains that written documents once existed. They are themselves fragile and subject to disintegration if they come in contact with water, unless they are found in a destruction layer during excavation. Then, there is a good chance that they have been baked hard by fire, which has burned the document under the sealings but ensured the survival of the bullae once attached to it (Deutsch 1999: 14-15).

The Elephantine papyri are a group of legal documents, records, accounts, lists, letters, and literary and historical texts written in Aramaic on scrolls made of overlapping layers of pounded papyrus stems. They bear dates that range from 495–399 BCE in the Persian period. They were found at or near the island of Elephantine in Egypt, in the middle of the Nile River, just downstream from (north of) the modern Aswan Dam, in the nineteenth and twentieth centuries CE. There was a walled settlement there containing a fort, housing for the soldiers and their families, businesses, and temples. The Aramaic name of the settlement was Yeb, and it is referred to in some of the correspondence as a *birah*, a walled settlement with a fort and civilian population. Some papyri were found by chance by locals and others were recovered through excavations (Porten 1992).

The Wadi ed-Daliyeh papyri were found in 1962 by Ta'amireh bedouin who were camping in the vicinity of the nearby spring at Fasayil in the central Ephraimite hill-country, during Ramadan. The specific name of the cave containing the papyri is Mugharet Abu Shinjeh; it is one of many that line the canyon. The scrolls were found among the personal possessions of a group of people who appear to have fled from Samaria, the capital of the adjoining province to the north, probably at the time that Alexander attacked the city in 331 BCE. Their hiding place was discovered; over 300 bodies were found on mats in the cave. Dates on the papyri range from 375–335 BCE (Lapp 1974; Cross 1974: 16-18).

Time to get down to business!

Generation 1

Iddo	Head of priestly family at the time of the return; grandfather of prophet Zechariah	Ezra 5.1; Neh. 12.4, 16
Kadmiel	Head of Levitical family at the time of the return; father of Yeshua	Neh. 12.8, 24
Yeshua ben Yehozadak	High priest	Neh. 3.2; 12.1, 7, 26

Members of this generation would have been elderly at the time of their return, between c. fifty-five to seventy-five years old. They would have been the eldest of the three generations that returned simultaneously, the 'grandparents', so to speak.

Iddo

A number of priests returned under the leadership of Zerubbabel and Yeshua to Yehud. One of these was Iddo, who was listed as one of twenty-two chief priests during the high priesthood of Yeshua (Neh. 12.1-7). These chief priests then became the ancestral heads of the main priestly families of the second temple, as indicated by the list of their descendants who had inherited their offices under the high priesthood of Yoiakim (Neh. 12.12-21). It is noteworthy that Iddo was the grandfather of Zechariah the prophet (Zech. 1.1), who succeeded him as head of the priestly family of Iddo (Neh. 12.16). Zechariah's designation as 'son of Iddo' in Ezra 5.1 is an example of the use of the term son to mean 'descendant' rather than 'son' literally. This implies that Iddo would have been quite aged when he returned to Yehud with his grown son Berekiah (Zech. 1.1) and grandson Zechariah. Thus, he would have belonged to generation 1, which represented the eldest of the three generations involved in the return. The main leaders and officials of the *golah* group probably belonged to the second generation, although it is possible that some of the other heads of the priestly houses would have belonged to his generation as well. They would have functioned as leaders for a brief period of time before their deaths.

Kadmiel

Like Iddo, Kadmiel appears to have been elderly at the time of his return. He was head of one of the eight Levitical families that had arrived with Zerubbabel and Yeshua. At the time of the subsequent registration of heads of Levitical families under the high priesthood of Yoiakim, Yeshua's son and successor, Kadmiel had been replaced by his son Yeshua. More heads who had arrived at the same time as him were still active: Shereviah, Mattaniah, and Bakbukiah (Neh. 12.8-9; 24-26). Thus, it is likely that he had been in his twilight years when he had made the trip from Babylonia. In comparing the two lists of head Levites under Yeshua and Joiakim, it can be noted that like Kadmiel, Binnui, Yeshua, Judah, and Unno disappear. They may also have belonged to the oldest generation.

Yeshua ben Yehozadaq

The genealogies for the second temple priesthood all begin with Yeshua, which suggests that he served as the first high priest of the rebuilt temple. This in turn implies that the temple was completed while he was still alive and able to perform his duties. There is the possibility that his title was honorary; Yeshua had returned to Yehud with Zerubbabel as the intended future high priest, but he could have died before the temple was actually completed. The prophecies of Haggai and Zechariah take place at the beginning of the building of the new temple, while both Zerubbabel and Yeshua were serving as appointed officials, but they do not indicate how long the process took. Although his death before the rededication of the temple seems highly unlikely; however, it is possible that he exercised the office only a short time before his death and succession by his son, Yoiakim.

It is not necessary to assume that Yeshua and Zerubbabel were members of the same generation. While it is likely that the Persians would have chosen a younger man to serve as governor, probably someone in his thirties with some life experience but also plenty of energy and an interest in endorsing higher policies in the interest of the advancement of his career, the selection of the high priest would have been dictated by other concerns and circumstances. The priesthood was a hereditary office held for life once it was filled by a person. Whether we assume that Yeshua was a blood descendant of Seraiah, the last acting head priest of the temple in Jerusalem in 586 BCE, or the patriarch of one of a number of priestly families who were active in the various communities in Babylonia under the Neo-Babylonians who was selected for the position by Zerubbabel or a Jewish council, his age would not have been the determining factor in his selection. It would have been his politics, his theological views, his pedigree, his popularity/reputation, or a combination of these factors. An older high priest would probably have earned more respect and cooperation than a younger, more inexperienced one.

Some consideration needs to be given to Yeshua's pedigree in light of his status as the first high priest to officiate in Jerusalem after a sizeable time gap. His father's name is given in Hag. 1.1, 12, 14; 2.2, 4; Zech. 6.11 as Yehozadaq. This is not particularly suspicious, although it is noteworthy that most of these passages belong to the editorial framework of the book in Haggai, while the passage in Zech. 6.11 has been suspected of having been altered, with Yeshua's name added secondarily. However, what needs questioning is whether Yehozadaq had been the biological son of the last main priest to officiate in the monarchic-era temple in Jerusalem, Seraiah (1 Chron. 6.14), before his execution at Riblah in 586 BCE (2 Kgs 25.18-21; Jer. 52.24). The Chronicler has claimed that this was the case in 6.15, but he may have been motivated by a desire to eliminate holes in his genealogy and, more importantly, by a desire to claim there had been continuity in the high priestly line between the two temples (so, e.g., Kosters 1895: 49; Dequeker 1993: 85). Thus, he may have taken the information he had about the first high priest to officiate after the temple was rebuilt, which was the name Yeshua son of Yehozadaq, and linked that to the last information available from the monarchic period, the name of the final priest, Seraiah.

Since there had been no high priest of Jerusalem in the inter-temple period, however long that lasted, there may not have been any genealogical materials preserved about Seraiah's biological descendants. In addition, there is no guarantee that Yeshua, the first high priest in the Persian era, had any ties to the lineage of Eleazar or of Seraiah. Once the Judahites were resettled in various regions of Babylonia, each town could have had its own temple to Yahweh, with a priestly line officiating locally and no hierarchy that would favor one group over another. In this situation, it is hard to determine if the former pre-eminence of the house of Seraiah would have been maintained so that the priestly line selected to return to Jerusalem would have been this historic house or not.

Even if Seraiah's line were put back in power, however, there is no guarantee that we have the genealogy of that family in its complete form in 1 Chron. 3.4. Hugh Williamson thinks that the expression 'was the father of' in the priestly genealogy is a metaphorical expression for the succession of office and should not be taken literally (Williamson 1982: 70-71). Yehozadaq may have been the grandson or great-grandson of Seraiah, rather than his son, if he was a blood relative at all.

Generation 2

Zerubbabel ben Shealtiel/ ben Pedaiah	Governor, Davidide	Neh. 12.1; 1 Chron. 3.19
Yoiakim	Son of Yeshua, high priest after father, father of Eliashiv, high priest	Neh. 12.10, 12
Shekaniah ben Arah	Father-in-law of Tobiah the Ammonite and possible father of Shemaiah, keeper of the east gate	Neh. 3.29, 6.17-18
Berekiah	Son of Iddo, father of prophet Zechariah	Zech. 1.1; Neh. 12.16
Yeshua	Son of Kadmiel	Neh. 12.24

The second generation also would have been born in captivity in Babylonia but would have returned to Yehud as adults, many accompanied by wives and children. It makes sense to assign them to the middle-aged bracket, around twenty-six to fifty-five years old, at the time of their return. Prominent members who figure in the Nehemiah narrative include Zerubbabel, the governor, Yeshua's son Yoiakim the high priest, Shekaniah ben Arah, and Iddo's son Berekiah, the father of the prophet Zechariah (1 Chron. 3.19; Neh. 12.4).

Zerubbabel
While the material is clear that Zerubbabel was a descendant of the royal house of David, there are two different patronymics given for him in Nehemiah and Chronicles. In Neh. 12.1, he is named as the son of Shealtiel, while in 1 Chron. 3.19 he appears to be the nephew of Shealtiel; his father is Pedaiah, the brother of Shealtiel. Different solutions to this problem have been proposed. The most widely adopted one suggests that Shealtiel died childless but that his widow contracted a levirate marriage with her husband's younger brother Pedaiah and that Zerubbabel, the first male offspring of that union, was considered the son of Shealtiel under the conditions of levirate marriage (so, e.g., Ryle 1893: 17; Rudolph 1949: 18; Brockington 1969: 53; William-son 1985: 32; Tollington 1993: 133-34 n. 4). Had this been the case, however, Shealtiel should have been listed as the only legitimate father since the purpose of levirate marriage was to secure a male heir for a line to maintain inheritance rights.

Four other proposals have been made. The first is that we are dealing with two separate Zerubbabels within the royal family; one was the son of the heir to the throne, Shealtiel, the other was the son of the third in line to the throne, Pedaiah, and both happened to be involved in the rebuilding of the temple (Talmon 1976: 391). This is too coincidental for me. The second suggests that the naming of Pedaiah as the father in the Masoretic text is simply an error and that the Septuagint text preserves the more original reading here; it makes Shealtiel the biologi-cal father (Mitchell *et al.* 1912: 43). However, it is likely that the Septuagint translator took the opportunity to 'correct' the text in 1 Chron. 3.19 so that it conformed to the information else-where in Haggai, Zechariah, Ezra and Nehemiah. In this case, it is better to maintain the more difficult reading as original.

A third option proposes that Pedaiah was the throne name assigned to Shealtiel prior to his accession, which would allow an equation of the two figures and which would eliminate any contradiction in the traditions (Meyers and Meyers 1987: 10). We have no evidence that throne names were pre-assigned before accession, however, and in this case the genealogy in 1 Chron. 3.17-18 should have given one name or the other but not both, which strongly suggests we are dealing with two separate individuals. Finally, it has been suggested that Zerubbabel was the biological son of Pedaiah, the third son of Yekoniah, but that a desire to aggrandize him and his position in later tradition led to his being made the eldest son of Shealtiel to put him in a more direct line to have inherited the throne of Judah (Chary 1969: 18). It could be argued that most or all of the uses of this patronym occur in the editorial sections of Haggai and so reflect this later aggrandizement, although it is unclear that this is the case in Hag. 2.23. Of the four solutions, this one is most plausible to me, but still lacks cogency.

There is a slightly odd wording in the list of the sons of Yekoniah in 1 Chron. 3.17-18. It begins in the standard way, naming Shealtiel, who is designated as 'his son' – almost as though he were the only male heir. It then goes on in v. 18, however, to name six additional males, Pedaiah, Shenazzar, Yekemiah, Hoshama and Nedeviah, without specifying that they are also sons of Yekoniah or clarifying their relationship to Shealtiel. No descendants of Shealtiel, the first-born, are given; instead, the two sons of Pedaiah are given: Zerubbabel and his brother Shimei. It is possible that Shealtiel had died as a youth, without producing male heirs, but the phrasing in vv. 17-18 also leaves room for the suspicion that there has been some sort of corruption or deliberate tampering with the text.

The six males named after Shealtiel could originally have been his sons; we would expect an enumeration of the sons of the eldest male in such a genealogy. However, this does not square with the subsequent enumeration of the sons of Pedaiah, who would have been Shealtiel's second eldest. The sons of Malkiram should have been named instead. Thus, unless it is also postulated that Malkiram had not produced male heirs, this reconstruction would not be plausible.

An alternative would be to emend vv. 17-18 to read: 'the descendants of Yekoniah the captive: Shealtiel, his son, Malkiram [his son], and [the sons of Malkiram]: Pedaiah, Shenazzer, Yekamiah, Hoshama, Nedeviah [five]'.[3] It would provide a reasonable rationale for why the Chronicler made Zerubbabel the son of Pedaiah and would reflect the expected practice of inheritance through the line of the eldest male. It would mean that historically, Zerubabbel had been the eldest son of Pedaiah, who in turn, had been the eldest of five sons of Malkiram, the eldest son of Shealtiel. If this reconstruction is correct, it would place Zerubbabel's birth sometime close to 500 BCE, assuming an interval of thirty years between each father and Shealtiel's birth shortly before his family's removal to Babylon in 597 BCE.

Four administrative texts found in the palace in Babylon among documents that dated between years 10 and 35 of Nebuchadrezzar, or between 595–570 BCE, mention Yehoiakin and his five sons (Oppenheim 1969: 308). They refer to oil rations that were given to Yehoiakin, king of Judah, and to his five sons, who are not named, but designated collectively as the sons of the king of Judah. Whereas Yehoiakin receives ten silas of oil in each case, his sons are allotted half a sila each.

It is not certain how much information can be deduced from these lists. It is likely that the sons were old enough no longer to be living in the harem with their mothers, but it is not clear if they would have all reached the age of majority, whatever that was at this time. This means that the texts probably date from close to 570 BCE, and it is possible that the five would have all been eighteen and older at that point. What is most significant here, however, is that Yehoiakin appears to have had only five sons, not seven, unless two more were still minors being included in their father's ration. Thus, these texts may be put beside the unattached list of six names in v. 18 as signaling some sort of irregularity in the genealogy at this point and the need for caution when relying on the list for reconstructing history.

It is well known that the term *ben*, 'son', can mean descendant, so there is not a problem really in Neh. 12.1 in Zerubbabel's designation as 'the son of Shealtiel'. Even so, it can be asked why Shealtiel was considered a more illustrious Davidic ancestor whose name should be linked with that of Zerubbabel in Neh. 12.1 than that of his actual father, Pedaiah, or even the last Davidic king, Zedekiah, or the first king-in-exile, Yekoniah.

A possible answer would be that Shealtiel, Yehoiakin's eldest son, had already been born before he and his family were taken captive to Babylon in 597 BCE (2 Kgs 24.15; 2 Chron. 36.9-10) (so, e.g., Meyers and Meyers 1987: 10). Jeremiah 22.28 seems to indicate that Yehoiakin had already fathered more than one child before he went into exile, although we cannot know how many would have been sons. In Hebrew, the word 'sons' could be used literally to refer to all male offspring of an individual, or in a more general way to refer to children of mixed gender. As the eldest son and heir to the throne, Shealtiel would likely have been considered the hope for the continuation and future restoration of the Davidic dynasty among those who had gone into exile at that time. Jeremiah 22.30 seems to be an attempt to refute this view.

The neo-Babylonians appointed Yehoiakin's uncle, Zedekiah, to succeed, him on the throne of Judah (2 Kgs 24.17) but slew all his sons as punishment for their father's rebellion in 586 BCE (2 Kgs 25.7). With the final king's family gone, those who went into exile subsequently in 586 BCE may well have focused their hopes on Shealtiel as well. Thus, Zerubbabel's designation as 'the son of Shealtiel' may have been done to draw on this association in the mind of a post-exilic audience that had inherited the idea themselves.

Yehoiakim

A son of Yeshua the high priest, Yehoiakim succeeded his father as high priest. He would already have been middle-aged when he arrived in Yehud, but could not have assumed office until the death of his father. During his eventual tenure as high priest, records were made of the heads of the father's houses of the priests that show the transfer of leadership responsibilities from generation 2 to generation 3, most of whom would have returned to Yehud as children (Neh. 12.10, 12). During Yehoiakim's high priesthood, there was a fully operational temple with priests, Levites, and gatekeepers (Neh. 12.12).

Berekiah

The son of the chief priest Iddo and father of the prophet Zechariah (Zech. 1.1), he appears to have had a second, younger son named Meshullam (Neh. 3.30) who would have been a contemporary of Zerubbabel. He apparently had already died when the list of acting chief priests of the original priestly families was compiled during the office of Yehoiakim. This accounts for Zechariah's having assumed leadership of this family (Neh. 12.16).

Shekaniah ben Arah

While the book of Nehemiah indicates that he was an important and well-connected personage in Jerusalem, his origins and function within the restored community of Yehud are not clear. His biggest claim to fame was his status as the father-in-law of Tobiah the Ammonite, who had married his unnamed daughter (Neh. 6.17-18). He may also have had a son named Shemaiah, who was keeper of the East Gate (Neh. 3.29).

It is plausible to think that this Shekaniah was one of the 22 chief priests who had returned to Yehud with Zerubbabel and Yeshua (Neh. 12.3), even though the lack of a patronymic in the list of chief priests makes it impossible to be certain. Thus, this must remain an unconfirmed but strong possibility. It would, however, explain his respect within the *golah* community (Neh. 6.18).

It cannot be ruled out that he belonged to the local non-*golah* community and had been given a position of authority by Zerubbabel as part of a plan to build bridges between the recent returnees and the leadership of those who had remained in the land. But this option seems less likely. Shekaniah may or may not have shared the political views of his son-in-law, so not much can be inferred from this marriage alliance concerning Shekaniah's status as a member of the *golah* or non-*golah*. In addition, there does not appear to have been any objection to marriages to 'foreign' or non-Jewish (?) women in the early years after the return; to the literature, this issue was only raised by Nehemiah later on (Neh. 13.23-29).

> In theory, it was raised by Ezra as well, possibly before Nehemiah (Ezra 9.10–10.35) but the historical status of Ezra is uncertain, as is the date of his alleged mission – is it portrayed to have preceded that of Nehemiah's or followed it? Scholars continue to debate this point, although the chronology found in the two books would seem to indicate that Ezra was meant to be seen as Nehemiah's predecessor, who had made it clear to the community that mixed marriages were against the law of God. Thus, any that allegedly had been contracted after the first set of dissolutions would have been egregious violations of the law.

If Shemaiah were, in fact, Shekaniah's son, it seems unlikely that he would have been entrusted with a position that involved the security of the city. Such a position which would have required implicit loyalty to the new regime, and sons of *golah* notables would probably have been selected first, had eligible candidates been available. On the other hand, it is hard to judge how strong tensions were between these two factions in the early years of the return. This could have led to his reassignment to the civilian police force in Jerusalem as a gate-keeper. We do not have sufficient evidence to know the details and reconstruct the situation with any amount of certainty.

Generation 3

Eliashiv	Son of Yoiakim, high priest after father	Neh. 3.1; 12.10, 22; 13.28
Meshullam	Son of Zerubbabel	1 Chron. 3.19
Hananiah	Son of Zerubbabel; appointed commander of the fort in Jerusalem by Nehemiah	1 Chron. 3.19; Neh. 7.2
Shelomit	Daughter of Zerubbabel, wife of Elnatan	1 Chron. 3.19; seal

Elnatan	Husband of Shelomit, daughter of Zerubbabel	Seal
Daughter of Shekaniah ben Arah	Married to Tobiah the Ammonite	Neh. 6.17-18
Shemaiah	Son of Shekaniah (ben Arah?)	Neh. 3.29
Zechariah the prophet	Head of priestly house of Iddo (grandfather) under high priesthood of Yoiakim, his contemporary	Neh. 12.16
Meshullam	Brother of Zechariah, son of Berekiah (ben Iddo)	Neh. 3.30

Locals who intermarried into the Yehud community or who were active politically, who would have been contemporaries of generation 3.

Tobiah the Ammonite	Son-in-law of Shekaniah ben Arah, adversary of Nehemiah	Neh. 2.10; 4.3, 7; 6.1, 12, 14, 17-19
Sanballat the Horonite/Sinuballit the Harranite	Adversary of Nehemiah; governor of Samerina	Neh. 2.10; 4.1, 7; 6.1, 5, 12, 14; Elephantine letter AP 30; Wadi Daliyeh bulla 22; Samarian coins
Geshem the Arab	Adversary of Nehemiah	Neh. 2.19; 6.1, 2, 6

Most if not all of the third generation would have been born in Babylonia. They would have returned with their parents to Yehud as young children or as young adults. These include: Joiakim's son, Eliashiv, who succeeded his father as high priest (Neh. 12.10), Zerubbabel's two sons Meshullam and Hananiah (1 Chron. 3.19) and his daughter Shelomit (1 Chron. 3.19), Shekaniah's probable son Shemaiah, keeper of the East Gate (Neh. 3.29), and Zechariah the prophet, son of Berekiah son of Iddo (Zech. 1.1) and his brother Meshulllam (Neh. 3.4, 30). Tobiah the Ammonite was a local contemporary of this group, who probably married a sister of Shemaiah to become the son-in-law of Shekaniah ben Arah (Neh. 6.17-18). Sanballat the Horonite, the likely governor of Samerina, appears also to have belonged to this generation, as did Tobiah the Ammonite and Geshem the Arab.

Eliashiv

Eliashiv succeeded his father Joiakim (Neh. 12.10) as high priest of the temple in Jerusalem. According to Neh. 3.1, he was serving as high priest at the time that the city walls were completed under Nehemiah's direction, presumably soon after the twenty-first year of Artaxerxes (Neh. 2.1). He is said to have occupied a sizeable house worthy of his office inside of Jerusalem, near the Angle and the ascent to the armory (Neh. 3.19-21).

During his term in office, there was a reported registration of the representatives of the chief Levitical families (Neh. 12.22-26), whose names were said to have been recorded in the book of Chronicles. This was the practice through or until the priesthood of Eliashiv's son Yoiada (12.23). Yet, interestingly, the ensuing list of names is said to date to a registration that had been conducted under Eliashiv's father, Yoiakim, not under Eliashiv, and this registration is then also placed during the administration of Nehemiah the governor (and Ezra the scribe) (Neh. 12.26). While Shereviah has continued in office, Kadmiel has been replaced by his son

Yeshua and Binnui, another Yeshua, Judah, and Unno have disappeared. In their place we now find Hashaviah, Mattaniah and Bakbukiah have been transferred from singing duties to gate - keeping duties, alongside other new appointees named Ovadiah, Meshullam, Talmon and Akkuv (Neh. 12.8-9 vs 12.24-25). There is a possibility that the Meshullam in question was the brother of Zechariah, though this is not at all certain.

A further tradition that seems to be out of place with Eliashiv's status as high priest appears in Neh. 13.4-9. Here, at some point prior to the rededication of the city wall, a priest named Eliashiv, who had been assigned a chamber in the temple or had been entrusted with oversight of the chambers of the temple, had 'drawn near to' Tobiah. He had converted one of the store-rooms inside the temple into a private chamber for the use of Tobiah the Ammonite. The claim that he had 'drawn near to Tobiah' (*qarov le*) seems to indicate that he had joined forces with him, perhaps like others within the community who had become bound by oath to him (Neh. 6.18).

Though Nehemiah was reported to have been angry over the incident, the end result was that Tobiah's household furniture was thrown out and the chamber was rededicated to ritual use (Neh. 18.8-9); no consequences are said to have befallen Eliashiv. Had he been a minor priest, one would have thought that he would have been banned from service.

The failure for anything to have happened to him could imply very different things. It might simply mean that Nehemiah had decided not to make a big issue of the situation and alienate other supporters of Tobiah, who apparently were many within the city (6.18). In this case, the Eliashiv in question may or may not have been the son of Yoiada.

Alternatively, it might imply that the Eliashiv in question was the incumbent high priest whom Nehemiah felt he had better not alienate if he wanted to gain support amongst influential members of the resident community in Jerusalem. Once in office, Eliashiv would wield a lot of authority and be untouchable politically, so it would not have been a good idea to get on his bad side.

A third possibility would be that Eliashiv had already become the high priest at this point in time but that the author of Nehemiah was either confused or was trying to disguise this fact. If either of the latter options was the case, then his omission of the title 'high priest' would have been designed to make Eliashiv look as though he were not the same person as the son of Yoiada. Perhaps this was done out of respect, to deflect any criticism from him. The decision to assign this incident to sometime after the thirty-second year of Artaxerxes, after Nehemiah had gone to Susa for some unspecified reason but had returned to Yehud subsequently, seems designed to eliminate any connection in the readers' minds between this Eliashiv and the high priest bearing the same name. The underlying historical reality, however, may have been quite different.

If these various traditions are taken at face value, they indicate that Yoiakim had been the high priest when Nehemiah had begun his governorship in c. 445 BCE. Eliashiv had assumed the reins of the office of high priest by the time the city walls were under repair (Neh. 3.1, 20-22), but perhaps this had not been the first task undertaken by Nehemiah after all. While it features as his primary task in the current narrative, chronological telescoping may have occurred in the account of his governorship, which has moved this task to the beginning of his appointment because it has made it his central concern and accomplishment. The walls appear to have been completed by year 32 of Artaxerxes I, but this allows up to twelve years for the completion of the task if one wants to discount the claim made in 6.15 that the walls were completely restored within 52 days of the work's commencement, which began almost immediately after Nehemiah's arrival in Jerusalem.

Meshullam, Son of Zerubbabel

Not mentioned in the books of Ezra or Nehemiah, he is listed before Hananiah as the apparent eldest son of Zerubbabel in 1 Chron. 3.19. Ordinarily then, he would have been groomed to succeed his father as governor of Yehud. His fate is unknown, although it appears that he died without issue. The line of succession was traced through Hananiah rather than through him. It is not even certain that he returned to Yehud with his father and siblings; he might have been detained by the Persian authorities in Babylonia or at the Persian court as a safeguard to guarantee the loyalty of his father and younger brother.

Hananiah, Son of Zerubbabel

Nehemiah 7.2 attributes two positions of influence and authority in Jerusalem to an individual named Hananiah. Although no patronymic is given, it seems likely that the individual in question was Zerubbabel's second son (1 Chron. 3.19). The absence of the patronymic in this case may well be due to his well-known status in the community.

The first position is that of chief of police for Jerusalem (*sar habbirah*) (Neh. 7.2). It is unclear when he had received this appointment. His title reflects Jerusalem's status as a garrison-city or *birah* (for this term, see Lemaire and Lozachmeur 1987), but it should not be construed to mean that he was commander of the garrison itself. A Persian would have been charged with that duty, one who had power independent of the local governor, in a check-and-balance system (Briant 2002: 340-41, 352). Hananiah's office was the equivalent of the monarchic office of *sar ha'ir*, chief of city police (for an extended discussion of this term, see pp. 216-22). This means that he would likely have been at least a teenager, if not a young adult in his twenties when he returned to Yehud.

Hananiah's second appointment gave him co-responsibility for Jerusalem with Nehemiah's 'brother' Hanani. Nehemiah is said to have commissioned these two 'over' or 'concerning' Jerusalem. They were to oversee the opening and closing of the city gates and post wall sentries (7.2-3). It is to be noted that no official title is reported for this job. The text uses the phrase *'atsavveh 'al* to describe Nehemiah's actions, which simply means, 'I *commanded* Hanani my "brother" and Hananiah, the commander of the *birah, concerning* Jerusalem'.

The text in v. 2 goes on to give a reason for the appointment of one or both men: 'for he was like a man of truth and he feared Elohim more than most'. This phrase occurs after the naming of both men and its referent is unclear. Syntactically, it should describe Hananiah, who is the closest preceding noun, but it might just as well be a dangling modifier intended to refer back to the qualifications of the first person, Hanani. While being in the third person singular, 'he', it might also be intended to be taken distributively to describe both men, in the sense of 'each man was like a man of truth and each feared Elohim more than most'.

This uncertainty makes it difficult to decide if Hanani were literally Nehemiah's brother or a peer. In the first instance, it might have been felt that Hanani had not been particularly qualified for the post but had received it due to the common practice of nepotism so his sterling qualities were emphasized to claim competency in spite of this. In the second instance, the individual's honesty and loyalty to the new religious regime would have been noted as the decisive factors that had led to his assignment to oversee the opening and closing of the gates. In the Elephantine correspondence that dates slightly later, c. 419–406 BCE, the term 'brother' is used in the latter way regularly, with no intimation of a blood relative.

Was Hananiah chosen for this additional assignment because of these two traits? As chief of police in Jerusalem, one might have expected him to be ultimately responsible for the opening and closing of the city gates, which were a primary element in the settlement's security system. Why was there a need for two men to be involved in this task?

The similarity in the names of the two men raises another possibility: the author of Nehemiah or a subsequent editor has found variant forms of the name of a single individual, the shortened form Hanani and the full form Hananiah, and has mistakenly associated them with two separate individuals. The person who had contact with Nehemiah in Susa (1.2) and who was subsequently appointed to oversee the operation of the city gates was Zerubbabel's son, the commander of the Persian garrison. In fact, it could be suggested that Hananiah had been summoned to Susa to receive his commission to be made commander of the newly finished garrison in Jerusalem when he met Nehemiah.

The suggestion that these two individuals were actually one person, but the physical brother of Nehemiah rather than the son of Zerubbabel, is unlikely (e.g. Tuland 1968: 158-59). As already noted, the term 'brother' was regularly used in this period at Elephantine to refer to a colleague and so need not signify a blood kinship. Nevertheless, it would be possible to argue that the conjunction 'and' that links the names Hananiah and Hanani should be translated instead 'that is' and that the text is referring to a single individual, who was the son of Zerubbabel, who was also being identified as a 'colleague' of Nehemiah.

Nehemiah's reported actions in 7.2 are, unfortunately, opaque. Nevertheless, the information in the verse indicates that a Hananiah was serving as chief of police of the recently rebuilt Persian garrison in Jerusalem when Nehemiah arrived and it appears that he was reconfirmed in that post by Nehemiah, who commanded him to oversee the opening and closing of the city gates as well. This situation would be consistent with the claim in Neh. 2.9 that Nehemiah had arrived in Jerusalem accompanied by cavalry and army officers, who would have been destined for service in Persian forts and relay-stations in the province, including the *birah* in Jerusalem itself. This point will be argued more fully in Chapter 6; I will argue against the common assumption that the cavalry and army officers simply formed a military escort. Nehemiah's actions in 7.2 put a Jew in charge of city security, in contrast to the Persians, who were to control the military garrison.

The seal impression found on a jar at Ramat Rahel that reads *yhwd hnnh*, 'Yehud Hananiah' (Davies 1991: 251, #106.009), along with three bullae with the same legend (Avigad 1976: 4-5, #3, pl. 5) might belong to this same person (so, e.g., Talmon 1976: 325).

Figure 1.   *Seal impression of Hananiah found on a jar handle*
Y. Aharoni, *Excavations at Ramat Raḥel Seasons 1961 and 1962* (Serie arche-
ologica, 6; Rome: Universita' di Roma Centro di Studi semitiei, 1964): pl. 20.7.
(Drawn by author.)

Figure 2.   *Bulla that reads Yehud Hananiah*
N. Avigad, *Bullae and Seals from a Post-Exilic Judean Archive* (Qedem, 5; Jerusa-
lem: The Insitute of Archaeology, The Hebrew University of Jerusalem, 1976): 5.
Reproduced by kind permission of the Israel Exploration Society.

However, there is no consensus on their dating. Most such seals and bullae are found outside of their original, stratified contexts, where accompanying pottery can be used to date them within a time span of about 100-150 years. As a result, dates from the late-sixth century to the second century BCE have been suggested (Stern 1982: 202, 205) and Hananiah was a popular name in the Persian period.

These seals and bullae belong to a specific subtype that includes the name of the province, Yehud, in Aramaic, and then a personal name and sometimes, in addition, the title *phw'*. The precise meaning of the latter is debated but it probably was used to designate a range of officials serving in the local Persian administration (see below under Elnatan for details). Nahman Avigad has suggested that the person in question was an official in charge of fiscal matters rather than a governor in his own right, but gives no rationale (1976: 4-5).

Joseph Naveh has proposed that two more seal impressions should be identified with this same person. Both read *lhnwnh yhd*. One was found at Tel Harasim in the Shephelah and the other in Babylon. He reads the personal name as Hanuna and proposes that she was a female minor official in the Persian administration (1996: 45-47).

Figure 3. *Seal of Hanunyah*

J. Naveh, 'Gleanings of Some Pottery Inscriptions', *Israel Exploration Journal* 46 (1996): 46. (Drawn by author.)

But a few observations can be made. Although the more frequent way to shorten names that ended with one of the theophoric forms *yah/yahu* was to make *y* (*yod*) the final letter of the name, using the first letter of the divine name, there is a small group of names that end in *heh*, using the final consonant of these two forms of the divine name. All are names of males: *mykh*, *ml'kh*, *'dnh*, and *qr'h* (all taken from the index in Davies 1991). Thus, if this is indeed the same person, his name appears to have been Hanunyah(u). These two additional seals are unique among the *yhd* collection; they mix the personal seal format that attaches an initial *lamed* of ownership with the provincial designation.

The seals that read 'Yehud Hananiah' do not indicate, however, that Hananiah served specifically as governor; they merely confirm that he held some sort of official post within the regional administration. No title appears beside his name; rather, it is the inclusion of the provincial name that strongly implies that he was serving in an official capacity.

The seal impression and bullae would be consistent with Hananiah's appointment as police chief of Jerusalem, whether or not they actually belonged to this individual. The holder of this office would have been entitled to receive government food rations as well as to oversee their distribution to men on active duty who were under his jurisdiction. In addition, it appears as though Hananiah was second in line by birth to succeed his father Zerubbabel as governor (1 Chron. 3.19), so unless his brother Meshullam had predeceased him, Hananiah would not have been groomed to become governor. His civil appointment would have been a logical option for a younger son from an influential family who was not in line to inherit the family estate and profession directly.

A letter from the Elephantine archive dated to the fifth year of Darius II Nothus, 419 BCE, AP 21, is written by one Hananiah to his 'brethren' Yedoniah and his colleagues in the Jewish garrison ordering them to keep the Passover, including the Feast of Massot, in the Egyptian month of Tybi (Cowley 1923: 60-65, #21). It has been proposed that the Hananiah in question was the relative of Nehemiah, mentioned in Neh. 1.2 and 7.2 (Tuland 1968: 161; Porten 1968: 130 as one of two options considered). Papyrus #38, which lacks a date, mentions in passing that Hananiah had personally visited Egypt and that ever since his departure, the God Khnum, the local deity of Elephantine, had been against the Jews in the garrison (Cowley 1923: 135-38).

Although it might have been possible for Hananiah still to have been serving as chief of police in Jerusalem in 419 BCE, it is not clear why he would have written such a letter to men serving in the military in Egypt. One might expect a temple official to have been involved in the order concerning Passover, since it was a religious issue under discussion, but not the head of civilian security in the capital of another province. It is unlikely that a police chief would have felt compelled to travel to a neighboring region outside his official jurisdiction to visit 'colleagues' in conjunction with a Persian order to observe Passover and Massot. In this case, the Hananiah in question seems to have been a member of the temple staff and not the son of Zerubbabel.

Shelomit

Zerubbabel's daughter Shelomit is the likely owner of the unprovenanced seal that reads *lshlmyt 'mt 'lntn phw'*), 'belonging to Shelomit, wife/maidservant of Elnatan, official' (Avigad 1976: 11-12, #14, pl. 15; Davies 1991: 253, #106.018). The seal was probably kept in the same place as the hoard of bullae that was found somewhere in the region of Jerusalem in 1974. The same Arab villager supplied the hoard and the seal within weeks of one another. If not found together, the seal almost certainly would have come from the same site, close to the bullae (Avigad 1976: 1-2). The connection with Zerubbabel's daughter has been widely accepted (e.g. Talmon 1976: 325; Lemaire 1977: 130; Meyers 1985: 33*-34*; Williamson1988: 75-76; Laperoussaz 1989: 61).

Figure 4.   *Seal of Shelomit*
            N. Avigad, *Bullae and Seals from a Post-Exilic Judean Archive* (Qedem, 5; Jerusa-
            lem: The Insitute of Archaeology, The Hebrew University of Jerusalem, 1976): 11.
            Reproduced by kind permission of the Israel Exploration Society.

It would have been logical for the daughter of the governor, and a Davidic descendant as well, to have been married off to an influential member of the community. It can be noted that two of the officers named in the so-called Solomonic district list in 1 Kgs 4.7-19 were said to be sons-in-law of the king: Ben-Abinadav (v. 11) and Ahimaaz (v. 15).

Among the corpus of Hebrew and Aramaic seals and seal impressions that is known, 23 belong to women. Of these, two are specified to have been royal daughters (Deutsch 1999: 79-80). The remaining seals belong either to daughters (nineteen total to date)[4] or wives (three total to date)[5] of influential men.

Elnatan

As the husband of Shelomit, the governor's daughter, Elnatan must have belonged to an influential family. While it is likely that he would have been a member of generation 3, whether born in Babylonia or locally, the possibility cannot be ruled out that he might have been an older man who was more the contemporary of the important individuals in generation 2 than of generation 3. A seal belonging to Elnatan himself has been found as well, which reads *l'ltntn phw'*, 'belonging to Elnatan, official' (Davies 1991: 253, #106.017).

Figure 5. *Seal of Elnatan*
N. Avigad, *Bullae and Seals from a Post-Exilic Judean Archive* (Qedem, 5; Jerusalem: The Insitute of Archaeology, The Hebrew University of Jerusalem, 1976): 5. Reproduced by kind permission of the Israel Exploration Society.

As noted in passing in the discussion of Hananiah above, the meaning of the term *phw'* on this and other contemporary seals from Yehud has been debated. The problem is that in the biblical text and other inscriptions and correspondence dating from the Persian era, we encounter the term *phh(')* as a title for various officials, but never *phw'*. So it is unclear if the spellings on the sealings from Yehud are meant to represent this same title or something else. In both cases, the final letter represents the definite article 'the' and is not the final consonant of the title. It appears as though *phw* was meant to be pronounced 'pehu' or 'pahu', while *phh* has been vocalized in the Bible as 'peha'. In each case, the final letter was assumed to be representing a vowel and not a consonant.

Until recently it had commonly been assumed that *phw'* was a variant spelling of *phh'* and that it specifically was used to designate the governor in Yehud (e.g. Avigad 1976: 6-7; Blenkinsopp 1988: 263; Petit 1988). Two other proposals, however, have disassociated *phw'* from *phh'*. Eduard Lipiński has suggested that it designated the official charged with guaranteeing, protecting, and distributing provisions from government stores to those entitled to them (Lipiński 1989). He argued that it was a loanword from Akkadian *pehû*, meaning 'to close up or seal'. While this derivation for the term may be correct, it need not imply that a person was sealing up provisions; it might rather refer to a person who was authorized to apply his seal on behalf of the crown, where the seal was a guarantee of the contents under seal. This could apply to official documents as well as provisions, and so the term could have been used in a more general sense to designate a person in a position of authority who was responsible for decisions.

Frank Cross, on the other hand, has argued that the third letter is to be read as an *R* instead of a *W*, yielding the familiar word *phr*, 'potter' (1969: 24-26). He has suggested that it reflects the practice seen on some imported Greek pottery of having potters sign or mark their work. However, the rarity of such seals in Yehud would require them to have been added sparingly, which would seem to go against the implied desire of potters to mark the work they had done. The pots bearing these seals were ordinary storage jars, and not highly decorated, unusual or unique creations, which might have prompted a special signature. In addition, we have no other indication that potters were so influential in ancient Yehud that their marks would have been required or desired on the pottery they made. More importantly, however, the reading of the third letter as *H* has been specifically upheld in subsequent discussions after a re-examination of the shapes of these two letters in examples dating to the sixth–fifth centuries BCE, so this proposal has not found acceptance.

While many scholars continue to assume that *phw'* is a variant spelling of *phh'*, there is growing recognition that this title should not be limited in meaning to 'governor' (e.g. Blenkinsopp 1988: 173; Naveh 1996: 44-47; Bedford 2001: 90 n. 4). Uses in other Persian-era administrative texts indicate that it was borne by a range of lesser officials as well. In the archive of the Murashu family from Borsippa, for example, it describes an officer in charge of the Simmagir Canal and another in charge of the left side of the Sin Canal (Stolper 1985: 39). In an Elephantine papyrus, the plural form occurs in reference to officers or treasurers responsible for the payment of salaries (Bresciani 1960: 13-14). Thus, this title seems to designate a person who has been appointed to oversee the interests of the government and could be applied to a range of specific assignments; it was not limited to a governor.

In the current situation, it is unlikely that Elnatan, Zerubbabel's son-in-law, would have succeeded him as governor rather than one of his two sons, Meshullam or Hananiah. It makes more sense to assume that once married to the daughter of the governor, he was appointed to some sort of administrative post and that the title *pehu/pehah* was used as it was at Borsippa and Elephantine to designate a lesser government official. While this argument goes against the common view, which understands Elnatan to have succeeded Zerubbabel as governor, most of those who espoused the common view were still also assuming that the title was limited in its meaning to 'governor' (e.g. Avigad 1976: 35; Talmon 1976: 325; Widengren 1977: 510; Stern 1982: 206; Meyers 1985: 34*; Williamson 1988: 74; Lemaire 1990: 35). If writing today, a number of them might alter their views.

Zechariah

According to Neh. 12.12, the prophet Zechariah had become head of the priestly family of Iddo sometime during the time that Yehoiakim had succeeded his father Yeshua as high priest. Thus, by the time that generation 3 had taken over the reigns of leadership in Yehud, both his grandfather Iddo and his father Berekiah had died. This suggests in turn that Iddo had been quite elderly when he had returned to Yehud, with a grown-up son and a grandson who was perhaps already a teenager or a young adult. Zechariah would likely have been at least in his twenties when he prophesied concerning the rebuilding of the temple during the governorship of Zerubbabel and the high priesthood of Yeshua. He would have had to have reached the age of majority for his pronouncements to have been taken seriously. He was from a well-connected, influential priestly family, so that his prophetic call to rebuild the temple would have echoed the interests of the *golah* party leadership.

Meshullam, Son of Berekiah and Brother of Zechariah

According to Neh. 3.30, Berekiah had a second son, Meshullam, who had a chamber within the walls of Jerusalem, not far from the Horse Gate. He almost certainly would have served as a priest, following in the family tradition that traced back to his grandfather Iddo, who had been one of the 22 chief priests of the second temple after it had been inaugurated. His other claim to fame seems to have been that his daughter married the son of Tobiah the Ammonite, both of whom were members of generation 4 (Neh. 6.18).

Shemaiah ben Shekaniah

The son of an influential member of the second generation, Shemaiah was appointed keeper of the East Gate (Neh. 3.29). This job would have been predicated on loyalty to the city officials and a reliable personality. Responsibility for opening and closing an access point to the newly resettled city would not have been entrusted to someone who lacked the ability to think and react quickly or who did not command the respect and cooperation of the city's chief of police. He was put in charge of repairing a segment of the city wall near the Horse Gate (Neh. 3.29). It is not certain that his father was Shekaniah ben Arah; it is possible that he was the son of the chief priest Shekaniah, who might have been a different individual. His patronymic is not given. Nevertheless, it seems likely that these two Shekaniahs are one and the same.

Tobiah the Ammonite

The son-in-law of Shekaniah ben Arah, an influential member of generation 2, Tobiah is logically assigned to generation 3. His wife was the probable sister of Shemaiah, the son of Shekaniah ben Arah. The Tobiads apparently were, or became, a powerful local family centered in the region along the Wadi es-Sir, above the east bank of the Jordan River opposite Jerusalem. In the third and second centuries BCE their family estate was located at 'Iraq el-Amir west of Amman and perhaps also as early as this period, though it is not known how early this land had become their private domain.

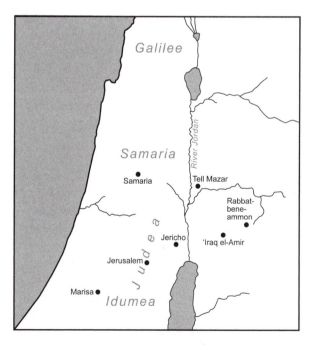

Figure 6.   *Location of 'Iraq el-Amir*

An individual named Tobiah/Toubias lived there under Ptolemy II Philadelphus (285–246 BCE). Zenon papyrus 13, dated to 256 BCE, mentions that Toubias was sending several tamed animals to the king as a gift (Edgar 1919b: 231-32). This same Toubias is named in papyrus 3 as commander of a colony of soldiers of the *birah* in Ammon, revealing him to be a local official (Edgar 1919a: 164-66). However, it is uncertain if this individual was related to the Tobiah who was named as one of Nehemiah's three primary enemies in the 440s–430s BCE, who had a great amount of influence in Jerusalem and Yehud. It has commonly been assumed that the two were members of the same family because both have Ammonite associations, but as will be seen in the ensuing discussion, there may be reasons to question this supposition that lacks tangible proof.

At his first introduction in Neh. 2.10, Tobiah is called 'the servant, the Ammonite' or 'the Ammonite servant'. Either translation is grammatically possible. Thereafter, he is once identified by the gentilic 'the Ammonite' (4.3), but otherwise, is simply referred to by his first name (4.7; 6.1, 12, 14, 17-19). The term 'servant' has a range of connotations and may have been deliberately used here to exploit its ambiguity. On the one hand, it designates a servant and has associations with humility and low social standing; on the other, it can be used to designate a person in a position of great authority, who was an appointed servant of the king and so of high social standing and very influential and powerful due to his office. Thus, while it could have been a legitimate title of Tobiah that would have commanded respect within his official circles, the author of Nehemiah may have intended his Jewish audience to conclude from its use that he was a servile person of no import (so, e.g., McCowan 1957: 72; Mazar 1957: 144; Brockington 1969: 129; Clines 1984: 145; Williamson 1985: 183-84; Blenkinsopp 1988: 218).

It has been suggested further that while Tobiah may have been born in Ammon or may have had an Ammonite mother, he was not Sinuballit's counterpart, or governor of this region, but instead, was a junior official in Samerina under Sinuballit (so, e.g., Rudolph 1949: 109; Widengren 1977: 529; Clines 1984: 145; Williamson 1985: 183). He has even been equated with the Samarian official named Tabeel in Ezra 4.7, on the assumption that Tabeel would have been the Aramaic equivalent of Tobiah, where the god-element El was substituted for that of Yahweh at the end of the name (Kellermann 1967: 168). Thus, some have accepted the genuineness of the label 'Ammonite' but have not understood it to designate the seat of Tobiah's power but rather, his ancestral roots.

The latter two ideas differ in their plausibility. The proposed linking with Tabeel is not convincing. There would have been no need to change the deity element from Yah(weh) to El in a personal name when writing in Aramaic instead of Hebrew; a name was a name. The proposal that Tobiah was an official in Samerina is also not very convincing since nothing in the text suggests his location there. However, the premise that the label 'the Ammonite' does not necessarily indicate his current place of residence or of power bears further consideration.

A final view challenges both Tobiah's status as an Ammonite and the view that he was governor of Ammon. Gösta Ahlström suggests that he would have been a Judean and an employee of the temple, evidenced by his having a special storeroom there, and who was put in charge of Jews living in Ammon. As such, he would have been a subordinate of the governor of Yehud, who gained the allegiance of a number of people in both Jerusalem and Transjordan and became an opposition leader to Nehemiah (1993: 824). This suggestion accounts for the secondary nature of the label 'Ammonite' as a result of Tobiah's role as official liaison to this region. However, it does not adequately explain why the temple or the governor of Yehud would have had the authority to place someone in charge of 'Jewish affairs' outside of the province. The nature of this alleged office needs further articulation in order for this position to be convincing.

All three ring-leaders of the reported outside opposition to Nehemiah's efforts in Yehud are identified by geographical or 'ethnic' gentilics rather than by their official titles of office. This may stem a desire to attach negative associations to them, to downplay their influence in the community by using labels that would have negative connotations to a Jewish audience. It is noteworthy that with the possible exception of 'the Ammonite', none of the gentilics is specifically the name of an adjoining province. Thus, in spite of widely-held scholarly opinion, it does not necessarily appear that the writer has tried to belittle three governors of adjoining regions who may have opposed Nehemiah by referring to them by their seat of influence instead of their official titles.

It has been suggested that this individual's grandfather and namesake may have been the Tobiah mentioned in Zech. 6.9-15 (Mazar 1957: 229; Meyers and Meyers 1987: 341-42). The context suggests that he was a wealthy member of the *golah* community who, along with three other individuals, supplied silver and gold for a crown for 'the Branch', who would rebuild the temple, bear royal honor, and sit and rule upon his throne. According to chronological and genealogical considerations, however, this individual would have belonged to generation 2 or 3, just like Tobiah the Ammonite. Assuming he would have returned with Zerubbabel and Yeshua, he would have been a member of the older generation 2 who could have afforded to contribute towards the cost of the crown. Thus, Mazar's argument needs to be amended: either this Tobiah was a contemporary of Tobiah the Ammonite, or the two were the same individual.

The latter option is intriguing in light of various comments in the book of Nehemiah concerning one or more Tobiahs. The claim is made in Neh. 6.18 that many in Jerusalem were bound by oath to Tobiah who, from the context, is clearly meant to be Tobiah the Ammonite. The exact implications of this bonding are unclear, but at the very least, it shows that Tobiah was a very influential individual. The oaths may have involved financial loans he had made, thereby spreading his influence and power within the community, or it may have had to do with his serving as a patron who was able to use his position of authority to secure governmental jobs for those who voluntarily became his clients (Lemche 1995). In the first case, he could have returned as a very wealthy man and used the bad economic conditions that had prevailed in the early years of the return to his advantage. In the second, he would have had to have held some sort of official post himself that had given him power and influence that could have been used to garner additional favors. His position as governor of the adjoining province of Amman would have fit the bill, but it is unlikely, then, that he would have been a member of the *golah* community that had returned to Yehud under Zerubbabel and Yeshua.

The further claim is made in 13.4-9 that Eliashiv the priest had prepared a chamber in the courts of the temple for Tobiah to use as living quarters, which Nehemiah returned to use as a storeroom. In this case, Tobiah is not called 'the Ammonite' or 'the Ammonite servant', but the statement that Eliashiv was 'connected to' Tobiah in v. 4 certainly implies that the same individual was being envisioned as the one mentioned above in 6.18. The assigning of living quarters within the temple precincts to Tobiah implies that he had some sort of claim to priestly status that entitled him to be resident while on duty.

This circumstance then needs to be put beside the comments in Neh. 7.61-65 concerning those who could not prove their Israelite heritage. Verses 61-62 name three families, including the 'sons of Tobiah', who had returned among those who had been registered as having lived in Telmelah, Telharsha, Keruv, Addon and Immer but who could not prove their affiliation within the traditional lines of Israel (v. 64). This seems to correspond to the earlier summary in 7.6-38 of the lay men who had returned to Yehud but who, in contrast to these three groups, had been able to prove their ancestral links. Verse 63 then details priestly families whose blood-lines could not be traced while vv. 64-65 proceed to explain that those who could not prove their genealogical links to Israel were excluded from the priesthood as unclean. These verses correspond to the second half of the earlier summary in 7.39-60 of cultic personnel who had returned and who, unlike their unfortunate brethren in v. 63, proved their Israelite heritage. Thus, the section in 7.61-65 that details those of dubious heritage is framed in the same way as the list of 'legitimate' members of the *golah* community. Both detail lay families before cultic families. The dubious Tobiads appear to be placed among non-cultic personnel (so, e.g., Rudolph 1949: 24; Myers 1965: 20; Fensham 1982: 55; Blenkinsopp 1988: 92).

It might be possible to argue, however, that vv. 61-65 all apply to cultic personnel and that this summary section does not parallel the structure of the earlier list. There would not have been a pressing reason to single out lay families whose historic affiliation with Yehud was not demonstrable, and on the assumption that vv. 61-62 deal with such families, no consequences are given for their lack of clear status. The reason for singling them out is, therefore, unclear, beyond the obvious desire to indicate that they were not to be considered legitimate members of the children of Israel. By contrast, however, the need to determine priestly 'legitimacy' would have been important since this bore privilege and was an occupation entered into by birthright. Consequences are given for the lack of proof of membership: exclusion from receiving (earning) or consuming priestly portions.

Can we therefore infer that the consequences also apply to the three families listed in v. 62, which include the Tobiads, and that they also were considered cultic personnel of some sort who were excluded from working and food rations? The third group, the sons of Nekodah, is listed among the families of the temple servants in 7.50, which might tend to favor the view that the three families in v. 61 were all nominally cultic rather than lay. The name Nekodah means 'the sheep-raiser' and seems to indicate members of a common profession more than of a kinship group, but they still could have been temple personnel, caring for the temple herds.[6]

The profession of *noqed* is also known from the texts found at Ras Shamra, ancient Ugarit on the coast of Syria, and from Babylonian texts. In all cases, it involves animal husbandry. One law from the Code of Hammurabi indicates that a *naqidu* could be in charge of cattle as well as sheep and goats (LH 261.21-27 in Roth 1995: 129), which is consistent with the claim that the prophet Amos was a *noqed* (Amos 7.14). At Ugarit, the profession is listed in a series of vocational groups that precede classes of cultic functionaries; some have concluded from this situation that the profession was loosely associated with the cult (e.g. Kapelrud 1956: 5-7, 69) or with temple/court service (Hayes 1988: 44; see Yamashita 1975 for a survey of opinions). Others explicitly have denied any cultic connection (e.g. Murtonen 1952; Craigie 1982; Paul 1991: 34). Neo-Babylonian texts have likewise been cited to support a cultic connection (e.g. San Nicolò 1948) but have not won wide support. It seems best to understand the term as designating the profession of animal-breeder, normally of small flocks like sheep and goat but by extension, of cattle as well. The profession was not limited to a temple or court setting, but both of these institutions would have needed to employ the services of *noqedim* to manage the flocks that were paid as taxes-in-kind and which may also have been administered by the temple so as to be able to have a ready supply of animals for the mandatory, daily sacrifices.

A further observation may be germane; two of the three families whose ancestry is claimed to be dubious bear names that relate to Nehemiah's traditional enemies. Delaiah was the name of one of the two sons of Sanballat, governor of Samerina, who was asked c. 410 BCE to become a patron of the temple to Yau in Elephantine and secure permission for its rebuilding after its destruction by the priests of Khnum (Cowley 1923: 108-32). It may be more than coincidental that both the Tobiads and the Sanballids were connected to the Jerusalemite priesthood through marriage (Neh. 12.3; 6.18; 13.28). The possibility needs to be considered that vv. 61-62 reflect attempts to exclude both of these influential families from claiming priestly prerogatives within Yehud (Eskenazi 1992: 584). Whether they were an integral part of the list or were added at a subsequent date to reflect tensions that became more pronounced later in time is unclear, but in either case, the reference to the sons of Tobiah in 7.62 may well able to be linked to the Tobiah who had been given a chamber in the temple in 13.4-9. Having married into the family of an influential priest, Tobiah may have pushed for this privilege to which, strictly speaking, he would not have been entitled by birth. Thus, it may be an oblique reference to the individual called Tobiah the Ammonite (servant) elsewhere in Nehemiah (e.g. Brockington 1969: 129).

Tension still remains, however, in equating all the references to Tobiah in the book of Nehemiah with the Tobiah in Zech. 6.9-15. The claim is made explicitly in the latter work that Tobiah was a member of the *golah* community and so had recently arrived in the region of Yehud with Zerubbabel and Yeshua from a home in Babylonia. The designation of Tobiah as 'the Ammonite (servant)' in Nehemiah, on the other hand, tends to suggest that he had been a member of the non-*golah* community whose family had perhaps fled to Ammon at the fall of Jerusalem in 586 BCE and become established there. As the probable 'servant' or appointee of the Persian king within the province of Ammon, it is unlikely that he would have returned with Zerubbael and Yeshua, unless he were one of the military officers who had been sent back with Zerubbabel (1.9) to command one of the forts that were to be built within Yehud and ended up being reassigned to duty in Ammon and eventually being made the local civil authority in charge there and not merely a military official. Nehemiah 1.10 implies that Tobiah was already a Persian appointee in place at this time, but the situation being depicted in the narrative world may have telescoped certain actual events that had transpired in Yehud during the reign of Artaxerxes I.

The possibility cannot be ruled out that these two individuals were one and the same person, even though it cannot be clearly demonstrated that they were. If one were to posit that the labels 'the Ammonite' and 'the Ammonite, the servant' were added subsequently by a scribe living in the time of the subsequent Tobiah or his son Hyrcanus in an attempt to link this earlier individual with the well-known personage of his day, then the biggest obstacle to the equation of the two individuals would be overcome.

Tobiah 'the Ammonite' in the book of Nehemiah was probably the contemporary age-wise of generation 3, although the possibility remains open that he was much older than his wife and was more a contemporary of generation 2 than of generation 3. He is reported to have been an adversary of Nehemiah, alongside Sanballat the Horonite (Neh. 4.3, 7) and Geshem the Arab

(Neh. 6.1). Many in Yehud were said to have been bound by oath to him because of his status as the son-in-law of Shekaniah ben Arah (6.18). It is unclear how or when he might have received the designation 'the Ammonite (servant)', but the possibility needs to be left open that this epithet had not been used of him during his lifetime.

Sanballat the Horonite/Sinuballit the Harranite

Best known in the book of Nehemiah as an adversary of Nehemiah, he is depicted to have banded together with Tobiah the Ammonite (2.9; 4.1, 7; 6.12, 14) and Geshem the Arab (6.1, 6) along with unspecified Arabs, Ammonites and Ashdodites (4.7) to be an active thorn in the side of Nehemiah during his term as governor.

The name Sanballat is a mis-vocalization within biblical tradition of the Babylonian name Sinuballit, 'Sin [the moon god] gives life'. The specific location of the place reflected in the gentilic 'Horonite' has been disputed. The most common view links it with Bet Horon, a town in the border region between Yehud and Samerina (Josh. 16.3, 5) (so, e.g., Torrey 1928: 387; Rowley 1963: 246; Rudolph 1949: 108). However, other proposals have included the site of Horonaim in Moab (Isa. 15.5; Jer. 48.3) (e.g. Hölscher 1923: 529; Kellermann 1967: 167), the Hauran region east of Galilee (Kraeling 1953: 107 n. 17) and the Syrian site of Harran, a center of the worship of the moon-god Sin (so, e.g., Feigin 1926: 58 n. 2; Galling 1935: 87; Meshorer and Qedar 1999: 27; Lemaire 2001a: 104). Another proposal would see it to be a contemptuous reference to his being a devotee of the god Horon (e.g. Myers 1965: 100). Of these options, an origin in Harran is the most attractive, which was a strong center for the cult of Sin. This individual's name suggests that he originated in an area outside of Samerina and was sent there subsequently as an appointee of the Persian crown.

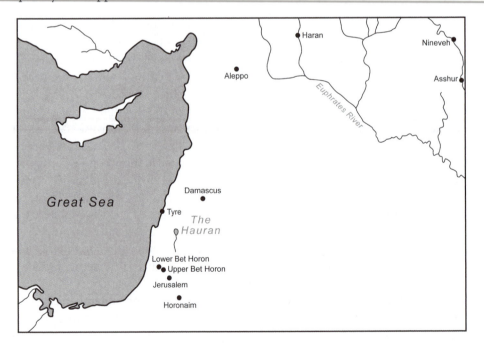

Figure 7.   *Proposed sites of origin for Sanballat/Sinuballit*

The label 'Harranite/Horonite' that is always attached to Sanballat/Sinuballit in the biblical narratives may have been used deliberately as an alternative to 'governor of Samerina', in an attempt to belittle him (e.g. McCowan 1957: 72). Nehemiah 2.9 could be taken to be an indirect reference to his status as governor of Samerina at the time Nehemiah arrived if one assumes that he was among the governors of Across-the-River who would have received a royal letter delivered by the hand of Nehemiah. Even though these details take place in the narrative world and so do not necessarily reflect real events, the situation being depicted seems to assume that in real life, Sinuballit was a person of high official standing. This, in turn, has influenced how he has been depicted in the story. In the narrative world, the royal letters announce Nehemiah's appointment and order the recipients to supply him with the raw materials he needs to fulfil his commission.[7]

I have already noted in connection with Tobiah that the use of a geographical or ethnic label to categorize or characterize all three of Nehemiah's reported enemies seems to stem from a desire to belittle them. In the contexts of the books of Ezra and Nehemiah, these labels could have been a way to imply that all three were 'foreigners' and therefore not eligible for membership in the religious assembly associated with the temple and the worship of Yahweh Elohim. Such a strategy would have been particularly effective in the cases of Sinuballit and Tobiah, since both were likely Yahweh-worshippers. Tobiah's name contains the divine name element *–yah*, as do those of Sinuballit's two sons, Delaiah and Shelemiah. As mentioned in the earlier discussion of Tobiah, the sons of Delaiah and sons of Tobiah who were to be excluded from cultic participation in Neh. 7.62 may well be references to the descendants of Sinuballit and Tobiah.

Elephantine papyrus AP 30, line 29, dated to 408 BCE, states that representatives of the Jewish community at Elephantine had already sent a letter to Delaiah and Shelemiah, sons of Sanballat/Sinuballit, governor of Samaria, *pht smryn*, asking them for help in securing permission for the rebuilding of the temple of Yau in the fortress located on the island of Yeb near Aswan. The letter also indicates that Yohanan was high priest in Jerusalem at this time. Yohanan represents generation 5 of the high priesthood. He is the grandson of Eliashiv and great-grandson of Yehoiakim, the two high priests in office when Nehemiah is rebuilding Jerusalem.

This valuable piece of information allows us to date generation 5 as adults in 408 BCE and also forces us to think carefully about Sinuballit's status at this time. A straightforward reading would suggest that a Sanballat/Sinuballit was still the governor of Samerina in 408 BCE with two grown sons who were thought to have had enough clout with the Persian government to be approached to help with the temple-building instead of the governor himself (so, e.g., Rowley 1963: Williamson 1985: 168). Thus, in 408, this Sanballat/Sinuballit would have been at least in his late fifties and more likely in his sixties. This means that he would have been at least in his late twenties but probably in his thirties when Nehemiah had arrived in Jerusalem as governor in 445 BCE. Such dating dovetails with the biblical claim that Sinuballit was an influential person in Samerina, if not already governor, who was able to oppose Nehemiah during his governorship.

However, it is more likely that Sanballat/Sinuballit was already dead at the time Elephantine letter 30 was written (an option raised by Schwartz 1990: 178). The central issue here is whether the title 'governor of Samerina' is functional, reflecting the actual status of Sanballat/ Sinuballit in 408 BCE, or whether it is honorific, reflecting his status achieved during life, which then accompanied him after death as well. So, for example, it is common to refer to Queen Elizabeth I or President Roosevelt, even though they both are long gone.

It may be significant that neither Shelemiah nor Delaiah are assigned the title *pehah*, meaning 'official' or 'governor', in Elephantine papyrus 30. As Yahweh-worshippers, they are being asked to help sponsor the rebuilding of the temple and as sons of the existing or former governor, have power within the local community and should carry some clout with the Persian administration as members of a local elite. But they hold no specific office in the administration of Samerina according to the letter, unless their status was so well known that it did not need specification.

The chronological implications that can be drawn from the designation of Sanballat/Sinuballit as 'governor of Samerina' in papyrus 30 from Elephantine are ambiguous; he may or may not have been alive in 408 BCE. Nevertheless, had he been alive, he would probably have been at least in his sixties, with grown sons old enough to have had clout with the Persian administration. This means that he would have been at least in his thirties when Nehemiah had held office in Jerusalem. Had he already have been dead in 408 BCE when the letter was written, he could have been in his forties or fifties when Nehemiah had been active in Jerusalem.

Three series of Samarian coins confirm Sinuballit's role as governor of Samaria with the authority to mint money for his province. As of 1999, seven different coins minted under the authority of someone whose name is variously represented as *SN'B*, *SB*[8] and *S* have been found (Meshorer and Qedar 1999: 92-93, #49-56).

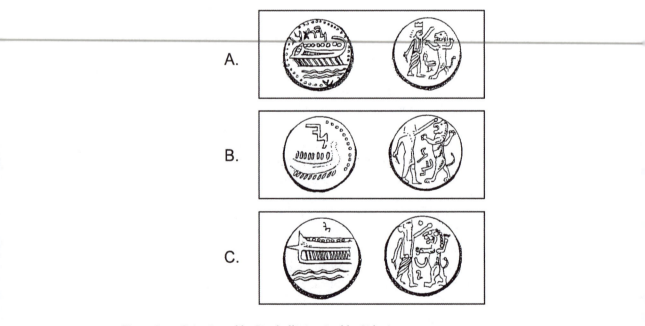

Figure 8.   *Coins issued by Sinuballit inspired by Sidonian prototypes*
             Y. Meshorer and S. Qedar, *Samarian Coinage* (Publications of the Israel Numismatic Society; Numismatic Studies and Researches, 9; Jerusalem: The Israel Numismatic Society, 1999): 93, #55, 56; 120, #201. Reproduced by kind permission of the authors.

One series has imitated common Sidonian coins belonging to series D that were minted in that city by successive rulers beginning at least by 430 BCE. Three examples, all *obol*-weight, are known (Meshorer and Qedar 1999: #55, 56, 201) (Fig. 8A-C). The first represents the name of the minter by *SN'B*,[9] the second by *SB* and the third by *S*. All feature a warship on the front, with shields displayed along the side of the boat and oars extending into the water. The reverse side features the Persian king in his kandys robe on the left, facing a lion standing up on its hind legs. He grasps its head with his left hand and has a dagger in his right hand. In between the two figures are (1) a bird, (2) the letters *S-B* and (3) a crescent, possibly the letter *'ayin*, and an uncertain letter.

The warship with oars above two lines of waves first appeared on Sidonian coins in series D, one example of which was found in the Massayaf hoard dated to 425–420s BCE. In spite of this evidence, J. Elayi prefers to date Series D to c. 400–375 BCE (1990: 212, 217); in my opinion, the dates of series A-D need to be raised higher than her current proposed scheme. The ship over waves, but without oars, had also appeared on the first series of coins minted in Aradus/Arvad in the late-fifth to early-fourth century BCE (Hill 1965: 1-4, pl. 1), and it is likely that the Arwadian image was derived from earlier Sidonian coins, as were the ships found on coins minted in Samerina.

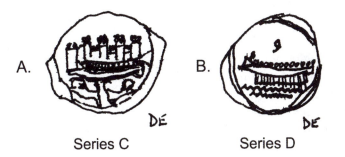

A.   B.

Series C   Series D

Figure 9.   *Series C Sidonian coin and Series D Sidonian coin*
J.W. Betlyon, *The Coinage and Mints of Phoenicia: The Pre-Alexandrine Period* (Harvard Semitic Monographs, 26; Chico, CA: Scholars Press, 1982): pl. 2.1, 4. (Drawn by the author.)

The war galley with oars in the water of series D (Fig. 9A) replaced a warship docked in front of the walls of Sidon in series C (Fig. 9A). Below these two images were two mirror-images of lions, their tails in the middle and their bodies and heads pointing left and right (Betlyon 1982: 6; pl. 1.7, 8). Boats had figured on the front of Sidonian coinage since its inception; a boat with an open, triangular sail had been featured in series A (Fig. 10A), while one with furled sails had appeared on series B (Fig. 10B) (Elayi 1994: 23). The innovative imagery of series C was introduced by Ba'lshillem I, the first king to put his name on Sidonian coins, which he abbreviated *B-SH*.

Series A

Series B

Figure 10.   *Series A Sidonian coin and Series B Sidonian coin*
           J.W. Betlyon, *The Coinage and Mints of Phoenicia: The Pre-Alexandrine Period*
           (Harvard Semitic Monographs 26; Chico, CA: Scholars Press, 1982): pl. 1.1, 4.
           (Drawn by the author.)

The image of the king slaying the lion found on the reverse side of the coin from Samerina first appears on a coin probably minted by 'Abd'eshmun, the likely successor to Ba'lshillem I. Both kings would have ruled at least in the last decades of the fifth century BCE, if not earlier. 'Abd'eshmun continued the imagery of the walls of Sidon, the galley and the two lions introduced by his predecessor on the front of his coins, but introduced this new scene on the back. He replaced the scene of the Persian king shooting a bow that had appeared on smaller denominations (1/2 shekel and 1/16 shekel) already in series A and B (Betlyon 1982: pl. 1.1, 4, 5), although he continued this image as well on at least one issue (Betlyon 1982: pl. 2.3).[10]

It is logical to argue that the series of coins minted by Sinuballit under discussion were copied from a prototype issued by 'Abd'eshmun, unless a future coin appears that shows that the imagery from both sides already was introduced by Ba'lshillem I in series C or one of his predecessors, appearing in Series A or B. No 1/6 shekel coins are yet known from Ba'lshillem I. Alternatively, one could argue that the prototype was the 1/16 shekel coin minted by B (Ba'ana? Ba'lshillem II?), a third king who would have ruled near the end of the fifth century. He appears to have been the first Sidonian king to feature the galley with oars on its own on the front of his coins (Hill 1965: pl. XVVIII.12-14; Betlyon 1982: pl. 2.6) and also used the image of the king slaying the lion on the reverse (Betlyon 1982: pl. 2.6).[11]

Sinuballit would have been the first to introduce the Sidonian imagery of the trireme with oars on coins minted in Samerina and was probably the first person authorized to mint coins for his province. Had he used the coinage of 'Abd'eshmun for inspiration, however, his engraver would have chosen not to include the city walls of Sidon or the two lions in this particular series, but to focus solely on the boat.

The boat imagery was copied by two successive local governors. The name of one is abbreviated *D-L* (#22) (Fig. 11A). The other appears to have been named *BDYH* (#7) (Fig. 11B), who also probably abbreviated his name *B* (#131, 195, 196, 199).[12] It should not be assumed that these two individuals would have been the immediate successors of Sinuballit. A review of the known Samarian coins shows a rich variety of imagery, implying that governors often preferred to innovate rather than maintain a standard, recognizable coin type, even though they did return to older images from time to time.

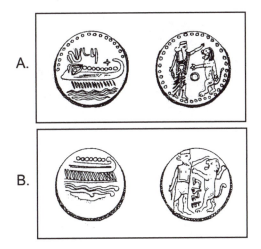

Figure 11. *Other Sidonian-inspired coins minted in Samaria*
Y. Meshorer and S. Qedar, *Samarian Coinage* (Publications of the Israel Numismatic Society; Numismatic Studies and Researches, 9; Jerusalem: The Israel Numismatic Society, 1999): 84, #7; 87, #22. Reproduced by kind permission of the authors.

The satrap Mazday minted money under his own name for Samerina sometime subsequent to 345 BCE, after he had suppressed the rebellion of King Tennes of Sidon and had been made satrap of Across-the-River in addition to satrap of Cilicia (*Diodorus Siculus* 16.40-46; Barag 1966: 7-8).[13] He, too, chose to reuse this same image of a Sidonian ship that had been in place for decades (#96). In his case, however, it carried a double meaning: it commemorated his victory over Sidon in addition also to being an existing type in circulation in Samerina. Leo Mildenberg has noted from a study of Mazday's coins that he had a tendency to adopt existing coin types initially when he issued new local coins under his authority in Across-the-River (1990/91: 10-15).

Mazday went on to introduce some new types as well that drew on imagery typical of coins of Tarsus, particularly the seated deity Baaltars (#100) and the deity Ahura Mazda (#84, 100). These may have been copied subsequently by later governors (#13, 14, 37, 40, 98, 123; #124), as were also his trademark lion vanquishing a stag (#19, 77, 99, 103), lion attacking a bull (#146, 147, 204), and striding (lion) (#19, 101) (Mildenberg 1990/91: 11, 16; see Meshorer and Qedar 1999 for coins).

The other two coin series thought to have been minted under the authority of Sinuballit contain a variety of imagery, much of it borrowed from existing Sidonian and Athenian coins in circulation.

A second series that contains issues in the drachm and obol denominations features on their front sides the head of the Persian king, wearing a crown and sporting a beard. The reverse side of the larger, drachm-weight coin (Fig. 12A) features a (winged?) lion rearing up on its hind legs, facing right, with its right paw suppressing a Bes figure. The abbreviation *SB* appears above the wing, which might rather be an ear of wheat or leafy branch. The scene is framed by a square border of dots (Meshorer and Qedar 1999: 93, #51).

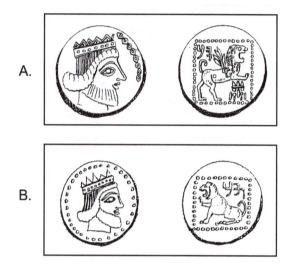

Figure 12.   *Persian-inspired coins of Sinuballit*
Y. Meshorer and S. Qedar, *Samaritan Coinage* (Publications of the Israel Numismatic Society; Numismatic Studies and Researches, 9; Jerusalem: The Israel Numismatic Society, 1999): 93, #51 and 52. Copyright permission granted.

An almost identical version of this scene appears on a coin of unknown provenience from the western Levant (Babelon 1910b: pl. CXXIII.23) (Fig. 13). The difference is that the lion is seated, the Bes face under the front right paw is drawn differently, and there is no writing. The front side of this latter coin has the helmeted head of Athena.

Figure 13.   *Coin featuring a winged lion with its paw over a satyr's face*
E. Babelon, *Traité des monnaies grecques et romaines . Troisième partie, album des planches. Planches LXXXVI à CLXXXV* (Paris: Ernest Leroux, 1910): pl. CXXIII. 23. (Drawn by the author.)

The reverse side of the small obol-weight coin (Fig. 12B) features a seated lion facing left and the abbreviation *SB* inside a square border composed of dots (Meshorer and Qedar 1999: #52). The image of the lion is very similar to the one on the coin of unknown provenience just described, except that it faces the opposite direction and has no image of Bes under the raised paw. It also resembles some of the depictions of lions on a series of animal stamps used to impress jar handles in Yehud in the early Persian period (see Chapter 4 for details). These impressions probably predate 450 BCE.

The portrait of the king's head, on the other hand, resembles one known from a rare 1/12 of the golden daric (Dressel 1904: 87-89, pl. IV.5; Babelon 1910a: 47-48) (Fig. 14). Although E. Babelon assigned it to Artaxerxes I, there is no way to confirm the date; there are no markings on it to support such an attribution. These small denominations of the darics are so little known that they cannot be tied in with the typological development of the daric series (Carradice 1987). It is uncertain whether these fractional issues were made from the start of minting under Darius I or were only subsequently introduced under a later king (Dressel 1904: 89). Nevertheless, in principle, it would be possible for this prototype to have existed prior to, or during the reign of, Artaxerxes I.

Figure 14. *Golden quarter daric*
E. Babelon, *Traité des monnaies grecques et romaines. Deuxième partie, description historique. Tome deuxième* (Paris: Ernest Leroux, 1910): 48, #6. (Drawn by the author.)

The image of the Persian king's head in profile was used by Mazday on his coins minted in Tarsus (Babelon 1910b: pl. CXIV.8-10) and possibly also on coins from Sidon (Babelon 1910b: pl. CXX.4, 5; CXXI.20, 21). In the latter case, however, the crown is not the standard Persian one with four or five points, but a local one, so it is possible that these coins feature a portrait of the Sidonian king instead, or have depicted the Persian king wearing the native crown. Neither the Cilician nor the Sidonian portraits appear to be a possible prototype for the one on the coin in question. It appears instead that Mazday, the Phoenician king responsible for using this image, and Sinuballit all drew independently from smaller denominations of the golden daric or possibly from similar imagery on smaller denominations of the silver siglum (shekel) and that there were multiple forms of the portrait on these coins. Ours has a closely trimmed beard; the others have a full beard.

The third series is represented by an obol and hemi-obol coin only. The front sides of both feature a head of a satyr. On the obol coin (Fig. 15A), the letter *S* appears on the right side of the face and the letter *B* on the left. The reverse of the obol coin, two lions facing forward stand above two sets of waves. The reverse of the hemi-obol coin (Fig. 15B), on the other hand, sports a single lion facing forward, with the Greek letters *A*, *TH*, and *E*, standing for Athens, written along the left of the body and the letter *S* written on the right side, with an olive sprig above (Meshorer and Qedar 1999: #54, 55).

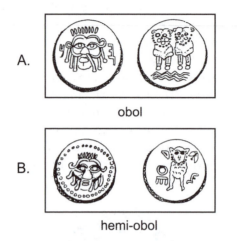

obol

hemi-obol

Figure 15. *Coins of Sinuballit featuring a satyr's face and lions over waves*
    Y. Meshorer and S. Qedar, *Samarian Coinage* (Publications of the Israel Numis-
    matic Society; Numismatic Studies and Researches, 9; Jerusalem: The Israel Numis-
    matic Society, 1999): 93, #53 and 54. Reproduced by kind permission of the authors.

The obol coin is based on imagery drawn from two sets of Sidonian coins. The full face of the satyr is copied from an early coin belonging to Series B (Fig. 16). On the front is a ship with furled sails and on the reverse is the full-faced satyr (Betlyon 1982: pl. 1.6).

Figure 16. *Series B Sidonian coin with a satyr's face*
    J.W. Betlyon, *The Coinage and Mints of Phoenicia: The Pre-Alexandrine Period*
    (Harvard Semitic Monographs, 26; Chico, CA: Scholars Press, 1980): pl. 1.6.
    (Drawn by the author.)

This coin dates at least from 440–430 BCE, but probably earlier. The image of the two lions above the waves, on the other hand, is likely to be an adaptation of the imagery first introduced by Ba'lshillem I, already described above. The creator of the image on the coin of Samerina has eliminated the city wall and war galley but has made the two lions the main feature. They stand side by side instead of being mirrored in profile. The carver decided to add waves under them that were typical of Sidonian coins, even though the coin that he adapted did not display them.

The designer of the hemi-obol coin has combined the early Sidonian satyr with standard Athenian imagery. He has merely substituted the lion for the owl. The standard Athenian imagery he copied had appeared on coins in circulation already by the mid-fifth century.

Yaakov Meshorer and Shraga Qedar have proposed that Sinuballit issued a fourth series of coins, but this is questionable. It includes two coins of drachm and obol weight that feature on the back sides in both cases opposing figures in profile (Meshorer and Qedar 1999: #49, 50).

Figure 17. *Coins assigned to Sinuballit featuring opposing figures*
Y. Meshorer and S. Qedar, *Samarian Coinage* (Publications of the Israel Numismatic Society; Numismatic Studies and Researches, 9; Jerusalem: The Israel Numismatic Society, 1999): 92, #49 and 50. Reproduced by kind permission of the authors.

On the reverse side of the drachm coin (Fig. 17A), a Bes-head appears on the shield of the soldier on the right. The style of shield is Boetian. On the reverse of the obol coin (Fig. 17B), on the other hand, the shield held by the figure on the right is round, with a round boss in the center. While the obverse side of the smaller coin features two soldiers with round shields standing side by side, the front side of their entire bodies depicted, the reverse has a figure of authority facing right, as in the drachm coin, and a soldier opposite him, facing left.

André Lemaire has suggested that the entire scene on the back sides might have been copied from a coin minted in Tarsus (Lemaire 1989: 149 n. 78; pl. 2.14; Babelon 1910b: pl. CVI, 6-7). There are two denominations of this coin. On both (Figs. 18A and B), the reverse sides feature two male figures facing one another. Both are bearded and dressed in Persian robes. Each has his hands on his javelin, which is held upright in front of him. They have bows and quivers on their backs (Babelon 1910a: 361-62, #526, 527). On the larger denominational coin, the letter *T* appears before the person on the right, and the place name *TRZ* (Tarsus) is written between the two javelin shafts in the center of the image (not included in the drawing).

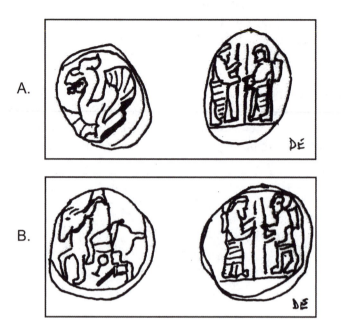

Figure 18.   *Cicilian coins from Tarsus*
          E. Babelon, *Traité des monnaies grecques et romaines. Troisième partie, album des*
          planches. Planches LXXXVI à CLXXXV (Paris: Ernest Leroux, 1910): pl. CVI.6-7.
          (Drawn by the author.)

While it is the case that the layout is similar between these coins from Tarsus and the two under discussion, the imagery is different. On the badly-worn Tarsus drachm, neither figure has a bow or quiver; the figure on the left, in relief, holds only a javelin, although it is possible that there is a hint of a quiver; the figure on the right, cut in negative, holds a Boetian or Theban-style shield with the head of Bes in his left hand and a javelin in his right. The shield is in relief, though the body of the person holding it is concave. While the scenes on both sets of coins might portray the commissioning of the figure on the right or his investment with power by the figure on the left, the coins from Tarsus seem to portray the king commissioning the satrap, while the Cicilian ones seem to portray the satrap commissioning a soldier/ mercenary. The scene on the front of the Tarsus coins depicts a sword fight between two individuals while those from Cilicia sport a griffin and a mounted horseman.

Another example of this same coin, of uncertain provenience, is known, though it lacks any writing on the front (Babelon 1910b: pl. CXXIII.1) (Fig. 19). It is unclear if the head of Bes appears on the Boetian shield in this version; the image is too small to decide. Ernest Babelon has noted that the technique used on the reverse side of drachm coin under discussion and the second example of the same coin, with the left half in relief and the right half in negative outline, was used on the oldest coins of Sidon (1910a: 629-30, #1018). This might provide some indication of date parameters.

Figure 19. *Coin of unknown origin featuring opposing figures*
E. Babelon, *Traité des monnaies grecques et romaines. Troisième partie, album des planches. Planches LXXXVI à CLXXXV* (Paris: Ernest Leroux, 1910): pl. CXIII.1. (Drawn by the author.)

Figure 20. *Coin from Tarsus with a single royal figure in profile*
E. Babelon, *Traité des monnaies grecques et romaines. Troisième partie, album des planches. Planches LXXXVI à CLXXXV* (Paris: Ernest Leroux, 1910): pl. CVI.8. (Drawn by the author.)

If the two coins under discussion are related in some way to the coins from Tarsus, it is unclear to me which way the dependency has gone; the ones with the soldiers/mercenaries could have been earlier than those with the king and satrap, which were adapted from the former. There is another series of coins whose imagery is closely tied to that on the reverse side of these coins. It features a single royal, crowned figure in profile, wearing a quiver, facing right. He holds a javelin in his right hand and a circlet on a short pole that sits on a horizontal bar or base (Babelon 1910b: pl. CVI.8).[14] Below the left hand, running along the outside edge of the spear is the legend TERSI in Greek letters, while the legend *TRZ* appears in Aramaic letters behind the back of the figure (not included in the drawing). The commissioning scene could easily have been inspired by this image, although the presence of Greek and Aramaic legends might suggest a date in the early Greek period, in which case this third coin would be later than the other two.

More crucially, it is uncertain whether the two letters on the front of the drachm coin read *S-N*, as proposed by Y. Meshorer and S. Qedar (1999: 92). The second letter is almost certainly a *B* or an *R*, not an *N*, and the first letter is not readily recognizable as any standard letter, but might conceivably be a *P* (*peh*). It is not clear if the letter has a very long tail or if it ends on the same base-line as the second letter. Thus, it is quite possible that this series has nothing to do with Sinuballit at all and it seems appropriate, under the circumstances, not to assign it to this governor until more evidence can confirm such an attribution. If the first letter on the drachm coin is *P*, then both it and its corresponding obol with no writing might have been issued by the satrap Pharnabazus in either 385–383 and again in 378/7-374/3 BCE in order to finance military expeditions. In this case, the home mint may have been Tarsus; there is no indication that these coins were minted in Samerina; the abbreviation *SH* does not appear on either one.

The assumption that coins were not minted in Samerina until about 375 BCE has no firm foundation (e.g Meshorer and Qedar 1999: 14-15). It is based on a consideration of styles of writing, which are poor indicators of dates since they tend to change slowly. Elephantine papyrus 30 indicates that Sinuballit must have been governor perhaps as late as the 410s. The Sidonian prototypes from which coins bearing his abbreviated name were copied were already in circulation during his governorship, and the relative chronology that we have for Ba'lshillem I and 'Abd'eshmun requires them to have lived and ruled at least in the second half of the fifth century BCE, but one of them probably already in the first half (Peckham 1968: 78-87; Dunand 1975-1976; Betlyon 1982: 6-11; Coacci Polselli 1984; Elayi 1990: 235-54). Sidon was a center of ship-building for the Persian navy from the time of Cambyses (Davison 1947; Wallinga 1987: 47, 54);[15] it appears that the trireme was introduced c. 530 BCE at the time of Cyrus' death and Cambyses' assumption of the throne (Wallinga 1987: 67; 1993: 103-104). Phoenicia also appears to have supplied rowers for the completed ships (*Herod* 3.19.3). The latter had to be paid regularly, which is thought to have been an influencing factor in the development of coinage (Wallinga 1987: 71). Thus, it seems likely that coinage was already introduced in Sidon by the end of the sixth century, allowing the placement of the three kings Ba'lshillem I, 'Abd'eshmun and Ba'ana/Ba'lshillem II probably in the last seventy-five years of the fifth century, not just the last half.[16]

None of the coins attributed to Sinuballit was found in a coin hoard, where the surrounding coins can provide some indication of date parameters for the lesser-known pieces found within them. Thus, their relative date cannot be established in this way. However, even in the case of hoards, it should not be assumed that all the coins date from about the same time. With larger denominations, there can be an heirloom factor in place, where the family wealth was invested in coins that were simply passed on from generation to generation if the money was not needed for an emergency. But this strategy could also have applied to smaller denominations as well, where the coins, once in the household, were stashed away for a rainy day and so taken out of circulation and handed down within the family.

A hoard of coins from Susa contains Sidonian coins that date from the end of the fifth century, Arvadian coins that predate 340/339 BCE, and coins of Alexander III, which means a date prior to 311 BCE (Elayi and Elayi 1993: 276). It thus spans a time period of a century, or about three generations. A similar situation could apply to hoards that contain primarily local coins as well if, as suggested above, the purpose of the hoard was an investment of family wealth, literally in hard cash, which was passed on over generations. As J. and A.G. Elayi note, however, some hoards might have been amassed by smiths with the intention of melting down defective and well-worn coins to recast new money and in such a case, it is likely that some of the coins would be older mints that had been in circulation a long time (1993: 231). So hoards can be collected for different purposes. Even if in the future some coins of Sinuballit are found in hoards, their date will need to be assessed carefully, bearing in mind these caveats.

A final reference to Sinuballit is found on Wadi ed-Daliyeh bulla 22, which was attached to the barely preserved papyrus 16 found in cave 3 (Gropp 2001: pl. XVII; called papyrus 5 in Cross 1974: pl. 61). This is only one of two bullae that were made with a seal bearing a personal name in the entire collection; the others are all impressions made from seals that bear images (Leith 1997: 21). The letters are paleo-Hebrew and the inscription reads *[...]yhw bn [...]blt pht smr[.]*.

Figure 21. *Bulla 22 from Wadi ed-Daliyeh*
P.W. Lapp and N.L. Lapp (eds.), *Discoveries in the Wâdi ed-Dâliyeh* (Annual of the American Schools of Oriental Reseach, 41; Cambridge, MA: ASOR, 1974): pl. 61. (Drawn by the author.)

The bulla is small and incomplete. A single photograph was taken when it was still attached to the papyrus soon after discovery and it gives the impression that some 'tails' of downstrokes of initial letters were preserved below a divot in the clay. After a personal inspection of the bulla at the Israel Museum in June, 2004 however, using a 10× magnifier, it is clear that there are no such tails.[17] Even more of the left top part of the bulla appears to have been broken off when it was removed from the papyrus. There is space for, at most, three letters before –*yhw*, and all of them would have had to have forms that normally were written above the base line, without long 'tails'. The fracture above which the right corner of the bulla is missing runs about halfway up the letter *Y (yod)*, so if any of the first three letters had been written with a long downstroke, there would have been visible traces present below the fracture, reaching the baseline. The ridge of the edge of the facture is irregular; there is one possible raised area on its edge that could belong the very bottom of the letter *L (lamed)* or *' ('ayin)*. This would have been the letter immediately preceding the *Y (yod)*.

In light of this fresh examination, F.M. Cross' initial proposed reading of *[lhnn]yhw*, 'belonging to Hananiah', can be eliminated as a possible reconstruction (1963: 111; adopted by, e.g., Mowinckel 1964b: 126; Ahlström 1993: 899). Only three letters can be restored, not four, and there is no evidence of the bottom portions of the downstrokes of the two *N* letters (*nuns*). It also rests on an unsupported, conjectural reading of 'Hanan the prefect' after '[...] a son of Sinuballit' in papyrus 11 and the further assumption that this Sinuballit was governor and that both individuals mentioned were his sons. See the discussion in the text below.

Frank Cross subsequently suggested that the bullae should be reconstructed instead as *[lys']yhw*, 'belonging to Yeshayahu'; this personal name appears by itself on the only other bulla in the collection of papyri that contains writing and not simply imagery (1974: 18 n. 10). This proposal, too, can be eliminated as a possible reconstruction since it requires four letters. The letter *Y (yod)* would normally have been visible had it been the second of four missing letters, although there are examples where *yod* has been written as though a raised letter, well above the baseline, especially when it has occurred in a grouping of raised letters, as it would here (Avigad and Sass 1997: #70, 71, 93, 119, 130). Thus, it would be possible to restore *ysh'yhw*, without the initial *L (lamed)*, as the original reading. Such a situation would go against the prevailing use of this letter on seals before the personal name to indicate ownership, however, which Cross recognizes, since his proposed restoration includes the initial *L*. Thus, it is unlikely that the name should be restored as Yesha'yahu.

What is the most likely name? The first letter almost certainly was *L (lamed)*, meaning 'belonging to'. The third letter was either another *L (lamed)*, or ' *('ayin)*. We are left to fill in the middle letter, which would have been the first letter of the personal name. Bearing in mind our need for a letter that could be written above the baseline, there are two options that yield attested Hebrew names: ' *('ayin)* and *D (dalet)*.[18] The name *'lyhw* has appeared in onomastic materials and would be possible to read here (Zadok 1988). But the name *dlyhw* is known from Elephantine Papyrus 30 as the name of one of Sinuballit's two sons: Delaiah, and so is the most plausible reading.

To read the name as Delaiah, we would need to posit that the letter *D (dalet)* was written with a short tail, which was one of its two forms in paleo-Hebrew. There are numerous examples of a raised *dalet* with a short tail on existing Hebrew seals and bullae, however, which demonstrate that this reading would be consistent with ancient practice (Avigad and Sass 1997: #8, 23, 33, 34, 40, 59, 239, 279, 288, 411, 692). In addition, there are a number of examples where the raised *dalet* with short tail was used when it occurred next to one or more letters that normally was written above the baseline (Avigad and Sass 1997: #29, 30, 39, 130, 286, 294, 323, 421). In the present case, it would appear between two *lameds* and so might easily have been written with the short tail to fit neatly on an imaginary upper baseline. In light of our current knowledge, it is most plausible to restore the name on Wadi Daliyeh bullae 22 as Delaiah (*[l]dlyhw*). He appears to have been the elder of Sinuballit's two sons, since he responded eventually to the petition of the Elephantine community, not his brother Shelemiah.

Papyrus 16, to which bulla 22 was attached, might be one of the oldest in the collection found in the cave, probably dating somewhere between 420–380 BCE when Delaiah is likely to have been an adult. Unfortunately, it is heavily worm-eaten, so only a few words in a narrow band running down the middle of the document remain, giving almost no clues as to its contents. Only three of the published documents found in the caves preserve legible dates (#1, 2, and 7), which range from 375–335 BCE in modern terms, so it is appears that the documents cover a time span of about ninety years or three generations.[19]

In support of his theory of papponymy, F.M. Cross Jr has seen the appearance of a son of Sinuballit whose name he read as [Yesh?]u'a as a witness on papyrus 11 from Daliyeh cave 3 to support the existence of a second governor named Sinuballit (1974: 18 n. 10; 21, commenting on papyrus 14; for the papyrus, see Gropp 2001: pl. XI). This name cannot be restored as Delaiah or as Shelemiah, the two known sons of Sinuballit the Harranite.

First, an examination of the published photograph of this papyrus allows for the last letters to be read [...]s'a, [...]p'a or [...]r'a with as much probability as [...]u'a (J. Dusek, oral communication). Cross' proposal to restore the name as Yeshu'a because this was the name that was found on the only other paleo-Hebrew bulla is so speculative it should not be taken seriously, and yet it has been adopted by a number of others (e.g. Tuland 1966: 177; Davies 1991: 381, 449; Leith 1997: 10; Avigad and Sass 1997: 176, #419; Briant 2002: 714).[20]

Great caution must be taken in deducing anything from this heavily damaged text. It could be that Sinuballit, governor of Samerina, had fathered more than two sons and that this one was a minor at the time of the composition of Elephantine papyrus *AP* 30 c. 410 BCE and so had not been named in that context. On the other hand, it is equally possible that the Sinuballit who was the father of the witness was unrelated to the governor but had been given his name by a parent who had admired the historic Sinuballit or who simply liked the sound of the name.[21] The text does not go on to state that the person in question was governor of Samerina, as we seem to find otherwise on bulla #22, where the name of the son is likely to be restored as Delaiah. Instead, in papyrus 11 two more names of witnesses immediately follow the son of Sinuballit: Hanan, and another, whose name seems to contain four letters and ends with *N'*, but otherwise, is illegible (J. Dusek, confirmed after inspecting the original papyrus; email communication). The affixed seals of the witnesses or parties to the transactions all bore imagery, which by Cross' own arguments, would make them ordinary citizens, not governors or prefects (1974: 18 n. 10).

Frank Cross' suggested reading of 'Hanan, *signa*' ('the prefect') immediately after the name of Yeshu'a son of Sanballat (1974: 18 n. 10; 21) is not supported by my examination of the photograph of the manuscript (Gropp 2001: pl. XI). The first letter of the new word after *hnn* looks like a *W* (*waw*), which means 'and' and so is introducing the name of a second witness. The second letter looks like an *'* (*aleph*), whose diagonal top stroke has overlapped with the top of the *waw*. In addition, it seems unlikely that the prefect would have been listed as the final witness; one would have expected distinguished witnesses to have been placed first, in order of their relative ranking.[22] After these last two names there is a third illegible word before a new section begins that, on the basis of standard practices for formatting such legal documents, seems to give the date, though nothing can be made out, followed by the place of writing. Part of this section is legible as 'in Samaria it is written' (Cross 1974: 19, confirmed by J. Dusek). In this light, it seems likely that the Sinuballit in question was not governor Sinuballit, but a namesake who may or may not have had any family connection.[23]

Geshem the Arab
The third named adversary of Nehemiah alongside Sinuballit and Tobiah, this individual has been identified with the Geshems found in two inscriptions. A silver bowl found in the Egyptian Delta at the site of Tell-el-Mashkuta bears the inscription, 'that which Qainu, son of Geshem, king of Qedar, brought near [as an offering] to [the goddess] Han-'Ilat'. Stylistically, the bowl is a type that appears in metal and glass from the Assyrian period onward (Dumbrell 1971: 37 n. 11), so a more specific date is hard to assign. However, it was found alongside a number of other bowls, three more of which bore dedicatory inscriptions in Aramaic, and a hoard of Athenian tetradrachm coins. The other bowls can be shown to have parallels in the Persian period, as can the bowl under discussion, even though all four forms have a longer time

span (Dumbrell 1971: 34-38). The coins seem to have been deposited during the fourth century BCE, before the rise of Alexander the Great (Dumbrell 1971: 33 n. 2). The latest minted coins date from 400–375 BCE, and it seems likely that they had also been votive gifts, chosen because on one side they bore the head of Athena, who had been equated with the deity Han-'Ilat (Rabinowitz 1956: 4).

The shapes of the letters contained in the inscription are not able to pinpoint the date of the bowl any more accurately since handwriting styles change slowly. The letters are in 'official Persian Chancellery hand' or 'conservative cursive', a style that tended to resist popular traits that began in other Aramaic cursive styles in the fifth century BCE and took hold rapidly during the fourth century BCE (Rabinowitz 1956: 6 n. 41; Dumbrell 1971: 38). Thus, the letters reflect a style of writing that was deliberately kept unchanged over time, making it very difficult to assign a date of composition. The coin hoard provides the strongest evidence for dating, although it is not known how many years before or after their deposition Qainu would have dedicated his bowl. Thus, it is possible that Qainu's father was the same person who is referred to in the book of Nehemiah as 'Geshem the Arab', but a firm identification of the two is beyond the scope of the current evidence.

Qedar was known in Persian-era biblical texts for being a region or tribe of consummate sheep-breeders (Isa. 60.7), a role that they had played already under the Neo-Babylonians. According to Ezek. 27.21, the princes of Qedar were trading sheep to Tyre. Thus, their leaders most likely profited well from extensive sheep-trading with both the Phoenicians and eventually, the Egyptians. Isaac Rabinowitz, however, has suggested that the north Arab allies, whom Darius I claims on the remains of a fragmentary stele found at Maskhuta to have garrisoned at that site to guard the frontier and police the canal zone, were Qedarites (1956: 9). In his view, the shrine had been established to serve their religious needs, so that the dedications were not made by traders but rather, by soldiers. Traders would have visited the fortress, however, to sell familiar wares to the mercenaries serving there, so it is hard to know what the status of the gift-givers was.

A second inscription, JS 349, has been thought to refer to the same individual. It was found at the edge of the oasis of al-'Ula in the territory of ancient Dedan in the northwest Arabian peninsula. It reads, 'Nuran the son of Hadiru inscribed his name in the days of Gashmu the son of Shahar and 'Abdu, the governor of Dedan...' (Winnett and Reed 1970: 115). The wording suggests that Nuran was under the immediate political authority of a leader named Geshem son of Shahar, but that Geshem was in turn under the authority of a man named Abdu, who was the officially appointed *pehah* of Dedan. However, in light of the use of the title Abdu/Ebed, 'Servant/slave' to describe a high-ranking political appointee, it would be worth considering whether Nuran intended the final phrase to list two official titles of Geshem or his father Shahar: the more local title, 'servant', and its official equivalent in the Persian administration, *fht/pehah* ('governor' or a lesser official). The 'and' before 'servant' would have functioned like a comma in English, to introduce the phrase that was placed in apposition. In this case, then, the inscription would indicate that either Geshem or his father Shahar had been the duly appointed Persian official in charge of Dedan when Nuran had carved the inscription.

Figure 22. *Ancient Arabia*

The style of script has been identified as early Lihyanite, but the date is unclear: somewhere between 450 BCE–100 BCE (Caskel 1954: 101-102; Winnett and Reed 1970: 116; Graf 1992: 122). The earlier date has certainly been influenced by the assumption that this Geshem is Geshem the Arab named in Nehemiah; the later one by Caskel has been deemed idiosyncratic, with a date in the fourth century BCE considered more likely (e.g. Eph'al 1982: 181 n. 612; 204 n. 693).

The name Geshem occurs in three Safaitic inscriptions as well, where it is used in dating formulae: twice it appears in the phrase, 'in the year of Geshem and Hann'il' and once in the phrase 'in the year of Geshem'. These uses of an individual to identify a particular year reflect the Assyrian system of dating by eponyms (for a discussion, see Chapter 2). JS 349 may do the same, even though the expression used there is not 'year' specifically but 'days'. Nevertheless, the two might be synonymous if the Assyrian custom had been adopted and used over time, even into the Persian and Hellenistic periods. Otherwise, if one assumes that these tribes would have adopted the dating formulae in vogue at the ruling imperial court, then these inscriptions would need to be dated to the Assyrian period. It can also be noted that the term *fht/phh* appears to have been used in the region throughout the Neo-Babylonian period and so was not unique to the Achaemenid administration (Graf 1992: 123, contra Winnett and Reed 1970: 116). A date prior to the Persian period is possible for the Lihyanite and Safaite inscriptions that contain the name Geshem if one is willing to allow the existence of these tribal groups among the Arabs who are mentioned in the Assyrian or Neo-Babylonian records (for details, see Dumbrell 1971; Eph'al 1982: 21-59, 181).

Militating against an equation of the biblical Geshem with either his Qedarite or Lihyanite namesake are dialectical spelling practices. Nehemiah 6.6 spells Geshem's name with a final *U* or *vav*, suggesting the actual pronunciation was something like Gashmu. The occurrence of final *U* in Arabic names is common in Nabatean inscriptions, less so in Palmyrene inscriptions, and extremely rare in South Arabic, Dedanite and Lihyanite inscriptions (Eph'al 1982: 211). Thus, it appears that he was not Dedanite or Lihyanite, and the spelling on the Maskhuta bowl lacks the final *U* as well, suggesting he was not Qedarite either. However, in the majority of instances his name is spelled without the final *U* and if these are taken as more accurate, then he could have been Qedarite, Dedanite or Lihyanite. Perhaps the final *U* was added inadvertently by a copyist in the one instance because he was more familiar with this form of the name from Nabateans active in his day.

Another occurrence of the name Geshem is in tomb inscription 177 from catacomb 15 at Bet She'arim (Vattioni 1973). The person buried there bore the name, Lazarus son of Gosam. Gosam is likely a variant vocalization of the name Geshem. This individual probably lived in the third century CE and so has nothing to do with the individual under consideration but the inscription testifies to the ongoing use of the name among individuals, probably of Arab origin or descent, centuries after the time of Nehemiah.

In the end, nothing definitive can be said about Geshem the Arab. The name was not rare among Arab tribes; the five inscriptions in Arabic languages discussed above, when set beside the references in Nehemiah, may show that it was borne by at least four individuals of high social and political standing: one a king of Qedar, one a governor(?) of Dedan, one an important official used in dating schemes, and one who was an influential person in the time of Nehemiah. The one inscription in Greek shows the ongoing use of the name.

The common assumption that Geshem was governor of Arabia, whose domains included southern Judah, southern Jordan, Edom, north Arabia, Sinai, and some portions of Egypt lacks corroboration (so, e.g., Wright 1962: 206-207). Since he cannot be definitively equated with the individual named in the al-'Ula inscription, his seat of power cannot be said to have been centered in this oasis site (contra e.g. Eph'al). The suggestion that he may have established a residence at Lakish is equally speculative (Wright 1962: 206-207). Wherever he might have been based, it is logical to conclude that, if he were a contemporary of Nehemiah as the text claims, disputes between the two could have arisen over control of the trade routes that passed through the Beersheva Valley (Eph'al 1982: 212) (For a fuller discussion, see Chapter 4). The possibility also needs to be kept open that Geshem's name has been added secondarily to the list of adversaries in the book in light of subsequent conflicts with Arabs in the later Persian or Hellenistic periods.

The use of the gentilic 'Arab' to characterize Geshem rather than a more geographically specific word like 'Qedarite' or 'Dedanite' or a political title like 'king' or 'servant' or 'governor' seems to be consistent with the writer's desire to downplay the importance of Nehemiah's adversaries. The strategy was either to give them gentilics that had bad associations for a Judean audience or to make them seem like ordinary men of foreign origin, who were not to be called by the usual patronymic because they were not native-born. Instead, they were to be labelled by their 'ethnic' or geographical places of origin. If Geshem had been alive in the 440s–430s and had opposed Nehemiah's policies, he could have been a member of generation 2 rather than generation 3; the texts in Nehemiah give no indication of his age other than his status as an adult with power and influence at this time.

Generation 4

| Yoiada/Yehoiada | Son of Eliashiv, high priest after father | Neh. 12.10-11, 22; 13.28 |
| Daughter of Meshullam ben Berekiah | Married to Yohanan, son of Tobiah the Ammonite | Neh. 6.18 |

Locals who intermarried into the Yehud community or who would have been contemporaries of generation 4.

Yohanan ben Tobiah the Ammonite	Married to daughter of Meshullam	Neh. 6.18
Delaiah	Son of Sanballat/Sinuballit	Elephantine papyrus 30, 31; Wadi Daliyeh bulla 22?; Samarian coin?
Shelemiah	Son of Sanballat/Sinuballit	Elephantine papyrus 30, 3; Samarian coins?
Bagohi	*Pehah* of Yehud in 410 BCE	Elephantine papyrus 30

The fourth generation, probably the first to be born in Yehud, included Yoiada, the son of Eliashiv, who had not yet inherited the office of high priest during Nehemiah's work in Jerusalem, the daughter of Meshullam son of Berekiah, who was married to Yehohanan, son of Tobiah the Ammonite (Neh. 6.18), the two sons of Sanballat the Horonite/Sinuballit the Harranite, and Bagohi, who was governor of Yehud in 410 BCE.

Yoiada/Yehoiada

Eliashiv's successor in the office of high priest was his son Yoiada/Yehoiada (Neh. 12.10-11; 13.28). A record of the heads of the Levitical father's houses was made during his term in office, as had been done under his father and was done subsequently by his son and successor Yohanan/Yonatan (Neh. 12.10, 22). It was allegedly recorded in the scroll of the Chronicles. One of his sons is said to have married the daughter of Sanballat the Horonite (Neh. 13.28), resulting in his banishment by Nehemiah. In theory, this union took place in the time when Nehemiah was away in Susa, beginning in 432 BCE (Neh. 13.28).

The Daughter of Meshullam ben Berekiah

The niece of the prophet Zechariah was apparently married to Yehohanan, the son of Tobiah the Ammonite (Neh. 6.19). The marriage had already taken place prior to Nehemiah's arrival, which means that generation 4 had reached the age of majority by the time Nehemiah arrived as governor. This in turn indicates that Tobiah would have been in his late forties or his fifties during Nehemiah's stint as governor of Yehud.

Meshullam would have been a priest like his grandfather, father, and brother. Thus, the marriage between Yehohanan and the daughter of Meshullam would have cemented the ongoing alliance between the Tobiad family and the influential priestly houses of the *golah* community. Tobiah had married into the house of Shekaniah and his son had now married into the house of Iddo.

The Sons of Sanballat/Sinuballit

Two sons of Sanballat/Sinuballit the 'Horonite/Harranite' are known from Elephantine papyrus AP 30: Delaiah and Shelemiah. In the year or so before 408 BCE, the temple authorities of the Jewish community at the Persian fortress on the island of Yeb near Aswan had written to them to request their help in securing permission for the rebuilding of the temple of Yau. In the letter, they are addressed as 'the sons of Sanballat/Sinuballit governor of Samerina' (Cowley 1923: 108-32). For them to have been able to help, they would have had to have reached an age of majority and so would have been at least in their twenties at the time. This, in turn, means that Sanballat/Sinuballit would have been at least in his late fifties. The petition makes more sense, however, if the sons were in their thirties, since they would have had more influence the older they became. This, in turn, would mean that Sanballat /Sinuballit would have been in his sixties probably c. 410 BCE. As already discussed in the section on Sanballat/Sinuballit, however, the use of the title '*pehah* of Samerina' does not necessitate this individual to still have been alive in 410 BCE; it may have been an honorific title that had been carried over into death. Thus, it would even be possible for these two sons to have been in their forties or fifties at the time they were asked to help use their clout to gain permission for the temple at Yeb to be rebuilt.

The likely appearance of Delaiah's name on bulla 22 from Wadi ed-Daliyeh has been discussed above in the section about Sinuballit. It is important to note, however, that Delaiah is not necessarily named as governor on this seal; it may be his father who had borne this title. The name of the office follows Sinuballit rather than Delaiah. It is difficult to decide if the layout of this and similar seals has placed the title of office of the first person to be named in final position to avoid interrupting the details of the father-son relationship, or whether it placed it there because it had been borne by the father. In the latter case, it would be a means of using the family's name and importance to gain personal respect.

A review of Hebrew seals bearing personal names or their imprints in bullae shows a preference for individuals who held office not to include patronymics; they gave their own name, followed by the title of their office. Particularly helpful are two seals that may have belonged to the same individual. One is a personal seal that reads 'belonging to Pela'yahu (son of) Mattityahu' that would have been used for personal business affairs (Avigad and Sass 1997: #20A). A second, however, reads 'belonging to Pela'yahu "who is over the corvée"' (Avigad and Sass 1997: #20B). This seal seems to have been designed for official use by its owner when he was sending out correspondence relating to his function as head of the corvée labor force. Thus, it seems as though we need to distinguish between official and personal seals. A telling example of personal seals are those belonging to royal sons. Two examples include 'belonging to Neriyahu son of the king' and 'belonging to Pedayahu son of the king' (Avigad and Sass 1997: #18 and 19). In these instances, the sons are proclaiming entitlement to respect and authority by virtue of their royal birth but are not holders of any specific office.

It is revealing that the other seals with the identical layout to the one under discussion, with a name, a father's name, and a title, all involve fathers who bear influential administrative posts. For example, we have 'belonging to Ga'alyahu son of 'Adayahu the scribe' (Avigad and Sass 1997: #21) and 'belonging to Hanan son of Hilqiyahu the priest' (Avigad and Sass 1997: #28). In these instances, the individuals would have probably followed in their father's footsteps professionally, but these are personal seals, not professional ones (contra Avigad and Sass 1997: comment on seal #28). Their professional seals would simply have given their name and their office. On this basis then, we should conclude that bulla 22 contains the imprint of the personal seal of [Del]aiah who was the son of Sinuballit, governor of Samerina. He was announcing his strong family pedigree on the seal he used for personal business transactions. As a result, we cannot know if he also eventually served as governor in his own right, or whether his father was still alive when he affixed his seal as witness to papyrus 16.

Figure 23.   *Coin of Delaiah*
Y. Meshorer and S. Qedar, *Samarian Coinage* (Publications of the Israel Numismatic Society; Numismatic Studies and Researches, 9; Jerusalem: The Israel Numismatic Society, 1999), p. 87, #22. Reproduced by kind permission of the authors.

It is possible, however, that Delaiah did succeed his father in office as governor. The Samarian obol coin that bears the name abbreviation *D-L* (Fig. 23) on the front above a Sidonian galley over three lines of waves is plausibly attributed to him.[24]

On the reverse is a depiction of a Persian hero/king slaying a rearing lion, with the letter *'ayin* between the two bodies (Meshorer and Qedar 1999: 22; 87, #22). Delaiah would have continued the imagery of the series of imitation Sidonian coins first introduced by his father. However, if this is the case, then we must also assume that he held office from 408 BCE or earlier (Elephantine papyrus 30) to at least 370 BCE. His imitation Sidonian obol coin is copied directly from a coin of 'Abd'astart I, who was king of Sidon from between 375–372 and 364–361 BCE. The 'circle' on the reverse between the king and the lion he is slaying is the letter *'ayin*, which appeared regularly on the latter king's coins weighing 1/16 shekel (Hill 1965: pl. XIX.9-14; Betlyon 1982: pl. 2.9; 3.1). Thus, in order to argue that Delaiah followed his father in office, it would also have to be argued that he minted this coin toward the end of a long career. If he already were in his thirties in 410 when he was asked to help sponsor the rebuilding of the Jewish temple at Elephantine, he would have been in his seventies when he minted this coin.

Ten Samarian coins bearing the abbreviation *SH-L* have been tentatively assigned to the governorship of Shelemiah (Meshorer and Qedar 1999: 28) (Fig. 24).

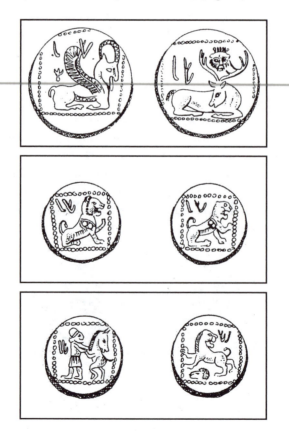

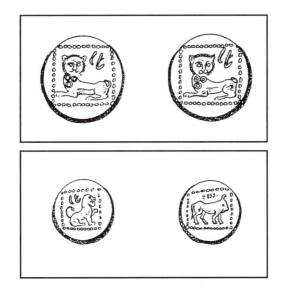

Figure 24. *Coins of Shelemiah*
> Y. Meshorer and S. Qedar, *Samarian Coinage* (Publications of the Israel Numismatic Society; Numismatic Studies and Researches, 9; Jerusalem: The Israel Numismatic Society, 1999): 94, #61; 95, #64 and 65; 96, #69 and 70. Reproduced by kind permission of the authors.

All have images on both sides enclosed in a square border of dots. According to Y. Meshorer and S. Qedar, the convention of using a square border of dots was in use on coins prior to c. 351 BCE, when it disappeared in Cilicia (1999: 28; for the coins, 94-96, #61-70). Assuming that its use was abandoned quickly thereafter in other parts of the western empire, its presence on these two coins would require a date of minting prior to 350 BCE. How much earlier than that date this convention began is uncertain. There is little else to help us pinpoint the date.

It is not certain, however, that this abbreviated name represents Shelemiah; typically, two-letter abbreviations either represent the first two consonants in a word, the first consonants of each component of a name, or the first and last consonant using the letters.[25] Thus, it could represent Shelemiah, but could equally represent, for example, Shallum, Shilhi, Shelami'el, Shilshah, or Shalti'el if the letters stand for the first two consonants (all found in Zadok 1988, where more options are available). Or, if they represent the first and last consonants, the name could have been Shobal, Shemuel, or Sha'ul, to give a few options. In this particular case, it is unlikely they would be the first consonants of two components in a name; there are no known west-Semitic names that would fit. Even if the name is restored as Shelemiah, there is no guarantee that this was Shelemiah the son of Sinuballit I, who is named in Elephantine papyrus 30. It can be noted that in the end, it was Delaiah who formulated an official response guaranteeing support for the rebuilding of the temple of Yau there with Bagohi, the governor of Yehud. Thus, it would be possible to argue that Delaiah's eventual answer in 408 BCE was rendered in his official capacity as governor of Samerina.

It would have been odd for two brothers to have held the office of governor in succession, but not impossible. Darius II (423–405 BCE), Artaxerxes II (404–359 BCE) or the satrap of Across-the-River, who may have overseen the appointments of his subordinates in charge of the various provinces that fell under his jurisdiction, could have decided to remove one brother from office and replace him with his sibling for any of a number of reasons. Or, it is possible that the person who minted the ten coins under discussion merely happened to have been given the same name as Sinuballit's second son but had no blood ties at all to this family, if he even bore this name and not another altogether. There is no reason to assume that the governorship of Samerina would have been hereditary; Yehud's was not, and elsewhere in the empire, the practice was to change families on the death of a satrap so that they did not gain too much power, with very few exceptions (Briant 2002: 338-44). Dynastic governorships could have bred troublesome revolts as much as dynastic satrapies.

Bagohi

Elephantine papyrus *AP* 30 clearly states that immediately after the destruction of the Yahwistic temple in Elephantine in 410 BCE, the governor of Yehud was named Bagohi and the high priest at that time was Yohanan. This was during the reign of Darius II Nothus (423–405 BCE), the successor to Artaxerxes I. It is likely that a stamp that reads *B'*, found at 'En-Gedi in the fill of building 234, belongs to him (Fig. 25) (Stern 1982: 209; Davies 1991: 256 #107.001; Edelman 1995b).

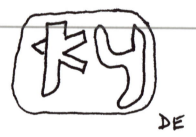

Figure 25.   *B' stamp from 'En-Gedi*
          E. Stern, *Material Culture of the Land of the Bible in the Persian Period 538–332*
          B.C. (Warminster: Aris & Phillips; Jerusalem: Israel Exploration Society, 1982): 208.
          (Drawn by the author.)

It also is probable that the tetradrachm coin in the British Museum with the depiction of Yahweh seated on a wheeled throne was minted in Yehud under his authority (Edelman 1995b: 190-98). It would be possible to assign Bagohi to the preceding generation 4 as well if Yehoiada had been a young man in his twenties when he became high priest. Bagohi could have been in his forties or fifties while serving as governor; we have no additional information that can help us establish his age or length of office.

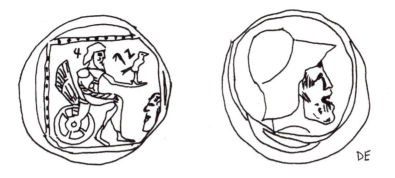

Figure 26. *Tetradrachm depicting Yahweh*
Y. Meshorer, *Ancient Jewish Coinage*. I. *Persian Period through Hasmonaens* (Dix Hills, NY: Amphora Books, 1982): pl. 1.1. (Drawn by the author.)

Generation 5

Yohanan	Likely son of Yoiada, high priest after father	Neh. 12.22 Elephantine papyrus AP 30
Son of Yoiada the high priest	Married to daughter of Sanballat/Sinuballit; possibly Yohanan	Neh. 13.28
Yonatan	Either son of Yoiada and brother of Yohanan, or son of Yohanan; father of high priest Yaddua	Neh. 12.11

Locals who were contemporary to generation 5.

Daughter of Sanballat/Sinuballit	Married to son of Yoiada the high priest	Neh. 13.28

The fifth generation features Yohanan, son of Yoiada (Neh. 12.11), who would have succeeded his father as high priest, and a son of Yehoiada who married the daughter of Sanballat (Neh. 13.28).

Yohanan ben Yehoiada
There is some question about the name of the fifth-generation high priest. In Neh. 12.11, his name appears as Yonatan, while in 12.22 it reads Yohanan. These are not variations of the same name; Yohanan means 'the Lord has been gracious' while Yonatan means 'The Lord has given'. Although they both begin with a form of the divine name, *yo*, the second elements represent different roots in Hebrew with different meanings.

A second anomaly is introduced by the claim in Neh. 12.23 that Yohanan was the son of Eliashiv rather than the son of Yoiada, as strongly implied but not specified in the immediately preceding verse. The father-son relationship is generally assumed because Yohanan followed Yoiada in office. However, unlike the statement in 12.11 that specifies that a father-son relationship had existed between Yoiada and Yonatan, none is explicitly confirmed for Yoiada and Yohanan. Thus, some have chosen to take the claim in v. 23 literally and have assumed that Yohanan had been the physical son of Eliashiv and thus, Yoiada's brother who had succeeded him in office (so, e.g., Marquart 1896: 33; Hölscher 1923: 553; Rudolph 1949: 192-93; Schneider 1959: 243; Mowinckel 1964a: 160; Kellerman 1967: 109; Clines 1984: 225; Williamson 1985: 363; Blenkinsopp 1988: 339). Others have construed the term 'son' in the less specific sense of 'descendant' and have concluded that Yohanan had been the physical offspring of Yoiada (so, e.g., Ryle 1893: 296; Batten 1913: 277; Brockington 1969: 200 if not a scribal error).

Richard Saley has proposed that two different high priests named Yohanan have been confused. One was the son of Eliashiv and the other the son of Yoiada, who in turn was the son of another Eliashiv. The first Yohanan lived in the fifth century BCE under Artaxerxes I while the second lived in the fourth century BCE under Artaxerxes II (404–359 BCE). The inclusion of an Eliashiv in the lineage of both priests led to the mistaken assumption that the two were a single individual, while at the same time creating the confusion over whether Yohanan was the son or grandson of Eliashiv (1978).

This theory presupposes the theory developed by F.M Cross Jr that papponymy, or the naming of a grandson after his grandfather, was a regular practice within the high priesthood of the second temple (1975). However, the proposed reconstruction does not yield strict papponymy since Yoiada, the son of Eliashiv II, is not named after his grandfather and has no descendant named after him either. In addition, the names of the first two high priests, Yeshua and Yoiakim, were not given to subsequent generations. Both of the preceding explanations for understanding Yohanan's genealogy offer plausible solutions to this dilemma without resorting to the multiplication of individuals without any firm proof of their existence.

Such an unusual succession as proposed by those who argue that Yoiada and Yohanan were brothers would only have likely taken place had Yoiada died childless or had he died leaving a son who was not old enough to assume office. Nehemiah 12.11 states that Yoiada had fathered at least one son, named Yonatan, who had lived long enough to father a son in turn named Yaddua, who eventually became high priest. Thus, for this reconstruction to be viable, one would need to assume that after Yohanan assumed office, he did not step down when the rightful heir reached an age of majority but continued to hold power until his own death. At that point, the rightful heir, Yonatan, had either died or been disqualified from holding office, so his son, the grandson of Yoiada, was put in office instead of a son of Yohanan, thereby maintaining the line of Yoiada as the legitimate and preventing the line of Yohanan from usurping the rights of the eldest male and his descendants.

If one adopts the position that Yohanan was a second son of Yoiada, a brother of Yonatan, then light might be shed on the story told in Neh. 13.28 about a son of Yehoiada, the high priest, who had been chased out of Jerusalem by Nehemiah because he had married the daughter of Sanballat/Sinuballit. Yohanan could have been the eldest son of Yehoiada, who had succeeded his father as high priest, but who had subsequently been dismissed from office because of his marriage alliance to Sanballat/Sinuballit (Vanderkam 2000: 179 n. 6, contra Schneider 1959: 243, who proposes that Yonatan would have been the elder brother). He would then have been replaced by his younger brother, Yonatan, who functioned as high priest until his own death, when his son Yaddua inherited the office. Nehemiah 12.11 specifies that Yonatan was the father of Yaddua. In this instance then, the office of high priest would have been permanently removed from the line of an elder brother who had been disqualified and transferred permanently to a younger brother's line.

Elephantine letter AP 30, dated to 408 BCE, is addressed to 'Bagohi, governor of Yehud, Yohanan the high priest and his priestly colleagues in Jerusalem, Ostanes, the brother of Anani, and the nobles of the Jews' (Cowley 1923: 108-32). This invaluable reference indicates that Yohanan was serving as high priest at this time, as well as in 409 or 410 BCE, according to the content of the letter. In addition, Neh. 12.22 claims that the names of the heads of Levitical families were recorded during his term as high priest. Thus, these two pieces of evidence make it certain that an individual named Yohanan served for a time as high priest and was in office in the year 409 or 410 BCE. The chronological ordering in v. 22 also indicates that he would have been high priest after Yoiada and before Yaddua.

A coin bearing the inscription *ywhnn hkwhn* has been found that may have been minted under the authority of this high priest (Fig. 27) (Davies 1991: 255, #106.049; Eph'al 1998: 113), although it appears more likely that the Yohanan in question was a subsequent high priest who shared the same name: Onias (Barag 1985).

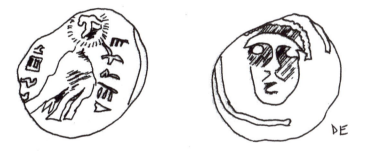

Figure 27. *Coin of Yohanan the priest*
Y. Meshorer, *Ancient Jewish Coinage. I. Persian Period through Hasmonaens* (Dix Hills, NY: Amphora Books, 1982): pl. 2.11. (Drawn by the author.)

In Sir. 50.1, the Hebrew form of the name of this later individual is given as Yohanan while the Greek version renders it as Onias (Vanderkam 2000: 198 n. 40). Julius Morgenstern, however, has pointed out that the Syriac version of Sir. 50.1 reads Netanyah rather than Yohanan, which could in turn be construed as a reference to Yonatan instead of Yohanan and linked to the Yonatan in Neh. 10.11 and 2 Macc. 1.23 (1938: 362 n. 107). According to Josephus, the high priest named Onias served after Yaddua and was in office during Alexander's reign in the Levant (so between 332 and 323 BCE). Stylistically, the coin is said to resemble others minted in nearby regions between 335–331 BCE (Betlyon 1986: 636, 642) and on this basis, is more likely to have been minted under the authority of this later Yohanan than his earlier namesake. Even without the coin, however, the literary evidence cited above confirms that Yohanan was high priest in 410 BCE.

The Daughter of Sanballat/Sinuballit and the Son of Yehoiada

An unnamed daughter of Sinuballit, governor of Samerina, was married to a son of Yehoiada, the high priest in Jerusalem. As discussed in the previous section, it is possible that this son was Yohanan, who had succeeded his father as high priest for some time until he was relieved of his post by Nehemiah.

Josephus reports a similar marriage but places it during the high priesthood of Yaddua during the reign of Darius III, the final king of Persia (335–330 BCE). He claims that the marriage was between Nikaso, the daughter of Sanballat, and Manasseh, the brother of Yaddua. Manasseh left Jerusalem rather than divorce his wife and went to live with Sanballat, who promised to build him a temple where he could serve as high priest (*Ant.* 11.302-12; 321-25).

It is highly improbable that two different daughters of Sanballat, governor of Samerina, were married to members of the family of high priests in Jerusalem within the span of a few decades. It is likely, then, that Josephus' story is a version of the tradition found in Neh. 13.28 (so, e.g., Rowley 1955–56: 170-72; Grabbe 1987: 237; Schwartz 1990: 198-99). A closer look suggests that there may have been confusion between the high priest Yoiada of generation 4 and the later high priest Yaddua of generation 6, which could have led to the displacement in time. The names sound similar, especially if the shortened form Yoiada is used over the longer form Yehoiada.

The giving of names to the bride and groom is consistent with a desire to provide details where an earlier tradition was vague and the variation in the status of Sanballat's son-in-law, who becomes the brother of the high priest instead of the son as in Neh. 13.28, is something that is found in oral story-telling. Thus, Josephus either drew on a popular version of this story that had been embellished and altered over time, or he was personally responsible for these changes, which he would have made for theological reasons.[26]

As discussed at length above in the section about Sinuballit, it is likely that he was born c. 480 BCE since his sons were adults considered to have influence in 410 BCE. Yehoiada's son Yohanan had assumed the high priesthood by 408 BCE and presumably had reached the age of majority by that time; how much prior to this date he had come to power is not known, but we can probably assume he was fresh in office since he or his brother had a long, subsequent career that probably spanned the first four decades of the fourth century. The final high priest under Persian rule, Yaddua, was still alive when Alexander took over the empire in 332 BCE, but would have also had to have had a long career that covered some thirty-five years.

Bearing all this in mind, it is plausible to conclude that the marriage would have take place close to 410 BCE, especially if the groom had been Yohanan. The daughter would have been a minimum of sixteen years old, and possibly closer to twenty, which would have made Sinuballit in his fifties at the time of her birth. This is possible, especially in a situation where the father was a man of power and influence. His first wife could have died in childbirth or he could have taken a young second wife or divorced his first wife in favor of a younger partner to boost his aging male ego. This would explain her probably belonging to a different generation than her older brothers. There is nothing that would have required either father to have been alive at the time of the marriage, although one or the other might have been.

Josephus appears to have taken a tradition dating to the time of Sanballat/Sinuballit that involved a political marriage between his family and that of the high priest in Jerusalem and confused the time setting and possibly also the family relationships of the husband and high priest. It is quite possible that this was a deliberate move in light of the part of the story that relates how Sinuballit promised to build his new son-in-law a temple if he stayed married to his daughter and moved to Samerina. Shortly thereafter, we are told that the temple on Mt Gerizim was built at the beginning of the reign of Alexander. The most recent finds from ongoing excavations there strongly suggest that the temple was built before 450 BCE, probably before or about the same time as the temple in Jerusalem (Magen and Stern 2000).

It looks as though Josephus was deliberately changing the past to conceal the fact that that the temple on Mount Gerizim had been in existence as long or longer than the second temple and possibly, that its priesthood had had blood ties to the Jerusalemite high priestly line that could claim equal legitimacy for its understanding of the proper way to worship and conceive of Yahweh.[27] A third possible influencing factor may have been the story's illustration of the contraction of a mixed marriage among the highest echelons of Yehudite society in the early years of the 'post-exilic' community without condemnation. When the issue of intermarriage became more heated, he may have felt that it would have cast aspersions on the high priestly line of the Jerusalem temple to have it be known that such a marriage had occurred at that early date and so transposed it in time so that he could properly condemn it while also moving the building of the temple on Gerizim much later in time and associating it with the evils of Hellenistic sponsorship and ideas.

Yonatan ben Yehoiada

Nehemiah 12.11 claims that the high priest Yoiada was the father of Yonatan and Yonatan of Yaddua. Yet in 12.22, the claim is made that the heads of Levitical houses were registered in the days of the high priests Yoiada, Yohanan and Yaddua, and as seen in the discussion of Yohanan in generation 5, Elephantine papyrus *AP* 30 shows that Yohanan was high priest in 410–408 BCE. No such evidence exists to date for Yonatan. Either we must assume that a scribal error has crept in to the text and was never corrected (so, e.g., Torrey 1969 [1910]: 321; Rudolph 1949: 190; Schneider 1959: 243; Rowley 1963: 248 n. 5; Cross 1975 by implication, though not stated explicitly; Saley 1978: 158; Vanderkam 2000: 179 n. 6) or we must accept Yonatan as the correct reading in v. 11 and work out the historical implications that the name implies.

If a scribal error is assumed, two mistakes would have been made. The letter *H* in *ywhnn* would have had to have been mistaken for a *T* (*ywntn*), which could have happened fairly easily in the later Hebrew square script but not in the older Hebrew script, where these two letters do not resemble each other at all. So any such error would have had to have crept in after the square script had become standard. Then, there has been a metathesis or interchange of the third and fourth letters, from *ywtnn* to *ywntn*. Once the *H* had been mistaken for a *T*, however, it would have been natural to assume that the name was Yonatan and reverse the order of the two letters; this was a common name, while *ywtnn* was not. Thus, scribal error is a possible explanation of the reason why there are two different names for the son of Yehoiada who followed him in office. However, I do not think it is the most likely explanation, since this discrepancy would have been noted in subsequent reading and copying and could have been corrected easily enough.

If we maintain the more difficult reading, we are left with the two options outlined above in the discussion of Yohanan. (1) Yohanan was the younger brother of Yehoiada and was made high priest temporarily when his elder brother died leaving a minor son. He refused to relinquish the priesthood to Yoiada's rightful heir, Yonatan, when he reached an age of majority, but the priesthood rectified the situation at Yohanan's death by placing Yaddua, Yonatan's son, in office. (2) Yonatan and Yohanan were brothers, both sons of Yehoiada. Both had successively held the office of high priest after their father. Yohanan had been the elder of the two and first in office, but he had subsequently been disqualified and removed from his post, which had resulted in his descendants also being barred from assuming the role of high priest. The younger brother, Yonatan, had replaced him in office and then his son, Yaddua, had become the final high priest during Persian hegemony upon his death (contra Vanderkam 2000: 179 n. 6).

Two other scenarios that were not considered earlier can now be explored as additional options. Assuming that Yonatan and Yohanan had been brothers, it could be argued that Yonatan had been the elder of the two (so, e.g., Ryle 1893: 296) but had died after a short term in office, before any official registrations of priests and Levites had been conducted. This would account for his failure to show up in the list of high priests, which appears to have been derived in large part from census lists that had been recorded during the Persian period. He had left a young son, Yaddua, who had not been old enough to take on the responsibilities of office. As a result, Yonatan's younger brother, Yohanan, had been put in office until Yaddua had been deemed ready and able to take on his rightful role. He then succeeded to the office either at the death of his uncle, or at some point after he reached the age of majority.

A final, but less likely alternative would be to propose that Yonatan had not been Yohanan's brother but his son, who had succeeded his father at his death (so, e.g., Morgenstern 1938: 362 n. 107). In this case, however, one would need to argue that Yohanan's name was inadvertently dropped from the list in Neh. 12.11, perhaps because of its similarity to the following name, while Yonatan's was dropped from the list in 12.23 for the same reason. This option would have the advantage, however, of adding another full generation who could have held office in the seventy-year period from 410 BCE, when Yohanan was high priest, to 335 BCE, when his alleged son Yaddua was high priest. If Yohanan and Yonatan were brothers, one could at most attribute a ten-year gap, while as father and son, a twenty-five-year gap is possible.

Josephus reports that Yehoiada had had a third son named Yeshua, whom Yohanan had killed in the temple during a fight over who would be high priest. Bagohi, the governor at the time, had been backing Yeshua, the younger sibling, and had promised to make him high priest instead of Yohanan (*Ant.* 11.297-301). There is no reason to set this incident in the reign of Artaxerxes III on the assumption that the Bagohi in question was the army general of that king rather than the governor of Yehud named in *AP* 30 alongside Yohanan the high priest (Williamson 1977: 58; 1985: 152). As J.C. Vanderkam has argued, the incident reflects local politics in which the governor was a friend of the murdered brother and was trying to interfere with the normal order of succession to the high priesthood by supporting a younger son over the eldest, who was entitled to succeed to the office. He was not an outsider who knew nothing of the situation (2000: 193-96).

The only consequence of this murder that Josephus reports was the imposition of a steep tax for seven years on every lamb sacrificed in the temple. Nevertheless, this incident might have led to Yohanan's immediate or eventual deposition from office in favor of the next eldest surviving son, since the high priest would have been polluted by the blood of his murdered brother. This story tends to support option 2 above because it confirms Yohanan's status as the eldest son of Yoiada.

Josephus' report about sibling murder among the sons of Yehoiada and the report in Neh. 13.28 of the expulsion of one of Yehoiada's sons for having married the daughter of Sanballat provide two provide different but equally plausible explanations for how as brothers, Yohanan and Yonatan could have served successively as high priests in Jerusalem. Yohanan, the eldest, could either have been banished for a marriage to Sanballat's daughter, or he could have been put to death for the murder of his brother or deposed by Bagohi, who had wanted him ousted in favor of Yeshua anyway. In either case, Yehoiada's next eldest son would have assumed the office and it is likely that the line of the disgraced son would have been eliminated from succession after that, with the rights passing on to the sons of the next eldest son.[28]

The inclusion of Yonatan in the list of *bona fide* high priests would help alleviate an otherwise awkward chronological gap between 410 and 335 BCE. It is hard to imagine that only two individuals served as high priest in this period of seventy-five years, although it is not impossible (Vanderkam 2000: 198-200). A few more years would need to be added to this figure as well because we do not know how much before 410 Yohanan had become high priest. By adding Yonatan as a functioning priest between Yohanan and Yaddua, the lengths of tenure in office become slightly shorter and so more believable. Thus, the more difficult reading is attractive because it provides a more likely historical scenario. But we cannot be certain about Yonatan's status as high priest until specific evidence turns up, like a seal, a coin, or a letter mentioning his name. Until then, his inclusion in the list of high priests in Jerusalem during the Persian period must remain a plausible hypothesis.

Generation 6

Yaddua	Son of Yonatan, high priest after father	Neh. 12.11

Yaddua

A final, sixth generation takes us until or through the reign of Darius III (335–330 BCE) and the end of Persian rule (Neh. 12.22). It includes Yaddua, the son of Yonatan, as the final high priest under the Persian administration. He continued on in office after the Greeks took over control of Yehud.

Until recently, it was commonly assumed that the imitation Attic coin bearing the name *ydw'* was minted under his authority (Spaer 1986/87; Meshorer 1990/91: 115, no. 6; Davies 1991: 256, #106.050). It is an imitation of the standard Attic issue with the head of Athena on the front and her owl, with an ear of wheat and the name of Athens abbreviated in Greek letters (*A-TH-E*) Fig. 28) (Meshorer and Qedar 1999: # 39; 126 bearing the letter *Y* might also belong to him).

Figure 28.   *Coin of Yaddua*
            Y. Meshorer and S. Qedar, *Samarian Coinage* (Publications of the Israel Numis-
            matic Society; Numismatic Studies and Researches, 9; Jerusalem: The Israel Numis-
            matic Society, 1999): 90, #39. Reproduced by kind permission of the authors.

André Lemaire was perhaps the first to challenge this attribution: he suggested that the coin should be assigned instead to a *pehah* of Samerina, the son of Sanballat named Yaddua, whose partially damaged bulla was attached to papyrus 16 from the caves at Wadi ed-Daliyeh and whose damaged name was also written on the papyrus 11 (1990: 66 n. 209).

Apparently unaware of Lemaire's argument, Y. Meshorer has now also decided that the coin was minted in Samerina rather than in Yehud. His new attribution rests on a number of considerations, including the discovery of two hoards of coins from this province that have provided a much-needed comparative data base. The motifs on the Yaddua coin are very similar to those used on another series from Samerina, the fabric is different than Yehud coins, and the style of writing is closer to that used on other coins of Samerina than to that found on coins from Yehud. In addition, a coin from the same series has been found now in Sebastiye/Samaria, the capital of Samerina (Meshorer and Qedar 1999: 23). While he has not drawn the explicit link to the person named on papyrus 14 from Wadi ed-Daliyeh that Lemaire proposed, he has made a strong argument for the coin not being from Yehud. The attribution of the Yaddua coin to a Samarian governor eliminates the somewhat awkward anomaly of having a priest as the minting authority rather than the governor.[29] In light of my earlier discussion of Sinuballit, where I argued that the witness on papyrus 11 was not a governor nor a son of the only attested Sinuballit, who was governor, I would reject Lemaire's proposed identification but would uphold the existence of a governor of Samerina named Yaddua, of unknown patronymic

Chronological Implications of the Genealogies

What does the foregoing analysis of the six generations reveal about the relative dating of Zerubbabel and Nehemiah?

Establishing Date Parameters
There is a single, reliable extra-biblical chronological peg: Elephantine letter *AP* 30, dating to the year 408 BCE. It indicates that slightly earlier, sometime between the destruction of the temple in 410 and the writing of this second letter, two adult sons of Sinuballit, Shelemiah and Delaiah, were active amongst the local elite of Samerina. Sanballat may still have been alive, but not necessarily. His description as governor of Samerina may have carried on after his death

since the office he had held while alive had been the highest in the province. At this same time, Bagohi was governor of Yehud and Yohanan was high priest. This means that generation 4 was active; its members were adults, probably in their forties and upwards at this time, and that generation 3 was mostly dead. A member of generation 5, Yohanan was the high priest, suggesting that he was part of the youngest generation just coming into majority.

Working backwards, we can conclude that this Sanballat, though probably dead, would have been at least in his sixties in 410 BCE, but perhaps older, placing his date of birth in the 470s. We cannot push it back too far because of the late birth of his daughter who married a fifth-generation son of Yoiada. This in turn would mean that he would have minimally been in his twenties or his thirties when Nehemiah is said to have begun his mission in the twentieth year of Artaxerxes in 445 BCE, but quite possibly more mature, even in his forties.

Active as a middle-aged adversary to Nehemiah during the latter's early term of office, generation 3 would have been in power alongside members of generation 2 who were still alive and active, and generation 4 were just beginning their political careers. On this basis, most of Nehemiah's contacts should have been with members of generations 2 and 3 and 4. Does this correspond with the textual tradition?

Yes. The narrative names Eliashiv of generation 4 as high priest during Nehemiah's term of office (Neh. 3.1) and possibly also his father Yehoiakim of generation 3 (Neh. 12.26). There is no trace of Yehoiada of generation 5 being high priest yet.

The wording in Neh. 13.28 could be seen to indicate that Eliashiv had served as high priest into a ripe old age, preventing his son from assuming the office as a young adult or even as a young middle-aged person, when he would ordinarily have officiated. It mentions that one of the sons of Yehoiada, the son of Eliashiv the high priest, became the son-in-law of Sanballat. The phrasing indicates that Eliashiv was still serving as the official high priest at this time, even though he had a grandson in his twenties, of marriageable age. Thus, he must have been in his late sixties or early seventies at the end of Nehemiah's governorship. When Yehoiada finally assumed the role as high priest, he would have been in his late forties or fifties already and may have had a relatively short stint in office before his death. While it is generally assumed that life spans were much shorter in the ancient world than today, the office of high priest would have involved little manual labor and a solid diet, so its holders may have lived well beyond the average person. This information, therefore, is basically consistent with the generational chart; Yehoiada would have been more or less contemporary with Sanballat, at most ten years or so his senior. Josephus' report about the marriage of Sinuballit's daughter Nikaso to Manasseh during the high priesthood of Yaddua has been misplaced in time.

If we accept the accuracy of both Neh. 3.1 and Neh. 12.26 and conclude that there was a change in the office of high priest during Nehemiah's governorship, with Yoiakim ending his term and his son Eliashiv beginning his, then we can deduce that Eliashiv would already have been in his late forties, fifties, or early sixties when he assumed the office from his father. This in turn means that during his priesthood under Nehemiah, he would have been working with members of his own third generation, who were ending their careers, alongside those of generation 4 and 5 who were young adults beginning their public careers in their twenties and those slightly more seasoned, in their thirties.

Other passages also indicate that Nehemiah had dealings with members of generations 2 and 3 during his governorship. Nehemiah 7.2 claims that Nehemiah had confirmed Hananiah, the probable younger son of Zerubbabel and a member of generation 3, in his previously appointed post as police chief in Jerusalem. This would only have been possible had Hananiah been a member of generation 3 or 4, since it is unlikely that an elderly man would have been entrusted with the oversight of the police force of the provincial seat. Thus, Hananiah and Nehemiah are more likely to have been contemporaries age-wise, although Nehemiah might have belonged to the next younger generation to Hananiah.

Tobiah the Ammonite figures as a member of generation 3 because of his marriage to the daughter of Shekaniah ben Arah. This means that during Nehemiah's governorship, Shekaniah would have been quite aged, like the high priest Yoiakim, his contemporary. Yoiakim had probably been in his sixties or seventies when he died in office under Nehemiah since his son was already in his fifties or sixties when he had assumed the office. Even if we were to make Tobiah Yoiakim's junior by ten years, Tobiah would still have been in his late fifties or early sixties when he opposed Nehemiah's policies.

If Tobiah, a representative of generation 3, were born c. 503–507 BCE, then members of generation 2, those who constituted the younger members of the leadership of the party that was repatriated to Yehud under Zerubbabel and Yeshua, would have been twenty-five to thirty-five years older, born c. 542–528 BCE. The more elderly members of the leadership, belonging to generation 1, like Iddo, Kadmiel, and Yeshua, would have been born at the earliest another twenty-five to thirty years prior to that, c. 572–553 BCE.

Assuming the calculated dates, the return to Yehud would have to be dated c. 480 BCE at the earliest. This is required by the circumstances of the prophet Zechariah of generation 3, his father Berekiah, of generation 2, and his grandfather Iddo, of generation 1. Zechariah prophesied while both Zerubbabel and Yeshua were still in office concerning the need to rebuild the temple (Zechariah 3 and 4). He must have reached the age of majority at this time to have been respected as a prophet within the community.

This suggests in turn that he would have had to have been a teenager at least or a young adult in his twenties when he had returned under the two leaders, if we assume that the temple was begun soon after the arrival. The prophecies of Haggai indicate that the temple was not begun immediately; the notables were already settled in panelled houses, presumably in Jerusalem although this is not specified, before work began on the temple (Hag. 1.4). Thus, Zechariah's prophetic activity may only have begun after some five years of the return and life under Zerubbabel's governorship.

An even later date, however, could be suggested by the datum of Zechariah's registry as head of the priestly family of Iddo during the high priesthood of Yehoiakim (Neh. 12.16). At some point during Yehoiakim's tenure of office, his father and grandfather had both died. Yehoiakim is reported to have still been in office when Nehemiah began his governorship; the question is, then, how close to the date of 445 BCE was this census made? When did Yehoiakim become high priest?

If he were in his sixties when he died, as was deduced earlier, the earliest Yehoiakim could have assumed office would have been c. 480 BCE, when he would have reached the age of majority. But his tenure would have been determined by when his father Yeshua died, not by his biological age. And, as seen earlier, both Eliashiv and Yehoiada probably lived to ripe old ages. So, he might not have assumed office until close to 460 BCE, when he would have been middle-aged.

Some indication of how long Yeshua held office may be provided by the list of the heads of the 22 priestly families that were compiled under Yeshua, on the one hand (Neh. 12.1-7), and the list of the leaders of these same houses under Yoiakim. All the lineages have new leaders, indicating that the members of generations 1 and 2 had died off and had been replaced by members of generations 2 and 3. Generation 3 had thus already reached the age of majority. A review of the list of changes in the Levitical lineages between the initial registration under Yeshua (Neh. 12.8-9) and a subsequent registration under Yoiakim (Neh. 12.24-26) shows less of a time gap. Kadmiel has been replaced by his son Yeshua, but Shereviah, Mattaniah and Bakbukiah have continued in service. The latter two have been shifted to positions as gate-keepers instead of singing songs of thanksgiving. Yeshua, Binnui, Judah and Unno have disappeared, probably due to death, while new faces have appeared: Hashaviah, a chief, and the gatekeepers Ovadiah, Meshullam, Talmon, and Akkuv.

It is noteworthy that there was no need for gatekeepers in the first registration conducted under Yeshua; this implies that the city gates, fortress gates and temple gates had not yet been completed during his tenure as high priest. It is only under Yoiakim that some gates become operational and Levites are appointed to guard them. It is unclear if these are fortress gates, temple gates, city gates, or some combination thereof. Mattaniah and Bakbukiah are transferred to this duty, presumably because they are still young enough to carry it out efficiently. This implies that there was not a big gap in time between the arrival under Zerubbabel and the rebuilding of the city walls – perhaps only about twenty to thirty years at the most. The data also implies that the registry of Levites was conducted earlier in Yoiakim's high priesthood than the list of priests, since some of the Levites of generation 2 are still at their posts but none of the priests of generations 1 and 2 are.

A review of the priests who are said to have been present at the dedication of the city walls under Nehemiah is also revealing: it includes a mixture of names of the heads of the twenty-two priestly lineages of generation 2 and generation 3. Members of generation 2 include Ezra (12.1, 33), Jeremiah (12.1, 34), Miniamin (12.5, 16, 41) and Shemaiah (Neh. 12.6, 18, 34, 42), while those of generation 3 include Meshullam (12.16, 33), Uzzi (12.19, 42), Zechariah (12.16, 41), Hananiah (12.12, 41) and Yehohanan (12.13, 42). This list of participants in the dedication ceremony that took place during Nehemiah's governorship suggests that some of those who had arrived under Zerubbabel and Yeshua as adults, who had headed the main priestly families, were still alive and able to function at the time the walls of Jerusalem were rededicated after repair. It confirms the impression given by the list of Levites that there was only about a twenty to thirty year gap between the arrival of the *golah* party led by Zerubbabel and Yeshua and Nehemiah's rededication of the city walls, which would have led to the appointment of Levitical gate-keepers to guard the storehouses located in the gates (Neh. 12.25).

The dedication of the city walls may also have been the occasion when the registry of the Levites was conducted by Yoiakim to record the new assignments needed to cover the gate storehouses, although it is possible that the list was made at the time of the completion of the temple instead, or of the completion of the *birah* or fortress complex inside the city, on the acropolis. These other two structures would also have had gates. In view of the above considerations, it can be concluded that Yeshua did not remain high priest for more than twenty to thirty years, since he was dead by the time Nehemiah dedicated the walls of Jerusalem, and he may have died much earlier.

The list of those who are reported to have set their seal to a covenant initiated during Nehemiah's governorship include familiar names from generations 1, 2 and 3 amongst the heads of the main priestly and Levitical families. Generation 1 and 2 priests include Seraiah (10.2; 12.1), Jeremiah (10.2; 12.2), Amariah (10.3; 12.2), Hattush (10.4; 12.2), Malluk (10.4; 12.2), Shevaniah (10.4; 12.14), Harim (10.5; 12.15), Meremoth (10.5; 12.3), Ginnethon (10.6; 12.4, 16), Abijah (10.7; 12.4), Miyamin (10.7; 12.5), Bilgai (10.8; 12.5), Shemaiah (10.8; 12.6) and Maaziah/Maadiah (10.5; 12.8), while generation 3 priests include Meshullam (10.7; 12.13, 16). Generation 1 and 2 Levites include Yeshua (10.9; 12: 8), Binnui (10.9; 12: 8) Kadmiel (10.9; 12: 8), and Shereviah (10.12; 12.8), while generation 3 Levites include Hashaviah (10: 11; 12.24). If any credence is to be given to the historicity of the list of those who witnessed the written covenant initiated by Nehemiah, then one would need to argue that Nehemiah succeeded Zerubbabel as governor and that the two successors were at most twenty to thirty years apart. This would account for the continuance of so many of the generation 2 head priests in office.

A similar picture emerges from a cross-referencing of the names of those who are reported to have rebuilt segments of the city walls and the lists of various officials in Nehemiah 10 and 12. Most belong to generations 2 or 3. Hasshuv (3.21) is said to have been one of the chiefs of the people who set his seal on the covenant written by Nehemiah (10.23). He is likely to have been a member of generation 2 or 3. Binnui son of Henadad (3.24) who also set his seal on the same covenant is almost certainly the Binnui listed as the head of a Levitical house in the days of Yeshua, who had disappeared in the time of Yoiakim's high priesthood. Thus, he most likely was a member of generation 2. Pedaiah ben Parosh (3.25) is probably a member of generation 2 or 3 since he bears the gentilic of the village of his origin in Babylonia (7.8). He also sealed the covenant. Shemaiah son of Shekaniah, keeper of the East Gate (3.29) is a member of generation 3, as is Meshullam son of Berekiah (3.30) and Eliashiv the high priest (3.21). Only Azariah son of Maaseiah son of Ananiah (3.23) might be a member of generation 4. The latter person would belong there on the assumption that his grandfather had belonged to generation 2 and had returned under Zerubbabel and Yeshua, but this is not certain; if his grandfather had been a member of generation 1 at the time of the return, Azariah would belong to generation 3 rather than generation 4.

The implications of the lists of the generation 2 and 3 priests, Levites and chiefs of the people and their reported involvement in activities under Nehemiah's governorship would suggest a date for the arrival of the *golah* party under the leadership of Zerubbabel and Yeshua closer to 460 BCE than to 480 BCE. The earlier date was the result of allowing generously for the life spans of the highlighted individuals discussed earlier.

Nehemiah as a Member of Generation 3

Nehemiah could not have had dealings in his reported twelve-year career from year 20 to year 32 of the reign of Artaxerxes with members of generations 2 and 3 on the one hand, and also with members of generation 4 and 5, on the other. There is a time span of 100–120 years covered by these four generations. It would have been possible for him to have done so, however, in a career that spanned decades, since he would have begun work as a member of the middle of the three living generations and completed it as a member of the oldest of the three living generations. Thus, to accommodate all of the chronological implications found in the book of Nehemiah, he could only have been a member of generation 3. When he began his post in Jerusalem he would have worked with generations 2, 3 and 4, and by the end of this career, he would have been working with generations 3, 4, and 5.

As a member of generation 3, he would have been the contemporary of Hananiah son of Zerubbabel, Tobiah the Ammonite, Geshem the Arab, and Sinuballit the Harranite. The priests, Levites, and officials of generation 2 who are said to have set their seal on his covenant, helped rebuild the city walls, and who were registered under the high priesthood of Yoiakim, could fit historically, as could the high priesthoods of both Yoiakim and Eliashiv, who belonged to generations 2 and 3, respectively. Yoiakim was just completing his career in the early years of Nehemiah's work in Jerusalem. In his twilight years as a senior bureaucrat, Nehemiah could even have chased the son of Yehoiada of generation 5 from his presence sometime after 432 BCE, as claimed in Neh. 13.6, 28. By this point, he would have been among the eldest of three living generations, with members of generation 5 coming of age. Whether he did so or not is another question, but the timing of the incident as portrayed in Nehemiah is not impossible; the account in Josephus, on the other hand, is irreconcilable with the dating of both Sinuballit, the governor of Samerina, and Nehemiah.

Conclusion

After weighing the various factors laid out above, it seems most plausible to associate Nehemiah with generation 3 age-wise. The writer claims to have had access to records of officials under each of the high priests who served in Yehud under the Persians, from the time the temple was rebuilt to the end of Persian rule with Darius III. Thus, had he had information that Nehemiah had been governor during the high priesthood of either Yoiada of generation 4 or Yohanan and Yonatan of generation 5, he could have used lists from their times in office instead.

If Nehemiah has been correctly situated as a contemporary of the youngest generation that was born in Babylonia but returned to Yehud as children and teens, generation 3, he was only one generation younger than Zerubbabel. This means at most a gap of twenty–thirty years between them, and possibly no gap at all in terms of their holding office. It is uncertain whether Nehemiah was a governor in his own right or whether he was a special envoy sent by Artaxerxes I to oversee the completion of the rebuilding of Jerusalem as a fortress city and district seat. In the latter case, he would have worked alongside the existing governor of the city, which could have been Zerubbabel. We have no firm indication of how long Zerubabbel held office.

There are major ramifications of this generational sequencing. The return under Zerubbabel and Yeshua would have taken place either at the beginning of the reign of Artaxerxes I in 465 BCE, or at the end of the reign of his predecessor, Xerxes, (486–465 BCE). The latter is only mentioned in the biblical texts in Ezra 4.6 and in the book of Esther, under the name Ahasuerus. The temple would only have been begun sometime close to 465 BCE. Thus, Haggai and Zechariah could not have been active during the reign of Darius, some sixty-five years earlier, as the dates in those books claim. The city walls would have been repaired soon after the temple was completed, not some seventy years later, as is currently thought. Then the possibility is also raised that the temple-building was part of a larger, coordinated plan for the rejuvenation of Jerusalem as the provincial capital, which included the establishment of a fortress on the acropolis, the resettling of the city with a civilian population to man the fort and provide the economic base for its sustenance, and the building of a temple for the local citizens to worship their preferred deity. In the next chapter, I will explore how the dates in Haggai and Zechariah erroneously arose.

Endnotes

1. The Bible provides no indication of what was considered an age of majority and the average age at marriage. It appears that men were eligible for military service beginning at the age of twenty (Num. 1.23), and yet this does not mean that they had already established an independent household at this time; they appear to have lived under their fathers' roofs until they married and set up their own households. Genesis 11.12-24 tends to suggest that men were between the age of twenty-nine and thirty-five when they had their first children. This fits in general with the information that M. Roth has gleaned from Neo-Assyrian and Neo-Babylonian documents about the average age of marriage for men in Mesopotamia as twenty-six to thirty-two (1987: 737). In the latter documents, women seem to have been married the first time between fourteen–twenty, although given the patriarchal society, we should reckon generations by the age of fathers rather than mothers.

2. The title, 'Artaxerxes, King of Babylon' is unattested in historical documents (Wilson 1915: 183-88), suggesting this section may be a late addition by someone well removed from the time period. It can be noted, however, that the title 'King of Babylon' had been used by Cyrus, Cambyses, and Darius, so it was a title used by the early Persian kings and might turn up in future documents (Wilson 1915: 183-84). The titles 'king of Babylon, king of the lands' and 'king of Babylonia and of the lands' were used by Cyrus, Cambyses, Smerdis, Darius, and Xerxes (Wilson 1915: 184-85).

3. Alternatively, if one adopts the reading in the Syriac version that has 'the son of' Yekoniah instead of 'the descendants of' Yekoniah, the text could be reconstructed: 'And the son of Yekoniah the captive (was) Shealtiel [and] his son (was) Malkiram; [and the sons of Malkiram]: Pedaiah, Shenazzer, Yekemiah, Hoshama Nedeviah [five]. The tendency in these genealogies is to place the qualifier 'his son' after the name of the individual in question rather than before it, however, so I would favor the reconstruction I have given in the main discussion. It can be also noted that the Syriac version adds the qualifier 'first-born' after the name of Hoshama. If adopted as reliable, it would suggest yet another reconstruction that would make Yekemiah the father of Hoshama and Nedeviah, the last two names in the list. Yet in light of the implication that Pedaiah should have been a first-born in his own right, the modifying phrase would have made better sense had it followed his name in the list.

4. Deutsch 1999: 43, #10.9; 82. Add to these 15 #34, *lbqst bt 'bdyrh*, which Deutsch may have decided was owned by a non-Israelite or Judahite because of the names, even though the script is in Hebrew, #664, *lhnh bt 'zryh*, #756 *l'ht brt nsry*, #1071 *lyhwsm' bt swssr'sr* (Avigad and Sass 1997: 62, 244, 283, 403).

5. Avigad and Sass 1997: 61, #31, *l'bygyl 'st 'syhw*; 62, #33, *l'dt/'dt' 'st pshr*; 417, #1103, *l'htmlk 'st ys'*. The two closest seals to the one under discussion are both Ammonite; both use the term *'mt* to describe the relationship between the female owner of the seal and the male responsible for her: #874, *l'lyh 'mt hnn'l*, and #875, *l'nmwt 'mt dblbs/rblbs*. The remaining Ammonite seals of women all specify a relationship of 'daughter', raising the possibility that *'mt* was the local equivalent or substitute term for 'wife'. The same term appears in the royal steward tomb inscription in Silwan. It has been suggested that the term designates either a concubine/secondary wife, or is an honorific title equivalent to *'bd* that has been used of the wife of a royal official. For a full discussion, with bibliography, see Avigad and Sass 1997: 11-13.

6. It may be noteworthy that Isa. 60.7 considers the Qedarites to be paradigmatic sheep-breeders, and a Persian-era silver bowl from Tell-el-Mashkuta in Egypt bears a dedicatory inscription that refers to Geshem,

king of Qedar. Is it possible that Geshem the Arab was Geshem king of Qedar and that the family of Nekodah excluded from temple service were Qedarite sheep-breeders? This would then provide a link between all three excluded groups in Neh. 7.62 and the three named enemies of Nehemiah.

7. The reference to Sanballat's displeasure at 'hearing' about Nehemiah's arrival with letters and/or army officers and cavalry, as opposed to his reading about it, can then be understood in two ways. In the narrative world, the displeasure could have been over the presence of the officers and cavalry, knowledge of which had been passed on orally via rumor or spy report and not specified in the letter. Alternatively, if the displeasure had been prompted by the arrival in general, his 'hearing' could refer to the official letter he had received that had been read to him, as was customary.

8. Although Meshorer and Qedar have suggested that the second letter on coins 49, 51-53 and 56 is an *N* (1999: 92-93), it consistently is shaped as a *B*. Thus, it appears as though the name has been abbreviated not by using the first two letters, *SN*, but by using the first letters of each component, assuming that the weak letter *'alef*, which begins the second verbal element *'uballit*, was skipped over in favor of the first strong consonant *B*, producing *SB*.

9. The photograph of the coin does not support the proposed reading of a final letter *L* by Meshorer and Kedar (1999: 93). If this is a letter, it is probably a *Y*. However, it appears instead to be part of the figurehead on the prow of the boat, which is regularly depicted on Sidonian coins that feature the trireme with oars on the front side of coins of varying denominations.

10. The royal archer image was standard on the golden darics and silver shekels that were the official coinage of the Persian kings. The form of depiction found in series A and B does not correspond to any of the standard types on Persian coinage, however. It features the king with quiver on his back, standing, facing right, and shooting his bow. Types II-IV all feature a king kneeling or running, and only Type II has him shooting a bow; in Type III he carries a bow and a spear, while in Type IV he carries a throwing stick(?) and a bow. Type I features the king holding his bow in his right hand and arrows in his left; he faces right, but is only depicted from the waist up (Carradice 1987: 78). Thus, unfortunately, nothing can be deduced at this point about the possible date of Series A or B from comparative Persian imagery. It may be that the archer on Series A and B was copied from a royal Persian seal instead of from coins in circulation.

11. I see no reason to assume that this abbreviation represents Ba'lshillem II rather than Ba'ana (contra Betlyon 1982: 9).

12. In addition, the imagery appears on coins #12, 152, 200 and 205 without any writing that provides a clue about the governor under whom they were minted.

13. J. Elayi and A.G. Elayi have claimed that his appointment over Phoenicia, if not all of Across-the-River, began already in 354 BCE, at the beginning of the reign of Tennes, before the rebellion (1993: 230). They do not provide any support for this idea, which makes it hard to assess its plausibility.

14. This symbol is described by Babelon as a croix ansée (Babelon 1910a: 361-62, #528. The symbol is found on many Sidonian coins (Babelon 1910b: pls CV.3, 5; CVI.11-46).

15. With J. Elayi (1994: 180), I have reservations about whether Tyre and Sidon were building ships for a Persian navy that was funded from royal coffers or were building ships at their own expense that remained their possessions, but were used by the Persians when the need arose for naval warfare or the transport of troops or horses being used otherwise for commercial purposes. In either case, however, there would have been an investment in such galleys with three decks of oars beginning at the time of Cambyses and continuing thereafter. Wallinga's comments about the need for money to pay the crews when the ships were used in war or for troop transport would still hold, regardless of who owned the boats, so it seems likely that coinage would have been introduced in Sidon already at the end of the sixth century BCE.

16. This allows room for Ba'lshillem II to have ruled immediately before 'Abd'astart I, whose dates can be set from c. 375–352 BCE. It also accommodates a reign for Bod'Astart, the son of Eshmunezer II, at the beginning of the fifth century, as well as his son Yatonmilk. All of the proposed dates for the beginning of Sidonian coinage need adjusting upwards in my opinion.

17. I am greatly indebted to Jean-Baptiste Humbert and Hagit Maoz for helping me to arrange to view the

bulla, and to Michal Dayagi-Mendels for giving me physical access to the bulla outside of its display case and allowing me to inspect it under good lighting conditions with a magnifier.

18. Two other letters would be possible: *SH (shin)* and *TS (sade)*, but neither can be placed before *L* or *'* and produce a name that is attested in the currently known body of writings.

19. The claim by F.M. Cross Jr that the oldest manuscript bears a date of 375 BCE(1974: 19) has been upheld by J. Dusek, who has re-examined the original papyrus. Published as #22 by D. Gropp, the document is very fragmentary, but the final line refers to [...] year 20 + 10 [...], which seems to refer to a regnal year between years 30–40 for a king named Artaxerxes . Artaxerxes II (405–359) is considered the only viable candidate since Artaxerses III only ruled twenty-one years. However, Artaxerxes I (465–425 BCE) ruled forty years, and it is not beyond the realm of possibility that this document could have been written c. 430 BCE. It would mean that the documents in the cave spanned transactions that involved three generations, which is plausible, since three generations are alive at a given time.

20. The alternate proposal of A. Lemaire to restore the name as Yaddu'a instead has more merit since it links the name with a subsequent governor of Samerina who minted a coin (1990: 66). Nevertheless, it is not even certain that the final two letters read [...]u'a, and his reconstruction also rests on the unproven and unlikely assumption that the governorship of Samerina became virtually 'dynastic'.

21. The name is regularly vocalized as Sanballat in the book of Nehemiah, so it may be that the connection of the name with the deity Sin was lost in the Jewish environment and the name became 'neutral' and acceptable, especially in Samerina, where a governor had borne it.

22. After re-examining the actual papyrus, J. Dusek has concluded that the reading *sgn'* is possible. He notes that there is a small vertical pen stroke that touches the top of first letter that is inconsistent with a standard *waw*. On this basis, he prefers to read the initial letter as *samek* (email communication). Even if the text reads 'Hanan the prefect...' with a final word after this witness, there is no reason to assume with Cross that this Hanan was also a son of Sinuballit II, who was continuing the family legacy as hereditary governors of Samerina by being put in office as second in command, from which he would graduate to the governorship on the death of his father.

23. It is possible that the individual on papyrus 11 whose father was named Sinuballit was, in fact, the great grandson of Sinuballit the Harranite, governor of Samerina who had lived during the reign of Artaxerxes I. There is evidence of the practice of papponymy among some families at Elephantine, for example, although this might have been a localized phenomenon. It is likely that those who had fled to the Wadi Daliyeh caves belonged to the upper classes of Samerina, so the Sinuballit whose son witnessed the transaction in papyrus 11 probably was of aristocratic background. We do not know, however, how witnesses were chosen for such transactions. They may simply have been those on hand at the time who were free citizens, and not always friends of those named in the transaction. In any event, if the witness named here were the great grandson of Sinuballlit, governor of Samerina, there is no evidence to support the view that his father or grandfather had also served as governors after Sinuballit the Harranite.

24. Next to the abbreviated name are either the poorly executed letters *SH-N*, which would represent an abbreviation of the provincial name Samerina, or a lotus flower and the number 1 (Meshorer and Qedar 1999: 67). In the former case, the *shin* has been drawn very much like a flower by someone who may not have been literate. Going against the suggestion that these two symbols are an abbreviation of Samerina is the fact that the only instances when the provincial name has appeared on coins alongside the abbreviated name of a minting authority are when a satrap, Megabyzos or Mazday, has minted coins in Samerina. There is no example where a local governor has included it alongside his abbreviated name. Thus, it appears more likely that the symbols, a lotus flower and the number 1, were added secondarily by a banker who guaranteed the weight and perhaps the purity of the metal by overstamping the coin with his countermark. Other examples are known where the lotus flower has been used in this way (Babelon 1910a: 45-46, #3 [pl. LXXXVI, fig. 6]; Hill 1922: 152, #29 [pl. 24.18]; 154, #49 [pl. 25.3]).

25. The first two options are nicely illustrated by name abbreviations on Sidonian coins. *B'* stand for Ba'ana; while *B-SH* stands for B'alshillem (Betylon 1982: 6-11). The final is illustrated on the coins themselves, where

the provincial name of Samerina is abbreviated *SH-N* (for the two clearest examples, which include the abbreviated name of the minting authority as well as the province, see Meshorer and Qedar 1999: #22 (*D-L* and *SH-N*) and #100 (*M-Z* and *SH-N*).

26. L. Grabbe has suggested he added the name Manassas in order to link this renegade priest with the worst apostasizing king of Israel, Manasseh (1987: 237) while D.R. Schwartz thinks that he was responsible for setting the narrative under Yaddua, changing it from the high priesthood of Simon the Just, who had appeared in his source (1990: 187-88). For Schwartz, Josephus drew on independent traditions that spoke of Sanballat and Manasseh on the one hand, and of Alexander and Sanballat, on the other (192) . For Grabbe, he was creating a midrash that was not based on any independent traditions.

27. My understanding overlaps with that of L. Grabbe. He has proposed that the intention of the passage is to dismiss the rival temple and priesthood of Gerizim by arguing that they originated with disaffected members of the Jerusalemite priesthood (1987: 241).

28. It has been suggested that Yeshua was the eldest son of Yoiada, who had been married to Sinuballit's daughter (Snaith 1934: 13-14; Cross 1974: 20). The claim in Neh. 13.28 that he was chased out of Jerusalem, however, does not square well with his murder by Yohanan over who would succeed to the high priesthood.

29. This leaves only the coin minted by Yohanan the priest as an anomaly, which can perhaps be explained by unique historical circumstances that required money for use at the temple or a temporary appointment of the high priest to the office of governor.

Chapter 2

WHAT'S IN A DATE? THE UNRELIABLE NATURE
OF THE DATES IN HAGGAI AND ZECHARIAH

Introduction

The analysis of the genealogical information in the book of Nehemiah in the foregoing chapter has shown that Zerubbabel and Nehemiah were not separated by some seventy years but rather, were either a generation apart or possibly even members of the same generation. They either succeeded each other in office or they had contemporaneous commissions within Yehud. This information has various implications for recreating the historical circumstances under which the temple was rebuilt in Jerusalem.

In this chapter, I will examine why the books of Haggai and Zechariah were assigned their current, erroneous dates that set the temple rebuilding during the reign of Darius I (521–485 BCE) rather than during the reign of Artaxerxes I (445–432 BCE). In Chapter 3, I will examine how and why the account of the temple rebuilding in Ezra 1-8 assumed its present form, which begins the rebuilding process under Cyrus but dates its completion also to the reign of Darius instead of the reign of Artaxerxes. Since, as I will argue, the author of Ezra 1–6 has used the dates in Haggai and Zechariah as a primary source for his recreation, it is necessary to gain a clear understanding of how these dates, which assign the temple-rebuilding to the early years of the reign of Darius, first arose before proceeding to an analysis of the Ezra narrative. While I am presuming that the year assignments are secondary, I am leaving open the possibility that the month and day elements might have been original and that an editor might have added the year at a much later date. I will look at context clues within the various prophecies to try to determine if they are consistent or not with the day and month dates assigned to them.

Three inter-related quotes from P.R. Ackroyd are appropriate to introduce the tasks at hand.

> It is a well-known fact that later amplifications of historical material tend to be more precise in their details than the earlier records... It may be that the years of the prophetic activity of Haggai and Zechariah are correctly given as from about 520 B.C., but there is no guarantee that the record is correct as it stands. We should need independent evidence to confirm it... It is much more probable that the dates in Haggai (and presumably also in Zech. i-viii) are the work of the compiler of the book, and his dating may be based either on some reliable historical record, which gave the date of the rebuilding of the Temple, or on a reconstruction of history which is no more to be relied on for historical exactness than that of the Chronicler in Ezra-Nehemiah (1951: 172-73).

Three main issues need to be addressed in this chapter. First is the probable secondary nature of all or part of the dating schemes within the books of Haggai and Zechariah. It is generally assumed that the dates had already been added or filled out before Haggai and Zechariah

1–8 was incorporated as a combined literary unit into the Book of the Twelve. This larger work contains the twelve books of the minor prophets but, in Jewish tradition, is considered a single composite work rather than twelve individual works. As a result, it is likely that editorial work has affected each of the works that have been incorporated to create the Book of the Twelve in order to highlight certain motifs or link the parts together more closely (for details, see Nogalski 1993a and 1993b). I will not do an independent assessment of these potential alterations, however, since they would have had minor impact on the already existent dating scheme that had created a new composite account of temple-rebuilding by interweaving traditions in Haggai and Zechariah 1–8.

Secondly, the reason why the prophecies of Haggai and Zechariah specifically have been dated to the opening years of the reign of Darius I needs to be examined. An adequate rationale for the removal of the temple-building from its historical context under Artaxerxes I and its placement almost seventy years earlier must be found.

Finally, the impact that the addition of the dates had on the internal logic and patterning of Haggai and Zechariah 1–8 when they were independent literary units will be explored. Both works will be analyzed as accounts of temple-building, using the standard ancient Near Eastern pattern for organizing such accounts as a basis of assessment. Afterwards, the organization of the new literary unit that chronologically interweaves the various subunits of text within both books to create a new narrative of temple-building will be examined against the standard template.

The books of Haggai and Zechariah contain the following dates:

Hag. 1.1	year 2 of Darius, month 6, day 1
Hag. 1.15	(year 2 of Darius), day 24, month 6
Hag. 2.1	year 2 of Darius, month 7, day 21
Hag. 2.10, 20	day 24, month 9, year 2 of Darius
Zech. 1.1	year 2 of Darius, month 8
Zech. 1.7	day 24, month 11, month of Shebat, year 2 of Darius
Zech. 7.1	year 4 of Darius, day 4, month 9

When seen in chart form, the variations in formulation become apparent: some begin with the year and then give the month followed by the day, while others begin with the year and give the day before the month. Two dates begin with the day, next give the month, and finally, the year. One of these also includes the name of the month in addition to its number within the calendar year. One, on the other hand, gives only the year and month, omitting the day.

It is customary today in most countries to use a single format for writing a date; in the western world, this takes one of two forms. In Europe, the practice is to begin with the day, then the month, and finally, the year. In America, one begins with the month, next gives the day, and then the year. What significance should we attach to these different ways of giving a date in the books of Haggai and Zechariah?

It is also noteworthy that the dates suggest that the prophetic activity of the two prophets overlapped. According to the dating scheme, Zechariah's first prophecy was delivered after Haggai had already made three pronouncements. After Zechariah's initial contribution, Haggai spoke on a final occasion. Then Zechariah spoke two more times. Six of the seven prophecies were allegedly delivered within the second six months of year 2 of Darius, or September 520–March 519 BCE; the remaining one took place two years later, in year 4, or 518 BCE.

We need to see if the contents of the prophecies make sense in terms of the dates that have been assigned or not; this will be one of two strategies we will use to try to determine if the dates are original or secondary. Since a later editor would logically have also used context clues to assign the dates, this method will not be foolproof. However, when used in conjunction with an analysis of the internal structure and coherence of each book and a consideration of whether the dates disrupt this coherence or affirm it, we should be able to make an informed decision about the original or secondary nature of the dates.

In analyzing the possible significance and origin of the dates in Haggai and Zechariah, a number of variables need to be addressed independently. To this end, it seems prudent to begin with a general overview of date formulas as known from the late monarchy in Judah, from the neo-Assyrian empire, from the Neo-Babylonian empire, from the Persian empire, and from the Ptolemaic and Seleucid empires. This covers the sequence of political regimes that controlled the region of southern Cisjordan that was known variously as Judah, Yehud, and Judea from the later monarchy, c. 750 BCE, to the end of the Hellenistic period, c. 33 BCE. The overview can allow us to see if there are chronological, regional, or political differences and preferences. Next, it would make sense to break down the given dates and analyze their components separately: the year-element, on the one hand, and the month and day elements on the other. The latter two need to be taken in conjunction since certain festivals fell within certain months and since 'lucky' and 'unlucky' days varied from month to month, as did days when certain restrictions were in force. Without such correlation, the significance might be overlooked. Finally, the results of the findings can be assessed and conclusions drawn about the origin and function of the dates in these two prophetical books. In light of the previous chapter, I will be seeking to find a plausible explanation for why a later editor would have chosen to assign specific dates within years 2 and 4 of King Darius to the temple-building prophecies, rather than the actual dates they would have been delivered within the reign of Artaxerxes I.

Dating Formulae Used from the Seventh–Second Centuries BCE

The most efficient way to present the following overview is in a table that allows one to scan the data and see the similarities and differences. I will use the single, arbitrary date of day 19, month 6 (Elul), year 2 of Artaxerxes to illustrate all of the formulas, even though he was a Persian king who lived well after the time of the first three political regimes. Since all were headed by kings, however, and most counted years according to the length of the reign of the living king, this approach will not interfere with the larger process; it just will not reflect the reality of when Artaxerxes actually lived. The Assyrians had the unique practice of naming years not numerically by the regnal years of their kings but by the *limmu* system. Each year a new name was selected from among the important court officials and it was to be used in all records written within the ensuing twelve (or thirteen)-month period.

All the countries and empires to be discussed except Egypt reckoned their months from new moon to new moon. As a result, it was necessary from time to time to introduce an additional month into the calendar so that the months would fall approximately within the regular seasonal cycles associated with the 365-day solar calendar. On average, six to eight such intercalary months (a thirteenth month) were needed over a nineteen-year span. It was not until the fourth century BCE during the reign of Artaxerxes II (c. 380 BCE), however, that is was formally recognized that 235 lunar months were equivalent to nineteen solar years and a standardized schedule of intercalations was introduced in fixed years (Addaru [month 12] II in years 3, 6, 8, 11, 14 and 19; Ululu [month 6] II in year 17).

Three systems of dating were used in the southern Levant from c. 750-33 BCE by the different rulers and their scribes. Most nations had a civil year that was calculated from new year to new year. I have indicated in the second column of the chart below whether the new year began in the spring or in the autumn in each instance. Problems arose when this system had to be harmonized with the common means of calculating the year in terms of the amount of time a ruler had been on the throne.

Two solutions were used. The most common was postdating or accession-year calculation (Parker and Dubberstein 1956: 10-24). When a king died, the remaining portion of the civil year was still counted as part of his last, official regnal year. Thus, even though the new king would have been crowned shortly thereafter, the months still left in that calendar year were counted as year 0 of his reign, or his accession year. The official expression used in texts to describe this interim period is 'the beginning of the reign' (Bickerman 1968: 66). The new king's first year began officially at the following civil new year. This system was used by the Assyrians and the Neo-Babylonians and was adopted as well by the Persians (Depuydt 1995: 193; Tadmor 1999: 407) and the Seleucids for use in their western provinces.

The second approach to the problem of harmonizing the civil year with the regnal year was ante-dating. Once a king assumed the throne, the remainder of the civil year in which this occurred became year 1 of his reign, regardless of when the coronation took place within the calendar year. Practically speaking, this meant that some civil years would have been counted as belonging to the reigns of two different kings since one portion would have fallen in the final year of a king who died and another in the first year of his successor. The Ptolemies used this system when they chose to date according to the Egyptian calender rather than the Macedonian calendar.

Finally, the Macedonians and perhaps also the Persians, when they used their native calendrical tradition rather than the Babylonian one, opted for a third system. They chose to ignore the problem of harmonization altogether by not adjusting the regnal year to the civil year. Documents were dated by regnal years, which began on the day a king was crowned and officially took control of the throne (Bickerman 1968: 28, 90, 106 n. 74; Dandamaev and Lukonin 1989: 291; Depuydt 1995: 193-99; Williamson 1985: 169). This practice is sometimes called absolute dating.

Country/empire	System of dating; start of the new year; type of months	Date formula(e)
Judah	Postdating; spring new year at end of monarchy; possible that there was an autumnal new year earlier	19 of sixth (no year) on ostraca; year 2 of Artaxerxes, sixth, 19 in book of Kings
Assyria	Postdating; spring new year; lunar months	Elul 19, *limmu* Beltashazar; Elul 19; Elul, *limmu* Beltashazar
Neo-Babylonia	Postdating; spring new year; lunar months	19 Elul, year 2 of Artaxerxes in economic texts; year 2 of Artaxxerxes, Elul, 19 in narrative and annals
Persia	Postdating; spring new year; lunar months	19 Elul, year 2 of Artaxerxes; 19 Elul, year 2; year 2 of Artaxerxes, 19 Elul in cuneiform narrative; year 2 of Artaxerxes, Elul 19 in old Persian narrative
Seleucids	Macedonian: year began at coronation and was not adjusted to the civil year; autumn new year; lunar months Babylonian: postdating; spring new year; lunar months	Macedonian: year 2 of Artaxerxes, Elul 19 Babylonian: year 2 of Artaxerxes, 19 Elul
Ptolemies	Egyptian: antedating; autumn new year; solar months Macedonian: year began at coronation and was not adjusted to civil year; autumn new year; lunar-based	Egyptian: year 2, Elul 19 of Artaxerxes; year 2, Elul 19 Macedonian: year 2, Elul 19

I will now discuss in more depth the calendrical systems used by the six nations listed in the table. In some instances, multiple systems were used, requiring further explanation, and in the case of Judah, our information is very fragmentary and so our conclusions are uncertain. In addition, relevant bibliography citing examples from ancient documents as well as synthetic studies will be provided for those who are interested in pursuing this topic more fully.

Judah

Little is known about the Hebrew calendar that was used during the time of the Judahite monarchy (c. 975–586 BCE). It is presumed to have been luni-solar, which means it was based on twelve lunar months of twenty-nine to thirty days each, calculated from the observation of the new crescent. The day probably was thought to begin at sunset. An adjustment to the solar year was made through the practice of intercalation. It is likely that the need to add the additional month was based on the observation of the heliacal rising or setting of a fixed star or constellation before the tenth day of month 1 in the spring and of month 7 in the autumn, possibly the Pleiades (Segal 1957: 273-74). If it was not visible, then an additional month was intercalated at this time, usually in the spring, before the grain harvest (Segal 1957: 275-76).

There is some debate over whether the new year was calculated from the autumn or from the spring; the majority of passages currently presuppose a spring civil new year, but it has been proposed that this reflects the adoption of the Assyrian calendar during the time that Judah was a vassal (Thiele 1965: xv; Lemaire 1998: 66-67), or of the neo-Babylonian calendar during the time that Judah was a vassal (Morgenstern 1924: 16-18, 76; Auerbach 1952: 336; de Vaux 1961: 281), or slightly later, when it became a Neo-Babylonian province (Malamat 1968: 144-50). Prior to that time, the civil new year may have begun in the autumn (Kaufman 1954: 313; Thiele 1965: 30),[1] although it has been suggested that it might always have been calculated from the spring (Clines 1974; Galil 1991: 371-72). The regnal year in Judah seems to have been calculated using the system of postdating or accession-year calculation.

The Arad ostraca, dating from the late-seventh century BCE in Judah, show the month in some cases, and the specific day of the month, in others, but give no year dates. The months are given numerically, not by using names, as are the days: tenth = month 10; on the second of the month or on XX IIII of the month specifies the day within the month after the sighting of the crescent (Aharoni 1981: inscriptions 7, 8, 17; Lemaire 1998: 66). No year dates are included.

In the biblical texts, there is a tendency to give only the regnal year in the book of Kings until the end of the seventh century BCE or occasionally, to refer to the year in which a remarkable event took place (Isa. 6.1; 14.28; 20.1; Amos 1.1). It is only in texts dating from the end of the monarchy that the month and day are also included. A full date formula then gives the regnal year, the month indicated by its number, and then the day of the month (2 Kgs 25.1; Ezek. 1.1; 20.1; 24.1; 29.1, 17; 30.20; 31.1; 32.1; 33.21; Jer. 32.9; 52.4, 5-6). Shortened versions provide only the regnal year and month (Ezek. 32.17; Jer. 28.1, 17; 36.9; 39.1) or the month and day (2 Kgs 25.8, 27; Ezek. 45.18, 21, 25; Jer. 52.31) (Lemaire 1998: 59-66).

Neo-Assyria

The Neo-Assyrian calendar was based on twelve lunar months of twenty-nine or thirty days each that was adjusted to the solar year through the addition of between six and eight inter-calary months over a nineteen-year span. The new year began around the spring equinox (Galil 1991: 372; Depuydt 1995: 194). The day began at midnight. Regnal years were adjusted to the civil calendar through the practice of accession or postdating, as they had been in Judah. Assyrian scribes employed the unusual *limmu* system for designating years.

Date formulas were given in legal documents beginning with the month, which was designated by its formal name, followed by the day of the month and ending with the annual eponym (Luckenbill 1975: §428; §695; §840; §873; §1137; S. Dalley and J.N. Postgate 1984: tablets 6-12, 15-17, 29-32, 34, 36-41, 43-45, 49, 51-55, 57, 59-61, 63, 70). So, for example, a grant made by Sargon II that renewed one made earlier by Adad-Nerari III to provide offerings for the god Asshur has the clear date of month Sivan, ninth day, eponym year of Asshur-bani, governor of Calah (= 713 BCE).[2] Shortened forms included the month by name + day of the month (Luckenbill 1975: §229; Dalley and Postgate 1984: tablet 91), and the month by name + annual eponym (Luckenbill 1975: §1142; §1155; Dalley and Postgate 1984: tablets 13). A cuneiform tablet found at Gezer on the border of Judah has the expected full date formula: month by name + day of the month + annual eponym (Johns 1905: 208; Lemaire 1998: 68).

Neo-Babylonia

The Neo-Babylonian calendar year and starting time of the day were calculated in the same way as the Assyrian practice. The *limmu* system was not used in Babylonia, however. Instead, years were calculated in terms of the length of the reign of the living monarch of the time, using the accession or postdating system.

The custom for recording dates on economic texts was to give the day element first, then the month element, using its name, and finally, the regnal year and the name of the king in power. Thus, there were significant differences between the Neo-Assyrian and Neo-Babylonian dating system. Not only were postdated regnal years used to designate the year element instead of the annual eponym/*limmu* system, but the order of the day and month elements was reversed. Examples of this date formula have been found, for example, in documents recovered from the regions of Nippur (Joannès 1982: 69-70) and Uruk (Joannès 1982: 138, 147, 164, 181, 185, 187, 201).

In the Babylonian Chronicles, within the narrative framework, year dates and month dates were given. A summary of important events within a given regnal year were grouped together. The account for the tenth year of Nabopolassar began, for example, 'In the tenth year, Nabopolassar', and then moved on to the first calendrical month that had a significant event: 'in the month of Aiaru'. After describing the event, a new subsection reported on noteworthy events in the next calendrical month when something important transpired: In the month of Abu...; in the month of Ululu...; in the month of Tashritu (Luckenbill 1975: 417-18). Thus, in the context of a narrative, the order within the standard date formula was reversed. The regnal year and name of the king were given first rather than last.

Persia

Since the Babylonian calendar had been used throughout the neo-Assyrian and neo-Babylonian empires by subject peoples, the Persians probably found it simplest to continue its use when they conquered the Babylonians and became the new empire rulers. While it is accepted that this calendar was used in the western part of the Persian empire, there has been debate about whether the eastern empire and the Persian court used a system of absolute regnal reckoning rather than postdating to count regnal years simultaneously while using the Babylonian calendar to determine the civil calendar.

Economic texts from the Babylonian city of Nippur from the Persian period give full dates in the following order: day of the month + month by name + regnal year + name of the monarch, with titles (Joannès 1982: 18, 38-39, 49, 59, 62-64, 71, 74). In some instances, the name of the monarch and titles are omitted (Joannès 1982: 56). Exceptionally, in one instance, the named month precedes the day in the full formula, and the scribe may have forgotten the day and added it out of place in this instance (Joannès 1982: 65). Texts from Shatir (Joannès 1982: 91, 94, 96, 98, 103, 105) and Uruk (Joannès 1982: 154, 165) use the same convention for full dating.

As was the case with the Babylonian Chronicles, in the longer versions of the Behistun inscription, which is in narrative format, the regnal year is given as the first element of a section that details what happened during that time period. 'Said Darius the king: This is what I did in both the second and third year after I became king...' Unfortunately, no additional day or month dates occur in the preserved segment (Kent 1953: DB V). However, in the body of the main inscription, such dates do occur. In the cuneiform version, they give the day element and then the month element by name (von Voigtlander 1978: §§10, 12, 17, 18, 22-26, 28, 31, 34, 37), while in the Old Persian, they give the month by name first and then the day (Kent 1953: §§11, 13, 25, 26-29, 35, 41-42, 46, 50). No year element is given, but the summary sections make it clear that all the dates pertain to the first regnal year: 'This is what I did by the favour of Ahura Mazda in one and the same year after I became king. XIX battles I fought...' (§52).

Dates contained in the papyri found in the caves at Wadi ed-Daliyeh from the fourth century BCE during Persian domination give dates in the following manner: day of the month + month by its proper name and not a numeral + regnal year + name of the king, in certain instances. Inscriptions from Beersheva from the same time period use the same formula, except they do not specifiy the name of the king. Ones from a site near Hevron in Idumea from the same time period use the same formula, occasionally with the name of the king but usually without it (Lemaire 1998: 71-75). Shorter forms of dating are also found. The Aramean ostraca from Arad that probably date to the Persian era give one element of a date using numbers rather than ordinals. While J. Naveh thinks that the numbers designate either days of the month or months (1981: 175), A. Lemaire thinks that they represent years (1998: 72). Their different interpretations highlight the ambiguity of the situation. A jar from Tell Jemmeh gives the month by name + the regnal year, but no name of the monarch.

Within the books of Ezra and Nehemiah, which are set within the Persian era, the standard Persian practice for writing dates in western Asia is followed. The book of Esther, which also is set in the Persian period, is particularly interesting because it has given the month numerically, but then glossed that by adding the name of the month secondarily.

The Ptolemies

After Alexander's death, in 323 BCE, Yehud became part of the Ptolemaic empire until 200 BCE, when it fell under Seleucid jurisdiction. It seems warranted to examine the dating formulas used in each of these dominions as well, in case the editor who created the dates lived in the Greek period. He would have been far enough removed in time from the rebuilding of the temple that he either would not have known the actual date, or, for ideological reasons, may have wanted to associate the dating with the early years of the reign of Darius.

The Ptolemies used two dating systems concurrently in Egypt until the beginning of the second century BCE: the Macedonian, and the Egyptian. In some documents dates are given using both formulas side by side, apparently to avoid any confusion. Soon after 200 BCE, the Macedonian calendar had become completely subservient to the Egyptian and no longer existed independently (Samuel 1962: 31, 138).

The Egyptian civil new year was composed of twelve months of thirty days each, plus five 'epagonal' days added at the end of the year for a total of 365 days. The months were not determined by phases of the moon; however, a true lunar calendar with months of irregular length was used for religious purposes. The year began in late autumn (November) in the month of

Thoth and the day began in the morning (Samuel 1962: 30-31, 39, 41). However, the financial year was calculated from the spring month of Mecheir, which was the sixth month in the traditional civil calendar (Edgar 1931: 50-51). Unlike in Judah, regnal years were antedated (Samuel 1962: 64).

The vast majority of Demotic papyri used the Egyptian civil year in its date formulas. The order of giving the date was regnal year + month by name + number of the day + name of the king (Adler 1939: §§2, 4, 6-7, 13, 116, 20). Some omitted the name of the king as the final element (Adler 1939: §§17, 19).

The Macedonian calendar was lunar-based, beginning when the crescent was first visible in the evening. The day began in the evening, and the civil new year appears to have begun in the autumn (Lemaire 1998: 79). Intercalations were done biennially to bring the calendar in line with the 365-year solar year. The first regnal year of a new king began immediately from the death of a predecessor and was not adjusted to the civil year. The new regnal year began on the anniversary of the coronation (Edgar 1931: 50). The Zenon papyri, which date to the reigns of Ptolemy II (286–246 BCE) and Ptolemy III (246–236 BCE), tended to use either this Macedonian dating system or the one based on the Egyptian financial year that began in Mecheir (Edgar 1931: 50-51). The order of giving the date in the Macedonian system was year + month by name + day of the month (Samuel 1962: 20, 50, 60).

In formal contracts written in Greek that used the Egyptian fiscal year for calculation, the opening sentence began with the standard date formula (year, month, day) and a summary of the transaction. After that, a narrative account giving the details of the transaction ensued. This began with a restatement of the date, which gave the regnal year and the name of the relevant king with corresponding formal titles, and then the day of the month and the month by its formal name (Adler 1939: §§G3, G9, G13). In some narratives, however, the same order appeared in both sections (Adler 1939: §§G5, G11, G21). Some contracts omit the opening summary and begin with the narrative. Both forms of ordering the date elements are found in these shortened formats, suggesting they were considered to be interchangeable (for year, month, day see Adler 1939: §§G10, G14, G17, G18; for year, day month, see Adler 1939: §§G1, G2, G7, G11, G16).

The very limited epigraphic evidence from Palestine that dates to the Ptolemaic period suggests that the Babylonian calendar had remained in force there and that the Egyptian calendar was not adopted. A bilingual Aramaic and Greek ostracon from Khirbet-el-Qom bears the double date: on X II of Tammuz, of year III III=on (day) 12 of Tammuz, year 6/year 6, 12 of month of Panemos. It is thought that the date falls during the reign of Ptolemy II and that the corresponding date in our calendar would be 25 July, 277 BCE (Lemaire 1998: 77-78). The first date clearly follows the Babylonian system, using the Aramaicized form of the Babylonian month name.

Three Greek inscriptions painted in tombs at Maresha in Idumea carry the Greek year dates 1, 2, and 5. These may reflect the reign of Ptolemy V (204–180 BCE), who lost control of Palestine to Antiochus III of the Seleucids in his fifth regnal year.

The Seleucids

The Seleucids appear to have used two calendrical systems as well: the Macedonian, for documents written in Greek, and the Babylonian, for documents written in Aramaic. However, it is thought that Seleucus I endorsed the use of the Babylonian system of date calculation but ordered that the Babylonian names be replaced by their Macedonian equivalents. The day began at midnight, the standard system of intercalations introduced under Artaxerxes II was followed, the year began in the spring, and postdating was used to date regnal years (Bickerman 1968: 25). In writing a complete date, the year was put as the first element, then the day of the month, and finally, the month, called by its formal name in Macedonian.

An ostracon from Maresha bears the date: month of Siwan, year 136 Seleu[cus] (Lemaire 1998: 79). While part of the last name has been restored, the initial consonants suggest that the name is indeed, Seleuchus. This ostracon would seem to indicate a slight change in the regnal scheme was in force; instead of the regnal year of a specific king, the regnal year of the dynasty, calculated from the time of its founding, seems to be used. It is significant, however, that the Aramaic form of the Babylonian month name is used, and the month preceded the year, as was standard in Babylonian practice, but not in Macedonian dates, where the year would have preceded the month.

Date formulas in the books of Maccabees, which relate events that took place under the Seleucids, show a range of options: (1) day of month + month by name + year of Seleucid dynasty (1 Macc. 1.54; 14.27); (2) day of the month + month by number + dynastic year (1 Macc. 13.51); (3) day of month + month by number and by name + dynastic year (1 Macc. 4.52); (4) month by name + dynastic year (1 Macc. 4.59; (5) month by number + dynastic year (1 Macc. 9.3; 10.21); (6) day of month + month by name (Mac 10.5); (7) day of month + month by number and by name (2 Macc. 15.36); (8) dynastic year + month by number (1 Macc. 9.54); (9) dynastic year + day + month by name (2 Macc. 11.21, 30, 33, 38); (10) month by name + day of month (2 Macc. 1.9) . The last two categories are Macedonian and are used in citations of Seleucid or Roman documents in 2 Maccabees; Category (8) has mixed the Macedonian format of the dynastic year as the first element with the Aramaic practice of numbering months rather than using their formal names to give the date of Alcimus' command to pull down the wall of the inner court of the sanctuary in 1 Macc. 9.54. The first eight categories reflect both the Babylonian system of date formulation that uses the formal names of months with the Aramaic practice of numbering months. The order of elements in the date formulation are otherwise the same in the two systems. Categories (3) and (7) harmonize the two systems by including the number of the month as well as its name. This same system was evident in the book of Esther.

Section Summary

Changes took place over time in the way full and partial dates were written by scribes in the territory of ancient Judah and later Yehud and Judea. At the end of the monarchy, the full formula began with the regnal year, next gave the month by number, and finally, the day of the month. This differed from the Assyrian practice on three points: in Assyria, the year stood last rather than first, it was reckoned by eponym rather than regnal year, and the month was given by name, not number. The Babylonian practice differed from the monarchic practice on four points: in Babylonia, the regnal year stood last rather than first, the month was designated by name rather than by number, the day preceded the month as the first element, and it was customary to specify the name of the king. Under the Persians, there was a continuation of the Babylonian practice. Under the Ptolemies, the Persian order was maintained for documents in

Aramaic, while documents written in Greek employed the Macedonian system, which began with the regnal year, then gave the day of the month, and finally, the name of the month. These same two systems remained in effect in Yehud and Idumea under the Seleucids. It is possible that in the latter era, Jewish scribes decided to revert to the use of numbers to designate the months rather than names, which were Babylonian in their origin. The Hasmonean coinage shows an attempt to resurrect the older Hebrew script and the decision to count months rather than designate them by name might have been a similar return to past practice as reflected in the received tradition.

The Dates in Haggai and Zechariah 1–8

A brief survey of the dates contained in Haggai and Zechariah 1–8 shows a mixture of forms (see chart on p. 81). Haggai 1.1 and 2.1 superficially seem to reflect the old monarchic system that began with the regnal year, then gave the month numerically, and ended with the day of the month. By contrast, Hag. 2.10, with one exception, reflects the standard Persian practice of beginning with the day of the month, then giving the month, and ending with the regnal year. However, instead of using the name of the month, it gives the number of the month. The shorter dates in Hag. 1.15 and 2.20 that give day and month would be consistent with either the Persian or Greek practice except for the same anomaly found above: the month is numbered rather than named. The date in Zech. 1.8, on the other hand, of numerical month + regnal year, would be Persian except for the use of the numbered month.

Zechariah 1.7 and 7.1 exhibit the same double designation of the month element that is found in the books of Esther and Maccabees. The former reflects the standard Persian order for giving a complete date: day, month, regnal year, while the latter follows the Macedonian (Ptolemaic) date system: regnal year first, then day of the month, and finally, the named month.

Can any significance be attached to the use of these different date formulations? Were it not for the two that employ the system in vogue at the end of the Judahite monarchy, it could be suggested that all the dates were added by different editorial hands in the Persian and Ptolemaic/Seleucid periods. This position could still be maintained if one would also argue that the two monarchic-style dates are part of a deliberate archaizing program introduced under the Maccabees. However, two considerations suggest that caution is in order. The first is a need to explain convincingly why months are predominantly given by their number rather than by name in both these texts and in other late biblical texts, in contrast to the opposite, more standard practice that is reflected in the limited epigraphic evidence available. In light of these two points, a modified form of this position seems likely.

André Lemaire has noted that there are three tablets dating from the Neo-Assyrian era and written in Aramaic that employ the numerical system of reckoning months. One comes from Asshur, one from Tell Sheikh Hamad, and a third of unknown provenance is in Brussels. He suggests that this may have become an acceptable Assyrian practice in the western parts of the empire where Aramaic was used. By contrast, in documents written in Assyrian, long-standing Sumerian logograms were used, making it difficult to know if this system was native to Assur itself or not (1998: 67-68). If he is correct, the practice of numbering months, if not the native custom within Judah, would have become the standard way of representing months in the Levant during Assyrian vassalship.

Although the Neo-Babylonians preferred to use month names at home, they may have allowed the existing system of designating months numerically to continue to be used as well by scribes in western Asia. When the Persians became the world rulers, they could have left the same dual system in place in the West, leaving it to the discretion and training of individual scribes to decide whether to refer to a month by the Aramaic form of its Babylonian name or by the number of its new crescent moons from the beginning of the civil year. Before this explanation is accepted, however, we should await the finding of an ostracon or other document from the territory of Judah or Yehud and Idumea dating from the sixth century BCE, when the area fell under direct Babylonian administration, which uses this system of reckoning the month by number rather than by name.

The second consideration is our lack of knowledge about the range of variation allowed in representing dates depending on the genre in which they appear. So for example, was it acceptable in a narrative to begin a paragraph that would give a date with the regnal year and the name of the specific king, even if it were standard practice otherwise to place the year in final position when writing the specific date on a receipt or in a contract summary? As seen in the Neo-Babylonian Chronicles, the longer versions of the Behistun inscription that include regnal years 2 and 3, and legal documents written in Egypt under the Ptolemies, this practice was used in narrative sections. Could this account for the three instances where the regnal year appears first in Hag. 1.1, 2.1 and Zech. 7.1? These two issues need resolution before a final proposal can be made concerning the range of dating styles in Haggai and Zechariah 1–8.

The Year Dates

Two year dates are found in Haggai and Zechariah 1–8: year 2 and year 4 of Darius. The entire book of Haggai is currently dated to reflect the beginning of the temple-building process, from the initial clearing work (Hag. 1.15) to the laying of the building's foundation (Hag. 2.18). Zechariah 1–8, on the other hand, has a number of prophecies and visions dated to year 2 in the early stages of the rebuilding (1.1–6.15) but also includes others dated to year 4 (7.1–8.23).

Zechariah 7.1-7

Although Ezra 6.15 provides the exact date of day 3 Adar (month 12), year 6 of Darius for the completion of the temple-building, Zech. 7.1-7 strongly implies that the building process was already completed by year 4. There is a difference of some twenty-four months between the dates implicitly or explicitly given for the completion of the Persian-era temple in the two books. The historical reliability of the temple-building account in Ezra will be analyzed in Chapter 3, but it can be noted here that the author of Ezra has not drawn his explicit date for the completion of the temple rebuilding from an existing date in either Haggai or Zechariah, even though he has otherwise drawn on these books as primary sources for his account of the temple's rebuilding.

In Zech. 7.1-7, Bethel-sharezer,[3] a royal official,[4] and his men send (a messenger or representative) to Jerusalem[5] from an unspecified location to entreat the favor of Yahweh and to ask the priests of the house of Yahweh and the prophets if they should continue to mourn and fast in month 5. The fast was in commemoration of the destruction of the monarchic-era temple in 586 BCE (Jer. 52.29) and the name of the royal official strongly suggests that the delegation had arrived from somewhere in Babylonia or from the Persian court, where Jews who had been born in Babylonia and given local names were now serving. Such diaspora Jews, nevertheless, would have had an interest in maintaining ties to their ancestral homeland and the re-established temple of Yahweh.

> Theophane Chary (1969: 121) and Joyce Baldwin (1974: 142-43) have suggested that the group's arrival three and a half months after the annual fast in month 5 reflects the average time it took to journey from Babylonia to Yehud. In their opinion, this provides implicit evidence that the delegation had been sent from Babylonia immediately after the annual fast to learn if it would need to be kept the next year since the temple was almost completed. There is no need to assume this scenario, however. Rather, once word of the completion of the temple had reached Babylonia or any other diaspora group, it would have been natural for a delegation to have been sent to offer sacrifices on behalf of their local Jewish community and to establish whether the annual fast in commemoration of the destruction of the temple, which evidently was observed in the diaspora, could be ended since the temple was once again functioning.

Verses 2-3 could be seen to imply that the temple was already rebuilt and functioning at this point, with its own cultic personnel. The phrase 'entreat the favor of the Lord', found here and elsewhere in Exod. 32.11; 1 Sam. 13.12; 1 Kgs 13.6; 2 Kgs 13.4; Zech. 8.21, 22; Mal. 1.9; 2 Chron. 33.12; Jer. 26.19; Dan. 9.13, is an idiomatic expression for an action that places a case or request before the deity in some ritual manner. It refers to cultic acts and so presumes the existence of a cult, but is probably not, strictly speaking, technical cultic language that describes a particular action within a ritual (Seybold 1980: 407-409). Thus, the claim by Baldwin that it is an idiomatic expression for the sacrifice and worship offered in the temple is not fully correct (Baldwin 1974: 143). Nevertheless, the phrase seems to indicate that the men were intending to make a formal request to Yahweh at the re-established temple.

It might have been possible to offer sacrifice at the altar in the temple courtyard before the temple building itself had been completed, but this seems an unlikely situation. With workmen all over the construction site, there would have been little decorum and dust and debris would have settled over the altar, creating physical pollution. The sacred zones within the temple precinct would not yet have been enforced, with laymen working inside the temple itself. Thus, the delegation's stated intention to 'entreat the favor of Yahweh' would seem to require that the temple had already been completed and dedicated by the time of their arrival, or that the delegation had timed its arrival to coincide with the rededication of the building.

In either case, the question about whether the annual fast that had commemorated the destruction of the temple could now be ended suggests that it had been less than a year since the last fast had been observed. Thus, the temple had recently been completed (Ackroyd 1958: 19, 26; Mason 1977: 66) or was expected to be finished (Smith 1908: II, 258-59; van Hoonacker 1908: 638; Baldwin 1974: 143; Hoffman 2003: 187) before the next fast in month 5.

The Seventy-Year Figure in Zechariah 7.4
The rationale for the dating of the temple completion in year 4 of Darius is conveniently provided in Zech. 7.4. Yahweh tells Zechariah to say to all the priests and the people of the land, 'When you fasted and mourned in the fifth month and in the seventh for these seventy years, was it for me that you fasted?' The seventy years in v. 4 represent the length of time

between the destruction of the temple in year 18 or 19 of Nebuchadrezzar (Jer. 52.29; 2 Kgs 25.8-9) and the completion of its rebuilding in year 4 of Darius.

As already noted, the fast in month 5 commemorated the destruction of the temple on day 7 of that month in 587/586 BCE. The fast in month 7, not mentioned in the delegation's question in v. 3 to which v. 4 allegedly was providing an answer, commemorated the murder of Gedaliah (2 Kgs 25.25; Jer. 41.1-2) in that month in 582 BCE.[6] While this date may have become an annual fast day within Yehud, members of the diaspora had not lived under Gedaliah in Yehud and would not necessarily have supported his appointment to oversee the new neo-Babylonian province since he was not of Davidic royal ancestry. It is unlikely, therefore, that they would have observed the fast in month 7.

This apparent contradiction is easily eliminated if the suggestion made by C.F. Whitley is adopted (1954: 64). He has argued that the text in v. 4 originally read, 'When you fasted and mourned in the fifth month on the seventh day of the month' and that the word 'day' somehow dropped out of the text in transmission. In this case, the date reference would have been to the exact day on which the temple had been burnt and desecrated by Nebuzaradan, Nebuchadrezzar's officer, as recorded in 2 Kgs 25.8. Following this lead, Yahweh's reply to the question asked by Bethel-sharezer's representatives about the ending of the annual fast commemorating the destruction of the temple would make perfect sense; it would not introduce a secondary, unintelligible reference to a fast that commemorated the assassination of Gedaliah. Instead, it would give the actual date of the annual fast relating to the temple destruction that was about to be removed from the cultic calendar because of the rededication of the temple in Jerusalem.

Why has the figure of seventy years been used, and is it to be taken figuratively or literally? The suggestion that it represents a lifetime and that the message being conveyed was that those who had experienced the destruction of the temple and fall of Jerusalem would not live to see its rebuilding is not likely (Baldwin 1974: 97; Achtemeier 1986: 114; Tollington 1993: 187 as one of two options). While Ps. 90.10 claims that a lifetime lasts three score and ten or even four score by reason of strength and Isa. 13.15 claims seventy years is the life-span of a king, it is generally thought that the average life-span in the ancient world was only forty-odd years. Thus, someone who lived to be seventy would have been extraordinarily old. Members of the elite and priesthood would have enjoyed longer lives by virtue of their better diet and lack of performance of manual labor throughout their lifetimes, which almost certainly is reflected in the higher figures in Ps. 90.10. Nevertheless, the majority of people would have died well before the age of seventy. Thus, while it is the case that almost no one other than the exceptional infant or toddler would still have been alive seventy years later, this does not appear to have been the reason why the figure of seventy was used to describe the length of the predicted period of ruin in Zechariah (so also Waterman 1954: 75).

The number seventy appears in Mesopotamian and biblical texts in the seventh and sixth centuries BCE as the length of time a land was to lay waste due to the anger of a deity (Ackroyd 1958: 23-27; Lipiński 1970: 38-40; Baldwin 1974: 97; Fishbane 1980: 355-58; Meyers and Meyers 1987: 117; Hurowitz 1992: 140-43; Tadmor 1999: 403-404; Bedford 2001: 165). An inscription of Esarhaddon (681–669 BCE) states that Marduk ordinarily would have been angry with his land for seventy years but had shown mercy and reduced the period to eleven years (Luckenbill 1924/25: 166-67; Borger 1956: 15, §10). There is a numerical play in this particular text:

Marduk renounced the decree by reversing the order of the two numerical signs for seventy, which yielded the number eleven. Isaiah 23.15-18 predicts that Tyre will be laid waste for seventy years, after which Yahweh will restore it to its fortunes, which will be used to feed and clothe those who dwell before him. These two applications, one extra-biblical and one biblical, employ the seventy-year figure of ruination to nations other than Judah. The first highlights the conventional nature of the figure in connection with the motif of the devastation of a city in the wake of divine anger and its abandonment, while the second is used more atypically to refer to a non-native deity restoring the fortune of a foreign city, which will then come under his dominion. In these uses, seventy appears to represent 'a very long time'.[7]

Jeremiah 25.11, 12 employs this same literary convention. The verses have Yahweh state that he is bringing Nebuchadnezzar and all the tribes of the north against the land of Judah, its inhabitants and the surrounding nations. As a result, the entire land will become a ruin and a waste and Judah, along with nations round about, will serve the king of Babylon for seventy years. Afterwards, Yahweh will punish the king of Babylon and make his land an everlasting waste. Jeremiah 29.10 then reiterates the seventy-year figure as the length of time that Babylon will rule the world, before which the exile will be ended. The statement is set in the context of the battle of Carchemish, which took place in 605 BCE, and assigns the Neo-Babylonians world dominion for a period of seventy years. If the number is taken literally, Neo-Babylonian dominion should have ended in 535 BCE. However, Cyrus' conquest of Babylon in 538 BCE effectively ended Babylonian dominion in 538 BCE, three years shy of the seventy-year figure. The lack of an exact seventy-year interval emphasizes the figurative use of the number in the prediction; it was sheer coincidence that the Neo-Babylonian empire ended sixty-seven years later. The central message of the prophecy is that Assyria will have world dominion 'for a long time' but then will be destroyed by another, and this was certainly the case historically.[8]

Nevertheless, it would be easy for a later person reading Jer. 25.11-12, who was not familiar with events in the late-seventh century BCE, to assume that the seventy-year period would have begun with the final destruction of Jerusalem in 586 BCE (Tadmor 1999: 405; Hoffman 2003: 188). Mention of the land becoming a waste for seventy years would naturally be associated with the final Neo-Babylonian devastation and second round of deportations in 586 BCE rather than with the first set of deportations in 597 BCE, which did not result in the destruction of Jerusalem or the temple (contra Achtemeier 1986: 114), or with the earlier, lesser-known battle at Carchemish. The proposal of G.A. Smith to take as a starting point the average of the two exiles, 590 BCE, which would then make year 2 of Darius, 520 BCE, exactly seventy years later is unnecessary and is seeking to historicize what was a figurative number to begin with (1908: 258 n. 1).

An echo of Jeremiah's prediction of seventy years of divine wrath against Judah and Jerusalem occurs earlier in the book of Zechariah in 1.12. The messenger of Yahweh asks, 'O Yahweh Sebaot, how long will you have no mercy on Jerusalem and the cities of Judah, against which you have had indignation these seventy years?' This comment, placed near the beginning of the book, is part of the traditional lament genre. The reference to the completion of seventy years signals the end of the proscribed period of punishment and the proper time for Yahweh to cease his anger and for the temple to be reinstated. The standard question of 'how long?' is found in Mesopotamian lament literature and is included in the ritual used to assuage the deity on the eve of repairing, rebuilding, or rededicating a temple.[9] Thus, Zechariah ben Iddo and/or a later editor of the book appear to have associated the rebuilding of the temple with the ending of a seventy-year interval of destruction that had been initiated by Yahweh against his people.[10] In his view, the Babylonian conquest of Judah had been designed by Yahweh as a temporary punishment for his people's transgressions, which would be reversed after seventy years of foreign rule and exile. Yahweh's restoration to his temple could only be accomplished once his divine wrath had ended and he was ready to return to his traditional sanctuary.

It seems likely that the person responsible for the original claims in Jer. 25.10-11 and 29.10 that the land of Judah and, by implication, its destroyed temple would lay in ruins for seventy years was using the standard ancient Near Eastern conventional figure for the length of time devastation would endure in the wake of divine anger and punishment through foreign oppression. It was meant to be taken figuratively and symbolically, not literally.

Was Zechariah or the editor of his book independently using the same standard convention of seventy years to express a long period of foreign oppression brought on by divine wrath? Or, was he specifically alluding to the two prophecies in Jeremiah that had applied this convention to both Assyria's dominion over Judah and its assigned length of world dominion in general? An answer to these two questions has important repercussions about whether the dating of the temple's rebuilding has been set in years 2–4 of Darius because either the founding date or the completion date was nearly or precisely seventy years after the destruction of the monarchic-era temple.

Before tackling this important question, however, we need to know if the length of time between the destruction of Jerusalem and the beginning of its rebuilding in year 2 of Darius or its potential completion in year 4 of this king was exactly seventy years or not. This can help us make a more informed decision about the writer's motivations in using the figure of seventy years.

The Date of the Destruction of the Temple by Nebuchadrezzar

Assigning modern dates to year 18 or 19 of Nebuchadnezzar and to years 2 and 4 of Darius' reign is not a simple task. There are three primary issues that must be resolved before calculation can occur. I will discuss each and illustrate how they potentially affect the reckoning of either set of dates. Drawing on the observations made in the course of these presentations, I will then address specifically the date of the final destruction of the temple and the beginning of Darius' official reign before surveying the range of years between the destruction of the first temple, the start of its rebuilding in year 2 of Darius, and its probable completion in year 4 of Darius.

Preliminary Considerations. A central issue in reckoning ancient Near Eastern dates in terms of our current calendar is determining whether the civil new year began in the spring or in the autumn, which effectively adds a six-month difference to dates calculated one way versus the other. It has been suggested that the different year dates found in 2 Kgs 25.8/Jer. 52.12 (year 19) and Jer. 52.29 (year 18) for Nebuchadnezzar's destruction of Jerusalem, the temple, and the deportation of a large portion of the local population could derive from the use of two different dating systems. The local Judahite system may have calculated the new year from the autumn while the Babylonian calendar was based on a spring new year, accounting for the discrepancy if both dates refer to the same cluster of events (so, e.g., Thiele 1965: 27; Borowski 2002: 42). Year 18 of Nebuchadnezzar would be 586 BCE and year 19 585 BCE. While the Jeremiah passage only explicitly refers to a deportation in year 18, it has generally been assumed that this would have taken place immediately after the capture and destruction of Jerusalem so that both dates should coordinate and agree. Only the year is given in Jeremiah, however, so we cannot determine for certain whether the difference in dating reflects the use of different beginning dates for the civil year or not.

It should be noted that Ezek. 33.21 supports both dates, depending which manuscript tradition is followed. The verse states that in the twelfth/eleventh year of the first exile, in the tenth month, on the fifth day of the month, a man who had escaped from Jerusalem arrived at Ezekiel's house and told him that the city had fallen. The Babylonian Chronicles confirm that the first set of deportations took place in month 12 of 597 BCE (Wiseman 1956: 47, 73), so year 11 would place the fall of Jerusalem in 586 BCE while year 12 would set its fall in 585 BCE. Although the majority of manuscripts read 12 in v. 21, one group reads 11. The difference between the two is a single consonant: *bshty* (12) versus *b'shty* (11). It is possible that the original reading was 11, which included the letter *'ayin* ('), and that it secondarily became 12 when the *'ayin* was inadvertently dropped in copying (Lipiński 1970: 40 n. 3).

In this case, Ezekiel would agree with the date given in Jer. 52.29 for the second deportation. However, it seems equally possible that the *'ayin* could have been added secondarily by a scribe who wanted to harmonize this date with the one given in 2 Kgs 25.8, which explicitly dates the burning of the temple by Nebuzaradan, captain of Nebuchadnezzar's bodyguard, to day 7, month 5 of year 19–585 BCE. Thus, this third text does not help establish whether 586 or 585 is the most likely year for the destruction of the temple, or whether one or two texts has miscalculated the year by assuming the Judahite civil year that began in the autumn instead of the Babylonian civil year that began in the spring.

A second crucial issue is the need to determine if the dating scheme in use follows a civil calendar to which the king's reign has been adjusted using postdating or whether it is based on royal regnal years that run from the time of accession to the time of death. It is thought that the native Persian system followed the latter practice. Elias Bickerman (1981: 28) has suggested that the native Persian calendar based on absolute dating was used simultaneously in the empire alongside the postdated Babylonian calendar. Thus, even though it has generally been assumed that the dates in Haggai and Zechariah assume a civil year that begins in the spring and follows the postdating practice, (e.g. van Hoonacker 1908: 545), the accuracy of this assumption remains unconfirmed and different date equivalencies would result if one used the hypothesized Persian royal court reckoning method instead. It also should be noted that the Macedonians used this same system of calculation of the year from the day of royal accession, without an adjustment to a civil calendar (Samuel 1962: 24-30, 64-65), so that a subsequent editor living in the Hellenistic period might have reckoned dates in previous eras via this method, on the assumption that it had been standard in earlier periods as well.

Although it is generally believed that the traditional system of regnal calculation in Judah had used postdating, some have argued that the person responsible for the regnal dates of Darius in Haggai and Zechariah may have unknowingly used the system of antedating, which had been used by the Persian court to deny any legitimacy to the brief reign of Cambyses' successor, his brother Bardiya (so, e.g., Waterman 1954: 76-77; Bickerman 1981: 25-27). In the particular case of Darius' accession, which took place irregularly, it has been argued that the officials responsible for maintaining the Persian court calendar may have altered normal practice and antedated the reign rather than postdating it as they would have done customarily in order to eliminate Bardiya from the history of succession. His accession regnal year had begun in month 12, day 14 of year 7 of Cambyses, 11 March, 522, according to §11 of the Behistun inscription (see Appendix 1), but Darius killed him and assumed the throne on 29 September, 522 (§13). By making the year that began a few weeks after Bardiya's claim to be king, from the end of March 522–spring 521 BCE his first regnal year rather than an accession year, Darius would have followed a common practice among those claiming to have overthrown a usurper and restored the throne to legitimate succession (Bickerman 1981: 25-26).

The plausibility of this proposal is seriously challenged, however, by Darius' own propagandistic account of his accession to the throne on the Behistun monument (von Voigtlander 1978) (see Appendix 1). Yes, it is the case that he has specifically claimed that Bardiya was being impersonated by Gaumata, a *magus* (wise man) from Media, and so had no legal right to the throne of Cambyses (§11-13), while he did, as a member of a collateral royal line (§3). Thus, he proclaims himself to be the restorer of legitimate succession (§14-15). However, he also specifically states that he only became king after he killed Bardiya on the tenth day of Tashritu, 29 September, 522 (§13) which then would make the remaining six months of 522–21 BCE his accession year according to normal practice. Unlike a normal usurper/restorer, he has chosen to 'tell all' in a carefully orchestrated account that immortalizes Bardiya as a villainous liar rather than trying to erase all memory of him from future generations.

A second objection to this proposal is that all of Bardiya's short 'reign' took place in years 7–8 of Cambyses. The last known private documents that are dated to Cambyses are all from Babylonia and all derive from month 1 of his year 8 (Parker and Dubberstein 1956: 14). This means that all of the year that ran from the end of March, 522 to mid-March, 521 BCE would have officially been assigned to his year 8, regardless of when he died during the course of the year. According to the Behistun monument, Gaumata had begun his claim to be Bardiya and king of Persia on day 14 of Adar, month 12 (year 7 of Cambyses) (§11). Although no private documents have yet turned up a date to that month with his name attached, documents dating to months 1–7 of either accession year or year 1 of his reign are known from various cities in Babylonia, which clearly demonstrate he was accepted as king there from April 14, 522–September 20, 522 BCE, within a month of his first declaration (Parker and Dubberstein 1956: 14-15). Thus, none of his ten-month reign would have taken place in a civil year that would not have been counted officially as a regnal year of Cambyses.

Because of this situation, there would have been no need to antedate to cover up or eliminate Bardiya's reign from the official records. Had Darius assumed the throne immediately upon the death of Cambyses sometime in the civil year that ran from spring 522–spring 521 BCE, the balance of that year would have been reckoned his year 0, or accession year. Thus, Bardiya's ten-month reign had no impact on the official length of Darius' reign in the normal postdating system (so, e.g., Wolff 1988: 75-76; Kessler 2002: 84).

However, had the Persian court used absolute regnal dating in which the regnal year was reckoned from the date a new king assumed the throne in Persia alongside the Babylonian system, then this argument could still have merit. The gap in succession would have been greater than normal and would have left room to include Bardiya's brief reign in the records. As argued above, however, there was no apparent intention to write him out of the history books, so even if the system of absolute dating was used, Darius' claim that he assumed the throne only after Bardiya's death signals an intention not to backdate to the death of Cambyses and eliminate any record of Bardiya's kingship.

The antedating argument is built upon the presumption that Haggai's references to Yahweh's intention to overthrow the world kingdoms and restore Zerubbabel in 2.6-8 and 2.20 only make sense within the context of the widespread rebellions against Darius that took place in 521 BCE. With the new proposed dating, they would have been proclaimed on 28 October and 30 December, 521 BCE. The first would have coincided with the second rebellion of Babylon and the second with the third revolt of Elam. While this certainly would be more logical than the standard date that would place the sayings in 520 BCE when peace had been restored throughout the empire and Darius was in firm control, it is not clear that these two sayings of Haggai were triggered by specific historical events (as noted by, e.g., Bentzen 1930; Ackroyd 1958: 21; Kessler 2002: 85).

Temple-building was traditionally the task of kings, and after a temple was (re)dedicated, the king's status as his god's earthly vice-regent was reaffirmed, and a long and prosperous reign was promised by the god. If Zerubbabel were indeed of the Davidic line, which seems to have been the case, then it would have been logical for a local or pro-Davidic prophet to include some words of encouragement to him. The promise that he will become like a divine signet ring is vague enough to signal him as receiving some sort of divine favor, but does not shout out 'you will become king of an independent Judah'. The claim that Yahweh is about to shake the heavens, the earth, the sea, the dry land, and all the nations so that the treasure of all nations will fill his temple with glory is more a motif associated with the divine manifestation of power and claim that Yahweh is universal sovereign than with an expression of political realities in year 2 of the reign of Darius. Similar ideas and language are found, for example, in Ezekiel 38–39, Joel 3.4 (Eng. 3), and Zechariah 12–14, which are not likely to stem from the same historical situation.

A problem that results from adopting this chronology is that Bardiya would have authorized the rebuilding of the temple and sent Zerubbabel to be the new governor of Yehud (Bickerman 1981: 27-28). This contradicts the standard understanding that Darius is the logical person to have authorized the project because of his claim on the Behistun monument to have restored temples throughout the kingdom (§14) (see Appendix 1) and the claim in Ezra 6.8 that he authorized the use of royal revenue to pay for the rebuilding. Logically, the search should have been made for the edict of Bardiya that had given permission to rebuild the temple, not one of Cyrus. Thus, if one wants to follow the earlier dates and their historical implications, one also has to be ready to accept the logical consequences that stem from them, which call into question the historicity of the account in Ezra. This topic will be explored in more depth in Chapter 3. Either Bardiya or Darius could have authorized the temple's reconstruction if, in fact, the project began in this time frame. However, the genealogical information in Nehemiah makes it unlikely that this was the case historically.

Finally, there is the issue of whether years are being counted inclusively or not. So, for example, the period from year 5 to year 10 can be considered to cover five years, if only one of the two end dates is included, but six years if both the starting and ending dates are counted. 2 Kings 18.9, 10 states that the period of time between the seventh and ninth regnal years of Hosea covered three years, providing a clear illustration of inclusive counting within the book of Kings. Depending which system is used, a difference of a year can result. The one-year discrepancy in the year of Nebuchadnezzar's reign during which Jerusalem and the temple were destroyed may have arisen from the use of inclusive counting in the case of year 19, and non-inclusive counting in the case of year 18.[11]

Year 18 or Year 19 of Nebuchadnezzar? Concerning the date of the final destruction of the monarchic-era temple, the Babylonian Chronicle records the date that Jerusalem was first seized by Nebuchadnezzar and Yehoiakin was deposed in favor of Zedekiah as day 2, Adar (month 12), year 7, or 15/16 March, 597 BCE (Wiseman 1956: 32-35). 2 Kings 24.12 claims that this event took place in year 8 of Nebuchadnezzar, without giving a month or a day, rather than year 7. By contrast, Jer. 52.28 correctly places these events in year 7. Like the author of Kings, the compiler has not specified a month or day. These events took place in the final month of year 7, allowing for the possibility that the biblical writer has based his date on deportations or subsequent looting actions that took place just after the turn of the year. Alternatively, G. Galil has noted that year 7 of Nebuchadnezzar was intercalary in Babylonia and an extra month (Ululu 2) had been inserted at the beginning of the second half of the year. If Judah had not made this year intercalary, then month 12 in the Babylonian civil year would have corresponded to month 1 of the new year in the Judahite calendar (1991: 376).

However, neither of these explanations is fully convincing, because 2 Kgs 25.8 similarly gives a year date one year higher than the one in Jer. 52.29 for the final capture and destruction of Jerusalem: year 19 versus year 18. In this instance, the specific date for the fall is given as month 5, day 7, which occurred in the middle of the year, precluding any question of a mistaken date because the operations took place at the turn of the year.

It is most unfortunate that no copies of the tablets of the Babylonian Chronicle recording events in the empire between years 594/93 and 557/56 BCE have yet been found, allowing us to confirm the exact date of the final capture of Jerusalem and destruction of the temple. Nevertheless, it would appear that the author of Kings has consistently miscalculated his Babylonian dates of Nebuchadnezzar by one year, whereas the compiler of Jeremiah probably has them correct. (For a detailed analysis of biblical dates, see Freedy and Redford 1976: 462-85.) The best way to account for this phenomenon would be to assume that the author of Kings has counted inclusively. This being the case, it would be better to accept the year date of 18 in Jer. 52: 29, which would place the fall in 586 BCE and not year 19, which would place it in 585 BCE. The date given in Ezek. 40.1, which supports the reckoning in 2 Kings, strongly suggests that the person responsible for its addition to Ezekiel was following the dating given in 2 Kings over that given in Jeremiah and/or was using inclusive counting, as was the editor of Kings.

Year 1 of Darius
Let us now turn to the date at the other end: Darius' accession to the throne of Persia. Once again, there are problems. In this case, they stem from a series of usurpations and revolts that

had to be overturned before Darius was firmly ensconced as king. He was not the natural son of Cambyses or the designated heir to the throne. He claims to have belonged to a collateral royal line (Behistun monument, §2-4; Appendix 1), but it is suspected that these claims are false and part of an attempt to legitimate his acquisition of the throne. Three factors are telling. The first is the certain knowledge that his father had been a local Persian administrator, not a king, so his claim to have come from a long line of kings is false (Briant 2002: 110, contra Olmstead 1938: 394). The second is the series of subsequent traditions about the group of the seven that all explain how he was chosen as a first among equals to kill Bardiya. None of these traditions appeals to his royal background to explain his choice among the others, which would have been the obvious reason for his selection had it been the truth. As a member of the royal family, he at least could have been able to claim some sort of legitimacy as successor, which the others could not have. The final involves his reported marriage to Cyrus' two daughters, Atossa and Artysone, which, if reliable, in retrospect certainly looks like a bid to use marriage into the ruling family to solidify an otherwise shaky claim to a legitimate right to the throne (for this tactic, see Morgenstern 1929).

> The extant sources provide contradictory accounts of the events that transpired, complicating matters further (Behistun I §§10-13 in Appendix 1; Ctesias *Persika* §§10-13; Justin 1.9.4-11; Herodotus 3.30.61-78). Thus, since Darius' rise to the throne was beset by a number of problems, there is room for debate about when his official reign would have begun, regardless of whether it was counted from his date of accession or from the ensuing new civil year after his official assumption of the throne.

> Cyrus had two male heirs: Cambyses, his eldest son, and Smerdis/Bardiya/Barziya his second son, both by the same mother. The rendering of the name of the second son varies tremendously. In the Behistun inscription, one finds Bardiya, while in Babylonian tablets, the name is written Barziya. Greek sources, on the other hand, have Smerdis, Tanyoxarkès, Tanoxarès, Margis, and Mardos. The variations seem to reflect attempts to render a foreign name into other languages using what would be familiar combinations of syllables and, in some instances, standard ways of taking over certain consonantal sounds. Cyrus chose Cambyses to succeed him and made him King in Babylon in 538 BCE. According to Xenophon, he made Bardiya *satrap* of Media, Armenia, and Cadusia in consolation (*Cyrop* 8.7.11). Cambyses assumed the throne in 530 BCE. He conquered Egypt in 525 BCE and spent some three years there physically, winning its loyalty and establishing its Persian administration. At some point either before his departure or during his stay, he is said to have ordered the execution of his brother Bardiya, for varying reasons. While Cambyses was en route home from Egypt, his brother allegedly declared himself king of Babylon or all of Persia, depending which source is followed. However, the person who did this allegedly was not the actual brother, but a *magus* named Gaumata who bore a physical resemblance to the prince, but who was able to perpetuate the ruse because Bardiya's execution had been done in secret so that most people in the empire thought he was still alive.

> Darius, Cambyses' spear-bearer, then allegedly departed immediately for Persia, while the rest of the army remained in camp with the king. He set up an alliance with six others, all from aristocratic families. Bardiya was killed by these seven on day 10 of month 7 in 522 BCE, and Darius was proclaimed the new king instead. Cambyses had no children at this point and the only other heir to the throne from the line of Cyrus had been Bardiya.

Documents from Babylon have dates assigned to both Cambyses and Bardiya in April of 522 BCE,[12] indicating this is when Bardiya had declared himself king in that city and was accepted as such by the populace (Parker and Dubberstein 1956: 14-15). The titles assigned to him in the documents are 'king of the lands' and 'King of Babylon, king of the lands'. These dates seem to be in line with the date given in the Behistun inscription of day 14, month of Viyaxna (month 12), or 11 March, 522 BCE, for the beginning of his revolt (§11 in Appendix 1). They can be seen to agree also with the subsequent claim that Bardiya assumed the reins of power over the entire Persian empire officially on Garmapada (month 4), day 4 of the following year, 1 July, which ran from the end of March, 522–March, 521 BCE. It is implied that this is the month in which Cambyses had died (§11), though without the specific date of death provided, it is difficult to know which occurred first.

It is clear that the account of events that was endorsed by Darius and publicly declared has been shaped to depict him as the suppressor of an illegitimate usurper, on the one hand, and a legitimate candidate to inherit the throne, on the other. This official account was written in Old Elamite, Old Persian, and Akkadian on the Behistun monument and it was subsequently translated into other languages used within the Persian empire and distributed widely for public consumption. Its version of the 'facts' is not likely to be fully reliable.

In particular, Darius' claim that the real Bardiya had been executed and that a *magus* had assumed the prince's identity in his place sounds like an attempt to circumvent the fact that he had, in fact, executed the royal prince who had led a revolt against this brother Cambyses in an attempt to take over the throne but had subsequently inherited the throne legally. It seems likely that the failure to give Cambyses' specific date of death is deliberately designed to cover up Bardiya's legitimate succession to the kingship of Persia upon the death of his brother in July of 522 BCE. This, in turn, allowed the perpetuation of the view that a *magus* posing as Bardiya had illegitimately usurped the kingship of all of Persia shortly before Cambyses' death. As a result, Darius' execution of the rightful successor to the throne with the backing of members of six powerful aristocratic Persian families three months into his legitimate kingship could be seen to be a righting of injustice by one who allegedly could lay claim through kinship to be a legal heir to the throne after the death of the legitimate claimants in Cyrus' line. It seems likely, then, that Darius usurped the throne after sizing up the situation at the time of Cambyses' death and seeing an opportunity to gain power for himself in light of Cambyses' childlessness and Bardiya having been passed over as king by Cyrus (for a sustained discussion see Briant 2002: 97-128).

Assuming the standard Babylonian practice of postdating, Darius' first year of reign would have begun at the civil new year in March, 521 BCE, after having become king on day 9 of month 4, or 1 July, 522 BCE. He would have reigned eight months during his accession year, from 1 July, 522–March, 521 BCE, which was officially counted as year 8 of Cambyses (for various reconstructions of the events and dates in the accession year and year 1 see, e.g., Olmstead 1938: 397-409; Poebel 1938; Cameron 1941: 314-19; Parker 1941; Hallock 1960; Briant 2002: 97-128). The former is the general date assigned for year 1 of his reign, which is why it is generally thought that the prophecies of Haggai and Zachariah, dated to years 2 and 4 of Darius, correspond to 520 and 518 BCE.

However, as soon as he had assumed the throne in Persia, his control over Babylon was contested by Nidintu-Bel, a high tax officer who declared himself king of Babylon. He assumed the throne name of Nebuchadrezzar III, presenting himself as the son of Nabonidus (Behistun monument, §16). Tablets from Sippar and Babylon have been uncovered that date his reign to month 7, or October, 522 BCE, three months after Darius' coronation as king of the Persian empire (Parker and Dubberstein 1956: 15). The Behistun inscription claims that Darius personally led his army against the rebel and after two successive routings of the enemy, he caught Nidintu-Bel and put him to death on day 2, month 10, or 18 December, 522 BCE (§18-20). Tablets from Babylon, Sippar and Kutha reflect Darius' reassumption of power in the area by month 11 of his accession year February, 521 BCE and his ongoing control at Sippar into months 5 and 6 of his first regnal year, August-September, 521 BCE (Parker and Dubberstein 1956: 15). The inclusion of year 1 on the latter tablets strongly suggests that after the revolt, his rule in the Babylonian region was synchronized with his ongoing rule in Persia as though there had been no interruption. Thus, it appears that there was no decision within Babylonia to begin the reckoning of his reign anew from the termination of the revolt.

Darius claims to have quashed nine rebellious lands after regaining control of Babylon in the course of the ensuing year (§21). He claims to have left Babylon in mid-January, 521, but had to send a general back there to suppress a second claimant to the throne, an Urartian named Arkha, who took the throne name of Nebuchadrezzar IV. He had arisen initially in Ur but after winning the support of the Babylonian army, had taken possession of Babylon (§49). Tablets from al-Gadiete and Uruk are dated in his name for month 5, August-September, 521 BCE while some from Uruk, Babylon, and Sippar are dated in month 7, or October-November, 521 BCE (Parker and Dubberstein 1956: 16). However, it is possible that the latter documents are to be assigned to the first rebel rather than the second (Briant 2002: 120).

Vindafarna, one of the six who had helped Darius assassinate Bardiya, quashed the second Babylonian rebellion on 27 November, 521 (§50, 68) and a document from Borsippa dating from the ensuing ninth month, December, 521 BCE, and ones from Sippar and Babylon in month 10, demonstrate that Darius was re-accepted as official king almost immediately (Parker and Dubberstein 1956: 16). All of these tablets are dated to year 1 of Darius, which implies that, as had been the case after the first revolt, the Babylonian dating system was correlated with Darius' ongoing, uninterrupted rule in Persia once the revolt was put down (contra Olmstead 1938: 402). According to longer versions of the text found at Behistun, however, rebellions continued into years 2 and 3, so that it was only in 519 BCE that peace was fully established and Darius' authority was recognized in all parts of the Persian empire (for details, see conveniently Briant 2002: 127-28; for the Old Persian version of these two years, see Kent 1953: 134 [DB V]).

So from what date would Darius' reign have been calculated by the person responsible for the dates in the book of Haggai and Zechariah? Would he have used the dates in vogue in the Persian capital, which probably would have reckoned Darius' reign to have begun from the date of his coronation after Bardiya's death on 29 September, 522 BCE, or would he have antedated it to begin at the end of March, 522? Alternatively, would he have used the Babylonian system, which would have begun Darius' year 1 at the new year in spring, 521 BCE? Is it possible that multiple dating systems were used for Darius – one by the royal Persian court and the other(s) by scribes in the various lands, which calculated his reign according to their local customs?[13] Would the Babylonian system have been used in the province of Yehud at the time of Darius' accession, and would the same system have continued in use throughout Persian rule and into the Greek era, so that a later editor would have used the same system?

As noted above, the extant documentary evidence indicates that local Babylonian scribes had counted both rebellions as blips within Darius' ongoing reign, which had begun with an accession year during the latter half of Cambyses' year 8. Nevertheless, it could be argued that someone living a generation or more subsequent to these events who used the Behistun inscription or information derived from it as a source for dating Darius' reign could have done otherwise. He might have found it more logical to count Darius' first regnal year in Babylonia from after his quashing of the second revolt there. In this case, the date would be one year lower than his normal first regnal year: spring, 520 rather than spring, 521 BCE. Might he have then assigned this date to Darius' reign in Persia as well?

The Seventy-Year Tradition Revisited

If we stay with the traditional dates assigned to various events and reigns, there is a sixty-six-year gap between the destruction of the temple in 586 BCE and the laying of its new foundation in 520 BCE, or year 2 of Darius, and a sixty-seven-year gap if that time period is counted inclusively. There is a sixty-eight-year gap between the destruction of the temple and the possible completion of the temple in the fourth year of Darius, in 518 BCE, if counting non-inclusively, and sixty-nine years if counting inclusively (Zech. 7.1). If we were to lower Darius' first regnal year to 520 BCE, presuming that the later editor calculated Darius' reign only from his successful suppression of the second revolt in Babylonia, but maintain the traditional date of 586 BCE for the destruction of the temple, we arrive at a time gap of sixty-seven/sixty-eight years until the laying of the new temple foundation and one of sixty-nine/seventy years until the completion of the building.

The range of figures from the above possible calculations, taken together with the direct reference to seventy years in Zech. 1.7 and 7.1, allows for the possibility that the person who created the dates in the books of Haggai and Zechariah intended the completion of the new temple building to have occurred exactly seventy years after the date of the destruction of the first temple. While not impossible, this does not seem likely for three reasons. First, in order to arrive at the exact figure, it is necessary to postulate that a later scribe miscalculated the first year of Darius, using information from a copy of the Behistun monument showing when he had gained firm control of the throne in Babylonia and then assuming that this date would also have been used throughout the empire. Secondly, it requires the same editor to have used non-standard, inclusive counting as well, which the writer/editor of Kings had used, but not the editor of Jeremiah. Neither assumption can be demonstrated and since both are needed in order to arrive at the figure of seventy years, it seems more logical to take the traditional dates for both the destruction of the temple in Jerusalem (586 BCE) and the first year of Darius (521 BCE). When this is done, a time lapse of sixty-six years between the destruction of the first temple and the laying of its new foundation results, and one of sixty-eight years until its completion.

Thirdly, the failure to include a specific date for the rebuilding of the temple in either book would seem to downplay any attempt to emphasize seventy years exactly. Without the date, the audience would not have been able to do the calculation themselves to confirm that the span had lasted seventy years. It is the case that the editor was limited to the material he had inherited, which did not seem to include any prophecy that could be directly associated with the rededication of the completed sanctuary. Thus, it could be argued that the lack of a date for the dedication is incidental here, but that the editor was still attempting to create an exact seventy-year period between the destruction of the monarchic-era temple and the completion of the Persian-era temple. He understood the prophecies in Zechariah 7–8 to relate to the completed temple and dated them accordingly, indirectly providing a completion date seventy years after the destruction.

If he were deliberately assigning prophecies that seemed to deal with the completed temple to year 4, however, one would need to ask why the editor did not assign a similar date to the prophecy in Hag. 2.1-8. It also presupposes that the structure has been completed and is operational or is about to be rededicated. It would have been easy enough for him to add an additional sentence about the completion and rededication of the building in one or both of the books, had this been a priority, which it does not appear to have been. Taking his failure to give an explicit date for the completion of the project, his assignment of Hag. 2.1-8 to year 2 rather than year 4, and the need to assume both hypotheses outlined above in order to support an exact seventy-year span between the destruction of temple 1 and the completion of the temple 2, it seems wiser to assume the time gap of sixty-eight years, as above.

Even so, this time gap is close enough to the literal figure of seventy years for an ancient writer to have considered Jeremiah's prophecy of seventy years of desolation in Judah to have been fulfilled, especially if he were understanding seventy to represent a round number symbolizing 'a long time' (so, e.g., Mitchell 1912: 98, 125, 200; Cohen 1948: 274; Ackroyd 1958: 24; Baldwin 1974: 97; Mason 1977: 37, 67; Hoffmann 2003: 188). By drawing an explicit link between the seventy years mentioned in Zechariah's two prophecies and a date early in the reign of Darius I that placed the temple's rebuilding nearly seventy years after its destruction, two messages would have been able to be conveyed: (1) Jeremiah was a genuine spokesperson of Yahweh, and (2) Yahweh kept his prophetically mediated promises.[14] The dates for year 2 and year 4 of Darius strongly signal that the person responsible for them understood the figure of seventy years used in Zech. 1.12 and 7.5 to represent the period of Yahweh's divine anger against his land, as proclaimed in Jer. 25.11, which had ended early in the reign of Darius, allowing the temple to be rebuilt and Yahweh to return to his traditional home.

Why Year 2 of Darius and Not Year 1?
A final issue needs clarification. Why would a later editor have chosen to place the beginning of the rebuilding effort only in year 2 of Darius and not in year 1 if the figures were artificial anyway? Why not have the non-native king concentrate his efforts immediately upon Yahweh's needs and desires? After all, this is what the author of Ezra does by having Cyrus issue an edict for the rebuilding of the temple in his first year as king (Ezra 1.1-4). In a similar fashion, the author of Kings strongly implies that Hezekiah undertook religious reforms as soon as he ascended the throne, although in his case he does not specify that the changes were accomplished in year 1. The Chronicler explicitly claims that this king initiated temple repairs in the first month of his first regnal year (2 Chron. 29.3). It was a customary practice in Mesopotamia as well to ascribe an important act to a king in his first year, which often was either the building of a temple, a war, or the decision to found and build a new temple. This custom is found in the inscriptions of Tukulti-Ninurta, Tiglath-Pileser I, Esarhaddon, Ashurbanipal, Sin-shar-ishkun and Nabonidus.[15]

The most plausible answer to this question is that the editor was familiar with Darius' widely circulated account of his rise of power. Although the fullest preserved text is known from the Behistun monument, which gives the account in Elamite, Persian, and Akkadian, two copies of an Aramaic version are known from the Jewish military colony at Elephantine (von Voigtlander 1978: 67; Greenfield and Porten 1982). The latter, though fragmentary, indicate that one segment of the Jewish community had first-hand knowledge of the document some 100 years after its promulgation and testify to its intentional translation into the various main languages of the empire for wide dispersal and consumption.

A single reading of the text gives the firm impression that Darius had been preoccupied with quashing fourteen rebellions in nine countries in his first regnal year. Thus, he would not have been likely to have turned his attention to the rebuilding of any temple until the second year of his reign. In §14 he claims to have rebuilt the temples of the gods that Gaumata had torn down, restored to the army the property that had been confiscated and redistributed, and restored the populace to its place. The reference to the restoration of temples, like that to the resettlement of the populace in its place in the same section, may simply be literary motifs borrowed from the Cyrus Cylinder (Oppenheim 1969: 316), which in turn were standard Babylonian motifs associated with the duties of a king in building or restoring a temple (for an analysis of the ideological nature of this proclamation, see Kuhrt 1983). It is thus unclear if Bardiya had, in fact, damaged any temples or confiscated their lands for redistribution to his loyal supporters. Nevertheless, had some damage to temples occurred during Bardiya's ten months in power, it is not likely that restoration work would have begun by Darius before year 2 of his reign, after he had secured firm control over the entire empire. Available manpower would have been diverted into the army in year 1 and the quashing of revolts would have taken precedence over building works.

The reference to Darius' restoration of temples may well have inspired the person who created the dates in Haggai and Zechariah to assign the rebuilding of the temple in Jerusalem to this particular monarch. A general reference to temple-rebuilding under this king would have provided a logical basis for association. A similar process seems to have led the author of Ezra 1–6 to set the initial rebuilding of the temple in the time of Cyrus, whose public edict known from the Cyrus Cylinder claims that he restored temples in Babylonia. This will be discussed more fully in Chapter 3.

A second consideration may also have influenced the decision to assign the start of the temple rebuilding to year 2 of Darius rather than year 1. The account of the building of the first monarchic temple under Solomon in 1 Kgs 4.24-25; 5.3-5 emphasizes that peace must prevail before temple-building can be undertaken. If this can be assumed to be a standard motif associated with the literary genre describing temple-building in ancient Judah, then the editor responsible for the year date elements in Haggai and Zechariah would likely have deliberately chosen to postpone the temple building until year 2 of Darius, after peace would have prevailed in the empire. The motif of peace as a prerequisite to temple-building is found in the first vision in Zech. 1.15-17, where Yahweh confirms that now that the nations are at ease, he has returned to Jerusalem with compassion and his house is to be rebuilt. The editor could have taken his cue from the contents of the vision itself or could have shared the conviction that peace needed to exist before temple-building could take place.

Why he would have assumed that the temple project would only have taken three years to complete is unclear. The wording of Hag. 2.3 strongly implies that the new building was smaller and plainer than the earlier temple had been, so three years would not have been an unreasonable length of time to assume would have been needed to complete such a task. However, there may be more to the figure. Had the editor gained access to the longer form of Darius' proclamation or heard rumors about additional military actions that had taken place in years 2 and 3 (for the Old Persian text, see Kent 1953: 134 [DB V] in Appendix 1), he might have decided to be prudent and to assign the completion of the building only to year 4, when complete peace would have prevailed.

Section Summary

To conclude this section, its seems likely that the assigning of the various prophecies in Haggai and Zechariah 1–8 to years 2 and 4 of the reign of Darius has been done deliberately in order to demonstrate that Yahweh's seventy-year anger against his land and people had ended, allowing the rebuilding of the temple and the deity's return to his traditional home. It is probable that the person who assigned the year element had in mind Jeremiah's prophecies in 25.11-12; 27.6-7 but transposed them in time and circumstance to apply to the exile of his own people and not the length of time that Babylonia would rule the world. He either formulated this connection independently, or was led to it by the two references to seventy years made in Zech. 1.12 and 7.5. It seems likely that Zechariah, or the editor of the book bearing his name, already had made a specific link to the prophecies of Jeremiah in both instances, transposing the original situation to the exile, although this is not certain. He could also have drawn on the motif of seventy years of divine punishment independently as a necessary element to include in any argument designed to persuade listeners that the time of declared punishment was now over and it was necessary to rebuild the temple so Yahweh could return home and bless his people.

Using the figure of seventy years as a rough guideline, the editor would have had a choice of making either Cambyses or Darius the royal sponsor of the temple's rebuilding. He appears to have chosen to place it under Darius rather than Cambyses because according to the available sources and traditions about these two kings, Darius had rebuilt temples while Cambyses had desecrated them. The latter information is reported in Herodotus (3.1-38), so if one assumes that similar traditions and rumors would have floated around Palestine, Egypt, and/or Babylonia, our editor may have known them as well.

Assuming that the restoration of Yahweh's temple in Jerusalem would have been a top priority of the world king and perhaps also employing the Assyro-Babylonian convention of assigning such a project to the opening year of a king's reign, the editor chose to delay the beginning of the rebuilding to year 2. He may have felt compelled to do so by his knowledge of the contents of Darius' proclamation. Darius had spent the first year of his reign securing control over various rebellions in the empire and peace was a prerequisite for the undertaking of temple-building. He may have decided to place the completion or imminent completion of the construction process in year 4 because of rumors or text that claimed that additional military actions had taken place in years 2 and 3 before absolute peace had prevailed. For the editor, it seems as though temporary peace had allowed the initiation of the project, which had seen its completion by the time total peace had been achieved.

Month and Day-Elements in the Date Formulae in Haggai and Zechariah 1–8

While in theory it might seem logical to separate the analysis of the month elements of the dates from the day elements, in practice the two need to be taken together as a unit. This is because specific days within certain months were festival days, and their significance would not be immediately clear if the discussion of the month were to be separated from the specific days within a given month. In the ensuing discussion, I will work systematically through the dates as they occur first in Haggai, and then Zechariah rather than rearranging them into their chronological sequence. This will allow the inner logic of the chronology of each book to be explored more efficiently.

There is no evidence to date of a strong astronomical interest or system of recording celestial movements in ancient Israel or Judah, although Gen. 1.16-17 is aware of the function of the stars in the keeping of time. As mentioned above, the calendar was lunar-based and was adjusted to the solar cycle through the practice of intercalation, as occurred in most of the ancient Near East. It is most likely that priests determined when the intercalations were to be made or on what specific basis, as they did in other surrounding cultures. However, once Judah became part of the Neo-Babylonian empire, both those who were relocated to the Babylonian region and those who remained in Yehud would have become more directly familiar with both the Babylonian calendar, which was based on careful observation and recording of the heavens, and with presuppositions of good and bad days. The latter system, detailed in writing known as menologies or almanacs, determined what activities could and could not take place on a given day of the month and within certain months. Judeans resident in Babylonia would have been directly affected by such monthly patterns/rhythms, since they would not have been able to buy or sell on certain days, or even leave their homes on certain days.

Even though such a system may never have prevailed within Yehud and so may not have influenced day-to-day life in the early Persian community there, it nevertheless may have had an impact on the schedule for the rebuilding of the temple. The Persians employed the Babylonian calendar within the western part of the empire since it was the system already in place. Since the Persian king was officially in charge of the rebuilding of the temple in Jerusalem, his representatives almost certainly would have followed the tradition detailed in the Babylonian almanac called *Iqqur Ipush* that dictated when a king should and should not build a temple. This series of texts, whose name means 'If he demolishes [or] builds', is a collection of menologies that focus on favorable and unfavorable months in which commoners should undertake activities relating to domestic housing. However, mixed in with these rules are sections detailing favorable and unfavorable months during which a king should begin and complete the construction or repair of a temple and sanctuary.

At the beginning of Darius' reign Yehud was part of the larger area comprising Babylon and Across-the-River that was administered by an individual named Ushtani. Texts dating to years 1, 3 and 6 of Darius name him as governor (*pehah*) of this combined unit. It would be logical to expect all building work being done on behalf of the king within this province to have followed the long-standing guidelines for the conduct of the king and the people as laid down in the almanac. In addition, since a sizable portion of the work-force used in the project was to have recently arrived with Zerubbabel and Yeshua from Babylonia, there would have been familiarity with the cycle of propitious and unpropitious days and knowledge of what activities were and were not allowed in what months. It can be noted that in the Hellenistic period, Antiochus Soter followed this prescription by laying the foundations of the temple Ezida in Asshur on day 20 of Addaru in the forty-third year of Seleucus (Oppenheim 1969: 317).

In the ensuing analysis, I will include a consideration of how the day and month dates assigned to various oracles and visions in Haggai and Zechariah 1–8 would have fit within the Babylonian almanac tradition. Since it is likely that this almanac developed in conjunction with the agricultural cycle of sowing and harvesting in Babylonia proper, with the corvée labor schedule also determined by periods of lesser activity in relation to crops and animal-tending, it is necessary to establish what differences might have existed between the cycle in Babylonia and the one in Yehud. Should the almanac tradition have been used in some way in Yehud, it would have had to have been modified to fit the local rhythm of life.

The Agricultural Cycles in Babylonia and Yehud

In Babylonia, the new agricultural cycle began in late summer, when the field that had lain fallow the previous year needed to be irrigated to loosen the soil and the ground broken up. Barley was sown first, then emmer and wheat. Harvest in the territory of southern Iraq today takes place in late April and May, and probably did so in antiquity as well. Although the barley should have ripened earlier than the wheat, they tended to ripen simultaneously, making the months of April and May the busiest in the farmer's year. It is thought that in antiquity, the temple and palace would have mobilized all available members of the population over which they had rights in order to ensure that these fields were harvested first and thoroughly. As a result, private lands would have been harvested secondarily, whenever its owners could manage (Postgate 1992: 167, 169). Land-owning citizens were required to work for free for the state a certain number of days in the year. This practice, called corvée, would have included harvest work as well as work on public works like road-building and large-scale construction projects.

Pulses (lentils, peas, beans), vetch, onions, garlic, flax, and sesame were also regular crops. The pulses, vetch and flax were winter crops, like the cereals. While vetch, peas and chickpeas were sown in the autumn and broad beans in mid-October, lentils were sown later, in February. Yet the lentils had the shortest growth season and were ready for harvest in April-June, alongside the cereals and vetch. Chickpeas were picked in May–June but could last into July, while broad beans were picked in February–April (Charles 1985: 56-57). Onions were planted after the cereals, probably in December or January, as is customary today, but harvested before them. Figs, apples, and pomegranates are mentioned in texts and almost certainly were culti- vated already in the second millenium BCE. Sesame, millet and flax were also regular cultivars. Sesame was usually planted in April/May (month 2) and harvested usually in September and October (Charles 1985: 58-59; Postgate 1992: 170-71. It is possible that an early planting was also done in mid-March, with a harvest in mid-July, as is the case in present-day Iraq (Stol 1985: 119). Millet likewise was harvested at this time, providing work in what otherwise would have been dead time in the agricultural cycle (Postgate 1992: 170-71). Flax was planted in October and harvested in May (Charles 1985: 58-59).

In Yehud, agriculture was dependent upon rainfall and not irrigation, as in Babylonia. The annual cycle began after the first rain fell in mid- to late-November usually and softened the ground enough that it could be plowed and seed sown. The main grain crops were sown at this time, in late November and early December: wheat, barley and oats, along with vetch. Then, afterward in December, pulses (peas, lentils, chickpeas) and flax were sown and garden vegetables in January–March. As in Mesopotamia, millet and possibly sesame were planted in the spring; millet first, in March–April, and sesame later, in April (Borowski 2002: 34).

Harvesting, threshing, and winnowing of the three main grain crops then took place usually in April-May, with the barley ripening first ahead of the wheat and oats. Vetch was also harvested in these two months, as were the peas and lentils. The chickpeas tended to be ready for harvest in June. Grapes could be ripe as early as June and tended to be harvested and processed over the summer months, from June to September. The first harvest of figs took place in June. In July, the flax, sesame, and millet was ripe and needed harvesting. August then saw the second round of figs and pomegranates reach maturity, and they were generally harvested late August and into September, depending on a given year. These figs were dried for storage and used over the winter months. The olive harvest and oil production then occupied the autumnal months of September-November, as did the pruning of the grapevines, until the rains arrived once again and the cycle began anew (Borowski 2002: 37, 109, 115).

Comparing the two cycles, it is apparent that there was not much difference in the planting and harvesting seasons. Actual planting and harvesting times varied from year to year, depending on the length of time it took for crops to mature. While regular irrigation may have made the variability in this process less pronounced, it did not guarantee success. Drought, disease, and insect infestation would have affected the outcome in both areas. Thus, there might not have been a need to adjust the monthly activities as prescribed in the Babylonian almanac if such a practice had been transposed to Yehud.

The Iqqur Ipush *Almanac*

It is time to examine more closely the Neo-Babylonian text, *Iqqur Ipush*. In spite of the fact that the series appears to have been set school texts learned and copied by scribes and so should have been prevalent, the examples that have been recovered in excavations are rarely undamaged, so we do not know the full contents of this tradition (Labat 1965: 5). Fortunately, we have information about which months were good and bad in which to do repair work or construction work on a sanctuary, shrine, interior dais, or a deity statue (Labat 1965: 89-97, §§29-33). For the present investigation, sections 32 and 33 are central.

The first section, §32, details, month by month, the results that will ensue if the king of the land constructs a temple or restores a sanctuary of the land, gives a gift to a god, celebrates (for a god) the feast of the New Year, or places a brick platform (in the temple of his god). Positive results will ensue in Nisan (month 1) (the prayers of his land will go the heart of god), Siwan (month 3) (god will hear his prayer) Elul (month 6) (god will hear the prayer of this man), Teshrit (month 7) (this man/king, his days shall be long), Shebat (month 11) (the gods will be his friends), and Addar (month 12) (this king/this man will conquer his enemy). Negative results will result if the work takes place in Aiar (month 2) (this man will have to deal with his adversary), Du'uzu (month 4) (his days will be short), Arahsamma (month 8) (the army of his land will be put into disorder; var. his heart will [not be content]), Kislev (month 9) (a revolution […] his land), or Tebet (month 10) (the gods will distance themselves from this land), while the text is too broken to know the effects for the month of Ab (month 5) (Labat 1965: 93-95).

The second section, §33, gives the results if the king constructs a chapel, or a square socle, or a sacred city, or if he restores a temple. Apparently work in Nisan (month 1) could yield both positive and negative results, depending on various manuscripts (his days will be long; var. he will not have joy). Positive results will otherwise ensue in Siwan (month 3) (greed [?] from the one who possesses [?] income; var. this king will obtain victory), Ab (month 5) (a critical situation will be resolved for him; cheerfulness), Elul (month 6) (god will treat this man with benevolence), Teshrit (month 7) (with his brother he will [re]take possession of that [by] which he had been frustrated), Arahsamma (month 8) (the king will triumph over his adversary; var. he will lose his temper because of his enemy), Shebat (month 11) (a good reputation he will have during his life; var. by the will of his god, he will overcome [all obstacles] toward happiness) and Addar (all that he has in view will return to him; var. will become his). Negative results will befall him in intercalary Nisan (his assets will be lost), Aiar (month 2) (this man will have to deal with his adversary), Du'uzu (month 4) (a matter will become an obstacle to his projects), intercalary Elul (he will lose what he has), Kislev (month 9) (the constraint of [sickness] will seize him; var. the constraint of the palace will seize him), and Tebet (month 10) (the god Adad will play havoc with his house by sending heavy rain) (Labat 1965: 95-97).

Comparing the two, the months that would have been most favorable for constructing the temple in Jerusalem would have been Siwan (month 3), Elul (month 6), Teshrit (month 7), Shebat (month 11) and Addar (month 12). These are the positive months found in both lists. Nisan is only fully positive in the first list and so has been removed, while Arahsamma is only positive in the second list. However, since the second list specifically deals with the restoration of a temple, it would be wise to stray on the side of caution and maintain Arahsamma (month 8) in the list as a favorable month. The verdict for Ab is missing in the first section, but is favorable in the second, which deals specifically with temple restoration, so it also will be included. That yields seven positive months in the year for rebuilding the temple in Jerusalem for any authorities who were following the almanac tradition.

It is not specified if the listed months in §§ 32 and 33 relate to the beginning of the project only, to work during the course of the project as well, or to its beginning and its completion.[16] Other sections of this collection that deal with the construction of private houses break the process down into a number of more specific components. They include the opening of foundations and placing of the first brick, (§1) the building of the house (§5), the destruction of a house (§7), dealing with a decrepit house (§8), the excavation of a house site (§9), the piling up of the excavated dirt at a house site, (§10) alterations made to the house by the owner (§ 11), alterations made by another followed by an inspection (§13), or not (§12), and the inspection of the house (§14). How much we can safely conclude from this comparison is unclear, however. The collection includes tablets that summarize month by month the entire range of everyday activities concerning houses, marriage, birth, death, religious observation and personal hygiene that are otherwise detailed in individual sections in the collection and their expected results (Labat 1965: 211-39. Tablets for months 4, 5, 6, 10 and 11 had not yet been found intact as of 1965).

Unfortunately for us, the king's efforts in building and repairing religious structures are not included, since the listed activities relate to activities of the common person rather than the king. So it may be that the list of royal building activities is incomplete; some segments may have been added to this collection because it detailed activities associated with destruction and construction, but these were summary in nature. They did not break down the building process into component parts, although such lists may well have existed in other menological collections. On the other hand, there may not have been a need to break royal building projects into component parts since, once begun, they would have been worked on steadily until their completion. Private houses, on the other hand, may have been built in stages, over time, as resources and labor became available. We thus are no further in knowing if §32 and §33 refer only to the beginning and end points of temple building and repair or if they also include intermediate stages in the process.

A comparison of the favorable months for work on a temple with the months that were favorable for the construction of a house shows a large amount of agreement, although the appropriate months for the latter activity were more extensive. While a temple could only be built safely in Siwan, Ab, Elul, Teshrit, Arahsammu, Shebat and Addar, a house could be built with a good result during Siwan, Du'uzu, Ab, Elul, Teshrit, Arahsamma, Kislev, Shebat and Addar. The results in Tebet have not been preserved on any tablet recovered (Labat 1965: 63, §5). A house's foundation, on the other hand, could be laid with good results in Siwan, Du'uzu, Ab, Elul, Teshrit, Arahsamma, Shebat, Addar and intercalary Addar (Labat 1965: 61, §2). The only difference was that a house foundation was not to be laid in Kislev. Since the months listed for the construction or repair of a temple correspond to favorable months for either the laying of a foundation and first brick or for more general construction work, we cannot draw any further conclusions about whether the royal activities listed in §32 and §33 meant construction only, excluding the laying of the foundation or final dedication, or whether these activities were subsumed under the more general heading of 'construction'.

We can note, however, that the exclusion of months 1 and 2 from all building activity is consistent with that time of year being the spring rainy season, when the ground was thawing and much soft mud was produced. Foundations laid at that time would likely have been unstable and any walls built on top of them would have been liable to collapse relatively quickly. The exclusion of Kislev may have been motivated by a similar concern. The autumnal rains generally started in November but, if delayed, would have arrived in December. In a mild winter, there would have been a lot of soft mud at this time as well, creating the same problems for the laying of a house foundation. The same weather conditions would have made these months inopportune for work on public buildings, including temples.

Two tablets have been found that detail which days in specific months are considered generally favorable, unfavorable, or good or bad for a specific activity. The first, published as KAR 177, includes on the front side a compilation of hemerologies from seven Babylonian sites. The reverse bears the hemerology of the city of Asshur, the capital of the Assyrian empire (Ebeling 1920: 5-12). These are both abbreviated lists that only give the days of the month that are favorable and unfavorable, without additional comments, and then give summaries of favorable days within each month in a summary form at the end. The second, KAR 178, is much fuller, giving prescribed and proscribed activities on each day of each month (Ebeling

1920: 13-28). It is Assyrian in origin, but is a compilation of texts and sometimes gives conflicting information about a day being both favorable and unfavorable (Labat 1939: 30). Neither text can be dated precisely; the sections that give the name of the scribe and the date when the text would have been composed or copied are both illegible.

René Labat believes that the almanac tradition is Babylonian in origin but was adopted by the Assyrians during the reign of Tiglath-Pileser I (1116–1090 BCE) along with the Babylonian calendar (1939: 25, 33). While originally the list of favorable and unfavorable days would have coincided in the Babylonian and Assyrian traditions, over time, the days fell out of sequence by one, two, or three days in some cases, probably due to careless copying by Assyrian scribes. Partially cited passages and duplicate copies of the Babylonian hemerologies and menologies show that their tradition had been standardized and did not change (Labat 1939: 33).

The status of a given day varies between the Babylonian and Assyrian traditions. None of the three hemerologies is undamaged; many lines of text are broken and illegible and unfortunately, information on the six specific dates found in Haggai–Zechariah 8 is missing in some instances. Nevertheless, all information recorded on the two tablets will be considered as each date is discussed in the ensuing section.

Day and Month Elements in the Book of Haggai
Day 1, Month 6 (Haggai 1.1). Haggai 1.1, dated (year 2 of Darius) day 1, month 6, is set at the new moon (e.g. Amos 8.5; Isa. 66.22). According to 2 Kgs 4.23, new moon and shabbat were favorable times for the people to inquire of a man of God. The claim made by A. Cohen that this verse supports an ancient custom of making pilgrimages to the temple on these five days during the month is incorrect (1948: 255). In the immediate context, the Shunamite woman is seeking the man of God at Mount Carmel, not at the temple in Jerusalem, and the husband mentions these days as times when it would have been logical to consult a prophet. He says nothing about them being times to offer sacrifice at the temple.

The Bible gives no explicit evidence that there was a festival celebrated at the local temple or sanctuary at the new moon. 1 Samuel 20.5 deals with a new moon, but simply says that that members of the royal court would have been expected to join the king at table (1 Sam. 20.5). However, this does not preclude a temple ceremony; it might simply presuppose it, with the royal banquet following for members of court.

In this regard, two inscriptions from Cyprus are instructive. They are on both sides of a limestone tablet that was found near a large Phoenician temple north of Kition and are thought from the style of handwriting to date probably to c. 450 BCE, during the Persian period. They detail expenses incurred by the temple administration in connection with the celebration of the new moon in two different months, Etanim and *p'lt* (Gibson 1982: 123-24). Fees are paid in Etanim to, among others, the leaders of the new moon festival, to the singers from the city who were in attendance on the Holy Queen this day, to the two pages, two sacrificers, two barbers working at the service, two bakers who baked the basket of cakes for the Queen, and to the chief scribe on duty this day (Gibson 1982: 125). Fees in the month of *p'lt* are paid to, among others, the leaders of the new-moon festival, the masters of the procession around the deity, to the [temple] girls and twenty-two girls [employed] at the sacrifice, and to three pages (Gibson 1982: 127).

These texts indicate clearly that there was a new moon temple celebration that included sacrifices in Phoenician colonies during the Persian period. While this does not require there to have been a similar practice in Judah, it is likely that other ancient Levantine cultures that calculated their months by the appearance of the new crescent moon would have similarly marked the occasion with some sort of cultic celebration. The assigning of the prophecy(ies) in Hag. 1.2-11 to the first day of the month seems to presume that there was a group gathered at some sort of event on the first of that particular month, if not the first of the month in general, where the prophet could easily have addressed a large group of people. Thus, while not made explicit anywhere in the biblical texts, it is likely that there was, in fact, a regular cultic cele-bration at the beginning of every month in Judah.

According to the Babylonian hemerological system on the front of KAR 177, day 1 of month 6 was a favorable day. No information is preserved in the Assyrian tradition on the reverse side, and the relevant segment of text on KAR 178 is broken. Nevertheless, the available information would indicate this would have been a propitious day and any message received from God would have been favorable (Labat 1939: 103, 161). It should also be noted that quite apart from its status as a propitious or unpropitious, day 1 of every month was considered one of nine monthly days of 'danger'. The list included days 1, 7, 9, 14, 19, 21, 28, 29, and 30, although at some subsequent point in time the number was reduced to five days (day 7, 14, 19, 21, and 28) (Labat 1939: 44). On these days, the doctor was not to relieve the groaning of a sick person, the diviner (*mar baruti*) was not to pronounce a word, and these days were not suitable to achieve a wish (Labat 1939: 147). Divining was a different form of determining the divine will than prophecy, however, so the prohibition against divination on day 1 did not necessarily preclude a prophet from delivering a message received from a deity. The situation in 2 Kgs 4.23 involving the Shunamite woman who sought the man of God at the new moon would thus be consistent with the Babylonian almanac, perhaps coincidentally.

Month 6 was known in the Babylonian calendar as Ululu, or Elul in Aramaic. It would have fallen in August–September in 520 BCE, with day 1 being 29 August. This was the time close to the autumnal equinox and of the approaching fall fruit harvest. In Yehud, the harvest of grapes, figs and pomegranates would likely have been about to begin, if not already underway. The olive harvest would have still been looming ahead (Borowski 2002: 37). The people would have already begun long days of labor with the harvesting of the flax and millet in July–August, while coping with high temperatures and dry, parching heat.

Although Elul was one of the seven propitious months in which to construct or repair a temple, it would not have been the most logical time to begin clearing the rubble from the temple site. It would have been poor planning to expect the labor force to divert attention from the fruit harvest, whose success was critical to having adequate food and drink supplies for the upcoming year. Joyce Baldwin has suggested that this is the reason why the work was not begun until twenty-three days later, on 21 September, 520 BCE. The intervening weeks would have been devoted to the harvest (1974: 43). But the people would have been equally tired at this point, having just completed the harvest, so that the inner logic of the dating remains questionable. The olive harvest would have occupied their full attention in Septem-ber unless the olives had matured late that particular year. The production of oil would have been the priority through September and October, so the population would not have been free to work on the temple repairs even in September.[17]

The original rationale that had led the people to proclaim that the time had not arrived to rebuild the temple is no longer recoverable. Being handed down without a date and firm historical context, such an attitude could have been prompted by the lack of financial resources, the ongoing drought and famine that made hard labor too taxing on already weakened bodies or the need to determine when the period of Yahweh's wrath would end. The drought and famine would have been interpreted by the locals as a sign of ongoing anger (so, e.g., Bedford 2001: 172-78). The term *'et*, which is commonly translated 'time' or 'appointed time', can refer to a larger era or epoch, or a divinely designated moment, but its most common meaning is 'an appropriate or suitable time' for a given activity (see Kessler 2002: 122-27). If the menological tradition for temple-building and repair was being followed, however, then it could be suggested that the authorities had proclaimed that one of the seven propitious months had arrived and the people were objecting and countering.

The editor who assigned the current date seems to have been prompted by two considerations. On the one hand, he selected a month when such work would have been very hard to begin anyway due to the heavy harvest responsibilities. Thus, he apparently assumed the saying partially reflected an attitude by the people that it had been the wrong time of year for public building works in light of the impending harvest.

However, a second more crucial consideration that appears to have dictated the larger dating scheme for Haggai–Zechariah 8 to years 2 and 4 of Darius has been pointed out by H. Tadmor, though his specific argument needs modification. He has noted that the slogan, 'the appointed time has not yet arrived', *lo' 'et-bo'*, seems to play off the statement in Jer. 27.7, 'until the appointed time of his own land comes', *'ad bo' 'et 'artso gam hu'*. Thus, upon reading v. 2 in Haggai, the editor was reminded of the passage in Jer. 27.6-7 and was prompted to link the rebuilding of the temple with the ending of Yahweh's seventy years of wrath against Judah and Jerusalem that is found in the related traditions in Jer. 25.11-12; 29.10 (1999: 402-403). However, this argument cannot stand, because the crucial phrase, 'until the appointed time of his own land comes', is missing in the Septuagint version of Jer. 27.7, suggesting that it was a later expansion in the Masoretic text. The expansion may well have been prompted by a desire to have an explicit catchword link back to Hag. 1.2 to make a direct link in this book as well as the two in Zech. 1.12 and 7.5.

Notwithstanding, Tadmor's insight can still be adopted by modifying the argument. Upon reading Hag. 1.2, the editor, in seeking to understand what the underlying referent would have been to 'the appointed time' in the people's slogan, was reminded of Jeremiah's prophecies in 25.11-12 and 29.10 of a period of seventy years of destruction and abandonment of Judah and Jerusalem. This then provided him with a key for placing the prophecies concerning the temple-building in Haggai and Zechariah 1–8 in a historical context. It was not a historically accurate key ultimately, but it allowed him to show how Yahweh's prophecies as mediated by Jeremiah had been fulfilled in historical time, which apparently was a central concern to him and his audience.

A third possible consideration, however, needs to be added. The editor may have assumed that the people's insistence that the time had not arrived may have been partially countering a claim by the authorities that month 6 was in fact, a propitious time to begin the work. If there had been awareness of the almanac tradition amongst even a segment of the population in Yehud, this situation could have developed, or could have been assumed to have done so, by the subsequent editor, had he shared familiarity with it.

The date of day 1, month 6 might have been chosen because it marked the beginning of the final month of the first half-year and so was intended to set the tone for activities that would have needed to be undertaken in the remaining half of the year. However, according to the Babylonian almanac, it would also have been an ideal time to undertake temple building and restoration. By announcing to the citizenry in month 6 that the time had come to rebuild, five–six months of planning, preparation, and gathering of materials could have ensued so that work could theoretically have commenced in month 11 or month 12, the last of the seven propitious months for such activity in a given year.

While it has been postulated that the Babylonian year was divided into halves (Langdon 1935: 51, 157), this has not been accepted as significant by many scholars. Nevertheless, Y. Kaufman (1954: 312-13) and J.B. Segal (1957: 275-76) have pointed out that the Judahite calendar had a similar biennial split, with week-long festivals that shared a number of characteristics in months 1 and 7. In addition, intercalary months were added at the end of month 12, or at the end of month 6, indicating that there was some importance to two half-year segments. Whether or not one thinks the calendar was deliberately structured in two halves, it can be asked whether it would have been more logical for the pronouncement to have been dated to the first day of month 7, at the holy convocation. This would have been the actual start of the second half of the year, and month 7 was also propitious for such building activity. In this case, the call for rebuilding would have been programmatic for activities needing completion within that half-year period.

On the other hand, however, the date might have been chosen specifically because Elul/Ululu was not a month when people were supposed to spend time in their homes. If a man entered his house, hostility would be continual (§16); if he returned to his house at this time, he and his wife would die (§15). If he moved into a new house, he and his wife would torment each other daily (§17) and if he made his wife enter his house, his heart would not [be content] (§62) (Labat 1965: 75, 77, 133).

Month 6 in Babylonia would have been just after the sesame and millet harvest and during the harvest of figs and pomegranates, as would have been the case in Yehud. Perhaps the almanac expected people to leave their homes in month 5 and help harvest the extensive royal and temple estates during months 5 and 6, before returning home in month 7 to harvest their own mature crops. They would have been mobilized again for further public harvesting in months 8 and 9 before being allowed to return home and tend to their own late harvest in month 10. Thus, it is unclear if month 6 was a time that the people were to be tending to their own plots, or were expected to be away from their homes helping with the royal harvest.

Elul was a good month in which to buy fallow land [inside the city] and transform it into a field. Anyone who did so would realize his [desire]; his name would be esteemed (§42). If a man restored or renewed a garden inside the city in this month, a god would lead him always in view of happiness (§§48, 49) (Labat 1965: 109, 115, 117). These three examples suggest that the month of Elul was a time that people spent outside, either working on their own lands or on the royal harvest.

The people's claim that the time had not come to rebuild would be consistent with their preoccupation with harvesting duties at hand, since theoretically, month 6 would have been one of the seven favorable times to work on the temple. The references to the sowing but inadequate harvest in 1.6 and little yield in 1.9 are part of a larger object lesson that generalizes bad living conditions that seem to have existed for more than the immediately preceding months of the current year. Nevertheless, both shortfalls would be consistent with a grain harvest that had ended in month 3 (May–June), a barley harvest that had ended in month 2 (April–May), and an oat harvest, lentil and vetch harvest that had ended in month 3 during the heat of the summer, before the fruit and olive harvest. Thus, the person responsible for the day and month notice in Hag. 1.1 may have decided on month 6 on the basis of the agricultural references within the ensuing prophecy, which presuppose the recent completion of the grain harvest (1.6). He may secondarily, however, have been aware that Elul was one of the propitious months to build, and, in light of the comments in 1.2, 4, found month 6 the logical setting for vv. 1-11. By selecting the new moon, the prophet would have had a ready audience at the cultic celebration of the appearance of the new crescent moon.

Day 24, Month 6 (Haggai 1.15). The statement in 1.15 that under the influence of the divine spirit, the people worked on the house on day 24 of month 6 would represent a logical redirecting of the assembled work force from harvesting to work on the temple. Day 24 of Elul was not among the propitious days for that month in either the Assyrian or Babylonian hemerology on KAR 177, and according to KAR 178, a person who would curse or swear an oath on this day would be seized by a god (Labat 1939: 109, 165, 177). Thus, if the person who added the dates was familiar with the Babylonian almanac tradition, he either would have been critiquing the diversion of the people's energies to work on the temple on a day when Yahweh would not have rewarded their efforts or he was deliberately selecting an unpropitious day to show that Yahweh was not bound by this foreign system and would look favorably on positive action initiated on any day. In the latter case, he would have been launching an oblique attack on the almanac tradition, implying it was not relevant to life in Yehud.

The scenario as presented, however, is very unlikely to have taken place at the date specified. No work could have been done on the temple without the performance of preparatory rituals by the priests. This would have included even the clearing of rubble from the structure. Thus, unless these had in fact been performed prior to day 24 and were simply being presupposed here, no work would have happened spontaneously. In light of this situation, it seems likely that 1.12-15 are part of the editorial framework designed to demonstrate that the people had responded to Haggai's prophecy, emphasizing that the prophetic word was acted upon and fulfilled, as is commonly recognized. It is possible that vv. 12-15 were added by the same hand that had created the date in v. 1.

Day 21, Month 7 (Haggai 2.1). Haggai 2.1, dated to day 21, month 7 (Tashritu) of year 2 of Darius, is set on the last day of the Feast of Booths/Sukkot. There was a solemn convocation on that day, which would have provided the prophet with a ready audience (Lev. 23.34, 36, 40-42).

Though this was the final day of the celebration of the fruit harvest and olive harvest that had just been completed, which would have been the primary focus of attention, historically, it was the time when, according to tradition, the monarchic-era temple had been dedicated (1 Kgs 8.2, 65; 2 Chron. 7.8-10). Thus, it is would have been an apt time for a prophet to speak on the topic of temple restoration, whether the date reflects the actual day on which the ideas in 2.2-10 were delivered or whether it represents a later contextualization of the prophecy.

In the Babylonian hemerological tradition, the status of this day has not been preserved; the list of favorable days in Teshrit on the face of KAR 177 is broken. In the Assyrian tradition on the reverse of KAR 177, the day is listed as favorable, while this date falls in a section of twelve illegible lines in KAR 178 (Labat 1939: 119; 163, 165). It also is one of the nine and subsequent five 'days of danger' when divination was prohibited. Teshrit was a favorable month in which to do temple construction; with the harvest over, work could have focused on the temple.

In its current sequencing, with 1.12-15 in place, the question asked concerning the current state of the temple in comparison to its physical appearance before 586 BCE presupposes that preliminary work has been undertaken at the temple site, perhaps some clearing, but that the main building effort remains to come, and Yahweh himself will provide the funds so that the new structure will surpass the former temple in its glory.

If the contents of 2.2-8 are considered in relation to the contents of the first prophecy in 1.2-11 without the editorial framework that gives the dates and talks of the people responding to Haggai by undertaking work, however, a different impression results. The saying is comparing the existing ruined temple to its former glory before 586 BCE. No work has yet begun, but there is a promise that the funds for the effort will be provided by Yahweh himself so that the work should begin. The final effort will be even more glorious than before.

The impression gained by P. Ackroyd that the temple-rebuilding has been completed but is nothing like the monarchic-era temple in its physical trappings and gilding would be equally valid were it not for Yahweh's command to the people in v. 4 to work (Ackroyd 1958: 19, 26). This imperative is hard to explain if the work has already been completed and is the primary determiner of the temple's ongoing state of ruination in the context. It can be noted, however, that Ackroyd believes that vv. 4-5 originally were part of the first prophetic unit in 1.2-11, which itself combines two oracles. They provided reassurance of Yahweh's presence so there would be no need for the people to fear once they began rebuilding (1952a: 4). Others have proposed that v. 4 belongs to the editorial framework and v. 5 is a later gloss (so, e.g., Beuken 1967: 57; Mason 1977: 19-20). If one were to accept either proposal, there would be no obstacle to the prophecy comparing the completed new temple to the former temple and attributing to Yahweh a promise that gilding and more lavish decoration would follow in the future.

The second option, that no work had yet begun, is more logical because, as mentioned above, it is unlikely that work could have been undertaken without some sort of preliminary purification ritual, which is often thought to be described in the third prophecy in 2.11-19. In addition, the report that the people worked in 1.12-15 seems to have been designed to show that they had obeyed the prophetic command. Assuming that the command from Yahweh to the people to work in v. 4 is original, the larger context implies that no work had been undertaken as of yet, rather than that the work had been completed. This is the understanding reflected in all the commentaries.

The rhetorical question in v. 3 addressed to the septagenarians and octagenarians in the audience about the former glory versus present devastation of the temple is specifically designed to remind the entire audience of the monarchic-era temple that was supposedly dedicated at the same festival in the distant past. There would have been almost no one still alive in 520 BCE who had seen the former temple in its glory who would have remembered the former structure, so for most of the intended audience, the question would have had no direct relevance. Paul F. Bloomhardt has suggested that the handful who would have seen the first temple would have idealized their reminiscences and, because of their age, would, at the same time, have been pessimistic about the time at hand (1928: 169). Leroy Waterman, on the other hand, has suggested that the real comparison being made would have been between the foundation of the new structure and the two splendid temples of Babylon and Borsippa, which the returnees would have known (1954: 75). In my opinion, the primary function of the question lay rather in acknowledging that the structure had once been glorious and after rebuilding, it would be even more so.

If the day and month elements are not original, they were likely selected because of the reference to the former temple and the need for an event that would have had all the people assembled at the temple site so that Haggai could point to the temple and ask the audience how 'this temple' appeared to them now. The festival of Booths was the logical choice because it had been the occasion when the first temple had been dedicated. In addition, if the editor were aiming to arrange his narrative in chronological order, he would have needed a date later in time than the one he had given to the first prophecy. The date needed to be transitional between 1.1-11 and the subsequent prophecy in 2.11-19, when either the temple's foundation stone was ritually laid in conjunction with a purification ceremony, or when the temple was dedicated. Finally, it can be noted that month 7 was one of the seven favorable months in which to do such work.

Day 24, Month 9 (Haggai 2.10, 18). Haggai 2.10 and 18 in their present dated form suggest that the cornerstone of the Persian-era temple was laid on day 24, month 9 (Kislev), or 18 December, 520 BCE.[18] According to the Babylonian almanac, this would not have been an acceptable month in which to set the stone; it should have been done in months 3, 5, 6, 7, 8, 11 or 12 on a propitious day. If a king accomplished a rite in Kislev, he would be in the grip of a fiend (§38) (Labat 1965: 103). The status of day 24 of this month has not been preserved in the Babylonian hemerology on the face of KAR 177. It was not one of the propitious days of Kisilimmu in the Assyrian tradition on the reverse of KAR 177 and in KAR 178, it was not a day to take a woman (Labat 1939: 133, 163, 167).

No project was undertaken in the Persian empire without official permission. There must have been indirect royal sponsorship of the temple, in the form of a writ giving authorization, even if funds and supplies were not necessarily included (see the example of the temple built using local funds by soldiers stationed at Xanthus in Teixidor 1978). One would have expected the building work in Jerusalem to have been done in conformity with the restrictions imposed upon the Persian king by the Babylonian almanac since, as already noted, at the beginning of Darius' reign Yehud was part of the larger area comprising Babylon and Across-the-River that was administered by an individual named Ushtani.

If both date references are removed from their present contexts, however, a different situation is presupposed by the contents of the prophecy in 2.11-19. Using a case of Torah legislation concerning pure and impure as a kind of parable, the change of the people's status from impure to pure is emphasized. The pivotal event that has transformed their ritual status and that has initiated the return of divine blessing has been either the laying of the foundation stone, or the completion of the repairs and the possible rededication of the temple for sacrifice. In the first case, there is a concomitant presumption of the end of 'exile' and the disappearance of divine anger, both of which are necessary prerequisites for the commencement of physical labor on the temple structure.

The crucial phrase in this regard is the remaining statement in v. 18 once the date is removed from the first half of the verse: 'since the day when the temple of Yahweh was *yussad*, consider'. The common translation, 'from the day that the foundation of the temple of Yahweh was laid' derives from an assumption that the verb *yussad,* in its active voice, means 'to lay a foundation' (so, e.g., Smith 1908: 248; Mason 1977: 23; Petersen1984: 88-90; Bedford 2001: 97). However, there is no noun signifying 'foundation' in the underlying text, even though there is a wide range of such nouns in Hebrew that could have been used (i.e. *yesud, yesôd, yesûdah, mûsad, môsad, massad*). A review of the use of the verb *yissed* reveals that it has less technical meanings as well. The basic idea seems to be 'to make firm or durable' (i.e. Pss. 104.5; 119.152; Prov. 10.25). Significantly, it is used in 2 Chron. 24.7 to describe the restoration of the first temple during the reign of Joash, as a synonym for the verb *hiddesh*, 'make new, repair, renew', in v. 4. It is equally, possible therefore, to translate the phrase in question, 'since the day that the temple of Yahweh has been repaired/renewed' (as done by, e.g., Galling 1964: 130; Gelston 1966: 235; Eybers 1975: 19-20; Baldwin 1974: 53; Busink 1980: 804; Meyers and Meyers 1987: 63; Verhoef 1987: 130; Wolff 1988: 64; Kessler 2002: 209).

Thus, was Hag. 2.18 originally a reference to the re-laying of the temple foundation, or to the completion of the reconstruction of the temple and, therefore, a possible dedication ceremony? The person who added the dates has decided to make it refer to the re-laying of the foundation and so assigned it a date three months after the initial clearing work began, but was he correct in his deduction? A survey of commentaries reveals advocates of both positions and no consensus. If it is the former, then the prophecy relates to the beginning of the rebuilding process. The removal of impurity would presuppose the performance of a purification ritual in which the cornerstone of the former structure was rededicated, whether or not the entire foundation was physically removed and reassembled. Part of the larger process would have involved the recitation of lamentations to appease the deity and to remove ritual impurity. If the latter, then it could imply the beginning of the repair process, which would in turn involve the same set of rituals. However, it might more logically refer to the process in general, which would then presuppose its completion and a set of dedication rituals that would have taken place well after the initial purification ritual.

The choice of date appears to have been influenced by the implications of the time of year when the prophecy would have been delivered, found in 2.19. The translation of this verse varies widely, although there is general agreement that it represents a change for the better, in contrast to the situation in vv. 15-17 prior to the ritual ceremony involving the temple foundation or the rededication of the structure. Two rhetorical questions are asked in a single, compound sentence: Is the seed still in storage? Have the vine, the fig tree, the pomegranate and the olive tree still not produced? The implied answer to both questions is no.[19]

The first question has no explicit verb, being a nominal sentence, but the only tense that makes sense is the present. The question indicates that the new cycle of plowing and planting has already taken place.[20] This normally took place with the autumnal rains that softened the ground, which even today usually arrive in November and December. Wheat, barley, oats, and vetch were and are traditionally sown in November and December, while peas were sown in December and January and lentils and flax were sown in December only (Borowski 2002: 34).

The second question is expressly placed in the past tense in the Masoretic text, and in spite of some translations, does not use a noun for 'nothing' but instead, negates the verb: 'has not given forth/produced'.[21] The translator of the Septuagint appears to have construed the verb as a participle rather than a perfect, which may have influenced the majority of English translators to render the question with a future meaning (Clark 1983: 438). However, if this had been the actual intention, then an imperfect verb form would have been used rather than a participle.

It is likely that both the translator into Greek and many of those rendering this phrase into English have been influenced to use the future tense here by the promise of change for the better that comes at the end of the verse. Most commentators and translators are already pre-suming the stated change in conditions at the end of the second question as they reread both questions and try to understand their import. As a result, they tend to see both as illustrations of the promised blessing. However, it seems better to maintain the perfect verb tense found in the Masoretic Text and to see the promise of future blessing to be for the future. The sown seeds will produce in the coming year as a result of Yahweh's blessing, unlike in the past, and the fruit harvest will yield its normal abundance in the coming year, unlike the recent partial yield, which was at least better than no yield at all, which may have occurred in the past.

The verb is in the singular, which has led to the speculation that three of the four items listed from the autumnal harvest have been added editorially (so, e.g., Wolf 1988: 62; Kessler 2002: 210). Grammatically, there are a few examples where a plural subject can follow a singular verb (see examples in Kautsch and Cowley 1982: §146; Jöuon 1947: §150 g, p, q, contra Kessler 2002: 201), but in this particular phrase, the subjects all precede the verb. This also is not a situation with a collective noun as the subject, where the plural subject can be linked to a singular verb. We have instead a compound, four-element subject, which is unlikely to have been considered a collective subject unit that could govern a verb in the singular.

James Nogalski has suggested that the original item in the list was the olive tree, which immediately precedes the verb and is singular and masculine, like the verb. He argues that the vine, the fig tree and the pomegranate have been added secondarily in order to bring to mind the images in Joel 1–2, providing an intertextual link within the Book of the Twelve (1993a: 228-29). Joel 1.7 and 2.22 mention both vines and fig trees, while 1.12 mentions the vine, the fig tree, the pomegranate, palm and apple. While oil is mentioned twice in these chapters (1.10; 2.24), there is no reference to the olive or the olive tree explicitly. Thus, his argument provides a plausible explanation for the addition of the references to vines, fig trees and pomegranates in v. 19 while providing a rationale by which to deduce that the original text read 'olive tree' alone.

Grapes are harvested over the four-month span covering months 4–7 (June–September), while figs and pomegranates are only harvested in months 6 and 7 (August and September);

olives, on the other hand, tend to have a later harvest in months 7–9 (September–November) (Borowski 2002: 37). Assuming the above argument for the originality of the olive tree as the subject of the verb 'has not yielded' in v. 19, a date at the end of month 9 would have been envisaged originally. The wording makes it clear that the harvest had been completed and had not been a total failure. There is then a promise of blessing in the forthcoming season of growth.

A date for the delivery of the original portions of the prophecy in 2.12-19 after or at the end of month 8 or month 9 is implied by the first question and one after or at the end of month 9 by the second. These textual clues embedded in the prophecy itself may well have led an editor to select a date toward the end of month 9 as the likely time for the prophecy to have been delivered if no day or month were attached to the original prophecy. Day 24 was a 'lucky' or propitious day and also was a day on which seers could prophesy. From the seventh century BCE onwards, they were forbidden to prophesy on days 7, 14, 19, 21, and 28 (Langdon 1935: 80, 83, 87); prior to that time, days 1, 9, 29 and 30 had also been days of rest when no prophecies had been allowed. Thus, the choice of this particular day toward the end of the month may have been more random, although it may reflect the deliberate choice of a propitious day within the monthly cycle.

Finally, it should be noted that the logic expressed in 2.12-19, once the dates are removed as secondary additions, does not necessitate that the prophecy was given on the day of the ceremony that is referenced in v. 18. It can be taken to imply that the ceremony had taken place in the recent past, probably just before both the autumnal harvest and the planting that had been done thereafter. On the other hand, the wording does not preclude the delivery of the prophecy at the ceremony either.

Some comment should be made about the logic of dating the final prophecy in 2.21-23 to the same date as the preceding one, day 24, month 9. This prophecy echoes the sentiments expressed in 2.6-8. Both portray Yahweh as a divine warrior who controls the resources and course of events in the world. Whereas the first focuses on how Yahweh would provide the resources to finance and gild his new house, this prophecy focuses on how he is going to overthrow the throne of the world empire and then make Zerubbabel, his chosen one, like a signet ring. It has been seen to resonate with the series of rebellions that took place throughout the empire at the beginning of Darius' reign and to express the hopes for a new independent kingdom (Bloomhardt 1928: 167; Thomson 1932: 116; Morgenstern 1938: 191; Olmstead 1938: 410; Waterman 1954: 76-77; Bickerman 1981: 23-25).[22] At the same time, it has been seen to express eschatological hopes, removed from present time and set at the end of time and the final judgment (e.g. Driver 1906: 168; Smith 1908: 250-52; van Hoonacker 1908: 575; Mitchell 1912: 77; Bentzen 1930: 503; Siebeneck 1957: 317; Chary 1969: 33; Baldwin 1974: 53-54; Rudolph 1976: 54; Mason 1977: 25; Japhet 1982: 76-77; Smith 1984: 182; Achtemeier 1986: 105; Meyers and Meyers 1987: 83; Verhoef 1987: 140; Tollington 1993: 136; Sérandour 2001: 271-72. George A. Smith and Hinkley G. Mitchell emphasize how the saying would have been triggered by political unrest at the beginning of Darius' reign, which could have fanned old messianic hopes).

James Nogalski has argued that v. 22 is a secondary insertion in this unit, intended to provide intertextual links forward to Zechariah and backward to Joel. The words 'rider', 'horse', and '*ish*, 'man', appear here and in Zech. 1.8, the opening verse of the first night vision. The 'nations', which have no other presence in Haggai, also play a prominent role in the first vision in 1.11 and 15. Chariots, on the other hand, appear prominently in the final vision in 6.1, 2, 3, 4, and 6, while a throne appears in 6.13. The imagery of v. 22 creates a battle scene that reverses the one of the attacking enemy in Joel 2.4-11, which includes horses and chariots. Here the enemy is in utter chaos and 'each man will fall by the sword of his brother', while in Joel it marched in a straight, orderly line where 'each man does not crowd his brother'.

In addition, Nogalski has proposed that the opening phrase in v. 23, 'on that day', was added in conjunction with v. 22. It appears only here in Haggai and seems to be consistent with the eschatological battle imagery presented in v. 22 detailing the conflicts that will take place at the end of time, before the final judgment day and the arrival of the messiah. It is inconsistent with the theophanic imagery presented in v. 21 of shaking the heavens and the earth as a form of divine manifestation and with the direct address to Zerubbabel in v. 23, which does not presume an eschatological setting. It is a phrase frequently found in the Book of the Twelve, however, and, like v. 22, is more likely to be a redactional element here than an original part of the prophetic saying (1993a: 234). In this case, both theories of political rebellion against Darius and eschatological hopes would be eliminated as contributing factors that motivated the pronouncement of the original textual unit comprised of v. 21 and v. 23, without the initial phrase, 'on that day'.

As an alternative to both proposals above, it would make sense to propose that the statements concerning Zerubbabel were either directly triggered by the ceremony referenced in 2.18, whenever it took place, or were thought by a later editor to have been logical within such a setting. Once the date of that ceremony was explicitly designated as day 24 of month 7, rightly or wrongly, it made sense to place the final utterance about Zerubbabel in the same context, on the same day.

I would like to propose the following historical scenario. The ceremony referred to in 2.18 involved the rededication of the temple after the completed repairs and took place in month 7 at Sukkot, as had the dedication of the monarchic-era temple as well. The prophecy now placed in 2.3-9, without vv. 4-5, could have been uttered on this occasion, as could have the prophecy concerning Zerubbabel being chosen, whom Yahweh was going to make like a signet ring.

The week-long autumnal fruit harvest was a time to celebrate Yahweh's bestowed bounty and was a logical time also to install him in his temple and emphasize his role as king of heaven. As part of the Babylonian temple dedication ceremony, the king traditionally was affirmed as the god's earthly vice-regent and promised long life, wisdom and blessing for his having built a suitable dwelling place on earth for the deity. This can be seen particularly in Gudea Cylinder B, §§xxiii.10–xxiv.9 (for a recent translation, see Jacobsen 1987: 386-44). Although technically, Yahweh's earthly vice-regent who had built the temple was the king of Persia, some sort of acknowledgement of his representative at the ceremony, Zerubbabel, who himself was a descendant of the former royal house of Judah, may have been deemed logical or desirable. By claiming that Yahweh would make Zerubbabel 'like a signet ring', the prophet was signaling that Yahweh considered him to be a visible expression of his divine ownership of the earth.

This is not the same as claiming that Zerubbabel was his earthly vice-regent; in v. 22 Yahweh claims that he will overthrow all human rulers and world empires. There is no promise to place Zerubbabel on the throne in place of the Persians here. Rather, there is an implicit assertion that Yahweh will take over the rulership himself and establish a theocracy. In this new situation, Zerubbabel will not be his earthly vice-regent, but instead, as a descendant of the former royal family of his special people, his lack of restored royal status will visually reinforce Yahweh's direct kingship over the earth. Practically speaking, the utterance accepts that Judah will no longer have a king or be an independent political unit, but the saying is not primarily eschatological either. It is not pointing to the end of time, but rather is asserting that Yahweh controls the throne of the world empire.[23]

Section Summary
In examining the five day and month combinations found in the book of Haggai, I have left open the possibility that these elements might have been attached to the various prophecies without the year element as I have undertaken my investigation. However, in examining context clues provided within each utterance, I have concluded that all of the day and month elements are later editorial additions that have been deduced on the basis of information drawn from the prophecies themselves. Thus, while I did not presuppose their editorial origin, I have come to accept that they are editorial in the end.

Many of the sayings are ambiguous when examined outside of their current assigned dates and could point to a completed temple rather than to the ritual dedication of the foundation at the beginning of the building process, which seems to be what the editor envisioned by placing all of the prophecies within a three-month time span. In particular, 2.3, 6-8; 2.21-23, and 2.18 can all be plausibly associated with the dedication ceremony of the completed structure, which might well have taken place during the Feast of Booths in month 7, as had the dedication of the monarchic-era temple according to tradition. Haggai 2.11-19 could have been pronounced shortly after the cult had been reestablished, in month 9, after the autumn fruit harvest had been completed and the seed had been sown, while 1.2-11 could come from some point prior to the commencement of the repair process. The description of the agricultural conditions includes most seasons and so is of little help in knowing when it would have been proclaimed. The actual length of time represented, which would cover the entire building process according to my analysis, beginning at some point before repairs began and ending a few months after the temple's rededication, cannot be determined from contextual clues. As already discussed in the previous section, the assignment to year 2 of Darius is not trustworthy either.

Day and Month Elements in Zechariah 1–8
Month 8 (Zechariah 1.1). The opening date in Zech. 1.1, month 8 without a specific day, introduces a call to the people to return to Yahweh and not to follow in the footsteps of their fathers. If they do, Yahweh will return to them. Month 8 in the Babylonian calendar was Arahsamma, or Heshvan in Aramaic, and was one of the propitious months for a king to restore a temple. In Yehud this would have been a time when the olive harvest was concluding or just completed and the rains were beginning, allowing the wheat, barley, oats and vetch to be sown once the ground had been softened by the water. It thus represents the month when the former agricultural cycle is complete and a new cycle is beginning. As such, it would have been a logical time to call the people to repent so that they could be ready to work in months 11 and 12.

According to §32 of *Iqqur Ipush*, it was not a propitious month to construct a temple or restore a sanctuary; but according to §33 it was a propitious month in which to restore a temple (Labat 1965: 92-96). Thus, it cannot be rejected out of hand that the editor was following the proscriptions of §33 and considered month 8 also to be propitious for work on the temple in Jerusalem, though I suspect the considerations outlined in the text were primary in his mind.

The logic of the arrangement is evident: the people must repent and express their desire to return to Yahweh so that Yahweh can end the seventy-year period of punishment and announce his desire to return to his home in Jerusalem. A call to repentance necessarily must precede the divine announcement of the desire to rebuild the temple. By delivering or placing this call for repentance at the beginning of the agricultural year, the prophet or editor would also be emphasizing the appropriateness of a fresh start after a full confession of wrong-doing, with the hope for divine blessing in the upcoming agricultural year.

While today this 'fresh start' would more logically take place at Yom Kippur on day 10 of month 9, when the congregation confesses their wrongdoings in the previous year so that the new year can bring a 'clean slate', the format of Yom Kippur in ancient times seems to have been different. It was a time to cleanse the sanctuary and so remove all communal sin (Leviticus 16; 23.26-32). Without a dedicated sanctuary, however, such a ceremony would not have been possible in the envisaged context. But it was still necessary to alert the people to the need of a communal confession of sin in order to dissipate the divine anger.

Day 24, Month 11 (Zechariah 1.7). The date in Zech. 1.7, day 24, month 11, which introduces a series of eight night visions in 1.1–6.15, is consistent with the Babylonian menological tradition; its status in the hemerological tradition is unknown because the list of propitious days for this month is broken on the face of KAR 177. Month 11 was one of the seven favorable months in the year for a king to restore a temple. Day 24 of this month was not among the propitious days in the Assyrian tradition on the reverse of KAR 177 and was specifically deemed unpropitious or unlucky in KAR 178 (Labat 1939: 141, 167, 177).

Whoever is responsible for this particular date felt that the contents of the prophecy signaled the correct time to begin the rebuilding process had arrived. He may have been working within the menological tradition that defined this time as months 3, 5, 6, 7, 8, 11 or 12 of the civil year that began in spring. With the prior date set in month 8, he may have moved to the next propitious month. His choice of an unpropitious day to have received the visions would then need to be seen in the same light as already discussed above for the unpropitious date of the twenty-fourth of Elul.

Herbert May has proposed that this specific date was determined by Zechariah's plan to hold a secret coronation of Zerubbabel at the imminent new year festival. He considers the contents of the eight visions to have been drawn from the new year ritual that Zechariah would have known from having grown up in Babylonia (1938: 174). In his estimation, time was needed to create the crown and plan for the coronation before the arrival of the new year. This argument assumes that the date is an integral, original element and ignores the logic of the other two dates in the book as well as their relationship to the dates in Haggai.

The first vision, 1.7-17, announces that Yahweh's seventy-year wrath has ended and that his house in Jerusalem shall be rebuilt (1.7-17). This is the logical consequence of the people's repentance in 1.6 and also emphasizes that the requisite condition of peace now exists, allowing the temple-rebuilding to begin (1.11). As a result, Yahweh confirms that his wrath has ended (1.14-16) and that he is ready for Jerusalem to be rebuilt, including his temple therein, and for his cities to prosper (1.16-17).

The remaining seven night visions contain a variety of themes. Vision 2 (1.18-21; 2.1-4 in Hebrew) deals with the defeat and punishment of those who had scattered Judah. Vision 3 (2.1-13; 2.5-18 in Hebrew) takes up again the theme of the rebuilding and future prosperity of Jerusalem, in which Yahweh will once again dwell. In its present form, vision 4 (3.1-10) deals with the purification of Yeshua, the high priest, the divine placement of a large stone before him and the promise of the future removal of the guilt of the land in a single day.

Vision 5 (4.1-14) moves on to Zerubbabel and his role as the rebuilder of the temple. Verse 9 states that his hands will rebuild this house and his hands will 'finish' it. The same verb that was discussed above in Hag. 2.18, *yissed*, is used here again, in a future meaning. The second verb, *bitstse'*, also a *piel*, has the basic meaning of 'to cut off, break off, or gain by violence'. There are three passages, however, where the *piel* conjugation seems to be used in the derivative sense of 'to carry out; to finish' without the negative overtones otherwise associated with the other meanings. These are Isa. 10.12; Lam. 2.17; and our passage, Zech. 4.9. Perhaps significantly, Isa. 10.12 refers to Yahweh's future restoration of Zion and Jerusalem after its destruction and so is very similar to the use here. The temple lampstand represents the eyes of Yahweh, and Zerubbabel and Yeshua are Yahweh's two anointed ones.

Vision 6 (5.1-4) deals with the establishment of Torah law throughout the land, while vision 7 (5.5-11) deals with the elimination of the worship of Asherah from the land. The final vision in 6.1-15 returns in imagery to the first vision, asserting once again that peace has been established in the north. It then commands the making of a crown of silver and gold for Yeshua, although the ensuing language makes it clear that the original name here was Zerubbabel (e.g. Thomson 1932: 110). He was to rebuild the temple, bear honor, and sit and rule upon his throne with a priest beside him (vv. 13-14).

The series of night visions are all set in the future and deal with aspects of the impending temple-rebuilding process (contra May 1938: 174; Sérandour 2001: 265). A fuller detailing of how the various elements fit into the standard template for describing the rebuilding of a temple will be done in the next section. The suggestion of B. Halpern that the series represents a reverie on the ritual involved in the rededication of the foundation stone is not fully tenable (1978: 167-90). It is the case that some elements may relate to that ritual, especially the stone mentioned in 3.9 (3.13 in Hebrew) (so, e.g., Petitjean 1966: 53-58), the 'former stone' in 4.7 (so, e.g., Lipiński 1970: 30-33), and Zerubbabel's role as builder in 4.9-10. Many, however, have seen the 'former stone' to be the finishing stone rather than a foundation stone (Smith 1908: 299; Cohen 1948: 285; Baldwin 1974: 121-22; Mason 1977: 55; Achtemeier 1986: 126; Hurowitz 1992: 261 n. 2) and tend to link it with the stone of tin or lead in 4.10.

I consider the object in Zerubbabel's hand in v. 10 to be the 'separated stone' that he had ritually removed from the former temple and set aside. I prefer to construe *habbedil* as an adjective describing the stone and not a second noun meaning 'the tin' or 'the lead'. I am uncertain, however, whether this stone was ceremoniously reincorporated into the foundation or was made the final stone to be laid at the dedication ceremony at the completion of the temple, though the former seems likely. David L. Petersen (1974: 368-71) and Antti Laato (1994: 66) have suggested that the object was a foundation deposit of precious metal that had no connection to the 'former stone', while E. Lipiński thinks it was a block of lead that had been removed from the first temple structure as 'the former stone' (1970: 33). Arnaud Sérandour thinks it is identical to the stone in 3.9 and 4.7, which he thinks was a copy of the tablet inscribed by the finger of God with the law. It either was deposited in the temple or in the building foundations (2001: 276-77). His views come close to the earlier proposal of H. May that the stone represents the covenant or law (*'edut*) inscribed on a stone tablet that was to be placed before Zerubbabel at his planned coronation during the new year's festival (1938: 181). Finally, P. Haupt has suggested that the stone was a record of acquittal given to Zerubbabel at his trial for treason by the presiding judge, Ushtani, governor of Across-the-River (1913: 114-15). Our lack of firm knowledge of the ceremonies used to dedicate a temple foundation or the symbolism of the items that have been included in foundation deposits in temples in the ancient Near East allows room for a range of proposals.

We know that in Assyria and Babylonia, inscribed commemorative cylinders and prisms were enclosed within temple walls and inscribed tablets of various materials were sometimes placed under or beside the foundations of the walls (Ellis 1968: 94-107, 113-20). There was also a strong tendency to lay the foundation over bits and scraps of precious metals, rocks, and plant material or to sprinkle these items over the lower courses, allowing various kings to claim that they had built the house on or with precious items like gold, silver, copper, tin, lead, precious stones including jasper, lapis lazuli and white limestone, and aromatic plants.[24] Occasionally, a few special bricks were made that incorporated these items, probably for laying in the foundational course (Ellis 1968: 131-35). Otherwise, we have one text from Warka in the Seleucid period that gives the ritual to be used by the *kalu*-priest when a new temple is built or during the repair of a temple wall. The latter includes the removal of a brick from the old structure by the builder of the new house dressed in pure clothing and its deposition in a restricted place. Offerings are then made to it (Thureau-Dangin 1921: 9, 41-45 [O.174]. See esp. face O.174, 13-14, p. 41. For an earlier version of the text from Babylon, see Weissbach 1903: 32-35, [no. XII]). While it is better than nothing, this information is insufficient to understand the ceremonies used when a temple foundation was laid for the first time or uncovered and reused.

Many other elements in the night vision represent motifs that both precede and follow the rituals involved in the (re)laying of the foundation and so relate to the larger process of temple-building. These include, for example, the establishment of peace (1.8-11), the overthrow of enemies (1.18-21 = 2.1-4 in Hebrew; 2.6-9), the purification of Zerubbabel/Yeshua (3.1-5) and the use of labor from far away (6.15) prior to the commencement of the rebuilding, and the establishment of justice (5.1-4) and the coronation and enthronement of Zerubbabel (6.9-14) afterwards (so noted also by Laato 1994: 67), while peace continues to exist (6.1-8). The date assigned in month 11, a correct time for undertaking temple restoration or rebuilding, is quite logical for this overview of the anticipated process of restitution.

Day 4, Month 9 (Zechariah 7.1). The final date in Zechariah, day 4, month 9 (Kislev) of year 4 of Darius (7.1), covers all the material in Zechariah 7–8. In the Babylonian almanac tradition neither this month nor this day in Kisilimmu (Kislev) were propitious for temple-building. Month 9 was not one of the seven lucky months for building or restoring a temple and day 4 was not among the favorable days of Kisilimmu in either the Babylonian or the Assyrian hemerological lists on KAR 177. The relevant section on KAR 178 is broken and illegible (Labat 1939: 129, 163, 167).

If the writer has deliberately chosen an unpropitious date for these two chapters, then he would be continuing his critique of this Babylonian system and asserting that Yahweh was not bound by it. However, it can also be noted that in the Babylonian tradition, day 4 of every month was a feast day for the god Nabu (Labat 1939: 42). Nabu was the patron god of scribes and was responsible for justice and recording the decisions of the gods. His worship was widespread; his temples at Calah and Nineveh had libraries, and the author of Isa. 46.1 was aware that he was second in importance to Bel-Marduk in Babylon (Millard 1995). There also was a temple to Nabu in Egypt at the military fortress opposite the Elephantine island at Syene and one probably also in Memphis (Porten 1968: 165-66). Nabu was invoked in a greeting on ostracon 277 from Syene (Dupont-Sommer 1944). Thus, a person who knew that day 4 was the feast day of Nabu might have chosen this day to assert Yahweh's superiority over Nabu and to undermine the Babylonian belief in predetermined fate. Nabu's reputation would have been well known within Jewish scribal circles. Be that as it may, the decision to date these two chapters to month 9 also could have been prompted in part or entirely by context clues contained in any of the three subunits within the two chapters, so all will need to be examined before any conclusions can be drawn.

The first subunit, 7.2-7, is associated with a prophecy made on the occasion when the representatives of Bethel-Sharezer had arrived in Jerusalem, perhaps for the temple rededication ceremony. Month 9, December, fell in the darkest time of the year. The processing of olive oil would have been completed by this time and the new round of sowing wheat, barley, oats, peas, vetch, lentils and flax would have been well underway, if not already complete. It was a time traditionally associated with rituals honoring the gods of the dead and was a time to stay at home according to the *Iqqur Ipush* almanac.

A reason for associating this event with the ninth month is not readily apparent. Had the date been added as late as second century BCE during the Hasmonean era, it could be readily explained, but it was already in place earlier than that. It appears in the Greek translation of the Book of the Twelve that was made sometime around 250–225 BCE and so was in place by then. In 2 Macc. 1.18-19 Nehemiah is said to have relit the altar fire of the temple on day 25 of month 9 (Kislev). The claim that Nehemiah rather than Yeshua or Zerubbabel dedicated the temple altar is quite surprising, but it is the date in particular that could potentially provide a rationale for how an editor decided to date the section in Zech. 7.2-7. He could have assumed that the delegation that had arrived to 'entreat the favor of Yahweh' was sent to be present at the rededication of the altar and the temple, which was to take place later in the month. He may well have been working with 25 Kislev in mind as the date for the altar dedication and simply selected a propitious date earlier in the month for the question of the delegation to be posed.

The problem with this scenario, however, is that it presumes that the date of 25 Kislev accurately records that date when the altar of the Persian-era temple had been rededicated. It is likely, however, that this date has been set back in time from the date when the Maccabees rededicated the temple and its altar after it had been desecrated by Antiochus IV. As J.C. Vanderkam has shown, the first sacrifices made to the emperor at the temple as part of the newly-imposed emperor cult had been made on 25 Kislev. This was also the date upon which his birthday was celebrated throughout the Seleucid realm. It is likely, then, that Judah Macca-bee deliberately timed his rededication ceremony to begin on this day, to overturn its imposed significance and replace it with a legitimate Jewish association (2000: 142-44). The author of Maccabees appears to have taken the date of 25 Kislev from his own time and assumed that this is when the Persian-era altar had also been dedicated. Thus, this date is not a reliable remem-brance of when the altar of the second temple had been rededicated and would not have been part of the common tradition available to the earlier editor to draw upon as a resource for dating.

The second subunit in Zech. 7.8-14 commands those living in Yehud to live according to Torah and so avoid the fate that their ancestors had met when they had failed to do so. The establishment of justice and social equality is a regular motif within temple-building accounts, whose position within the larger account can vary, occurring both as a prerequisite for building and again as a condition that prevails after the completion of the temple. In the current situa-tion, then, it would appear to describe the post-building state. This provides no clue for the choice of month 9 to head Zechariah 7–8.

The final subunit, Zechariah 8, seems to hold the key to the date selection. In 8.2, Yahweh declares, 'I have been jealous for Zion with great jealousy and with a great wrath I have been jealous for her'. Verse 3 then continues, 'I have returned to Zion, and I will dwell in the midst of Jerusalem and Jerusalem will be called a city of truth, and the mountain of Yahweh Sebaoth, the holy mountain'. The remaining verses through to v. 7 then go on to detail additional future benefits that will accrue as a result of Yahweh having already returned to Jerusalem. In v. 8, Yahweh announces that he is saving his people from the east and west countries and that he will cause them to enter and dwell in Jerusalem. They shall be his people and he their God. Many English translations render the verbs in vv. 2 and 3 in the future tense, which is not an accurate reflection of the underlying Hebrew text.

According to the author, Yahweh has already returned to Jerusalem and set in motion a positive change there that will bring prosperity in the future. The same verb tenses are found in Zech. 1.14-17; Yahweh has been jealous and still is, allowing a translation of 'I am jealous' in both cases, and 'I have returned'. The difference is that in 1.8, the temple is to be rebuilt, whereas in 8.3, Jerusalem will be called 'The City of Truth' and 'The Mountain of Yahweh'. The latter two designations will be used after the rebuilding of the temple. Zechariah 8.1-8 pre-sumes the recent completion and rededication of the temple.

The next subunit, 8.9-17, seems out of context in its present wording. Like Hag. 2.11-19, it details the changes for the better that are now to take place as a result of the state of the temple, with abundant harvests and material wealth. However, J. Nogalski has noted that the links to Joel 2.18–3.5 are so deliberate that the current shape of Zech. 8.9-13 needs to be seen to have derived not simply from the initial combination of Haggai with Zechariah 1–8 to form a single literary unit, but rather, from editorial work that integrated this block of material into the Book of the Twelve (1993a: 265-66). The turning point again is the fact that the temple has been *yussad*, 'repaired/renewed', or its 'foundation relaid'. Verse 9 reads, 'Thus Yahweh Sebaot has said, 'Strengthen your hands, those of you hearing in these days these words from the mouth of the prophets who were [there or speaking] on the day of the repair/relaying of the foundation of the house of Yahweh Sebaot the temple to (re)build'.

The syntax is very contorted and the sense is not fully clear. The command might be to strengthen your hands to rebuild the temple, in which case the situation presumed is one in which the foundation has been laid but the final project is not finished: the people are to complete the work that remains. Editorially, it is two years into the project and things are flagging. On the other hand, the command might be to strengthen your hands now that the temple is already rebuilt, implying the need to gear up for the regular cycle of agricultural work in the upcoming months, With the project complete, there will be a change in fortunes. In this case, the last word, 'to rebuild', would be eliminated as a secondary editorial expansion, while 'the temple' would be in apposition with 'the house of Yahweh Sebaot'.

Neither above alternative uses the phrase 'strengthen your hands', in its typical sense of performing a military deed, or fighting. Wim Beuken in particular has emphasized how this expression, alongside 'fear not', which is used in v. 13, derives from a military context; he has labeled it a formula of encouragement (1967: 158-61). This use is seen, for example, in Judg. 7.11; 1 Sam. 10.7; 2 Sam. 2.7; 16.21. Thus, it is worth considering a third option: now that the temple work is completed, the male citizenry should turn their attention to their primary role as resident soldiers who have been posted to the fortress in Jerusalem and to other forts throughout the province. The Persians had rebuilt Jerusalem to serve as a *birah,* a fortress settlement whose primary function was defensive but which also contained a civilian population, especially the families of the soldiers stationed there (Neh. 1.8; 7.2). It also appears to have been intended to replace Mizpah as the provincial seat. The men had been assigned land to produce food but also were expected to perform rotations of military duty in the relay stations. This option would allow the military connotation to be maintained and would also be consistent with the emphasis on Yahweh Sebaot, Lord of Hosts, in both books, which seems to have been the title used of the deity particularly in his capacity as a god of war.

The first rendering is inconsistent with a temple that is about to be rededicated or has just been rededicated (7.2-7), while the second requires the deletion of a word. The latter option seems the stronger one, however, especially in light of the very awkward wording of v. 9. Technically, the direct object marker is missing in front of 'the temple' in the phrase 'the temple to rebuild', so the first option lacks correct grammatical support. The inclusion of the need for justice in vv. 15-17 is consistent with the recently completed project, or with one that has recently begun, but not with one that has been underway for two years. The call for justice either precedes the beginning of the work or follows in the wake of the finished, operating temple.

When the date superscription is left aside, it appears that the tradition in 8.9-17 originally served the same function as its counterpart in Hag. 2.11-19; both were meant to signal the completion of the temple repairs, allowing the bestowal of divine blessings to ensue directly. They seem to refer to the same occasion and so could be considered variants of a single tradition or prophetic declaration made on that occasion. On the other hand, one promises agricultural success to the citizens in their capacity as farmers while the other focuses on the role of the male citizens as both soldiers and farmers, so they may have been two separate pronouncements made in connection with the dedication of the completed temple structure.

Zechariah 8.18-19 also seems to presuppose the recent completion of the temple. Yahweh announces that the four fasts in months 4, 5, 7, and 10 that have been observed since the destruction of the temple in 586 BCE are to become seasons of joy. This statement picks up on the question asked by the representatives of Bethel-Sharezer in 7.3 concerning the termination of the fast in month 5 that commemorated the destruction of the temple. Yahweh's response in vv. 4-7 is ambivalent; it is a criticism more than a reply. However, the answer finally comes clearly in vv. 18-19 and includes all fasts associated with the past punishment of Judah, signaling that Yahweh's wrath has ended and a new era is beginning as a result of his return to his home in Jerusalem.

The final verses, 8.20-23, assert Yahweh's status in the near future as the universal god. Peoples of foreign nations will seek out Yahweh at his new temple in Jerusalem and entreat his favor. Newly installed in his home, the world will recognize his sovereignty and become his devotees. This is a logical consequence of the completion of the temple, which allows Yahweh's ritual worship to begin again. This theme, which includes a positive attitude toward the foreign nations, is echoed elsewhere within the Book of the Twelve in Jonah 3, Mic. 4.1-5 and Mal. 1.11, 14.

What does Zechariah 8 suggest would have motivated the editor to assign it and the two units in Zechariah 7 to month 9? It seems as though he would have selected this date as a way to deal with what otherwise appeared to be parallel traditions in Hag. 2.15-20 and Zech. 8.9-12. For some reason, he did not want his readers to gain the impression that any of the units of tradition in Haggai and Zechariah 1–8 had been delivered on the same occasion and so dealt with the same stage in the rebuilding process. Having dated Hag. 2.10, 20 on the basis of internal clues about the agricultural harvest, he decided to place the entire unit of Zechariah 7–8 two years later to pick up where things had left off in Hag. 2.16-17. In this way, he could imply that there had been a two-year hiatus in the building process and avoid two accounts of either the laying of the temple foundation or of its dedication. This point will be expanded in later discussion.

Section Summary

The day and month elements in the book of Zechariah seem to have been derived with the book of Haggai in mind. The assigning of the series of night visions that anticipate various stages in the temple rebuilding process to month 11 (1.7) seems to presume the dates already assigned to what were taken to be earlier events in the larger temple-building process in Haggai. Having used a date in month 9 in Hag. 2.10 to imply when the temple foundation had been laid, it was necessary to assign the sequence of dreams about the entire process, including its completion, to a later time. It is probably not coincidental that the next propitious month for temple restoration was month 11. There is no other apparent reason that would have led the editor to skip over month 10 in favor of month 11.

The assigning of 7.1–8.23 to day 24 of month 9 (Kislev) (of year 4) seems to have resulted from a decision that the promises made in Hag. 2.18-19 had not been fulfilled, as evidenced by Zech. 8.10-13. This second set of promised blessings, together with the two commands for the people's hands to be strong in vv. 9-13, seems to have prompted the editor to posit that a delay in the building process had occurred immediately after the laying of the temple foundation, which had then led Yahweh to delay action on his initial promise. He decided to place the resumption of activity in the same month that it had ended, as a convenient way to pick up the story thread and bind the two narratives more closely into one with the repetition of month 9, but two years later.

The first date in Zech. 1.1 seems to have been chosen above all in order to allow Zechariah 1–8 to be interwoven with Haggai and the two considered a single literary unit. With dates already decided in Haggai, this opening call for repentance needed a date prior to the alleged laying of the temple foundation in month 9. The message was consistent with the one that opened Haggai, but the writer appears to have decided not to assume that any prophecies in the two works would have been delivered at the same historical occasion. He therefore had the option to date this call for repentance before events in Hag. 1.2-11, or after them. He chose the latter, and in so doing, felt the call made better sense after events in Hag. 2.3-9 as well. Like month 11, however, month 8 was a favorable month for temple restoration and so this might have been a motivating consideration as well.

The Internal Organization of Haggai and Zechariah 1–8 as Temple-Building Accounts

It is generally accepted that Haggai and Zechariah 1–8 were included in the Book of the Twelve as a single, pre-existing unit. Thus, these two texts that both deal with the rebuilding of the Persian era temple would already have been interrelated through the dates. Whoever added them used the principle of intercalation in order to combine two originally separate works, Haggai and Zechariah 1–8. This principle interweaves material by assigning dates that force a segment of one work to be read within the context of another. Haggai 1.1 begins with a date in year two of Darius, month 6, day 1; 2.1-9 continues with a date of year 2, month 7, day 21. Zechariah 1.1-6 then is inserted into this account by its date of month 8, year 2. Then one is to return to Hag. 2.10-23, before returning to the series of visions and their interpretations in Zech. 1.7–6.15, which are dated day 24, month 11, Shebat, year 2. Finally, Zech. 7.1 ends the entire corpus with a date of year 4, day 4, month 9, Kislev.

Bearing in mind, then, that the dates are secondary and are used in part as a way to interrelate the two texts, it is logical to examine each work to see what sort of internal logic may have originally determined their sequencing as independent compositions. Both texts, though associated with a prophet, are considered narratives that focus on the rebuilding of the temple. It is therefore justified to compare them with other temple-building texts from the ancient Near East to see how they measure up and if their presentation might follow a standard template for this subject matter. Once this is done, the logic of their combination into a single literary unit via the dates can also be evaluated.

The most complete study to date of literary accounts of temple-building has been done by Hurowitz (1992), although much of the ground for his discussion had already been laid by Bewer (1919), Kapelrud (1963), Petitjean (1966), and Lundquist (1984) and subsequent work has been done by Laato (1994: 56-62). Victor Hurowitz has deduced a standard six-part pattern that has a few established variations. The elements are as follows: (1) The circumstances of the project and the decision to build are given, which can either be the initiative of a deity or of a king. In the latter case, confirmation of divine approval must be sought. When the god takes the initiative, it can be the result of a decision of a divine council that has allowed that deity to have a temple. In addition, the god can use divine inspiration to aid in the task. In Sumerian and Neo-Babylonian accounts, the god frequently reveals the plan of the temple. Also included here can be background information about the earlier history of a site being restored, and/or an account of the defeat of nations. In this case, there often will be an appeasement or reconciliation of the god after a set period of alienation or abandonment of the city and temple. (2) Preparations, such as drafting workmen and gathering materials, are detailed. Common sub-elements here include (a) the acquisition of wood for the project, (b) the imposition of peace and social equality prior to commencing the work, and (c) the flow of materials from the ends of the earth, freely given by foreign nations for the project. Often, foreign labor is used in the building as well. (3) A description of the building is given. (4) Dedication rights and festivities, which involve the entry of the god into his or her new home, sacrifices, purification, music and feasting, the establishment of the temple personnel in their posts, and the establishment of justice are described. These last two motifs are found particularly in Gudea Cylinder B, §§vi.10-xii.25; xvii.12-17 (Jacobsen 1987: 430-36, 444). (5) The blessing of the king by the god(s), with promises of prosperity, long life, and a stable dynasty, is related, or a prayer by the king to the deity for these blessings. (6) Blessings are pronounced on those in the future who will renew the temple and curses on those who profane it (Hurowitz 1992: 32-64, 137-38, 209-15, 220).

Not all of the elements occur in every account, and there is a tendency to emphasize 1 or 2 over the others. In Neo-Assyrian accounts, the idea of a divinely revealed temple plan as a motif of element 1 was not standard. On the other hand, Assyrian building accounts usually began by giving background to the history of the building's earlier construction and destruction when it was not a totally new project (Hurowitz 1992: 85). In Neo-Babylonian inscriptions, it was standard practice to omit element 4, the dedication, and element 6, the blessings and curses for those in future generations who would respect and disrespect the building and the inscription (Hurowitz 1992: 91).

Finally, it can be noted that in both Neo-Assyrian and Neo-Babylonian accounts, there is a strong tendency to recount how the king had defeated his enemies prior to beginning the actual account. This seems to reflect the idea of the successful human warrior who had proven his entitlement to build a house for his god(s), on the one hand, and on the other, the successful divine warrior behind the earthly vice-regent, who, by defeating the gods of the enemies, was entitled to an earthly temple in which he or she could be made manifest and dwell (Hurowitz 1992: 82) It should be observed that in the Old Babylonian account of Samsuiluma, the king's suppression of a rebellion is recounted between elements 1 and 2, which is simply a variation of this motif. Here, also, the king has to show his worthiness to carry out the divine command to build the Ebabbar temple (Hurowitz 1992: 64).

Haggai as an Independent Account of Temple-Building
The book of Haggai contains elements 1, 2 and 5, and may contain element 3, depending on how one analyzes the section in 2.2-8. Haggai 1.2-11 contains elements 1 and 2. The rhetorical question in v. 4 is Yahweh's indirect command to build his temple, while v. 8 contains a direct command to the people to build the house so that he may take pleasure in it and appear in his

glory.[25] Thus, in this case, the project is initiated by the deity. Hurowitz has pointed out that Hag. 1.2 contains the motif of reconciliation after a set period of destruction, while 1.3-10 exhibits the god's initiation of the temple project and Hag. 1.14 divine inspiration for the work (1992: 142, 149, 153). All three are integral parts of element 1. The absence of a native Judahite king who was Yahweh's vice-regent, to whom Yahweh ordinarily would have revealed his will, has lead to a 'democratization' of this element, with a prophetically mediated command directed to the entire community. The command in v. 8 to bring wood so that the temple can be repaired is part of element 2, the gathering of materials. Also, in all of vv. 2-11, the people are being commissioned to be the work force for the project.

Haggai 2.2-9 may also belong to element 2, the gathering of materials. Verses 7-8 refer to all the treasures of the nations that will come to Jerusalem, including the silver and the gold, which belong to Yahweh. It exhibits the motif of the voluntary contribution of materials by the foreign nations (Hurowitz 1992: 208).[26] At the same time, however, it may allude to the normal use of bits of these precious metals in the laying of the temple foundation. This custom was practiced by the Hittites, the Neo-Assyrians and Neo-Babylonians (Ellis 1968: 131-40), so it is likely that it was a common ancient Near Eastern ritual procedure that also was used by the Judahites and Judeans. The issue is whether the three questions in v. 4 are to be taken to refer to the situation before the repairs are begun, or after the completion of the project. If they refer to the existing ruins, before their reconstruction, then the incoming treasures, gold and silver could be seen to be additional elements relating to the gathering of the building materials. If, on the other hand, the questions are seen to reflect the completed building, then the predicted treasures, gold and silver would be intended to help with future adornment, but not with the construction of the edifice itself. In this instance, items that normally would belong to element 2 would be used in a novel way, to refer to additional future work, and the questions would give an indirect indication of the nature of the completed structure, touching on element 3, a description of the building.

Haggai 2.11-19 can either be related to the ritual resetting of the temple's foundation stone, or to the dedication of the completed structure. The theme of the removal of impurity from the people is logical in the wake of the relaying of the foundation or in the wake of the dedication of the completed temple. The theme of blessing in v. 18, on the other hand, tends to make better sense in the context of the completion of the structure, since it belongs to elements 5 and 6.[27] However, in Gudea cylinder A, §11, the deity promises to send agricultural abundance, surplus cream and surplus wool as soon as the temple foundations are laid, so it would be possible to associate the blessings promised in v. 19 with the re-laying of the foundations rather than the completion of the building (Hurowitz 1992: 322-33). This kind of agricultural blessing on the land is normally part of the deity's blessing of the king after his completion of the project, but without a local king in place who had been responsible for the temple's rebuilding, this element, like element 2, has been 'democratized' and now is bestowed directly on Yahweh's chosen people.

The final textual unit, Hag. 2.21 and 23, clearly relates to element 5. Zerubbabel, the Persian-appointed local leader who also is a descendant of the former royal Davidic house, is singled out for recognition by Yahweh; he will become like a signet ring. The usual blessing that was bestowed on the king who built or rebuilt the temple could not be given to Zerubbabel; the

Persian king was the official temple-builder in this case. Nevertheless, in deference to tradition and the local Davidide, a vague sort of favorable pronouncement was made to Zerubbabel, who, had Judah continued as an independent kingdom, would have been the temple-restorer.

The book of Haggai can be interpreted as having been organized on the basis of the standard ancient Near Eastern template for temple-building. As in all building accounts, some elements have been highlighted and others just touched on or passed over in silence completely, but presumed. In this instance the beginning and end of the process have been the two areas of focus.

Zechariah 1–8 as an Independent Account of Temple-Building
Zechariah 1–8 also stresses the beginning and ending elements. Zechariah 1.2-21 give an extended presentation of element 1, the circumstances of the project and the decision to (re)build. Verses 2-6 begin with a statement of the need for the people's repentance as a pre-requisite to the deity's ending his anger and returning to Zion and his temple there. They thus exemplify the motif of reconciliation after a set period of alienation (Hurowitz 1992: 143). Haggai 1.12 specifies the nature of the set time. Verses 7-17 then announce Yahweh's reversal of his anger and his decision to return to Jerusalem,[28] where his house is to be built according to preset measurements.[29] Thus, as in Haggai, Yahweh himself has declared his desire to have his temple rebuilt. In addition to the people's repentance, it is necessary for peace to exist before the task can begin, and v. 11 declares that the earth is at rest.[30]

Verses 18-21 (2.1-4 in Hebrew), which feature the four horns that will terrify and cast down the horns of the nations that scattered Judah, work together with v. 15 to illustrate the motif of the defeat of the enemy as a prelude to temple-building. Nogalski has cautiously argued that 1.14b, 15 is a later editorial insertion designed to integrate the literary unit, Haggai–Zechariah 8, into the Book of the Twelve (1993a: 250-22). It introduces imagery and language from Joel 2.18. Even if this is the case, however, the verses work together with 1.18-21a to illustrate the motif of the defeat of the enemy within the context of the temple-building template.

Zechariah 2.1-13 (2.5-18 in Hebrew) takes up for a second time three points from chapter 1. In vv. 1-2 the measuring of Jerusalem in anticipation of its rebuilding echoes the same motif that was used briefly in 1.16. In addition, the defeat of enemies in 2.7-9, 13 states anew this general motif previously developed in 1.15, 18-21. Finally, Yahweh once more affirms that he will dwell in the midst of Zion and again choose Jerusalem in vv. 10-12, an idea already introduced in 1.16-17.

Element 2 of the standard building template, preparations and the gathering of materials and workmen, is addressed at length in Zechariah 3–6. Chapters 3 and 4 deal with the appointment of the one(s) who will oversee the building work. It is likely that 3.1-5 originally told of the purification of Zerubbabel and that Yeshua's name has been substituted for Zerubbabel's secondarily (e.g. Haupt 1913: 114). It is not necessary to see this section as a later addition (for details, see Redditt 1992: 253). The reference in v. 8 to 'my servant the branch' is more suitable to the Davidic descendant, whose Hebrew name may have been 'Branch', than to a priest (Lemaire 1996: 50-51). In addition, the specific words addressed to Zerubbabel in 4.7-10 identify him alone as the temple-restorer, and the term used to describe the turban placed upon the head of the figure is not the usual one used to describe the turban of the high priest. Here the term *tsanîf* is used, whereas the priestly turban is called a *mitsnefet*. The noun *tsanif* occurs only three times in the Hebrew Bible: here in Zech. 3.5, in Job 29.14, in connection with a robe to describe a costume of nobility or royalty, and in Isa. 62.3, where it says that Zion will be like a royal turban in the hand of its God. In the latter passage, the noun *m^elukah* is used explicitly to specify that the turban is one associated with royalty. Thus, it seems likely that the clothes being placed on the figure after his cleansing are symbols of royalty rather than the costume of the priestly office. The absence of other typically priestly apparel, like the linen girdles (Exodus 2; Leviticus 8), is suspicious and points toward clothing of high office rather than priestly apparel. It also seems likely that the references to the two olive trees representing Zerubbabel and Yeshua in 4.3, 11-12 are a secondary addition to include Yeshua alongside Zerubbabel as a leader of the rebuilding.

The reference to the stone that Yahweh placed before Yeshua (probably originally, Zerubbabel; so, e.g., Wellhausen 1893: 181) in 3.9 sounds as though it is a reference to some sort of foundation deposit to be used in the ritual relaying of the foundation (so, e.g., Petitjean 1969: 190-236, who equates it with the *h'vn hbdyl*, 'separated stone' in 4.10; Lipiński 1970: 33; Halpern 1978; Laato 1994: 63). Whether it is different from, or identical to, the 'head stone' or 'former stone' in 4.7 is unclear. Eduard Lipiński has proposed a specific linkage and has proposed further that it was a large stone, at least the size of a grown man. He does not think, however, that it had anything to do with seven 'eyes' or 'facets' or engraving. Instead, he thinks the text has Yahweh promise that 'all at once, seven sources' will flow from it, similar to the rock from which Moses made water flow in the desert in Exod. 17.6 and Num. 20.7-11. He relates it also to the similar idea found in Ezek. 47.1-12 of a river that will flow eastward from below the threshold of the temple (1970: 29-30). Charles H.H. Wright identified it as the foundation stone that had been laid under Cyrus, taken from the previous temple to symbolize continuity (1879: 71-73).[31]

At the same time, the stone in 3.9 has also been seen to refer to the 'coping stone' that will be the last stone put in place, so signaling the completion of the temple building rather than its beginning (Smith 1908: 297 implicitly; van Hoonacker 1908: 612; Cohen 1948: 282; Siebeneck 1957: 320). Like Lipiński, Le Bas has equated the two stones in 3.8-9 and 4.7, but considers the stone in question to be the finishing headstone rather than a key foundation stone. He links it with the stone mentioned in Ps. 118.22 and Ezek. 28.16, the triangular headstone from the first temple that was buried in Mt Zion (1950: 102-106). However, he then contradicts himself by suggesting it was a small stone that David was able to carry when he approached God in prayer and was possibly a sculpted jewel of surprising beauty and value (1951: 143). In his opinion, the seven eyes in v. 10 are a figure of speech for the seven angelic beings who attend upon God (2 Chron. 16.9; Rev. 1.4; 5.6) and they are not engraved on the stone; the LXX has correctly represented Yahweh to be digging a trench to uncover the former headstone (1950: 115-18).

Some remove the stone in 3.9 from the building context altogether, however, and interpret it to be an ornament for the costume of the high priest (e.g. Wellhausen 1893: 181; Mitchell 1912: 157-58; Baldwin 1974: 117; Petersen 1984: 211-12; Achtemeier 1986: 123; Tollington 1993: 165). While Carol and Eric Meyers equate the stone with a decoration on the high priest's garb like those above, they also think it anticipates the foundation stone associated with Zerubbabel in 4.7, 10 and was deliberately used in this dual sense to allow the insertion of 4.6b-10a into vision 4 (1987: 225). James C. Vanderkam has suggested a variation on the ornamental theme. In his opinion, the stone symbolically represents the fourteen stones of remembrance that were on the costume of the high priest: the two on either shoulder of the linen apron called the ephod and the twelve on the breastplate. Collectively, they reminded Yahweh of his complete people when the high priests wore them in his presence and bore their judgment. Vanderkam assumes that the seven inscribed 'eyes' on the stone in v. 9 were seven pairs of eyes, representing the fourteen stones (2000: 172-76). Chary has proposed that the stone in 3.9 represents the temple (1969: 79) while Rudolph thinks it was a flat stone slab to be placed in front of the holy of holies (1976: 102). Given the range of proposals, the meaning of the stone is far from established. The significance of the lampstand with seven bowls in 4.2, 10 is less clear, but might also have something to do with the ritual re-laying or rededicating of the foundation.

Zechariah 5.1-4 symbolizes the need to establish justice before the temple-building can proceed, which is a standard motif within element 2. However, in this particular context, it may also be emphasizing the central role that Torah will play in the renewed temple cult. This would be part of the redefinition of the nature of Yahweh within the cult in Yehud. The establishment of justice can also be emphasized as an immediate consequence of the completion and dedication of the temple, however, so it would be possible to associate it with element 4 as well.

Zechariah 5.5-11 seems to refer to the need to remove the worship of Asherah permanently from Yehud. She is not to be beside Yahweh in the restored temple. Like the previous vision, this one seems to be addressing the understanding of the nature and functions of Yahweh in emerging Judaism in Yehud. On a more symbolic level, however, in the context of the template for temple-building, her removal can serve as an illustration of the need to ritually purify the city and building site before the rebuilding/repair work can commence (see Edelman 2003b for a summary of views about the meaning of this vision).

Zechariah 6.1-6 then picks up the earlier image of the four horsemen who patrolled the earth in 2.8-11 and found it at rest. These now become horse-drawn chariots, and the report comes back that the North country, which had been punished in 2.6-13, was now at rest again. Thus, the condition of rest, a necessary prerequisite to the temple repairs, which had been temporarily disturbed, has been reinstated. Verses 9-14 command the formation of a crown for the one named 'Branch', who will build the temple, bear royal honor, and sit and rule on his throne. Picking up on the cleansing and investiture of Zerubbabel in 3.1-5, his role as the temple-rebuilder is once again emphasized. As in the earlier passage, so too here, Yeshua's name has replaced Zerubbabel's in subsequent editing of the text (e.g. Wellhausen 1893: 185; Mitchell 1912: 185-86; Haupt 1913: 112-13; Siebeneck 1957: 322-23 with some hesitation; Chary 1969: 110 contra e.g. Beuken 1967: 275-82; Ackroyd 1968: 198; Baldwin 1972: 134; Petersen 1984: 275; Meyers and Meyers 1987: 350-53; Redditt 1992: 252-53). Verse 15 then claims that those from far off will come and help build the temple. This is a form of the motif concerning the use of foreign labor and materials willingly donated to the cause, which is found as part of element 2 of the temple-building template.

With Zech. 7.1–8.23 we jump to element 4, the dedication ceremonies. They are only alluded to rather than described directly. The question posed by the representatives of Bethel-Sharezer concerning the ending of the fast that commemorated the destruction of the temple, together with their intention 'to entreat the favor of Yahweh', imply the dedication ceremonies for the completed temple that included sacrifices, feasting, and rejoicing. The same idea is reinforced in 8.18, where there will be feasting instead of fasting in the future on the anniversary of the rededicated temple. As discussed earlier, 8.9-13 is probably to be associated with the completion of temple repairs, even though the person who created the dates has interpreted it otherwise.

Element 5, blessings on the king that result from the successful installation of the deity in his or her new home, appear in a more democratized form as blessings on the people in Zechariah 8. This is a bit surprising since there is an explicit mention in 6.9 of the coronation and enthronement of Zerubbabel in the final night vision, which seems to presume that this process would have taken place at the end of the temple restoration. Nevertheless, the very presence of such a coronation in the vision indicates that this was the normal element in the standard template for temple-building. It is the reality of the situation, where Zerubbabel is merely the local representative of the Persian king and not king in his own right, which has led to the decision to have Yahweh bestow his blessings directly on his people, who have rebuilt his temple, even though ordinarily they would have been given directly to the king and would have filtered down indirectly to his subjects as well.

The subunit in vv. 20-23 concerning the turning of people of many cities and nations to the worship of Yahweh may be an integral part of element 5, the blessings that flow from the building of a temple. In the pseudepigraphical inscription of Lugalannemunda (Güterbock 1934; 1938; Longman 1991: 92), the dedication ceremonies are described as having included eight rulers who sacrificed seven sacrifices each. People arrived for the ceremony from great distances (IV.8) and were entertained with song, were honored by being placed on golden thrones, and given golden vessels to use for drinking. In the concluding prayer to the goddess of the new temple, she is asked to bless the lands of these kings if they will offer continuous sacrifices in her temple (Hurowitz 1992: 62-63). Here is expressed the idea of the adoption of the worship of a particular deity by those from far away. She will bless their lands if they become her devotees. While Zech. 8.20-23 does not specify that the people from afar participated in the temple dedication ceremony, they will seek out Yahweh now that the temple exists, because they have heard that God is with the Jews. The latter phrase may be an allusion to the prosperity that can be expected when a god favors his worshippers.

Peter Marinkovic has argued that Zechariah 1–8 contains only a few verses that deal with the rebuilding of the temple and that these are marginal or part of pronouncements that express other concerns (1994: 90). In his opinion, these chapters deal with three main themes: (1) the recognition that Yahweh's return to Jerusalem and his abode is the turning point for his people's return to Jerusalem; (2) leadership of the community of Yahweh in Jerusalem; and (3) the main features of the rules of conduct that order daily life in the Yahweh-community in Jerusalem (1994: 91-96). His arguments have been accepted by M.C. Love (1999: 82).

The first and third themes are integral elements of the temple-building template, while the second addresses the unusual circumstances raised by the temple's builder being the Persian king, who was not a participant in the cult of Yahweh. The king normally had prescribed roles to play in the rebuilding process, which in the present instance, were to be accomplished instead by his representative(s), Zerubbabel (and Yeshua). I disagree with Marinkovic's assessment that Zechariah 1–8 deals tangentially and in a very limited way with the rebuilding of the temple; in my estimation, the entire composition speaks explicitly to this topic.

Haggai–Zechariah 8 as a Single Account of Temple-Building
Both Haggai and Zechariah 1–8 are internally organized to reflect the temple-building process. They tend to detail the same elements within the building process: 1, 2, and 5, while Haggai touches on element 3 and Zechariah on element 4. It was probably this overlap in subject and presentation that led a later editor to combine the two works into a new literary unit through the addition of the dates.

The dates provide the following chronological ordering for the new combined work: Hag. 1.1-11; Hag. 2.1-9; Zech. 1.1-6; Hag. 2.10-23; Zech. 1.7–6.15; Zech. 7.1–8.23. This is consistent with the larger pattern for temple building. Element 1, the decision to rebuild and background information giving the circumstances that had led to the prior destruction, together with element 2, preparation for the building project, including the gathering of the work force and materials and correct situation of peace and justice, are clustered in the first three textual units. Haggai 1.2-11 combines elements 1 and 2, while Hag. 2.2-9 focuses on element 2 and Zech. 1.2-6 returns us to element 1. Perhaps the writer chose to insert Zech. 1.2-6 after Hag. 2.2-9 to create a kind of chiastic symmetry involving elements 1 and 2 (A + B, B, A).

Whereas Hag. 2.11-19 probably originally represented the completion of the repair work, and 2.21 and 23 would have represented element 5 after the dedication of the temple, the editorial date given to this section changes that situation. It implies that 2.11-19 deals with the re-laying of the foundation instead, since it is dated to the first year of the work. Yet is it probably significant that the day and month are identical to that assigned to Zech. 7.1–8.23, but with a two-year gap. The editor appears to have wanted to demonstrate that the people responded quickly to Haggai's prophetic message in a desire to emphasize their new obedience to Yahweh, unlike the past generations. A new era was beginning in their relationship with their God with the rebuilding of the temple. As noted earlier, the references to seventy years of wrath as predicted by Jeremiah may also have been a deliberate attempt to emphasize that God fulfills his prophetically mediated promises.

Given the chronological parallel established between Hag. 2.11-19 and Zech. 7.1–8.23, the close parallel between Hag. 2.15-20 and Zech. 8.9-12 particularly needs consideration. The awkward wording in Zech. 8.9 refers to the words from the mouth of the prophets who were [speaking] on the day the temple was *yussad*, making an explicit reference back to the situation and prophecy in Hag. 2.15-20 exactly two years earlier. Given the assigned date, this reference must now also be construed as one to the re-laying of the foundation.

It then talks about the poor conditions that had pertained before the temple work had begun, in v. 10, as did Hag. 2.16-17, although each emphasizes different things. Whereas Haggai focuses on the drought and lack of adequate harvests, Zechariah focuses on the lack of wages and safety within the city. Now, after the foundation has been laid, there is an implied change in fortunes for the better in both cases. In Haggai, we find the two rhetorical questions concerning the seed and the olive trees whose status as positive or negative imagery is disputed in v. 19, but after which one finds the clear assertion, 'from this day on I will bless you'. In Zech. 8.12, on the other hand, there is no ambiguity but a clear assertion that the vine will yield its fruit, the ground its increase, the heavens will give dew, and that Yahweh will cause the remnant of his people to possess all things.

What went on in the editor's mind with these two traditions? In many ways, they seem to be doublets that arose from the same occasion. However, the editor has not construed them in this way since he has dated them exactly two years apart. It would seem that he has focused on the repeated command in Zech. 8.9 and 13, 'Let your hands be strong' and the slight difference in the conditions as depicted prior to what he took to be the re-laying of the foundation, with no wages for man or beast and lack of safety in the city (Zech. 8.10) and deduced that work had ceased on the building project soon after the laying of the foundation. As a result, the promised blessings in Hag. 2.19 had not materialized.

It is possible that, given the two similar traditions, he also had construed the initial *H (heh)* on Hag. 2.19 not as the introduction to two questions but as the rarer exclamatory *heh*, as proposed by P. Jöuon (1947: §161b). In this case, he would have taken the two statements to reflect the *status quo* rather than a change: Indeed, the seed is still in the storage pit and the olive has not produced, but things are about to change. The fact that they apparently had not would have been the result of the cessation of work. Thus, the renewed promise of the end to the drought in Zech. 8.12 in the wake of the resumption of work on the temple would have been logical.

This means, however, that the editor considered neither Hag. 2.11-19 nor Zech. 8.9-13 to represent the final completion of the temple project. Given the ambiguity of the meaning of the verb *yussad*, however, such an understanding is possible. Whether it was the originally intended meaning in either case is another question. Regardless of this potential misconstrual of the function of both of these units in the larger temple-building process, in both cases the promised blessings (Hag. 2.19; 21 + 23; Zechariah 8) can still be considered to be democratized, anticipatory examples of element 5. The laying of the foundation signaled the beginning of a project that would see completion eventually, and the end of the divine wrath would have signaled the return of divine favor and a hope for immediate improvement in conditions even before the completion of the building, when such blessing were traditionally bestowed.

The series of eight night visions that ensue in Zech. 1.7–6.15, two months after the re-laying of the foundation, summarize various stages of the anticipated rebuilding process, some of which has already taken place. It focuses particularly on Zerubbabel's role as temple-builder and develops in the visions the traditional scenario that would have transpired had he been king of the independent nation of Judah: his cleansing and dressing for the ritual rededication of the foundation and his coronation and enthronement after the completion of the temple structure, affirming his status as Yahweh's earthly vice-regent.

The final unit in Zech. 7.1–8.23 then returns to the reality of work that the editor deduced had lapsed soon after the completion of the foundation and focuses primarily on element 5, anticipating the blessing that will ensue once the project is completed. In the editor's interpretation, the delegation sent by Bethel-Sharezer to inquire if the commemorative fasts can now end emphasizes the tragic cessation of the work. Had it continued steadily after the re-laying of the foundation, the temple would have been completed within two years in the opinion of the editor. By implication, with the new start, it can be completed within two years.

Chapter Summary and Conclusion

The addition of day, month, and year dates to the books of Haggai and Zechariah 1–8 seems to have been prompted in large part by a desire to bind these two independent units into a larger, literary whole. Both dealt with the rebuilding of the temple in the Persian period. We have seen that each had its own internal structure that seems to have followed the general outline of the standard ancient Near Eastern template for the construction of a temple. Both concentrated on elements 1 and 2, the commissioning of the project and the gathering of materials and the workforce, on the one hand, and on element 5, the blessings that normally would be bestowed by the deity upon the king after the successful completion of the project. Both books appear to have originally used the verb *yussad* in its broader sense to describe the larger process of renewal and repair as opposed to its more narrow sense of laying a building's foundation.

The person who interwove the prophecies from the two parts to create a new composite literary work broke the internal logic of each book in the process of creating a new entity. In particular, he decided that the verb *yussad* was used in its more technical sense for the laying of the temple foundation and, as a result, lost what was originally probably intended to be traditions that related in both books to the completion of the temple structure. Since he felt he could not have doublets, or variations of a single tradition in both books, he was forced to conclude that the two references to what he construed as the laying of the temple foundations in Hag. 2.15-19 and Zech. 8.9-12 must have meant that that the temple-building process had ceased shortly after the re-laying of the foundation. As a result, he introduced a two-year hiatus in the building process, removed the former references to the completed, dedicated structure, and made the blessings that ordinarily are bestowed after the successful completion (Hag. 2.19, 21, 23; Zech. 8.12, 13, 20-23) into anticipated future blessing contingent upon the completion of the structure.

A review of the day and month dates suggests that the editor may have been familiar with the Neo-Babylonian almanac tradition that assigned the undertaking of temple-building or repair strictly to months 3, 5, 6, 7, 8, 11 and 12 during the year, but this is by no means certain. If he did know it, he did not seem to consider this tradition to be binding in Yehud. Of the six dates, the four placed in months 6 (Hag. 1.1, 15), 7 (Hag. 2.1), and 11 (Zech. 1.7) are consistent with propitious months for temple restoration as detailed in the *Iqqur Ipush*, but the two in month 9 are not (Hag. 2.10, 20; Zech. 7.1).

There is no explicit claim in 2.10-19, however, that the foundation was laid on day 24 of month 9; the context allows for that possibility but also for the foundation to have been completed in the recent past. Thus, a date in the preceding month 8, would be possible, and that was a propitious month. Haggai 2.10-19 is pointing out the change in fortunes that has arrived after the completion of the olive harvest; there has been at least a partial harvest. Verses 20-23 then anticipate events in conjunction with the completion of the process. The contents do not require a date within a propitious month since they are not dealing directly with the need to work.

I have argued that the date in Zech. 7.1 has been derived from the prior date assigned in Hag. 2.10. Like the Haggai tradition, there is no explicit reason why the three units of text associated with that date would have had to have been dated to a propitious month. Once the editor had decided that this section was a new call for work to resume, he could logically have placed it in a non-favorable month to allow time for the people to respond and be ready to work at the next viable opportunity, in month 11.

Nevertheless, it is odd that all of the other dates are set in propitious months. It seems likely to me that the editor intended the unit in 2.10-19 to have taken place at the ceremony for the laying of the temple foundation, even though he appears to have derived his date for the ceremony from the reference to the recent completion of the olive harvest in v. 19. It may be sheer coincidence, however, that all the other dates happen to fall in propitious months for temple restoration. There are better than fifty/fifty odds of this happening since seven of the thirteen specified months (intercalary Nisan is included) were propitious. Thus, it is not clear whether or not the editor knew the Babylonian almanac tradition that outlined the favorable months for temple restoration.

By tradition, work on the Solomonic temple had begun in month 2, with the laying of the foundation at that time (1 Kgs 6.1, 37), demonstrating that Judah had had no almanac tradition that dictated propitious times to begin certain kinds of projects. Thus, even if historically, restoration work might have begun and taken place in months 3, 5, 6, 7, 8, 11 or 12 in order to comply with the tradition current in the province of Across-the-River, the series of dates in Haggai and Zechariah do not clearly presume its primary use by the editor to select appropriate dates after the fact. It appears instead that days and months were derived primarily from contextual clues about the agricultural cycle within each unit of tradition, whether rightly or wrongly. Whether the almanac tradition was a secondary consideration must remain an open question since the evidence is ambiguous.

The situation with the days of the month yields a different picture than the months alone, however. Only two of the six days are propitious according to the three Assyrian and Babylonian hemerological texts examined. Day 1, month 6 (Hag. 1.1) and day 21, month 7 (Hag. 2.1) are favorable, but the remaining four are not. Even if there were no need for the prophecies in Hag. 2.10, 20 and Zech. 7.1 to be placed in a propitious month for work on the temple since they are calls to resume work, we would still expect them to have been delivered on lucky days within month 9 to convince the people that this was really what Yahweh wanted. Day 4 and day 24 were not lucky. The remaining two dates, day 24, month 6 (Hag. 1.15) and day 24 of month 11 (Zech. 7.1) were similarly unpropitious for any undertaking and so would not have been logical choices by someone who was sympathetic to the almanac tradition.

The preponderance of unpropitious dates can be explained in two ways. (1) The writer had no interest in the almanac tradition and was not working with it in mind but simply selected random days after having deduced logical months from context clues. (2) The writer was working with the almanac tradition in mind as he used context clues to deduce plausible months for his dates. He then adjusted those in which building activity took place to fall in propitious months to go along with the menological tradition. However, he then subtly undercut his own position, deliberately, by having four of the six dates fall on unpropitious days. In this way, he could assert that Yahweh was not bound by the menological or hemerological tradition in spite of opinions to the contrary among a portion of those who had been moved from Babylonia to Yehud. If certain positive events fell on propitious days, it was coincidence, and when positive events took place on unpropitious days, it demonstrated that this system had no effectiveness in the world of Yahweh. In order for the latter situation to have prevailed, we would need to assume that this conflict between those who believed in the efficacy of the almanac tradition and those who did not lasted a number of generations, possibly because of ongoing contacts with Jews in Babylonia and handed-on family traditions within Yehud.

The dating of the larger rebuilding process to years 2 and 4 of Darius appears to have been prompted also by a contextual clue: the reference in what would have been the opening verse of Haggai to the people's claim that 'the time has not yet come'. He took this to be a reference to Jeremiah's prediction of Yahweh's seventy years of wrath against Jerusalem (25.11-12; 29.10) and made this link explicit by adding the references to seventy years in Zech. 1.12 and 7.5. Though meant to be a symbolic number representing a long time, the editor appears to have taken it as an approximately literal figure, though not an absolutely literal one. This led him to the reign of Darius (521–486 BCE).

Fortunately for the editor, there were written (the trilingual Behistun inscription and two Aramaic versions known from Elephantine) and oral traditions readily available about this Persian monarch. These indicated that while Darius had rebuilt temples in his empire, he had spent his first regnal year suppressing a series of fourteen rebellions in nine countries, and had been forced to continue these activities even into years 2 and 3. Respecting the biblical tradition that required peace to prevail before temple-building could begin (2 Sam. 7.1; 1 Kgs 4.20), the editor was able to harmonize his interpretation of a hiatus in the building process of the Jerusalem temple with the information concerning peace and its disruption in Darius' first three regnal years. His decision to place the initiation of the rebuilding process only in year 2 of Darius appears to have been prompted by the tradition of widespread rebellion and its suppression in year 1 of Darius. Year 2 then became the earliest point in the reign of this Persian monarch that peace was temporarily achieved and attention could have been turned to temple-building. However, rebellion broke out again in year 2 and lasted through year 3.

It seems likely that the decision to date in year 4 the call to end the hiatus in the building process that the editor deduced to have taken place after the re-laying of the foundation was motivated by knowledge of the new rebellions that had taken place during years 2 and 3 of Darius' rule. It was only at this point that peace prevailed fully throughout the empire, signaling an opportune time to reinitiate the building process, with the prerequisite peace back in place. It is uncertain whether the editor had a written copy of Darius' self-justification concerning his first three regnal years or was dependant on oral tradition that had been handed down concerning this monarch. However, in either case, the content of the tradition would have covered the same material concerning years 1–3, so it makes little difference.

After the creation of the interwoven, new, single literary unit that combined Haggai and Zechariah, a few minor expansions were added when the unit was incorporated into the Book of the Twelve. Specifically, it seems likely that Hag. 2.17, 19, 22; Zech. 1.14b, 15; 8.12 were added at this time, as argued by J. Nogalski. They were designed to link this unit more tightly with Joel especially. These had little impact on the existing unit comprised of Haggai–Zechariah 8, with its dates already in place and its assumption that a hiatus had taken place in the building process.

The date formulations in Haggai and Zechariah are consistent with practices used in the Persian and Hellenistic periods, but are specific to Yehud in the preference for designating the month by number rather than by name. The date of day 24, month 9, year 2 of Darius, found in Hag. 2.10, 20, reflects what would have been normal Persian-era practice within Yehud. The two dates in Hag. 1.1 and 2.1, however, that begin with the regnal year and then give month and day, follow the standard Macedonian order for dating used by the Ptolemies, as opposed to the Persian order or the Seleucid order. The date in Zech. 7.1 of year 4 of Darius, day 4, month 9, on the other hand, could be either Persian, Ptolemaic, or Seleucid. If Persian, then it was following the convention used in a narrative of pulling the year date in front as the first element; if Ptolemaic, then it was following the convention of reversing the month and day elements in a narrative context, and if Seleucid, it followed the normal order.

The two dates with only two elements are arguably Persian in their formulation. Month 8 of year 2 of Darius in Hag. 1.1 looks Persian rather than Hellenistic since the year element is last and not first. Day 24, month 6, found in Hag. 1.15, follows the normal order for the day and month that was used in Persia and by the Seleucids. If the regnal year is implicitly made the first element by carrying it over from 1.1, then the resulting order could be deemed Persian in a narrative context, or Seleucid in any context. If it is understood to be the final element of the date, then it would imply a normal Persian date.

The remaining date of day 24, month 11, month of Shebat, year 2 of Darius reflects the normal Persian order for a date, but gives the month both by number and by its name. This practice is seen elsewhere, in the book of Esther, which is set in the Persian period, but whose date of composition may be as late as the Hellenistic period.

Various hypotheses can be posited concerning when the person responsible for adding the dates lived. He could have lived in the Persian era, in which case the two dates in Hag. 1.1 and 2.1 would need to be seen as subsequent scribal errors where the day and month elements were reversed by mistake because it was the common practice in the scribe's time to place the month before the day at that time. Or, he could have lived in the Hellenistic period but, aware that under the Persians, the elements in the date formula were written in a different order, he could have deliberately archaized. He may have done so successfully, only to have two of his dates later reversed by scribal error during subsequent copying, or he may have reversed them himself, following the conventions of his own day, and not noticed the error.

The final issue to be addressed is whether the author knew the date of the rebuilding of the second temple and deliberately moved it back in time by almost seventy years or had no such tradition and so deduced the date under Darius on his own, tying the reference to the wrong 'time' in Hag. 1.2 to Jeremiah's prediction of seventy years of Neo-Babylonian rule but reinterpreting the latter to refer to the exile. This issue is difficult to assess. I have argued above that it is unlikely that tradition had preserved the date of 25 Kislev for the dedication of the Persian-era temple altar. This date reflects the rededication of the temple under the Maccabees and was secondarily set back to the Persian period on this basis by the author of Maccabees (2 Macc. 1.18-19). Ezra 6.15 states that the temple was finished on day 3 of Adar (month 12), year 6 of Darius. In the next chapter, I will consider whether the author of Ezra derived this date from tradition, oral or written, or from other considerations. To anticipate my conclusions, which are germane to the present issue, I think this date has been derived indirectly from the dates in Haggai–Zechariah 8 and directly from a literal calculation of seventy years from the destruction of the temple in 586 BCE to show how Jeremiah's prophecy was literally actualized. I do not think this date was handed down in written or oral sources.

It appears that the dates in Haggai–Zechariah 8 resulted from an earnest desire by the editor to demonstrate that Jeremiah's prophecies had been actualized in history. Understanding them to apply to the predicted length of time Jerusalem would remain destroyed and uninhabited after 586 BCE, he was able to calculate forward approximately seventy years and ended up in the reign of Darius. Written and oral traditions associated this king with temple-building, but also with a first regnal year of rebellion suppression and subsequent conditions of unrest again in years 2 and 3. As a result, the editor chose to place the Haggai traditions in year 2, when peace would have begun, and to place the recommencement of work after a break, which he deduced from Zech. 8.9-13, in year 4, when peace, the necessary condition for temple-building, prevailed.

If the editor had deliberately altered the date, he did so out of pious motivations. He felt it was more important for Yahweh's word as spoken through Jeremiah to have been fulfilled more literally, almost seventy years later, instead of almost 140 years later. For him, the demonstration that his God kept his promises and was once more on the side of his people he had abandoned would have been reason enough to stretch the facts. After all, the temple had been rebuilt, so it did not matter when exactly.

Did the editor know that the temple had been rebuilt under Artaxerxes I and not under Darius I? Yes, he probably did, because the knowledge that Nehemiah had dedicated the temple altar appears still to have existed at the time the letter found in 2 Macc. 1.10–2.18 was composed, some 300 years after the rebuilding of the temple. 2 Maccabees recounts events that transpired between c. 180–160 BCE leading to the establishment of the Hasmonean dynasty in power as a backdrop to its central focus on Hanukkah as a legitimate Jewish festival that was to be observed annually. It probably was written in Egypt sometime near the end of the second century BCE.

The attribution of the altar dedication to Nehemiah falls within the second introductory letter, whose authenticity as an independent document written by Judah Maccabee himself is heavily disputed. Whether the letter is genuine, stems from the author of 2 Maccabees, or stems from another later author and was appended secondarily to the book, its author seems to think that the temple was dedicated by the same person who had been entrusted with the rebuilding of the city walls. This author presumed that the temple was rebuilt when the provincial seat was moved from Mizpah to Jerusalem, under Artaxerxes I.

On the basis of existing biblical tradition in Haggai–Zechariah 8 and Ezra 1–6, we would have expected either Yeshua, the high priest, or Zerubbabel, the governor, to have performed the dedication. Thus, we must assess whether the Maccabees tradition reflects genuine historical memory or is deliberately contrived to alter the actual course of events in line with ideological concerns at the end of the second century BCE.

It would be possible to suspect that the author of 2 Macc. 1.10–2.18, who was a member or supporter of the Hasmonean dynasty, might have wanted to downplay the importance of Zerubbabel because of his Davidic lineage. The Hasmoneans were a priestly family belonging to the line of Yoariv, who also became the civil leaders of Yehud, making it into a vassal kingdom once again instead of a province. They eventually claimed the title of 'king', in spite of the long-standing tradition that only a descendant of David could legitimately occupy the throne of the kingdom. Thus, they might have wanted to remove the honor of the temple dedication from Zerubbabel, had he actually been the one to have performed this rite or under whose governorship it was performed by the head priest. But why transfer it to Nehemiah, with whom the Hasmoneans had no blood ties?

If someone had deliberately changed the name of the person who had dedicated the temple altar, it would have been most logical to have substituted Yeshua or his son Yehoiakim for Zerubbabel. Not only was a religious facility being inaugurated for use, but having the priesthood oversee such a ritual would have been in keeping with the priestly origins of the Hasmonean kings. This was one function where their priestly lineage could have been deemed more important and appropriate than a Davidic one. Using the same logic, if the author had decided to reject the testimony of Haggai–Zechariah 8 and Ezra 1–6 about the temple's dedication during the reign of Darius and associate it instead with the broader rebuilding of Jerusalem during the reign of Artaxerxes I, we might have expected him to have had Ezra dedicate the altar, rather than Nehemiah. Ezra is described as a priest and scribe of the Law of the God of Heaven in 7.12, and the priestly connection might have made him a more logical candidate or the high priest at the time of Nehemiah, Yehoiakim.

Jonathan A. Goldstein has argued that the story of Nehemiah's building of the temple and rededicating the altar was created by the author of the second letter found in 2 Macc. 1.10b–2.18. He was trying to convince Jews in Egypt that the post-exilic temple in Jerusalem had been the direct continuation of the first temple and endorsed by Yahweh as his selected place of worship. This had become an issue because a Jewish temple had been built in Egypt when the temple in Jerusalem had been temporarily defiled and had continued as a rival temple after the rededication of the Jerusalemite temple. The argument in the letter implies that some Egyptian Jews were claiming that Yahweh had not re-chosen Jerusalem as his central place of worship after its rebuilding. Specifically, because there had been no miraculous fire from heaven that had kindled the altar fire that had occurred when Solomon had dedicated the temple (2 Chron. 7.1), the second temple had never been legitimate. It is noteworthy that no mention of this fire is found in the parallel passage in 1 Kgs 8.62-66, which traditionally is seen to be the older of the two accounts.

To counter this argument, the author created the story of how priests of the first temple had hidden some fire from the first altar in a dry well and that, when Nehemiah sent their descendants to retrieve it, they found naptha, or petrolium oil, instead. Some of this was poured on the wood when Nehemiah rededicated the second temple and, when the sun came out from behind cloud, a great fire flared up, to everyone's astonishment (1983: 173). According to Goldstein, the author found no miracle to quote from extant tradition and felt he could not add it to the account of Ezra 1–6, which already was known, so he created the current story, which drew on Neh. 1.20, 23-25 and 1 Kgs 18.30-39, appealing to archives and memoirs of Nehemiah (2 Macc. 2.13), in the hopes that some would be convinced that God had indirectly relit the fire of the second temple, signaling his acceptance of this traditional site as his legitimate place of worship (1983: 166, 173, 177).

Even if one accepts these arguments by J.A. Goldstein, they do not explain why the author chose to associate the rebuilding of the temple, the rededication of the altar, and the use of naptha to rekindle the altar fire with Nehemiah and not with Zerubbabel, Yeshua, or Ezra. Perhaps another contributing factor was the ability to appeal to Nehemiah's memoirs, where such a story could plausibly have been recorded, providing the illusion of a legitimate source from which it was taken. It is unclear whether the claims that additional archives of Nehemiah existed and that this individual founded a library that included books dealing with the kings and prophets, the writings of David and the letters of kings on the subject of offerings are fictitious or based on fact (2 Macc. 2.13-14).

Is it mere coincidence that 2 Macc. 1.18-19 has Nehemiah dedicate the temple altar, implying that the temple had been completed and was made functional during his term in office? I think not. It is more logical to assume that the temple was erected when the provincial seat was moved from Mizpah back to Jerusalem, as part of the larger construction project in which a fort and administrative buildings were erected alongside limited domestic housing, and the city walls were repaired than to adopt the biblical story that places its rebuilding in a deserted war-damaged former capital. Biblical tradition associates the last phase of this work with Nehemiah: the completion of the *birah*-garrison, the temple, the city walls, and the governor's palace (Neh. 2.8; for a full discussion of the grammar of this verse, see Chapter 6, pp. 344-46). The temple altar would have been the last item to be dedicated in the temple complex, since it inaugurated the sacrificial cult, which could only be effective once the rest of the temple complex had been completed, ritually purified, and set apart from profane presence. The claim made in 2 Macc. 1.18-19 may be grounded on genuine historical recollection, in spite of the reshaping of history that took place within biblical tradition in Haggai–Zechariah 8 and Ezra 1-6 (for further thoughts, see Edelman 2005c).

When the editor who combined Haggai and Zechariah 1–8 into a single narrative lived cannot be pinpointed, but some general parameters can be set. Ben Sirah, writing about 200 BCE, refers to the Book of the Twelve, showing that Haggai–Zechariah 8 had been incorporated into the larger sequence of minor prophets by this date (Sir. 49.10). It is also found in the Septuagint, the translation of the Hebrew writings into Greek. Unfortunately, the translation of the Book of the Twelve was probably not completed at the same time as that of the Pentateuch, which was deemed more important. The latter is traditionally dated to the last quarter of the third century so at most, we might be able to push the date for the Book of the Twelve back slightly into the last decade of the third century (contra Wolfe 1935: 118). Regardless, we have no clear idea about how early the two writings would have been combined through the addition of the dates. If the temple were, in fact, built under Artaxerxes I c. 450 BCE, then we would need to allow sufficient time to elapse so that this fact were no longer widely known within the common collective memory and could be altered without immediate resistance or repercussions. This suggests to me that the editor must have lived in the early Hellenistic period, c. 300 BCE, though this date could be adjusted twenty-five years either way and I would not protest.

Endnotes

1.   Neh. 1.1; 2.1 has been seen to reflect an autumnal New Year in place in Yehud as late as the fifth century BCE, unless these dates represent the calendar used at Susa (Segal 1957: 284).

2.   Kataja and Whiting 1995: 20-22, document 19. Similar complete month designations are found in documents 1, 10, 25, 26, 69, 85, 92, 94. The translators have used the Hebrew form of the month names and have supplied the number of the month afterwards in Roman numerals to help their readers, but no such designation by number exists in the original texts.

3.   I consider the most likely reading here of the first three words of v. 2 to be 'Bethel-Sharezer sent' and not 'Bethel sent Sharezer'. The personification of a town in this way, making it the source of messengers, is otherwise unattested, while the proper name Bethel-Sharezer is. The common translation, 'the men of Bethel' or 'the people of Bethel', would require the presence of another word before Bethel to represent either term, which is not present in the underlying Hebrew text. Thus, it is not an option grammatically. For the personal name, Bethel-sharezer, see Wellhausen 1893: 186; Hyatt 1937.

4.   The term *regemmelek* can be construed either as a royal title or as a personal name. For a discussion of the title *regem-melek*, see Lipiński 1970: 36-37.

5.   This translation of the MT text requires no emendations and assumes there was no need to specify that a messenger or representative was sent because this was implied by the verb. Alternatively, the next best translation would be: Bethelsharezer sent (via) Regemmelek and his men to entreat the favor of Yahweh. This requires the deletion of one letter, the *waw* before Regemmelek, which otherwise would mean 'and' in this particular context. In my first translation, it is being construed as a *waw explicativum* that is introducing an appositive, with the force of 'i.e'. If Regemmelek and his men are taken to be direct objects of the verb 'sent', then they should have both been introduced by the direct object marker, *'et*. However, if the phrase 'by the hand of, via', *beyad*, is understood to be assumed after the verb 'sent', which is a common idiom, then the direct object markers would not be lacking. For helpful discussions of the various options for reading this verse, see, e.g., Baldwin 1974: 142-44; Mason 1977: 65-66.

6.   Jer. 52.30 claims that there was a subsequent deportation in year 23 of Nebuchadrezzar, or 582 BCE, which many assume would have resulted from Gedaliah's murder (e.g. Ackroyd 1970: 36-37; Lindsay 1976: 27 n. 30, 29; Miller and Hayes 1986: 125). However, 2 Kgs 25.25 and Jer. 41.4 imply that he was assassinated only two months after his appointment in 586 BCE. No year is given with month 7, however, so the actual time of the killing could have been year 23.

7.   G. Larsson has argued that the number needs to be taken literally and that it reflects the period from Jehoiakim's surrender and removal to Jerusalem at the beginning of the reign of Nebuchadrezzar in 605 BCE and the return of the first group from Babylon to Yehud in 538 BCE. He uses the lunar year of 354 days to arrive at his figure of seventy years exactly (1967: 417-23). He has failed to discuss the secondary nature of this meaning for the seventy years, however, which was originally applied to the length of Babylonia's rule over the world.

8.   So emphasized by Van Hoonacker 1908: 595. The argument by C.F. Whitley that the number seventy is secondary in all its occurrences in biblical texts and has its origin in the fact that there were exactly seventy years between the destruction of the first temple in 586 BCE and the rededication of the second one 516 BCE (Ezra 6.15) is misguided. He has failed to understand that the date given in Ezra was specifically selected to produce an exact seventy-year differential but is artificial and derivative. The author of Ezra has used Haggai and Zechariah as sources and has picked up on the references in Zech. 1.12 and 7.5 to seventy years but has taken them literally, rather than symbolically (1954: 66). As A. Orr has correctly pointed out in his response to Whitley, the two uses in Jeremiah are older than the other uses in Zechariah, Isaiah, and Daniel, which all are dependent upon the Jeremiah passage. In its original setting in Jeremiah, however, the figure did not describe the length of the Judahite exile but rather, the length that Babylonia would be the world empire. The application of the symbolic figure to Judah is derivative (1956: 304-306).

9. Stephanie Dalley informs me that the five Old Sumerian city laments were written on the eve of the rededication of their respective city temples and not at the time of destruction (oral communication). For a discussion of these laments, see Edelman 2005b.

10. C.F. Whitley has made a strong grammatical case for assigning both references to seventy years in 1.12 and 7.5 to the editor (1954: 62-63). A. Orr has accepted this as probable in spite of his objections to other parts of his argument (1956: 304). In light of the probable date of the temple's rebuilding under Artaxerxes I, I would also agree that these references should be assigned to the editor who created the year date elements.

11. The proposal by W.F. Albright that the discrepancy over the fall of Jerusalem in year 18 versus year 19 of Nebuchadrezzar can be resolved by assuming that the Palestinian historian reckoned his reign from 605 BCE rather than the official 604 BCE because he had led the neo-Babylonian forces alone at the battle of Carchemish, leading to his recognition as *de facto* king from that event, is unlikely (Freedman 1956: 57). Scribes would have needed to employ the regnal year reckoning system that was used at the Babylonian court in official documents.

12. Documents from Hubadishu (?) are dated to Bardiya in month 1, while ones from Babylon date to month 3 and from Sippar to month 4, or April, May and June of 522 BCE. Documents from Sippar, Uruk, Nippur, and Shahrinu are dated to month 1, year 8 of Cambyses, indicating that the rebellion had taken hold by month 2 (Parker and Dubberstein 1956: 14-15).

13. Multiple dates are assumed by, e.g., Olmstead 1938: 409-10; Bickerman 1981: 28, but not based on different accession dates due to revolts. Instead, Bickerman assumes in all cases the same assumed date of accession, which yielded different dates either because of antedating, postdating, or a late autumnal new year. He proposes an official Persian date beginning year 1 on 1 Nisan (14 April), 522 BCE, which was also used in Syria and Yehud, but states that the same date would have been considered 1 Nisan (3 April), 521 BCE in Babylonia and 31 December, 522 BCE in Egypt.

14. The second is probably the more important of the two because of its theological affirmation of the principle of prophetic fulfilment. This principle is heavily emphasized in writing associated with the so-called Deuteronomistic Historian.

15. In the case of Nabonidus, H. Tadmor has demonstrated that the phrase that originally meant 'in the accession year' came also to have a less specific chronological meaning of 'in the early part of the reign'. He is uncertain, however, whether the use of this expression in connection with the account of the rebuilding of the temple of Ehulhul in Harran was deliberate, to obscure the chronology of the events, or not. Thus, it is possible that this is not a relevant example of first year events, although I consider it to be one, since the dream requesting the rebuilding is set then, even though the actual rebuilding does not appear to have taken place until somewhere between years 8 and 13. At the time of the dream, Harran was in enemy hands, so it would not have been a serious option at the beginning of the reign. This demonstrates the ideological nature of setting the dream early (1965: 351-63; 1981: 21-25).

16. Since corvée labor would have been used as the main workforce, there may have been certain months when this mandatory service could not be imposed or was needed to be used to harvest crops on royal estates rather than for building projects.

17. If the temple had official authorization to be rebuilt and was a work project of the Persian king, then all who were subject to corvée labor would have been pressed into service according to their annual tax obligation. It is unlikely that there would have been a sizeable slave force available in this outlying province to do the construction and this temple to a minor regional deity would not have had a high enough priority for the king for him to have ordered the transport of slaves to do the work instead of the local free population.

18. Although this is straightforward, some have suggested that 2.15-19 should be moved forward and associated with the date in 1.15, which would result in the foundation stone being laid in month 6 rather than month 9; so, e.g., Rothstein 1908: 53-56, 63; Waterman 1954: 75; Mason 1977: 18; Achtemeier 1986: 99. As J. Baldwin has pointed out, however, month 6 was consumed with harvest activities and so would not have been a logical time for work to have started on the temple (1974: 43).

19. In the MT the first question begins with the prefixed interrogative *heh*, which clearly indicates that a question is being asked. The second question does not have the *heh* as well, but begins with the same word, *'ôd*,

written in the shorter form without the *waw* as a vowel marker (*'od*). The two questions seem to be contained in a single sentence, where the first *heh* would accordingly carry over to the second question as well. P. Joüon has proposed that the initial *heh* is not the standard interrogative *heh* but instead, a rare exclamatory *heh* (1947: §161b). He has not defended his suggestion, however, and his proposal is contradicted by the date, which presumes that sowing has already taken place. Thus, whoever added the date assumed that the *heh* was interrogative rather than explanatory. This does not ultimately mean that he was correct, however, or that Joüon is incorrect concerning the original prophecy. The second statement, 'The olive tree has not produced', taken as a presentation of fact rather than a rhetorical question, would be possible in an earlier context, from month 7-9, when the harvest normally would have taken place, before the autumnal rains. H.W. Wolff has adopted his suggestion, but recognizing the problem with the date, has moved the saying to immediately after the date in 1.15: 'Certainly, the seed is still in the corn pit'. Since the rains have not yet come, the grain cannot yet have been sown (1988: 58-59; 66).

20. G.A. Smith (1908: 249) takes this statement to say, 'Is there yet any seed in the barn?' He seems to think that the spring harvest had been so bad that the grain has already been eaten by December. H.G. Mitchell adds yet another twist: there has been no harvest since the work began (1912: 72).

21. Most commentators see the verse to be predictive of the future rather than a statement of what has already transpired, in spite of the clear grammar. So, e.g., Smith 1908: 249; Mitchell 1912: 72; Baldwin 1974: 52; Mason 1977: 23; Clark 1983: 439; Petersen 1984: 94; Achtemeier 1986: 104; Verhoef 1987: 134-35. P. Bloomhardt is in the minority. He considers the second question to indicate that the recently completed good vintage has given proof of the changed fortunes (1928: 174). I find no clear indication that the harvest was good.

22. In a variation on this theme, A. Lemaire proposes that it expresses the hope for a change in Yehud's status from province to vassal kingdom (1996: 55).

23. My position seems closest to that espoused previously by Petersen (1984: 100, 106). While I would agree with Wolff's assessment that the prophecy is not an appeal for warlike leadership or participation, I think that its intent goes beyond claiming that as Yahweh's seal, Zerubbabel would be the guarantor of the temple's completion (1988: 106, 108).

24. Section 6 of the almanac *Iqqur Ipush* details the calamities that will befall anyone unlucky enough to find any sort of precious metals or objects in the former foundation when they build a new house (Labat 1965: 63-65). It clearly has in view the uncovering of a temple foundation, which seems to have carried enough residual sanctity that ordinary houses were not to be built over it. The listed finds help illustrate the type of things that commonly were included in foundation deposits and confirms existing impression: silver, gold, copper, a stone, tin, lead, and 'something one cannot extract'.

25. Hurowitz argues that the reference to Yahweh's being glorified at the end of the verse alludes to the divine presence and the bringing of the god into the temple in element 4 (1992: 146).

26. Contrast Bloomhardt, who considers it to be an allusion to the future booty that the independent nation will take in war with Yahweh's aid, which was finally realized 350 years later under the Maccabees (1928: 170). D.J.A. Clines (1994: 64-65) and R.P. Carroll (1994: 41) take it literally to indicate that the temple was primarily a treasury rather than a cultic center for sacrifice. P. Bedford, on the other hand, links it to Zion theology stressing Yahweh's role as king (2001: 252). The latter point could be consistent with its function in the temple-building template since both share a common underlying mythic tradition in which the god defeats his enemy to become king of heaven, thereby earning a temple.

27. I am not convinced that Hag. 1.8; 2.7-9 also symbolize God's blessing within the account and thus, are additional examples of element 5 after the dedication of the temple, element 4, as suggested by Hurowitz (1992: 268).

28. Hurowitz suggests that vv. 12-17 might be a metamorphosis of the motif of the divine conference that meets to decide if a temple should be built for a given deity. The writer's monotheism has transformed the lesser deities into angels (1992: 140).

29. Hurowitz argues that the measuring imagery derives ultimately from the Mesopotamian practice of presenting a measuring rope and measuring rod to the king in preparation for temple-building (1992: 326).

30. Contrast this with the explanatory comment that the verse implies that all nations are enjoying security except Yehud, which is in a state of misery and oppression (Cohen 1948: 274).

31. At the same time, he adopts the interpretation of many of the church Fathers and the Reformers that the stone typified the messiah as the foundation of the eternal temple, upon whom the hopes of an everlasting peace depended (1879: 71, 73).

Chapter 3

IT'S ALL IN THE SOURCES: THE HISTORICITY OF THE ACCOUNT OF TEMPLE-REBUILDING IN EZRA 1–6

Introduction

In Chapter 1 I presented genealogical evidence from the book of Nehemiah that I think demonstrates that Zerubbabel and Nehemiah lived within twenty-five years of each other and were either successors to the office of governor in Yehud or had overlapping commissions, with Nehemiah serving as an overseer of public works during Zerubbabel's term as governor. Dates in the Elephantine papyri tend to indicate that Sinuballit I had been governor of Samerina during the reign of Artaxerxes I, not during the reign of Darius, which in turn suggests that the temple-rebuilding headed by Zerubbabel took place under Artaxerxes I, not under Darius.

In Chapter 2, I argued that the dates in the books of Haggai and Zechariah were added secondarily by an editor in order to interweave the two separate but parallel accounts of the rebuilding of the temple of Jerusalem in the Persian era. I proposed that he derived his dating to the early reign of Darius I by applying the principle of prophetic fulfillment. Specifically, he assumed that Jeremiah's prophecy of seventy years of destruction for Judah during Neo-Babylonian rule referred more broadly to the length of time that Jerusalem would lay devastated after its destruction in 586 BCE. Then, using oral or written traditions associated with Darius, which confirmed the king had rebuilt temples, he set the initial work in year 2, after Darius had managed to establish temporary peace in his empire, and used contextual clues within various prophecies to select day and month dates.

In the current chapter, I will investigate the third biblical account of the rebuilding of the temple in Persian-era Yehud contained in Ezra 1–6. I have left it to the end because it is a derivative account, based in large part upon the combined account in Haggai–Zechariah 1–8. Like both of the original compositions, its author has organized his material by using the standard template for temple-building. I will summarize the account to make its historical implausibility apparent. Then, I will lay out how its components correspond to the temple-building template. Finally, I will deduce the sources used by its author in its composition, to show that it is not a historically reliable account.

I will not include an analysis of the related temple-building account in the Greek work known as 1 Esdras in English Bibles, III Esdras in the Vulgate or Latin Bible, and Esdras A in the Septuagint or Greek Bible. This composition is widely recognized to have been based on Chronicles and the book of Ezra, if not the combined work of Ezra–Nehemiah. It wanted to emphasize the role of Ezra at the expense of Nehemiah and so its author probably deliberately chose not to include any traditions relating to Nehemiah. He is mentioned once in passing in

1 Esd. 5.40. Under these circumstances, it is difficult to determine whether its author only used a form of the book of Ezra that circulated before its combination with Nehemiah or knew the combined work of Ezra and Nehemiah but opted not to include any portions from Nehemiah to further his own ideological purposes (for a recent discussion, see Talshir 1999).

> The inclusion of information about Ezra found in Neh. 7.73b–8.13 need not indicate a knowledge of the combined work. This section may have been added secondarily to Nehemiah when the two works were combined into one to help tie them more closely together. The later editor might have removed it from its original context in Ezra and placed in Nehemiah.

> The use of a combined Ezra–Nehemiah narrative is more likely, however, because 1 Esdras includes the section found in Ezra 4.7-24, which I will argue below is a late editorial insertion that presumes the single, combined work. Its placement in a different location in the text in 1 Esdras was to further that writer's own agenda. Regardless of which way one argues about whether the author of 1 Esdras knew Ezra–Nehemiah as a single work or not, the derivative nature of 1 Esdras means that no new information of a reliable, historical nature can be uncovered from an analysis of this late work relating to the rebuilding of the temple under Artaxerxes I.

In the ensuing analysis I will not take a stand on whether the Chronicler also wrote Ezra and/or Nehemiah or whether the book of Ezra ever existed as an independent work before being combined with the book of Nehemiah. These are complex issues whose full scope I have not been able to investigate as of yet.[1] Thus, in the ensuing analysis, when I refer to 'the book of Ezra', I am not intending that phrase to refer to an independent composition that circulated alongside the book of Nehemiah before the two were combined into a single literary work, as I think was the case with Haggai and Zechariah 1–8. I am using it in a more neutral way to refer to the material currently contained in Ezra 1–10, reserving judgment on how it was created and whether it ever had an independent existence or was composed wholesale as an introduction to the formerly independent work of Nehemiah. At the same time and for the same reasons, I am reserving judgment about whether Ezra was a historical personage or a fictional creation.

Summary of Ezra 1–6 and Some Historical Problems It Raises

Summary
Ezra 1–6 claims the following sequence of events transpired in connection with the rebuilding of the Persian-era temple. The first monarch of the Persian empire, Cyrus, sent out an official proclamation throughout his empire in his first year that stated that Yahweh had charged him with building his house in Jerusalem. To that end, any member of his people was authorized to go to Jerusalem in Yehud to rebuild the house of Yahweh, taking with him freewill offerings from his neighbors who remained behind (1.1-4). Many Jews responded and gathered freewill offerings, while Cyrus returned the temple vessels that Nebuchadrezzar had carried off, entrusting them to Mithredath, the treasurer, and Sheshbazzar, the prince of Judah (1.5-11). A list of those returning at this time under the leadership of Zerubbabel, Yeshua, Nehemiah, Seraiah, Reelaiah, Mordecai, Bilshan, Mispar, Bigvai, Rehum and Baanah is then given, including their servants and animals. They settled in their towns (Ezra 2). The MT text lacks the statement in 2.70 that they lived in Jerusalem and its vicinity though this is implied; this claim is found

specifically, however, in the Greek book, 1 Esdras 5.46. That author appears to have made explicit what was implicit, for clarity.

In the seventh month, presumably of year 1 of Cyrus, the people gathered in Jerusalem and under the direction of Yeshua and Zerubbabel, built and dedicated the temple altar and observed the week-long Feast of Booths (3.1-6). Afterwards, they hired masons and carpenters and bought cedar from Sidon and Tyre, in accordance with Cyrus' grant, in order to be able to rebuild the temple (3.6-8). Work began in the second year of their arrival in Jerusalem, in month 2. Zerubbabel and Yeshua appointed the Levites to oversee the work, and the foundation was laid ceremoniously. Many priests and Levites and heads of fathers' houses wept when they saw the foundation of this temple, but were drowned out by those shouting joyfully at the ceremony (3.8-13).

When their adversaries, who had been settled in their current home by Esarhaddon, king of Assyria, heard that they were rebuilding the temple, they asked permission to help with the construction but were rebuffed. In retaliation, the people of the land discouraged the people of Yehud, made them afraid to build, and hired counselors against them to frustrate their goal all the days of Cyrus, king of Persia, until the reign of Darius, king of Persia (4.1-5). During the reign of Ahasuerus (Xerxes), they wrote an accusation against the inhabitants of Yehud and Jerusalem. In the reign of Artaxerxes, Bishlam, Mithredath, Tabeel and their associates wrote to the king in Aramaic. Rehum the commander, Shimshai the scribe and their compatriots whom Osnappar had deported and settled in the cities of Samerina and in the rest of the province of Across-the-River, also wrote a letter, warning the king that the Jews who had come up from him to them had gone to Jerusalem and were rebuilding that rebellious city. They were finishing the walls and rebuilding the foundations. They claimed that if the city were rebuilt, they would not pay tribute, custom or toll, which would impair the royal revenue. They urged the king to search the book of records to learn that the city had been a rebellious city, hurtful to kings and provinces, and that sedition had been stirred up in it from of old. That was why it had been destroyed (4.6-16). The king wrote back saying he had had the records searched and had confirmed their accusation. He commanded them to issue a decree making the men cease the work to prevent the city from being rebuilt, until he could make a decree himself (4.17-22). After receiving that letter, Rehum, Shimshai and their associates hurried to the Jews in Jerusalem and made them cease by force and power. The work on the temple ceased until the second year of Darius, king of Persia (4.23-24).

Then, after Haggai and Zechariah prophesied in the name of Yahweh, Zerubbabel and Yeshua began to rebuild the house of God in Jerusalem (5.1-2). But at the same time, Tattenai, the governor of Across-the-River, and Shetharbozenai and their associates asked them who had given them a decree allowing them to build the temple and finish it and what the names of those currently building were. Work continued on the edifice while a letter was sent to Darius and a response was returned (5.3-5). The report sent by Tattenai informed the king that the house of the great God was being built in Jerusalem and those responsible claimed to have had a decree from Cyrus, given in his first year, to rebuild the temple that Nebuchadrezzar had destroyed. He also had restored the temple vessels that had been carried away to the temple in Babylon. They had been entrusted to Sheshbazzar, who had laid the temple's foundation, and the temple had been in the process of reconstruction ever since, but had not yet been completed. He urged the king to have a search made of the royal archives in Babylon to confirm this story (5.6-17).

Darius then ordered the search and at Ecbatana, a scroll was found that recorded Cyrus' decree ordering the rebuilding of the temple and the re-establishment of the altar for burnt sacrifices. Certain of the temple's dimensions were specified, the cost for construction was to be paid from the royal treasury, and the gold and silver vessels were to be restored (6.1-5). He then ordered Tattenai, Shetharbozenai and their associates to leave the governor and elders of the Jews alone and let them rebuild the temple on its site. He also issued a decree to Tattenai to pay the construction expenses without delay from the royal revenue, the tribute from the province of Across-the-River, and also to provide whatever else was needed for the cult on a daily basis so that the priests could offer sacrifices to Yahweh, God of Heaven, and pray for the life of the king and his sons. Penalties for altering the edict followed (5.6-12).

Tattenai complied with the royal edict, and the building was completed by the decree of Cyrus, Darius, and Artaxerxes, king of Persia, on day 3, month Adar, year 6 of Darius (6.13-15). On day 14 of month 1, the returned exiles kept the week-long passover, along with the people of Israel who had joined them and separated themselves from the pollutions of the people of the land. Yahweh had turned the heart of the king of Assyria to them so that he helped them in the work of the temple (6.19-22).

Historical Problems

The account of events in early Yehud found in the book of Ezra is not convincing from a modern historical standpoint. Why would Cyrus have commissioned the rebuilding of the destroyed temple in a ravaged and uninhabited backwater city in an insignificant province or sub-province that already had a functioning capital at Mizpah? Why were the adversaries able to halt the temple-building, which had had official permission, during the balance of Cyrus' reign (559–530 BCE), during the reign of his son Cambyses (530–521 BCE), who appears to be unknown to the author, and under Darius I (521–486 BCE)? Why was it only finally at the beginning of the reign of Xerxes (Ahasuerus) (486–465 BCE) that the adversaries filed a formal complaint against the *golah* group led by Zerubbabel (4.6) and why have details not been given of this accusation? Why did they write again under Artaxerxes I (465–423 BCE) (4.7)? Why did Artaxerxes not send an official decree stopping the work on Jerusalem immediately, but instead, authorize the leaders in Samaria to issue a temporary decree to stop the work? Why would the king have ceased work on the reconstruction of Jerusalem when it was the site of an official fortress (Neh. 7.2), whose construction, manning, and supplies would have been the responsibility of the imperial crown? Was he not fully informed by his own advisors or scribes about what was transpiring during the transfer of the new regional capital in Yehud from Mizpah to Jerusalem?

Why did work then resume under Darius after the official response of Artaxerxes I had forbidden it? Which Darius is intended here, Darius I, who had preceded Artaxerxes, or Darius II Nothus (423–405 BCE)? And why did this Darius seem to overlook the decision of Artaxerxes and only find the original decree of Cyrus I concerning the temple, now allowing it to be completed in his sixth year (chs. 5-6)? Finally, what did the king of Assyria have to do with the rebuilding of the Persian-era temple when there was no longer a native king of Assyria?

Shemaryahu Talmon has suggested that the present account does not imply that there had been an interruption after an initial laying of the foundation in year 2 of Cyrus and a subsequent resumption of work on the foundations in year 2 of Darius; this is a false impression modern readers have developed by failing to understand the function of the information presented in 4.4. He proposes that the reference to the people of the land making the people afraid to build in v. 4 is meant to recapitulate the events of the preceding textual unit in 3.1–4.3. Thus, while the people built the altar, celebrated Sukkot and gathered the building materials (3.3-7) in year 2 of Cyrus, they did not actually begin to build and lay the foundation of the temple until year 2 of Darius (3.8-13) (1976: 322; adopted by Williamson 1985: 43-44). This reading is designed to get around the apparently contradictory reports that Sheshbazzar laid the temple foundation under Cyrus (5.16) while Zerubbabel and Yeshua laid it under Darius (3.8-12).

While this is a valiant effort to make sense out of the present form of the text and to eliminate two accounts of foundation-laying, it does not ultimately succeed (Halpern 1990: 105-106). The author has otherwise drawn on Hag. 2.3 for the content of vv. 12-13, so it seems strange that he overlooked the date contained in that larger narrative for the laying of the temple foundation: month 9, year 2 of Darius (Hag. 2.18). He reports instead that the temple foundation was laid in month 2 of year 2, which, in the flow of narrative events, is year 2 of Cyrus. The preceding chapters are set in years 1 and 2 of Cyrus, and the writer has not signaled a change of monarch in 3.8 by stating that the year 2 belonged to Darius instead of Cyrus. In addition, as will be discussed in more depth in the section concerning sources, it was crucial for the writer that the foundation had been laid during the reign of Cyrus, since that had been prophesied by 2 Isaiah (44.28). The placement of the event in month 2 of year 2 (of Cyrus) has been done deliberately to separate it from the subsequent work done in month 7 of year 2 of Darius and is patterned after the claim that work on the Solomonic temple had commenced in month 2 (2 Chron. 3.2). Thus, the author of Ezra 3–4 intends his audience to understand that the temple foundation was initially laid in year 2 of Cyrus under the close supervision of Zerubbabel and Yeshua while Sheshbazzar was governor of the province (5.16), but that worked ceased immediately after that and was not resumed again until year 2 of Darius, when Zerubbabel and Yeshua continued their oversight of the project (contra Halpern 1990: 109-110; 123).

One of the biggest problems in the current biblical account for modern historians is the chronological aberration introduced by 4.6-24. Some scholars have concluded that this section contains a digression that deals with events subsequent to the rebuilding of the temple (so, e.g., Talmon 1976: 322; Goldstein 1983: 174; Williamson 1985: 57; Eskenazi 1988: 55-56; Hurowitz 1992: 115; Blenkinsopp 1988: 106, 111; Dozeman 2003: 450). They think that a literary device known as resumptive repetition, which creates an envelope around a digression in the story line, has been used in vv. 5 and 24. The segment of text forming an 'aside' (in vv. 6-24a) is framed with the same statement, so that the reader knows where the digression ends and the main story line resumes. The repetition of the last verse or a phrase therein of the main story signals a return to that original topic.

Verse 12, falling within what those above consider to be a digression, states that the Jews who have returned from Babylonia to Cisjordan are completing the rebuilding of the city wall as well as doing some sort of work involving foundations (Smith 1945: 385-89; Tuland 1958:

269-71). The specific meaning of the Aramaic verb is not clear because this is the only place where it is used. The underlying root has been reconstructed as *yḥt, ḥtt* and *ḥyt*. All three would have been irregular in their conjugations, which explains why there have been the different proposals for its meaning, including 'dig', 'lay', 'repair', reinforce', 'search for', 'inspect' and 'join up' (for a detailed discussion see, e.g., Batten 1913: 175-76; Blenkinsopp 1988: 114).

Sidney Smith has argued that the word used here for foundations, *'ushayya'*, is Sumerian in origin and that its use indicates that the temple in Jerusalem was built according to Mesopotamian practices. Because there was little bedrock in Mesopotamia, double-thick walls were created to carry the weight of the superstructure. The interior space between these lower foundations was back-filled with rubble to create a level podium. The visible, upper walls were then built on the lower foundations and the floor level was set on top of the backfill (1945: 385-89).

Smith assumes that since the settlers in Jerusalem had recently returned from Babylonia, they would have used building techniques they had learned there. However, Jerusalem, unlike Babylonia, has plentiful stone and bedrock. He also points out that normally, the verb *y-sh-d* in Hebrew refers to the placing of foundations on bedrock, without resorting to the use of lower foundations, but still argues that in the case of Zech. 4.9 and Ezra 3.10, it is used exceptionally to designate the laying of the upper walls on top of a lower foundation. Since Ezra 4.10 is written in Aramaic, its use of the term *'ushshayya'* to describe foundations need not imply Mesopotamian building techniques (Smith 1945: 396). This term may have been broadened in its meaning in official Aramaic as well as local dialects to mean 'foundations' in general, especially in areas where lower foundations were not needed for structural stability.

We do not know if the Persian temple was rebuilt on its original foundations or not. If it were, then it is likely that those foundations had been placed directly on bedrock in the Iron II period; the builders were not Babylonian. If not, then two options are possible.

It is likely that the old walls would have been traced and some portions reused; this would have been done to maintain continuity at a sacred site as well as for practical reasons: readily available building materials that reduced the need for newly quarried stones. In addition, it is likely that a 'cornerstone' from the old structure would have been incorporated into the new, along with any old foundation deposits that may have been built into the earlier structure. In this case, it is likely that internal rubble and debris would have been cleared out to the level of the first course of foundation stones that had been set on bedrock, if not to bedrock itself.

If, however, one wants to argue that the tracing of the earlier foundations was not a priority, perhaps because a smaller structure was being built on the site of the former temple, then it might be possible to argue that to save time, the existing rubble and debris was compacted and leveled and that building was done over that layer, knowing that there was underlying bedrock that would support the weight of the new foundations without too much settling. In this case, however, it is not clear that time and effort would have been spent digging out a segment of the rubble so that double thick lower foundation walls could be sunk down into it; it is more likely that the first course of stones would simply have been set on the leveled building site.

There is no need to assume that Babylonian foundation techniques would have been used in the construction of the Persian-era temple, or that the verb *yashad* is being used in a non-standard way in Zech. 4.9 and Ezra 3.10. Smith has also overlooked the wider meaning of this verb to designate 'repair, ' as discussed in Chapter 2, that need not imply work specifically on foundations, whether upper or lower. It seems warranted not to limit the meaning of the Aramaic term *'ushshayya'* as used in Yehud to 'lower foundations' but to assume that it meant 'foundations' in general.

There is no explicit reference in v. 12 to the temple. Luc Dequeker has argued that there is an oblique reference to it, because the term *'ushshayya'* is used elsewhere in the book of Ezra exclusively to describe the temple foundations (5.16; 6.3) (1993: 79-80). However, Ezra 1–6 is focusing on the rebuilding of the temple, so one would expect any mention of foundations to relate to that project, even though the term can describe the foundations of a range of building types. In addition, Dequeker considers the use of the term in 4.12 to be part of a genuine letter written in the reign of Artaxerxes that has been cited verbatim (1993: 76), so the meaning of the term there would not necessarily be governed by the two uses that he attributes to the author of Ezra 1–6.

The fact that the subsequent authors of 1 Esdras and 3 Esdras interpreted the reference to the foundations to be to the completion of the temple is no guarantee that this was the original meaning. That interpretation suited the ideas that both authors wanted to convey. It is likely that the mention of the foundations, in the plural, is either to the foundations of houses being rebuilt within the city wall or to those of larger public structures being built inside the city. This is how Ben Sira construed it (Sir. 49.11-12). The suggestion that it refers to the rubble fill against the city wall that served as a substructure for dwellings (Clines 1984: 80) or to some segments of the foundations of the city walls would also be possible if the verb meant either 'reinforced' (e.g. Schneider 1959: 114; Blenkinsopp 1988: 109) or 'inspected' (e.g. Driver 1931: 364; Brockington 1969: 76). Verse 12 is introducing the narrative context particularly of the book of Nehemiah, whose main topic is the rebuilding of the city wall and the re-population of the city thereafter. Ezra 7–10, however, is also situated within the time period of Artaxerxes, so it sets the chronological scene for the second part of the book by taking the reader forward in time to this era briefly, in anticipation of later events.

Those who argue for the presence of resumptive repetition define its parameters by the repeated phrase 'the reign of Darius, king of Persia'. It ends v. 5, signaling the beginning of the digression in v. 6, and then is repeated at the end of v. 24, marking 5.1 as the resumption of the original narrative on the rebuilding of the temple. This device is often used editorially to insert information into a narrative but can equally be used by an author to provide background information deemed relevant for plot development immediately before a specific event (e.g. Berlin 1983: 126-28). In the current instance, it has been seen by some to introduce events that will be dealt with later in the combined literary unit comprising Ezra and Nehemiah.

It needs to be noted, however, that there are still irregularities within the current text that are not explained by the suggested use of resumptive repetition in 4.6-24 to introduce material anticipating later story developments. The first is the content of v. 24, which states that work on the house of God in Jerusalem ceased until year 2 of the reign of Darius, king of Persia. The content of the earlier verses is not focused on the temple-building, but on the reconstruction of the city wall and resettlement of the city. Thus, all of v. 24 is returning the reader to the situation in v. 5, even though only the final phrase is repeated. This is not normal within resumptive repetition. One would have expected v. 5 to have contained all the information found in v. 24 to have used this device effectively, or for the sentence order in v. 24 to have been reversed so that it started with the phrase, 'in the reign of Darius, king of Persia', and then went on to give the information concerning the cessation of work on the temple, returning to the original story line.

The theory offered by T. Eskenazi about the purpose of this section cannot easily account for the reference to opposition in the days of Ahasuerus in v. 6. She thinks that the larger narrative in Ezra–Nehemiah centers on the construction of 'the house of God', a term which is not to be equated with the temple proper, but which is used to designate the entire city of Jerusalem. For her, the references here to the building of the city walls and house foundations under Artaxerxes are designed to anticipate story-line developments; the story is only partially complete when the temple building itself is completed in Ezra 6.14 (1988: 56). But what, then, is the function of 4.6?

The current wording gives the clear impression that vv. 6-24 have dealt with the delay in the temple reconstruction. As noted by others, it provides what is intended to be a chronological listing of hindrances placed in the way of the Jews to build the temple and the wall of Jerusalem to illustrate how the community's loyalty was tested continuously (so, e.g., Coggins 1976: 30; Brockington 1969: 74; Michaeli 1967: 272-73; Fensham 1982: 70). Thus, it appears as though the person who created this section intended his audience to think that the foundations mentioned in v. 12 belonged to the temple. This person also seems to have thought that Artaxerxes I had ruled before Darius, since he was including this letter dating to the reign of Artaxerxes in this period when work had been interrupted. The argument of J. Trotter that the author deliberately telescoped the available materials and events of which he had knowledge does not account for the non-chronological arrangement (2001: 282). This is especially the case given the summaries in vv. 4 and 24 that claim there was an interruption in building from year 2 of Cyrus to year 2 of Darius. In vv. 5-23, Artaxerxes falls within this period.

The person responsible for 4.5-24 was probably also responsible for adding the reference to Artaxerxes in 6.13 where it is said that the temple was completed by the command of Yahweh and the decree of Cyrus, Darius and Artaxerxes king of Persia. In 6.12 the order of the three kings is chronologically correct, which is a bit surprising since the author seems to have thought that Artaxerxes would have ruled between Cyrus and Darius, but perhaps he simply inserted the name at the end, not intending to give a chronological order. Thus, in spite of the use of repetitive resumption, which could have introduced information that was anticipatory of later chronological or story developments, it is likely that the person who placed 4.3-24 in its current location was a subsequent editor and not the original author of Ezra 1–6.

This editor did not know much about the order of the Persian kings, but this apparently was the case by the end of the Hellenistic period, under the Seleucids. The book of Daniel gives the order of the Persian rulers after Belshazzar, the final Neo-Babylonian king, as Darius the Mede and Cyrus (Dan. 5.30; 6.28), showing a similar lack of knowledge of the correct order of the kings. This same order may be presumed in Ezra 1–6, if the Darius under whom the temple-building was resumed was presumed to be Darius II instead of Darius I the Mede (so, e.g., Dequeker 1993: 79). This would presume the following order of the Persian kings: Darius I (the Mede), Cyrus, Xerxes, Artaxerxes I, and Darius II (Torrey 1910 [1969]: 141, 160). The original author, on the other hand, was much better informed, since he was able to calculate an exact seventy-year gap from year 19 of Nebuchadrezzar to year 6 of Darius.

Understanding the later, editorial origin of 4.6-24 eliminates many of the questions raised above if we work with an earlier, hypothetical form of the text in which this section was not in its current location and Artaxerxes' name did not appear in 6.12. Artaxerxes I never forbade the construction of the temple. The temple was rebuilt under Darius I; the Darius in 4.5 is identical to the one in 4.24. This Darius knew nothing of events that would transpire almost seventy years later under Artaxerxes I but would have been able to order a search to be made for a decree of Cyrus I giving permission to rebuild the temple.

Nevertheless, four questions raised earlier remain to be answered. Why would Cyrus have commissioned the rebuilding of the destroyed temple in a ravaged and uninhabited backwater city in an insignificant province or sub-province that already had a functioning capital, probably with a functioning temple, at Mizpah? Why were the adversaries able to halt the temple-building, which had had official permission, during the balance of Cyrus' reign (559–530 BCE), during the reign of his son Cambyses (530–521 BCE), who appears to be unknown to the author, and under Darius I (521–486 BCE)? Finally, what did the king of Assyria have to do with the rebuilding of the Persian-era temple when there was no longer a native king of Assyria? We will return to these questions in the conclusion, after investigating the sources that were used to create the present narrative. If we work with the final form of the text, however, with 4.6-24 and 6.12 in their present locations, then all of the initial questions remain to be answered.

Ezra 1–6 as an Account of Temple-Building

The first 6 chapters of Ezra are primarily an account of the rebuilding of the temple in the Persian era. To appreciate their organization fully, it will be helpful to see how they agree or disagree with the standard ancient Near Eastern template for describing such an event, as was done in the previous chapter with Haggai, with Zechariah 1–8, and then with the secondarily created literary unit, Haggai–Zechariah 8.

To refresh your memory of the elements and motifs that constitute the template, I will represent them again here. (1) The circumstances of the project and the decision to build are given, which can either be the initiative of a deity or of a king. In the latter case, confirmation of divine approval must be sought. When the god takes the initiative, it can be the result of a decision of a divine council that has allowed that deity to have a temple. In addition, the god can use divine inspiration to aid in the task. In Sumerian and Neo-Babylonian accounts, the god frequently reveals the plan of the temple. Also included here can be background information about the earlier history of a site being restored, and/or an account of the defeat of nations. In this case, there often will be an appeasement or reconciliation of the god after a set period of alienation or abandonment of the city and temple. (2) Preparations, such as drafting workmen and gathering materials, are detailed. Common sub-elements here include a) the acquisition of wood for the project, b) the imposition of peace and social equality prior to commencing the work; and c) the flow of materials from the ends of the earth, freely given by foreign nations for the project. Often, foreign labor is used in the building as well. (3) A description of the building is given. (4) Dedication rights and festivities, which involve the entry of the god into his or her new home, sacrifices, purification, music and feasting, the establishment of the temple personnel in their posts, and the establishment of justice are described. The last two motifs are found particularly in Gudea cylinder B, §§vi.10-xii.25; xvii.12-17 (Jacobsen 1987: 430-36, 440. (5) Blessing of the king by the god(s), with promise of prosperity, long life, and a stable dynasty is related, or a prayer by the king to the deity for these blessings. (6) Blessings are pronounced on those in the future who will renew the temple and curses on those who profane it (Hurowitz 1992: 32-64, 137-38, 209-15, 220).

Element 1 is found immediately, in Cyrus' decree authorizing the return of Jews to Yehud to become the workforce that will rebuild the temple (1.2-4). It names Yahweh as the initiator of the project, who has charged the world king, his earthly vice-regent, with carrying out the task. Background information about the history of the site is given much later, in 5.11-13, in the context of Tattenai's letter to Darius repeating the explanation he had been given about why the temple was being rebuilt. It occurs briefly also in 1.7. Thus, while present, it is not in its more usual place within the account, at the beginning.

Element 2 is partially interwoven with element 1 in Cyrus' decree, since it authorizes Jews to return to Yehud to rebuild the temple and also to gather freewill offerings from others for the temple. Cyrus also contributes to the materials by restoring the former temple vessels (1.7-11). The list of returnees in 2.1-67 details the workforce that will undertake the restoration (so also Halpern 1990: 96). In addition to turning over the freewill offerings they had brought from neighbors to the treasury to help pay for the construction costs, some of those who returned also make personal contributions (2.68-69). Considering the contributions to have been gathered from Egyptians rather than Jews, B. Halpern links the free-will offerings with the motif of the flow of materials from the ends of the earth, freely given by foreign nations for the project (1990: 90). Though I disagree with his view that the source of money was Egyptians rather than Jews, if he were correct, his observation would be valid.

The altar of burnt offerings is rebuilt in its former location as part of the preparations for work on the temple building proper (3.1-3). This is in part so that the Feast of Booths could be observed correctly and immediately (3.4), but also probably so that Yahweh could be properly appeased and entreated during the reconstruction of his new house. The money given to the treasury is then used to hire masons and carpenters for the project, while cedar wood, probably for interior panelling, is secured from Sidon and Tyre in exchange for food, drink, and oil (3.7). Finally, the Levites are appointed to oversee the work (3.8-9).

The section detailing the building preparations is basically self-contained, although it is revealed later in 6.4 in the record of Cyrus' decree found in Ecbatana that Cyrus not only returned the temple vessels but also provided funds for the rebuilding from the royal treasury. It is curious that this alleged record or summary of Cyrus' earlier edict contains a number of details not found in the edict quoted directly in 1.2-4, including certain dimensions of the temple and the use of three courses of stone and one of timber in its construction. Darius then upholds the terms of Cyrus' original decree and instructs Tattenai to give money for the temple project to the Jews from the royal revenue, the tribute of the province of Across-the-River (3.8). He even surpasses it by ordering Tattenai to give them in addition whatever is needed for the daily ritual (3.9-10).

Element 3, a description of the building, is found primarily in the citation of Cyrus' supposed edict in 6.4, and then in the brief report of the ongoing work and completion of the project in 6.14-15. The beginning of the project is recorded in 3.8, however, and the laying of the foundation, with its accompanying dedication ceremony, is related in 3.10-13.[2] As already noted, the account of the building of the altar is deliberately set prior to the commencement of building work, as part of element 2.

It would have been more logical for the report of the building of the altar to have been part of element 3. This raises the possibility that the section in 3.2-6a detailing its construction and the celebration of the Feast of Booths immediately thereafter may be a later addition by the same hand responsible for 4.6-24. Its purpose would have been to allow the information in Ezra 7.15-23 to refer to events during the gap in construction between year 2 of Cyrus and year 2 of Darius, on the assumption that Artaxerxes had ruled during this interim period. The existence of a functioning altar even without a rebuilt temple would have allowed the offerings sent back with Ezra's group to be made, even though the wording in 7.15-23 strongly implies that the temple itself has been completed and has a functioning cult. But a person who assumed that Artaxerxes had ruled between Cyrus and Darius II and not after Cyrus, Cambyses, and Darius I would have taken all references to the temple to be anticipatory in 7.15-23.

Nevertheless, to make this section that would have struck him as odd and chronologically incoherent more intelligible, the editor may well have added the specific reference to the completion of the altar under Cyrus and the celebration of the Feast of Booths. He would have done so to help clarify the anticipatory references to the temple and to make the ability of the sacrifices to be offered without the temple in place obvious to readers. His placement of the altar's construction within the context of element 2 rather than element 3, however, betrayed his lack of attention to detail within the larger story-line.

Element 4, the dedication ceremonies at the completion of the structure, is briefly but explicitly mentioned in 6.16-18. The festivities included the offering of sacrifices and joyous celebration and confirmation of the priests and Levites for the now-established temple service (Halpern 1990: 121). Element 5 is missing, but element 6 is present in Darius' decree to Tattenai concerning the need not to interfere in the rebuilding of the temple in 6.11-12.

The account of the building of the Persian-era temple in Ezra 1–6 is more complete than the one created by the combination of Haggai and Zechariah 1–8 into a single literary unit, or either one individually. Unlike those, it contains explicit details of element 3, instead of alluding to the completion in passing. It also contains curses on those who will alter the royal decree commanding the completion of the temple or destroy the temple in the future. This element is totally lacking in the other three accounts. On the other hand, however, the present account lacks element 5, the bestowal of blessings, which was present, albeit in a democratized form, in the other three accounts. Finally, it should be noted that the present account explicitly states that the *golah* community remaining in Babylonia, together with some of the returnees, provided money to pay for the rebuilding, alongside the Persian king, who authorized the use of tribute funds from the province of Across-the-River, to pay for the work.

The account follows the standard template fairly closely in its ordering of events, but still has individualized this particular account in deviating from the norm. Specifically, elements 1, 2, 3, 4, and 6 occur sequentially in chs. 1–6. However, the larger account has been somewhat obscured through the addition of the long section dealing with opposition to the rebuilding of the city wall and resettlement in 4.6-24. In addition, the segment in 5.3–6.13 expands element 3 significantly, developing a twist in the otherwise straightforward plot. As a result, the description of the building comes in the form of a cited record that was intended originally as the blueprint for the project, and additional details of element 2 are revealed (6.4). A history of the building project, also normally part of element 1, likewise is given within the citation of a letter of complaint to the king (5.11-16).

Instead of having a description of the progress of the work and the building itself, we have a series of letters and records quoted in 5.3–6.13. While detailing an event that might well have thwarted the completion of the building project, they contain a mini-building account on its own that gives the background to the destruction of the temple, initial permission for its rebuilding, and ongoing patronage for its completion. At the same time, the expanded narrative within element 3 highlights the interruption in the otherwise normal building process that allegedly took place between its beginning under Cyrus and its completion under Darius. The reason for this ordering of the account will be explored in the next section.

Finally, it needs to be noted that Ezra 7–10 deals with the establishment of justice, which frequently is a subunit within element 4. As noted, element 5 does not occur at the end of the building account in Ezra 1–6, as would be expected on the basis of its inclusion in the accounts in Haggai, Zechariah 1–8, Haggai–Zechariah 8, 1 Kings 5–9, and 2 Chronicles 1–7. It appears to have been a standard element within Judahite and Judean accounts. Element 6 is found within Darius' decree to Tattenai concerning the need not to interfere in the rebuilding of the temple in 6.11-12. It is not found, however, in any of the other biblical accounts of temple-building and so does not appear to be a standard element in the Judahite and Judean scribal tradition. Perhaps Yahweh's claim in 1 Kgs 9.8, reflected also in 1 Chron. 7.20-21, that he personally will allow his house to become a heap of ruins to punish his people can be considered a variation on this theme. Bearing this in mind, it is likely that the temple-building template provided the author of the larger Ezra narrative with a logical segue into the account of Ezra's bringing of the law and establishing its observation in Yehud some sixty years after the establishment of the temple in chs. 7–10. Were it not for the sizeable time gap, Ezra's mission to establish the law would have made an extended treatment of element 4 in the temple-building account. Perhaps the author wanted to convey the impression that the temple was not fully initiated and functional until Ezra brought the law to Yehud, in spite of the lengthy time gap. If this is the case, then it could be argued that the entire book of Ezra was intended to be taken as a single temple-building account, with particular emphasis placed on elements 3 and 4, which receive extended development.

Sources Used to Compose Ezra 1–6

The author of the account of the building of the temple under Darius I has relied heavily on existing biblical tradition to formulate his narrative, as well as on a strong belief in the fulfillment of prophetic pronouncements. The latter point is explicitly stated in the opening sentence: 'in order that the word of Yahweh by the mouth of Jeremiah might be accomplished, Yahweh stirred up the spirit of Cyrus, king of Persia, in his first year so that he made his proclamation allowing Jews to return to Jerusalem to rebuild the temple'. In spite of the fact that the dating to Cyrus in 1.1 has been motivated by a desire to show the fulfillment of the prophecy found in Isa. 44.28 rather than in Jeremiah, the completion of the temple under Darius has been connected with the fulfillment of Jer. 25.11-12 and 29.10 in Haggai–Zechariah 8, making the initial statement proleptic and, therefore, still accurate. Hugh G.M. Williamson has suggested that the author had in mind Jer. 51.11, which states that Yahweh has stirred up the spirit of the kings of the Medes to destroy Babylon as vengeance for his temple (1985: 10). This certainly is possible, though it does not exclude the presence of proleptic references to Jer. 25.11-12 and 29.10 at the same time. I strongly disagree with the claim by T.C. Eskenazi that there is no allusion to Jer. 29.10 and the seventy-year limit to the exile in Ezra 1 or elsewhere in the larger Ezra–Nehemiah narrative (1988: 44).

2 Isaiah (Isaiah 40–55)

Cyrus as the Temple's Rebuilder. The claim that the temple foundation was initially re-laid during the second month of year 2 of Cyrus in Ezra 3.8-13 has almost certainly been motivated by a desire to demonstrate that the prediction found in Isa. 44.28 had been actualized in real time. '[I am Yahweh], who says of Cyrus, "He is my shepherd and he shall fulfill my purpose", saying of Jerusalem, "She shall be built" and of the temple, "Your foundation shall be laid".' Here, in Ezra 3.10-13, we explicitly have an account of the laying of the temple foundation during the reign of Cyrus. While a number of scholars have pointed out a direct echo of the prophetic text (e.g. Rudolph 1949: 3; Gelin 1960: 27; Myers 1965: 6; Michaeli 1967: 252; Coggins 1976: 11; Williamson 1985: 10), almost all have been reluctant to state explicitly that they consider Isa. 44.28 to be the source that has prompted the dating of the laying of the foundation to Cyrus. Rare exceptions are W.H. Kosters (1895: 27), C.C. Torrey (1896: 56) and G. Hölscher (1926: 107, 111).

The suggestion by J. Trotter that the placing of the initial work under Cyrus was an attempt to explain why work did not commence at the beginning of the Persian period (2001: 283) does not adequately account for the present narrative claim. Since Haggai and Zechariah dated the commencement of the work to year 2 of Darius, there was no reason for the author of Ezra 1–6 not to accept their testimony. He could easily have placed the arrival of the group headed by Zerubbabel and Yeshua in year 1 of Darius, which most consider to be the historical time frame when this event took place, and no troublesome construction gap would have existed. There must have been a stronger motive underlying the assigning of the initial work on the foundation to year 2 of Cyrus, and Isa. 44.28 provides the key.

It is likely that the author of Isa. 44.28, whom scholars refer to as 2 Isaiah, lived in Babylonia during Cyrus' reign (559–530 BCE) and was familiar with the story recorded on the Cyrus Cylinder (see Appendix 2). This was Cyrus' official account of how he had been given control of Babylon by the god Marduk to rescue it from the grip of the evil king Nabonidus and how he had restored many temples, returning to their homes all the gods that Nabonidus had alienated. While the account on the cylinder itself is written as a building dedication inscription and probably was placed as a foundation deposit in the rebuilt temple of Marduk in Babylon (Kuhrt 1983: 88), the version of history it propounded, which made Cyrus a divinely chosen deliverer, would have been widely circulated as official propaganda within Babylon and perhaps, more widely in the former Babylonian empire. In 538 BCE, Cyrus had taken control of Babylon, the capital of the former empire, and had placed his eldest son Cambyses on the throne, thereby ending the rule of the Neo-Babylonian empire and replacing it with the rule of the Persian empire. He then set about restoring deity statues to their traditional sanctuaries and reinstating their cults. Nabonidus had held them hostage in Babylon in an attempt to promote the worship of the moon god Sin throughout his realm. A comparison of the wording of the Cyrus cylinder on which Cyrus recorded his takeover of Babylon and his acts of deity restoration with ideas that 2 Isaiah expressed about Cyrus reveal a number of close overlaps. These seem to stem from his direct borrowing of ideas from Cyrus' propaganda of the day rather than from coincidence or from a shared world-view in which each was generated independently of the other.

In both, the native god selects Cyrus to be his human agent of change and restoration. '[Marduk] scanned and looked through all the countries, searching for a righteous ruler willing to lead him (i.e. Marduk) in the annual procession. Then he pronounced the name of Cyrus, king of Anshan, declared him to be ruler of all the world (Oppenheim 1969: 315; for the full text, see Appendix II). This same idea is echoed in Isa. 43.14 and 45.1-2. There Cyrus is called the shepherd, the anointed one of Yahweh, whom Yahweh has called by name to send to Babylon to break down all the bars and turn the shouting of the Chaldeans to lamentations. Yahweh has grasped Cyrus' right hand to subdue nations before him and ungird the loins of kings.

In both texts Cyrus' main job after conquering Babylon is to restore destroyed temples so that their gods can be returned to their habitations and to return exiled groups to their former homes. 'I returned to the sacred cities on the other side of the Tigris, whose settlements had been established of old (or abandoned previously),[3] the images which used to live therein and established for them permanent sanctuaries. I also gathered all their former inhabitants and returned to them their habitations. Furthermore, on the command of Marduk, the great lord, all the gods of Sumer and Akkad whom Nabonidus has brought into Babylon, to the anger of the lord of the gods, unharmed, in their former chapels, the places that make them happy. May all the gods whom I have resettled in their sacred city daily ask Bel and Nabu for long life for me...' (Appendix II). Similarly, 2 Isaiah predicts that Cyrus will fulfill Yahweh's purpose by re-laying the foundation of the temple and rebuilding Jerusalem (44.28). 'He will rebuild my city and set my exiles free' (45.13). Jerusalem shall be re-inhabited and the cities of Judah shall be rebuilt from their ruins (44.26).

It appears as though 2 Isaiah knew the wording of Cyrus' proclamations, one version of which was recorded on the Cyrus cylinder, and applied their logic to the situation of his own people, in the hopes that Cyrus' policies would eventually benefit them as well. The verses in 46.1-2 imply that this writer witnessed processions pass in which the statues of the gods Bel and Nabu were being carried back to their home sanctuaries, and these two gods are specifically named on the cylinder. It is easy to imagine how such a spectacle would have stirred up yearnings for Yahweh to be similarly returned to his home in Jerusalem, along with his worshippers.

However, Yahweh's cultic objects had been carried away by Nebuchadrezzar in 586 BCE, not by Nabonidus during his reign (555–539 BCE). The policies of Cyrus were limited to deities whom Nabonidus had recently removed from their temples. His restorations were intended to win the support of all those who were angry at the cultic reforms that Nabonidus had introduced. Yahweh was not included in this group of deities (Kuhrt 1983: 89-90; Williamson 1985: 13-14).

Nevertheless, 2 Isaiah could dream of repatriation and the rebuilding of Yahweh's temple in Jerusalem on the basis of the rhetoric contained on the Cyrus cylinder. He could pretend that Cyrus' actions would include the return of Yahweh and his people to Judah, prompted not by Marduk but by Yahweh. But to do so, he felt obliged to adapt the certainty expressed by the priests of Marduk about Cyrus' being the chosen divine agent, which had come from knowledge that Cyrus had ordered restoration work to be done on various temples and had sent home some deity statues. Knowing that no such edict had yet been issued on behalf of the temple in Jerusalem and the Judeans in exile, he was left to assert that Cyrus had been chosen and called by Yahweh but that he did not know this explicitly: 'For the sake of Jacob my servant and Israel my chosen, I call you by your name, I surname you, though you do not know me' (45.4). In this way, he could allow for a delay in Cyrus' decision to include Yahweh and Judah in the scope of his restoration efforts since the king was not fully aware of his status as Yahweh's agent. His logic could even cover the failure of the hoped-for repatriation to materialize, eventually, since Cyrus might never become aware of this duty he owed Yahweh. He might stop after his overthrow of Babylon as the world power since he did not recognize that he was acting as Yahweh's agent but, instead, wrongly believed he was Marduk's chosen agent. In this sense, Cyrus could develop 'Samson syndrome' (Judges 13–16); being unaware that he had been selected by Yahweh, he would misuse or misdirect his talents.

Evidence of Cyrus' restoration work on some temples has been confirmed archaeologically. Excavations at Uruk in the sanctuary named Eanna, which was dedicated to the goddess Ishtar, uncovered bricks bearing a stamp that read 'Cyrus, king of the lands, who loves the Esagila and the Ezida, son of Cambyses, the mighty king, I' (de Vaux 1972: 68). Esagila was the temple of Bel-Marduk at Babylon and Ezida was the main temple of Nabu at Borsippa. Every year the statue of Nabu was carried in procession from Borsippa to Babylon at the New Year feast to receive homage beside the statue of Bel-Marduk. A brick uncovered at Warka bears a similar stamp: 'Cyrus, builder of the Esagila and the Ezida'. At Ur, Cyrus restored the Enunmah temple complex that Nabonidus had altered. Bricks from that excavation bear a long inscription: 'Cyrus, king of all, king of Anshan, son of Cambyses, King of Anshan, the great gods have delivered all the lands into my hand; the land I have made to dwell in peaceful habitation' (de Vaux 1972: 68-69). Thus, Cyrus' claims to have restored sanctuaries were not fictitious. On the other hand, he probably limited such work to very important sanctuaries with long-standing traditions and high visibility, especially ones that Nabonidus had neglected, so that he could receive the maximum propagandistic benefit for the least investment of resources.

Cyrus' Return of the Temple Vessels. A second use of 2 Isaiah to shape the events reported in Ezra 1.2-6 is found in the references to the temple vessels that were sent back during Cyrus' reign (1.7-11). Isaiah 52.11 envisages the future departure of the vessels of Yahweh from Babylon, presumably, borne by priests: 'depart, depart, go out thence, touch no unclean thing; go out from the midst of her, purify yourselves, you who bear the vessels of Yahweh'. The explicit mention of the return of the temple vessels in 1.7-11, which were entrusted to Sheshbazzar, who is given the title, *nasi'* (prince or leader) of Judah, is the literal actualization of this prophecy (so, e.g., Williamson 1985: 16; Blenkinsoppp 1988: 78 sees an echo of Isa. 52.11-12), just as the report of the laying of the temple foundation under Cyrus is meant to illustrate the literal fulfillment of Isa. 44.28. The report of the return of the temple vessels is repeated in the account of the Jews to Rehum about the history of the temple-building in 5.14-15, right before the report that Sheshbazzar laid the temple foundations. Both references are intended to give credibility and confirmation to the earlier claims.

A third use of 2 Isaiah as a source by the author of Ezra 1–6 may underlie Cyrus' alleged command to those survivors who are returning to be assisted by the men of his place with silver, gold, clothing, beasts of burden, and freewill offerings for the temple (1.4). Isaiah 41.18-19; 43.16-21 and 48.21 refer to the exodus traditions and claim that Yahweh is about to initiate a second exodus, this time from Babylonia, to return the *golah* community located there to Yehud (Myers 1965: 8). This may have prompted the author to use the motif found in Exod. 3.21-22; 11.2-3; 12.35-36 of despoiling the Egyptians in v. 4 (so, e.g., Jahn 1909: 4; Gelin 1960: 28; Clines 1984: 38; Williamson 1985: 16; Blenkinsopp 1988: 75-76, although only Clines sees a possible allusion to 2 Isaiah), but if so, he modified it considerably in its application. It can be noted that Isa. 52.12, which is not routinely included in the examples of the use of the exodus motif, explicitly states that in the new exodus, the people will not go out in haste or in flight, unlike before. This idea of changed circumstances in the new exodus might have prompted the writer to alter the motif of despoiling the Egyptians deliberately, to illustrate the contrast between the first exodus and this second one, which he was describing to have taken place in the first year of Cyrus.

While the items being demanded of the Egyptians were items of silver and gold and clothing (*semalot*), here we have silver and gold alone, but not in the form of worked items (*kelim*). There is no clothing, but instead, moveable property, animals, and freewill offerings. In Exodus, it is made clear that the items are coming from Egyptians and are to be taken for the purpose of despoiling that nation. Here, however, the things are to be asked from 'the men of the place' (*maqom*), which implies local fellow Jews in the village, not Babylonians (so, e.g., Ryle 1893: 8; Batten 1913: 59, 66; Schneider 1959: 90; Myers 1965: 8; Fensham 1982: 44; contra Michaeli 1967: 252; Brockington 1969: 49; Clines 1984: 38; Williamson 1985: 16; Halpern 1990: 90).

More important, however, is the use of the term *maqom* to designate 'the place'. This word frequently is used to refer to a sacred place or sanctuary (Browne 1916; Cowley 1917; Gamberoni 1997: 539-44), so the royal decree might be commanding the Jews who were planning to return to Jerusalem to seek financial support for the trip from their local temple treasuries but also allowed them to gather additional funding for the project in the form of free-will offerings from other local Jews remaining behind. If v. 4 were intended to play off the motif of the despoiling of the Egyptians, it was not doing so by commanding the despoiling of the Babylonians. Instead, it was reversing that former motif from the first exodus by having non-returning Jews support their brethren to return to Yehud and rebuild the temple.

The Books of Chronicles

The claim in Ezra 3.8 that the rebuilding began in month 2 seems modeled on the initiation of work on the Solomonic temple in month 2 (1 Kgs 6.1; 2 Chron. 3.2) (e.g. Brockington 1969: 69 as one of two options; Williamson 1985: 47; Blenkinsopp 1988: 100-101; Halpern 1990: 102). The bartering of food, wine and oil for cedar from Sidon and Tyre probably also echoes Solomon's deal with Hiram of Tyre in 1 Kgs 5.8-11; 2 Chron. 1.3, 8, 15) (e.g. Batten 1913: 116 as one of two options; Myers 1965: 27; Clines 1984: 68; Williamson 1985: 47; Blenkinsopp 1988: 100). The tradition is expanded now to include Sidon, which was preeminent over Tyre in the Persian period. Its preeminence had been achieved by the early-fifth century BCE and continued until the closing years of the Persian eras (330s BCE) (Markoe 2000: 51-52). Reference to the purchase of the services of masons and carpenters presumes the widespread use of money, which only spread with the Persians but was not the norm in year 2 of Cyrus.

Specific echoes of the Chronicler's history are found in the claim that Cyrus returned the temple vessels that Nebuchadrezzar had carried off (1.7-11), that the rebuilding was funded both by private and royal funds, and that the laying of the foundations followed the prescriptions set by David in 3.10. In the first instance, the Chronicler has emended the claim in 2 Kgs 24.13 that Nebuchadrezzar had destroyed the golden temple vessels to state that all the temple vessels were carried away to Babylon (2 Chron. 36.10, 18). The second agrees with the Chronicler's account of the sponsorship of the Solomonic temple in 1 Chron. 29.9, as opposed to the one in 1 Kings 5–8, where the king alone bore the expense. Finally, the reference to David having established the Levites in their various roles of temple service in Ezra 3.10 is based on the account in 1 Chronicles 23–26. No comparable passage occurs in Kings.

Jeremiah
The End of Captivity and Return to Yehud. Ezra 1.1 refers specifically to a prophecy of Jeremiah that was accomplished when Yahweh stirred up the spirit of Cyrus to make his proclamation concerning the return of Judeans to Yehud to rebuild the temple. As discussed at the beginning of this section, it might be possible to see an allusion to Jer. 51.11 here, but if so, it is in addition to allusions to Jer. 25.11-12 and 29.10. The focus of 1.1 is Cyrus' proclamation to rebuild the temple, while that in Jer. 25.11 is on the destruction of Babylon by the kings of the Medes as vengeance for his temple. Jeremiah 25.11-12 has a similar focus. It is Jer. 29.10 that comes closest to the focus of 1.1 in its claim that after seventy years Yahweh will fulfill his promise to his people and bring them back to this place. It emphasizes the return of the *golah* to Yehud and Jerusalem but does not explicitly refer to the rebuilding of the temple. The same idea is voiced in Jer. 27.22: 'They shall be carried to Babylon and remain there until the day when I give attention to them', says Yahweh. 'Then I will bring them back and restore them to this place.' While Jer. 30.18 states that the city [Jerusalem] shall be rebuilt upon its mound and the palace shall stand where it used to be, there is no explicit focus on the rebuilding of the temple. The closest Jeremiah seems to come to such an idea is 31.23. Yahweh says, 'Once more they shall use these words in the land of Judah and its cities when I restore their fortunes: "Yahweh bless you, O habitation of righteousness, O holy hill"!' Thus, it is possible to see all of these texts from Jeremiah (25.11-12; 27.22; 29.10; 30.18; 31.23; 51.11) to have influenced the writer of Ezra 1–6 to frame his account of the rebuilding of the temple not only by using the standard template for a building account, but also as a demonstration of how Yahweh kept his promises to restore his exiled people to Judah and Jerusalem and to rebuild the destroyed cities there, including Jerusalem and its temple, as announced through his prophets.

The Date for the Completion of the Temple. The completion date for the temple in Ezra 6.15 of day 3, Adar, in year 6 of Darius, 516 BCE has almost certainly been derived by counting exactly seventy years from the destruction of the temple and Jerusalem in 586 BCE to actualize Jeremiah's predictions in 25.11 and 29.10. The author has explicitly referred to the prophecy of Jeremiah in the opening verse of the book. He also found likely references to it again in Zech. 1.12 and 7.5. They had been inserted by the editor who had already used it to derive his dates for the various prophecies in both books and wanted to reinforce his thinking by adding the two explicit mentions of seventy years to the text. Having found the dates for the rebuilding process in years 2 and 4 of Darius in his source but no clear date for the completion of the project in either book, the author of Ezra 1–6 simply decided to calculate a seventy-year interval between the destruction of the first temple and the completion of the new one (considered likely by Ackroyd 1951: 173; 1958: 27; Williamson 1985: 84; Blenkinsopp 1988: 130; Dequeker 1993: 83). In this way, he could illustrate how Jeremiah's prophecy had been fulfilled literally.

His placing of the termination of the project in Adar was probably deliberate. Adar was the last month of the year, so the completion of the temple was made to coincide with the very end of the seventy-year period of exile. This then would have reinforced his purpose of having seventy calendar years between the destruction and rebuilding of the temple. The completion during Adar has probably not been influenced by the Babylonian menological system, which considered this month ideal for initiating such a project, but would not have expected its completion within the same period of time. In addition, the author might have wanted the project completed in time for the celebration of Passover in month 1 of year 71. This would have been the first pilgrimage festival of the year, when Yahweh's self-imposed exile from his home would have ended and he would have been reinstalled in the temple, inaugurating a new period of favor and blessing.

However, as was the case with the account of the building of the altar and the celebration of the Feast of Booths in 3.2-6a, 6.19-22 may have been added by the later editor who was responsible for adding the section in 6.6-24. The wording has many correspondences to the description of the Passover celebrated under Josiah in 2 Chron. 35.1-19, though there is a difference in the description of the Levites slaying versus preparing the Passover. As such, it follows the general trend already seen to use the Chronicler's version of monarchic history as opposed to the version in the book of Kings. However, this could have been done either by the original author of the book of Ezra or by the later editor. The primary reason to doubt its originality lies in the designation of the king of Persia as 'the king of Assyria' in v. 22.

Scholars have long been stumped by the reference to the king of Assyria in v. 22 and have proposed a range of solutions. Four will be considered, leaving aside the view that it was a scribal or copyist's error (so, e.g., Ryle 1893: 86; Brockington 1969: 87). The first suggests that the reference is to a Persian satrap in the former Assyrian domains who had been instrumental in expediting the completion of the temple. He was being honored by being designated 'the king of Assyria', a title well beyond the scope of his office (e.g. Batten 1913: 154). Though not stated, the official in question would most likely have been Ushtani, the satrap of Babylon and Across-the-River, or Tattenai, the governor of Across-the-River. This proposal, however, is implausible within the framework of the Persian empire, where the title of king would have been used only of the Persian monarch and otherwise for the few puppet kings who were retained as heads of their vassal lands or newly created provinces, like the kings of Sidon and

Tyre. We have no evidence that any royal line was retained in power in the provincial heartland of Assyria. In addition, it goes against the common assumption that the reference is to an actual king, Darius, which is based on a straightforward reading of the text.

A second option proposes that the term is meant to allude to the Chronicler's version of Hezekiah's celebration of the Passover in 2 Chronicles 30 (e.g. Blenkinsopp 1988: 133). Specifically, v. 6 calls on the people to 'return to Yahweh so that He may turn again to the remnant of you who have escaped from the hand of the kings of Assyria'. This verse may have been in the writer's mind as he concluded his own story of the return and restoration. It seems to have been in the mind of the person who composed Neh. 9.32, but whether it underlies the composition of v. 22 is less certain. If it did, it must have been used in a similarly general way to refer to the first instance of exile, without focusing specifically on the northern kingdom versus the southern kingdom.

Ezra 6.22 mentions the king of Assyria in the context of the return of the descendants of Judah to Jerusalem and the rebuilding of the temple there. In 2 Chron. 30.6, on the other hand, the phrase 'the kings of Assyria' occurs in an address to the remnant of the population of Israel that had not been sent into exile in 721 BCE, who remained in the land. It does not seem likely that we are to see this verse as an attempt to include some portion of the population of Samerina within Jerusalem's form of emerging Judaism as opposed to that found elsewhere within Samerina, which comes to be associated with the Samaritans. However, it would be plausible to think that a writer could be intending to say that just as the kings of Assyria had caused the first of many exiles of the Jews' ancestors, so Darius, a much later ruler who could lay claim being a legitimate heir to the defunct neo-Assyrian throne, had ended the exile by restoring the temple. It was not the best analogy, but that does not mean it was not intended.

A third option is that Assyria is being used in a general sense to designate the eastern empire in Mesopotamia. Since it had been the first world empire from that location to have conquered Judah, it maintained a special place in the Judean pysche and could be used to mean 'Mesopotamian magnate' (e.g. Wolfe 1935: 100; Michaeli 1967: 280; Japhet 1982: 74). This idea fits with the depiction of the Medes as the immediate successors of the Assyrians in the early fifth century BCE by the Greek author, Hellanikos of Lesbos in his work entitled *Persika*. He either did not know that the Babylonian empire had existed (so Kuhrt 1982: 541) or had assumed that the neo-Babylonian rulers had directly continued the succession of neo-Assyrian rulers and had perpetuated this empire (so Dalley 2003). Herodotus, who wrote after him in the first half of the fifth century, considered Babylon to have been one of a number of great Assyrian cities; he refers to it at one point as the capital of Assyria (*Hist.* 1.178). He was unaware that it had been a separate political entity that had conquered Assyria and become the new master of the ancient Near East (*Hist.* 1.184) (Kuhrt 1982: 543; 550 n. 17). Again, however, this impression might have been derived from Babylonian inscriptions and propaganda, in which the Babylonian kings made no claim to have subdued Assyria or replaced it. Instead, they portrayed themselves as the legitimate, ongoing rulers of this political empire, having triumphed over Babylon in a civil war to become the sole holder of supreme power (Dalley 2003: 28*). Following the lead of these earlier works, Ktesias, writing his multi-volume work entitled *Persika* at the beginning of the fourth century BCE, has three volumes on Assyrian history and begins Median history from the fall of Nineveh, the Assyrian capital. For him also, the Neo-

Babylonian empire never existed. However, instead of its being subsumed in the neo-Assyrian empire as in Herodotus' history, he considers it to have been a part of the Median empire (Kuhrt 1982: 544). By the third century BCE this view had become widely adopted and was followed by the majority of later compilers of histories and writers of novels in the first century BCE–first century CE (Kuhrt 1982: 545).

This argument is not fully convincing, however, since Babylonia had eclipsed Assyria in importance and political prowess and a large portion of the former population of Judah had been deported to Babylon and its vicinity, not to regions within Assyria. Certain Persian kings, like Darius, were identified as the king of Babylon to show continuity with this former world power, which was central in Jewish thought. If any former empire would have been considered the parade example of the eastern Mesopotamian empire for Jews, it would have been Babylonia, not Assyria. In later Christian tradition, Babylon plays the role of the quintessential oppressive foreign ruler (1 Pet. 5.13; Rev. 14.8; 18.2).

There is no similar use of Assyria in this manner in Chronicles, for example, which is generally seen to stem from the same general time period as Ezra, so this phrase cannot be identified as a notion current at the time of composition by appeal to other biblical texts. As noted under option 2, the use of the expression 'Kings of Assyria' in Neh. 9.32 appears to be a proper historical allusion to the exile of the kingdom of Israel, prior to that of Judah, and so does not reflect a similar idea to the one expressed here in v. 22.

The fourth and most cogent suggestion is that 'the king of Assyria' reflects the Seleucid-era view of the succession of world kings, by which they viewed themselves and their Persian forebears to be the most recent in a unbroken line of kings that traced back to the first world empire, the Assyrians (e.g. Fensham 1982: 96-97). An example of such a list has survived from the Mesopotamian city of Uruk (Oppenheim 1969: 566). Unfortunately, the text is quite broken, so its full extent is not known. We cannot tell with which Assyrian king the list begins, but it concludes the section detailing Assyrian monarchs with Kandalanu, Sin-shum-lishir, and Sin-shar-ishkun. It then goes on to name the Neo-Babylonian monarchs from Nabopolassar to Nabonidus before turning to their Persian successors.

As is the case so often, this crucial section on the Persian kings is heavily damaged. It names three kings before being totally broken, and picks up on the reverse with two final monarchs before detailing the Greek world rulers from Alexander to Seleuchus (II). The first name ends in –rus, which is easily reconstructed as Cyrus. All that remains of the next two names, however, is –es and –us. The second name could be Cambyses, Xerxes, or Artaxerxes; the third name is probably Darius. In spite of the fragmentary nature of the three names, it appears that they reflect the correct historical order and not the order that was common in Yehud under the Seleucids, where the first name would have been Darius and then Xerxes and Artaxerxes would have followed Cyrus and preceded Darius. The list shows that Mesopotamian scribes kept accurate lists of past monarchs and the length of their reigns. Scribes in Yehud may have done so as well; the author of Ezra was able to calculate the seventy-year interval between year 18 of Nebuchadrezzar and year 6 of Darius and the person who added the dates to Haggai and Zechariah was also able to calculate that Darius was on the throne about seventy years after the destruction of the temple in 586 BCE. However, it seems as though something either happened to these lists by the Seleucid period, or that the editor of Ezra was not privy to such records and relied instead on the popular history of his day.

Since the Seleucid empire included the heartland of the former neo-Assyrian empire, its rulers would have found it ideologically expedient to portray themselves as direct descendants of that line of kings and emphasized the preeminence of Nineveh over Babylon. From a Seleucid perspective, then, it would not have been out of place to designate Darius as the king of Assyria, in a way that would parallel Cyrus' designation as 'king of Babylon' in 5.13, even though the Persians did not routinely spend time in Nineveh, the former capital of Assyria, the way they did in Babylon.

Charles Fensham (1982: 97) and David Clines (1984: 97) suggest that the use in v. 22 is ideologically driven by a desire to show how Cyrus (so Clines) or Darius (so Fensham) has finally overturned the evil committed against Israel by the Assyrian kings in turning Israel into an Assyrian province and exiling a sizeable portion of its population. This proposal does not illustrate the implied parallel, however; the reversal should be of the destruction of Jerusalem and the temple by the neo-Babylonian king Nebuchadrezzar in its rebuilding by Cyrus and/or Darius. Logically then, we should expect a reference to the 'king of Babylonia', which would be fitting since both Persian kings claimed such a title for themselves.

If the designation of Darius as 'the king of Assyria' in 6.22 is accepted to reflect a Seleucid perspective, then it would be logical to argue that the account of the celebration of Passover in 6.19-22 is a secondary expansion of the text from the same hand that placed 4.6-24 in its current location and possibly added 3.2-6a as well. Seleucid ideology wanted to glorify the former world empire of Assyria over that of Babylonia because, when Alexander's kingdom had been divided up amongst his generals, Seleucus had received the area that had been the heartland of the Assyrian empire. A person who would accept this ideology would be likely to refer to Darius as king of Assyria versus king of Babylonia if he wanted to indicate a link with the past. However, it might be possible that the link with the past that then came to mind as the counterpoint would have been the exile of Israel in 721 BCE under the Assyrians, rather than the exile of Judah in 598 and 586 BCE by the Neo-Babylonians. The logical conclusion of the account of the rebuilding of the temple occurs in 6.18; if vv. 19-22 are removed, there is no interruption in the narrative, which might also tend to point to their secondary nature.

The reason for the selection of day 3 for the completion of the temple is harder to explain. Donald Wiseman has suggested that it is derived from knowledge that the initial desecration of the temple had taken place on 2 Adar, year 7 of Nebuchadrezzar, in 597 BCE (1956: 73). The Babylonian Chronicles give this date as the occasion when he seized the city, captured the king, and appointed there a king of his own heart (choice). However, this date is not reported in the biblical account of these events, and there is no mention of the desecration of the temple at this time in the Babylonian source. In addition, while Wiseman is correct that 3 Adar would have been one day beyond the anniversary of this event, the time gap would have been eighty-one years, not seventy-one years. It is highly unlikely that the author of Ezra had researched this date by consulting the Babylonian Chronicles; there is no firm proof he was resident in Babylon or would have had access to such documents there.

It should be noted, however, that in 1 Esd. 7.5, the day of completion is given as day 23 rather than day 3. If one assumes a week-long dedication ceremony, as happened at the time of the first temple, then the final day of the festivities would have fallen on day 1 of the new year if the week of celebration had begun on day 24 and if the month had twenty-nine days in it. Had the month had twenty-eight days, then the celebrations would have concluded on day 2 of the new year. This dating seems timed specifically to coincide with the arrival of year 71 more so than day 3 and so better reflects the theology of an exact seventy-year period of divine exile between the destruction and rededication of the temple. On this basis, the suggestion that the day date in 6.15 originally was also day 23 but that the number 20 was inadvertently dropped from the text, leaving the current day 3, is probable (Ryle 1893: 82; Jahn 1909: 56; Myers 1965: 50; Brockington 1969: 85; Fensham 1982: 93; Blenkinsopp 1988: 129-30; contra Coggins 1976: 40; Clines 1984: 95).

Haggai–Zechariah 8

Dissatisfaction with the New Temple. The claim in 3.12-13 that many of the old men who had seen the first house wept aloud when they saw the foundation of this house being laid is commonly recognized to derive directly from the rhetorical question in Hag. 2.3, 'Who is left among you that saw this house in its former glory? How is it now? Is it not in your sight as nothing?' As discussed in the last chapter, it is quite possible that this saying, prior to the assignment of its current date, related to the finished temple rather than to its foundation and was meant to be instructive to its audience, none of whom would necessarily have seen the former temple but could clearly have seen that the current temple was small and basic, without lavish adornment, and perhaps considered inadequate. The author of the Ezra narrative has used the combined narrative of Haggai–Zechariah 8, with its dates already added, as his source of information about the re-laying of the foundation. It is perhaps worth pointing out that this assumption has led to the implication that the new temple's foundation was not rebuilt exactly over the old one but was reduced significantly in size.

In using the tradition of dissatisfaction expressed allegedly at the time the new temple's foundation was established, the author has removed the laying of the foundation from its 'original' assumed context of year 2 of Darius and relocated it in year 2 of Cyrus. He also has shifted the month from month 7 to month 2, the month when the first temple was begun. This is not an oversight but a deliberate, calculated move. Wanting to set the initial work on the temple under Cyrus so that Isaiah's prophecy could be confirmed historically, he used what he considered to be 'reliable' information about the laying of the foundation from his 'primary' source, Haggai–Zechariah 8, but relocated the action in time.

The Delay in the Completion of the Temple

The author has similarly relied on the narrative of Haggai–Zechariah 8 for his explanation of why the temple was not completed until the reign of Darius. The dates already had provided 'evidence' of a two-year hiatus in the building process (Hag. 1.1; Zech. 7.1), so that with some poetic license, the length of this hiatus could be broadened.[4]

The rather vague claim that work was stopped by adversaries in some unspecified way may be loosely based on the statement in Zech. 8.10 that before the laying of the foundation there had been no safety from the foe for those who went out and came in. Both passages use the term *tsar*, 'narrowness, stricture', to describe the troubling force that was opposing the local citizens.

Though most seem to accept the historical reliability of the events portrayed in 4.1-5, a few have argued that the explicit identification of the adversaries as Samarians who had been settled to the north in the neighboring province by the neo-Assyrian king Esarhaddon and the rejection of their request to help rebuild the temple and worship there was fueled by subsequent quarrels between Jews and Samaritans over the preeminence of Jerusalem (so, e.g., Rudolph 1949: 175; Noth 1967: 175; Williamson 1977: 67). This seems likely, in spite of the fact that in biblical tradition it is Shalmaneser (V) (727–722 BCE) rather than Esarhaddon (681–669 BCE) who is said to have conquered Israel and is implied to have been the 'king of Assyria' who settled deportees in the region of Samaria after it was made the province of Samerina in 721 BCE (2 Kgs 17.3-6).

As C.C. Torrey has astutely pointed out, however, the claim by the residents of Samerina to have been settled in their territory by Esarhaddon is a likely a deliberate strategy of the writer to give plausibility to his story. By having the locals claim to have originated under a neo-Assyrian monarch other than Shalmaneser, whom biblical tradition recorded as having resettled Samerina (2 Kings 17), he could emphasize their foreign, non-Jewish nature through their own claims of origin, which were manifestly independent of the biblical tradition (1896: 169). They condemn themselves by their own words, which not only confirm that they are non-Jews, but also imply to the writer's Jewish readership in Yehud and possibly Babylonia and Egypt that they are liars as well, since it was a well-known fact written in 2 Kings 17 that Shalmaneser, the 'king of Assyria', had settled them in Samerina, not Esarhaddon. The latter king is not mentioned anywhere in the biblical text. Thus, the author has drawn independently on a list of Assyrian kings or on oral or written traditions involving Assyrian kings to paint a negative portrait of those who initially caused the stopping of work on the temple.

Haggai–Zechariah 8 is the source underlying Ezra 5.1-3. Here the author has merely summarized the more complicated contents of the combined work in two sentences and not gone into the delay that allegedly took place in the process or the people's claim that the time had not yet come to rebuild the temple. In both cases, he was changing the information in his source and so would not have wanted to draw attention to his creative use of the material. In the former case, he was transposing the delay to span year 2 of Cyrus to year 2 of Darius to justify his setting of the work on the foundation under Cyrus. In the latter case, he was deliberately altering tradition in order to claim that the people began work on the temple immediately upon returning to Yehud. It apparently was inconceivable to him that the *golah* community would not have made the rebuilding of the temple its top priority immediately upon their arrival and so make the prediction in 2 Isaiah a reality.

My arguments go against the proposal by B. Halpern that the motif of the suspended building of the temple was part of the writer's strategy to integrate his account of the temple-rebuilding with that of the wall-building in Nehemiah (1990: 114-15). They agree with those of S. Japhet, who sees the writer idealizing the experience of restoration by having the community full of good intentions and commencing work right away. It was only matters outside their control that posed a threat to their wellbeing and prosperity and forced the official ceasing of work on the temple project: the scheming of 'foreigners' and 'adversaries'. The apathy and internal economic and political turmoil referenced in Haggai and Zechariah are not allowed to be factors that caused a delay in the rebuilding process (1991: 186).

The Date of the Completion of the Temple

As discussed at length in Chapter 2 and again in the preceding section, the dates in Haggai–Zechariah 8 have indirectly provided the author of Ezra 1–6 with his date for the completion of the temple in 6.15. It is likely, however, that he would have arrived at this date even without the dates in Haggai and Zechariah since he was looking to demonstrate the literal fulfillment of seventy years of ruin. However, finding the dates in the combined work of Haggai–Zechariah 8 may only have reinforced his belief that he was correct.[5] He probably was not aware that the same logic, applied less literally, had led the earlier editor of that work to place the beginning of the temple's rebuilding in year 2 of Darius.

It is likely that the account of Tattenai's inquiry about permission to complete the temple in 5.3-14 has been indirectly influenced by Zechariah 8. As already pointed out, the author of Ezra appears to have transferred an artificially-created hiatus in the building process after the initial laying of the foundations that spanned year 2 to year 4 of Darius in Zech. 8.9-13 to span the larger period from year 2 of Cyrus to year 2 of Darius. He also appears to have taken from Zech. 8.10 the concept of adversaries who created trouble. Using these two motifs, he created a new story line in which adversaries caused a long hiatus in construction after the initial laying of the foundations under Cyrus so that he could show the partial fulfillment of the prophecy of Isa. 44.28. He then apparently decided to create a kind of parallelism in the two halves of his story by having adversaries rise up again, after work resumed in year 2 of Darius, but this time unsuccessfully. Thus, the plot-lines in both halves of the temple-building account in Ezra 1–6 have been shaped by material derived from Zechariah 8.

Baruch Halpern has proposed that the writer based his account of the building of the temple altar in Ezra 3.1-6 on Zech. 2.1-4 (1990: 98). He has noted that the report of the erection of the altar before the laying of the temple foundation is not standard for the temple-building template but seems to reflect the vision concerning the four horns in Zech. 1.18-21 (= 2.5-8 in Hebrew), which immediately precedes the account of Yeshua's purification and the placement before him of the engraved stone in Ezra 3. In his opinion, while the four horns symbolize Judah's old oppressors, the image being played upon is that of a four-horned altar. In addition, he considers the prominence given to Yeshua over Zerubbabel in connection with the temple reconstruction in Zechariah 3 to have influenced the mention of Yeshua and the priests ahead of Zerubbabel in Ezra 3.1-6.

This proposed linkage is possible, but not fully convincing. While altars often were horned, it is not absolutely clear that these four horns are representing an altar. Horns were used as symbols of strength and the reference to four might have more to do with the four cardinal points, implying the wide scattering of Judah, than with an altar.

The report of the building of the altar as the first move to restore the temple seems to have been motivated by a desire to have a functioning altar available to celebrate the pilgrimage festival of Booths more than by a desire to follow the general outline of events in the night visions. It is difficult to know how much significance should be attached to the mention of Yeshua and the priests ahead of Zerubbabel in this account of the building of the altar. It may be due to the primary role they would have played in the physical building work and dedication of the altar, as opposed to the temple-building proper, which involved the king or his representative alongside the priests in key ceremonies, especially the molding and placing of the first brick. Thus, while the opportunity certainly existed for the writer to draw upon Zechariah 2–3 in the creation of his account of the rebuilding of the temple altar, a clear, straightforward echo of these chapters in Ezra 3.1-5 is not apparent.

Nehemiah

The List of Returnees. The list of returnees under Zerubbabel and Yeshua in Ezra 2 has either been taken from Neh. 7.6-73 (e.g. Batten 1913: 71; Rudolph 1949: 26; Allrik 1954: 26; Schneider 1959: 37; Myers 1965: L; Michaeli 1967: 262; Japhet 1982: 84; Williamson 1983: 2-7; 1985: 29-32; Clines 1984: 45; Halpern 1990: 95-96), or vice versa (so, e.g., Schaeder 1930: 19-24; Blenkinsopp 1988: 83). As a third option, both lists could have been taken from the same document preserved in archival material (so, e.g., Nikel 1900: 71-72; Brockington 1969: 49; Fensham 1982: 49).

The suggestion that both lists were derived from a single source presumes either that a single author composed Ezra and Nehemiah and repeated the list verbatim in Ezra 2 and Nehemiah 7, possibly to frame an account of how the community built the temple and the intramural city of Jerusalem,[6] or that two different authors wrote the two works at the same time, unaware of each other's narrative. Either alternative is possible, but not likely in my opinion. I agree with the proposal of H.G.M. Williamson that Ezra 1–6 is a late expansion of the Ezra narrative, added in order to give an account of the temple's rebuilding as the first act of the post-exilic community (1983: 28-30).

The person responsible for the composition and addition of Ezra 1–6 shared with the Chronicler a view that the temple was central to the life of the community in Yehud, but this seems to have been a common view among a prominent segment of the elite of that society. Many would have embraced this position. This editor almost certainly would have been familiar with the book of Nehemiah and was more likely to have derived the list from Nehemiah 7 than independently from the same archival source that the author of Nehemiah had used at an earlier period. He deliberately left out the mention of the gifts of the governor and the people in the summary in Ezra 2 in order to emphasize the contributions of the diaspora and the Persian king instead of those of local individuals and the governor, in addition to the heads of fathers' houses.

For those who favor Ezra 2 as the original setting, a primary factor is the inclusion of the contributions made to the treasury and temple fund by the heads of fathers' houses, the governor, and the people in the ending summary in vv. 68-69 (e.g. Blenkinsopp 1988: 43). These verses make more sense in the context in Ezra, where the account is dealing with the gathering of materials to rebuild the temple, than in Nehemiah, where the temple has already been built and a census is being taken to move people into the city. The list is serving the dual duty of showing the immediate, unified, full-scale response to Cyrus' edict (Blenkinsopp 1988: 83; Bedford 2001: 108) and to detail the workforce for the temple. Thus, those who favor this view would argue that the person who combined Ezra–Nehemiah into a single narrative chose to repeat this information at the end of Neh. 7.6-73 in vv. 70-73 to refer the reader back to its first use in Ezra 2 in the context of preparations for the rebuilding of the temple.

It is fairly easy to see, however, that the list of names is out of place chronologically in Ezra 2, where it is dated to the first year of Cyrus' assumption of control over the former Babylonian empire (538 BCE). These same leaders are still active seventeen years later in year 2 of Darius, according to the dating of Haggai and Zechariah 1–8. The latter prophecies imply that there was a return to Yehud at the beginning of the rule of Darius I led by Zerubbabel and Yeshua, while Ezra 2 claims that they were leaders alongside Sheshbazzar of a return in year 1 of Cyrus.

We have already seen that the author of Ezra 1–6 seems to have placed the initial return under Cyrus to show how the prophecies of 2 Isaiah had been actualized in history and that this probably does not reflect what actually happened. The author has similarly set the completion of the temple under Darius I on the basis of the dates that he found already attached to Haggai–Zechariah 8. As seen in the previous chapter, these are also probably not accurate; it is more likely that, historically, Zerubbabel and Yeshua led a group of settlers from Mesopotamia to Yehud at the beginning of the reign of Artaxerxes I.

Those who favor Nehemiah 7 as the original setting can point out that the dating of the list is more circumspect; it is said to detail those who came up initially, whenever that was. The summary in vv. 70-73 would have been an integral part of the list that was copied from some sort of archival source. While no specific date is given for the source, the context clearly suggests that it would have been compiled at the time that the completed temple was dedicated, with the money and basins being used for the cult and the priestly garments for those officiating at the newly restored rites.

In its current setting in Nehemiah 7, the list appears to have been correctly situated in the reign of Artaxerxes I, but it has been given a secondary context. It is not linked to the completion and dedication of the temple. Instead, it is placed in the context of the taking of a census of the people after the completion of the city walls and the appointment of various personnel.

Various proposals have been offered to explain this secondary setting. Joseph Blenkinsopp, for example, thinks it was placed in its current location in the story-line to provide a basis for the transfer of one-tenth of the population into the city and to serve as an appropriate introduction to the reading of the law before the entire community (1988: 83). Lester Grabbe, on the other hand, thinks that its function in the narrative is to emphasize that the increase in the city's population that is about to take place is justified by the original intent of the settlement for purposes of building the temple, while making Nehemiah the restorer of the city rather than Zerubbabel, as in Ezra (1998: 51-52). As a third option, Hugh G.M. Williamson suggests that it is intended to underline the lines of continuity between pre-exilic Israel and the community of the restoration (1985: 39). In terms of the development of the story line, the census provides Nehemiah with a means of determining his tax base to pay the Levitical workers, gatekeepers and the guards and also to determine how many men would have been available to serve as soldiers in the now completed *birah* or fortress city.[7]

Whichever option is chosen, the underlying source cited would probably have been a document dating to the reign of Artaxerxes. As seen in Chapter 1, it is likely that Zerubbabel and Yeshua were only a generation older than Nehemiah and that Zerubbabel either immediately preceded Nehemiah as governor or that Nehemiah may even have been a special envoy during Zerubbabel's governorship. The temple probably was built as part of the larger project that refurbished Jerusalem, making it the seat of a fortress city and the regional capital for Yehud, in place of Mizpah, under Artaxerxes and not under Darius. The dating to Darius is erroneous, deriving from a desire to show that Jeremiah's prophecy of seventy years of devastation for Jerusalem and Judah was realized in historical time.

The Identity of the Adversaries as Samarians. While it is likely that the general idea that adversaries caused work to cease after the laying of the foundation under Cyrus was derived from Zech. 8.10, the characterization of these adversaries as residents of Samerina in 4.1-2 is almost certainly derived from the explicit references to Sinuballlit as the leading opponent to the rebuilding of the city wall in Neh. 2.10, 19-20; 4.1-6 (= Hebrew 3.33-38); 4.7-8 (= Hebrew 4.1-2); and 6.1-14. Since the Haggai reference did not give any indication of the identity of the adversaries, the writer resorted to the more explicit information on adversaries presented in Nehemiah. Similarly, the reference to the hiring of counselors against the *golah* community in Ezra 4.5 appears to be derived from Neh. 6.10-14. Thus, both Haggai–Zechariah and Nehemiah appear to have been used as inspiration for the composition of Ezra 4.1-5. The two proposed sources for the adversaries seems more likely than the suggestion made by B. Halpern that they were developed secondarily from 4.6, 8-23 (1990: 104).

The Charge of Sedition in 4.8-22. In what is presented as an exchange of official correspondence between Rehum the commander and King Artaxerxes, the charge is made that Jerusalem has been a rebellious city in the past, which led to its destruction, and that if rebuilt, it would take control over the province of Across-the-River (4.11-16; 19-21). A similar accusation is leveled by Sinuballit and Geshem against Nehemiah and the Jews in Neh. 6.5-7. It is reported that their building the wall shows their intention to rebel and that they have had prophets proclaim that there is a king in Judah. The closeness of these two accounts cannot be coincidental; it is likely that the author of Ezra 1–6 has drawn upon Neh. 6.5-7 as an inspiration for developing what appears to be a plausible accusation against the Jews that would gain the attention of the King and result in an order to stop the work. Yet, with this accusation, the author is developing his story line by which foreign accusers initially thwart the intentions of the Jews by lying to the king, but the Jews are able to overturn this initial setback by lying themselves and they triumph in the end over their detractors. Thus, this account of lying on the part of Yehud's adversaries is integral to the larger plot and not likely to be information contained in official correspondence dating to the reign of Artaxerxes. It can be noted that the accusation in Neh. 6.5-7 may play a similar literary function in that narrative, developing a simpler form of this plot line in which adversaries rise up and create obstacles that must be overcome by the protagonist.

Artaxerxes' Future Decree in 4.21. The failure of the king to issue the decree immediately himself but to state he will do so in the future in his reported response to Rehum's letter in 4.21, has been understood to have resulted from editorial concerns. Once the narrative of Ezra was combined with that of Nehemiah, the decree forbidding the completion of Jerusalem conflicted with the authorization that Artaxerxes is reported to have given Nehemiah to rebuild the city (Neh. 2.5-8). Thus, some have proposed that Artaxerxes' reference to his future decree at the end of v. 21 is meant to be an anticipatory allusion to the one he will give Nehemiah to allow the resumption of work and not to concern one he will give to prevent the work as a back-up to Rehum's temporary decree (e.g. Jahn 1909: 43; Rudolph 1949: 43; Galling 1951a: 74; Brockington 1969: 77 [as one of two options]; Blenkinsopp 1988: 115; Dozeman 2003: 462). If they are correct, it would need to be seen as a secondary addition to the 'original' letter, unless one were ready to admit that the entire letter is a free composition, in which case it could be integral to it or a secondary expansion as well.

It is possible to see the second edict to be anticipatory, but also to be an integral part of the letter. It would reflect the king's decision to conduct an independent enquiry. He ordered the temporary halting of the work so that he could send trusted men to investigate the claims further and then make a final decision about whether to go ahead with his original plans to rebuild or to alter them. That decision would be rendered in the form of a subsequent edict. In the narrative world, this is a logical approach on the part of the king (Batten 1913: 179; Fensham 1982: 76; Blenkinsopp 1988: 115). The reference to a second edict would be plausible even if the book of Nehemiah did not exist, reflecting a statement of royal policy to gather facts more fully before making a final decision. It does not require an account of its fulfillment to make sense in the context. Thus, it cannot be argued decisively that the reference to a second edict has been created in anticipation of Artaxerxes' authorization and letters in Neh. 2.5-8. However, in light of the cumulative evidence of other uses of Nehemiah by the author of Ezra 1–6, this would seem to be the more likely situation.

Ezekiel 40–48
Sheshbazzar the Nasi'. A use of Ezekiel 40–48, with its vision of the restored temple, seems likely. The characterization of Sheshbazzar as *nasi'*, 'leader' of Judah in 1.8, is probably based on the use of this title to describe the future leader of Yehud after the return in Ezek. 44.3; 45.7-8, 16-17, 22-25; 46.1-18; 48.12-22. The point here would not necessarily have been to imply that he was a Davidic descendant (so, e.g., Williamson 1983: 13-14; Bedford 2001: 74 contra, e.g., Ryle 1893: 13; Caquot 1964: 19-20; Bodi 2001: 255). The title is used five times in Ezekiel 1–39 to describe the heir-apparent to the throne of the kingdom of Judah before 586 BCE (7.27; 12.10, 12; 19.1; 21.25), but these all fall outside this self-contained section of the book, which dates from after the destruction of the temple and the loss of political nationhood. Thus, there is no reason to assume that the title maintained this more narrow meaning in Ezekiel 40–48 and that the later author was assuming that the leader of Yehud under the Persians would be a member of the former royal house. In fact, Gedaliah had been made governor in 586 BCE, and he was not of royal blood.

It would make more sense to assume that the title was used in its more general sense of one 'lifted up' to a position of authority, as it is elsewhere within biblical tradition, where there is no explicit tie to the Davidic house either. The plural form is used in this broader sense in Ezek. 21.12 (Hebrew 21.17), 22.6 and 45.8, 9 to refer to the chief men of Judah, with no overtone of royalty. This same meaning, the chief men, is applied to leaders of the various tribes of Israel in Num. 1.16, 44; 2.3; frequently in chs. 2, 7, and 34 and in 1 Chron. 2.10; 4.38; 5.6; 7.40 and 2 Chron. 1.2 and 5.2. It is used to designate the rulers of the congregation in Exod. 16.22; 34.31; Num. 4.34; 31.13; 32.2; Josh. 9.15, 18, 19, 21; 22.30 (van der Ploeg 1950). Sarah Japhet has proposed that this was an early attempt to provide a native Hebrew equivalent for the Aramaic *peḥa*, which derived ultimately from the Akkadian title *paḥatu*, but that this attempt was quickly abandoned in favor of simply taking the foreign term over into Hebrew as *peḥah* (1982: 98).

It is the case that two passages in chs. 1–39, Ezek. 34.24 and 37.25, use the title *nasi'* to describe the future descendant of David who will once again rule over a restored kingdom of Judah. However, these passages express a future utopian vision of events that will transpire after the imminent demise of the present kingdom and form part of a standard Judahite literary pattern of sin, punishment, and restoration. It is not at all clear that the author of Ezekiel 40–48 was building specifically on these two passages when he used the term *nasi'* to describe the future political leader when the temple would be rebuilt. The limitations and duties he places on this figure could have been dictated by a belief that this figure might not have been of Judean origin. In addition, it is not clear that the temple restoration was anticipated only as part of the future restored independent kingdom, in spite of some of its less than practical visions of the distribution of land in chs. 47–48. Its author may well have been anticipating the rebuilding of the temple by a future king of the world empire in the not too distant future.

Whatever the intention of the person who added the visions of the restored temple in Ezekiel 40–48 concerning the Davidic or non-Davidic origin of the *nasi'*, the more important issue is whether the author of Ezra 1.8 assumed that this figure in those chapters had to be a Davidide. There is no guarantee that he construed this term in the sense that it had been intended in Ezekiel 40–48. His primary concern appears to have been to show that prophecies from the past had been actualized. Without an explicit tradition that had even recorded the name of the governor who was in charge of Yehud under Cyrus, the author of Ezra 1.8 was free to provide a name and to associate the title of *nasi'* with it, in addition to the more standard title of *peḥah* (5.14).

It does not seem as though the writer intended the title to have royal overtones, since this would have been much better accomplished by giving Sheshbazzar a patronymic that would have clearly linked him to the Davidic line, as we find used of Zerubbabel, son of Shealtiel, in Haggai–Zechariah 8. Thus, the characterization of Seshbazzar as *nasi'* in 1.8 could easily have been done to show a fulfillment of this prophecy concerning the future *nasi'* by having the first reported leader of the restored community bear the title predicted in Ezekiel. Such a view is consistent with this author's use of the same technique in connection with prophecies in 2 Isaiah, Jeremiah, and Haggai–Zechariah 8. Thus, claims that there is no connection with Ezekiel's use of the term in temple law in chs. 40–48 are premature (e.g. Brockington 1969: 51; Williamson 1983: 14; 1985: 18-19; Blenkinsopp 1988: 79).

The Dimensions of the Second Temple. A second use of Ezekiel's temple vision may be seen in the dimensions that Cyrus reportedly specifies for the new structure in 6.3. Its height is to be sixty cubits and its *petayeh* (breadth or thickness) sixty cubits. These dimensions have long confused interpreters for two reasons: (1) the lack of a specification of the length, and (2) the great size, which exceeded the monarchic-temple in Jerusalem, even though Hag. 2.3 strongly suggests that the new temple was smaller than the former one. In Ezek. 40.5-7, the man in the vision who is measuring the various elements of the temple uses a reed that measures six royal cubits long. The wall surrounding the complex was to be one reed thick, or six cubits, and one reed high, or six cubits. Here, as in 6.3, only two dimensions are given: height and 'breadth', which in the context means thickness of the wall. In Aramaic the root *pt'* means 'to be spacious'. It seems possible, therefore, that the two figures for cubits in v. 3 originally were 'six' as well, rather than 'sixty', and that a later scribe who did not recognize the allusion here felt that these were impossible for the dimensions of the temple structure itself. Assuming that the plural endings must have somehow dropped off, he added them to turn the number 'six' into the number 'sixty' and these figures were then perpetuated instead of the former ones.

If the above suggestion is correct, then no overall dimensions of the temple structure are given in the edict; just a specification of the thickness and height of the wall that will enclose the sanctuary and altar, and the general method of construction.[8] By citing the very first dimension given in the vision in Ezekiel 40–43, however, the author might have intended his audience to assume that the rest of the dimensions applied as well. In this way, he could maintain a more authentic flavor to his 'document' by not making the biblical allusion too explicit or obvious, but still steer a knowing audience to Ezekiel's temple vision and imply that Cyrus was commanding its realization.

It can be noted that later descriptions of the Persian-era temple complex indicate that such an enclosing wall had been built around the temple proper and the sacrificial altar. Hecateus of Abdera, writing about 300 BCE, mentions the existence of a stone wall, *peribolos lithos*, that surrounded the sanctuary and the altar. Although his work has not been preserved, this detail was cited from it by Josephus, the Jewish historian who lived in the first century CE (*Apion* 1.198).

The existence of the wall is corroborated by the edict of Antiochus III that prohibited all foreigners from entering the enclosure of the temple (*eis ton perbolon*) that was also forbidden to the Jewish laity. Both texts demonstrate that an enclosing wall had been erected to separate the sanctuary proper and the sacrificial altar, access to which was restricted to authorized temple personnel, from an outer court that had more public access. If T. Busink is correct, an outer wall would have been erected that enclosed both the walled temple-altar complex and the forecourt (1980: 832), to define the larger sacred complex as sacred space within the city. While the existence of an inner enclosing wall in the Persian-era temple complex does not prove the accuracy of my above proposal that the author of Ezra 6.3 derived his dimensions from the enclosing wall in Ezek. 40.5-7, it provides a plausible explanation for why there are only two dimensions given and opens up the possibility that the intended referent in 6.3 was the inner enclosing wall rather than the temple structure itself.

The Authenticity of the Six Documents Cited in 1.2-5; 4.11-16; 4.17-22; 5.7-17; 6.2-5; and 6.6-12
Written sources allegedly dating to the reign of Artaxerxes are cited in Ezra 4.9-23, whose authenticity will be scrutinized below. These verses partially anticipate events in both Ezra 7–10 and Nehemiah and also are partially designed to give a history of the opposition to the rebuilding of the temple between year 2 of Cyrus and year 2 of Darius. There is a good chance, however, that they are a later expansion of the text by an editor working after the initial composition of Ezra 1–6. It remains to be determined whether the original position of the two letters could have been somewhere in the book of Nehemiah, which someone subsequently moved to its current position, whether the editor derived them from genuine records from the time of Artaxerxes, or whether he composed them freely himself, using existing information in Nehemiah alone or possibly Nehemiah and other records from the time of Artaxerxes otherwise unknown to us.

The various edicts, reports and letters that appear cited in Ezra 1–6 remain to be scrutinized for their authenticity. This includes Cyrus' edict in Ezra 1.2-4; the letter from Rehum and Shimshai to Artaxerxes in Ezra 4.11-16; Artaxerxes' response to that letter in 4.17-22, Tattenai's report to Darius in 5.7-17, the record of Cyrus' decree in 5.2-5, and Darius' response to Tattenai in 6.6-12 (for a general overview of the various positions, see Williamson 1987: 31-34).

Ezra 1.2-5. A review of the titles and language used in the reported edict of Cyrus in Ezra 1.2-4 granting permission for the initial rebuilding of the temple reveals anomalies that point to the fictitious nature of this alleged 'official document'. Peter Bedford has recently highlighted four inconsistencies that continue to lack adequate explanations allowing them to be part of an authentic edict from Cyrus (2001: 114-29).[9] First, the claim that the edict was proclaimed 'throughout the empire', while plausible in terms of Persian administrative policy, is suspect in the present context that addresses the Jewish population only. The wording in v. 3 presupposes that all Jews live outside of Yehud and so need to return there to accomplish the rebuilding. This ignoring of the non-*golah* community already in Yehud reflects the tendentious interests of the author, a member or descendant of the *golah*-community, and not that of the imperial court, which is not likely to have been aware of the internal community fight over defining who was a true member of Israel (Bedford 2001: 114).

Secondly, it is unlikely that a Persian scribe or the Persian king himself would have used the phrase 'God of Israel', *'elohe yisra'el*, to describe the main god of the province of Yehud. Israel had ceased to be a political entity in 721 BCE and its core territory became the province Samerina, named after the former capital. The name 'Israel' would not have been familiar to a Persian. The phrase once again reflects an author who belongs to, or is a descendant of, the *golah*-community, which has appropriated the name 'Israel' to describe those who went into exile as the only true worshippers of Yahweh Elohim (Bedford 2001: 115-18).

Thirdly, the phrase *kol-hannihs'ar*, 'all the remnant', in v. 4 reflects the use of the noun *nish'ar* as a technical theological term to describe those Judahites who had gone into exile and their descendants. This specialized use of the term is found widely in the books of Ezra and Nehemiah and once again reflects an author who has strong sympathies with the *golah*-community and its ideology. It is unlikely to have been known to the Persian court, which would not have been bothered about such a distinction amongst its Jewish taxpayers (Bedford 2001: 118-20).

Finally, the use of the phrase 'the God of Heaven', *'elohe hashshamayim*, as an appellation of Yahweh, in v. 2, might be an anachronism in the reign of Cyrus. The phrase has been argued to have been a way to depict Yahweh similar to that used to describe Ahura Mazda, or possibly even in a way that would equate the two deities. 'God of heaven' does not appear in the biblical texts prior to the Persian period. It is debated, however, whether Ahura Mazda was the main Persian god before the time of Darius I, who is the first Persian king to name the deity in royal inscriptions. Cyrus' main deity appears to have been Mithra. Thus, if the title 'God of heaven' is meant to relate Yahweh to Ahura Mazda, then it is unlikely that Cyrus or one of his scribes would have chosen to use it to describe Yahweh and it is questionable whether the title would have even have been applied to Yahweh by Jews prior to the reign of Darius I (Bedford 2001: 122-28). Its use in the present context would once again betray a later Jewish author.

A sixth point can be added here: the unlikelihood that Darius' edict would have been written in Hebrew. The citation is made in Hebrew, with no claim made that it has been translated from an original in Aramaic. But any such historical edict would have been written in imperial Aramaic, the official language of correspondence in the western part of the Persian empire.

The six points briefly summarized above provide good reasons to doubt the historical reliability of the claim in Ezra 1.1-4 that Cyrus issued an edict for the rebuilding of the temple in Jerusalem by repatriated Judahites. This only confirms the observation already made that the assignment of the beginning of the rebuilding to Cyrus has been motivated by a desire to show that Isa. 44.28 was partially fulfilled by its commencement during his reign. The author of Ezra wanted his readers to believe that had it not been for unforeseen obstacles, whose nature is never clarified in the narrative, the rebuilding would also have been completed under Cyrus, according to the announced plan.

Ezra 6.2-5. If Cyrus' edict is fictional, then the subsequent memorandum from Darius I in 6.2-12 that is allegedly based on a copy of the edict kept in official records in Ecbatana is also likely to be fictional. It already is a bit suspicious that the narrative switches to Aramaic in 4.8 and remains in that language through 6.18. One would have expected the third-person narrative to remain in Hebrew and only the cited documents to appear in Aramaic. More suspicion is raised by the fact that the cited record contains information that is totally different from that given in the first edict. Whereas the one in 1.2-4 authorizes the return of the *golah* to rebuild the temple using private donations, this one gives permission for the house and altar for burnt sacrifice to be built and then gives two of its dimensions, the manner of its construction, and authorizes use of royal funds for the work and the return of the temple vessels removed by Nebuchadrezzar. There is no mention of the return of Jews here, so this cannot be the same edict, and the two different methods of funding reinforce this conclusion. One would need to presume that Cyrus issued two separate edicts in order to uphold the historicity of the given account.

A number of details within this edict are suspicious. I will examine them in the order in which they appear. First, as pointed out by L.W. Batten (1913: 142), the use of the year 1 of Cyrus in v. 3 presumes his first year as king over Babylonia. This was not his first year as king of Persia, however, and it is likely that Cyrus' regnal years would have been calculated from his assumption of the throne of Persia and that any official document promulgated at his court in his name would have used the Persian reckoning of his regnal years. Thus, we either have to assume that the date of the decree preceded his conquest of Babylonia in 538 BCE, or that this date has come from the author of Ezra, who erroneously considered his first regnal year to be 538 BCE, when he became king of the Levant.[10]

Second, it is unlikely that a king would dictate the dimensions of a temple to be rebuilt or the method of construction. Rebuilding was done usually by finding the foundations and reusing them. The king would not have known what the former dimensions of the temple would have been. The specification that there are to be three courses of stone and one of timber seems to derive from the use of this method in the construction of the first temple (1 Kgs 6.36) (Batten 1913: 142; Brockington 1969: 82). The Persian king would not have known of these local practices either.

It could be argued that the building dimensions were included here by the author in order to blame the allegedly smaller size of the new structure on Cyrus, trying to substantiate the claim in Hag. 2.3 that he had used directly in Ezra 3.12, but the dimensions given do not seem to bear this out. The former temple measured sixty cubits long × twenty cubits wide and 120 cubits high (2 Chron. 3.3) or sixty cubits long by twenty cubits wide by thirty cubits high (2 Kgs 6.2). Cyrus' temple is to measure sixty cubits in width, three times the original, and sixty cubits in height, half of the original, or twice the original. No length is given, which seems very odd. Unless the width dimension has dropped out of the text, we are left to assume that the length and width were identical and that the dimension was only specified once. This would have resulted in a huge cube of sixty cubits. Would an ancient reader have considered this much smaller than the original temple? Probably not.

As argued above, however, this text may have been secondarily edited to change an original figure of six cubits of breadth/thickness and the same in height into sixty cubits each by a later scribe who did not recognize the intended allusion to Ezekiel 40–43. By citing the first dimensions presented in that temple vision, those of the thickness and height of the enclosing wall of the temple complex, the author would have steered his audience to this text in Ezekiel and implied that Cyrus was going to make it a reality. In so doing, he would have been able to show the fulfillment of the words of both Isaiah and Ezekiel simultaneously.

Third, three details concerning Nebuchadrezzar raise eyebrows. As noted above, 2 Kgs 24.13 claims that Nebuchadrezzar had cut up the golden vessels; the current account agrees with the Chronicler's version, which has altered this information to claim that all the vessels, great and small, were carried off (2 Chron. 36.18), allowing their subsequent restoration. The omission of a title for Nebuchadrezzar would not have been likely in an official document and raises more suspicion about the authenticity of this alleged record. The use of the biblical form of his name, Nebuchadnezzar, rather than the more accurate form of his name, Nebuchadrezzar, reinforces this impression (Grabbe 1998: 131).

The detail about the document being found in Ecbatana rather than Babylon gives an initial impression of being historically reliable. However, it serves the purpose of explaining why Xerxes, Artaxerxes and Darius knew nothing about Cyrus' decree, allowing work to be interrupted for so long (Torrey 1910 [1969]: 151-52). Ecbatana had been the former capital of the Medes that Cyrus had captured in c. 550 BCE when he had defeated Media and added it to the Persian empire. It is not likely that this was a well-known fact, however. More likely, the author of this document was familiar with the popular tradition that was picked up by Xenophon at the beginning of the fourth century BCE that Cyrus spent the seven winter months in Babylon, the three spring months in Susa, and the two middle months of summer in Ecbatana/Hagmatana (*Anab.* 3.5.15; *Cyrop.* 8.6.22).

It can be noted that subsequent writers (Plutarch [*Moralia* 78D, 499AB, 604C], Dio [6.1], Athenaeus [513F], Aelian [*NA* 3.13; 10.6], and the Aristophanes scholiast [*Knights* 1089B]) also quote this tradition, though they do not agree on the lengths of time or the seasons in which the Persian kings were resident in their different palaces. They all concur, however, on the single point that the kings spent the summer in Ecbatana (Tuplin 1998: 64-66). Matthew Stolper claims the figure of Cyrus' seven months of residency in Babylon reflects the schedules of later great kings. A palace was maintained in Babylon as late as the reign of Artaxerxes III (1985: 9 n. 26).

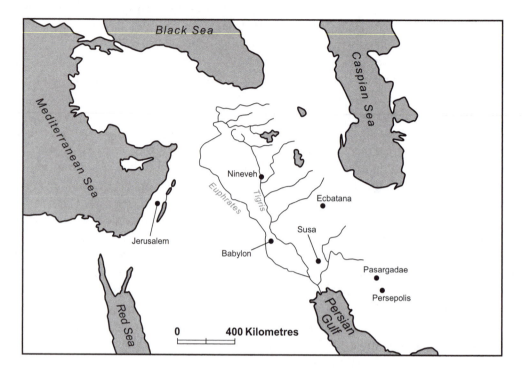

Figure 29.   *The capitals of Persia*

Why would the Jews have not had a copy of the authorization from Cyrus themselves that they could have shown Tattenai to resolve the situation on the spot? This would have been vital historically, and it is unbelievable that there would not have been a copy of such an important document kept on hand by the authorities in Jerusalem in the archives (so also Japhet 1991: 180, in slightly different context). Even the author of Ezra 1–6 is fully aware that nothing happened under the Persians without an official decree and written record. He has given great verisimilitude to his story by quoting a series of alleged official documents.

It has been pointed out that in Elephantine papyri 32.1, the term used here to describe Cyrus' commands, *dikronah*, which usually is translated 'record or memorandum', is used to describe the written record made by the bearer of a verbal message (Brockington 1969: 82). Perhaps this same meaning was intended here, as a possible excuse for why the Jews had no written edict to show Tattenai. However, some sort of equivalent memorandum would have been written down by a local Jewish scribe when the message had been conveyed, so this would not really solve the author's problem of the missing local record. The same term is used in 4.15.

A final argument that is met regularly in discussions of this alleged document needs to be addressed. Many scholars have pointed out that the policy voiced by Cyrus in 1.2-4 is consistent with his actions of temple restoration and repatriation reported on the Cyrus cylinder (see Appendix II). A few, however, have asserted that the cylinder corroborates the authenticity of the biblical 'edict' (so, e.g., de Vaux 1972: 78-79; Williamson 1985: 12). Consistency is not identical to corroboration, however, and as seen in the earlier analysis of the Cyrus cylinder, to claim that 1.2-4 is consistent with the Cyrus cylinder is inaccurate. Cyrus' actions were aimed primarily at the restoration of the cults of deities whom Nabonidus had temporarily shut down. This did not include the cult of Yahweh. The Cyrus cylinder is written after the temple and deity restorations have been initiated or have been completed, while 2 Isaiah is still anticipating Cyrus' inclusion of Yahweh and the Judean exiles within the scope of his actions as a future event. He has drawn on the text of the cylinder or on oral reports of its contents after it has been written to express his hope that Cyrus might yet also apply this policy to Yehud, yet he is not at all confident that it will happen and so claims that although Yahweh has chosen Cyrus for this task, Cyrus does not know it (Isa. 45.4). Thus, any attempt to use the Cyrus cylinder to argue for the authenticity of an edict issued by Cyrus for the rebuilding of the temple in Jerusalem and the repatriation of Judeans living in exile in Babylonia is misguided and should be dismissed as an unreliable argument.

Ezra 5.3-17. The next two documents to be examined are those associated with Darius: the letter from Tattenai to him reporting on the rebuilding of the temple and giving its history in 5.3-17 and Darius' reply in 6.6-12. Tattenai is introduced as *pehah* of the province of Across-the-River. It is known that the person who held this post in years 1–6 of Darius was Ushtani, not Tattenai. Three letters from a private archive excavated in Babylon refer explicitly to Ushtani, *pehah* of Babylon and Across-the-River (Leuze 1935: 192-93; Stolper 1989: 289). Although some would equate the two individuals (e.g. Nikel 1900: 130; Batten 1913: 131; Haupt 1913: 114; Olmstead 1938: 403; Michaeli 1967: 275; Grabbe 1998: 131), it is likely that Tattenai is a Babylonian name (Torrey 1896: 172; Eilers 1940: 35; Brockington 1969: 78; Fensham 1982: 80; Blenkinsopp 1988: 120) while Ushtani is a Persian name (Leuze 1935: 193; Eilers 1940: 35; Myers 1965: 44; Fensham 1982: 79; Blenkinsopp 1988: 120) and that the two individuals are separate. However, even though the title *pehah* is used for both Ushtani and Tattenai, we now know that this title could be used of a range of officials besides the main satrap or governor (Leuze 1935: 194-95; Stolper 1985: 39, 58). Thus, it would be possible to see Tattenai as a lesser official who reported to Ushtani. Shetharboznai, who accompanied him, might bear a Persian name (e.g. Eilers 1940: 34) but this might also be an altered form of the name Shatbarzan found in *AP* 5.16 at Elephantine (Brockington 1969: 79).

It has been suggested that the name of our Tattenai appears in a letter found in Babylon and dated to 502 BCE during the reign of Darius (Ungnad 1940/41: 243; Olmstead 1944: 46).[11] The text mentions that a person whose name begins with *Ta-at* had sent his slave to Babylon. The individual is identified by the title *pahat Abar-Naharâ*, 'governor or official of Across-the-River'. The last two signs of this individual's name are broken. The two horizontal wedges of *tan* can be read, while the last sign is likely to be read *nu* (Schwenzner 1923: 246; Ungnad 1940/41: 241, contra Olmstead 1944: 46). Olmstead has gone so far as to suggest the 'slave' Tattenai had dispatched to Babylon bore the very letter cited in Ezra 5.6 to Ushtani, his immediate superior, who would then forward it to the king, his immediate superior. As Ungnad as pointed out, however, the term 'servant/slave', used here of Bel-etir-an-ni, probably is being used to designate an official of high standing who was subordinate to the governor, rather than a personal slave.

The name found in this document is almost certainly Tattenai (so, e.g., Schwenzner 1923: 246; Ungnad 1940–1941: 241-42; Stolper 1989: 289, 291), which would indicate in turn that the author of Ezra had some sort of source that correctly named him as a *pehah* in Across-the-River at least in year 19 of Darius.

> The archive belonging to the Murashu family, found in Nippur, indicates that Tattenai was a common name in Babylonia during the reigns of Artaxerxes I, Darius II and Artaxerxes II. The archive contains about 330 intact cuneiform tablets, 400 or more damaged tablets and fragments, and twenty small clay tags with seal impressions (Stolper 1985: 1). The documents record business transactions carried out by members of the Murashu family or their agents. Dated documents span the range from 22/XII/10 Artaxerxes I = 17 March, 454 BCE to 28/VII/1 Artaxerxes II = 1 November, 404 BCE, with the bulk falling between year 25 of Artaxerxes I and year 7 of Darius II (440/439–417/416 BCE) (Stolper 1985: 18-19). The name Tattenai appears with two spellings, *Tat-tan-nu* and *Ta-at-tan-nu* in twenty-one of these documents and represents a minimum of eleven different individuals and as many as eighteen. Eleven can be distinguished by their patronyms, which clearly show they had different fathers. Four of the remaining seven are the fathers of various male offspring, some of whom might have shared the same father. The remaining three appear without a patronym, using a title of office instead, or without any additional information after their name (Stolper 1985: 300). Thus, it can be noted that if the author did not have reliable information that there had been an official named Tattenai serving in some sort of important administrative post within the sizeable satrapy of Across-the-River, he could have selected this popular Babylonian name to provide good ethnic flavor to his letter.

In 5.6, the associates of Tattenai and Shetharboznai are further identified by the Persian term *'atars^ekaye'*. This title is applied to two individuals in a late Akkadian text (Eilers 1940: 8) and possibly occurs in a fuller form, **frasakara*, in Persepolis Fortification tablet 3568 (Hinz 1970: 434). It probably is derived from old Persian **frasaka* (Eilers 1940: 30; Blenkinsopp 1988: 121) and designates either a 'subordinate agent of the governor of Syria' (Eilers 1940: 30) or a legal 'inquisitor' (Eilers 1940: 17; W.P. Schmid cited in Hinz 1970: 434; Dandamaev 1994: 232). Unfortunately, none of the surviving texts provide a clue about the specific duties associated with the title. As a result, we cannot determine if the author of Ezra has used this title to give Persian coloring to the document he was creating but did not know the actual function of the office connected with the title.[12]

If we were to assume that the entire letter were authentic, so that that Tattenai, Shetharboznai and a group of accompanying *frasaka*-officials had visited Yehud and Jerusalem, what underlying situation would have prompted the composition of the letter? One option would be that the group had passed by Jerusalem en route to the fortress and capital that would have been at Mizpah during the reign of Darius and happened to see the work going on, which then prompted their inquiries. Their visit could have been part of a tour of the larger province to inspect the roads and official administrative and military facilities to see that they were functioning adequately or to decide what improvements might be made.

A second option would be that the group had been making an inspection of the fortress established in Jerusalem as part of a larger tour of the region and in that context, saw that the temple was being built. The problem here is that no such facility is mentioned anywhere in the book of Ezra. However, Neh. 2.8 and 7.2 explicitly refer to the existence of a fortress in Jerusalem, but only in the subsequent reign of Artaxerxes. In addition, it looks as though Nehemiah put the finishing touches on its structure when he arrived in the latter part of the reign of this king and confirmed its commander in his post, so it is not likely that the fortress existed in the time of Darius to be inspected.

The patent lie contained in the report of the elders' version of the history of the building efforts is an effective use of a standard literary motif by which a person or group acquires what they want through lying. The effect is to highlight the gullibility of the Persians and the cleverness of the Jews, who were able to dupe their political superiors about the history of the rebuilding project and have the lie work to their advantage. Other illustrations of this device are found, for example, in Abraham's claim to Pharaoh that Sarah was his sister rather than his wife, which yielded him great wealth (Gen. 12.10-20) and David's lying to Achish, king of Gath (1 Samuel 27).[13] If this is the case, however, the letter and its version of events would be the creation of a Jewish writer and not an authentic document sent from him to Darius.

Some have pointed out that a non-Jew writing to the king of Persia is unlikely to have referred to the temple under construction in Jerusalem as 'the house of the Great God', as happens in 5.8 (e.g. Batten 1913: 135; Coggins 1976: 35). Since the king would not have been a devotee of Yahweh, to use such a title for a deity who was not the main god of the Persian empire would not have been politic. Grammatically, however, it is equally possible to understand the adjective 'great' to modify the temple rather than Yahweh, so this potential irregularity could be dismissed altogether. Notwithstanding, it is even more implausible to think that the Persian officials would have described the building under construction as 'the great house', since the temple would have been nowhere near the size or impressiveness of the temples in Babylonia. Thus, it is likely that the correct reading of the phrase is 'the house of the great God' and that the title of God betrays a Jewish hand in its composition.

Another irregularity in the correspondence is the failure to mention Zerubbabel and Yeshua as the leaders of the provincial government in Yehud in year 2 of Darius. Instead, the Persian officials question the elders (v. 9) and report their response (Grabbe 1998: 131). One would have expected the officials to observe the chain of command and deal directly with the superiors of the province rather than with those further down the hierarchy. The letter seems to presume that Zerubbabel and Yeshua were away at the time of the visit. There is nothing in the narrative or the confirmed extant sources, however, that would support this view, unless one were to suggest that the ancient writer had deduced from Haggai–Zechariah 8, like some modern commentators, that Zerubbabel had mysteriously disappeared before the completion of the temple. But if this were the case, then again we are dealing with a Jewish author who has used these two prophetic texts as his inspiration.

Since the communication purports to quote the words of the Jewish elders in 5.11-16, the details presented can all be seen to reflect a Jewish viewpoint and so their appropriateness is not easily challenged. The typical rehearsal of the biblical view of the reason for the exile presented therein, the use of the biblical spelling of Nebuchadrezzar, the reference to the continuing existence of the former golden temple vessels, and the claim that Cyrus had delivered the temple vessels to Sheshbazzar, whom he had made governor, who also laid the initial foundation, all can be explained as Jewish understandings and explanations of the course of historical events. Even the oversight of the hiatus in building from year 2 of Cyrus to year 2 of

Darius is logical since the elders were trying to make it appear that there had been no break and they had continued to act on the original decree issued by Cyrus.

Given the unlikelihood that Cyrus ever issued either decree now cited in Ezra 1.2-4 and 6.3-5, and the concomitant unlikelihood that any temple vessels were entrusted to Sheshbazzar, or that initial work on the temple took place during his governorship in year 1 of Cyrus, the contents of this letter betray its inauthentic nature. The purpose of the freely-composed letter was to provide seemingly independent confirmation of the initiation of the temple-rebuilding under Cyrus. Thus, it was part of the writer's strategy to bolster the credibility of his account of the two-stage construction of the temple. The lack of any knowledge of this earlier work on the temple foundation in Haggai or Zechariah 1–8, which reflect events and conditions at the actual time of the work, also highlights the fictitious nature of the course of events in Ezra 1–3 and belies the historical reliability of the alleged communication under consideration.

Why did the Persian officials simply not ask to see the written edicts giving permission for the work to confirm the claims of the elders on the spot? Why bother the king with this matter and suggest that he confirm the Jews' story, and why specify that he search the royal archives in Babylon?

There is nothing in the leaders' response that claims that Cyrus had issued his decree while in Babylon. There is a claim that the decree was issued in his first year as king of Babylon, or 538 BCE, but this is part of the official dating formula, indicating a use of the Babylonian system for reckoning his reign, which probably was used in local documents and contracts throughout the territory that had been under the control of Neo-Babylonia. It seems as though the reference in v. 14 to the return of the temple vessels from the temple in Babylon would have prompted an assumption that there would have been a record made and stored in the temple's archive at the time of the removal of the vessels by the command of Cyrus. This then could have confirmed a portion of the story at least, and perhaps by implication, a copy of the original decree would also have been filed with that record, to show why the vessels had been removed from the temple treasury.

More importantly, where would the author of Ezra 1–6 have gained access to this missive? There would have been no reason for Tattenai's party to leave a copy in Jerusalem; they were not stationed there and so would not have kept duplicates of their official correspondence in the local archives in Yehud as they passed through. Logically, it would have been stored in an archive in one of Darius' palaces since it was sent to him directly. The wording in v. 17 strongly suggests that the letter was sent to Darius while he was in Babylon: 'let a search be made in the royal archives *there* in Babylon'. Would the author of Ezra 1–6 have had access to the royal palace archives in Babylon? Would such a record from the time of Darius have survived until the time of the author, to be found by him?

Ezra 6.6-12. Darius' alleged response to Tattenai, Shetharboznai and their associates, the military commanders, in Across-the-River in 6.6-12 has a few irregularities that would lead one to question its authenticity even if examined on its own, without the cumulative weight of the evidence presented so far that points to its being a free literary creation by the author of Ezra, like the previous three documents.

The standard opening of the letter is missing, which gives the names of those being addressed and an initial greeting.[14] It is as though this is a second section of a letter that is continuing immediately after the citation of the Cyrus document, except that there is no standard opening prior to the cited document either. The omission of this opening undermines the air of authenticity that is trying to be achieved, but may not have disturbed its ancient audience as much, who would have known the convention of making up speeches and documents to give an aura of verisimilitude to a piece.

In v. 7, the king commands the group to leave the governor and the elders alone so that they can complete the temple. Here, all of a sudden, the governor is taken into consideration, even though he was not mentioned at all in the letter to which Darius is allegedly responding. His presence here is plausible and expected and, without the previous letter, would not look suspicious. Since he was not included in the prior missive, however, his inclusion here calls for a cautious evaluation of the source. Perhaps the writer did this deliberately, to maintain the integrity of Zerubbabel on the one hand, and to provide a potential 'out' should the officials have detected the lie. The governor could then have feigned ignorance about the whole matter and intervened on behalf of his community to straighten out matters.

Many have considered it historically implausible for Darius to have authorized the use of royal funds in the rebuilding project, in spite of the claim that he did in v. 8 (e.g. Jahn 1909: 54; Hölscher 1926: 112; Coggins 1976: 39; Blenkinsopp 1988: 127; Grabbe 1998: 131-32). The phrasing that specifies the source of the funding is somewhat cumbersome: 'from the riches of the king that are from the tribute of Across-the-River' (*minnikse malka' di middat 'avar-nah*ᵃ*rah*). The wording implies that the annual tribute collected in provinces included a certain percentage that was considered the personal income of the king. This may have been intended to have been sent to the capital directly, while the balance of the funds remained in the province to be used to pay soldiers and for whatever official expenses arose. Whether this is the case, however, is unknown.

It is also possible that the wording was simply intended to emphasize that the king was personally paying the building expenses so that he could become the patron of this particular temple and have prayers and offerings made on his behalf. This certainly is the intention expressed in vv. 9-10, where he commits to underwrite the costs of the daily sacrifices after the completion of the temple, so that the priests can 'pray for the life of the king and his sons'.[15] While we have an inscription demonstrating such a pious attitude of Cyrus toward the main temple of Esagila in Babylonia, this would have been done in order to allow him to be portrayed as the quintessential Babylonian king, following the stereotypical role of the king as temple-builder. But Babylonia was the center of the former world empire; would Darius have felt compelled to support the cult of a minor deity in an insignificant backwater of his empire, thereby losing valuable tribute money and taxes-in-kind that could otherwise have been used to feed military personnel stationed in Jerusalem? This seems unlikely to me.[16] The image of Darius as the pious servant of Yahweh, however, supporting his cult, exemplifies the theme expressed in Hag. 1.6-9 and Zech. 8.20-23 of the foreign nations seeking Yahweh in Jerusalem and so might have been composed in order to show the partial fulfillment of these prophecies.

Other telltale signs of Jewish authorship appear in vv. 9-10. The listing in v. 9 of sacrificial materials is in the order typical of the Chronicler (1 Chron. 29.21; 2 Chron. 29.21, 32) and found elsewhere in Ezra 6.17; 7.22 and 8.35.[17] A king devoted to the cult of Ahura Mazda, which did not use animal sacrifice, would not have known the details of the daily cult of a deity in Jerusalem. Similarly, the reference to 'pleasing sacrifices' in v. 10, *niḥoḥin,* which uses a technical term specific to the Yahwistic cult, assumes intimate familiarity with the cult of Yahweh that Darius would not have had (Blenkinsopp 1988: 127).

The designation of Yahweh in v. 12 as the God 'who has caused his name to dwell there' in the rebuilt temple reflects specifically Deuteronomistic theology (Jahn 1909: 55; Brockington 1969: 84; Fensham 1982: 91; Blenkinsopp 1988: 126). It is highly unlikely that the Persian king would have known this internal Jewish view of the divine presence that had only developed during the exile and was one of a number of competing ideologies in the early Persian period (for this topic, see Mettinger 1982). Its use here must either be considered a later scribal gloss or be seen to be one more piece of evidence indicating the inauthentic nature of this alleged official document.

Finally, we must ask once again where the author of Ezra would have accessed this document. It was sent to Tattenai, an official who would have been under the satrap Ushtani in year 2 of Darius according to the story line developed here. We have no way of knowing whether he would have been stationed in Babylon, like the satrap, or posted to one of the regional centers within the province. Regardless, he would have stored any correspondence he received from the king while away on official business in the administrative archive of his home city, after returning. Did our author live in that city and have access to its old archives?

It could be suggested that a copy of this letter would have been made by local Jewish scribes in Yehud once a favorable verdict had been rendered that authorized them to complete the work. This would then require the additional presumption that Tattenai would have shared the contents of the letter directly with Zerubbabel and the elders when it had arrived and would also have permitted a copy to be made for the local records. Given the reprimanding tone in the commands to 'Keep away' and 'let them alone', however, it is doubtful that an official could have shared the contents directly without losing face, so this option is not likely in the end.

Ezra 4.7-16. The last two documents whose authenticity needs scrutiny are the letter from Rehum, Shimshai and their associates to Artaxerxes and his reply to them in 4.7-16 and 4.17-22. It has been noted above that while their complaint does not explicitly deal with the rebuilding of the temple, the editor who has placed 4.3-24 in its current location seems to have assumed that the work on the foundations mentioned in 4.12 was explicitly work on the temple (Japhet 1991: 180, 183). The entire segment in 4.3-24 deals with opposition to the temple-building that had prevented work from year 2 of Cyrus to year 2 of Darius. This person also seems to have thought that Artaxerxes I had ruled before Darius since he was including this letter dating to the reign of Artaxerxes in this period when work had been interrupted (contra Japhet 1991: 183). He also was probably responsible for adding the reference to Artaxerxes in 6.13, where it is said that the temple was completed by the command of Yahweh and the decree of Cyrus, Darius and Artaxerxes king of Persia. From where, then, did he get these traditions?

Rehum bears the title, *bᵉˁel-ṭᵉˁem,* 'lord of (the) decree', indicating he was entrusted with overseeing the delivery and implementation of royal edicts. Shimshai was his scribe, who was responsible for reading and recording all official correspondence sent to Rehum to execute and for writing all of it that Rehum wanted sent to others. In v. 9 he says he is writing to the king on behalf of himself and Shimshai, as well as their colleagues, the judges and investigators ('*afarsatkaye*'),[18] and a host of ethnic groups whom Osnappar (Ashurbanipal) had deported and resettled in Samerina and elsewhere in the satrapy of Across-the-River.

Rehum appears to have been a popular name in the Persian period. It is used of five individuals in the Bible (Ezra 2.2; 4.8; Neh. 2.3; 3.17; 10.25 [Hebrew 10.26]), occurs as a personal name in three Aramaic papyri from Elephantine in the Brooklyn Museum (Kraeling 1953: 250 [10.19]; 260 [11.14]; 272 [12.34]) and once among Assyrian personal names (Tallqvist 1914: 185). It is Semitic and means 'has been shown compassion'.

While we are not informed where Rehum was stationed within the larger province, the focus in vv. 9-10 is on opposition centered in Samerina specifically. This is made clear by the enumeration of various ethnic groups that allegedly had been settled by 'the great and noble Osnappar' in cities of Samerina and then, more widely, in the rest of the province of Across-the-River. Three points are noteworthy. First, Osnappar's royal title as king of Assyria is not given, which is very suspicious in a letter that was supposed to have been an official correspondence. A writer in the time of Artaxerxes I could not have assumed that the king, who was of Persian origin, would have known that Osnappar, a king of Assyria, had settled deportees from various parts of his empire in his western provinces in Syria and Samerina some 200-300 years earlier.

Secondly, which king is meant by Osnappar is uncertain. This name does not correspond to any of the more familiar transcriptions of the names of Assyrian kings. It is thought to be closest to Ashurbanipal (669–626 BCE) (so, e.g., Schrader 1888: 65; Meyer 1896: 29; Ryle 1893: 57; Batten 1913: 172; Rudolph 1949: 36; Schneider 1959: 113; Michaeli 1967: 270; Brockington 1969: 75; Fensham 1982: 73; Clines 1984: 79; Williamson 1985: 62; Dequeker 1993: 81; Grabbe 1998: 20) but there are no records of deportations to Samerina during his reign (668–627 BCE). As a result, links with Shalmaneser (Josephus *Ant.* 11.2; Bewer 1922: 51-52; Torrey 1910 [1969]: 170), Sargon (722–705 BCE) (e.g. Marquart 1896: 59) or Esarhaddon (681–669 BCE) (e.g. Winckler 1892: 98; Howorth 1893: 77 as one of two options; Dozeman 2003: 461) have also been proposed.

The lack of inscriptional or annalistic accounts of such deportations under Ashurbanipal does not mean they might not have occurred. Bustanay Oded has pointed out that there seems to have been a de-emphasis on deportations in the scribal tradition under Esarhaddon and Ashurbanipal (1979: 19-22; Na'aman 1993: 116). Thus, they may well have taken place but were not described in the records. One was recorded, however; the movement of exiles from Kirbit to Egypt (Luckenbill 1975: 326, 346, 351), so it is likely that the policy remained in place throughout his reign.

If the list of nations is taken to reflect historical reality, then Ashurbanipal is the best candidate for Osnappar since he is the only neo-Assyrian king to have captured Susa, which he did in 641 BCE. He had conquered Elam in the previous year. Thus, the claim in 4.9 that the settlers included men from Susa, that is, Elamites, would point strongly to him (so, e.g., Malamat 1953: 28-29; Clines 1984: 79; Williamson 1985: 62; Blenkinsopp 1988: 113). In addition, he had suppressed a rebellion in Babylon in 648 BCE, which would account for the settlers from that city (Na'aman 1995: 110). He also campaigned in the west in 640–639 BCE, where he reportedly received the tribute of twenty-two rebel kings, which could account for the presence of Tarpelites if they are men from the Phoenician coastal city of Tripolis and for the decision to move new groups into Samerina while possibly removing some others from there, if they had been active in the rebellion. However, the reference to the men of Erech, if this is what is intended by the Archivites, does not fit easily. Erech had not joined in the Babylonian revolt in 652–648 BCE but instead, had fought alongside Ashurbanipal (Malamat 1953: 28). Assuming there was no subsequent disloyalty that led to deportation, the presence of the men of Erech here raises a problem for the assumption that the list reflects historical reality from the time of Ashurbanipal, unless one would want to try to suggest an alternative identity for this group.

It is easy to see how the name Ashurbanipal could have become corrupted to Osnappar. The intermediate consonants *R* and *B* were dropped since the name was already long and Hebrew did not normally have consonantal clusters where two consonants were to be pronounced without an intervening vowel. The *SH* (*shin*) became *S* (*samek*), which was a common phenomenon when Assyrian names were transferred into Aramaic (Millard 1976: 4), and the final *L* became an *R* through a common process of sound shift involving this dental sound and the guttural sound *R* (Brockelmann 1908: §84). The latter shift has also been seen possibly to reflect Persian influence since Old Persian had no *L* within its alphabet and so chose to render this sound as *R* (e.g. Meyer 1896: 29-30; Rudolph 1949: 36; Millard 1976: 11-12). However, it is more likely that the name was altered when it was transcribed from Akkadian into Aramaic in the neo-Assyrian period than when the name was transcribed into Persian, where there was no *L* and then passed back to Aramaic usage in this altered form in the Persian period. This Assyrian monarch had been long dead and there was little need for his name to have been current in Persian scribal circles. Egyptian similarly lacked the *L* sound and regularly transcribed this sound in foreign languages with *R*.

The Bible claims that Shalmaneser (V) (727–722 BCE) had ended Israel's existence as an independent nation, exiled its population, set up the region as the province of Samerina, and implies that he settled deportees from Babylon, Kuthah, Avva, Hamath, and Sepharvaim in the land (2 Kings 17). However, it is noteworthy that the less specific term 'king of Assyria' is used to describe the person responsible for the resettlements, and it is likely that historically, his successor, Sargon II, forcefully moved these groups into Samerina after his successful campaign against Merodach Baladan in 710–709 BCE. He conquered all these cities and areas at that time (Na'aman 1993: 110). He would, therefore, be the more likely historical referent in 2 Kgs 17.24, though the biblical writer may not have known this and so may have mistakenly assumed that Shalmaneser had carried out the deportations; the wording of the text tends to suggest this is the case.

The corresponding account in 1 Esd. 2.17 does not give the list of ethnic groups and does not mention Osnappar; it merely summarizes with the phrase, 'the magistrates in Coele-Syria and Phoenicia'. Josephus and the Lucianic Greek text, on the other hand, identify Osnappar with Shalmaneser. Both seem to be variant solutions to the same sticky problem: what to do with a non-intelligible reference to an Assyrian king. The first simply omitted it while the second ventured a logical identification by appealing to biblical tradition. Lucian's reading should not be seen to preserve an old, more authentic textual tradition that somehow was corrupted to read Osnappar.

If we were to assume that the list of deportees in 4.9 does not reflect reality in the neo-Assyrian period but, instead, is a partial list of conquered peoples and regions in the Persian era with which the Jewish author was familiar, or the origin of more recent groups sent by the Persians to boost the local population in conjunction with the incorporation of Samerina more fully into the Persian military, economic, and postal systems, then we would not need to try to find a plausible historical match for an Assyrian king who could have deported these various groups to Samerina. In this case, it could be suggested that the author intended Osnappar to be Shalmaneser and that he wanted to link the current claim to existing biblical tradition.

It would be possible for the name of Shalmaneser to have been corrupted into Osnappar (*'snpr*) if one assumed a series of steps. First, the second letter, *S* (*samek*), had rendered underlying Assyrian *SH*, which was standard. Then, the name was shortened, so that the *L* and *M* were dropped. The letter *L* was commonly omitted from foreign names. The final Assyrian element, *usur*, would have unusually been rendered *sar* with *samek* (*S*) instead of the more normative *tsar* with *sadeh* (*TS*): this *samek* would then have been mistaken as a *peh* (*P*), due to sloppy scribal handwriting. This interchange would only have happened in a manuscript written in the Hebrew square script; these letters were very distinctive in the earlier Hebrew lapidary script. The addition of the initial *'aleph* would have been due to the foreign origin (non-Hebraic) of the name, making it easier to pronounce. For a different reconstruction of the process, see C.C. Torrey (1910 [1969]: 170).

In light of the conflicting claim in 4.2 that Esarhaddon had been responsible for moving new population groups into Samerina, it is unlikely that the author was intending to corroborate biblical tradition in 4.9-10. He could have been consistent had he wanted to be and made Shalmaneser the king named in both 4.2 and 4.9-10, harmonizing both presentations with biblical tradition. There is no inscriptional or annalistic evidence that confirms or denies Esarhaddon's purported actions and as noted above, there seems to have been a deliberate decision to downplay forced deportation and resettlement policies in the official records of his reign as well as those written under Ashurbanipal. Thus, we need to seek an explanation within the narrative world and the author's strategy of why the author would have deliberately chosen to have the residents of Samaria/Samerina represent themselves as foreigners who were settled in their current home by two different Assyrian monarchs at two different occasions in the Persian period.

Hugh G.M. Williamson has proposed that in 4.9-10, the author deliberately had the adversaries distance themselves from the Jews so that they could imply their greater loyalty to the crown than the residents in Yehud and thereby curry favor (1985: 62). This is a plausible idea, but it fails to explain why the Samarians chose to represent their origins differently to the leaders of Yehud in the time of Cyrus (4.2) than to Artaxerxes I in their accusatory report in 4.9-10. After all, they had been resident in Samerina for at least two centuries at this point, so it is hard to understand why they would have emphasized their origin as 'foreigners' in their alleged correspondence with Artaxerxes at all; it did not have any bearing on their case and by this time, they should have considered themselves natives of this region.

In my opinion, this concern with the foreign origin of the populace of Samaria/Samerina betrays the concerns of the author of Ezra 1–6, who has deliberately portrayed the opponents of the temple-building process as foreigners in order to emphasize that they were not 'pure'

Yahweh-worshippers and so had no right to help rebuild the temple or to participate in the cult once it was established. It reflects a similar mindset to the one expressed 2 Kgs 17.24-40, where the resettled groups are portrayed as worshipping foreign gods and not following the statutes or laws or ordinances or commandments of Yahweh. It also echoes the attempt to cast dispersions on Nehemiah's three opponents, Tobiah, Geshur, and Sanballat, by assigning them geographico-ethnic labels that make them 'outsiders'.

Why are two different accounts of origins given by the residents of Samaria under Cyrus and under Artaxerxes I? As proposed earlier in connection with Ezra 4.2, the author of Ezra 1–6 may have wanted these adversaries to incriminate themselves in the eyes of his Jewish audience with their own 'lies'. Not only do they have their 'facts' incorrect to anyone familiar with biblical tradition about who resettled them in their current location, but they are not internally consistent; they claim Esarhaddon in one situation and Ashurbanipal in another. They clearly are not to be trusted, so that a Jewish audience can see that their claims, especially to Artaxerxes I about the rebellious nature of the city, are untrustworthy and slanderous.

Finally, the author wanted to emphasize the location of the opponents in the city of Samaria. The text of 1 Esdras reads 'cities of Samaria', in the plural, which is slightly more logical but perhaps an adjustment to make the text more believable. Sense can be made from the reference to Samaria alone since it was the administrative center of the province of Samerina, which adjoined Yehud to the north. There would not have been any need to mention one or more cities of Samaria because it or they were part of the province of Across-the-River. Thus, the person responsible for vv. 9-10 was singling Samaria out for specific attention by his audience. Some have seen this to have resulted from the fact that Rehum was stationed in Samaria (e.g. Torrey 1986: 171; Gelin 1960: 8).[19] For me, however, it raises suspicions that the writer has drawn on the book of Nehemiah for an identity for his opponent. Finding Sinuballit the most prominent 'bad guy' character, he made his opponents the people of Sinuballit's sub-province. Tamara Eskenazi has noted the striking narrative parallelism between Ezra 4.1-5 and Neh. 2.19-20: both exclude foreign opponents from participation in the building projects (1988: 79). I think this parallelism derives from the deliberate use of Neh. 2.19-20 by the author of Ezra 4.1-5 as the source of his opponent.

It is quite odd that there is a long detailing of those sending the letter in vv. 9-10, yet once the letter is finally quoted in v. 11, the senders are identified simply as 'the men of the province of Across-the-River', with no mention of Rehum or Shimshai by name. It is doubtful that in a genuine letter, the senders would be so vaguely identified. The names of those responsible and in positions of authority would be given, but not the anonymous masses. Even if this were meant to be 'an anonymous tip', if such things existed in the Persian era, the official who was passing the tip along would have been named so that he could have been questioned, if necessary, and further details about his source sought.

The main complaint in 4.13 is that if Jerusalem is rebuilt and the walls finished, the inhabitants will not pay tribute, custom or toll and the royal revenue will be impaired. When put beside the further warnings in vv. 15 and 16 that sedition has arisen in its midst before and that if it is rebuilt the king will have no possession in the province of Across-the-River, the underlying reasoning and intent of the message becomes clear. The informers are implying that once completed, a new king will be raised up in Jerusalem who will be strong enough to conquer most of the territory of Across-the-River from the Persians and rule over it as sovereign lord. As a result, all of the revenues that would have gone to the Persian king in Across-the-River will go instead to the new king of Jerusalem.

The suggestion in v. 15 that Artaxerxes search 'the book of the records of your fathers' in order to confirm that Jerusalem was a rebellious, seditious city in the past, hurtful to kings and provinces, seems to presume that Arxtaxerxes considered the kings of Babylonia and also possibly Assyria to be his forebears. The rebellion and sedition must refer to the history of rebellions that had taken place while Judah had been a Neo-Babylonian vassal, leading to its destruction in 586 BCE, but also possibly earlier rebellions when it had been an Assyrian vassal. Cyrus had legitimated his assumption of the throne in Babylon by claiming that the god Marduk had chosen him as successor, so it could be claimed that all of his Persian successors would have been able to claim that they were legitimate monarchs as well. The locals did not think so, however, as evidenced by the rebellion that had broken out when Darius took the throne after Cambyses' death.

It is noteworthy that the person who took over the throne briefly claimed to be the son of Nabonidus, the last legitimate Neo-Babylonian king. He clearly was not accepting any Persian claim to be the legitimate successor to the last royal line. However, it could be suggested that the senders were trying to flatter the king by accepting the royal ideology that claimed that the Persians were legitimate heirs to the throne of Babylon, to ingratiate themselves in the hopes of a positive response.

If my proposal that Zerubbabel returned to Yehud during the early part of the reign of Artaxerxes at the head of a large *golah* contingent is correct, then the concerns presented in this letter concerning the potential of an attempt to re-establish an independent nation of Judah once again would be partially defensible. Zerubbabel was a descendant of the royal Davidic house and could have become the focus of a nationalistic movement for independence within Yehud (e.g. Blenkinsopp 1988: 114). As already noted, many have interpreted certain sayings within the books of Haggai and Zechariah to indicate that such a situation was developing at the time the temple was being rebuilt, although others, including myself, have questioned the legitimacy of such understandings of the texts. Morton Smith has suggested that the two references in the letter of complaint in Ezra 4.12, 15 are specifically about Zerubbabel's planned revolt (1971: 116); his idea requires the revolt to have been real.

It is suspicious, however, that the warning does not name Zerubabbel explicitly as the potential rallying point for immanent sedition but, instead, urges the king to prevent the completion of the rebuilding of Jerusalem as a *bona fide* settlement. Who would have had a vested interest in keeping Jerusalem in ruins? The most likely group would have been the inhabitants and officials of Mizpah, the existing regional seat of Yehud. The rebuilding of Jerusalem, with its fortress and civilian population, would have meant that Mizpah would lose its status and privilege as the regional capital in favor of a return to the former seat of power. Officials in Samaria and elsewhere in Across-the-River had little vested interest in where the regional seat for Yehud would have been situated. Its transfer from one locale to another would have had no impact on their own districts or their revenues. Thus, in spite of a certain level of historical plausibility about possible rebellion developing around a member of the former royal family, this letter does not make sense in terms of the identity of the senders and the larger complaint. Unless one argues that Rehum and Shimshai were stationed in Mizpah and that the letter originally was written by them on behalf of the citizens of Mizpah, the contents do not reflect legitimate concerns of officials in adjoining districts.

Two additional considerations highlight the letter's lack of cogency. We know on the one hand that nothing was done in the Persian empire without official permission and on the other hand, that when Jerusalem was rebuilt, it housed a Persian fortress. Thus, it is not believable that the recently arrived Jews would have been rebuilding the city walls and laying foundations under their own initiative, without a royal remit and without royal provision of materials and rations. It is much more plausible to assume that this activity was done as part of the larger plan to move the provincial capital of Yehud from Mizpah back to Jerusalem and to make it a *birah*, a fort with a supporting civilian population. In this case, the accusations of the 'people from Across-the-River' would have been nonsense. They would not have dared to complain to the king about his decision to rebuild a city in a neighboring province as the new local seat and site of a new fortress. In addition, an argument that the site would become a seat of rebellion would be illogical when it was to house an official Persian fort with duly appointed Persian officers in charge. To question the wisdom of putting a member of the former royal line in charge of the civilian population would have called into question the king's good judgment, which would not have been a wise move. Such a policy had been followed elsewhere in the empire and would have been a calculated measure to prevent unrest and potential rebellion by giving ethnic groups the illusion that they had some measure of self-autonomy and control over affairs in their corners of the empire.

Someone, however, who did not know about the circumstances of the re-founding of Jerusalem and who overlooked the two references to the *birah* that Nehemiah had completed during reign of Artaxerxes I might use such an argument and think it persuasive. If one assumed that the Jews rebuilt on their own initiative, following the lead of Haggai and Zechariah, but extended that to include the re-founding of the city at large in addition to the temple, then the charge of potential sedition would make sense. Such an interpretation would be greatly reinforced by the claims in Neh. 2.11-16 that the plan to rebuild the walls had been Nehemiah's personal initiative and that there had been a physical threat of retaliation by neighboring groups that had forced the people to rebuild the walls under cover of armed guards (Nehemiah 4). The failure to name Zerubbabel as the potential focus of rebellion would have been due to the author's assumption that he had lived in the time of Darius, as the dates in Haggai and Zechariah indicated. According to his version of Persian chronology, this Darius succeeded Artaxerxes, so Zerubbabel had not become a point of royal aspiration until later. Thus, the contents of the alleged letter to Artaxerxes are consistent with the majority of Persian-era biblical traditions about the re-founding of the city. The historical reliability of many of these traditions, however, has already been seen as questionable.

Ezra 4.17-22. Artaxerxes' reported response to the letter does little to inspire confidence in its credibility. It basically is a report that the king has followed the advice of Rehum and his colleagues, has ordered a search, and has learned that the city has rebelled and been seditious in the past (4.17-19). As such, it is dependent totally on the former letter for its contents. The only new information is found in v. 20, where what was implicit in the previous letter is made explicit here: mighty kings have been over Jerusalem, who ruled over the whole province of Across-the-River, to whom tribute, custom and toll were paid. Here Artaxerxes appears to be confirming the biblical claim that David and Solomon had ruled from the Euphrates to the Brook of Egypt, receiving tribute and other income from the various subject nations in that vast territory that later would comprise the satrapy of Across-the-River.

The historical reliability of these boundaries for the kingdoms of David and Solomon is not accepted by the majority of current historians of ancient Israel and Judah (e.g. Herrmann 1975: 158-59, 175; Miller and Hayes 1986: 179-85, 214-16; Davies 1992: 86; Ahlström 1993: 480-486, 505-508) or by the majority of commentators (e.g. Rudolph 1949: 45; Gelin 1960: 41; Michaeli 1967: 270; Brockington 1969: 77; Fensham 1982: 75; Clines 1984: 81). It is only those who are religiously conservative and assume that the Bible is a history book written according to modern standards of evidence and critical assessment of sources who have maintained the accuracy of the boundaries and deeds attributed to David and Solomon in the books of Kings and Chronicles (e.g. Millard 1997).

It is highly unlikely that the Chronicles of the kings of Babylonia or Assyria would have mentioned either David or Solomon. No Chronicles have survived from the tenth century BCE in either Assyria or Babylonia, but it is generally doubted that either nation had any contact with Cisjordan at this time. What a search of the records in Babylon would have revealed, however, would have been that Yehoiakim had rebelled almost from the time he became a vassal (2 Kgs 24.1; Oppenheim 1979: 288, 563-64), that Zedekiah had tried again a few years later (2 Kgs 25.1) and that Nebuchadrezzar had destroyed the capital at Jerusalem as punishment, turned Judah into a province, and moved the new provincial seat to Mizpah (2 Kgs 25.22-25). Thus, the claims about sedition and rebellion would have been able to have been confirmed in the Babylonian Chronicles.

Apparently persuaded by the accomplishments of David and Solomon in the distant past that Jerusalem could successfully free itself from Persian rule and reconquer all of Across-the-River, Artaxerxes halts the rebuilding. He orders Rehum to issue a decree that will cease the work immediately until the king himself makes a decree. It is most unlikely that the king of Persia would have accepted this argument at face value, would have been fearful of the Judeans, and would have considered Jerusalem to pose a real threat to his throne by being able to mount a successful rebellion against him. As the most powerful man in the world, he would have considered himself invincible much of the time, especially against a backwater area not known for its culture which had never ruled an empire. Having said this, however, his paranoia about maintaining his position might well have led him to follow up on all potential sources of opposition, however remote, as a matter of course (for the royal psyche, see Lasine 2001). In addition, Yehud could have been considered a potentially sensitive area at this point in time, due to the rebellion that had begun in Egypt in 460 BCE (Blenkinsopp 1988: 111). Thus, the credibility of this first point is not as suspect as it might appear at first sight, though still not beyond doubt.

As noted in the discussion of sources, the reference to the second edict has the added benefit of allowing the subsequent granting of permission by Artaxerxes to Nehemiah in 2.5-8 to be taken as the ultimate resolution of the matter that was left pending. As such, the reference could easily have been included by an author who intended to allude to future developments in the combined Ezra–Nehemiah narrative, or even added by someone who wanted to make such a connection. Ultimately, then this anomaly is not of much help in deciding whether or not the letter in 4.16-22 is authentic.

In light of the dating of these two letters to the reign of Artaxerxes and their concern with opposition to the rebuilding of the city at that time, the possibility needs to be explored that they originally had been part of the book of Nehemiah and had been moved to their present location by the person who combined Ezra and Nehemiah into a single literary unit. The purpose would have been to use these letters to anticipate the problems that would arise later in the time of Artaxerxes and so bind the two books more closely together.

The first point that goes against this possibility is the failure of Rehum or Shimshai to appear within the Nehemiah narrative as active opponents. It is Sanballat, governor of Samerina, Tobiah the Ammonite, and Geshem the Arab who constantly oppose the rebuilding of the walls. Had these two letters been part of the original Nehemiah narrative, one would have expected either to find Rehum and Shimshai named as active opponents alongside these three so that their letter could eventually be put into context, or for them to have written on behalf of one or all three of the other governors. This latter situation would equally have drawn a connection between the section in 4.3-24 and Nehemiah 1–6. Thus, this lack of cross-referencing goes against an original location of the material in Ezra 4.8-22 in the Nehemiah narrative.

The tightly developed structure of Nehemiah 1-6, the account of the completion of the city walls of Jerusalem, leaves no room for the inclusion of these letters in an earlier form of the narrative. As V. Hurowitz has shown, the current narrative consists of a complete, coherent building account that has been punctuated with seven passages describing interference that took place during the process (1992: 120). These latter passages, 2.10; 2.19-20; 3.33-37; 4.1-8; 4.9–5.19; 6.1-14 and 6.16, divide into two groups. The first three (2.10; 2.19-20; 3.33-37) involve verbal opposition, and the third ends with a prayer by Nehemiah. The fourth (4.1-8), fifth (4.9–5.19) and sixth (6.1-14) involve violence and stratagem, upping the stakes and intensifying the opposition. The sixth, like the third, ends with a prayer by Nehemiah, which also intensifies the earlier sentiments expressed in the first prayer. The final, seventh passage, 6.16, describes the final failure of opposition and the downfall of all opponents, serving as a cry of victory. It is the fitting end to the seven-element series. The number seven is a symbol of completion, while it is common to use three-fold repetition with intensification as a device for plot development. In the current case, we have two sets of threefold repetition involved, with the second set intensifying the first, but also with internal intensification within each set as well that leads to the prayer ending each set.

Were the two letters in 4.8-22 to have been an original part of the account of the wall-rebuilding with its concomitant opposition, they would have disrupted this elegant pattern of 3 + 3 + 1, making an eighth example. Thus, the idea can confidently be rejected that an editor removed the two letters dated to the time of Artaxerxes in 4.8-22 from Nehemiah and inserted them into their present location in Ezra to anticipate the problems that would ensue upon the rebuilding of the city walls almost seventy years after the alleged rebuilding of the temple. This then leaves us with two main options. (1) They were freely composed by the person who combined the two works into one, to anticipate later events while simultaneously filling out developments that had taken place during the construction gap on the temple. (2) They were legitimate documents from the time of Artaxerxes that were inserted by a later editor into their current location in Ezra. This would have been done either to anticipate developments in Nehemiah or because the editor mistakenly assumed they related to the alleged delay in temple rebuilding between year 2 of Cyrus and year 2 of Darius. He may have retouched the contents in the process to suit his purposes better.

The first option is the more probable; the same charge of imminent sedition is also found in Neh. 6.5-7, which appears to have served as the inspiration for the contents of these two 'letters'. In one of the seven accounts of opposition, Sinuballit sends a letter to Nehemiah in which he states that it is reported among the nations, and Geshem also concurs, that he and the Jews intend to rebel. Nehemiah is explicitly accused of wanting to become their king, and Sinuballit charges that he has set up prophets to proclaim on his behalf that there is a king in Judah. The letter in 4.8-16 is implying that a king will rise up if the walls are completed, throw off the Persian yoke, and conquer the territory of the satrapy of Across-the-River to rule. Its author has almost certainly drawn on Neh. 6.5-7 for his main idea of a charge of imminent sedition by the citizens of Jerusalem in the time of Artaxerxes, in connection with the rebuilding of the city walls. He has freely composed both this letter and its response in 4.17-22.

The foregoing extended analysis of the six documents allegedly dating to the reigns of Cyrus, Artaxerxes and Darius has, in each case, revealed wordings and interests that are specifically Jewish. This led H. Graetz to deny their authenticity and declare them forgeries in the late-nineteenth century CE (1876: 87, 100). His minority position was supported by C.C. Torrey, who, however, argued against their characterization as forgeries (1896: 145-50). Pointing out that Hellenistic historiography and Jewish writing in the Hellenistic period regularly used freely-composed speeches, letters, and documents to make their accounts more interesting and effective by increasing their verisimilitude, he considers the composition of such pseudo-official sources to be a standard tool of Hellenistic writers. Their intent was not to deceive, as Graetz and others have assumed, but to enliven. The idea of deliberate deception implies a modern use of critical evaluation of sources and a reporting of the facts only, which was not a presumption or practice in the ancient world.

The majority view has tended to uphold the presence of genuine documents underlying the five documents written in Aramaic, but also has acknowledged that each has been overworked or retouched by the Jewish author or editor who incorporated them into the Ezra narrative (for early supporters of this position, see Torrey 1896: 142-45; for more recent supporters, see Blenkinsopp 1988: 42). This view reflects a strange combination of assumptions. On the one hand, it wants the documents to be genuine and reliable and so accepts an underlying genuine core. On the other, it recognizes that their contents reveal anomalies that would not have been part of genuine documents but reflect Jewish concerns and views. Thus, its adherents conclude that genuine documents were used, because the author of Ezra 1–6 would have sought out such documents to prove the historical accuracy of his account, but that they were deliberately altered at the same time to make an even stronger case. What would be the point in including genuine documents but then not quoting them verbatim? Here it should be noted that not one of these documents includes a date formula, which was standard in such official documents. Why would these have been omitted from citation when they would have been integral features of the documents that would only have strengthened the case of authenticity?

This position assumes modern standards of history-writing, on the one hand, that require the use of reliable sources, but then impugns the veracity of such sources, without seeing the resulting contradiction. If one is willing to concede that these six documents betray Jewish ideas and concerns, then why assume any sort of underlying 'original' core instead of their being free compositions by a Jewish writer to give an air of verisimilitude and Persian-era flavor to his narrative? After all, this was standard practice in his day. The variant view that Jewish scribes wrote these letters on behalf of the kings, so explaining the 'Jewishisms', or that the Persian kings would have consulted Jews about details of cult and Jewish concerns and so would have become informed about specifically Jewish ideas and concerns is no more convincing in its attempt to reconcile the strong Jewish overtones of these letters with an assumption that they still must be genuine (so, e.g., de Vaux 1972: 90, 92).

The above analysis has demonstrated that the contents of all six documents are based on views contained in Jewish tradition about the rebuilding of Jerusalem and the temple in the Persian period. In addition, they show knowledge of Hellenistic-era popular traditions concerning the locations of Persian courts and the extensive Persian postal system that kept the king in touch with developments throughout the empire while facilitating the delivery of official letters and edicts, without which nothing could happen. There is nothing within them that would not be able to be assigned to the hand of a Hellenistic Jewish author. More importantly, however, they betray a specific dependence on the *biblical* understanding of the events that surrounded the rebuilding of the temple. They assume the version of events found in Haggai and Zechariah and combine this with a desire to show that other prophetic predictions concerning the future rebuilding of the temple were actualized in history. Specifically, they draw on Jeremiah's prediction of seventy years of devastation for the land of Judah and on 2 Isaiah's prediction that Cyrus would re-lay the temple foundation.

Not only are there no date formulas given in any of these letters, which goes against normal convention, but explaining where the author of Ezra 1–6 would have gained access to the six alleged documents remains a major obstacle to anyone wanting to accept their authenticity. By the writer's own admission, the Jews did not seem to have access to a copy of Cyrus' original edict giving permission to rebuild the temple, giving the dimensions for the enclosing wall and promising royal funding for the project. Such a circumstance is unthinkable since this document would have justified their entire project and should have prevented any initial halting of the work by opponents in year 2 of Cyrus, unless we are also to assume that an official edict to that effect had subsequently been issued by Cyrus. The correspondence between Tattenai and Darius would have been kept in the archives of Tattenai and of Darius, while that between Rehum and Artaxerxes I would likewise have been deposited in the official archives of each individual. At most, one could hope for a copy of the edict that Rehum issued to the people of Jerusalem in Artaxerxes' name that ordered the immediate halting of work on the temple to have been kept in the provincial archives in Mizpah and then transferred to Jerusalem.

As noted by C.C. Torrey, the documents fit well into a larger narrative strategy to show how a villain who succeeds initially through deception will be defeated in the end (1896: 160-61). The two documents set under Artaxerxes in 4.8-22 show an enemy shrewd enough to halt the rebuilding of the temple by mentioning the threat that the rebuilding of the city as a whole would pose to the king. After the Jews resume the building process, however, under Darius, the second attempt to thwart the completion of the temple fails when the officials are less shrewd and reveal their true intentions to prevent the temple's rebuilding (5.6-17; 6.1-12). Their plan backfires and results in the recovery of long-lost documents that led the king to become the personal patron of the temple, thus allowing the Jews to triumph in the end, and even gain royal support for their enterprise.

An alternate narrative function for this section has been proposed by T.C. Eskenazi (1988: 55-56). She argues that the reference to the city wall and house foundations is not a ruse but an expression of the central view that the building of the house of God would not be complete with the reconstruction of the temple proper. It would only be accomplished after the completion of the city walls and community houses as well. Her proposal rests on the premise that there is a distinction in the combined narrative of Ezra–Nehemiah between the terms 'temple' and 'house of God'. She argues they are not interchangeable synonyms but rather, represent distinctive ideas. Whereas the temple refers to the temple complex proper, the 'house of God' is used metaphorically to designate the intramural area of the city of Jerusalem. My review of the uses of the two terms has not found this distinction to be present, however. Her proposed narrative strategy, while attractive, is not viable unless one can also accept her underlying premise, in which case both her proposal and that of C.C. Torrey could both be possible. Whichever functional option one adopts, the letters are instrumental in the development of the larger story line, creating suspense by introducing obstacles that must be overcome.

Chapter Summary and Conclusion

This detailed consideration of the account of the rebuilding of the temple in Ezra 1–6 has revealed that its author drew upon existing biblical tradition to compose it. He made primary use of the three accounts that involved the temple: the Chronicler's version of the building of the monarchic-era temple by Solomon in 1 Chronicles 22–2 Chronicles 7, the vision of the reconstructed temple in Ezekiel 40–48, and the account of the rebuilding of the Persian-era temple in Haggai–Zechariah 8. In addition, he used prophetic texts from Jeremiah and 2 Isaiah, whose predictions he wanted to show were fulfilled in historic time. From 2 Isaiah he specifically drew on the predictions that Cyrus would lay the foundation of the new temple (44.28) and that the temple vessels would be restored (52.11). From Jeremiah he drew on five texts that all dealt with the predicted destruction of Jerusalem and Judah for seventy years and its subsequent restoration and rebuilding by returned exiles at the end of the set time (25.11-12; 27.22; 29.10; 30.18; 31.23). Finally, he used the book of Nehemiah.

The reliance on Isa. 44.28 required a story line that told of Cyrus' granting permission to rebuild the temple and the initial laying of its foundation in his reign. Drawing on the literary convention of placing an important military deed or temple-building in the first regnal year of a king, he freely composed Cyrus' edict in 1.2-4 to represent element 1 of the temple-building template, and part of element 2.

The writer needed the name of an official within Yehud who would carry out Cyrus' mandate. He chose Sheshbazzar, a Babylonian name, to be consistent with his role as an official who would work with members of the *golah* community. He assigned him the title *nasi'* to equate him with the functionary who would oversee the temple in Ezekiel 40–48. Sheshbazzar is not named elsewhere in biblical tradition, so this name was selected to give appropriate coloring to the narrative. At the same time, the use of an otherwise unknown name would have heightened the narrative's plausibility by making it an unfamiliar quantity whose origin could not be readily traced. The choice of Mithredath to be the treasurer would have resulted from a similar thought process. Knowing that a Persian would have been entrusted with the transport of such a valuable collection of items, he selected a familiar Persian name to give the proper coloring to story details and enliven the narrative. The specific inclusion of details concerning the return of the temple vessels was motivated by a desire to show that this prediction in Isa. 52.11, like that of the laying of the temple foundation in 44.28, had taken place in real time.

A list of returnees to Yehud, probably originating in the reign of Artaxerxes and derived from the book of Nehemiah, was used to provide details of the workforce as part of element 2. Additional details drawn from the Chronicler's account of the building of Solomon's temple about the gathering of materials and the appointment of Levites as foremen were then given to complete element 2 (3.6b-9). A report of the explicit laying of the temple foundations then followed immediately, to fulfill Isa. 44.28 and to illustrate element 3, and a literary link to Hag. 2.3 was made (3.12-13).

In order to bridge the chronological gap that resulted from taking both Isa. 44.28 and Jer. 25.11; 29.10 literally, the author needed to explain why the temple was not completed until year 6 of Darius, seventy years after its initial destruction. He used the motif of adversaries who, by their own self-description, lived in Samerina, but chose not to name any leaders. His decision to do this appears to have been based on references to adversaries in two of his sources: Zech. 8.10 and the references to Sinuballit, governor of Samerina, in Neh. 2.10, 19-20; 4.1-3 (= Hebrew 3.33-36); 4.7-8 (= Hebrew 4.1-2); 6.1-14. Since the Haggai reference did not give any indication of the identity of the adversaries, the writer resorted to the more explicit information on adversaries presented in Nehemiah. The reference to the hiring of counselors against the *golah* community in Ezra 4.5 appears to be a direct allusion to Neh. 6.10-14, which has been expanded, however, to cover the gap between year 2 of Cyrus and year 2 of Darius.[20]

As a result, the author has judiciously not named Sinuballit as the leader of the opposition since existing tradition put his opposition specifically in the days of Artaxerxes, not under Cyrus or Darius. He apparently knew the correct order of the Persian kings. Nevertheless, he did not go out of his way to disguise the source of his adversaries, and by making the more anonymous group the residents of Samerina has drawn a link to Sinuballit, the later governor of this province. This author had access to a tradition that knew that Esarhaddon and Ashurbanipal had been kings of Assyria, which he used to allow the opponents from Samerina to condemn themselves unwittingly by admitting they were non-Jewish foreigners who did not even know their own history accurately.

Having brought his story to year 2 of Darius, the author used Haggai–Zechariah 8 to complete his account of the rebuilding of the temple (5.1-2; 6.14-22). He referred to it directly in 5.1-2; 6.14a. He calculated the date for the completion of the work on the basis of Jer. 25.11; 29.10 and the dates in Haggai–Zechariah 8. In order to allow the dedication of the temple to have taken place during the last week of year 70, from the year of the temple's destruction by Nebuchadrezzar, he set the completion date as 23 Adar, year 6 of Darius (6.15). His ability to make this calculation reveals his access to records that accurately recorded the order and regnal lengths of the Neo-Babylonian and Persian kings from Nebuchadrezzar to Darius I. He then gave a brief account of the dedication ceremony, element 4, drawing on the Chronicler's account of the dedication of the first temple for details, and concluded with the celebration of Passover, the first annual pilgrimage festival of the year, in the newly-dedicated temple fourteen days later (6.19-22).

It is likely that this same author is responsible for having freely composed the letter from Tattenai to Darius in 5.6-16 and Darius' reply in 6.1-12, although this is not certain. The author would have found a reference to Tattenai, *pehah* of Across-the-River, in some sort of records dating to Darius I, or learned of him from preserved oral tradition. The contents of both letters, however, betray their free composition with an eye to appear to give confirmation to the earlier narrative sequence in official documents. No dates are given to either correspondence, which would have been included in the body of any sort of official written document, and Darius' response in 6.6 begins even without an addressee and greeting. The person responsible for creating the segment in 5.6–6.13 would have known this, however, and so considered these formalities unnecessary for his purpose.

The author of these letters added good Persian coloring by referring to the first document as a *parshegen* (5.6) and a *pitgam* (5.7), both Persian technical terms for types of written messages or documents. The first seems to designate a copy and the second means 'written word'. At the same time, however, he revealed their contrived nature by having Cyrus allude to Ezekiel's predicted measurements of the outer wall of the temple complex metonymically, producing one more instance of suggested prophetic fulfillment.

The inclusion of Darius' curses upon future malefactors might also favor the assignment of the two letters to the original author. In 6.11-12 Darius curses those in the future who might dare alter his edict concerning the rebuilding of the temple or destroy the structure, which represents element 6 of the temple-building template. Its inclusion here, though proleptic, still allows the inclusion of this element from the pattern in a clever way. Since the king responsible for the project needed to issue these curses and, in the case of the temple of Jerusalem, the builder was not the native king but a distant lord who had not personally overseen the entire process or participated in the dedication, this letter overcame a number of problems.

A subsequent editor added the two letters set in the reign of Artaxerxes I in 4.3-24 and the name of Artaxerxes to the list of those who had given decrees concerning the temple in 6.15. Unlike the author, the editor did not know the historical order of the early Persian kings but presumed the one current in his own day, under the Seleucids: Darius I, Cyrus, Xerxes, Artaxerxes I, Darius II. On this assumption, Darius II would have completed the temple and would have been the king referenced in the dates in Haggai–Zechariah 8. In addition, the city walls would have been built before the temple was completed, since Nehemiah gave firm testimony that they had been built under Artaxerxes I. Picking up on the last point, this editor used Neh. 6.5-7 as an inspiration to compose freely the letter from Rehum and Shimshai to Artaxerxes in 4.11-16 and Darius' response in 4.17-22. He used names from popular culture for the two officials and set these in the context of ongoing opposition. He gave Persian color to the narrative by using three technical terms to describe the correspondence: *parshegen* (v. 11, 23), *pitgam* (v. 17) and *nishtewan* (vv. 18, 23).

He filled the larger time gap he thought existed between Cyrus and Darius II by alluding to opposition under Xerxes (4.6) and to two sets of opponents under Artaxerxes (4.7; 4.8-10). He then detailed the complaints of one of these latter two sets. By adding in this new section, he was able to develop the theme that the villain may initially prosper through deception but will fail in the end. He either played off the existing section with the letters to and from Darius in 5.6–6.13 or added these as well in order to develop this secondary theme in the otherwise straightforward account of the rebuilding of the temple. In complicating the story line, however, he would have simply been augmenting the motif of opponents that already was an integral part of the original account, either in its basic form in 4.1-4 or in the more developed form that included 5.3–6.13 as well.

It is possible that this same editor also added the two sections that report the keeping of the Feast of Booths in 3.2-6a and of Passover in 6.19-22. In the first instance, the placement of the building of the altar prior to the laying of the temple foundation, within the context of element 2 instead of element 3 of the temple-building template, might suggest its secondary origin. In the second instance, the use of the title 'king of Assyria' to designate Darius would seem to reflect a specifically Seleucid perspective rather than a Persian or Ptolemaic one.

As a final observation, it can be noted that this later, Seleucid-era editor may have been inspired by the artistic use of the threefold pattern of repetition and intensification used in Nehemiah to introduce the sub-theme of villains who do not ultimately succeed, however hard they try. The latter narrative is comprised of a building account that is punctuated at regular intervals with accounts of increasing hostility and opposition, which never succeeds in the end. The final form of Ezra 1–6 is also a building account that is punctuated by two main accounts of opposition. The adversaries are initially successful here, which is not the case in Nehemiah, but the editor could easily have used a variation on a theme in order not to be accused of slavish imitation or simply in the exercise of artistic license.[21]

The bottom line, then, is that both the author and the subsequent editor of the temple-building account in Ezra 1–6 have not drawn on any independent sources relating to this event beyond those they found in the Bible. As a result, the version of the events as depicted, which is a synthesis of a number of sources driven by a view that God fulfilled his promises made through the prophets in historic time, cannot offer independent corroboration of the views offered elsewhere within the biblical texts. This author and editor were no better informed than we are today about when and why the temple was rebuilt in Jerusalem, in spite of having lived much closer to the events than we do. As modern historians, however, we are compelled to evaluate critically the same sources that the ancient writer and editor used and take note of their underlying assumptions about the inclusion of the divine as an active agent in cause and effect. Then, after deciding what the reliable facts are, we are in a position to offer our own reconstruction of the event that we find most compelling in light of the given evidence.

It is time to revisit the list of ten questions that resulted from the initial reading of Ezra 1–6 in Section B. Some are able to be answered satisfactorily, but others remain, leading to a suspicion that the account of the rebuilding of the temple in Ezra 1–6 is not historically reliable.

The secondary origin of the section in 4.6-24 from an editor who lived in the Seleucid period explains a number of anomalies. His assumption that the order of the Persian kings had been Darius the Mede, Cyrus, Xerxes, Artaxerxes I, and Darius II, which apparently was the common perception of his day, gave rise to his placing of the first official letter of complaint against the inhabitants of Judah and Jerusalem under Xerxes. This was his own assumption; he had no documents to support it but also appears to have decided it best to imply a buildup and intensification of opposition over time. In this way, he could legitimately postpone giving specifics until the opposition reached a climax. He built on the received text which claimed that opposition had arisen during the time of Cyrus. The editor then illustrated how this opposition had continued under each succeeding monarch until year 2 of Darius. Speaking in generalities, he was able to build up the plot to a point where he then could give a specific example, in the form of the freely composed letters to and from Artaxerxes. This reduced his workload considerably from three sets of freely composed documents to only one.

The failure of the initial author to give full details about the nature of the accusations that the counselors made against the people of Judah to Cyrus probably was due to his similar lack of traditions that gave that information. This left him to improvise. He needed something that would have worried the king enough to halt the temple-building. Searching his existing sources, he came up with two plausible explanations: Zech. 8.1 had implied that intimidation tactics had been used, which he used in 4.4, while Neh. 6.10-14 had reported that adversaries in the time of Artaxerxes had hired counselors to prevent the rebuilding of the city wall. This then was used as a likely tactic by this earlier opposition group in 4.5. He felt no need to spell out the contents of the accusations that these counselors would have made; it was enough to indicate the means by which the opposition succeeded.

Artaxerxes' reported decision to issue a temporary decree in 4.21 served two purposes in the narrative. On the one hand, it allowed the king to undertake an independent investigation of the charges before making a final, informed decision. On the other hand, it allowed a tie to be made forward to his subsequent decree issued in Nehemiah 2.

Two different Dariuses are implied to have been responsible for the rebuilding of the temple. The original author had assumed that the dates in Haggai–Zechariah 8 had belonged to Darius I. He calculated the date for the completion of the work on the basis of the correct order of Persian kings, counting seventy years from the initial destruction of the temple in year 18 of Nebuchadrezzar to arrive at his date in year 6 of Darius I. The subsequent Seleucid editor, however, had assumed that the Darius referenced in Haggai–Zechariah 8 had been Darius II, as had been the one in whose sixth year the temple had been completed (Ezra 6.15). The person who had added the dates to Haggai and Zechariah 1–8 to unite these two compositions into a single literary unit had presumed that the temple had been completed under Darius I.

The later editorial insertion of 4.6-24, which presumed that Artaxerxes I had preceded Darius, produced a potential unresolved hiccup into the narrative in that neither Darius nor his officials seem to have known of the decree of his predecessor that had halted work on the temple. His officials did not happen to find it either when they were searching for the original decree. However, since no mention was made of that decree in the report of the Jews' account of the history of their rebuilding efforts (5.11-16), there would not have been any reason to search the records of Artaxerxes. In the larger plot, there is an ironic twist in that, whereas the opposition had been able to secure an official writ to prevent building activities by lying to Artaxerxes about the circumstances, the Jews were able to overturn that writ under Darius by lying about its existence! Thus, while the villain initially prospered by falsehood, he was defeated in the end by the same means: the lie that the Jews told to Darius.

The king of Assyria mentioned in 6.22 had nothing to do with the rebuilding of the temple. The use of this expression to designate Darius, however, seems to betray a world-view that prevailed under the Seleucids, which glorified the kingdom of Assyria because their current political realm coincided with the heartland of that former world empire.

Three key questions remain without adequate answers. (1) Why would Cyrus have commissioned the rebuilding of the destroyed temple in a ravaged and uninhabited backwater city in an insignificant province or sub-province that already had a functioning capital at Mizpah? (2) Why would Artaxerxes have ceased work on the reconstruction of Jerusalem when it was the site of an official fortress (Neh. 7.2), whose construction, manning, and supplies would have been the responsibility of the imperial crown? (3) Was he not fully informed by his own advisors or scribes about what was transpiring during the transfer of the new regional capital in Yehud from Mizpah to Jerusalem?

The three are interrelated in that they center on the issue of when Jerusalem was rebuilt by Persian command to house a fort and to serve as the new regional capital of Yehud, replacing Mizpah. In my opinion, the rebuilding of the temple would have taken place as part of this larger royal initiative, to provide the locally recruited soldiers who would serve within the fortress a place to worship their god. The Jewish soldiers serving in the Persian garrison at Elephantine in Egypt enjoyed the same privilege. The book of Nehemiah claims that the move of the capital from Mizpah to Jerusalem took place during the reign of Artaxerxes. When Nehemiah arrived, the fort was already in place, needing some final finishing touches. He then rebuilt the outer city walls to provide protection for the civilian population and government officials who would man the fort and carry out the administration of the province. The temple had either already been completed during the governorship of his predecessor, Zerubbabel, or was built during his term of office in Jerusalem when Zerubbabel was the governor and he was a special envoy overseeing the remaining building projects.

With an analysis of the relevant literary sources now complete, it is time to turn our attention to the artifactual remains, to see what light they can shed on when the temple was rebuilt, and why. No remains of the Persian-era temple exist in Jerusalem; when Herod rebuilt the temple, he removed all vestiges of the former structure in order to be able to build his new edifice on bedrock. Nevertheless, regional surveys of Persian-era settlement patterns and site sizes, combined with excavation reports from sites with Persian levels, can be used to suggest what imperial policy might have underlay the repopulation of Yehud. The next two chapters will address the boundaries of Yehud at the time of Artaxerxes I and then the artifactual evidence from within those limits during the Persian period.

Endnotes

1. For an introduction to the issues and various proposed solutions, see Williamson 1987 and Blenkinsopp 1988: 38-72. On the first issue, see also Eskenazi 1988: 21-34. I am suspicious of the theory that the Chronicler also produced Ezra–Nehemiah. I am open to the possibility, however, that either all of Ezra or at least chs. 1–6 were appended to the book of Nehemiah in an attempt to expand its horizon backward in time to include a specific account of the rebuilding of the temple alongside the completion of its walls. For me, this would not

require this material to have been a pre-existing literary composition that was combined editorially, however. I can easily envision its free composition, drawing on material within Nehemiah as well as other parts of biblical tradition.

2. Here I differ from V. Hurowitz, who includes the foundation-laying under element 2, preparations for building. Otherwise, my analysis tends to agree with his, although I am not convinced that 6.22b should be considered element 5, and he has not included element 6 in the account at all, which I point out is present in 6.11-12 in Darius' decree. His analysis has emphasized the existence of two parallel accounts, one under Cyrus and one under Darius, both of which contain difficulties that need to be overcome. Under Cyrus, the opposition halts the process, while under Darius, it is overcome and the building is completed (1992: 113-18). I think he is correct here, and that this plot line has been derived from the implied two-year hiatus in work on the temple that was created by the editor who combined Haggai and Zechariah 1–8 into a single account through the assignment of the dates.

3. The phrase that is rendered 'the sanctuaries of which had been in ruins for a long time' in Oppenheim is misleading (1969: 315). The two options given above have been proposed by P.N. Postgate in a private letter to H.G.M. Williamson (1985: 13).

4. S. Japhet has noted that both Ezra and Zechariah contain accounts of delays in the rebuilding process. She does not think that one is dependent on the other however; instead, she accepts this as evidence that there were such delays historically. She cites Zech. 1.14-16 and 6.12-15 as proof of a delay rather than the dates in Hag. 1.1 and Zech. 7.1 (1991: 179).

5. G. Hölscher has argued that the person who wrote Ezra 1–6 has based it on two 'givens': Isa. 44.28 and 45.1, and the dates in Haggai–Zechariah 1–8 (1926: 107).

6. So Eskenazi 1988: 88-95. She argues that the list brackets three subsections that detail this process: Ezra 1.7–6.22; Ezra 7.1–10.44; and Neh. 1.1–7.5. She makes no judgment about the origin of the list. It needs to be noted, however, that her description has a slight flaw in that in the first subsection, Ezra 1.7–6.22, the list of returnees is not the introductory element, as would be expected if it were a framing element as she suggests. To be consistent, one would need to begin the subsection at 2.1.

7. The numbers cited in the summary are not likely to be original; they sound as though they have been greatly expanded to show the generosity of the locals who supported the restored cult lavishly.

8. Here I would agree with Eskenazi that they are deliberately incomplete. However, we differ on our understanding of why. She thinks this was done to convey the idea that Cyrus had granted permission for a 'house of God' that went well beyond the boundaries of the temple complex to include the area contained inside the walls of Jerusalem. For her, the incomplete dimensions leaves much room for growth and expansion (1988: 57).

9. A fifth proposed inconsistency is invalid. Although Bedford claims that the title 'king of Persia' that is used in v. 2 to describe Cyrus is as yet unknown in official Persian documents dating to his reign (2001: 120-22), the phrase occurs on Cylinder B, line 15 and so was a legitimate contemporaneous designation (Wilson 1915: 183).

10. R.D. Wilson has pointed out that in 5.13, the title 'king of Babylon' is used explicitly of Cyrus in order to distinguish between his first year as King of Babylon and his first year as king of Persia (1915: 181). This tends to indicate that the author has presumed that distinction is still remembered by the reader and need not be repeated here. However, in a genuine document, such a distinction might have been expected to have been used to clarify the date. It is likely that scribes in Palestine would have adopted the Babylonian system of reckoning his first year from 538 BCE when he assumed the throne of Babylon since Yehud had been a province of the Babylonian empire.

11. For the cuneiform version of VAT 4559, see Delitzsch 1907: 48, #152, which is misidentified as VAT 4560.

12. E. Meyer proposed that the word here was an adjective meaning 'Persian', composed of the underlying name *prs* for Persia, with the suffix *ka*, which then turned the noun it into a gentilic designating a person from Persia (1896: 38). He wrote before the other texts containing the title were known.

13. Though this motif can be used where both parties are of the same ethnic background, in instances where the party being lied to is foreign, there may be an additional element of ethnic humor that emerges intentionally or unintentionally. By implication, the liar is more clever than the one who is duped and has not detected the lie.

14. The argument of Batten that the opening has been transposed to 5.6 is not convincing (1913: 145); the argument by Michaeli that there has been an editorial abridgement would be more logical were one to assume the authenticity of both the original edict and Darius' response (1967: 277).

15. While it is widely acknowledged that the offering of prayers on behalf of the king and his sons in non-Persian cults was an idea current in Persian thought, Jahn suggested that its use here reflected the spirit of later Macabbean Judaism rather than the Persian era (1909: 54).

16. Blenkinsopp finds this situation historically plausible in light of such detailed stipulations by Persian kings regarding the cult of Apollo in Magnesia, the temple at Xanthus, and the Jewish temple at Elephantine in Egypt (1988: 126). It needs to be noted, however, that the Gadatas inscription relating to the first temple is now considered a fraud, and in the case of Elephantine, the Persian king is not underwriting the daily offerings but responding to a specific inquiry brought to his attention concerning the celebration of Passover. At Xanthus, the people specifically funded the offerings, not the Persian king (Teixidor 1978). These examples are not relevant to the issue at hand.

17. So noted by Blenkinsopp 1988: 127. He also notes that the use of the phrase in v. 9, 'on a daily basis', *yom beyom*, is characteristic of the Chronicler. The attempts to explain away the Jewish nature of the details in vv. 9-12 by suggesting that Darius used a Jewish scribe to compose his letter, who filled in the specific details in vv. 9-12 on behalf of the king, or that he consulted Jews at his court for information, strikes me as an attempt to maintain the historicity of these documents for faith purposes in the face of logic (so, e.g., Myers 1965: 52; Fensham 1982: 90; Clines 1984: 93).

18. This term, if a title of office, would seem to derive from old Iranian **fraishtaka*, meaning 'emissary' (Eilers 1940: 40) or from **aparathraka*, meaning 'lower level escort or guard' (Scheftelowitz 1901: 82-84). It is not identical with the title used in Ezra 6.6 (contra Meyer 1896: 38; Fensham 1982: 72, 82). It has been suggested, however, that it might better be seen to be a corrupted name of one of the groups of people whom Osnappar had resettled in Samaria (Marquart 1896: 64; Meyer 1896: 36; Eilers 1940: 38).

19. Myers suggests that Mithredath may have been the Persian consul at Samaria instead, and Tabeel the chief local representative of the people. He thinks two separate letters have been telescoped here, accounting for the failure to have the letter of Mithredath and Tabeel cited in v. 7 but one by Rehum, Shimshai and their associates, a different group, given (1965: 37). He seems to be assuming that both letters came from groups in Samaria, which provided the common link between the two.

20. P. Ackroyd has proposed that the picture of strife in 4.1-6 represented the traditional view of the time of restoration, based on such texts as Haggai 1 and Zechariah 3 (1952b: 154). While I agree with his general observation, I do not think he has pinpointed the specific texts that inspired the contents of 4.1-6.

21. The possibility should be considered that this editor was responsible for the combination of the Ezra and Nehemiah narratives into a single larger literary work. In assuming that Nehemiah's account of the building of the city walls would have taken place in the gap when work had ceased on the temple, he could have intended the segment he added in 4.3-24 to have served double-duty: it developed the sub-theme of the wicked prospering initially but losing in the end while simultaneously anticipating the later account of the building of the city walls in its allusion to Neh. 6.5-7. In this case, he would have assumed that the offerings that arrived from Babylonia with Ezra in year 7 of Artaxerxes (Ezra 7.1-26) were able to be used immediately because the altar was already functional, even though the temple was still not built (Ezra 3.3). The references to the house of your God in Jerusalem in 7.17, 19, 23 would be anticipating its future completion, and Ezra 7–10 in general would illustrate the need to establish peace, justice and social equity before the building work could be resumed, following the typical building template. The Nehemiah narrative would then illustrate that the people had not been totally idle during the break in construction but had turned their attention to much-needed physical security as well as the implementation of the law so that when the temple-building resumed, it could be completed without any further delays, quickly.

Chapter 4

Setting the Bounds: The Territory Comprising Yehud under Artaxerxes I in the Mid-Fifth Century bce

Introduction

Our analysis of the relevant literary evidence concerning the rebuilding of the Persian-era temple is now complete. Genealogical information contained in the book of Nehemiah has indicated that Zerubbabel and Nehemiah were either contemporaries or a generation apart in age, not some sixty-five years apart. Thus, either Zerubbabel and the temple-rebuilding needs to be moved to the reign of Artaxerxes I, or Nehemiah and the rebuilding of the city walls of Jerusalem needs to be moved to the reign of Darius I. A fresh analysis of Haggai–Zechariah 8 and Ezra 1–6 has led to the conclusion that the dating of the rebuilding process in years 2, 4, and 6 of Darius I is not historically accurate. As a consequence, the logical deduction to be drawn is that the reconstruction of the temple is to be placed alongside the rebuilding of the city walls in the reign of Artaxerxes I. This date under Artaxerxes I is corroborated by the extra-biblical reference to the adult sons of Sinuballit, governor of Samerina, the 'adversary' of Nehemiah, in Elephantine papyrus *AP* 30, dated 408 bce. The father must have been active as governor in the 450-420s or 410s, during the reign of Artaxerxes I and his successor, Darius II.

Before this hypothesis can be explored further, however, we need to turn our attention to what we can learn from texts and artifacts about the physical layout of the province of Yehud at the time of Artaxerxes I (465–433 bce). We need to understand what the approximate boundaries of the province were, and whether the people tended to live in walled cities and towns, or in unwalled cities, towns, villages, and farmsteads. We need also to establish where forts, *birot* (walled sites with a fort and a civilian population), and relay stations were located. The latter three types of sites are crucial for our understanding of Persian policy within Yehud and why Artaxerxes would have decided to rebuild Jerusalem as the new provincial seat and bring in new settlers from Babylonia to increase the provincial population.

The current chapter will focus on defining the territory that was included within Yehud at the time of Artaxerxes. Specifically, we need to determine if the Negev was an integral part of Yehud under Artaxerxes that subsequently was reassigned to the province of Idumea when the latter was created, or whether it had lain outside the territory of Yehud since the destruction of the kingdom of Judah in 586 bce. In addition, we need to determine if Lod and Ono in the coastal plain were within Yehud at this time. Once these two issues are investigated, we can move on in Chapter 5 to examine the distribution and sizes of sites in Yehud during the fifth century bce. The critically evaluated archaeological findings can then be used in conjunction to the conclusions drawn in Chapters 1–3 to propose a new recreation of Persian imperial policy for the development of Yehud under Artaxerxes I, which will be presented in the final chapter.

The Boundaries of Yehud in the Fifth Century BCE

The Biblical Evidence

The lists in Nehemiah 3; 7.6-69 and 11.25-35 purport to provide information about where the people of Yehud lived in the time of Nehemiah; we need to consider if they are inventions of the author (so, e.g., Torrey 1896: 37-38), if they stem from genuine sources composed at the time of Nehemiah, or if they stem from sources created either before and/or after Nehemiah's term of office. The function and possible date of each list will be examined in turn, with an eye to information each might potentially provide about the nature and location of settlements in Yehud at the time of Artaxerxes I.

Nehemiah 3. Nehemiah 3 is an account of those who allegedly helped rebuild segments of the city walls under Nehemiah's direction during the reign of Artaxerxes I. Some of the individuals are identified by their patronymics (the names of their fathers), others by their towns of origins (gentilics), and a few by both. The last two categories provide a glimpse of areas that the writer of Nehemiah considered to have belonged to Yehud during the time of Artaxerxes I. The towns include Jericho (3.2), Hassenaah (3.3), Tekoa (3.5), Gibeon, Meron, Mizpah (3.7, 15, 19), Harim, Pahat-Moab (3.11), Zanoah (3.13), Bet-Hakkerem (3.14), Bet-Zur (3.16), and Keilah (3.17-18). None lies further south than the middle of the Judean hill-country; no sites in the coastal plain, the Negev, or the Shephelah are included.

It is widely acknowledged that the list of repairs and laborers is incomplete. Seven groups are said to have repaired two segments of the wall, but explicit details about both portions only appear in three cases (vv. 4 and 21; 18 and 24; 5 and 27). In four other instances, details about the work on the second portion have been given but no mention of the location of the first segment occurs earlier in the text (vv. 11, 19, 20, and 30). Since the same groups would have been involved in the four missing instances, their absence does not affect the southernmost settlement from which the workers originated. However, the incomplete nature of the present account leaves room for the possibility that groups who repaired a single segment of the wall may also have dropped out and that they might have originated from sites near Lod and Ono in the coastal plain or further south than Bet-Zur, in the central or southern Judean hills or the Shephelah.

Scholarly opinion varies on the date and purpose of the source from which the names in Nehemiah 3 was derived. It has been seen to have been a list of those who worked on the restoration of the walls that was created at the time of the work and kept in the city archives (so, e.g., Fensham 1982: 172; Clines 1984: 149; Grabbe 1998: 43), temple archives (e.g. Myers 1965: 112; Williamson 1985: 200) or just recorded (Brockington 1969: 37; Coggins 1976: 81; Blenkinsopp 1988: 232).[1] Its purpose has been understood, on the one hand, to have been to record for posterity those who had been involved so that their families could claim subsequent honor (so, e.g., Grabbe 1998: 43, 159). On the other, it has been proposed that the list was composed by those who had helped build the walls and who later became antagonistic toward Nehemiah, wanting to claim from him much of the credit for the work. It was drawn up under priestly influence, as demonstrated by the prominence of Eliashiv the high priest, and kept in the temple archives (Williamson 1985: 200-201).

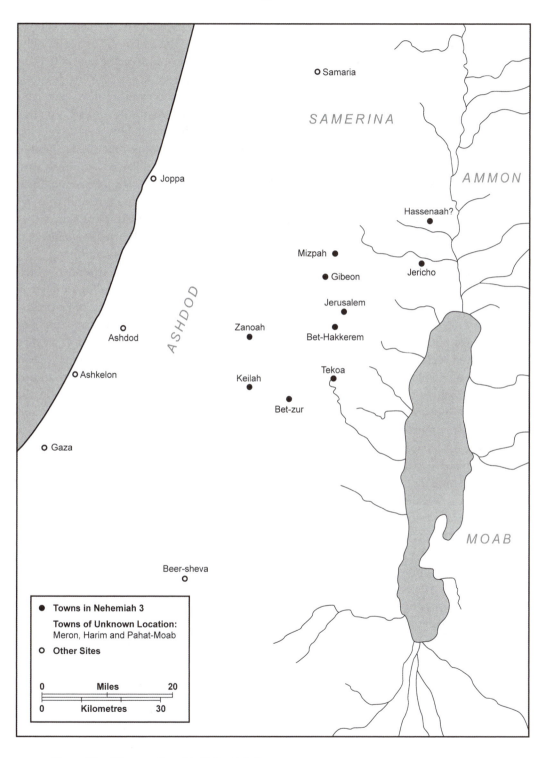

Figure 30. *Sites mentioned in Nehemiah 3*

Nehemiah 3.7 contains a curious comment concerning either the status of the men of Gibeon and/or Mizpah or the extent of the wall segment they repaired. The text of v. 7 states literally, 'Next to them repaired Melatiah the Gibeonite and Yadon the Meronothite, the men of Gibeon and Mizpah, to the seat of the governor of Across-the-River'. The wording of the final prepositional phrase is ambiguous. It might refer back to the men of Gibeon and/or of Mizpah, who belonged 'to' the seat, that is the jurisdiction of the governor of Across-the-River, as it is understood in the RSV translation (e.g. Myers 1965: 107). On the other hand, however, it could be understood to refer to the end-point along the wall to which two groups repaired: up 'to' the seat of the governor of Across-the-River, namely the newly constructed Persian administrative headquarters within the walls (e.g. Batten 1913: 211; Brockington 1969: 137; Fensham 1982: 174). This need not imply that the governor himself had a palace in Jerusalem; only that the *pehah* stationed in Jerusalem was under the authority of the *pehah* of the satrapy of Across-the-River. As seen in the earlier discussion of Tattenai, we know from official correspondence that this was, in fact, the case; Yehud was a province within the satrapy of Across-the-River.

However, the normal preposition that is used to express the idea of the extent to which something occurs (i.e. 'up to' a certain point), is *'ad*, not *le*. Thus, the understanding adopted by D. Clines (1984: 153), H.G.M. Williamson (1985: 197) and J. Blenkinsopp (1988: 235) is probably the most plausible: that the phrase 'to the seat of the governor of Across-the-River' modifies only the place-name it immediately follows: Mizpah. Thus, the sentence would read, 'Next to them repaired Melatiah the Gibeonite and Yadon the Meronothite, (and) the men of Gibeon and of Mizpah, (which had/possessed) the seat of the governor of Across-the-River'. In this case, the *le* would be seen to be used in the typical idiomatic way of expressing ownership or 'having' something in Hebrew: something 'is to' something else. As commonly occurs, the verb 'to be' has been omitted in this instance.[2]

Hugh G.M. Williamson has suggested further that the reason the phrase was used here was to clarify which Mizpah had been involved (1985: 197). The name means 'watchtower' and so was used of a number of sites descriptively. This is not likely, however, since we have no references to other Mizpahs within any of the lists of settlements of Yehud that purportedly derive from the Persian period. Thus, another explanation seems be needed. Since Mizpah had functioned as the provincial seat throughout the Neo-Babylonian and early Persian periods, the comment would make historical sense: it would still have served in that capacity until the completion of the rebuilding of Jerusalem, when all provincial administrative functions would have been transferred over to the new 'seat'. Thus, the comment would have been meant to give due honor to the former or existing provincial seat by identifying it explicitly.

In addition to identifying some people by their patronymics and/or gentilics, it can be noted that certain individuals in Nehemiah 3 bear a title that many think reflects administrative subdivisions within Yehud. Rephaiah son of Hur is *sar* of half of the *pelek* of Jerusalem (3.9) while Shallum son of Hallohesh, is *sar* of the other half-*pelek* of Jerusalem, with 'his/its daughters' (3.12). Malkiyah the son of Rekav is *sar* of the *pelek* of Bet-Hakkerem (3.14); Shallum son of Kolhozeh *sar* of the *pelek* of Mizpah (3.15), Nehemiah son of Azbuk *sar* of the half-*pelek* of Bet-Zur (3.16), Hashaviah *sar* of the half-*pelek* of Keilah (3.17), Bavvai the son of Henadad, *sar* of the other half-*pelek* of Keilah (3.18), Ezer son of Yeshua, *sar* of Mizpah (3.19). We need to determine the meaning of the terms *pelek* and *sar* so that we can understand the status of the five towns within this list that had one or two officials in charge of something called a *pelek*. Let us begin with the latter term.

The Meaning of Pelek. The term *pelek* as used above has been seen to designate two related, but distinctive ideas. The first is a 'district' within the larger administrative unit of the *medinah* or province of Yehud. The term would be a loan-word from Akkadian *pilku I*, meaning 'border, district, or boundary' (von Soden 1972: 863). Working with this definition, some scholars have proposed that the province of Yehud was subdivided into five districts, each named after their administrative 'seat': Jerusalem, Mizpah, Bet-Zur, Keilah, and Bet-Hakkerem.[3] Of these, the first four would then have been further subdivided into half-districts (so, e.g., Meyer 1896: 166-67; Noth 1960: 325; Herrmann 1975: 315; Fensham 1982: 175; Clines 1984: 150; Miller and Hayes 1986: 642; Ahlström 1993: 843; Milevski 1996/97: 20). Yohanan Aharoni has even proposed the identification of the sub-district seats in the first four instances: Gibeon was the sub-district seat of Jerusalem, Jericho of Mizpah, Tekoa of Bet-Zur, and Zanoah of Keilah (1979: 418).[4]

The second proposed meaning of *pelek* in Nehemiah 3 is 'mandatory annual labor tax' or corvée labor. In this case, the term would be a loan-word from Akkadian *pilku II*, which designated such annual tax labor (von Soden 1972: 863). Those who favor this definition have argued that Yehud was too small to have been subdivided into at least five districts (e.g. Demsky 1983; Carter 1999: 80). Whichever definition is adopted, it is clear that the underlying word was an administrative term that became part of local Judean vocabulary as a result of the experience of imperial domination. It was passed on from neo-Assyrian administration to Neo-Babylonian and Persian administrative language.[5]

If we adopt the second proposed meaning, we must ask why only certain parts of the labor force would have consisted of conscripted labor. Are we to believe that the others, representing the priests, Levites, and some professions like goldsmiths, shepherds, and perfume-makers, volunteered their labor? This seems unlikely. But so does the subdivision of the small province of Yehud into five sub-districts.

In neo-Assyrian administration, annual conscription for mandatory tax labor was levied by the same process used to conscript soldiers. Once called up, the men were divided roughly half and half into military service and civilian work service. In each case, they were put under the authority of a *rab kitsri*, a 'captain', who was a permanent officer and professional soldier. The contingents were then sent to their respective assignments. In the case of those assigned to civil service, the provincial governors were responsible for supervising their labor on behalf of the king (Postgate 1974: 224-27). Civil service typically took the form of building work, which could include the preparation of a site, the transportation of the necessary earth and straw, the manufacture of bricks, the laying of bricks, the building of walls, the digging of canals, and agricultural work (Postgate 1974: 228).

One text that seems to provide a nice parallel to the situation in Nehemiah 3 records that the governors of Kalhu and Arrapha were assigned a specified stretch of wall to complete in the building of the new city of Dur-sharruken, using conscripted labor from their home cities (ABL 486). The head of this royal project was the chief steward, a direct representative of the king; under him came the *rab pilkanu*, who supervised the sections of wall being built by the different contingents of conscripted laborers. Each civil work contingent was then headed by a *rab kitsri* (Postgate 1974: 227-29). The only other attested use of the title *rab pilkani* seems to confirm the function of the office as head coordinator of conscripted labor contingents. In ABL 91, in connection with the building of a structure to house the iron brazier in the palace at Asshur, the *rab pilkani* was to be in charge of clearing the site and the bricklaying, while the sons of the palace were to collect the *bitqu* and install the roof. *Bitqu* was a mandatory tax obligation that involved the supplying of manpower and animals for whatever was required in a given circumstance for the standing army and labor force of the empire (Postgate 1974: 44, 62, 250-51).

The Assyrian evidence indicates that *pilku* was mandatory labor for royal work projects that was done through annual conscription. While it dates centuries before the Persian period, it appears that the tax system and system of land ownership and rents that were established by the neo-Assyrian administration in its western provinces remained in place into the Greek period with little or no alteration (Limet 2000). Thus, the use of the term in a Persian-era context in connection with the rebuilding of the city walls of Jerusalem as part of a royal initiative should not be too surprising. If the term did not change in meaning, it indicates that in the case of the towns/settlements of Jerusalem, Mizpah, Bet-Zur, Keilah, and Bet-Hakkerem, the labor forces used to rebuild the walls were conscripted on the basis of their annual, obligatory service due to the Persian king.

It may be significant that at four of these five sites there is textual or archaeological evidence for the presence of a citadel in the Persian period. Nehemiah 1.8 and 7.2 indicates that when Jerusalem was rebuilt, a citadel or fort was included within the walls. Excavations at Bet-Zur, though initially completed prior to the adoption of modern stratigraphic methods, show evidence of a citadel that probably was used in the Persian period (Reich 1992a). A considerable number of Persian-era artifacts have been published in both Bet-Zur reports (Stern 1982: 36; Reich 1992a: 116), confirming that the site was occupied in this era. While we cannot know whether the fort was built at this time or had existed in an earlier period, this point is not important; its use in the mid-fifth century as a military installation is the crucial factor.

Bet-Hakkerem, identified with Ramat Rahel halfway between Jerusalem and Bethlehem, had housed a citadel from its initial founding in the eighth–seventh centuries BCE. In the late monarchic period in stratum VA, a palace that either housed an Assyrian official placed to oversee Assyrian interests in the region (Na'aman 2001: 270-73) or which was used by the king of Judah (O. Lipschits, oral communication) lay within the citadel complex (for the palace layout, see Reich 1992b: 207). The high-quality ashlar masonry from the late Iron Age suggests the building complex served more than a defensive purpose. The main structure was reused in the Persian era, stratum IVB, with a few alterations (Aharoni 1964: Fig 2; 1993: 1262-65). It likely housed a citadel once more, since Yehud was now a province under the governance of an appointed official rather than a vassal nation still headed by its own local dynasty. There was not longer any need to appoint an official to keep an eye on the local monarch, if that had been the function of the earlier stratum (contra Na'aman 2001: 272), nor the need for a royal villa.

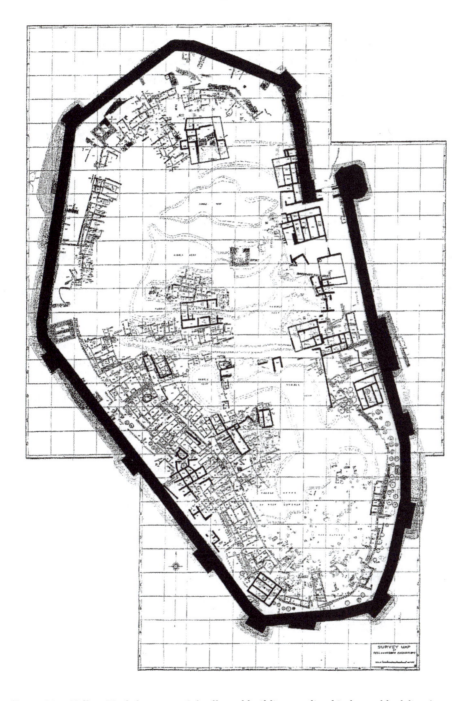

Figure 31. *Tell en-Nasbeh stratum 2 (walls and buildings outlined in heavy black lines)*
Copyright permission granted by Jeffrey R. Zorn, adapted from the 1:400 Site plan
published in C.C. McCown, *Tell en-Nasbeh*. I. *Archaeological and Historical Results*
(Berkeley, 1947). Copyright permission granted by the Badè Museum, Pacific
School of Religion.

At Mizpah, which was the seat of Yehud under the Neo-Babylonians and the Persians until the rebuilding of Jerusalem by Artaxerxes I, we can presume that there would have been a citadel. The existing Neo-Babylonian facilities of stratum 2 remained in use in the late-sixth century through the fifth century BCE, as indicated by the presence of twenty-six pieces of black-figure or black-slipped Attic pottery, eighteen Yehud stamp impressions, and an imitation early Attic bronze tetradrachm (Zorn 2003: 444). The lack of Greek pottery or coins dating to the fourth century, on the other hand, also confirms the termination of stratum II at the end of the fifth century BCE (Zorn 2003: 444).

Alongside a number of well-built, large four-room houses belonging to stratum 2 is courtyard building 7410 at the north end of the tell. Its exposed dimensions were c. 18 meters wide × over 15 meters long, with the actual dimensions undetermined (Zorn 2003: 423). While the four-room house is a local building tradition in the western Levant, the courtyard building belongs to Mesopotamian tradition and is frequently used of large administrative complexes or palaces. No citadel could be discerned from the original records of the digs that were conducted before modern methods of recording and excavations were introduced. It seems quite likely, however, that such a structure would have been included among the official buildings of the capital. Courtyard building 7410 is a possible candidate.

No excavations have been conducted at Khirbet Keilah, the fifty-dunam walled site thought to be ancient Keilah. However, Persian pottery was collected from the surface (Kochavi 1972: 48-49, site 70; Dagan 2000: #188), indicating occupation in this period. Whether the site was a fortress, a village or a farmstead, however, can only be determined through excavation.

It appears likely that the five sites that supplied *pilku*-labor for the wall-building project all housed forts. It raises the possibility that soldiers stationed there full-time or men who did rotations as soldiers there were temporarily reassigned to perform civil service. For full-time soldiers, this would have substituted for their normal duties. In the case of part-time soldiers, however, it may have counted as their annual mandatory labor owed to the king. Thus, the distinction made here between *pelek*-laborers and others may be one that, in this particular situation, was between military and non-military personnel. Those who were goldsmiths, shepherds, and perfume-makers may also have been conscripted labor fulfilling their annual duty to perform physical labor on behalf of the crown,[6] but they were not intermixed with the existing contingents of soldiers, who were supervised by their existing commanding officers.

The Meaning of Sar. The term *sar* designates a person in a leadership capacity, very often in a military setting. This is made clear from various extra-biblical ostraca and bullae. Four generic uses of this title of office are known from bullae of unknown provenance. All read *sr h'r*, '*sar* of the city' (Davies 1991: 100: 402, 510; Deutsch 1999: #13; Deutsch 2003: #42).

Figure 32.   *Bulla that reads* sar *of the city*
R. Deutsch, *Messages from the Past: Hebrew Bullae from the Time of Isaiah through the Destruction of the Temple* (Tel Aviv: Archaeological Center Publications, 1999): 78. Reproduced by kind permission of Archaeological Center Publications, Israel.

Figure 33.   *Bulla of Peqadyahu* sar *of the city*
R. Deutsch, *Messages from the Past: Hebrew Bullae from the Time of Isaiah through the Destruction of the Temple* (Tel Aviv: Archaeological Center Publications, 1999): 78. Reproduced by kind permission of the Israel Exploration Society.

Figure 34.   *Bulla of Hagav* sar *of the city*
R. Deutsch, *Biblical Period Hebrew Bullae: The Joseph Chaim Collection* (Tel Aviv: Archaeological Center Publications, 2003): 66. Reproduced by kind permission of the Israel Exploration Society.

Figure 35.   *Bulla of Shaphan* sar *of the city*
R. Deutsch, *Biblical Period Hebrew Bullae: The Joseph Chaim Collection* (Tel Aviv: Archaeological Center Publications, 2003): 68. Reproduced by kind permission of the Israel Exploration Society.

Three additional bullae, however, preserve the names of individuals who bore this office: 'belonging to Peqadyahu *sar* of the city' (Deutsch 1999: #12), 'belonging to Hagav, *sar* of the city', and 'belonging to Shaphan, *sar* of the city' (Deutsch 2003: #39 and 40).[7] Unfortunately, none of these seven bullae contains iconography that can help us define the function of the *sar* of the city, although it might be significant that the one belonging to Shaphan has used two lengths of rope with nooses at either end to separate the personal name from the title of office. This could symbolize the custom of binding prisoners.

Four bullae, however, bear graphics that illustrate the nature of the office of *sar*. The first, probably from the region of Samaria, bears only the title *sar*. It shows a man leading a captive, whose hands are bound behind his back (Avigad and Sass 1997: 170, #401). He may be grabbing the hair of the prisoner to restrain him. The imagery suggests that the office of *sar* involved fighting against enemies to protect the safety of others. A second example of this bulla is now known, but the impression was poorly done and is distorted (Deutsch 2003: #43).

The identical imagery appears on four other bullae, but instead of the title *sar*, the title *melek* appears in three cases (Avigad and Sass1997: #400, 1065; Deutsch 2003: #5) and the personal name Mar'iyavav in the other (Avigad and Sass 1997: #810). All of these bullae, including the one that reads *sar*, have smooth, convex backs, which indicate they were not used to seal a document but instead, were some sort of receipt, proof of payment, or token (e.g. Deutsch 2003: 71). It is probably significant that the bulla imprinted with the seal of Azaryahu the gatekeeper of the prison belongs to this same type or category (Deutsch and Heltzer 1994: #14). It seems as though they all were used to transfer prisoners under the authority of the named individual. In the case of the two generic titles, *sar* and *melek*/king, it appears that it was deemed expedient to use a more generic stamp that represented the authority of the chief of police who was responsible for the safety of the city or the king himself. By using the same iconography, the purpose would have been readily apparent, even to a soldier who may have been illiterate but who escorted the prisoner to the proper authorities, where he would have handed him over, along with the token.[8]

Figure 36. *Bulla depicting a captive figure that reads* sar
N. Avigad and B. Sass, *Corpus of West Semitic Stamp Seals* (Jerusalem: The Israel Academy of Sciences and Humanities; The Israel Exploration Society; The Institute of Archaeology, The Hebrew University of Jerusalem, 1997): 170, #401. (Drawn by the author.)

Figure 37. *Bulla depicting a captive figure that reads king (*melek*)*
R. Deutsch, *Biblical Period Hebrew Bullae: The Joseph Chaim Collection* (Tel Aviv: Archaeological Center Publications, 2003): 21. Copyright permission granted.

Figure 38. *Bulla of Mar'iyavav*
            N. Avigad and B. Sass, *Corpus of West Semitic Stamp Seals* (Jerusalem: The Israel
            Academy of Sciences and Humanities; The Israel Exploration Society; The Insti-
            tute of Archaeology, The Hebrew University of Jerusalem, 1997): 303, #810.
            (Drawn by the author.)

Figure 39. *Bulla depicting an investiture in office that reads* sar *of the city*
            R. Deutsch, *Biblical Period Hebrew Bullae: The Joseph Chaim Collection* (Tel Aviv:
            Archaeological Center Publications, 2003): 70. Copyright permission granted.

The other four bullae were made by the same seal. They feature two men facing each other.
The larger figure on the left has a sword in his belt. His right hand rests on the hilt of the
sword, while he holds a bow and arrows in his left hand. The smaller figure on the right is
unarmed. His left hand is by his side while his right arm is extended, bent at the elbow, toward
the other figure. Below his feet is a cartouche-like oval containing the inscription, *sr h'r*, '*sar
of the city*' (Avigad and Sasson 1997: 171, #402, 403; Deutsch 2003: #42). The scene seems to
reflect the delegation of military powers or the right to use force by the larger figure on the

left to the smaller one on the right, under whose feet is the title of office. The presence of the weaponry suggests once again the idea that the office of *sar* involved protection against enemies.

These two styles of bullae tend to indicate that the office of '*sar/sar* of the city' was equivalent to 'commander of protective forces' (so, e.g., Noth 1960: 324; Herrmann 1975: 312)[9] rather than 'governor of the city', as has been suggested in past discussions (contra, e.g., Lemaire 1988: 221; Avigad and Sass 1997: 170-71; Deutsch 1999: 76-78, but qualified in 2003: 71 to recognize that the title was administrative and military and probably involved command over a unit of soldiers to impose his rule in the city; Niehr 2004: 195). While firm dates are not known for any of the six bullae, the style of writing suggests a date in the Iron Age, probably prior to the imposition of Neo-Babylonian administration in the region in 586 BCE.

An ostracon from Mesad Hashavyahu, a fort in the coastal plain dating to the late-seventh century BCE, records a petition concerning the confiscation of a cloak, allegedly for the failure to complete the allotted amount of reaping required within a day. It is addressed to 'my lord, the *sar*', who has generally been assumed to have been the head official of the facility (Naveh 1960: 134; Davies 1991: 7.001; Niehr 2004: 195). If one adopts this interpretation of the function of the addressee, it would be best to render the title as 'commander' rather than 'governor', as has been done in the literature. However, it is possible in this instance that the petition is being addressed instead to the main overseer of a corvée labor project. The petitioner appears to have been performing mandatory work service at the time, and he might have been appealing to the superior of his work-gang boss to right the wrong that the latter had committed. Finding the letter in the fortress gate indicates only that the complainant had to go there to find a scribe to compose the document for him.

Four graffito from Quntillet 'Ajrud, a way station in the Sinai peninsula dating to the first half of the eighth century BCE, read *lsr 'r*, '(belonging) to the *sar* of (the) city' (Davies 1991: 8.007-10). It would appear that the latter facility, while established to oversee the trade route, was part of the military network of the kingdom of Judah and would have housed a contingent of soldiers to deal with attacks on the caravan traffic and to protect those stopping overnight at the facility from enemy raids (contra Niehr 2004: 195, who prefers to read the title as a personal name). Hananiah, who was reportedly appointed by Nehemiah over the *birah* or fortress within Jerusalem, similarly bears the title *sar* (Neh. 7.2).

The title '*sar* of the city' is used in the biblical texts as well. It describes Zebul, who allegedly served under Abimelek, the son of Gideon, who made himself king in Shechem (Judg. 9.30); of an individual named Ammon, to whom Ahab had the prophet Micaiah returned with orders that he be put in prison (1 Kgs 22.26; 2 Chron. 18.25), and of two different individuals who served under King Josiah: Yehoshua (2 Kgs 23.8), who was responsible for guarding one of the city gates, and Ma'aseyahu, who was entrusted with the task of delivering money to the temple for its repair alongside the recorder and another individual (2 Chron. 34.8). It is noteworthy that they confirm the role of the *sar* of the city as one in charge of prisoners. In addition, they illustrate two other functions that were overseen by the holder of this office: (1) guarding the city gates, and (2) providing an armed escort for the delivery of money, which would also have been a protective measure against ambush.

In the Bible, the term *sar* is used to designate a person of note or a leader (Niehr 2004: 196-98). It often is qualified, however, by additional administrative or military titles of office, like *sar* of the armed forces (1 Sam. 17.55; 2 Sam. 24.2-4), *sar* of the chariots (1 Kgs 22.32-33), *sar* of the footsoldiers (1 Kgs 14.27), *sar* of a troop or military division (1 Kgs 11.4), *sar* of a patrol or unit (1 Sam. 22.7), *sar* of the corvée (Exod. 1.11), *sar* of the herds (Gen. 47.6), *sar* of the movable property (1 Chron. 27.31), *sar* of the royal estate (1 Chron. 29.6), *sar* of the prison (Gen. 39.11; 1 Kgs 20.14-19), and *sar* of appointed officials (1 Kgs 5.30) (Koehler and Baumgartner 1996: 1351-52).

In the Persian period, it appears that the title continued its association with military and administrative offices. Hananiah was *sar* over Jerusalem; he appears to have functioned as the *sar* of the city or chief of police for the newly rebuilt *birah*. Part of his duties included overseeing the guard details for the gates (Neh. 7.1-4). In the case of the five individuals who bear the title '*sar* of a *pelek*' or '*sar* of half-*pelek*', it seems likely that a military connotation is also implied, rather than an administrative one. It does not seem likely that *pelek* is being used in these instances to designate a sub-district that then was divided a second time in some instances into 'half-districts'. It is more likely that it is being used in the sense of annual corvée-labor, but not necessarily as a standard administrative title for a person in charge of a forced labor group, although this is possible. Instead, it seems likely that Jerusalem, Mizpah, Bet-Hakkerem, Keilah, and Bet-Zur housed forts with commanders and assigned military personnel and detachments of soldiers from these sites were used as the labor force to reconstruct the walls.[10] They would have continued to work under their existing commanders (*sarim*), whose assignments were temporarily switched over to supervising their men in civil building activities on behalf of the crown (*pelek*).

Section Summary. A review of Nehemiah 3 has shown the widespread acceptance of its information to reflect accurately the names of individuals and settlements in Yehud at the time the walls of Jerusalem were constructed during the reign of Artaxerxes I. The southernmost town mentioned in the list is Bet-Zur, in the middle of the Judean hill-country, well north of the Negev. Mizpah was still acknowledged as the provincial seat, suggesting that the transfer of that function to Jerusalem could not take place until the walls and administrative complexes within them were completed. Nevertheless, a functioning administration was in place, as evidenced by the probable use of soldiers from the five sites of Mizpah, Jerusalem, Bet-Hakkerem, Keilah, and Bet-Zur to help rebuild the walls, possibly in fulfillment of their annual corvée labor duty.

If the list more or less reflects the towns from which people were pressed into service to help rebuild Jerusalem, it need not necessarily reflect the territorial limits of Yehud under Artaxerxes I. If this king had ordered a group of settlers to be sent to Yehud as part of an initiative designed to redevelop the region, groups assigned land in the more outlying areas of the southern Shephelah and the Negev may have been put to work building military installations at strategic crossroads near their new homes. The labor for the rebuilding of Jerusalem may have been drawn from locations that were fairly close to Jerusalem, to allow the men to return home from time to time.

It is curious that few settlements from Benjamin appear among the list of those who rebuilt the wall in Jerusalem. Benjamin had been heavily settled in the Neo-Babylonian period, consituting the northern portion of the province of Yehud. Perhaps men from these established farmsteads, hamlets, villages and towns were sent to help build the forts and relay stations in the more outlying areas to equal out the workforce and ensure the speedy implementation of the Persian directives for the province. In this case, however, they would not have been able to return home periodically as easily as those assigned to the construction work in Jerusalem.

Nehemiah 7.6-69. Nehemiah 7.6-69 contains a list of the men of Israel who were to have returned to Jerusalem with Zerubbabel and Yeshua. As stated in Chapter 3, it was reused by the author of Ezra 1–6, but it was originally designed to make sense in the context of the narrative setting in Nehemiah. In the subsection detailing the lay repatriates in vv. 7-38, the first segment lists men by their clans (vv. 7-24)[11] while the second lists men by their towns of habitation (vv. 25-38). The towns in vv. 25-38 include Gibeon, Bethlehem, Netophah, Anatot, Bet-Azmavet, Kiryat-Yearim, Kephirah, Beerot, Ramah, Geva, Mikmash, Bethel, Ai, Nebo, Elam, Harim, Jericho, Lod, Hadid, Ono, and Senaah.

There are a number of overlaps with the sites named in Nehemiah 3: Jericho, (Has)senaah, Gibeon and Harim. However, what really stands out is that the majority of the new sites in this list are located in Benjamin: Anatot, Bet-Azmaveth, Kiryat-Yearim, Kephirah, Beerot, Ramah, Geva, Mikmash, Bethel, Ai and possibly Nebo, Elam, and Harim. Two Nebos and two Elams are mentioned in this list (Ezra 2.29; Neh. 7.33, 34) and in both cases one of the two could be located within Benjamin, given their appearance after Bethel and Ai in the list. It also is possible that Harim, which is named immediately after them but before Jericho, was similarly located within Benjaminite territory.[12] Of the five remaining sites, Lod, Hadid, and Ono represent the spread of settlement westward beyond Benjamin into the coastal plain, while Bethlehem and Netophah lie immediately south and southeast of Jerusalem, just beyond the southern border of Benjamin.

As already noted, the settlements comprising Yehud in the Neo-Babylonian period were concentrated in the territory traditionally associated with Benjamin. On the one hand, then, it would be logical to assume that the newly-arrived groups might have been distributed among the established towns for easy integration into the existing system. On the other hand, however, if the Persian king were sending a group of immigrants to the area as settlers, it is likely that they would have been intended to have founded new villages and farmsteads in areas of Yehud that lacked population instead of augmenting the population of existing settlements and leaving the depopulated regions unoccupied. Thus, the list is curious in its heavy emphasis on settlements that lay north of Jerusalem.

The original purpose and date of Neh. 7.6-19 has been widely debated. It has been seen to have been drawn up initially to serve as (1) a tax list (Hölscher 1923: 303-304); (2) a list to restore land rights that had been confiscated by the Neo-Babylonians (e.g. Alt 1953b: 334-35); (3) a list of persons who were legitimate 'Israelites' versus Samaritans (e.g. Galling 1951b: 157; 1964: 89-91); (4) a list of heads of families at the time of the initial return under Darius (e.g. Clines 1984: 179); and (5) a genealogy to record where various families lived to be used to move

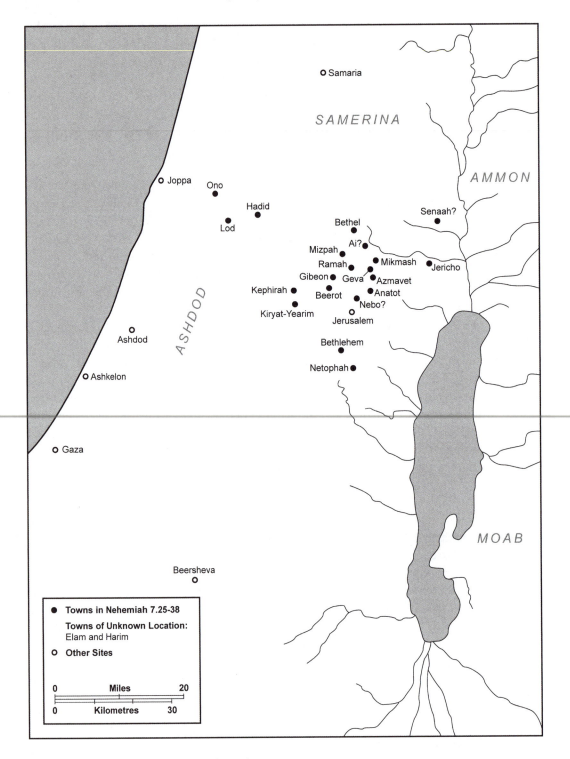

Figure 40. *Map of towns in Nehemiah 7.25-38*

a segment of the existing population into Jerusalem after the walls were complete (so, e.g., Myers 1965: 146; Fensham 1982: 211). Its date is equally disputed. These verses are thought by some to be a compilation of those who had returned during the first twenty years or so of Achaemenid rule (538–518 BCE) (so, e.g., Brockington 1969: 35; Williamson 1985: xxiv) and by others to be a composite that combines a list from the time of Ezra and Nehemiah with one detailing settlements that dates from the later-fifth century BCE (so, e.g., Mowinckel 1964a: 98-109). Still others date all of it specifically to the time of Ezra, as a compilation of all who had come to Yehud from the time of Zerubbabel to the present day (e.g. Batten 1913: 72-73) or claim it originally had not had a date but merely listed those in the *medinah* (province) who had come up out of captivity from Babylon with Zerubbabel (e.g. Galling 1951b: 157).

In spite of the range of proposed dates, there is a general feeling that the source from which information in Neh. 7.6-69 was derived was in existence no later than 400 BCE and reflected either directly or indirectly the extent of settlement within Yehud no later than the end of the fifth century BCE. Yet, when placed beside the list of settlements named in Nehemiah 3, which is thought by most to derive from the reign of Artaxerxes I, Neh. 7.6-69 implies that the southernmost settlement in Yehud was at Zanoah or Netophah. Both of these towns lie north of Bet-Zur, the southernmost site mentioned in Nehemiah 3. The Jordan Rift Valley still remains within Yehud, however. Unless we want to presume that territory had been lost between the time that the sources underlying Nehemiah 3 and Neh. 7.6-19 were composed, we need to acknowledge that the present list, like that in Nehemiah 3, does not reflect the full extent of the territory of Yehud at any point in history. The decision to place the returnees in sites primarily within Benjamin has been motivated by concerns other than an accurate reporting of events.

One underlying motivation may have been a desire to claim that those in Yehud who had returned from Babylonia were true heirs to the name Israel and represented this entity in its transformation into a religious community instead of a kingdom. It is noteworthy that Neh. 7.7 states that the list in vv. 8-69 details men constituting 'the people of Israel' and that they arrived in Yehud under the leadership of twelve individuals – the same in number as the traditional tribes of Israel. Thus, it is probably not coincidental that the 'returnees' are said to have settled primarily in the land of Benjamin. In the Genesis stories, Benjamin is portrayed as the youngest and favorite son of Jacob who was orphaned and 'taken in' by his big brother Judah. Half of the traditional territory of Benjamin lay within the kingdom of Israel and half within the kingdom of Judah when the boundary was set at Ramah during the reigns of Asa and Baasha (1 Kings 15). By the Persian period, however, the former half that had been part of Israel had become part of Yehud, according to Nehemiah 7. Thus, to have the people settle primarily in the territory of Benjamin, which was able to symbolize the former Israel because part of it had belonged to that kingdom, may have been a deliberate move by the author. He may have wanted to appropriate the name of Israel from the past but at the same time, he may have wanted to redefine its membership to include only those who accepted Yahweh Elohim as the sovereign king in Yehud (Edelman 1995a).

If the foregoing hypothesis is accepted, we would need to postulate a date of composition for Neh. 7.6-69 at some point after the rebuilding of the temple c. 450 BCE, when the cult of Yahweh Elohim would have been first reintroduced into the province as the official religion to be followed. In addition, we would probably need to posit a lapse of some decades during which the local population of Yehud that had always lived in the land would have resisted this new, exclusivist religion. Many of the attacks against ongoing, local religious practices voiced in 3 Isaiah (Isaiah 56–66) seem to reflect this conflict. It would have been in the wake of the failure of a significant portion of the population in Yehud to have adopted this new religion and the views of the political party backing it that the decision would have been made to appropriate the name of Israel to designate members of the cult of Yahweh Elohim and allow a distinction to be made within the province of 'insiders' (Israelites) and 'outsiders' (people of the land; resident aliens, and foreigners).

A date of composition no earlier than c. 425 BCE for Neh. 7.6-69 would seem to be warranted. However, due to underlying ideological motivations, its author has not given the full extent of the territory of Yehud at the time of Artaxerxes or in his own day. Instead, he has concentrated his attention artificially on settlements located primarily within the territory of Benjamin. Like Nehemiah 3, then, this list cannot be used with confidence or certainty to determine the boundaries of Yehud at the time of Nehemiah or Artaxerxes I.

Nehemiah 11.25-35. The final list to evaluate, Neh. 11.25-35, ostensibly enumerates the settlements of Yehud that were occupied after the completion of the walls of Jerusalem under Artaxerxes I. It is subdivided geographically into sites belonging to Judah and those belonging to Benjamin. The first group includes Kiryat-Arba and its 'daughters', Divon and its 'daughters', Yekavzeel and its 'daughters', Yeshua, Moladah, Bet-Pelet, Hazar-Shual, Beersheva and its 'daughters', Ziklag, Mekonah and its 'daughters', En-rimmon, Zorah, Yarmut, Zanoah, Adullam and its 'daughters', Lakish and its fields, Azekah and its 'daughters'. The second group includes Mikmash, Aiya, Bethel and its 'daughters', Anatot, Nob, Ananiah, Hazor, Ramah, Gittaim, Hadid, Zevoim, Nevallat, Lod, and Ono. There is a distinction made between sites that had 'daughters', that is, dependent farmsteads perhaps, and those without such associated lands. The significance of this distinction is not clear; it could indicate a difference in size, on the one hand, or function, on the other. It can be noted that in Neh. 3.12, Jerusalem is described also to have had 'daughters'.[13]

What is immediately apparent is the inclusion of eleven sites in the Negev region and two in the southern Shephelah within the territory of Yehud, unlike the situation in the two previous lists. On the other hand, there are no sites in the Jordan Rift Valley; Jericho and Hasenaah have disappeared, even though both were named in Nehemiah 3 and Neh. 7.6-38. Settlements continue in the coastal plain, however, around Lod and Ono. But most noteworthy is the almost total lack of overlap of sites located within the region of Judah among the three lists: the only town in common is Zanoah, found here and in Neh. 3.13. Conspicuously lacking from the settlements of Judah in 11.25-30 are Bethlehem, Bet-Azmaveth, Netophah, Elam, Harim, Jericho, and Senaah found in Nehemiah 7, and Keilah, Bet-Zur, Meron, Bet-Hakkerem, Pahat-Moab, and Tekoa found in Nehemiah 3. What are we to make of all of this?

The inclusion of the nine towns in the Negev among settlements allegedly occupied during Nehemiah's governorship has prompted a wide range of proposed dates for the underlying source. The earliest is placed at the end of the monarchy in 586 BCE, when the Negev would still have been under Judahite control and a list of military conscription was drawn up for the

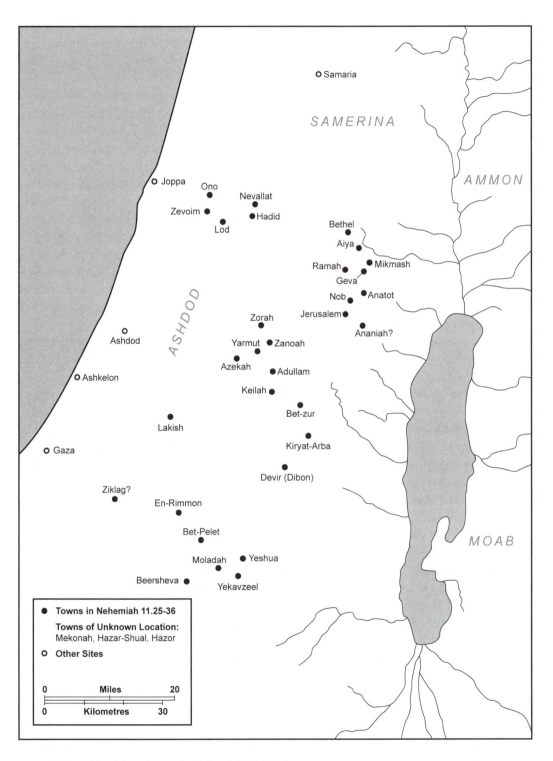

Figure 41. *Map of towns in Nehemiah 11.25-36*

defence of Jerusalem against the impending Neo-Babylonian attack (e.g. Kellerman 1966: 217-25). The latest is set in the Maccabean period, when the Negev, which was part of Idumea, was conquered by the Hasmonean kings and reincorporated into the vassal kingdom of Judea (1 Macc. 5.65; 11.34) (so, e.g., Meyer 1896: 105-108).

In between these two extremes, the underlying source has been seen to date from the time of Nehemiah, and, on the one hand, to provide an accurate list of the extent of the area covered by Jerusalem's jurisdiction (e.g. Batten 1913: 273; Coggins 1976: 128; Clines 1984: 220-21 as one of two options). On the other hand, it has been thought to be a list dating from the time of Nehemiah of Jewish settlements and not of the boundaries of Yehud. This then accounts for the presence of the Jewish settlements in the Negev and Shephelah that lay under Arabian control (Myers 1965: 191; Fensham 1982: 249; Clines 1984: 220 as one of two options).[14] Finally, the list has been seen to date from the generation after Nehemiah because of the rise to prominence of the children of those who were in power with him (Mowinckel 1964a: 149-50), or two generations later, since the grandfathers of some of those listed had participated in the work on the walls (Blenkinsopp 1988: 325). The middle positions tend to assume a date somewhere between c. 450–400 BCE for the source underlying Neh. 11.25-35, which is consistent with the date proposed for the source underlying Nehemiah 7.6-69 and also contemporary with, or slightly later than, the source underlying Nehemiah 3.

A growing trend in recent years has been to see the list in vv. 25-35 as a secondary expansion within the book, which also included Neh. 11.3-24 and which drew heavily on Joshua 15. The Chronicler (von Rad 1930: 21-25) or a later editor (Williamson 1985: xxxiii, 350; Lipschits 2002: 439) wanted to idealize post-exilic Israel and so extended its historical boundaries to reflect those of Judah in the days of the incomparable King Josiah (c. 640–609 BCE). Joseph Blenkinsopp argues along similar lines but does not consider the list to have been a secondary expansion. He has pointed out how the listing of towns seems to be drawn from the boundary lists for Judah and Benjamin in the book of Joshua, following their same organizational format that presents settlements along the cardinal boundary points before interior sites but omitting the border between Judah and Benjamin since the two were being considered a single unit (1988: 329-30).

Nehemiah 11.25-35 has clearly been shaped to reflect the boundaries of the former kingdom of Judah that are elsewhere found in the Deuteronomistic History (the books of Deuteronomy–2 Kings, except Ruth; see esp. 1 Kgs 15.22). These are described as running from Geva in the north to Beersheva in the south (2 Kgs 23.8). Verses 31-35 present the settlements of the people of Benjamin, which are restricted to sites north of Geva, with the implication that all sites to the south were occupied by the people of Judah. Similarly, in vv. 25-30, there is a summary stating that the people (of Judah) encamped from Beersheva to the Valley of Hinnom. In the list of settlements none that has been positively identified with a high degree of certainty lies south of Beersheva.

A Comparison of Nehemiah 11.31-35 and Nehemiah 7.6-38. The list of settlements of the people of Benjamin in 11.31-35 is particularly interesting when compared with the list in Neh. 7.6-38 of the sons of Israel, which was heavily concentrated in the territory of Benjamin. The first thing that is apparent is the omission of the four 'Gibeonite' settlements, Gibeon,

Kephirah, Kiryat-Yearim, and Beerot. While the first three lie south of Geva and so would have been excluded anyway, Beerot lies northwest of Geva and should have been included. Thus, the exclusion of the Gibeonite cities has not been motivated strictly by geographical concerns. Instead, it reflects the Deuteronomistic portrayal of the Gibeonites as foreigners, non-members of the people of Israel (Joshua 9; 2 Sam. 21.1-14).

Otherwise, there is a lot of overlap with the two lists in enumerating sites that lay north of Jerusalem: Mikmash, Ai/Aiya, Bethel, Anatot, Ramah, Hadid, Lod, Ono and possibly Nob/the other Nebo. The site of Ananiah might be mentioned in Neh. 3.23 in the identification of Azariah, son of Maaseiah, son of Ananiah. The first may be his father's name and the second his village. It was common biblical practice to use the term 'son' to refer to a member of a non-family group, like a profession or a place of origin. Yet it can be noted that, as currently identified, Anatot (Ras el-Kharrubeh) and Ananiah (el-Azariyeh) lie southeast of Geva (Abel 1967: 243-44, 266; May 1974: 122; Aharoni 1979: 430; Monson 1979: 15.2), so again, the proposed identifications of these two sites might need to be rethought.

If we look at the remaining sites in Neh. 7.25-42, it is apparent that in most cases, those located south of Geva have been eliminated: Bethlehem, Bet-Azmaveth, Netophah, Elam and Harim. The two that are exceptions, Jericho and Senaah, both lie in the Jordan Rift Valley and so may have been excluded because the eastern boundary was being set in the hill-country. Perhaps by the time this list was composed, that area had been made into a crown-owned *paradeisos* or park whose settlements were no longer included within the province's administration.

Theophrastus, writing toward the end of the Persian era (c. 350–300 BCE) said that the 'park' located in the 'Valley of Syria' (the Jordan Rift Valley) produced the best quality balsam in the largest quantity (*Inquiry into Plants*, 9.6.2-4), and this area continued to serve a similar function in Herodian times when there was a royal palace and orchard in the balsam *paradeisos* (Strabo 12.2, 41; Josephus, *War* 4.467-69; Heltzer 2000: 129). Diodorus Siculus claims that when Tennes decided to launch a revolt against Artaxerxes III and had gathered a navy and mercenary army, his first hostile act was the destruction of the *paradeisos* in which the Persian kings had liked to take their recreation (16.41). By implication, it was located near the Phoenician coast. Nehemiah 2.8 indicates that such royal parks were also a source of raw materials besides leisure (Schrader 1888: 71). According to Solinus, Artaxerxes destroyed Jericho, the capital of Judea after the destruction of Jerusalem (*Collactanea rerum memorabilium* 4.35). It has been thought likely that if this is a garbled account of a historical event, it involved Artaxerxes III on his return home from Egypt in 342/41 BCE. So perhaps it was at this time that the park mentioned by Theophrastus was first created. The site of Tell es-Sultan that had housed settlement at Jericho since the Natufian period was abandoned toward the end of the Persian period, which would be consistent with the turning of the area into a royal park at this time (Kenyon 1993: 680-81). It appears already to have been a crown domain at the time of the conquest of the region by Alexander the Great in 333 BCE and subsequently became the property of this king and his heirs (Foerster 1993: 681).

Balsam or balm is thought to derive from the shrub or small tree known as *commiphora gileadensis* which, in spite of its name, is never thought to have grown in Gilead. The shrub grows in hot deserts or semi-arid deserts and is native to southwest Arabia and Somaliland. Its small clusters of white flowers produce small fruits that contain a fragrant yellow seed. There are about 100 species of the *commiphora*, some of which exude a fragrant resin that can be obtained artificially by making incisions in the stems and branches of the plant. Initially bright green, the droplets that congeal into clumps turn brown when they harden and then fall to the ground, from where they are collected

(Zohary 1982: 198-99). Excavations at 'En-Gedi have unearthed the tools, vessels and furnaces that have been seen to have been used to produce balm commercially in the late monarchic period (Mazar, Dothan and Dunayevsky 1966: 17-21).

Turning to the list of 'Benjaminite' settlements in Neh. 11.31-35, there are five sites not found in Neh. 7.25-42 and not mentioned elsewhere in the Bible, except possibly Ananiah in Neh. 3.23: Gittaim, Ananiah, Hazor, Zevoim, and Nevallat. Of these, the proposed locations for Zevoim somewhere north of Lod and Nevallat at Beit Nabala north of Hadid are consistent with the specification that the settlements lay north of Geva (May 1974: 136, 143; Aharoni 1979: 440). Those for the remaining three sites, however, would place them south of Geva and so contradict the claim that the listed settlements lay from Geva onwards: Gittaim (Tel Ras Abu Hamid), Ananiah (el-Azariyeh), and Hazor (Khirbet Hazzur) (Abel 1967: 243-44, 266; May 1974: 122, 130; Aharoni 1979: 430, 435; Monson 1979: 15.2). New identifications might profitably be proposed.

What can we make of all of this? It seems as though the person who created the list in Neh. 11.31-35 has accessed some sort of list that reflected Persian-era settlement in the northern part of Yehud and has selected from it sites that lay north of Geva, excluding Beerot because it was Gibeonite. It is even possible that he worked with Neh. 7.25-42 directly, and that he added the five additional place names not otherwise found in that list because they existed in his day and fit the criterion of lying north of Geva. Of these five sites, Hazor and Nevallat occur only here, in a Persian-era context; Ananiah may appear in Neh. 3.23 but if so, only in a Persian-era context.

The remaining two sites, on the other hand, are depicted to have existed in the Iron II period as well. Zevoim is mentioned in 1 Sam. 13.18 as the Valley of Zevoim, which lay towards the wilderness. Gittaim is mentioned in 2 Sam. 4.3 as the site to which men of the Gibeonite town of Beeroth fled and remained as resident foreigners. It is to be distinguished from the Philistine city of Gath. A *gat* is a winepress and there are many place-names that include this element. In the present case, Gath means a single winepress while Gittaim means a double press, although it has been suggested that the *–ayim* ending in place names may not represent the dual, as it does with common nouns, but may be an old case ending expressing location. Of the five sites that occur in 11.31-35 but not in Neh. 7.25-42, three appear to be strictly Persian in date while two may have been settled previously in the Iron II period, during the time of the monarchy.

The limitation of the settlements of the people of Judah in the first section of the list in Neh. 11.25-30 to the Valley of Hinnom highlights the artificial use of Geva as the northern boundary point for Judah in the Benjaminite list. While it was a traditional boundary during much of the monarchic period for the political unit of the kingdom of Judah, that kingdom included within it much of the traditional tribal land of Benjamin (Josh. 18.21-28). The tribal boundary for Benjamin lay south of Jerusalem (Josh. 19.28). This is consistent with the placing of the northernmost point for the encampments of the people of Judah at the Valley of Hinnom, which runs immediately east and south of Jerusalem. By choosing to use Geva as a boundary point for Benjamin, however, the person who shaped this list created a territorial gap in the region north of Jerusalem and south of Geva that was unaccounted for. He was forced to eliminate a number of sites that fell within the traditional territory of Benjamin, which also are mentioned in Nehemiah 3 or Neh. 7.25-42: Mizpah, Bet-Azmaveth, Gibeon, Kephirah, and Kiryat-Yearim. We have already noted that the last three had to be eliminated because they were deemed 'non-Israelite'. The first two, however, seem to have been deliberately 'overlooked' for the sake of the larger ideology being expressed.

Thus, the strategy reflected here is slightly different than the one deduced for Neh. 7.6-69, though the two have much in common. The editor's desire to use the Deuteronomistic boundaries for the kingdom of Judah 'from Geva to Beersheva' forced him into an artificial truncation of the traditional tribal territory of Benjamin from just south of Jerusalem to the region north of Geva. As a result of this move, however, his list of settlements in Benjamin came to represent the reclamation of part of the former territory of the kingdom of Israel by members of the *golah* community. In this sense, he was doing something similar to what the person responsible for Neh. 7.6-69 had done in closely linking the *golah* community with Israel. At the same time, it is clear that, in his limitation of the settlements of Judah to the area south of the Hinnom Valley, this editor also was working with the traditional tribal allotment for Benjamin in mind, which ran as far south as the this valley. As a result of ideological considerations, an artificial 'no-man's land' was created between Geva and Jerusalem, which had not been the case with the person who created Neh. 7.25-37, and the Gibeonite towns were also excluded from the territory of Benjamin because they did not belong to 'the people of Israel'.

A Comparison of Nehemiah 11.25-30 and Joshua 15. A comparison of the settlements of the people of Judah in Neh. 11.25-30 with the tribal allotment in Joshua 15 is instructive. The latter subdivides the territory of Judah into four geographical zones: the extreme south (*negev*), the lowlands (*shephelah*), the hill-country (*har*), and the wilderness (*midvar*). The person who created Neh. 11.25-30 has organized his list by using the same geographical headings as in Joshua, but has not presented the materials in the same order; he begins with the hill-country, giving only two sites: Kiryat-Arba (Hevron) and Divon (a likely corruption of Devir). Both are also found in Joshua 15 alongside many other sites not mentioned here, but in reverse order in that latter list. He then moves on to the extreme south, or the Negev: Yekavzeel, Yeshua, Moladah, Bet-Pelet, Hazar Shual, Beersheva, Ziklag, Mekonah, En-Rimmon. Of these, all but Yeshua and Mekonah also are found in Joshua 15 as part of a much fuller list, in the same order. Next, he moves to the lowlands or Shephelah: Zorah, Yarmut, Zanoah, Adullam, Lakish, Azekah. All appear in Joshua 15, which again has a fuller list of sites, but not in this order. The final zone, the wilderness or Midvar, is not included at all, suggesting that in his mind, the Jordan Rift Valley lay outside the land of the people of Judah. This is consistent with his exclusion of Jericho and Senaah from the holdings of the people of Benjamin.

In light of the data just presented, the suggestion that the entire Nehemiah list has been derived in some way from Joshua 15 is unlikely. Joshua 15 is thought to reflect conditions towards the end of the monarchy in the Iron IIc period that have been set back in time to the period of the occupation of the land. It would be natural for some overlap in occupied sites to occur between the Iron IIC and the Persian periods; settlements were placed to take advantage of natural resources, like water, protective heights, and crossroads. The listing of settlements according to the natural ecological zones found within it is also logical, especially given the variety represented. The overlap of names between the two lists is 7.46 percent (15 of 112, excluding the Philistine sites in 15.45-47). It is more likely that Neh. 11.25-36 reflects an incomplete or idealized list of settlements within the province of Yehud at some point in the Persian period.

Notwithstanding, it is probable that the section in Joshua detailing the extreme south (Negev) has been used by the person who created Neh. 11.25-30, since the sites are in the same order as they occur there and all fall within Idumean territory. It seems too coincidental for nine sites to have been listed in the same order in both cases, especially when the same order does not occur for the other two geographical sub-regions where many fewer sites are involved. If the original southern boundary for Yehud lay at Bet-Zur, as is often assumed, then the author would have needed to include sites as far south as Beersheva to be consistent with his ideology that the southern border of Yehud lay at Beerheva and so could have used Joshua 15 as a ready source. He may or may not have selected sites from the list that were occupied once more in his own time (7 of 29). The presence of two in his list that are not found in Joshua (Yeshua and Mekonah) would tend to favor his selection of sites occupied in his own time from Joshua 15, which he then supplemented with two additional, contemporaneous sites he knew existed in the region.

Summary. It appears that the list of settlements for Benjamin and Judah in Neh. 11.25-35 has been heavily shaped by ideological concerns. It ostensibly reflects settlements known to the author at the time of composition, but does not accurately record the boundaries of Yehud in his own day. Instead, it has been influenced by Deuteronomistic views of the territory that had belonged to the kingdom of Judah and also by the anti-Gibeonite bias in that same work. The placing of the northernmost border for the new Yehud at Bethel may well have been a result of the claim that Josiah had shut down its impure cult in 2 Kgs 23.15, which in turn carried the implication that he had been able to move the boundary of Judah north beyond the traditional point at Geva to Bethel. Persian-era settlement at Bethel is likely; however, it can be noted that there was no Persian occupation at nearby Ai (et-Tell), in spite of its inclusion in v. 31 (Callaway 1993: 40). Thus, either the location of Ai was moved away from et-Tell in the Persian period to a nearby location, which might account for the variation in name as Ai/Aiya, or this is one more detail that betrays the idealized nature of the portrait presented in Neh. 11.25-35.

More significantly, there has been an artificial inclusion of the Negev within the southern bounds of Yehud, indicated by the use of Josh. 15.21-32 as a source for the list of nine sites south of Hevron, and the Jordan Rift Valley has been excluded from the territory of Yehud. Yet excavations at Jericho and 'En-Gedi have provided firm proof of the occupation of both sites in the fifth century BCE and their association with the province of Yehud. Both sites have yielded jars stamped with the legend *Yehud* (see below for details). Thus, it must be concluded that Neh. 11.25-35 does not reflect the boundaries of the province at the time of Artaxerxes I.

Section Summary. The originator of the list in Neh. 11.25-35 may have used Neh. 7.6-38 as a source in addition to Joshua 15. Although we saw there were some shared ideological outlooks in the two lists, there were also differences, which suggest that they derive from different hands and so have not been drawn from the same underlying source by a single author. The creator of 11.25-35 seems to have been motivated by a desire to have the borders of Persian Yehud overlap with the borders of the kingdom of Judah during the reign of Josiah. Not finding the Negev (or Shephelah) included in 7.6-38, he used the list of sites in the Negev in Joshua 15.21-32 to rectify this gap. In this case, however, the possibility remains open that the Negev had been part of the province of Yehud in the time of Artaxerxes I.

Ideological motivations seem to have led the author of Neh. 7.6-38 to limit the settlements of the *golah* community to the tribal area of Benjamin and the immediate vicinity of Jerusalem in the time of Nehemiah. The source he used to create his list of towns may well have included Negev sites, but he excluded them in his desire to associate the *golah* with Israel. Similarly, the list of the places of origin of the labor force that rebuilt the walls of Jerusalem in Nehemiah 3 is incomplete and may reflect the use of selective provincial labor to rebuild Jerusalem. Many settlements in Benjamin are not included, raising the possibility that their manpower was diverted to building projects elsewhere in the province, especially the construction and refurbishment of miliary posts in more outlying, under-populated southern areas. We must concede that the biblical texts do not preserve any accurate record of the boundaries of the province of Yehud during the reign of Artaxerxes I.

The Artifactual Evidence
Three sets of stamped jars have been found within the territory of Yehud that might potentially supply information about the extent of the province at the time of the use of each set.

m(w)sh-Stamped Jars. The earliest jar stamps read *m(w)sh*, which is the name of a site that was located due west of Jerusalem at Qaluniya . It is now becoming a common assumption that jars bearing these seals were part of the administrative distribution of some sort of foodstuff within the Neo-Babylonian province of Yehud (so, e.g., Zorn, Yellin and Hayes 1994: 182-83; Lipschits 1998: 475; Stern 2001: 335; Edelman 2004). Forty-three examples of jars with these stamps are known to date.

Figure 42.   *m(w)sh-stamp*
E. Stern, *Material Culture of the Land of the Bible in the Persian Period 538–332 B.C.* (Warminster: Aris & Phillips; Jerusalem: Israel Exploration Society, 1982): 208. (Drawn by the author.)

Thirty come from Mizpah, the district capital of Yehud under the Neo-Babylonians. The rest come from Gibeon (4), Ramat Rahel (1), Jericho (2) Jerusalem (4), Belmont Castle (1), and one of unknown provenance (Zorn, Yellin and Hayes 1994: 164-65). The site the furthest south is

Ramat Rahel, which is just south of Jerusalem. Thus, the stamps appear in a fairly circumspect area. Either they represent a limited distribution of whatever commodity they contained, or they indicate that the southern border of Neo-Babylonian Yehud was just south of Jerusalem (so, e.g., Lipschits 1998: 480). They provide ambiguous testimony for the southern boundary of Yehud at this time. Perhaps when more sites in the Judean hill-country and the south Samarian hill-country in the Occupied West Bank are excavated, we will be able to understand their distribution pattern more fully.

The function of these jars has been disputed. Nahman Avigad has proposed three possible functions: (1) they contained taxes-in-kind that were stored at the administrative center at Mozah; (2) they represented a local trademark identifying their contents, such as a special quality of wine, oil, honey, or the like, which was sent to market in stamped jars and eventually made subject to local taxes, or (3) they contained the contents of foodstuffs (olive oil and wine) produced at the crown estate located at Mizpah, whose incomes went to the Persian satrap (1958: 118-19). Frank M. Cross adopted the second proposal, arguing that the jars contained wine produced at Mozah (1969: 22-23), while Ephraim Stern adopted the third proposal: the stamps marked a food product produced at Mozah, which was one of many 'tax-exempt governor's estates' that existed in Yehud in the Neo-Babylonian and Persian periods (1982: 209).

All three proposals have drawbacks. It is unlikely that a second administrative center would have been established so close to Mizpah in the compact region of Benjamin. If the jars marked a special kind of local produce, why have no similar, contemporary stamps been found from other regions to mark their specialties? Finally, if the jars marked foodstuffs from one of many crown estates, why have we no similar, contemporary stamps from the other crown estates?[15] I have recently argued that the jars contain olive oil that had been processed at Mozah from olives that had been harvested using corvée labor from groves located in the uninhabited areas of the Shephelah (2004). Mozah had housed the olive presses used to produce oil from raw materials gathered from provincial land; the resulting oil would have belonged to the government storehouses of the province and would have been used as part of the food rations available for distribution to qualifying administrative personnel. If the number of stamps does not increase dramatically in future years after ongoing excavations, however, then I would need to modify my proposal, which presumes the large-scale production of olive oil similar to, but on a smaller scale than, the industry established at Ekron between 701–605 BCE. In this case, I would change my suggestion and propose that Mozah had been the private estate of a governor of Yehud and that the olive oil and wine contained in the jars marked the harvests of his private estate that he and his family members had used on various occasions in various sites within the province.

Animal-stamped Jars. A second set of vessels bear animal impressions, usually a lion in one of four stances (Stern 1982: 209-13). Sixty-six had been recovered as of 1982 from excavations at the following sites, with the quantity indicated in parentheses: Shechem (1), Mizpah (Tell en-Nasbeh) (5), Gibeon (2), Mozah/Qaluniya (1), Jerusalem (6), Ramat Rahel (45), Jericho (1), and 'En-Gedi (5).

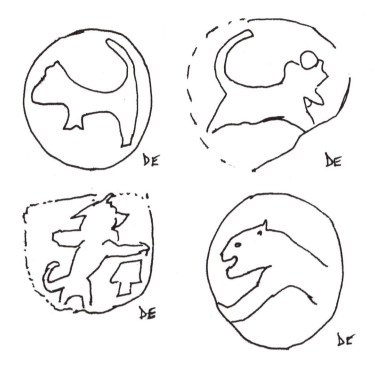

Figure 43. *Animal stamps*

E. Stern, *Material Culture of the Land of the Bible in the Persian Period 538–332 B.C.* (Warminster: Aris & Phillips; Jerusalem: Israel Exploration Society, 1982): 210-11. (Drawn by the author.)

While there is much overlap with the distribution of the *m(w)ṣh*-stamped jars, there is a definite shift toward Ramat Rahel, ancient Bet-Hakkerem, as the main recipient of the foodstuffs contained therein, as opposed to Mizpah, the district capital under the Neo-Babylonians. The lion imagery in particular recalls Persian royal iconography and may indicate that the foodstuffs distributed in the jars were either part of a rations system for administrative and military personnel or that they derived from a local estate that had been granted to a Persian who had been posted to Yehud to oversee its development and smooth operation. If their number remains relatively small after ongoing future excavations in Persian-era levels at various sites, then the second option would be preferable.

Ramat Rahel (ancient Bet-Hakkerem?) also yielded a jar bearing a seal impression that reads Yehud Hananiah, and a bulla with the same impression (see illustrations 1 and 2). As discussed in chapter 1, this Hananiah is likely to have been the Hananiah who was made *sar* of the fortress in Jerusalem. Both impressions come from fill or eroded deposits that may have washed down from a higher terrace onto the floor of a room, however, and so it cannot be demonstrated conclusively that they belong to the same chronological horizon. However, a date in the lengthy reign of Artaxerxes I (465–424 BCE) is likely and is consistent with the use of *pelek* labor-force under the leadership of Malkiyah the son of Rekav from Bet-Hakkerem to help rebuild a section of the city walls (Neh. 3.14).

The distribution of the animal-stamped jars is wider than that of the *m(w)ṣh*-stamped jars. Notably, they extend as far south as 'En-Gedi, an oasis that lies at the foot of the Judean foothills in the Jordan Rift Valley about halfway down the western shore of the Dead Sea. In addition, there is a single stamp from Shechem, located well into the province of Samerina. This latter example could have been the result of someone carrying food supplies while on a mission into the neighboring province, like the stray stamp that has been found at Nineveh, in Mesopotamia.

'En-Gedi does not appear anywhere in the book of Nehemiah or other Persian-era biblical literature. It is listed as one of the settlements in the wilderness of Judah in the tribal allotments in Josh. 15.62, which would be consistent with the group of buildings found there that date from c. 625–580 BCE, though the destruction date needs to be lowered closer to c. 550 BCE. The founding of the Persian-era settlement uncovered at Tell el-Jurn/Tel Goren, stratum IV, has been dated to 500–450 BCE, with a proposed destruction date c. 400 BCE. The pottery includes a small portion that is typical of the preceding stratum V, which was in existence in the Neo-Babylonian period, together with hallmark Persian-era sherds decorated with triangular, wedge-shaped and reed impressions and imported Attic ware. In addition to the animal stamp, two Aramaic ostraca were found as well as jar handles stamped with the legends *yhwd, yhd,* and *yh* in Aramaic. All three designate the province of Yehud (Mazar 1993: 402). Thus, it is plausible to view 'En-Gedi as a settlement that fell within the jurisdiction of Yehud, rather than Idumea, on the basis of the five animal-stamped jars found there and the three Yehud-stamped jars.

In addition, there is a stamp impression that reads *b'*, which I would tentatively associate with the governor of Yehud, Bagohi, whom we know from the Elephantine papyri was in office in 410 BCE (see illustration 25). The termination of Persian-era occupation at 'En-Gedi c. 400 BCE would fit well within the framework of the creation of Idumea as an independent province around this time and the resettlement of its inhabitants/personnel within the new borders of Yehud. Noting the imprecision of dating on the basis of ceramics, the date of destruction/abandonment could be lowered another twenty-five years without a problem. Should one choose, on the other hand, to locate 'En-Gedi within the territory of Idumea, then the two stamps would provide evidence that this territory had been administered by Jerusalem prior to 400 BCE.

The Yhd, Yhwd *and* Yh-*Stamped Jars.* The final sets of stamps to consider are those that bear the provincial name in Aramaic, spelled either *yhd, yhwd* with an internal vowel marker, or abbreviated as *yh*. We have already seen that one of each type was found at 'En-Gedi in the Persian-era stratum. In addition, examples have been uncovered as of 1982 from Jericho, Ramat Rahel, Mizpah/Tell en-Nasbeh, Mozah/Qaluniyah, Ophel outside of Jerusalem, the Tyropoeon Valley outside of Jerusalem, and Tell el-Ful (Stern 1982: 203) and one is also now known from Gezer (Stern 2001: 431). They thus have a similar geographical spread to the animal stamps. Only additional excavations, especially in the Shephelah and the central and southern Judean hill-country will help us understand the full range of their distribution.

Figure 44   Yhd, Yhwd *and* Yh-*stamps*
            N. Avigad, *Bullae and Seals from a Post-Exilic Judean Archive* (Qedem 5; Jerusa-
            lem: The Insitute of Archaeology, The Hebrew University of Jerusalem, 1976): 2.
            Reproduced by kind permission of the Israel Exploration Society.

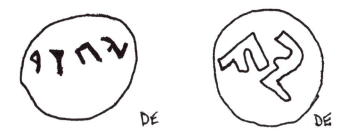

E. Stern, *Material Culture of the Land of the Bible in the Persian Period 538–332
B.C.* (Warminster: Aris & Phillips; Jerusalem: Israel Exploration Society, 1982): 203-
204. (Drawn by the author.)

The date of this series of stamped jars is uncertain, as is their function. While some have
assigned their initial introduction to the sixth century BCE, a majority of scholars favor a date of
introduction in the fifth century, while a minority position would see their introduction only in
the fourth century BCE (for a convenient summary, see Stern 1982: 205). The fact that a number
have been excavated in Jerusalem tends to favor a date after about 450 BCE, when the city had
been rebuilt as the provincial seat. Since they bear the name of the province, it is likely that they
contained foodstuffs that had been paid as taxes-in-kind and were being redistributed to those
who were entitled to receive government food rations. However, the possibility cannot be ruled
out that they contained foodstuffs that had been harvested from provincial lands using corvée
labor instead of from private lands, representing the percentage of the annual yield owed in
taxes. We know very little about the inner workings of Persian provincial administration, which
may have varied regionally.

Section Summary. The three sets of stamped jars do not provide us with any more reliable
information than the biblical texts about the boundaries of Yehud under Artaxerxes I. While
they constitute evidence for the existence of some sort of provincial administration in the Neo-
Babylonian and early Persian periods, we cannot be certain that any of them was used during
the reign of Artaxerxes I. In addition, since we do not know the full extent of their distribution
yet, due to the large number of unexcavated sites in the southern Judean hills, the Shephelah,

and Negev, and since we do not know their specific purpose(s) either, it is impossible to know if their distribution is likely to reflect the boundaries of the province or not.

If, for example, the jars contained government food rations used by civil officials and administrative personnel, then their find spots would likely reflect places where such personnel had been stationed. However, these sites might not have lain at the boundary points of the kingdom. If, on the other hand, they also were used by military personnel, then we could expect them to turn up in forts and relay stations and so reflect the strategic points of the province as well as its borders perhaps. However, since we are dealing with a province within an empire and not an independent kingdom, there may not have been a perceived need to secure the borders of an internal administrative unit, unless one or more of those borders adjoined a region that lay outside of the provincial system. Thus, even if some of the rations were used by military personnel, we cannot assume that the distribution of the jars reveals the provincial boundaries of Yehud at the time these jars were in use. We also need to acknowledge the possibility that some of these jars were used secondarily so that their final find spots may not reflect accurately the original site distribution for which they were intended. The possibility of secondary use makes the find spots even harder to correlate with Yehud's borders at any given time.

The Status of the Coastal Plain around Lod and Ono in the Mid-Fifth Century BCE

The inclusion of the towns of Lod, Ono and Hadid in both Neh. 7.37 and 11.34 requires us to consider whether this coastal region was made an integral part of Yehud as early as the time of Artaxerxes I or only later on. Even though, as we have seen, neither list in ch. 7 or 11 accurately reflects the boundaries of Yehud during this monarch's reign, it is extremely difficult to devise a strategy to test when this region might have been added. It lay outside the traditional boundaries of Benjamin and Judah so an appeal to earlier tribal lists, which, in the case of the Negev towns, helped us to argue that a secondary borrowing was likely, will not work in this instance.

Nehemiah 11.35 reports that Ono and Lod constituted the 'Valley of the Craftsmen'. Menashe Har-El has pointed out that the term 'craftsman' is generally used in the Hebrew Bible to refer to one of three occupations: stone-dressing, wood-working, and metal-smithing. Noting that the Sharon region, which includes Ono and Lod, contained a forest of Tabor oak in antiquity, he concludes that metal-smithing was what was practised in this region, even though he cites no evidence of smelting or refining remains in support of his idea (1977: 79-86). It is hard to believe that because the Gilead region was heavily forested and would have provided a ready source of charcoal for the process, unprocessed ore would have been shipped overland from the 'Ajlun region of Gilead to be processed in the coastal plain (1977: 83-85). It seems more appropriate to conclude that the region's primary industry was wood-working or stone-dressing.

A survey of the Lod region has revealed evidence for ancient quarrying at a number of sites. These include: Bareqet (1456 1581), Khirbet el-Bireh south (1468 1583), Khirbet Burnat (1469 1576), Shoham (1444 1566 [Byz]; 1451 1576), Nahal Beit Arif (1466 1555), el-Khirba (1455 1569), Horvat Tinshemet south (1467 1559), Horvat Nevallet (east) (1466 1548) and southeast (1465 1542), Khirbet Beit Kufa (north) (1467 1535), el-Haditha (west) (1441 1523) southwest (1447 1520) northwest (1452 1528) and south (1455 1524), and Abu el-Hubban (1465 1525).

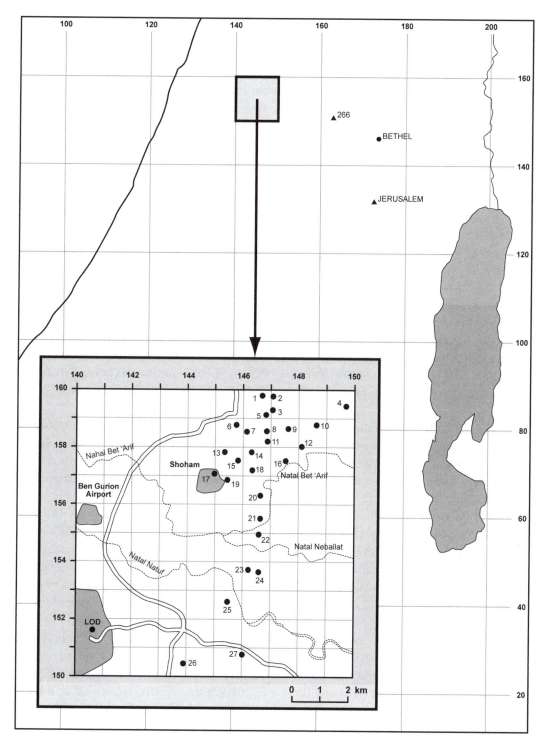

Figure 45. *Map of Lod and Ono settlements*

They all lie at the edge of the foothills where they adjoin the coastal plain. Modern quarrying has been carried out near Haditha southwest and Tirat Yehuda. Some of the older quarries seem to be attributable to the Byzantine period, but others are older (Gophna and Beit Arieh 1997). Thus, it would be possible to argue that the main attraction of the Valley of the Craftsmen was good-quality limestone and dolomite for stone-working (Gophna and Beit-Arieh 1997: 10*). The abundance of oak as well may have meant that both stone masons and woodworkers were drawn to the area to ply their trades and that the name arose from two industries rather than one.

Opinions vary on whether and when this region that contained the Valley of the Craftsmen became a part of the province of Yehud/Judea. Many think that it was only under the Hasmoneans, in the second century BCE, that this area would have been incorporated into the territory of Judea (e.g. Avi-Yonah 1966: 28-31; Aharoni 1979: 416 and ft. 125; Ofer 1993: 38*; Lipschits 1997). Another group, however, argue for its inclusion already during the monarchy. George A. Smith, for example, suggested that it was settled by Judahites as early as the time of Saul, the first king of Israel, c. 1000 BCE (1896: 161-62 n. 1). Zecharia Kallai (1986: 373 n. 89; 399, 495), Maxwell Miller and John Hayes (1986: 401) and Gösta Ahlström (1993: 765), on the other hand, have argued it first became Judahite when Josiah expanded the borders of the kingdom of Judah slightly north and allegedly also considerably west, as far as the fort at Mesad Hashayahu on the coast, c. 630–620 BCE. Albrecht Alt (1925: 110-111) and Ulrich Kellermann had already argued for a Josianic date prior to the discovery of the coastal fort (1966: 224) on the basis of the biblical text alone. Ram Gophna and Itzhaq Beit Arieh include it within the Persian province of Yehud (1997: 11*), as does Ephraim Stern (2001: 431).

It is very difficult to determine whether Mesad Hashavyahu was built and administered by the king of Egypt (so, e.g., Naveh 1962b: 99; Na'aman 1991: 46-47), by the king of Judah (so, e.g., Cross 1962: 42; Naveh 1962b: 98; Amusin and Heltzer 1964: 156), or by the latter in his capacity as a vassal of the former. The ostracon written in Hebrew that petitions the *sar* to return the cloak that was confiscated under false charges of failing to complete the daily quota of work in the fields need not indicate that the fort was Judahite (Naveh 1960; Yeivin 1962; Cross 1962: 42-46; Amusin and Heltzer 1964). It only indicates that Judahite corvée labor was being used to harvest fields near the fort (e.g. Mendelsohn 1962: 34; Amusin and Heltzer 1964: 156, though all three assume the fort was also Judahite).[16] Such a situation could have arisen from Judah having been the vassal of Egypt (Na'aman 1991: 46-47). It is known that Psammetichus I, king of Egypt (664–610 BCE), invaded Cisjordan as neo-Assyrian power waned in the region and re-established Egyptian control there briefly for the first time since the tenth century BCE. The fort may have been manned by Greek mercenaries employed by the Egyptian king. There is a lot of imported Greek pottery in the Middle Wild Goat style at the site, whose flourit was c. 630–600 BCE, and Herodotus reports that this pharaoh hired Greek and Carian mercenaries (2.152, 154). At the same time, it is possible that Josiah, as a vassal, had been ordered to supply food for the fort and so sent Judahite corvée labor to harvest the adjoining fields. It is premature to conclude that Josiah expanded his western border all the way to the coast on the basis of the Hebrew ostracon from Mesad Hashavyahu. The idea that he added

Lod, Ono and the Valley of the Craftsmen to his domain at this time is founded on shaky ground that is best avoided for fear of it giving way underfoot.

1 Chronicles 8.12 reports that Lod and Ono were settled by Shemed/Shemer, the son of Elpaal. It can be argued, but not proven, that the context implies the resettlement of the area in the post-exilic period (so, e.g., Abel 1967: 370) and does not refer to the initial settlement of the area during the monarchic era when it first came under the control of Israel or Judah or settlement in the seventh century during the time when the region was prosperous and free from war under the neo-Assyrians (Na'aman 1991: 49-50). When such settlement took place in the post-exilic period, however, remains an open question. At most, it might imply that by the Chronicler's day, such settlement had taken place but that he wanted to suggest that it had occurred when the *golah* group had first 'returned' with Zerubbabel and Yeshua. In this case, we could date the movement of Jews to these towns anywhere from 450 BCE to 250 BCE, depending on what date is favored for the Chronicler.

Oded Lipschits has argued that there was such movement in the early Persian period, but not as the result of the settlement of newly-arrived members of the *golah* in these areas. Instead, he argues that people who had never experienced exile, whose ancestors had lived in Benjamin under the Neo-Babylonians, decided to move out of Yehud after the arrival sometime between 538–520 BCE of the *golah* group. They objected to the policies put in place by the new government and so fled the jurisdiction (1997).

In this connection, the mention that Sanballat asked Nehemiah to meet together with him in one of the villages in the plain of Ono is interesting (Neh. 6.1-9). Many have assumed that this proposed meeting was to take place in neutral territory outside the jurisdiction of both men, within the province of Ashdod. However, it might be wondered whether instead, the purpose of the meeting would have been to discuss disputed villages in this region, due, perhaps, to the recent arrival of an influx of settlers from Benjamin into towns that belonged to Samerina. Could the governors of Samerina and Yehud have met in territory belonging to Ashdod without official permission from the local governor?

Alternatively, the settlement of Shemed/Shemer could be assigned to the Hasmonean period in light of the widespread argument that Lod and Ono lay within one of the three districts that Demetrius II reassigned from adjoining provinces to Judea in 145 BCE (1 Macc. 11.34, 57). It needs to be noted, however, that the explicit names of the three districts are not given in 1 Maccabees 11. Nevertheless, it is commonly assumed that they were the districts of Lod/Lydda, perhaps belonging originally to Ashdod, and Haramatha and Apharaema, which had belonged to Samerina (so, e.g., Avi Yonah 1966: 56). While it is probable that the area around the Valley of the Craftsmen was formally ceded to Judea at this time, we cannot assume it to be hard fact. And, it does not rule out the possibility that Jews could have settled earlier or even that this area had been controlled by Yehud at a previous point and been lost and regained. It has been suggested, for example, that the region might have been assigned to Yehud for a time by Alexander the Great and that Hasmonean claims to the area may have been based on this earlier grant (Lipschits 1997; 2004: 180).

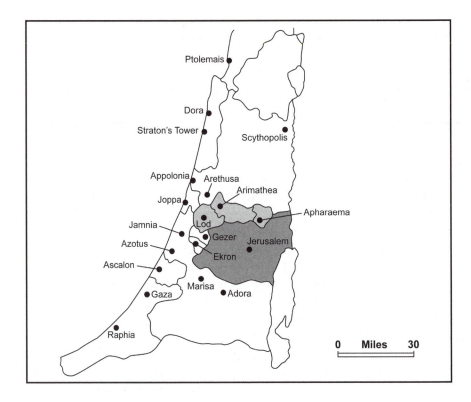

Figure 46.   *The districts of Lydda, Haramatha and Apharaema, thought to have been ceded to Jonathan*

A survey of the region of Lod has revealed extensive settlement in the Persian period. Twenty-eight sites were occupied in the western foothills of Mt Ephraim; none lay on the coastal plain proper. Of these, only four were newly founded in the Persian period; the remaining twenty-four were at sites that had been villages or farmsteads already in the preceding Iron II period (Gophna and Beit-Arieh 1997: 11*). Without excavation, however, it is not possible to determine if the settlement had been continuous and uninterrupted or whether there had been a gap in occupation and an influx of new settlers in the Persian period, most of whom chose to reoccupy former sites where they could renovate and which already had water cisterns dug so they would not need to begin from scratch (contra Gophna and Beit-Arieh 1997: 11*). It can be noted that settlement dwindled over time and that there were only nineteen sites occupied in the Hellenistic period, mostly at places that had already been established in the Persian period or earlier (Gophna and Beit Arieh 1997: 11*).

It is likely that some of the twenty-eight Persian sites were occupied in the mid-fifth century, so we need to try to determine whether they would have been counted as part of the province of Samerina, or Yehud, or possibly of the coastal province of Ashdod. Since they lay in the foothills, it makes more geographic sense to associate them with the western limits of either of the first two hill-country provinces. However, it is hard to know whether provinces were arranged strictly on the basis of geographical considerations, or whether economic considerations might have led to the deliberate incorporation of a range of mico-environmental niches in a province when possible, to allow for a greater range of diversity in resources and the spreading of risk factors over more crops and raw materials. Nadav Na'aman has argued, for example, that according to an inscription of the neo-Assyrian king Esarhaddon, Aphek, located in the coastal plain of Sharon north of Lod and Ono, lay within the province of Samerina (1995: 107). Thus, it would be possible to argue that Lod and Ono, also in the coastal plain, had remained part of Samerina in the Neo-Babylonian and Persian periods.

There is no easy way to resolve the issue of which province this area may have fallen within at the time of Artaxerxes. Perhaps when more excavations are done, some of the three forms of stamped jars will turn up that will give a more of an insight into the history of the area, although their presence will not automatically signal that the area was controlled by Yehud. As seen, sometimes these stamps end up well outside the boundaries of Yehud, probably as containers of provisions that were used en route.[17] Similarly, any ostraca found with personal names will not give a firm indication of administrative control since Yahwistic names could indicate a connection to Samerina or to Yehud, and it is likely that Jews were settled in this area, even if it were part of the province of Ashdod at some point in time. The pottery repertoire will be of some assistance in sorting out whether the population tended to use coastal forms or inland forms, however, and an analysis of the clay and inclusions used in their production will point to the location of the clay beds, which might help indicate their provincial affiliation.

On the basis of the current information, it seems best to exclude Lod and Ono, and any other sites that may be found on the coastal plain proper, from having been part of the province of Yehud during the time of Artaxerxes. It is likely that the lowland region was added in 145 BCE during the reign of Jonathan the Hasmonean. The fort at Mesad Hashavyahu is not unequivocally Judahite; it more likely was Egyptian, and there is no firm proof, textual or archaeological, that Josiah expanded the boundaries of Judah into the coastal plain. Thus, it is best not to assume that Lod and Ono were already included in the province of Yehud when its borders were initially established in 586 BCE by the Neo-Babylonians in the wake of the demise of the kingdom of Judah.

There is, however, a reason to exclude the twenty-eight farmsteads in the western foothills from lying within Yehud's provincial territory at the time the province was redeveloped by Artaxerxes I. They all lay north (and west) of Bethel, which appears to have been the northern limit of Yehud. Thus, it is more logical to assume that they fell within the jurisdiction of Samerina, representing the southwestern extent of settlement of Sinuballit's jurisdiction in the mid-fifth century BCE.

The Borders of Idumea

A number of the settlements listed under the heading of the people of Judah fell within the boundaries of Idumea in the Hellenistic period. The earliest reference to Idumea as an independent administrative and territorial unit is found in Diodorus Siculus in his account of events that transpired in 312 BCE. In the Hellenistic period, the northern border of Idumea ran between Bet-Zur, which lay in Yehud, and Alouros (Halhul), which lay in Idumea, while the southern border included the line of fortifications at Arad, Malhata, Beersheva and Aroer. The latter is known as the limes of Herod as well as the limes Palastinae. Interestingly, it is uncertain if the eastern boundary was in the Judean desert or in the Jordan rift. The western limit abutted the holdings of Gaza, Ashkelon and Ashdod and so probably ended in the Shephelah (Hübner 1992: 382).

How early the province was founded is disputed. Ephraim Stern thinks it was created by the Neo-Babylonians and was located at this time in the southern Judean hills, while the Negev and Edom were ruled alongside Gaza by Qedarite Arabs (1990: 221). Siegfried Herrmann, on the other hand, seems to think that it was created by the Persians c. 450 BCE, when the palace at Lakish was constructed as its capital. The Edomites had already controlled this territory, however, under the Neo-Babylonians, having been given control after 586 BCE (1975: 315, 324). Others date its creation to c. 400 BCE, in the wake of Egypt's successful rebellion against the Persian king, which moved the new southern boundary of the empire to the Beersheva Valley (e.g. Sapin 2004: 109-10; N. Na'aman, oral communication). A date at the beginning of the fourth century is also favored by C.H.J. de Geus, but in response to an increase of population in the Negev and southern Judah that made it profitable to impose taxation, combined with the rise to importance in the region of the Qedarites combined with the Nabateans. He thinks that the Hellenistic cities of Marissa and Gerar in the Shephelah were also transferred to the new province from the province of Ashdod (1979/80: 62). Of these options, I find Idumea's establishment about 400 BCE in response to the loss of Egypt the most plausible argument; however, it leaves open the status of this territory from the end of the kingdom of Judah in 586 until 400 BCE.

There are thirteen sites in Neh. 11.25-30 that fall within this Idumean territory. They include: Elam (Khirbet Beit 'Alam), Lakish, Kiryat-Arba (Hevron), Divon (probably a corruption of Devir or Dimonah), Yekavzeel, Yeshua, Moladah, Bet-Pelet, Hazar-Shual, Beersheva, Ziklag, Mekonah, and En-rimmon. This is two of the six sites in the lowlands and all of the sites in the extreme south. The crucial fact to determine, therefore, is when Idumea was established as a province in its own right. Specifically, we need to try to determine if the boundaries of Yehud initially encompassed the region that later became the separate administrative unit of Idumea and, therefore, if the Negev needs to be included in our survey of settlement patterns in Chapter 5.

Two Historical Scenarios Based on Nehemiah

Returning to our original three lists in Nehemiah 3, 7.25-42 and 11.25-36, let us consider which is the southernmost point within each. For Nehemiah 3, it is Bet-Zur, unless Pahat-Moab was located further south. For Neh. 7.25-42 it is Elam, if it has been correctly equated with Khirbet Beit 'Alam; otherwise, it, too, would be Bet-Zur. In Neh. 11.25-36, it is Beersheva.

This data can be reconstructed in two different ways. In one, the southern boundary for Yehud would have been set at Bet-Zur at the time that the provincial capital was moved to Jerusalem to implement new Persian policy, with the territory to the south being assigned to the province of Idumea. The assigning of thirteen towns of Idumea to the people of Judah in Neh. 11.25-30 would have been motivated by a desire to portray the borders of Persian Yehud to have coincided with those of Josiah's kingdom in 2 Kgs 23.8.[18]

In the second reconstruction, the boundary for Yehud would have been established at Beersheva at the time of the reconstruction of Jerusalem, when a possible change in Persian policy for the region was implemented. This may or may not have been the border already inherited from the Neo-Babylonian administration of the region. A southern boundary at Beersheva would be reflected in the list of sites in Neh. 11.25-30, though this list need not date from the reign of Artaxerxes I; it might reflect historical conditions before the creation of Idumea or might be reflect a desire to have the southern border of Persian Yehud coincide with the Deuteronomistic portrayal of the southern extent of the kingdom of Josiah.[19] This scenario would be consistent with the inclusion of Elam in Neh. 7.34, which lay south of Bet-Zur. In time, but perhaps right away, the territory just south of Bet-Zur to Beersheva would have been made a sub-district of the province for administrative purposes.

The primary role of groups living there would have been to produce food surpluses to be used by the administration as necessary, to man the few military and postal installations in the region, and oversee the safe passage of caravans along the routes through the territory. Any settlement located north of Beersheva would have lain within territory that received at least 200 millimeters (c. twelve inches) of rain annually, the minimum required for successful farming based on rainfall alone, without irrigation. Although there would have been years when crop yields would have been minimal or would have failed, in theory, all settlements would have been viable for producing grain, and those to the north of the Beersheva Valley could also have grown olives and grapes.

In order to choose between the two alternatives, some means of determining the boundaries of Yehud under the Neo-Babylonian administration needs to be considered, as well as evidence that might indicate whether sites within Idumea would ever have been administered by Jerusalem or not. Data from a number of sources is available to help with this task. We will begin by considering the status of the Negev at the end of the monarchy, using biblical texts, ostraca written in Aramaic that have been found at various Negev sites, and survey and excavation results that have uncovered the presence of Edomite and Arab pottery at a number of sites.

The Negev at the End of the Monarchy and Thereafter

The Biblical Texts

Various biblical prophetical texts suggest that there was hostility between Edom and Judah at the end of the monarchic period. It is noteworthy that there is no hostility reflected in the book of Zephaniah, whose prophecies seem to date to the reign of Josiah (c. 640–609 BCE). But clear animosity between Edom and Judah appears in literature that can confidently be dated to the closing years of the monarchy and the Neo-Babylonian period (Ezekiel) and the Neo-Babylonian and/or early Persian period (Malachi, Third Isaiah, and Obadiah).[20]

Ezekiel. In Ezek. 25.12-14, Edom is characterized as having taken revenge against the house of Judah. According to 35.10, Edom has claimed ownership of the land although Yahweh was there. And in 35.5, Edom is accused of having given the people of Israel over to the power of the sword at the time of their calamity, while in v. 12, they were to have said of Judah, 'They are laid desolate, they are given to us to devour'. These verses express the view either that Edom abetted the demise of Judah by letting it be given over to the sword of others, looted after the destruction, and then took over the land, or that it participated actively in the demise and looting before taking possession of the land.

The aftermath of the occupation seems to be reflected in Isa. 63.1-9, which is thought to date from the early Persian period, either just before or soon after the arrival of the Zerubbabel group to Yehud. Here, Yahweh is depicted to have personally and single-handedly destroyed Bozrah, the seat of Edom, for the sake of his people. No human agents are involved in this 'massacre'; Yahweh appears from Edom in bloody garments after his 'deed'. This scene may be wishful thinking on the part of the author, but in any case, it reflects the belief that Bozrah, the seat of Edom, had done something terrible to Yahweh's people, which the deity was now rectifying for the sake of his people. In the context of the imminent or recent arrival of the new Jewish settlers from Babylonia in Yehud, this vision could either reflect a desired future reversal of Edom's control over part of the former land of Judah or its recent reversal by the king of Persia as part of his plans for the development of the province of Yehud.

Malachi. In Mal. 1.4, Edom says, 'We are beaten down, but we will return and rebuild the ruins'. In response, Yahweh declares, 'They may rebuild but I will tear down'. This saying seems to reflect a situation in which Edom has lost control of Judahite territory against its own volition, but hopes to regain it in the future. Yahweh is reassuring his constituents that this will never happen. Thus, this verse might testify to the return of some portion of the former territory of Judah from Edomite oversight to Yehudite control, either by Persian writ or by Yehudite aggressiveness.

Obadiah. Obadiah offers the longest testimony of events that took place at the time that Jerusalem was destroyed in 586 BCE. Edom is characterized as Judah's brother, who stood aloof without offering aid and gloated over Judah's fate, but then entered the gates and looted, like the foreigners. It also is accused of having cut off Judahite fugitives and delivered them up on the day of their distress. After a predicted total annihilation of the house of Esau, it is asserted that the Negev shall possess Mount Esau, those in the Shephelah shall possess the land of the Philistines (and) shall possess the land of Ephraim and of Samaria, while Benjamin shall possess Gilead. Finally, the exiles of the army of the sons of Israel who are in Canaan as far as Zarephat/Zarepta and the exiles of Jerusalem who are in Sepharad shall possess the cities of the Negev. Saviors shall go up to Mount Zion to rule Mount Esau.

This version of events is the most explicit of all found in the prophetic literature. It suggests that Edom and Judah had been allies, but that Edom did not come to Judah's assistance in 586 BCE. It looted in the aftermath of the Babylonian conquest and handed over fugitives to the Neo-Babylonians, or perhaps, took them as captives that they sold on as slaves. It took control of the Negev and possibly part of the Shephelah; the Philistines may have taken over some, or all, of the Shephelah as well. The hope is expressed that Yehud will once more take over control of the Negev and the Shephelah.

This sequence of prophetical texts provides cumulative evidence that Edom took control of the Negev and perhaps also part of Shephelah after the destruction of 586 BCE (contra Bartlett 1982: 18-21). This implies in turn that they did so with the blessing of their Neo-Babylonian overlords, perhaps as a reward for not having honored their alliance with Judah and aided them during their revolt or during the Neo-Babylonian siege of Jerusalem. Even so, Edom eventually lost control of these territories to Yehud in the Persian period.

There are some interesting correlations between Obadiah vv. 19-21 and the list of the settlements of Benjamin and Judah in Neh. 11.25-36. Those in the Negev will possess Mount Esau, while those in the Shephelah will expand west to possess the land of the Philistines and north to take over the field land of Ephraim and of Samaria. Those in Benjamin shall possess Gilead. Here the two major ecological zones of Judah that share boundaries with other nations are expected to expand from their initial bases and occupy foreign territory in time, while Benjamin is to expand eastward into Transjordan.

Verse 20 makes the surprising claim that those who will repossess the Negev will be the exiles of the army[21] of the sons of Israel who are (in) Canaan as far as Sarepta, together with the Jerusalemite exiles in Sepharad. Sepharad is probably the city of Sardis on the River Hermus in ancient Lydia in Asia Minor, inland from the Ionian coast (Schrader 1888: 145 if a later addition; Wolff 1986: 63; Avalos 1992; Raabe 1996: 268 as one of two options), although it also has been equated with Hesperides, later Berenici (mod Benghazi) on the west coast of the Gulf of Suez, where Jewish mercenaries were stationed by the Ptolemies at the end of the fourth century BCE (e.g. Gray 1953: 57; Watts 1969: 66). According to Josephus, Ptolemy Lagos settled Jewish garrisons in Egypt and Cyrenaica (*Apion* 2.44). Additional, less plausible suggestions for its location include Spain and a site in western Media named Saparda (Schrader 1888: 146 if not a later addition; Gray 1953; Avalos 1992; Raabe 1996: 266-67). Both verses are in the future tense and indicate that Obadiah is envisioning an anticipated but as yet unaccomplished event.

The reference to the 'army' has been seen to be problematic and has led to a range of attempted interpretations and emendations of the phrase. This has been encouraged in part by the variant readings of the phrase in various manuscript traditions. The term in the Masoretic text is written *hhl*, which, technically speaking, means 'rampart' or possibly 'territory' (so Ben Zvi 1996: 220). However, the Aramaic Targums, the Latin Vulgate, the Syriac version, as well as manuscripts collated by Symmachus and Theodotion presume an underlying Hebrew text that read *hhyl*, in the sense of either 'army' of 'fort'. Apparently their translators assumed that the MT spelling of the word had left out the internal vowel marker (this meaning is adopted by, e.g., Thompson 1956: 866-67; Keller 1965: 262). Aquila, on the other hand, read this same underlying noun, but construed it in the rarer sense of 'property' (Bewer 1911: 44; Wolff 1986: 61). The possibility that this spelling could be interpreted as the adjective 'wealthy' instead of the noun 'army' has been raised but not adopted (Ben Zvi 1996: 217). The Septuagint presumes an underlying Hebrew text that read *hhl* but construed it as a *hiphil* infinitive from the root *hll*, meaning 'to begin', referring to the first group to be sent into exile. This interpretation has found some advocates (e.g. Wolff 1986: 61; Gray 1953: 53, who emends *hhl hzh* to *thlh zh*). Finally, two emendations have been proposed: (1) *hat(t)el* instead of *hahel*, which would mean the exiles of this 'tel' or city mound (e.g. Halévy 1907: 178-70) and (2) the rendering of *hhl hzh*, 'this rampart/territory/army' as *hlh zh*, 'Halah, that is', which requires the dropping of the initial *h* and a redivision of the remaining letters into two new words (e.g. Bewer 1911: 44-45; Rudolph 1931: 226; Horst 1964: 116; Watts 1969: 62-63). Halah was a site located northwest of Nineveh to which exiles from the northern kingdom were sent in 721 BCE (2 Kgs 17.6; 18.11).

Of this array of options, some can be eliminated on the basis of context clues and the principle of not emending a text unless it is impossible to make sense of the reading as it stands. Both proposed emendations can be rejected as unnecessary. In addition, the suggestion that the text refers to exiles sent to Halah presumes that the reference to the sons of Israel is to inhabitants of the former kingdom of Israel. This phrase, however, probably is being used to designate adherents to the new cult of Yahweh Elohim in Yehud, which had been introduced when the temple was rebuilt in Jerusalem. It is more likely that the phrase is being used to reflect the in-fighting within the Persian province of Yehud in the late-fifth or early-fourth century BCE, as reflected in the use of the term in the books of Ezra and Nehemiah, than to designate exiles of a kingdom that had disappeared in 721 BCE.

Of the remaining readings, all are possible, yet each is awkward. The reference needs to be construed in a context that can make sense of exiles from Judah or Yehud. Thus, the proposal by D. Barthélemy to understand 'this rampart' to refer to Samaria can be rejected (1992: 704). But it is hard to understand what a reference to 'the exiles of this rampart of the sons of Israel who are (in) Canaan as far as Sarepta' would mean if it was not talking about Jerusalem, which it cannot be because of the reference to the exiles of Jerusalem in Sepharad in the latter part of the verse. Thus, it seems better to opt for one of the three remaining meanings: 'the exiles of this army of the sons of Israel', 'the exiles of this territory of the sons of Israel, ' or 'the initial exiles of the sons of Israel'. In the latter case, the reference would seem to be to the deportations in 592 BCE.

No other biblical text indicates that members of the former Judahite army were reassigned to contingents elsewhere stationed in the coastal plain as far north as Zarephat/Sarepta, or that some of the Jerusalemite deportees were sent to Asia Minor. Nevertheless, these details are plausible. The Neo-Babylonian king Nebuchadrezzar (604–561 BCE) sent armies regularly to Hatti (Asia Minor) to control and collect tribute. Thus, it would have been possible for some of the captives removed from Jerusalem in 592 BCE or 586 BCE to have been sent there as settlers to break up local resistance. Tablets from Babylonia that date between 595–570 BCE mention the presence of captives, artisans, workmen, mariners and musicians from Judah (Yekoiakin and his five sons), Ashkelon (the sons of King Aga), Tyre, Geval, Arvad, Elam, Media, Ionia, Cilicia, and Lydia. The relocation of Judahite soldiers to Tyre, Geval or Arvad and of civilians to Lydia would be consistent with the areas from which Nebuchadrezzar had removed a segment of the native population to Babylon.

> It can be noted that a funerary stele has been found in Daskylium in the satrapy that adjoined Sparda/Sardes, which has been attributed to a wealthy Jewish family. It was dedicated by Elnaph, the son of either Eshyai or Eshyahu and is thought to date to c. 450 BCE (Dupont-Sommer 1966; Cross 1966; Lipiński 1973). While it does not prove there were Jews living in the adjoining satrapy of Sparda, it has been seen to confirm that Judahite or Judean exiles had been moved to Asia Minor (Lipiński 1973: 36).

> However, it is not certain that the final element of the father's name is *yahu*, reflecting the deity name Yahweh. The name might end in *y*, with the next word being *hu*, the masculine pronoun 'he'. It has been noted that Elnaph might be an Arab name, and Ishyai could also be Arab in origin (Dupont-Sommer 1966; Cross 1966: 9 n. 17). In this regard, it is significant that the deities Bel and Nabu are invoked on the stele to prevent passers-by from harming the tomb. This does not favor a

Jewish origin for either man. If both men were Arabs, one or both may have grown up in Babylonia, where they came to worship these deities, and were subsequently relocated to Asia Minor. Thus, this funerary stele does not provide clear evidence that Jews had been resettled in Daskylium.

Most scholars consider Obadiah vv. 19 and 20 to have come from the hand of a later editor, though they vary in the proposed date of its addition. Bert Dicou thinks they are the latest stage in the book's three-part development and were added in the early post-exilic period (late-sixth century BCE) (1994: 103-104). Hans Wolff (1986: 67), Alfons Deissler (1984) and Paul Raabe (1996: 17), on the other hand, consider the verses to be a commentary on v. 17b and to have been added no later than 400 BCE since they anticipate the return of exiles, which did not take place after the fifth century BCE. John Watts suggests a slightly later date, in the late-fourth century BCE, on the assumption that the exiles in Sepharad were placed in North Africa by the Ptolemies (1969: 68). A significant group, by contrast, considers some or all of vv. 15a, 16-21 to have been added in the Hasmonean period (e.g. Wellhausen 1893: 213; Duhm 1911: 178; Myers 1960: 150; Diebner and Schult 1975: 11, 13), possibly under Alexander Jannaeus (108–107 BCE). The latter consider it to have been a prophecy set back in time to anticipate the glory of the Hasmonean empire at its greatest territorial extent. However, Zarephat never lay within the Hasmonean boundaries, so this suggestion is implausible (e.g. Wolff 1986: 63). Those who consider the book to be a unity stemming from the prophet himself form a minority (e.g. Allen 1976; Stuart 1987).

If vv. 19-20 are a later addition, they would not necessarily reflect events that transpired at the end of the monarchy, so that the deportations could have taken place at a subsequent point in time. That would have to have been after the rebuilding of Jerusalem under Artaxerxes I, however, when there once again were soldiers or a rampart, and a civilian population to deport. There is no recorded incident that would serve as the likely referent in v. 19, however, so it seems logical to associate the two groups of exiles with people resettled in 586 BCE, whenever these verses were composed. The use of the phrase 'the sons of Israel' to describe members of the population of Yehud who identified with the belief system being represented by the rebuilt temple betrays the writer's setting in Yehud after c. 450 BCE.

Obadiah vv. 19-20 provide invaluable evidence that when the kingdom of Judah was turned into a province in 586 BCE, the Negev and the Shephelah were removed from its jurisdiction. The Negev was put under the control of Mount Esau, or Edom, while the Shephelah was either also ceded to Edom, or was added to the Philistine jurisdiction of Gaza and/or Ashkelon. Bearing this in mind, we must consider the possibility that the person responsible for the list of settlements of Judah in Neh. 11.31-36 has used Obadiah v. 19 as an additional source of inspiration for his depiction of the extent of settlement. This might also account for his failure to include any sites in the Jordan rift, which is not mentioned here, even though it would have formed the eastern boundary of both Judah and Yehud.

The Arad Ostraca in Hebrew from the Monarchic Era
Indication of Edom's more active participation in hostility against Judah at the end of the kingdom is found in one of the ostraca recovered from the Judahite fort at Arad, in the Negev. The reverse side of ostracon 24 is an order for the sending of fifty soldiers from Arad and an unpreserved number from Qinah under the command of Malkiyahu son of Qerav'ur, who is to

deliver them to Elisha' son of Yirmiyahu in Ramot-Negev 'lest anything should happen to the city'. The addressee, Eliashiv, is reminded, 'The word of the king is incumbent upon you for your very life! Behold, I have sent to warn you today: Get the men to Elisha' lest Edom should arrive there!' (Aharoni 1981: 46).

The ostracon was found outside the fortress on the western slope; on the basis of the form of the written letters, it has been assigned to stratum VI, which is thought to have been destroyed at the end of the monarchy (Aharoni 1981: 46). The contents seem to suggest that the fort is still under Judahite royal control.[22] The ostracon may reflect a policy instituted as early as 600 BCE by Nebuchadrezzar to enlist raiding parties from Moab, Ammon and Edom (not Aram) to work alongside a contingent of Neo-Babylonian troops to keep Yehoikim, the king of Judah who had rebelled at this time, in line until he could arrive with full forces and deal personally with the situation (2 Kgs 24.2). Nebuchadrezzar appears to have secured the Negev as a buffer zone between Egypt and Judah to isolate the former from the latter as a potential ally (2 Kgs 24.7; Jer. 13.19) before he laid siege to Jerusalem in 588 BCE.

Edom's Status in the Neo-Babylonian and Persian Periods

Edom's status during the Neo-Babylonian and Persian periods remains hazy. Opinions vary about whether its kingship was terminated during the neo-Babylonian period or not, and whether it continued to exist as a recognized administrative entity in the Persian period. Some scholars propose that Nebuchadrezzar would have attacked and destroyed its capital at Bozrah, modern Buseirah, in his military campaign in 582 BCE (e.g. Finkelstein 1992: 165). Josephus claims the offensive in the king's twenty-third year was targeted against Moab and Ammon (*Ant.* 10.9.7), which were converted into provinces at this time. We have no account of events in this year preserved in the Babylonian annals, however, so we cannot confirm whether this is historically reliable or not. There is no mention of Edom in Josephus' report, so if Nebuchadrezzar also campaigned there, he either simply destroyed this political unit and left its land outside of his official jurisdiction since most of the territory was uninhabited desert, or he converted it to a province as well but this was not reported, due to scribal oversight in the original source or because of Josephus' own ideological considerations.

Others think that Edom survived as a Neo-Babylonian vassal until 552 BCE, when Nabonidus destroyed it in the early part of his campaign to conquer and occupy Tema' in the Arabian peninsula (so, e.g., Smith 1944: 36-39; Lindsay 1976: 38; de Geus 1979/80: 53; Eph'al 1982: 188; Bartlett 1989: 159, 163; Beaulieu 1989: 168-69; Ahlström 1993: 833; Lee 1994: 32; Byrne 2003: 19; Lemaire 2003: 287-88). This is based on the reference to an attack against a city of [...] *dummu* during the march to the oasis at Tema' in the very fragmentary Nabonidus Chronicle and Royal Chronicle. Its ruler apparently escaped to another town named Shindini or Rugdini and was apprehended there and killed (Oppenheim 1969: 305). The name of the original city that was the home of the king has been restored either as 'Edom' or as 'Adumah/Dumah'. The latter is a site thought to have been located at Dumat al Jandal in the oasis of el-Jawf in a remote mountainous region known today as Jebel Nafud southeast of the Wadi Sirhan (Albright 1925) or, alternatively, near modern Azraq (Smith 1944: 38), on the main north–south road through Transjordan.

Three factors favor the view that the city in question was the capital of Edom and not the city of Dumah. First, the route south went from Babylon around the Fertile Crescent, with an initial battle somewhere in the region of Lebanon. After recuperating from an illness there for seven months, Nabonidus continued south, reaching the city in question. Buseirah was on the road to Tema' but not Dumah, which would have required a detour to the southeast. Secondly, it does not appear that the caravan route from the Arabian peninsula to Babylonia that cut across the desert around Jebel Nafud was used until Persian times (Byrne 2003: 12). So even though it is only a march of four days from Tema' to Dumah, at the northern edge of Jebel Nafud, this would not have been the route used by Nabonidus to reach Tema' from Babylonia (contra Albright 1925). Finally, it appears that Nabonidus ordered the carving of a rock relief at Sela' near at-Tafilah, close to Bozrah. Unfortunately, the writing is too eroded to be read so the purpose of the monument is not certain, but the manner of depicting the ruler and the accompanying divine symbols point strongly to Nabonidus as the source of the monument (Dalley and Goguel 1997). Thus, the relief corroborates the broken textual accounts of Nabonidus' campaign in Edom.

Although most seem to think Edom disappeared altogether after Nabonidus' expedition and that the area ceased to be administered officially, P. Bienkowski has suggested that Nabonidus installed a governor in Buseriah in 552 BCE after taking the city, making it an official province for the first time (2002: 478). He bases this proposal on his correlation of different occupational phases in different areas of Buseirah that have been dug, in an attempt to create a site-wide history of occupation. His final report on the excavations conducted by Crystal M. Bennett in 1971–1980 has revised some of her earlier preliminary conclusions (2002).

In his opinion, Nabonidus was responsible for the localized fires or destruction encountered in various areas of the city that he has designated 'Integrated Stage 2'. Deposits of ashy material were found in parts of the plastered courtyard and around the steps and in the interior sanctuary of the 'temple' in Area A, in the reception room/courtyard, bathroom and storage area of the 'palace' in Area C, and in the gateway in Area B. In Area D, some of the walls collapsed but there was no evidence of a fire having been lit there. He believes the majority of the city was left intact, and that the rebuilding of the 'temple', 'palace', gateway with new perimeter wall and the buildings in Area D in 'Integrated Stage 3' took place immediately, without a gap. New techniques were used to rebuild the walls, and a number of former spaces were partitioned to create smaller and more numerous rooms. He suggests this would be compatible with an altered use of the buildings by a governor instead of a king, acknowledging that the evidence cannot prove such a theory but is consistent with it (2002: 478). His observations concur with C.M. Bennett's preliminary understanding of the sequence of dates for Area A (1983: 15-16).

What can be made out from the fragmentary account of events that transpired in 552 BCE in the two Neo-Babylonian documents does not require us to conclude that Nabonidus destroyed Bozrah, 'the city of Edom', only that he damaged it. Since the king managed to escape from his seat of power, it could be argued that a full siege was not laid against the city and that it was not systematically burned, so that there is no need to seek a widespread destruction level to corroborate the story. The objective would have been the capture of a rebellious king and his punishment, but not necessarily the reduction of his city to ruins, especially if Nabonidus intended to reduce the area to provincial status. He would have needed a seat of adminstration. The localized destruction evident in four excavated areas is consistent with what P. Bienkowski has proposed concerning the end of Integrated Phase 2 and the alterations made in Integrated Phase 3.

As J. Bartlett has noted, the permanent destruction of Bozrah and Tell el-Kheleife on the Gulf of Aqaba would not have benefited Nabonidus had he been interested in controlling trade in the region (1989: 159). However, he may have decided to eliminate the Edomites as middlemen in a branch of the western trade that was able to move goods from India and southern Arabia through the port at Tell el-Kheleife and then to the coast. This move would have forced all subsequent trade to take instead the overland routes through the Arabian peninsula that could be controlled from Tema'. In either case, we can see that Bozrah was rebuilt and remained occupied throughout the Persian period so whatever action Nabonidus may have taken in 552 BCE, it did not result in the permanent elimination of the largest site in the Edomite heartland.

Until the published final report on Buseirah, there were no clear stratified remains from any site in Edom proper east of the Aravah that could confidently be dated to the Persian period, although a contract found at the site of Tawilan that was dated to the accession year of one of the Persian kings named Darius (Darius I [521 BCE], Darius II [423 BCE], Darius III [335 BCE]) had been seen to signify probable occupation at that site in the Persian period (Bienkowski 1995: 48-49). This was because none of the forms that were considered diagnostic of the Persian period in Cisjordan had been found at Edomite sites. However, the finding of three sherds of Attic ware in the final occupational phase at the Edomite capital at Bozrah (modern Buseirah), Integrated Stage 3, has made it clear that the Iron II pottery tradition in Edom continued in use throughout the Persian period without innovation or the introduction of western forms (Bienkowski and van der Steen 2001: 23 n. 3; Bienkowski 2002: 90; 478). This discovery has important implications for identifying and dating potential sites west of the Aravah that may have been controlled by Edom after 586 BCE.

Although one of the Attic sherds was found in topsoil, making it impossible to associate it with regular occupation at the site and not to view it simply as a piece of a discarded broken bowl by a passerby, the other two were found in stratified contexts in Area A. Both sherds belong to bowls whose shapes indicate a fourth-century BCE date (Bienkowski 2002: 90).

One sherd was in an ashy deposit of phase 4 (= Integrated Stage 3) that overlay a phase 4 plaster floor in a long narrow room of Building A. The ash was mixed with collapse or a burned deposit that was characteristic of the final destruction of this phase of occupation. Most phase 4 loci were overlain by thick deposits of black ash and burnt debris, suggesting an intense fire had ripped through the building. Then, in all areas but one, a layer of collapse fell on top of the ash, suggesting that the walls collapsed inward after the fire. In the one area that was the exception, the collapse occurred before the ash layer (Bienkowski 2002: 88-89).

The second Attic sherd was found in compact red-brown soil that lay immediately on top of the Phase 3 (= Integrated Stage 2) plaster floor in a long narrow room of Building B. It was probably part of the widespread earth or rubble fill that was used in the rebuilding and alteration of the latter building to create Building A in the final phase of Iron Age/Persian occupation. Thus, the second sherd is likely to date from the beginning of phase 4 (= Integrated Stage 3) (Bienkowski 2002: 88, 90). Three Hellenistic sherds belonging to saucers and bowls were also found in area A and one from a black-slipped bowl dating to the third century BCE was thought to have been within phase 4 fill. Two more, dating from the third or early-second century BCE, were found in black ash that overlay the phase 4 (= Integrated Stage 3) collapse and so, theoretically, belonged to use of the site after 300/200 BCE by Nabateans.

Whatever may have happened in 582 or 552 BCE, Edom's capital remained a functional, occupied site for over another 200 years, from the end of the Neo-Babylonian period and all through the Persian period. Bearing this in mind, three scenarios are possible for understanding Edom's status in the period from 586–332 BCE. (1) Buseirah served as the seat of a vassal kingdom under both the Neo-Babylonians and Persians, continuing the status it had had at the time of Judah's demise in 586 BCE. It was assigned control over the Beersheva Valley by the Neo-Babylonians and continued to exercise this control until the Persians either ceded control back to Yehud in 450 BCE, or until they created the new province of Idumea c. 400 BCE. (2) Edom became a province toward the end of the Neo-Babylonian period and remained so under the Persians. Its provincial seat was located at Buseriah, the capital of the former kingdom. As such, it had within its jurisdiction the Beersheva Valley until the Persians placed it under the jurisdiction of Yehud c. 450 BCE or created a new province in this region named Idumea c. 400 BCE (Eph'al 1982: 205-206; Bartlett 1989: 164). (3) Buseirah remained an occupied city but was viewed as part of the larger sphere of the Arabs (Lemaire 2003: 290). It was deprived of its status as an independent kingdom, stripped of its larger domains, which were assigned to 'Arab territory', and made simply one more 'Arab' settlement (*Herod.* 3.88, 97, 107). This could have happened under Nabonidus, who appears to have tried to gain direct control over the Arabian spice trade routes and may have eliminated Edom as a middleman in the western branch of this trade. Or, it could have happened under Cambyses, who granted the Arabs in the territory between Gaza and Egypt special privileges for their help in supplying his army with water that allowed them to invade and successfully conquer Egypt in 525 BCE (*Herod.* 3.4-5). As part of their reward, he may have decided to make them overseers of the Beersheva trade routes instead of Edom. To do this, he would have assigned the remaining Edomite settlements to Arab control.

Edomite Remains in the Negev in the Late Iron II Period

Edomite remains have been found at a number of sites in the eastern Negev that have been dated to the later monarchic period. The reason for their presence must be considered carefully, as well as the possibility that some of these sites continued in use after the Neo-Babylonians annexed Judah in 586 BCE and created the province of Yehud. The textual tradition just reviewed would suggest that the Edomites would have taken over control of existing forts at strategic crossroads as the new masters of this land after 586 BCE or would have built some new facilities themselves at points they needed to serve as caravan stations. We need to try to determine if the Edomite presence reflects physical control of the territory or merely the presence of traders as part of the terms of the alliance struck between Judah and Edom sometime before the former's demise.

It seems likely that before the end of the monarchy, the Edomites were using the trade route that went from their capital city at Bozrah to a terminal point at Gaza on the Mediterranean coast and which crossed through the Beersheva Valley (Finkelstein 1995: 152-53; Singer-Avitz 1999; Bienkowski and van der Steen 2001: 24). Their main, locally-produced commodity would have been copper, retrieved and smelted in the Wadi Feinan and then traded on, possibly to Judah as well as the coast and Egypt. Edomite 'painted ware' has been found in mining and smelting sites in this region (Knauf-Belleri 1995: 113). Secondarily, however, Edom would have controlled the northwestern portion of the Arabian spice and incense trade from Buseirah to Gaza, or at least the portion that crossed through its territory. Camel statuettes that likely were votive offerings of long-distance traders have been found in Buseirah, the capital of Edom (Knauf-Belleri 1995: 114). After the fall of Jerusalem, the primary interest of the Edomites in the Negev would have been the safety of this road system as they continued to traverse the territory with their own goods or escorting Arab caravans to Gaza or possibly Tell Jemme and Tell Ajjul in the same vicinity (Lindsay 1976: 30). In addition, they might have wanted a population base in the area to produce food that could be used by the caravans to replenish their supplies en route.

There is no record of Nebuchadrezzar having captured or destroyed Gaza. A text from his reign that details his officials ends with a section that mentions the kings of Tyre, Gaza, Sidon, Arvad, and Ashdod (Oppenheim 1969: 308). Unfortunately, the text is broken immediately after the list of names, so the context in which they were being mentioned in uncertain. However, since the larger list names officials within his empire, this subsection is most likely indicating that these Levantine coastal cities of Phoenicia and Philistia were allowed to maintain their native kings as Assyrian vassals instead of being made into provinces.

Jacob Katzenstein has argued, however, that the business archives of the Murashu family, which date from 454–404 BCE, provide indirect evidence for the reduction of Gaza from an independent Neo-Babylonian vassal with its own king to a provincial city. The texts refer to three suburbs around Nippur named for Ashkelon, Gaza, and Bit Arsa. This can only mean that people had been removed from these areas on the coast of Palestine and forcefully resettled in the vicinity of Nippur. He identifies two possible occasions when such military action and deportations could have been accomplished: 586 BCE, when Nebuchadrezzar made Judah into a province and there were large deportations of its population, some to the same region, and 582–581 BCE, when this same king campaigned against Moab and Ammon and reduced them to provinces (1994: 46-47). In his opinion, the kings of all the Philistine cities were systematically removed from power and sent to Babylon with their families to live out their days under house arrest at the royal court, like King Yehoikin of Judah. Their towns were put under direct military administration (1994: 47).

The presence of deportees from Gaza and Ashkelon in the vicinity of Nippur does not automatically mean that their home cities were reduced to provinces. There was a deportation from Judah in 598 BCE, but the monarchy was left intact, with a new king being put on the throne by the Babylonians who continued to serve as a vassal to the Babylonian empire. A similar thing could have happened in the case of Gaza. There are no firmly-dated written records that refer to events in southern Transjordan or along the southern Mediterranean coast from Nebuchadrezzar's campaign against Ammon and Moab in 582 BCE and the beginning of the Hellenistic period.[23] Thus, we can only speculate about Gaza's status as a Neo-Babylonian vassal or provincial city in this period, and arguments can be made either way. In either case, however, it is likely that Gaza remained a functioning terminus for Arabian and Edomite trade in the Neo-Babylonian period.

The following sites in the Negev have yielded characteristic Iron II Edomite pottery: 'En Haseva, Tel Aroer, Tel Malhata, Horvat Qitmit, Horvat Radum, Horvat 'Uza, Tel Arad, Tel 'Ira, Tel Masos, and Qadesh Barnea (Beit Arieh 1995a: 33, 35).

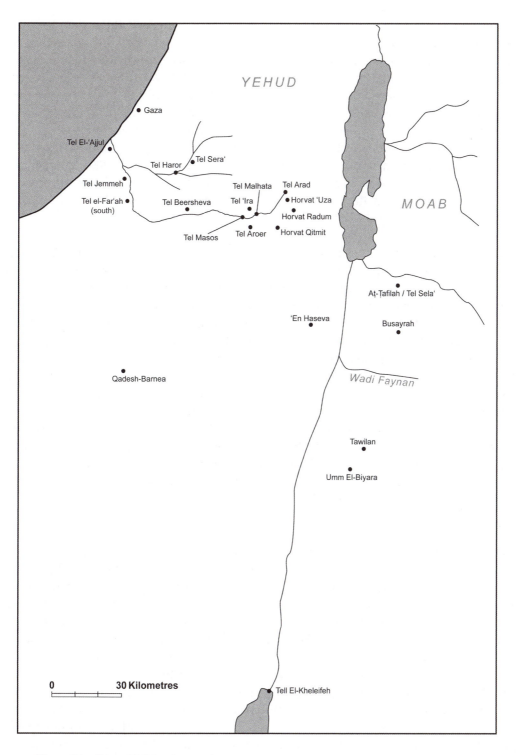

Figure 47. *Sites with Edomite remains*

Cooking pots tend to be a good indication of their users' origins in the ancient Levant. It seems as though people were most comfortable using the style of vessel with which they had learned to cook, if possible. An analysis of the type of clay used to make the Edomite cooking pots found at Tel Malhata, for example, tends to indicate that they were not made locally in the Negev, even though other Edomite pottery forms were made of the distinctive green-white local clay, as were many of the Judean forms (Bienkowski and van der Steen 2001: 27).[24] Thus, while people may have been more open to adopting local forms of serving and eating vessels, they appear to have preferred to use their traditional cooking pots from their homeland if given the opportunity (e.g. Finkelstein 1997: 230; Bienkowski and van der Steen 2001: 27). Edomite pottery found at sites where the cooking pot tradition is predominantly 'Judahite' can probably be tied to trade relations in the closing decades of the Judahite monarchy. This would include, Tel Sera', Khirbet 'Uza, Tel Masos, Tel 'Ira, and Qadesh Barnea.[25]

Tel es-Sera'/Tell esh Shari'a. At Tel es-Sera' some Edomite pottery was found in the stratum IV fortified settlement, along with east Greek imported ware, Assyrian palace ware and its local imitations, mortaria, basket-handled jars, Egyptian-style fertility figurines, a late-seventh century Middle Corinthian aryballos, two Hebrew ostraca, and a single, large Aramaic ostracon (Oren 1974: 265; 1982: 160-61; 1993b: 1333). The site housed a citadel and almost certainly was a military installation. It had a number of circular grain storage pits and refuse pits, and installations for cooking and baking (Oren 1973: 252; 1974: 265). In addition, there was evidence of iron-working in a spacious, open courtyard east of the citadel, including iron slag, charcoal, broken crucibles, clay tuyeres and a pit lined with bricks and coated with vitrified clay (1982: 160). The site appears to have been destroyed sometime near the end of the seventh century and was not reoccupied until the fifth century. The site has never been published so it is unknown how many Edomite sherds there were, if any were cooking pots, and whether the majority of the pottery repertoire belonged to the Judahite tradition. Nevertheless, it seems likely that the Edomite sherds arrived as a result of trade. The site is believed to have housed an Assyrian garrison (Na'aman 1995: 112).

Khirbet 'Uza. Khirbet 'Uza was built as a Judean fort that dominated the 'Way of Edom', in the late-seventh or early-sixth century BCE. A small, extra-mural settlement covering seven dunams was located outside the gate, built on terraces stepping down the steep wadi slope. It probably housed soldiers and their families. An analysis of the cooking pots from this occupational level showed that twenty-five percent were Edomite, twenty-five percent were coastal, and fifty percent were Judahite, while the overall assemblage was otherwise typically Judahite (Beit-Arieh, personal communication).[26] The coastal and Edomite forms were probably acquired from Edomite caravans passing by the fort en route to Gaza or returning to Tell el-Kheliefe.

An Edomite ostracon was found in the first room adjoining the outer wall of the fort, on the east (Room 336). Four Hebrew ostraca were found in the same locus; the Edomite one was ten centimeters higher than the others and presumably deposited later (I. Beit Arieh, personal communication). It lay at the top of the destruction debris. Lumalak or Elimelek writes to Blbl, greets him in the name of Qos and instructs him to give some food/grain that someone named Ahima/o[ ] 'stood'. After an illegible section, the instruction comes to have A[]iel lift to... A final bit reads ...The food become leavened(?) or become bitter(?) or a homer of the food/grain (Beit Arieh and Cresson 1985).

The contents of this ostracon would tend to suggest that control of the fort was take over by the Edomites at some point, were it not for the fact that in the few rooms in the fort that had not been cleared by the subsequent Greek occupants of the site, the Edomite pottery was found in the destruction level, not above it (Beit Arieh and Cresson 1991: 132). Since it is unlikely that the Edomites would have chosen to live full-time among the ruins, with thick destruction debris underfoot, it appears likely that the ostracon was left by an Edomite official, messenger, or soldier who either was temporarily stationed there to secure the region after the destruction of the site or who was in transit through the region and who stopped at the ruined fort for the night or to rest and discarded the order just inside the gate.[27] The Edomite pottery found at Khirbet 'Uza is best seen to be the result of trade at the end of the monarchy, as at Tel es-Sera' and Beersheva.

Horvat Radum. The situation at Horvat Radum is similar. This appears to have been a single-period site[28] that was a fort/rest house measuring 21 × 25 meters, located only two kilometers south of Khirbet 'Uza along the Nahal Qina. Two cisterns were located outside the fort, near the northern wall. The interior space had ovens and what appears to have been a stepped altar immediately inside the entrance, to the right (Beit Arieh 1993a: 1254). It appears to have been abandoned rather than destroyed (I. Beit Arieh, personal communication). The few sherds found during excavation belonged to Judahite pottery types and also included a restorable Edomite cooking pot, which could have been purchased from passing caravans. Five Hebrew ostraca were found in various locations inside the structure, indicating that it had belonged to the administrative system of Judah until the end of the monarchy (Beit Arieh 1993a: 1255). It is possible that the site was used after its abandonment by Edomites as a stopping place en route. There is no evidence of an attempted permanent occupation by Edomites. One would have to argue that they took all but one of their pots with them when they left and that they broke almost none while in residence to try to make a case in favor of such an occupation. This is unlikely.

Tel Masos. Tel Masos Area G also housed a late Iron II Age fort, whose pottery assemblage places its abandonment anywhere from c. 605–586 BCE (Zimhoni 1983: 130). The cooking pots were Judahite except for one type that tended to be found in southern coastal sites and in the northwest Negev at Gerar. Some Edomite ware was also found. The assemblage closely resembled those found at Tel Malhata and Khirbet el-Garra, both in the neighboring vicinity (Zimhoni 1983: 129). Three Hebrew ostraca found in various room in the fort confirm that the site belonged to Judah's fort system in the region (Fritz 1983). The names of the individuals mentioned on them are Hebrew: Zakaryahu, Shema[yah] and Hananyahu (Fritz 1983).

Tel 'Ira. Tel 'Ira was built as a walled settlement with public administrative buildings as well as domestic housing probably at the end of the eighth century. Located on a flat hill that divided the Arad Valley from the Beersheva Valley, it could oversee two trade routes that cut through the region. It was definitely occupied in the first half of the seventh century BCE (stratum VII).

After destruction, it was rebuilt in stratum VI. The finds suggest this took place immediately, within the seventh century. There was a final destruction and abandonment of the site probably in the closing decades of the monarchy c. 600 BCE (Beit Arieh 1999: 172-74, 177). Edomite bowls cups, and jugs were found in stratum VII (Freud 1999: 194-96), while some sherds of Edomite and coastal cooking pots were found in stratum VI (Freud 1999: 218). The site has a predominantly Judahite pottery assemblage, otherwise, and the presence of rosette-stamped jars in the stratum VI destruction indicates that the site fell under Judahite administration (Cahill 1999). The Edomite pottery is best explained as the result of trading caravans passing en-route through the area.

Qadesh Barnea. Qadesh Barnea was a Judahite outpost in the late-monarchic period. An Edomite krater was found in the Upper Fortress, which contained a number of pottery vessels typical of the Judahite repertoire in the seventh and sixth centuries BCE as well as some local, handmade 'Negevite' pottery (Cohen 1983: 12). A number of ostraca written in Hebrew were also found in the destruction debris, indicating that the site was administered by Judah. Its destruction date cannot be firmly established but it is likely that it did not survive the collapse of Judah in 586 BCE (Cohen 1993: 846-47). The Edomite ware is likely to have arrived with caravans passing en route and stopping to replenish water supplies at the oasis.

Five remaining sites with Edomite remains, Tel Malhata, Horvat Qitmit, 'En Haseva, Tel Aroer, and Tell el-Kheleife, have a different profile than the others that could suggest Edomite occupation in the Beersheva Valley and northern Sinai during the Neo-Babylonian period, as successors to Judah.

Tel Malhata. Tel Malhata stratum III has two sub-phases. The later one is of interest to us; it dates from the late-seventh to some point in the sixth century BCE. The pottery is still being restored and awaits final analysis. However, preliminary examination has indicated that the majority of the cooking pots were Edomite (I. Beit Arieh, personal communication). Other pottery belonging to the Edomite sphere was included in the larger assemblage, which also contained Judahite and coastal forms.[29] In addition, two figurines like those found at Qitmit were uncovered (see next subsection), clearly from the same workshop, and it is likely that they were manufactured in Malhata, where there is water readily available, and secondarily distributed to the latter, open-air cultic center (Beit Arieh 1995a: 37).[30] Six Edomite ostraca are now known; one was found during excavations undertaken by M. Kochavi (Kochavi 1993: 936); the remaining five, as yet unpublished, were uncovered in the subsequent excavations conducted by I. Beit Arieh and B. Cresson (I. Beit Arieh, personal communication). Due to the presence of a Bedouin cemetery on top of the tell and protests against its disturbance lodged by local tribesmen, only areas on the perimeter of the tell were able to be excavated during the 1990s (I. Beit Arieh, personal communication).

The limited evidence currently available indicates that in its final occupational phase, a segment of Malhata was settled primarily by Edomites and belonged to that politico-cultural sphere of influence, rather than to the Judahite one. Thus, it is plausible to suggest that Malhata provides evidence for Edomite settlement in the Beersheva Valley during the Neo-Babylonian period, when formal control of this area had been ceded by the authorities to Edom. With this is mind, I would tentatively suggest that the site was not destroyed in 586 BCE at the end of the monarchy, but rather was ceded to the Edomites without resistance or an armed conflict. The destruction of stratum III may be associated instead with Nabonidus' possible decision to eliminate the Edomite role in the western branch of the spice trade in 552 BCE, by other Neo-Babylonian initiatives in the region whose events have not been preserved, or by Arab military action in an attempt to take over control of these routes from the Edomites at some point in the Neo-Babylonian or early Persian period.

Horvat Qitmit. The site is located on top of a hill that runs beside an ancient road that paralleled the main east–west route through the eastern Beersheva Valley but lay south of this main road, and then cut southwest to intersect with the main north–south road through the Negev highlands, at Tel Aroer. There were and are no wells there; the closest water is five kilometers northwest at Tel Malhata (Beit Arieh 1995b: 1-3). It is a single-period site with two building phases discernible, consisting of two building complexes, each with several rooms, a courtyard, and installations. Complex A consisted of a three-room building measuring 10.5 × 5 meters, an oval platform surrounded on three sides by a stone wall, a stone basin, and an altar (Beit Arieh1995b: 9-20). Complex B, about fifteen meters to the north, contained a structure whose inner dimensions were 8.5 × 8 meters, with inner rooms whose configurations changed over time. A large ovoid enclosure (13 × 11 meters) lay to the west, between the two buildings but closer to complex A, and a smaller one (6.5 × 3.5 meters) lay southwest of the same complex (Beit Arieh 1995b: 20-26). Extensive figurines, statues, cultic vessels and votive offerings were found at the complex, suggesting it was an isolated, open-air shrine.

The bulk of cooking pot fragments (eighty-three percent) are of the typical Edomite type with a stepped rim and nuclear activation analysis has shown that the sand mixed into the clay to tempering the pots and prevent them from cracking under the heat of a fire originated in the central Edom region (Beit Arieh 1995b: 225). Otherwise, large quantities of sherds from domestic vessels common in Judah and Transjordan were found beside the cooking pots (Beit Arieh 1995b: 303).

Those frequenting the shrine were most likely Edomites who carried their cooking pots with them and were traversing the trade routes through the Beersheva basin (so, e.g., Finkelstein 1992: 162). The site might also have been frequented by residents of Tel Malhata, where two figurines from the same workshop as those at Qitmit were found in excavation (Beit Arieh 1995b: 315) or by Edomites who dwelt as traders and mercenaries in the various towns in the region (Finkelstein 1992: 158-59).

A total of eighteen cowrie shells that had been made into beads were found at the site. They belong to the species *cypraea annulus*, which are rarely found in the Gulf of Aqaba or the Gulf of Suez, but which becomes more common toward the extreme end of the Red Sea along the southern and eastern shores of the Arabian peninsula and only abundant east of India and along the east coast of Africa (Beit Arieh 1995b: 277). Their presence suggests trade links with the Gulf of Aqaba or the Arabian peninsula and this is consistent with Edomite finds at Tell el-Kheleife, a port in the northern Gulf of Aqaba.

The cultic assemblage belongs to the same tradition as the one at 'En Haseva, about 100 kilometers to the northeast, although the large figurines were not made at the same workshop (Beck 1996: 104). Influences from southern Philistia, around Gerar and Mefalsim are apparent in the iconography, style, and technique of three figurines, which were probably made there, while the closest parallels to the small, open-topped figurines or stands and the solid handmade ones are from Ashdod (Beck 1995: 185). Some of the iconography, gestures, and the use of masks are thought to reflect Phoenician influences, and the shape of the jars on which the large statues were formed as well as the distinctive goatee on male figures are thought to be of Transjordanian influence (Beck 1995: 186).

Establishing the founding date of the shrine and the length of time it was used is difficult. It could have been established as early as the the end of the eighth century or the beginning of the seventh century BCE, when the Assyrians seem to have taken an active interest in this trade route through the Beersheva Valley and built a number of Assyrian installations near the terminus on the coastal plain at Tel Jemme, Tell el-Far'ah and Tel Haror, and Tel es-Sera' (Na'aman 1995: 111-12). However, this seems unlikely to me. The indications are that Qitmit lay within the territory formally controlled by Judah until 586 BCE, and while the royal court might have given permission for the building of such a shrine to be used by traders in the region, it is more plausible to assume that the shrine was built after the demise of the kingdom, when formal control of the area was ceded to the Edomites by the Neo-Babylonian king. At that point, the shrine was a means of their laying claim to the land as part of the domain of Qos and his control over the local trade routes.

'En Haseva. 'En Haseva contained the largest spring in the western Aravah and was located almost due west of Bozrah, the capital of Edom. It would have been a natural stopping point for travellers and caravans in the area. Two building complexes were located near the spring. One was a fort, whose full dimensions in its final Iron Age phase have not been determined but one side of which measured 36 meters from corner watchtower to corner watchtower, and was 1.5 meters thick (Cohen and Yisrael 1995: 224). The other was a rectangular building measuring 6.5 × 2.5 meters, located outside the walls of the fort. It did not have a typical domestic floorplan and appears to have been a shrine. A favissa (pit) close by contained more than seventy cultic vessels, these appear to have been removed from the shrine and deliberately broken by having segments of ashlar blocks thrown on top of them. The blocks had probably also been removed from the shrine.

The two buildings need not have been in use simultaneously since they were free-standing, independent units. The date of the shrine needs to be determined by the contents of the favissa and any finds within the sanctuary building itself and not by the adjoining fort. A preliminary analysis has been made of the finds from the favissa by P. Beck. She has noted that the assemblage is not as rich or varied as the one at Qitmit. Lacking, for example, are small hollow human figurines, human figurines with a hollow body and solid head, solid human figurines, composite creatures, musicians, and musical instruments (Beck 1996: 105). She concluded that the articles do not belong to the Judahite sphere, for which no parallels are known, but rather, to the Edomite sphere. There are no comparable parallels from the Edomite heartland either, but by inference, Edom is a more viable candidate than Judah (1996: 112).

Rudolph Cohen and Yigal Yisrael have assumed that the shrine was Edomite and have suggested that it was destroyed at the time the stratum IV fortress was erected by King Josiah, as part of his wide-ranging religious reforms (1995: 225). Their proposal is not convincing; favissae with deliberately broken figurines and altars have been found at a number of sites in the Levant in various time periods. They probably reflect an attempt to desacralize cultic objects when a temple or shrine is abandoned.

There is nothing to prohibit the shrine from being dated to the Neo-Babylonian period, after the abandonment of the fort. Had the Neo-Babylonians ceded control of this area to Edom after 586 BCE, there may not have been much need for the series of protective forts as there had been when Judah had controlled the region. The Negev was primarily a transit zone for the northwestern branch of the Arabian trade and for the movement of Edomite copper. The Edomites had posed the biggest threat to Judah at the end of the monarchy and they now were in charge; there may not have been enough free-lancing predators in this environmentally marginal region to warrant the manning of forts regularly along the route. More important for the Edomites would have been safe camping points en route, with access to water and food, if possible.

On the other hand, the stratum IV fort might have been used to house a small contingent of Edomite soldiers as well, or some merchants. It can be noted that what have been dated as seventh-century BCE deposits at 'En Haseva have only Edomite cooking pots, no Judahite cooking pots, although there is other Judahite pottery found inside the stratum IV structure. This strongly suggests the presence of people of 'Edomite' background as the permanent residents, not Judahites (Bienkowski and van der Steen 2001: 27). As noted above, the Iron II Edomite pottery assemblage continued in use through the Neo-Babylonian and Persian period, and the local Iron IIC Judahite tradition likewise remained unchanged until the mid-fifth century BCE. This allows the Edomite occupation to be dated in the Neo-Babylonian or early Persian period. Stratum IV was destroyed, perhaps by Nabonidus' troops in 552 BCE, or by Arab marauders (Cohen 1994: 208)

It should also be noted that a full-time priest apparently was in service at the shrine. A seal was found outside the fort that belonged to Mskt, the son of Whzm. It depicts two figures facing each other on either side of a horned altar. One is making a gesture of offering and the other of blessing, suggesting that one is a priest and the other a deity (Cohen and Yisrael 1995: 224).

Tel Aroer. It is possible that the Edomites took over control of the stratum II settlement at Aroer in the Neo-Babylonian period. At some point during the late seventh or early sixth century, a tower or fortress was built to protect the unwalled settlement of stratum II that had existed already since stratum IV, which probably was settled in the first half of the seventh century BCE (Biran 1993: 90-91). A growing Edomite influence is seen, particularly in phase 2 of this stratum, especially in Area A south of the fort and outside the earlier walls of stratum I (Biran 1993: 91). Much Edomite pottery was found here. The site has no destruction levels in levels IV, III, or II, so the date of its abandonment is unclear but need not be tied to the Babylonian conquest (contra Biran1993: 91).

Figure 48.   *Seal of Mskt bn Whzy*
            R. Cohen and Y. Yisrael, 'The Iron Age Fortresses of 'En Haseve', *Biblical Archae-
            ologist* 58 (1995): 224. (Drawn by the author.)

Perhaps a priest could have survived on the offerings made by passers-by, but it seems more likely that his presence signals a deliberate manning of the site as a whole by a central authority, which would also have guaranteed food rations to those in service there. Neither of the names on the seal is Yahwistic, and while neither contains the name of the Edomite deity Qos either, the names are not Judahite. Perhaps after the Edomites assumed control of the fort, it became more of a caravanserai, with some permanent residents who included government employees as well as private citizens.

Surveys of the Southern Judean Hills. The southern Judean hills contained nineteen sites that were potentially settled continuously from the end of the monarchy, through the neo-Babylonian period, and into the Persian period (see #243-45, 247-50, 252-61in site chart in Chapter 5). Of these, twelve had been established already in the Iron IIA period and have evidence of occupation in each subsequent sub-phase of the Iron II period. Three had been first established in Iron IIB (# 243, 253-54), while just two had been founded in Iron IIC, either at the end of the monarchy or during the Neo-Babylonian period (#258, 261). The settlement history of the two southernmost sites (#263, 264) was not broken down into sub-phases within the Iron II period so, unfortunately, nothing more specific can be said about them.

Ten of these sites had most likely been towns in the Iron IIC, measuring sixteen dunams (four acres) or more: Dura (#244), Khirbet Bani Dar/Khirbet Yukin (#245), Khirbet Marajim (#247), el-Hadab (#248), Tel Keleikh (#249), Tel Zif (#250), Yatta east (#253), Khirbet Rabud (Hevron) (#256), Khirbet Ma'in (#259) and Khirbet 'Anim (#261). Seven were farmsteads or hamlets measuring less than sixteen dunams (four acres): Khirbet Kan'an (#243), Khirbet Bism (#252), Khirbet Umm el-'Amad (#254), Khirbet Umm Lispa (#255), Khirbet el-Karmil (#257), Khirbet 'Unnab es Saghir (#258) and Khirbet Shuweike (#260). It is unclear whether there would have been a population decline in the ten towns, some or all of which might have been targeted for destruction or looting by the Neo-Babylonians, with limited reoccupation in the Neo-Babylonian period. The sizes of the two southernmost sites, Tel Shoqet (#263) and Horvat Yattin (#264), were not given in the published survey; it is likely that the first was a town, since it is identified as a tel, but the nature of the second is harder to assess. Some sites that bear the designation *horvah/khirbeh* are well over sixteen dunams (e.g. Khirbet Madras: 120 dunams; Khirbet Shahah: thirty-five dunams; Khirbet Batan: thirty dunams; Khirbet el-Tujeirah: thirty dunams) while others are the size of farmsteads (e.g. Khirbet Alia: five dunams; Horvat G'rish: three dunams; Khirbet Abu Shun: two dunams).

Careful thought needs to be given to whether all of these sites belonged to the province of Yehud after 586 BCE and were administered from Mizpah, or whether any would have been reassigned to the jurisdiction of Edom at this early period. Bearing this in mind, it could be significant that the two settlements immediately north of the Beersheva Valley, Tel Shoqet (#263) and Horvat Yattin (#264), are isolated from the other cluster of seventeen sites in the region of Hevron. They lie a noticeable distance to the south, much closer to the valley basin. Neither has been excavated, so it cannot be determined if there was destruction in the Iron IIC period, presumably at some point between c. 602–586 BCE, and a subsequent occupational gap until resettlement in the Persian period, or whether there was continuous occupation through the Iron IIC period into the Persian period, with or without a destruction layer. Of all the sites in the southern Judean hills, however, they are the most likely of any to have been within the Edomite domain. Lying just north of the valley, in the southernmost reaches of the Judean hills, they could have grown surplus food supplies for caravans passing through the Beersheva Valley.

It is not clear, however, if such food supplies would have been needed. It is possible that the caravans carried adequate food supplies to cross the entire valley without replenishing supplies en route, purchasing new supplies in Gaza or the coastal plain, and in Buseirah. Water could have been secured en route at 'En Haseva and Malhata, and possibly also at the well at Beersheva. Camel caravans that operate today in the Sahara average thirty-six miles or fifty-seven kilometers a day (Rainier 2003). It is about 120 kilometers from Gaza to 'En Haseva, so it would only have taken a little over two days to cross the Beersheva Valley. It seems unlikely, then, that food supplies would have been needed to be purchased on this leg of the route. Thus, it might be wiser to view both of these sites, if occupied in the Neo-Babylonian period, as the southernmost settlements of the province of Yehud, with the northern edge of the Beersheva Valley where it adjoined the hill-country and southernmost Shephelah marking the boundary between Neo-Babylonian Yehud and the territory of the vassal kingdom of Edom.

Tell el-Kheleife. Stratum IV at Tell el-Kheleife consisted of a walled settlement whose main gate complex faced the sea, indicating an orientation to the port (Pratico 1993a: 34; 1993b: 870). Its date, based on the pottery finds, was between the eighth and sixth centuries, although new, limited excavations conducted in 1999 found pottery that, on preliminary inspection, dated only to the seventh and sixth centuries BCE (Mussell 1999: 6). Grooved-rim cooking pots with necks, Edomite cooking pots and painted pottery were among the remains beside 'Assyrian'-style bowls, carinated cups, bottles and censers and Negevite ware (Pratico 1993a: 39-50). A number of rooms contained large storage jars whose handles were stamped with a seal that read, 'Belonging to Qos-Anal, servant of the king' (Divito 1993: 53-55). Qos was the national god of Edom. Other Edomite inscriptions were found, including ostracon 6043 from room 70, which contained a list of ten names, three of which contain the element Qos and two more of which might have done so. The remaining five names were West Semitic. No name was Arab

(Albright 1941: 13-14; Divito 1993: 55-57). A jar graffito and an inscribed sherd were similarly written in Edomite script (Divito 1993: 53-58). One jar from room 40 that bore two characters believed to be in a south Semitic language, possibly Minean or proto-Dedanite (Divito 1993: 62). This occupational level was ended as a result of an attack, which destroyed the site.

The date of the final destruction of stratum IV is debated. Nelson Glueck, the orginal excavator, had suggested it was destroyed by the Neo-Babylonians in 586 BCE (1993: 869). John Lindsay, on the other hand, has proposed that it was destroyed during Nabonidus' campaign to conquer Tema' c. 552 BCE (1976: 38). In the latter case, the king's goal might have been to gain control of the Arab spice trade and make this the only viable route for moving goods to and from Arabia. For this reason, he would have ended Edom's competing trade network; by destroying the port city, he would have prevented the arrival and departure of goods by sea and forced the use of the overland route through Arabia instead.

William Albright has made the conflicting proposal that the final phase of stratum IV should be associated with Nabonidus' mercantile activity in northwest Arabia c. 552–545 BCE, when the site remained under Edomite control. In his opinion, it would have been destroyed in the closing years of the latter king's reign (1941: 14). However, it is unclear by whom.

Section Summary. Evidence for the physical presence and control of the Negev by Edom after 586 BCE is difficult to pinpoint. It seems as though their primary interest in the region would have been in the roads that caravans traversed from Arabia, the Feinan region, and the Gulf of Aqaba to markets in Gaza and the immediate region. While the territory south of the Beersheva Valley was marginal for successful agriculture and not conducive to widespread settlement, the hills north of the valley were able to sustain viable farmsteads, hamlets, and possibly some towns. However, it is uncertain whether the nineteen settlements that lay in the southern Judean hills in the vicinity of Hevron and down to the Beersheva basin were ceded to the formal control of Edom after 586 BCE or whether they remained within the administrative control of the newly established province of Yehud. Since there does not appear to have been an increase in settlement in this region during the Neo-Babylonian period, the common idea that Edomites and Arabs infiltrated the southern hill-country that was more or less empty and eventually settled down, being no part of any organized administration but constituting a sort of self-regulating frontier region, lacks credibility.

It makes more sense to me to propose that the border between the newly established province of Yehud and the expanded territorial state of Edom, which maintained its vassal status until at least 552 BCE, was placed at the northern edge of the Beersheva Valley where it adjoins the southern Judean hills and the southern Shephelah. Perhaps Tel Shoqet and Horvat Yattin were abandoned during the Neo-Babylonian period and only resettled after 400 BCE, after the province of Idumea was created and the forts at Arad (#283), Harei 'Anim (#284), Beersheva (#285) and Nahal Yattir (#286) were built along the northern edge of the valley.

The strongest evidence for Edomite presence is found at the two open-air sanctuaries at 'En Haseva and Horvat Qitmit, even though there is nothing that specifically dates their use after 586 BCE in the Neo-Babylonian period. Otherwise, there may have been some post-586 Edomite occupation at Malhata, at Aroer, and at the former fort building at 'En Haseva, that was made instead into a caravanserai. Although Malhata and Aroer lay within the marginal zone that received less than 200 millimeters of rain annually; nevertheless, even here, grain crops could have been successfully grown on a seasonal basis by channelling the little rain that fell into fields located along wadi banks. Such a strategy had been used much earlier during the Middle Bronze period in the Hauran region in southern Syria and northern Jordan (Eames 2003: 97-2000) and was used subsequently by the Nabateans in southern Jordan and the Negev. Food could have been grown using irrigation at 'En Haseva had the fort been made into a caravanserai.

The biggest impediment to positing more extensive Edomite settlement is the widespread occurrence of Edomite pottery in destruction levels at a number of sites. One has to posit one of two explanations. (1) Many of these sites were abandoned without a struggle at the end of the monarchy, administered for a time by Edomites, and then destroyed in 582 BCE by Nebuchadrezzar, in 552 BCE by Nabonidus, or at some other point by a Neo-Babylonian king or perhaps an Arab tribe, details of which have not been preserved in the few sources that have escaped the ravages of time. Or, (2) one has to accept the traditional destruction dates between 600–586 BCE. In the latter case, however, the Edomite pottery must be associated with Edomite trade and presence in the region in the closing decades of the Judahite monarchy.

Aramaic Ostraca from Persian-Era Idumea

We only have circumstantial evidence to determine when Idumea became a separate administrative province. The most relevant is more than 1,000 Aramaic ostraca that have been found over the last twenty years from somewhere near or in Khirbet El-Qom, a site located west of Hevron that is thought to have been ancient Makkedah (Lemaire 2002: 197). In addition, however, we have Aramaic ostraca from Persian-era Arad, Beersheva, and Tell es-Sera', and a single ostracon from Tell 'Ira. They all provide vital information about the administration of the Idumean region during the latter part of the Persian period (c. 363–332 BCE).

Khirbet El-Qom/Makkedah. None of the 1,000 plus ostraca recovered so far from the region around Khirbet el-Qom has been excavated legally so their find spots are as yet unknown. While one ostracon mentions the site of Idna (Lemaire 2002: #365), others refer to the storehouses of Makkedah so they might well originate from one or both of these settlements (Lemaire 2002: #35, 85, 127). They date between 363-313/312 BCE and probably are connected with the administration of this region (Lemaire 2000; 2003: 291).[31] These ostraca provide strong testimony that Idumea had been made into its own administrative unit by this time. How much before this time it existed is not certain; however, Lemaire's conclusion that Idumea first became a province at the beginning of the fourth century BCE is plausible in light of the ostraca (2003: 291).

The ostraca detail the delivery of various foodstuffs, straw, materials, and workmen to governmental warehouses and officials. They illustrate nicely the working of the local tax system (contra Eph'al and Naveh 1996: 15). Villagers were required to pay taxes-in-kind, including animals and animal products. In addition, they were required to supply materials for public projects, and corvée labor. All of these requirements have parallels in the Assyrian provincial taxation system, which many believe remained in place under the Neo-Babylonians and the Persians (e.g. Briant 1981: 22; Limet 2000).

The Neo-Assyrian administrative system assessed various types of taxes on crops for human consumption. Those from cultivated land were called *nusahe*, those on straw were called *shibshu*, and those on domestic animals and animal products called *tsibtu* (Postgate 1974: 171-72, 189, 208). Taxes-in-kind that were delivered by individuals to local officials were designated by the general term *pirru*, while taxes collected by administrators who went out to round them up from those owing them in their regions were known as *bitqu*. *Bitqu* is more widely attested than *pirru* in the texts that have been preserved from the Neo-Assyrian empire (Postgate 1974: 59-60, 166). Beams were included among *bitqu* items in Assyria (Postgate 1974: 62)

Ilku was the term used in the Neo-Assyrian administration to designate the personal service men owed the king in exchange for landholding, although it may have been widened over time to include mandatory labor to be supplied by male citizens, whether landholders or not. It could only be levied on humans, not on animals (Postgate 1974: 62, 86, 91). Men called up to perform their *ilku* were either sent to do military service or were put into labor gangs (Postgate 1974: 206-208, 221-22, 227). It was possible for some landowners to equip substitutes to stand in for them or to pay a certain amount of money instead to the proper authorities, which was known as *kasap (rikis) qabli*, 'money for (the outfitting of) the soldier' (Postgate 1974: 91).

The main crop in Idumea was barley, though wheat was also grown (e.g. Eph'al and Naveh 1996: #29). Taxes were paid both in measures of winnowed grain and also in lesser amounts of ground, fine flour (e.g Eph'al and Naveh 1996: #30) and barley groats (e.g. Eph'al and Naveh 1996: #41, 42, 49, 50). In addition, olives (Eph'al and Naveh 1996: #186; Lemaire 2002: #132, 294), oil (Eph'al and Naveh 1996: #17, 32; Lemaire 2002: #56, 70, 140, 232) and wine (Eph'al and Naveh 1996: #150; Lemaire 2002: #90, 253) were delivered to the local authorities. Villagers were also expected to supply straw (e.g. Eph'al and Naveh 1996: #23), probably for the horses used in the postal system and by military patrols, and wood (Eph'al and Naveh 1996: #25, 129, 158, 167). There are a few examples of the payment of animals (Eph'al and Naveh 1996: #46; Lemaire 2002: 251, 167) and animal skins (Eph'al and Naveh 1996: #151). Examples of materials that locals had to supply for public works include pegs (Eph'al and Naveh 1996: #28), a beam (Eph'al and Naveh 1996: #86) and possibly ladders (Eph'al and Naveh 1996: #135). It appears that in Idumea, the *pirru* system of tax collection prevailed for straw, foodstuffs, and building materials, while animals, animal hides and wool products may primarily have been collected by using the *bitqu* system.

Finally, there are records of the local villagers supplying laborers (Eph'al and Naveh 1996: #69, 87, 95, 118; Lemaire 2002: #114, 130) and artisans (Lemaire 2002: #15). In addition, the lists of personal names on certain ostraca may detail contingents of men doing their compulsory annual *ilku* labor, either as workers on public projects or as soldiers (Eph'al and Naveh 1996: #178, 181-83; Lemaire 2002: #154-84). Some of the instances that record the delivery of money may reflect the practice of allowing required corvée labor to be paid for in silver instead (Eph'al and Naveh 1996: #140-41).

The ostraca demonstrate that villagers could borrow grain from the local storehouses; when they did they paid back the interest in kind (Eph'al and Naveh 1996: 47, 92). Some of the ostraca seem to be records of the amount of seed needed to plant certain allotments; they imply that the land was owned by the crown but leased to locals (Eph'al and Naveh 1996: 13, #185-95; Lemaire 2002: #258-83). The seeds might have been supplied annually, with the tenants then being responsible for their planting, weeding, and harvesting. The labourers would have been allowed to keep a percentage of the yield for personal consumption but would have turned over the majority of the harvest to the local storehouses, designated officials, or provincial facilities.

Arad. About 100 Aramaic ostraca have been excavated at Arad; only forty-two have at least one legible word intact. Their style of handwriting indicates they were written in the fourth century and were contemporary with those found at Khirbet El-Qom. All bear incomplete date formulae that give only the day and month, but no regnal year; this indicates their use as informal, internal records. Presumably, the information was transferred to a more formal, official ledger that contained the year dates. The ostraca reflect the payment of taxes-in-kind on grain, and, in addition, give us some insight into the workings of a fort. There are two references to a *degel*, which was a military unit or regiment (Naveh 1981: #12, 18; Porten 1968: 29-35).

Some ostraca appear to record the delivery of quantities of barley and wheat to officials at the site by local farmers (Naveh 1981: #1-6, 17, 20, 27). More interesting, however, are the number of deliveries or assignments of horses (Naveh 1981: # 3, 12, 14, 15, 16, 26, 32) and donkeys (Naveh 1981: #1, 2, 14, 21-25) and, in one instance, a camel (Naveh 1981: #24). The horses were apparently used by the military to patrol the local region and some may have been used by postal agents and messengers in transit. The donkeys, on the other hand, seem to have been used as pack animals by military regiments and officials in transit (Naveh 1981: #12, 37).

There are two references to 'the horsemen of Eliashiv' and one to an unnamed horseman who received rations of crushed barley, probably to be eaten during tours of duty (Naveh 1981: #7, 8, 11). It is possible, therefore, that in some of the instances that refer to horses they are being 'signed out' for official use rather than delivered as taxes-in-kind.

On the other hand, however, the reference to the twelve colts in inscription #6 that were delivered in conjunction with one seah, three qabs of barley must be understood to reflect a tax payment; colts cannot be ridden but would have needed breaking in and training. It could be taken as indirect evidence that horses and donkeys were entrusted to local tax-payers, who may also have been soldiers assigned to the fort in many instances, to groom and feed when they were not being used. The practice of 'loaning out' horses used for chariots to men who were charged with their feeding and care fell under *iskaru* in the Neo-Assyrian empire: materials or equipment issued by the administration to men working for it (Postgate 1974: 210).

Such a practice would have cut down on the amount of stable space and straw storage needed at the fort proper. There is a reference to a straw-shed and another, larger storage building for straw ('house of straw') owned by a person named Anani, who also had a cave (Naveh 1981: #38). This does not seem to refer to facilities within Arad itself but to privately owned buildings, which would be consistent with the 'farming out' of animals for a period of rest. Be that as it may, some straw would have been needed at the fort to feed incoming and outgoing animals so it is likely that the locally assessed taxes-in-kind included some obligation to furnish straw to the fort, even though not one of the legible ostraca has provided firm evidence of this practice.

Two lists of names occur, as at Khirbet El-Qom (Naveh 1981: #39-40). They are likely duty rosters, either for military service or for corvée labor to undertake building or repair works at the fort.

Beersheva. During eight years of excavations, fifty-seven Persian-era ostraca dating to the fourth century were found. Many were found in pits located inside the city walls, around the Persian-era fort. Initially, J. Naveh argued that they had been discarded into refuse pits (Naveh 1973: 79), presumably after their details were transferred into a larger ledger. However, in a subsequent study, he changed his mind and argued that they were labels that had been placed in the storage pits along with the grain, indicating their origins and dates of delivery (Naveh 1979: 193). Ze'ev Herzog thinks that the pits may originally have held grain but subsequently were used for refuse (personal communication). All the ostraca are in a poor state of preservation and many are illegible.

A number record the delivery of quantities of barley and wheat by various individuals to Beersheva, presumably as payments of taxes-in-kind (Naveh 1973: #1-9; Naveh 1979: #26-30). Their names suggest that one third were of Arab background, one third of Edomite background, and one third of Semitic origin (Jews and Arameans) (Naveh 1979: 194). Others are lists of names (Naveh 1979: #32-44), which, as noted at Khirbet El-Qom and Arad, might detail corvée laborers who either were assigned to military rotations or to manual labor gangs. Those that include amounts of money after names or quantities of grain either record the payment of 'salaries' to these individuals from government warehouses and funds or record the payment of taxes-in-kind and in silver by various individuals.

Tel es-Sera'. Four Aramaic ostraca were found during three seasons of excavation at Tel es-Sera'. Two were found in Area B in the first season of excavations. They were inside two pits, which also contained whole or restorable domestic vessels and imported Attic ware dating to the fifth–fourth centuries of the Persian period (Oren 1972: 168). Two additional ones were found in one of the two subsequent seasons. Ostracon 5607 from locus 2193 contains a list of fourteen names, although six of them have disappeared completely. Two names are probably Hebrew, two possibly Arab, and the remaining three with more than a single letter appear to be west Semitic (Cross 2003: 162-63). After the names comes the abbreviation *b*, probably representing the cubic volume measure known as a 'bath', and then a number varying between 1 and 3. This list seems to have recorded the delivery of tax payments of a food commodity, probably barley or wheat, by the named individuals. The Persian-era stratum featured a grain storage pit that measured 7 meters wide x 3 meters deep, and another brick-lined installation whose diameter was 5 meters (Oren 1973: 252; 1993b: 1334). Since the site has never been published, we cannot determine if this list might have been associated with either feature.

Ostracon 1246 from locus 2170 bear the name *Nahashtab*, meaning 'good omen', while ostracon 1034, whose locus is apparently unkown, bears the name *zbydw*, with the Arabic ending *–w*. It is a nickname that means 'bestow upon', whose full form would have ended with the name of a particular deity (Cross 2003: 163). Finally, ostracon 305 from locus 2005 bore two lines of writing, but only the first is legible, and incomplete; the right part of the sherd is missing. What remains reads *Jhw b'srn*. The second word might be part of a date formula; it means 'on the twentieth' (Cross 2003: 163). The first and third are thought to reflect writing styles of the mid-fourth century BCE while the last could be mid- or late-fourth century BCE. No comments about date are given for the third one (Cross 2003: 163). Nothing definitive can be said about the purpose of these last three ostraca, though the two names are likely to have been borne by Arabs.

Tel 'Ira. Two Aramaic ostraca dating to the Persian period have been found in excavations. One was found inside a house in Area C in stratum V, the Persian-era occupation at the site, while the other was found in fill above a Byzantine structure in Area M but can be dated by its style of handwriting to the fourth century BCE. The first is fragmentary and has some blurred letters, but seems to read in its three lines, (1) goat, wild goat, (2) [.]*sm'* (a personal name) 1 *sh*(*eqel*), (3) Wa'el (a personal name) 2 q(uarters of a sheqel). It is likely that the ostracon records two sums of money paid by two individuals for hides of domesticated and wild goats. The hides would have been used to make leather clothes (Naveh 1999: 412-13).

The second also has blurred letters, especially in its second line, but seems to read, (1)Natnu (a personal name), barley: 11 *seah*, 2) 2[+] D (Biran and Cohen 1979: 125). It is a record for the delivery of the specified quantity of barley by a person named Natnu, and of some other abbreviated commodity that cannot be read, in the smaller amount represented by the abbreviation D. This abbreviation appears in Beersheva ostraca 1, 3, and 4 and so was a standard measure amount of the time (Naveh 1999: 413). Both are consistent with the types of ostraca from Khirbet El-Qom, showing the paying of taxes-in-kind and the resale of non-edible raw commodities that probably had been delivered as taxes-in-kind to private individuals.

Section Summary. The various ostraca that have been recovered from sites in the southern Shephelah and Negev provide evidence of an efficient administrative system operating within the province of Idumea. Local farmers produced foodstuffs that fed them and their families, as well as government officials, both civil and military. The latter received food rations that were received from the farmers as taxes-in-kind. The dates recorded on the bulk of the sherds from Khirbet El-Qom indicate that this system was in effect in the course of the fourth century BCE during the reigns of Artaxerxes II and Artaxerxes III. A portion of the personnel stationed at the forts may have been professional soldiers and mercenaries, but it is likely that their ranks were regularly augmented by local farmers who were performing mandatory annual *pilku* labor. It may well be that these local inhabitants had been granted land in a *ḥatru*, a communally held allotment, in exchange for the obligation to furnish able bodies for military duty when called upon to do so (Briant 2002: 405), in addition to other taxes-in-kind on their produce. Horses were a vital part of military operations in the Negev.

The earliest recorded date in these ostraca is 363 BCE. On the one hand, this allows us to move back the creation of Idumea as an independent province by a little more than fifty years from the otherwise earliest literary reference to its existence by Diodorus Siculus in 312 BCE (19.95.2). On the other hand, however, it does not help us know how much before that date Idumea may have been established, or if it is merely coincidence that no earlier texts have turned up so far.

Geshem the Arab and the Northern Border of Arabia

André Lemaire's claim that the ostraca from Khirbet El-Qom confirm that the southern border of Judah did not change from 582 BCE, when Gedaliah, the first appointed Neo-Babylonian governor of Yehud, was assassinated until the annexation of Idumea by John Hyrcanus in 112/111 BCE goes beyond the evidence of the ostraca. He asserts that Bet-Zur was the southernmost

Judean fortress, while Lakish, Maresha and Hevron already were in Edom/Idumea or Arabia (2003: 291). The last uncertainty is revealing. A few sentences earlier in his argument, Lemaire states that the territory south of Beth-Zur had already been assigned to neo-Babylonian Arabia and later, by implication at the time of Nehemiah, was part of the Arab kingdom of Qedar before being made into the Persian province of Edom/Idumea at the beginning of the fourth century BCE (2003: 291). But at no point has he explained why the border with Arabia in the neo-Babylonian period would have been moved north to Bet-Zur from the traditional southern border of the kingdom of Judah before its demise. There is no proof that the traditional southern border of Judah was changed before the creation of Idumea as a province and it is just as logical to assume that the traditional border was left intact. The governor of Yehud could have been made responsible for maintaining a few military outposts in the Negev to oversee the roads, even though there was little settlement in this area.

Lemaire voices a common view concerning the fate of the southern half of the kingdom of Judah shortly after its conquest by the Neo-Babylonians in 586 BCE. It is widely assumed that after the elimination of the kingdom of Judah in 586 BCE, the southern portion of the former kingdom, which eventually becomes Idumea, was counted as part of the large Arab domain (so, e.g., Dumbrell 1971: 44; Aharoni 1979: 414-15; de Geus 1979/80: 60-61; Blenkinsopp 1988: 329 implicitly; Stern 2001: 369). This idea tends to be based in turn on the prior assumption that, since Geshem the Arab controlled it in the time of Nehemiah, Arab control must have been established by the Neo-Babylonians and simply inherited by the Persians. Yet as discussed in chapter 1 in connection with Geshem, it is not certain that the three adversaries, Sinuballit, Tobiah, and Geshem, were all governors of the regions adjoining Yehud to the north, east, and south. Since Sinuballit is known from the Elephantine letters and from bullae to have been *pehah* of Samerina, it has been assumed by analogy that the other two were as well. There is no firm ground for this this assumption, however.

Israel Eph'al has argued that Geshem's conflicts with Nehemiah would have been over trade routes and rights and that his kingdom would have lain around al-Jawf in the Arabian peninsula, not contiguous to Yehud (1982: 212; contra Graf 1990: 139-43) (see map 22). Tobiah, on the other hand, seems to have gained his influence in Yehud from marriage into an influential family, but, as discussed above, may have been a returnee himself, and if not, need not have been the governor of Ammon. Although Sinuballit became linked to the high priestly family of Jerusalem through marriage, as discussed in Chapter 1, he would have been quite elderly or even dead at the time of the actual marriage, so it would not have provided a basis for his meddling in local affairs during the rebuilding of the city in the mid-450s BCE. It is not clear that governors of adjoining provinces would have interfered in the affairs of Yehud, especially when plans for expansion and development would have had imperial authorization. Nevertheless, it is possible that disputes over settlements in the border region between the two provinces caused some friction between Sinuballt and the local governor of Yehud, whether that was Zerubbabel or Nehemiah. Perhaps Sinuballit also chose not to faciitate the transporation of raw materials from or through his territory that were intended to be used in the rebuilding of Jerusalem. Finally, we need to give serious consideration to the possibility that Sinuballit's role as adversary, especially his opposition to the rebuilding of the temple, may have been expanded by a later redactor, who considered him to be a respresentative of the Samaritans and the competing Samaritan temple in Samerina.

The Loss of Egypt and the Creation of a New Southern Levantine Border
for the Persian Empire in Idumea

Political developments in the first quarter of the fourth century may have led the ruling Persian king to decide that the southern territory of Yehud needed much fuller development and would be best administered as an independent unit. Specifically, the loss of Egypt from the empire after its successful revolt in 401 BCE now placed the southern boundary of the Persian empire at the Beersheva Valley. This would have been a logical time to establish Idumea as a separate province, with its own seat of power and internal administration, which could build additional forts in the Beersheva Valley to secure the new southern border of the empire. The traditional southern border of Yehud could then have been moved north to Bet-Zur at this point.

The Status of Lakish

A monumental, Persian-era building measuring 36 × 45.5 meters was excavated atop the podium that had formerly housed a palace–fort complex at the end of the monarchic period, when the site was part of the kingdom of Judah. The Persian structure appears to have been a governor's palace that was built around an open, central courtyard measuring 18 × 18 meters, surrounded by groups of rooms. The southern wing had an audience room for receiving dignitaries and tribute-bearers and messengers (Tufnell 1953: 131-35; Reich 1992a: 116-19). Such a building would only have been found in a provincial capital, sub-district capital, or on a governor's estate. This suggests in turn that Lakish became the seat or sub-seat of a province at the time that this building was constructed on site, or a governor's villa in the western part of the province of Yehud.

In the final publications of the excavations conducted from 1932–1938, O. Tufnell concluded that this building in Level I was constructed c. 450 BCE and remained in use until c. 350 BCE (1953: 48, 133) on the basis of the pottery found on or just above the plastered floors of the building. The locally-made jars and mortaria were characteristic of the sixth–fourth centuries BCE, while the Red-Figured sherds had an equal proportion of fifth and fourth century types. In addition, Black Glazed and Black Attic sherds dating from 475–425 BCE were lying on or close to the original floor surfaces in several rooms (1953: 133).

In order to build the Residency, the earlier walls of the last monarchic structure on the citadel podium, Palace C of Level II, had been reduced to a common height and then the entire area had been covered by c. twenty centimeters of humus before the new building was erected (1953: 131). Outside the southeast corner of this new building and extending along its eastern side were more than fifty pits that had been dug into the fallen debris from the collapsed walls of Palace C (1953: 151). The contents tend to suggest that the pits were dug as the need arose during the occupation of the Residency, although some may date to the later Level 1 occupation. Their function is unclear; they may have stored grain; some had traces of straw (1953: 151; 153).

Alexander Fantalkin and Oren Tal have recently proposed that the Residency was built c. 400 BCE (2005), not 450 BCE, as argued by Olga Tufnell. They base their redating on a fresh examination of pottery that was found in the earlier seasons as well as in subsequent excavations in 1973–1977 directed by David Ussishkin. They report that pits were found to underlie the IB Residency building containing locally made Persian pottery and Attic imports dating predominantly to the first half of the fourth century BCE. According to their interpretation, the site had been occupied in the early Persian period, which they call Level IA, prior to its being made the new provincial seat in Level I B (Fantalkin and Tal 2005).

In cross-referencing their discussion with the first preliminary report of the later excavations, it appears that the pits in question were rather a single large pit, locus 3248, which underlay the the the pillar bases in the western portico of the building, by which one passed from the courtyard to Room U. The sub-bases of the two pillars had been embedded in the fill of this large pit, which was found to extend over the line of the outer southern foundation wall of podium A that had belonged to the construction of the first Iron Age palace on the site. The pit appears to have been dug in order to rob out stones from the earlier podium wall that could be reused in the new Residency building. A similar robbing was discovered along the northern Podium wall (W250) in pit 3017. The backfill in both pits contained burnt brick rubble, probably destruction debris from Palace C, and Persian pottery fragments (Ussishkin 1978: 31, 41). Only pit 3248 underlay the residency building, however, so this must be the source of the sherds used by A. Fantalkin and O. Tal in their analysis.

They state that the dating of plain Attic ware and painted Black and Red figure ware has been refined in the decades since O. Tufnell's original publication and that most of the imported forms she thought were equally distributed between the fifth and fourth centuries are now dated to the first half of the fourth century. Only a miniscule number of Attic sherds found in the building date to the fifth century BCE. For them, these are best seen as heirlooms, with the date for the founding of the residency being determined by the latest materials contained in the pit and fill underneath the residency's floors. While the pits (Pit 3248?) contain primarily fifth-century forms, there was one sherd from the 1938 season that they say was found below the floor level of one of the rooms in the Residency that dates to the first half of the fourth century BCE (Fantalkin and Tal 2005).

Assuming with Fantalkin and Oren that the single sherd of the ware found underneath the floor of a room belongs to the initial phase of building the Residency and not a subsequent alteration done to the building, it would have been deposited before or at the time of building. Thus, it can be seen to indicate that the residency was built in the first half of the fourth century BCE (Level IB) as they propose. However, it is also possible that it was deposited during subsequent alterations to the building in Level IC in the late-Persian and early-Hellenistic period. Some drums of dismantled columns were reused in a secondary context, indicating that there was a subsequent phase of occupation in the complex that involved changes to the building. The latter option needs serious consideration since sherds of several transitional late-fifth century or early-fourth century Attic imports were found on the floors of the building. How would a later sherd end up under the floor?

Alexander Fantalkin and Oren Tal have suggested that the one (?) or two (?) late-fifth century sherds found on the floors are better understood to be heirlooms than chronological anchors for the date when the residency was built. This is possible. It would presume that a few pieces of pottery owned by someone's parents had been brought by the new administrative personnel to the completed complex when it was occupied. These forms would not have been readily available for purchase from local merchants since they were no longer in regular production and circulation. High-ranking Persian officials are likely already to have had such luxury goods in their existing surroundings, however, so this explanation is logical.

Having said this, however, they go on to contradict themselves in their suggestion that Attic ware was not widely distributed inland from the coastal plain and its presence should be seen as an indicator that Lakish was an administrative center. This point does not square with the presence of late-fifth century Attic forms in the pits of level IC, underneath the floors of the Residency. According to their proposal, the various pits excavated in the 1930s and the 1970s under and around the Residency indicate that Lakish had been resettled in the early Persian period prior to the construction of the Residency and the pits represent a distinctive phase of occupation they have labelled 1A. But this means that the Attic ware found in them had already been obtained by the earlier residents at the site, perhaps because Lakish lay on a major road between the coastal plain and the Hevron hills. Such forms apparently would have been more readily available at sites bordering the coastal plain than they have assumed and was not only used by elite administrative personnel.

If the argument of Fantalkin and Tal is followed to its logical outcome, it would need to be presumed that the imported late-fifth century Attic pottery in the pit(s) underneath the floor(s) of the Residency was deposited at the time of the construction of the structure, having perhaps been broken in transit when the personal belongings of the new officials had been shipped. While such a scenario could allow for a construction date c. 400 BCE as Fantalkin and Tal have proposed, it is not the only explanation. It is equally plausible to argue that the Attic ware in the pits underlying the building were not heirlooms but contemporaneous pieces, suggesting a construction date c. 450 BCE, as O. Tufnell originally argued. The one sherd that dates from 400–350 BCE either was deposited during subsequent alterations or may have been an early example of the type of vessel to which it had once belonged. Fantalkin and Tal do not say what type of ware it is or which room its was found under so we cannot check to see if the date range of this particular vessel might have had a slightly earlier date of introduction or if this room might have evidence of subsequent alterations.

It seems more logical to argue in light of the limited information presented in their article and the information published so far from the two sets of excavations in Area P that housed the Residency and earlier Iron Age palace-citadel complexes that there was no stratum 1B. Pit 3248 was part of a robber's trench dug at the time the Residency was built to secure stones for the new foundation, while the fifty pits outside the southeast corner of the Residency walls are likely to have been dug and used after the building was completed. No pits like those outside are reported to have been found by either team under any part of the Residency proper, just the single robber's trench. Neither the exterior pits nor the single interior robber's trench provides evidence for a reoccupation of the site c. 450 BCE, on the assumption that the reference to Lakish in Neh. 11.30 as a site that was resettled after the return to the land is historically reliable.

The cogency of their proposal and my counter-proposal will need reassessment when the final publication report for the excavations at Lakish conducted from 1973–1987 is published. Its appearance is supposed to be imminent. Only then can scholars and the general public gain access to the full details needed to make a reasoned judgment about the history of the reoccupation of the site in the Persian period.

Until this report is released, I do not feel able to make an informed decision about which anomalous sherd is more significant: the late one under the floor or the earlier one(s) above the floor. Sound explanations can be given to account for either, but it is necessary to know exactly how many of the later sherds there are, where the earlier sherd was found, where the reused column segments are located and what other evidence there might be of secondary alterations to the building and their nature and location, and the date of all the imported pottery found in the robber's trenches and in the pits beside the Residency structure. Thus, I will refrain from making a decision about the date when the Residency was first constructed.

Notwithstanding, the founding date of the Residency is crucial for our ability to deduce when Idumea became a separate province. The Residency was almost certainly a governor's seat or a governor's villa, and since Lakish lay within the territory that became Idumea, it is logical to conclude that it became the provincial seat for Idumea when it was made into a province. According to the traditional dating of the building's foundation, Idumea would have been established at the same time that Jerusalem was being rebuilt and Yehud reorganized. As such, it could have been part of a larger master plan for the development of Cisjordan that Artaxerxes I instituted. According to the revised dating of Fantalkin and Tal, however, it would have been established about 400 BCE. This would have been in the wake of the loss of Egypt from the Persian empire and the need to strengthen the new southern border of the empire, which now ran through the Beersheva Valley.[32]

Both are plausible scenarios; however, two considerations favor the later date for the creation of Idumea. First, there was no particular need to establish Idumea before the loss of Egypt; this area could have been effectively administered by the newly redeveloped Yehud or by Gaza or by the Arab tribes who controlled the stretches of desert south of the Negev highlands. The trade routes that ran through the Beersheva Valley were the main source of income, but lay well within the boundaries of the empire and so were not under unusual threat. Second, the ostraca found so far within Idumea date from the fourth century (363–311 BCE), which is more consistent with the establishment of Idumea as a province in 400 BCE than 450 BCE. It would be odd to have no signs of internal administration in a province for eighty-three years; it is already odd that there are thirty-seven years without records. However, it may well be the case that future finds of ostraca will close both gaps.[33]

Alternatively, it needs to be asked whether the presence of a governor's palace at Lakish requires us to conclude that this was the seat of an independent province. There is nothing to prevent the view that Lakish served as the seat of a sub-district within Yehud and that a palace was constructed on site where the governor of Yehud or the visiting satrap could have resided while touring the province regularly. Thus, it is not absolutely necessary to conclude that the existence of a palace signals the existence of an independent province with its own governor. If the traditional date for the building of the palace is maintained, this alternative option needs serious consideration.

Charles Carter has argued that the palace was built c. 450 BCE and served as the seat of an independent province that included the Shephelah; as a result, he excludes the Shephelah from lying within the terrritoy of Yehud. He argues on the one hand, on the basis of Central Place theory, that it was unlikely that a governing body with limited resources and autonomy would have been able to extend its influence beyond certain natural topographical boundaries. He accepts the application of Christaller's Central-Place theory (1966) by K. Hoglund to southern Palestine, which identifies Gezer, Lakish, and Jerusalem as central administrative complexes, each surrounded by a hinterland with a radius of twenty kilometers (1989). In this analysis, the Shephelah falls under the domain of Lakish (1999: 92-93).

On the other hand, Carter argues that, since the Shephelah was an independent geographical zone, the Neo-Babylonians would have made it into a separate province, which the Persians inherited and left in place, building the palace complex at Lakish to serve as its seat. He does not discuss whether the seat had been there originally or if this was a new development (1999: 91). This area had been part of the kingdom of Judah until 701 BCE, when Sennacherib reassigned it to the control of Ashdod, Ekron, and Gaza after Hezekiah's rebellion. However, it had been regained before the end of the monarchy, perhaps during the reign of Manasseh (697–642 BCE), but probably by the end of the reign of Josiah (639–609 BCE). Ekron, the center for the processing of the olives from the Shephelah into oil, was destroyed in 605 BCE so that any land it might have still controlled at that time would have been open for the Judahite kings to reclaim. Since this area would have been under Judahite control in 586 BCE when the Neo-Babylonians converted the former kingdom to the province of Yehud, it is logical to include it within the borders of the new territorial unit administered from Mizpah.

The applicability of Central-Place theory to Persian provincial structure is questionable. In a situation where adjoining territory belonged to the same empire so that there was no need to worry about the constant threat of invasion, the amount of area that would have been administered from a provincial seat could have varied greatly, but could easily have covered significantly more territory than a twenty-kilometer radius.[34] In addition, larger territories may have been subdivided and administered from satellite regional or district seats. The number of unexcavated sites within the Shephelah and Judean hill-country precludes our knowing where these satellite facilities existed and so prevents a responsible application of this model. We cannot rule out the possibility that Lakish may have served as a sub-provincial seat or may simply have housed a governor's villa, in which case it would not have served as a central place, but as a site of secondary rank, dependent ultimately on the provincial capital.

Chapter Summary

Our examination of the three lists that purport to reflect settlements within Yehud at the time of Artaxerxes I, Nehemiah 3, 7.6-69, and 11.25-35, has led to the conclusion that none is a reliable indicator of the extent of the province's historical territorial holdings. In trying to determine the date when Idumea was created as a separate province, it was observed that certain passages in the prophetical books of Ezekiel, Obadiah, and Malachi, especially Obadiah vv. 19-20, indicate that control over the Beersheva Valley and the Negev was ceded by the Neo-Babylonians to Edom after 586 BCE. This is consistent with Edom's hostile activity in the region in the closing days of the monarchy as revealed in Arad ostracon 24. Evidence of the physical presence of Edomites in the region as Judah's successors has been argued to exist in the archaeological record at 'En Haseva, Malhata, Qitmit and Aroer. Additional Edomite presence might be found at Nahal Haro'a and possibly at Tel Shoqet and Horvat Yattin at the edge of the southern Judean hill-country, if these sites are excavated in the future. The latter two sites lie just north of the Beersheva Valley and are well removed from the sites that cluster around Hevron, inland in the southern Judean hills.

It is uncertain how long Edom maintained control of the Beersheva Valley and the Negev. Excavations at Buseirah, the capital of Edom, seem to show that the site was occupied until the end of the Persian period. In theory, then, it could have controlled the area throughout the Neo-Babylonian and Persian periods (from 586–332 BCE) if no changes in policy were introduced after the initial Neo-Babylonian policy had been implemented. However, this does not appear to have been what transpired historically. Specifically, Mal. 1.4 could be taken to indicate that Edom lost control of this region in the early Persian period to Yehud, though this is not the only possible interpretation of the verse. More importantly, the building of the governor's residency at Lakish either c. 450 BCE or 400 BCE probably provides evidence for the establishment of Idumea as a sub-district of Yehud or the governor's western villa in the middle of the fifth century, or as a new Persian province in its own right at the end of the fifth century BCE.

It is my suggestion that Artaxerxes I was the first Persian monarch to alter the status of the Beersheva Valley and the Negev that the Neo-Babylonians had instituted. Initially assigned to Edomite jurisdiction in 586 BCE, it was transferred to the jurisdiction of Yehud when this province was reorganized and redeveloped in the mid-fifth century. Part of the redevelopment of the region included the importation of new settlers from Mesopotamia to be settled in the under-populated areas of the southern hill-country and the Shephelah. They were to be given farmsteads near fire-relay stations and forts that were to be established along the main roads of the province. Since this area had been controlled from Jerusalem in the past, it could be done so again efficiently, and the food supplies needed to feed authorized Persian agents in transit along the more southerly routes could be made readily available from taxes paid in kind by the local settlers.

There would not have been much need to move new settlers into Yehud from Mesopotamia had the southern border of the province been established just south of Jerusalem. The resulting territory would have been quite circumspect and of little strategic or economic value. In addition, there already was a sizeable population located in the region north and northwest of Jerusalem, as well as in the central Judeans highlands, with a modest presence in the southern Judean highlands in the vicinity of Hevron. The most important road running from east to west within the region would have been the route through the Beersheva Valley from Arabia to Gaza, while the most important route running north to south would have been the coastal road, which lay outside the jurisdiction of Yehud. Thus, for me, it is the account in the book of Nehemiah of a large number of 'returnees' to Yehud, which undoubtedly included many non-Jews who were settling the region for the first time, that strongly implies that Artaxerxes I intended to include the development of the southern Judean hill-country and the southern Shephelah as part of the larger plans for the full incorporation of Yehud into the Persian administrative, economic, and military systems. If one wants to argue that this account is unreliable historically and has been created to demonstrate the actualization of prophetic announcements of a large-scale return to the land of Judah as found, for example, in 2 Isaiah (43.4-6, 19-20; 44.26; 45.13; 49.8-13, 19; 51.3; 54.1-3), then it would be possible to set the boundary of Yehud under Artaxerxes I further north, as proposed by most scholars. Yet these same scholars all accept the accuracy of the biblical account.

We cannot be certain if Idumea would have been made a sub-district of Yehud or would simply have been considered an integral part of the newly expanded province. Had it been made a sub-district, it would be possible to argue that Lakish was chosen to be its seat and that the governor's residency and other public buildings belonging to Level 1B were built about the same time that Jerusalem was rebuilt as the provincial capital, c. 450 BCE. Otherwise, it would be possible to suggest that Lakish was selected to house a governor's villa in the western part of the provincial territory.

If Lakish were not already a sub-district seat or governor's western residency, then it became the official seat of Idumea c. 400 BCE, when, in the wake of the successful revolt of Egypt, the boundary of the Persian empire effectively became the Beersheva Valley. Whatever its status while it was under the jurisdiction of Yehud, c. 400 BCE it became a fully-fledged, self-sufficient province whose primary role within the empire was to protect the new boundary and ensure the ongoing movement of trade caravans from Arabia to Gaza and oversee the safe passage of Persian agents and troops, if necessary, along the southernmost road within the empire's firm control. Undoubtedly, more forts and garrisons would have been established in the area at this time, both to boost protection and to stockpile supplies for the inevitable attempts to reconquer Egypt. The mixed Arab, Edomite, Aramean and Jewish population that became resident in the fourth century reflects the various interest groups who originated primarily from the adjoining regions. Only the Arameans are a surprise element, although some may have arrived as new government settlers at this time. The Jews would already have been present for fifty years at some sites, while the Arabs and Edomites may have been operative in the area for generations, leading caravans through the Beersheva Valley. Some may have decided to settle to protect family trading interests while others may have been induced to settle in exchange for serving as seasonal soldiers or scouts for the newly built forts.

In the upcoming survey of settlement patterns in Yehud in the second half of the fifth century BCE, the southern Judean highlands north of the Beersheva Valley and the southern Shephelah will be included as integral parts of Yehud.

Endnotes

1. The possibility that two separate sources have been combined, one for vv. 1-15 and one for vv. 16-32, has been considered but rejected by M. Burrows (1933/34: 117-19) and H.G.M. Williamson (1985: 199-200). The change in formula from 'at his hand' in the first part to 'after him' in the second prompted the consideration of this possibility.

2. The decision of the Greek translator of the book to construe the preposition *le* in the sense of 'up to', using the preposition *eos*, only reflects his best guess to make sense within the context and he has undoubtedly been influenced by the giving of the limits of segments elsewhere in the chapter.

3. M. Avi-Yonah has added a sixth district centered at Jericho, with its sub-district at Hasenaah (1966: 19-22). He has proposed that the sub-district seat of Jerusalem was Ramat Rahel rather than Gibeon, which he thinks was the sub-seat of Mizpah, instead. Likewise, he has disputed the sub-seat of Keilah, which he makes Adullam in place of Zanoah. The latter site he names instead as the sub-seat of Bet-Hakkerem. It is now widely thought that Ramat Rahel was Bet-Hakkerem, however, so his proposals for two of the districts are contradictory.

4. L. Batten, following the lead of the Greek translator's decision to render *pelek* not as a district but as 'the country around', has proposed that in Nehemiah 3 the term refers to the 'suburbs' of each of the five towns so listed. Each named *sar* had a domain not in the city proper in each case, but in the suburbs (1913: 212). The problem with this view is that none of these sites were cities; they were towns or fortresses, so there were no suburbs. It would be possible, however, to think of the farmsteads that lay outside the town/fortress walls to have composed the *pelek*. However, only Jerusalem is said to have had 'daughters' in the list in Nehemiah 3, and none of these five are among the nine settlements that are said to have 'daughters' in the list in Nehemiah 7.

5.   The objection voiced by M. Weinfeld that in Akkadian, both 'district' and 'tax' derive from the same root *pilku*, with the meaning 'district' being primary and 'service'being derivative, does not address the fundamental point raised by Demsky that the two meanings are distinctive and that 'service' is what is being designated here, not 'district' (2000).

6.   In Mesopotamia, an institution called *ḫatru* was developed in the Persian period whereby land was redistributed as fiefs to soldiers and artisans in exchange for mandatory annual corvée labor (Dandamaev 1994: 233; Briant 2002: 405). Thus, it is possible that the goldsmiths, shepherds, and perfumers were also pressed into service to help rebuild the wall as part of their annual corvée labor. In their cases, however, they were overseen by one of their own, who was not regularly a military commander.

7.   R Deutsch proposed that a fourth example was Tobshalem, but the lower left portion of the seal was broken, making it uncertain what followed *sr h---* (Deutsch 1999: #11). A subsequent complete impression made by the same seal has now been found and it indicates that Tobshalem bore the title '*sar* of the army' instead (Deutsch 2003: #7).

8.   The possibility should be left open that *sar* on these tokens stands for 'head of the prison', but this is not a necessary conclusion. Since such an individual would have been under the authority of the *sar* of the city and the king, the tokens can easily be representing the higher authorities rather than the specific one.

9.   Both were specifically commenting on the title '*sar* of the *birah*' used in Neh. 7.2 and so might have rendered the title '*sar* of the city' differently if they were relying on the military imagery associated with the *birah* or fort to guide their interpretation. I consider the two offices to be equivalent; a *birah* could also have a civilian population and was the equivalent of a city when it was not an isolated, self-standing fortress building.

10.   It is likely that Mizpah, Jerusalem and Keilah had civilian populations that lived alongside the local fort, who would have been liable to perform corvée labor. It is less certain that Bet-Hakkerem and Bet-Zur would have housed such people, however. Given their size, especially Bet-Hakkerem, they may have housed a fort and its personnel only.

11.   It appears as though some of these listings are names of settlements rather than clans: Arah, Pahat-Moab, Elam, and Ater. In these instances, clans may have taken on a geographical name rather than giving their name to the geographical region.

12.   Thus, the proposed southerly locations for Nebo (Nuba) and Elam (Khirbet Beit 'Elam) in the central Judean hill-country, both of which are based on name preservation, could stand as references to the 'other' two towns of this name. The equation of Harim with Khirbet Horan, in the western Judean hills close to the Shephelah, however, would need to be rethought, however (May 1974: 127, 130, 136).

13.   It can be noted that there is no overlap in site names with the five locations that supplied *pelek* labor in rebuilding the walls in Nehemiah 3: Mizpah, Keilah, Bet-Zur, Bet-Hakkerem and Jerusalem. However, Nehemiah 3 indicates that Jerusalem supplied two divisions of *pelek*-labor and also had 'daughters', so that it could stand as the single point of overlap between these two forms of administrative organization.

14.   Sitting on the fence on this issue, L.H. Brockington has suggested that it was copied from official archives in the Nehemiah-Ezra period and reflects 'the gradual reoccupation of Jewish (or formerly Jewish) territory in post-exilic times' (1969: 39). Without giving a date, C. Carter argues that the intended function of the passage is not to delineate the boundaries of the province, but to list sites to which Jews had returned in the years after Cyrus' decree or in which returnees had real or fictional ancestral connections, whether or not they lay within the borders of the province (1999: 81).

15.   It has been suggested by a number of Harvard-based scholars that jar handle stamps from Gibeon that include the name of Gibeon and a personal name provide contemporary evidence of the same practice proposed in options 2 and 3. However, the date of these stamps is disputed; a number of French and Israeli epigraphers date them to the late-eighth century BCE rather than to the sixth century BCE, so they do not provide firm corroboration of either point (Edelman 2003a: 156).

16.   Five additional ostraca in a poor state of preservation were also in the vicinity of the guardroom where four of the five pieces of the petition were found, the last one having been found just outside the room (Naveh 1962a: 27-28). One bore the personal name Hoshavyahu son of Yesh... inscribed on a jar (Naveh 1960: 136); a

second of eight lines contains the name Ovadyahu; a third seems to read 'four shekels'; a fourth 'shekel' or 'he weighed', and a fifth, '(Ne)tatsbaal weighed four (shekels) of silver, *after the king's weight* (represented by a symbol) as a (religious) donation' (Naveh 1962a: 29-31).

17. E. Stern has argued, for example, that the Yehud-stamped jar found at Gezer means that this site, which he believes would have belonged to the sub-district of Lod, was part of Yehud (2001: 431). Such an argument is highly speculative.

18. C. Carter sets the southern boundary as follows: from 'En-Gedi, moving northwest, toward Tekoa and then west to Bet-Zur and onwards to Keilah (1999: 98). He claims that in the second half of the Persian era, this border moved further south, just below Hevron and west to the western border of the hill-country. While he rejects the view that the area between Bet-Zur and Hevron had been under Edomite control in the first half of the Persian period, he does not state who had alternatively controlled this region at that time (1999: 99).

19. It should be noted that Judahite forts were located in the Negev highlands, south of Beersheva, in the Iron IIC, which were destroyed at the end of the monarchy. It is possible that they were built and in use already by the time of Josiah, in which case the southern border would have extended south of Beersheva.

20. To this list can be added Lam. 4.21-22; Joel 4.19 and Ps. 137.7 that corroborate hostility. None explicitly claims that Edom took part in the siege.

21. The word for army is written without the internal *yod*, although it is not intended to be in construct state since the modifier *hazzeh* follows it and disrupts what otherwise would be a four-element construct chain. However, perhaps this should be seen as one of the exceptions to the rule, where a modifier has been allowed to break up the construct chain. Another option would be to understand the phrase *hl-hzh* to be a misheard rendering of the place name that appears in Neh. 11.5 as Kol-Hozeh. *Kaph* would have been misheard as *ḥet* and *heh* as *ḥet*. I see no reason to render the term *ḥayil* in the less technical sense of a 'company' or 'large group' (so, e.g., Raabe 1996: 264).

22. Ostracon 40 is a message sent from Gemar[yahu] and Nehemyahu to Malkiyahu concerning the failure of a letter detailing demands being made by 'the man' to be conveyed from them to Malkiyahu by [E]shi[yahu]. The demands have something to do with Edom. Apparently, these two had already given some letters concerning or from Edom to Malkiyahu before sunset, but their latest response had failed to be relayed. They state at the end that 'the king of Judah should know that they cannot send...; this is the evil that Edom has done'. The ostracon was found in a room in the center of the fortress and has been assigned to stratum VIII; it may be that trouble with Edom was recurrent in the last 150 years of the kingdom of Judah because Arad was watching over the main trade route from Arabia and Edom to Gaza on the coast, but it might be worth rechecking the stratigraphy of this find. Malkiyahu is a person of authority and could well be the same individual who was entrusted with the important task of delivering the troops from Arad and Qinah to Ramoth Negev 'lest Edom come there'. He could easily have had a son named Shemaʻyahu old enough to have done military service or corvée labor at Arad, who appears in a roster of names on ostracon 39. Found outside the fort on the western slope, it has been assigned to stratum VII on the basis of its script; should all three ostraca be assigned to stratum VI and the slight differences in style be put down to the quirks of individual handwriting (Aharoni 1981: 68-74)?

23. Katzenstein places the list of court officials c. 570 BCE, though others place it closer to 590 BCE (1994: 46). He also thinks that Nabonidus' campaign to Temaʻ in the Arabian peninsula in 552 BCE was launched from Gaza (1994: 48), but there is no specific mention of this city in the badly preserved accounts of that campaign. The route taken may well have gone down through Transjordan rather than down the coast, further west, and then back east across the Beersheva Valley (so, e.g., Ephʻal 1982: 187-88).

24. Edomite wares from Beersheva stratum II, which was probably destroyed in 701 BCE, were found to have been manufactured from local loess soil in the valley and from an orange-colored *terra rosa* clay that originated in Judah that L. Singer-Avitz suggests was imported and also made into pots at production centers in the Beersheva Valley (1999: 38). None were cooking pots. She believes that the local potters imitated forms they had seen being used by caravaneers passing by; they tend to be small vessels like bowls, jugs, and bottles used for pouring and drinking (1999: 53).

25. The situation at Tel Beersheva is unclear so it has not been included in the discussion. Stratum II, thought to have ended in 701 BCE, contains some Edomite ware, but all the cooking pots are Judahite (Bienkowski and van der Steen 2001: 27). No information is given about the pottery from stratum 1 in existing publications, which would be the one more likely to cover the end of the monarchy. It is suggested that the site may have housed a fort and some domestic structures that were enclosed within a new retaining wall meant to strengthen the older wall (Aharoni 1973: 6-7).

26. Although two phases were able to be discerned in this occupational level due to the raising of the street in the gate entrance by 0.6 meter and minor alterations made to some of the rooms within the facility, there was no destruction separating the two (Beit Arieh 1993b: 1496 and oral communication).

27. If one were to suggest that the fort had been abandoned c. 586 by the Judahites when the kingdom fell and was subsequently occupied by Edomites, the final destruction might be able to be placed in 552 BCE. This would be on the further supposition that Nabonidus destroyed key Edomite forts along the trade routes to and through the Beersheva Valley in addition to whatever he might have done to the capital at Bozrah. However, this proposal is not likely in light of the very few sherds of Edomite painted ware in the overall assemblage and the presence of only twenty-five per cent Edomite cooking pots These figures would likely have been higher had the site been occupied for thirty years by Edomites (I. Beit-Arieh, oral communication).

28. There is evidence that the width of the thresholds of the outer and inner gates or entrances were narrowed from 1 meter to 0.6 meter (Beit Arieh 1993a: 1254) but this need not indicate a separate occupational phase; only minor building alterations in a single occupational phase.

29. The initial estimate by M. Kochavi that twenty-five per cent of the entire assemblage was Edomite must now be revised in light of the later excavations (Kochavi 1993: 936; I. Beit Arieh, personal communication). If the Rhodian jug was found in the final destruction layer, it may be able to provide some helpful dating parameters once it is analyzed (Kochavi 1993: 936).

30. The figurines from the favissa at 'En Haseva belong to the same iconographic tradition but were not manufactured at the same workshop as those at Qitmit and Malhata or at least, were not made by the same potter. For the latter, see Beck 1996.

31. The Greek-era ostraca specify the name of the reigning king when they give the regnal year, while the Persian-era ones only give the year. However, by a process of deduction and working backwards in time, the earliest date of year 42 must fall under the reign of Artaxerxes II, the only Persian king to have reigned that length of time. In addition, a jar that probably was found in the same location as the ostraca bears a Phoenician inscription dated 'to year 35 of the king'. The king in question is probably Azzimilk of Tyre, given the long reign, and the corresponding year would be 313/2 BCE, which coincides with the latest ostracon dated to year 5 of Antigonus (Lemaire 2002: 75).

32. Their suggestion that Level IB was built as a garrison to protect imperial interests in the area that was prone to territorial quarrels between Judeans and Edomites/Arabs is unlikely. The residence is much more than a 'garrison'; by their own description, the entire Level IB settlement was walled, and other monumental buildings besides the governor's residency were inside the walls (Fantalkin and Tal 2004).

33. It could also be argued that the loss of Egypt in 404 BCE led to the development of a much more active administration in the wake of the Beersheva Valley road becoming a much more important route as the southernmost imperial road of the kingdom in the western Levant.

34. If we applied this model to the kingdom of Judah in the Iron II period, it is doubtful that we would be able to identify the boundaries of this political entity, which included the Negev highlands at certain points in time, as well as the Shephelah, or be able to link up all the subsidiary administrative districts with their hinterlands.

Chapter 5

EXCAVATING THE PAST: SETTLEMENT PATTERNS AND
MILITARY INSTALLATIONS IN PERSIAN-ERA YEHUD

Introduction

We are finally in a position to turn to the archaeological data and to examine the possible settlement patterns in Yehud in the mid-fifth century BCE during the reign of Artaxerxes I. It is impossible, however, to determine if a site was occupied specifically during the period from 565–532 BCE, even if it has been excavated, because our dating methods are not that precise. We can generally determine if a site was occupied within a time span of 100–150 years, and this will have to serve as the basis for the current investigation. Site sizes, functions, and locations will be considered, but our final conclusions in terms of any policy for the redevelopment of Yehud during the reign of Artaxerxes I will not be able to be decisively confirmed by artifactual remains since those that were in use or produced during his reign cannot be identified with any certainty.

Preliminary Issues in Using Survey and Excavation Results

Before examining Persian-era remains that have been uncovered during excavations and others that have been identified through surface surveys, we need to be aware of a number of problems that tend to be associated with the retrieval of artifactual remains. These problems impact on the responsible use of archaeological data for the recreation of the past.

Absolute versus Relative Dating

The periods when different sites were occupied are determined in the ancient Near East primarily by the pottery that is found inside the buildings and in pits associated with a given stratum or level of occupational use. After more than a century of excavations in the western Levant, records of the forms of pots and their types of decorations that have been found in each successive layer of a site have been compiled. The result is a sequence detailing the life-span of each individual form and type of vessel. The further down one excavates, the earlier the time period one encounters, although one must always be aware of pits and building foundations that may have been sunk into earlier layers. By noting in which layers a certain type of vessel occurs and which other types are found with it in each layer, it is possible to assign a date for a given layer that should be accurate within 100–150 years. This appears to be the general length of time that a type of vessel remained part of the local repertoire.

The chronological sequence that serves as the current basis for dating is relative in that it places a given form either earlier than another, later than another, or contemporary with it. Our ability to place this relative sequence within some sort of dating framework that assigns segments to certain centuries rests ultimately on the finding of written materials in conjunction with the pottery. In ancient Israel and Yehud, Egyptian scarabs that routinely bore the names of pharaohs have allowed the defining of the pottery used during the Middle Bronze Age and Late Bronze Age periods. The Iron Age has been less fortunate in this regard, although ostraca and bullae have been found that have assisted in the process. For the Persian period, coins have helped date primarily the fourth century, when they first appear to have become widely minted in the region. For the sixth and fifth centuries, however, dating has depended heavily on the finding of imported Greek pottery, the dates of which are also relative within their native traditions, but which are supported in part by written sources. The local pottery tradition did not change much from the end of the monarchy in 586 BCE, through the period when Yehud was a Neo-Babylonian province (586–538 BCE), into the early Persian period (538–450 BCE). People continued their ordinary lives and routines, regardless of who their overlord was. Nevertheless, there were certain developments that allow some forms to be identified as diagnostic for the Persian period (for a full discussion, see Stern 1982: 93-142).

Even when objects with absolute date implications such as coins or scarabs are found, they do not automatically yield an absolute date for the accompanying artifacts. Both are subject to the 'heirloom factor', in which valued objects are handed down for generations within a family. Thus, the final level in which they are deposited might be a century or so later than the time when the object was manufactured. This same factor is operative with imported pottery as well. In addition, every effort has to be made to determine if the objects are in their original place of deposition, even if that was a century after their production. They may have been disturbed and moved due to animals digging on site or due to the shifting of materials on site by ancient occupants in the process of digging a pit, excavating a foundation trench for a later building, robbing out stones from earlier levels to reuse in later buildings, or leveling an area for building, either by removing materials to create a level surface or by bringing in fill to create a level surface (Lapp 1977).

Absolute dates are almost non-existent in the archaeological record in Yehud; the few we have tend to come from destruction layers that can be definitively associated with a written claim to have destroyed a site. An example of this would be the destruction of level III at Lakish, which is recorded on the walls of room 36 of Sennacherib's palace at Nineveh and which is reported to have transpired during the third of eight military campaigns conducted by this king in his annals that were summarized on the Taylor Prism and on the Oriental Institute Prism of Sennacherib (Luckenbill 1975: 115-28, esp. 118-21). Sennacherib reigned from 704–681 BCE; this event is usually dated to 701 BCE.

Using Epigraphy to Date Artifacts

Sometimes when objects with writing on them are found in an occupational level, attempts are made to date the accompanying pottery by looking at the shape of the letters on the inscription. This approach assumes that styles of writing change over time in a given region. A look at documents written only 100 years ago will confirm that handwriting styles do indeed shift over time and differ from region to region. The problem, however, is that they shift at about the same pace as pottery forms do, so they are not any more reliable as date indicators than pottery. There also is the added factor that individuals tend not to conform absolutely to the norms of the day in their particular region, due to idiosyncrasies and experience, so even though there is a standard within every age, there is a huge variation from that norm. Some individuals might stray toward older trends or anticipate later ones. Thus, unless an inscription contains specific information like the name of a king or another known individual or event that we can place into an established chronological framework, epigraphy is not any more reliable a date indicator than pottery is, and at times, can be misleading. Examples of writing remain quite limited for many periods, creating a small comparative data pool that might not be representative (for various problems with dating by epigraphy, see Zuckerman and Dodd 2003). Pottery, by contrast, is found in great abundance at most sites and since its sequence is better established, it is the better factor to use at this point in time and knowledge for dating on a regular basis.

Limitations of Remains Retrieved through Excavation
Excavations provide us with invaluable glimpses into the past through the unearthing of artifacts and associated life activities that have been preserved from various cultures. Yet those glimpses are only as good as the methods that have been used to retrieve them and to interpret them. The cost of excavation almost always precludes the excavation of an entire site in the Middle East down through all of its layers of occupation to bedrock or sterile soil. At large tells, which are the remains of millennia of occupation of an ancient walled settlement, it is unusual for more than twenty percent of the site to have been excavated by one or more teams who have been granted a license to do so. The resultant picture of activities that took place in a given layer of occupation is thus quite fragmentary, and might be very unrepresentative of the nature of the site at that time. If, for example, the only buildings that are excavated are large, public structures, we will derive a very different understanding of the nature and function of the site than if we were only to uncover private houses. Digging in an elite zone will reveal information about the lifestyles of the rich and famous of the day but not help us to understand how the ordinary people lived or what percentage of the population was wealthy. While this is less of a problem at a small village site, where the size allows a greater percentage to be dug and the extremes in social hierarchy found in urban areas are probably less, though still existent, it still applies to some degree; it is dangerous to reconstruct the history of a given period of occupation at any site based on limited exposed remains.

Only extended excavation can determine the extent of settlement in a given time period. Wall systems tend to remain intact for centuries and provide an easy definition of the edge of a tell. However, these walls do not always define the extent of the settlement at any given time. In times of prosperity or high population density it can spill outside the walls into additional urban sectors or into farmsteads or unwalled, dependent villages. On the other hand, it can contract within the city walls to a restricted sector, like the upper walled portion of the city, as happened at Hazor, Tel Miqne and Tel Rehov, for example. Or, less drastically, more peripheral quarters may be abandoned as the population declines. Thus, it cannot be assumed that the surface area defined by the city walls accurately reflects the extent of settlement in any period.

The reliability of archaeological findings depends entirely on the skill of the square supervisors, field staff, and volunteers or paid workers in identifying new features as they are encountered in a systematic peeling back of the soil in designated, surveyed grids by ten centimeter increments. It is easy to miss packed earth floors, intrusive pits and foundation trenches, and to distinguish secondary additions to buildings from original constructions or repairs to structures. If very fine screens are not used in sifting dirt removed from a locus, many small animal bones will be lost as potential data. If soil samples are not taken regularly and with care not to have been walked over by someone removing dirt from another area or having just returned from dumping a wheelbarrow, with dirt from the balk or another area on his or her shoes, then the results of the botanical analysis may be contaminated. If volunteers mistakenly put pottery sherds from one locus in the bucket being used to collect those from another locus, future attempts to reconstruct activities that took place in the locus will be compromised unless the mistake is caught. The failure to record the top and bottom levels for a special find and to mark its exact find spot on the daily top plan can affect the ability to interpret its significance after the fact, since no context clues can be used. The failure to photograph regularly can lose valuable visual records that might help sort out a stratigraphic problem after the fact. The failure of supervisors to keep detailed daily diaries where they indicate their goals for the day, their strategies used to accomplish them, problems that occur, and tentative thoughts about a locus as it is being dug makes it much harder for other researchers not present at the dig to reconstruct the dig process and make decisions about whether the final interpretations given to artifacts and loci are likely to be correct or not. Yet, in spite of so many potential things that can be done shoddily at an excavation, most are done proficiently and yield results that are largely dependable.

A final drawback of excavation is the failure to publish the results in a format that makes the data useful for other researchers or in a timely manner. Oral reports with slides at annual professional meetings are no substitute for written final publications that make the results of seasons of work readily available to anyone who is interested. In addition, the final report needs to be as complete as possible, providing information for each locus, extensive drawings, photographs and pottery plates, registries of all small finds and top plans that allow all finds to be located easily, as well as maps that clearly mark the locations of all loci.

Popular accounts of the excavations should be produced secondarily after the more 'scientific' reports have been disseminated. They are not detailed enough to be used by colleagues to evaluate the plausibility of an excavator's interpretation of the materials. This peer evaluation is a normal part of scholarly debate and allows reconstructions that include an interpretive dimension to be challenged and refined and gain a level of consensus among experts before being shared with the wider public. Popular treatments usually present interpretations as 'fact' rather than as hypothesis.

Limitations of Remains Retrieved through Surveys

Surveys provide vital information about settlement patterns in a region without the intrusiveness and expense of excavation but, nevertheless, have their own drawbacks. They cost money, but much less than excavations on the whole, and require trained supervisors and volunteers or workmen, just like excavations. It is not always possible to get permission to survey segments of privately owned land or, in Israel, of military installations that fall within the desired scope of the study. The identification of features and the collection of pottery can be hampered if the survey is done at times of the year when vegetation may cover over potential finds, and erosion processes in the area may not regularly deposit remains from all the periods in which a site was used on the surface. Different pottery results have been obtained when the same site has been surveyed more than once, illustrating the latter phenomenon. So, for example, when Khirbet et-Tuqu' was surveyed in1968 in the first systematic survey of the land of Judah, Persian pottery was collected (Kochavi 1972: 47, #62); in a more recent survey, no Persian finds were recorded (Hirschfeld 1985: 37).

In areas that experience annual soil deposit from spring rains washing eroded rock, soil and silt down from adjoining mountains, ancient remains will be buried under centimeters or meters of soil. No evidence will lie on the surface. In such areas, if the survey is to be effective, it is necessary to use one of the many indirect exploration techniques like ground-penetrating radar, magnetometry, magnetic susceptibility, electromagnetic conductivity or electrical resistivity to discern buried buildings and pits and other non-natural features that lie beneath the ground (see Banning 2002: 44-45; Collins and Molyneaux 2003: 77-98)

Surveys generally cover many square miles or kilometers, making it impractical to explore every square inch or centimeter of surface area. A number of approaches are used, all of which involve the physical walking over of only a portion of targeted fields or terrain. Usually, this involves the establishing of a grid for the entire targeted area and the selection of regularly shaped units, often rectangles (quadrats) or long narrow corridors (transects) to explore. The number selected will be determined by the funding, available labor, time constraints, and the size of the targeted survey area. The selected grid units will then be walked over, often by people spaced a predetermined distance apart in parallel lines. The distance between them will be set according to the larger goals of the survey, with the aim to have few, if any, of the type of features being examined fall completely between the lines (Banning 2002; for a specific application see, e.g., Shennan 1985: 9-17). Such approaches, however, leave room for the failure to see and record features present in the landscape.

Pottery remains are collected at identified sites in one of two ways. In the first method, they tend to be gathered selectively, especially at large sites, by those who know which sherds are diagnostic of certain time periods. This is done by walking around the site and collecting various sherds, which are examined immediately afterwards. The results are then recorded and the sherds often left at the site. When this method is used, there is always the possibility that certain forms and time periods are overlooked as the eye strays to the more interesting sherds. At smaller sites, it is possible to try to collect all surface pottery for analysis.

In the second method, a random sampling is taken by placing a grid over the site and collecting all the pottery from selected units. The combined sherds are then dated and the percentages of the various types calculated, on the assumption that pottery from all periods has been distributed randomly over the site and that it occurs on the surface in the same proportion as in the ground. Thus, users of this method presume that the percentages found in the surface survey give an accurate representation of the percentages deposited in the occupational layers underground. Experience has demonstrated that this is not the case at tells, however, where sherds from the deeper, earlier levels do not work their way to the surface as readily as those from the later periods; the walls act as a 'girdle' that holds the remains in place with little movement. In addition, if occupation was limited to certain sectors, it will be concentrated in certain areas only and not randomly distributed over the entire site.

Finally, it needs to be noted that survey results cannot confirm if a site that has sherds from two succeeding periods was occupied continuously between these two periods or had a break in habitation. So, for example, a site that has Iron IIC sherds could have been occupied for any part of the sixth century. At the beginning of this time, the kingdom of Judah was on its last legs. Then, from 586–532 BCE, Judah/Yehud became a Neo-Babylonian province, and, immediately after 538 BCE, a Persian province. Occupation at the site could have covered any part of this tumultuous century.

The finding of Persian sherds at the same site, which would be the next period identified by distinctive pottery, does not mean that the site remained occupied from the monarchy through the Neo-Babylonian period and into the Persian period. The loss of the capital city of Jerusalem in 586 BCE meant that many outlying sites in the Judean wilderness and the Negev, where subsistence was always a challenge, would have lost their support network in cases where there was not enough rainfall to support a local crop in a given year. Strategic sites had been conquered and destroyed by the Neo-Babylonians, and the Shephelah had never fully recovered from its having been under Philistine control from most of the seventh century BCE, where there appears to have been a deliberate policy of depopulation. It has been thought that very few sites south of Jerusalem continued to be occupied after 586 BCE, while many to the north, by contrast were occupied, forming the core of the Neo-Babylonian province of Yehud (e.g. Miller and Hayes 1996: 416-17; Ahlström 1993: 795; Barstad 1996: 47-48; Stern 2001: 321-23).

More recently, however, O. Lipschits has challenged this view, noting that in the central Judean hills north of Hevron, no site above five dunams appears to have been abandoned after 586 BCE (2003: 355). While there was a drastic decline in the larger sites in the area, there was a marked increase in small and medium-sized sites (2003: 353). But only excavation at a site can confirm if there was uninterrupted occupation or not, and not always, especially if a site was abandoned rather than destroyed, so we need to be very careful about concluding the extent of continuous or non-continuous settlement from survey results.

Surveys are useful tools for identifying the range of settlement and for determining the approximate size of occupied sites, even though excavation is needed to determine what percentage of a site is likely to have been occupied in a given time period. In the case of unwalled sites, how far beyond the core of a settlement artifacts belonging to it may have been scattered over time by humans scavenging for building materials and erosional forces needs to be considered. Nevertheless, if the remains of an unwalled site cover an area of four dunams (one acre) while those of a walled site cover fifty dunams (twelve and a half acres), we are able to learn something about comparative size even before excavation. The first site was never larger than four dunams at any point and represented a different model of settlement from the urban center, no matter what percentage of its interior space was occupied in the same time period. Thus, while relative size may not accurately reflect the extent of historic settlement, it is still a reliable indicator of site hierarchy within a region and provides a means of plausibly suggesting which smaller sites in a given region might have been considered dependent upon larger, central sites, being considered their 'daughters'.

Persian-Era Sites Identified by Survey or Excavation

The first systematic survey of the territory that would have fallen within Yehud was conducted by Israeli archaeologists after 1967, when this land was occupied after the Six-Day War. The results were published in 1976. In the survey of Judah, thirty-four sites were identified as having Persian-era pottery. Seven had a predominant number of sherds collected dating to this period, while three had so few as to be questionable as having been occupied in this period. The survey of Benjamin yielded nine sites with Persian pottery, none of which represented a dominant period of occupation at the site, and one of which was questionable. The survey of the Judean desert yielded as single, non-dominant site (Kochavi 1972).

Subsequent surveys of the same areas were conducted by PhD students at Tel Aviv University in the 1980s and 1990s, the results of which were presented in their doctoral theses (written in modern Hebrew). In addition, new surveys are currently being conducted by the Department of Antiquities of Israel that are tied to the Israel Survey Maps. These are ongoing, but some results have been published. The following presentation of sites is culled from the results of all these various surveys to the extent that they were available as of June 2004. I am accepting the judgment of what constitutes diagnostic Persian forms that have been made by the experts who have analyzed the pottery that was collected from surface survey. However, in most cases, the survey results will not allow a distinction between sixth–fifth century forms and fourth-century forms unless imported Greek wares happen to be found.

I will present the following collation of site information using somewhat non-standard categories. While it is usual to group material by geographical sub-regions in survey reports, we are primarily interested in a site's size, probable function, and whether it was a new foundation in the fifth century or had possibly been occupied continuously. This data will allow us to examine any possible change in the settlement pattern that might have taken place in the fifth century BCE in Yehud, when Artaxerxes I moved the capital of Yehud from Mizpah to Jerusalem and appears to have ordered the transferral of new settlers to the area, which is reflected in the biblical text as the return of the *golah* from exile. As already noted, however, the new settlers were not all Jewish in origin, and no doubt included people of other ethnic origins.

In the ensuing categorization, my suggestions for the function of a given site that has been surveyed but not excavated will be based on a combination of the site size and the percentage of Persian pottery collected on site during the survey. Some of the more recent surveys give percentages for the different time periods the pottery represents. In particular, the survey of the hill-country of Benjamin made on behalf of the Department of Antiquities and the survey of the hill-country of Judah in A. Ofer's PhD thesis has done this. In many cases, the spread of the remains might cover as many as ten to fifteen dunams, yet the Persian pottery represents only two to five percent of the total pottery collected. Even taking into consideration the caveats expressed above about surveys, it is likely that during the Persian period, only a small part of this site was occupied, probably by a single farmstead. In the Greek, Roman, and Byzantine periods, additional farmsteads appear to have joined the original one, creating an unwalled hamlet or village over time. This is a consistent phenomenon at the sites in the hill-country of Benjamin.

In cases where pottery percentages are not given, I have had to remain cautious and suggest that smaller, unwalled sites might have contained one or more farmsteads, a hamlet, or a village; there is insufficient information to decide amongst the three options. It might be possible to argue by analogy with the situation in Benjamin that most of these small sites throughout the province would have been farmsteads. However, caution is once again needed, since the settlement pattern in the region of Benjamin might have been established already in the Neo-Babylonian period, when most of the inhabitants of Yehud were concentrated in the territory of Benjamin. The changes made by Artaxerxes I when he ordered the redevelopment of the province could have introduced a different settlement pattern into the previously unoccupied areas of the province, or a mixture of farmsteads, hamlets, and villages, depending on their location and function within the larger administration.

Similarly, it is impossible to state the nature of settlements that were located on tell sites from survey alone. Without excavations, the extent of the settlement cannot be determined, and there are known instances where only a small percentage of a tell was occupied in a given period. I have indicated when a site is a tell to alert readers to this problem.

To help readers with their own assessments of the data, the following information will be helpful. There are about four dunams to an acre of land. I use the term 'farmstead' to refer to a cluster of buildings that would include a main residence as well as outbuildings and facilities used for agricultural purposes. The latter would include barns, storage shed, silos, and wine and olive presses. A hamlet would include a collection of five to fifteen residences and their accompanying outbuildings, while a village would be even larger, with sixteen to about thirty houses and associated buildings. A town would be the next size up, including residences and some public structures. In towns, residences would have been grouped more tightly and would not have had the same sort of out-buildings found in the smaller, more rural organizational layouts. They might have been walled; most sites that would qualify as towns lie on tells that had city walls that, though centuries old, were still able to afford protection to those living within. Towns would be the first level in which I would expect administrative personnel to be headquartered and working.

Any site that is listed in survey results as having Persian/Hellenistic pottery I have omitted. I am assuming that this reading reflects Persian pottery that postdates 400 BCE and belongs primarily to the fourth century BCE. Our interest lies in fifth-century pottery.

I have decided to include any site that has even a single sherd of Persian pottery collected during survey since much of the Persian-era occupation seems to have been in farmsteads. We should not expect large quantities of broken pottery from a single household, and if the site had been abandoned after a period of time, the occupants would have taken their possessions with them, reducing potential finds even further. In addition, given the subsequent occupation at many of these sites in the Hellenistic and Roman periods, earlier remains would undoubtedly have been removed from the premises and dumped elsewhere. Thus, even a single sherd seems a significant find under the circumstances.

I have also included sites where the pottery readings for the Persian period have been inconclusive but thought likely. These have been signalled in the reports either by a question mark or by placing the Persian period in parentheses. It is unclear if such a reading has been prompted by finding only one or two diagnostic sherds; in some reports, we are told there was one sherd, two sherds, or a few sherds, so this might be a variant way to present and assess the significance of such findings. I feel it is better to include all the potential sites that were inhabited in the Persian period, although I have deliberately omitted tomb sites, caves (Wexler 2002) and springs with no evidence of regular, settled habitation.[1]

Sites That Were New Foundations in the Persian Period
The following table includes three types of sites. The first were established on virgin soil for the first time in the Persian period, while the second had been occupied in the more distant past, after a gap of at least four centuries, in the Iron I period (1200–1000 BCE) or earlier. The third had been occupied in the Iron II period (1000–586 BCE) but had been destroyed or abandoned either in 701 BCE, when Sennacherib had destroyed many settlements in the kingdom of Judah, or in 586 BCE, when Judah had been turned into a Neo-Babylonian province. In the latter case, sites where excavations have demonstrated an occupational gap are included, as well as sites from the survey of Avi Ofer where no Iron IID pottery is found. Assuming that the Persian-era settlement would not have taken place before the arrival of new settlers with Zerubbabel during the reign of Artaxerxes I, there would have been an occupational gap of at least 120 years at the sites abandoned after 586 BCE and of 236 years at the sites abandoned after 701 BCE.

In cases where percentages are given, if the numbers do not add up to 100 percent it is because there was occupation either before the Iron Age or after the Roman period. To save space, I have chosen to give statistics only for the Iron Age–Roman periods. This allows us to see trends in a site's development in an adequate manner for our chronological interests. I have arranged the sites according to decreasing latitude, moving from North to South.

I	Iron Age	1200–538 BCE
I I	Iron Age I	1200–1000 BCE
I II	Iron Age II	1000–586/538 BCE
I IIA	Iron Age IIA	1000–900 BCE
I IIB	Iron Age IIB	900–700 BCE
I IIC	Iron Age IIC	700–586 BCE or 700–538 BCE if not using Iron IID or Iron III
I IID	Iron Age IID (Neo-Babylonian period)	586–538 BCE
I III	Iron Age III (equivalent to I IID)	586–538 BCE
P	Persian period	538–332 BCE
H	Hellenistic period	332–37 BCE
R	Roman period	37 BCE–324 CE
R I	Roman period I	37 BCE–132 CE
R II	Roman period II	132-324 CE

A review of the time periods highlights confusion over how to describe the period of time in the sixth century after 586 BCE when Judah became the Neo-Babylonian province of Yehud. While it is recognized that the local pottery traditions would not have ceased overnight, it is also widely assumed that the regions of the southern Judean hills and the Shephelah were largely empty of settlement after the fall of Jerusalem in 586 BCE. There is evidence of destruction at tell sites certainly, but this does not mean that the many farmsteads in these regions would have been abandoned as well, leaving a more or less empty land. No larger site has been excavated in the region of Benjamin or Judah where there was no destruction in 586 BCE, whose stratigraphic results were recorded carefully enough to allow a pottery typology for the sixth century to have been developed. The results from Bethel, Tell-en-Nasbeh and El-Jib/Gibeon, where there was continuous occupation, cannot be used.

Under the circumstances, then, archaeologists are uncertain about what diagnostics can be used for certain to identify post-586 sixth-century occupational levels or if these can be distinguished from seventh-century levels. This has led in turn, in some instances, to the use of Iron IIC to cover the Neo-Babylonia period, while in other instances, the new category Iron III or Iron IID has been introduced to designate the Neo-Babylonian period, but without clear indication of what the diagnostics are that allow it to be distinguished from the preceding and succeeding phases.

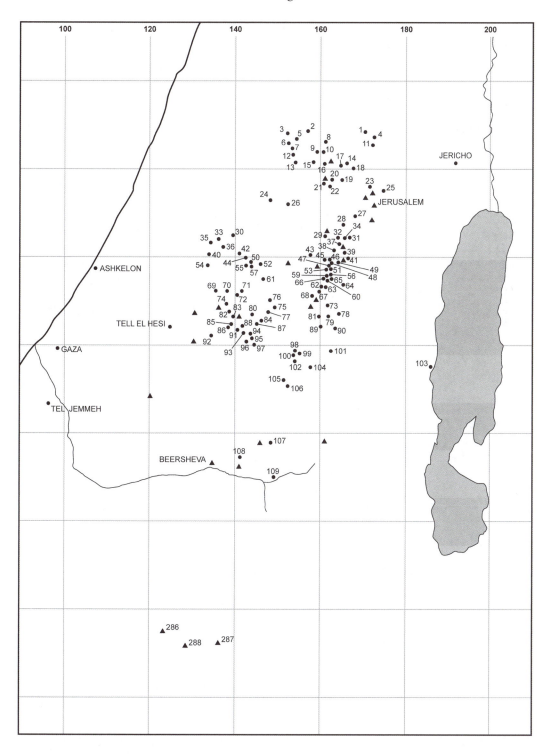

Figure 49.   *Sites newly founded in Yehud in the Persian period*

#	Site name(s)	Israeli grid coordinates; size	Pottery finds	Type of settlement	Bibliography
1	------	1696 1479 3 dunams	P.13% H.13% R.71%	Farmstead	Finkelstein and Magen 1993: #70; Finkelstein, Lederman and Bunimovtiz 1997: 358
2	Khirbet Kureikur	1535 1475 3.5 dunams	P.13% H.23% R.13%	Farmstead	Finkelstein and Magen 1993: #7
3	Shilta	1520 1472 7 dunams	P.14% H.29% R.24%	Farmstead(s)	Finkelstein and Magen 1993: #2; Finkelstein, Lederman and Bunimovitz 1997: 135
4	------	1738 1463 6 dunams	P.1 sherd H-R.67%	Farmstead(s)	Finkelstein and Magen 1993: #204
5	Khirbet Kafr Lut	1541 1458 5 dunams	P.2% H.2% R.2%	Farmstead	Finkelstein, Lederman and Bunimovitz 1997: 143
6	el-Burj	1521 1455 ?? Arab village	P.15% H.12% R.7%	Farmstead(s)? Hamlet? Village? On tell	Finkelstein and Magen 1993: #117
7	Khirbet Najmat el-Hadali	1545 1453 4 dunams	P.few H.29% R.21%	Farmstead	Finkelstein and Magen 1993: #11; Finkelstein, Lederman and Bunimovitz 1997: 145
8	Khirbet es-Sanjaq	1611 1451 4 dunams	P.2 sherds H.13% R.39%	Farmstead	Finkelstein and Magen 1993: #34
9	Khirbet L'isa	1598 1443 1.5 dunams	P.few H.7% R.24%	Farmstead	Finkelstein and Magen 1993: #25; Finkelstein, Lederman and Bunimovitz 1997: 166
10	------	1618 1442 2 dunams	P.5% H.38% R.57%	Farmstead	Finkelstein and Magen 1993: #32
11	------	1720 1429 13 dunams	P.2% H.53% R.24%	Farmsteads? Hamlet?	Finkelstein and Magen 1993: #190
12	Khirbet 'Ajanjul	1523 1420 ??	P.32% H.8%	Farmstead	Finkelstein and Magen 1993: #112
13	Khirbet esh-Sheikh Suleiman	1520 1418 10 dunams	P.1 sherd H.9% H/R.9%	Farmstead	Finkelstein and Magen 1993: #111
14	Khirbet el-Latatin	1660 1417 4 dunams	P.?? R.18%	Farmstead	Kochavi 1972: 181, #112; Finkelstein and Magen 1993: #60
15	Khirbet el-Judeira	1588 1416 ?? ruin	P.2 sherds H.8% R.14%	Farmstead?	Finkelstein and Magen 1993: #136

16	Khirbet Jifna	1604 1414 5 dunams	P.few H.13% R.few	Farmstead	Finkelstein and Magen 1993: #141
17	Khirbet el-Jufeir	1653 1411 5 dunams	P.?? H.10% R.15%	Farmstead	Kochavi 1972: 181, #111; Finkelstein and Magen 1993: #153
18	Khirbet 'Id	1675 1402 16 dunams	P.4% H.11% R.14%	Farmstead(s)? Hamlet?	Finkelstein and Magen 1993: #160
19	Khirbet Abu Leimun	1661 1370 11 dunams	P.30% H.23% R.15%	Farmstead(s)? Hamlet?	Finkelstein and Magen 1993: #306
20	Beit Surik	1642 1367 ?? Arab village	P.few H.21% R.15%	Farmstead(s)	Finkelstein and Magen 1993: #284
21	Khirbet el-Bawaya	1629 1364 9 dunams	P.4% H.5% H/R.13%	Farmstead(s)	Finkelstein and Magen 1993: #274
22	------	1631 1359 1.5 dunams	P.1 sherd H.45% R.40%	Farmstead	Finkelstein and Magen 1993: #277
23	Ramat Shelomo (Rekhes Shu'fat) and Khirbet Er-Ras	1710 1352 1709 1354	I II gap P H R	Farmsteads or Hamlet	Onn and Rapuano 1995 Kloner 2001: [102]#114
24	Khirbet Shobab	1488 1337 55 dunams	I IIB gap P H R	?? on tell	Dagan 2000: #3
25	Ras Tumeim	1754 1332 5 dunams	P H R	Farmstead?	Dinur 1987/88
26	Eshtaol	1511 1320 60 dunams	I IIB gap P	?? on tell	Dagan 2000: #6
27	Sharafat	1681 1278 12 dunams	P.27% R.33%	Farmstead(s)	Kochavi 1972: 36, #2 Ofer 1993: #334
28	Khirbet Abu Shun	1646 1263 2 dunams	P.6% R.91%	Farmstead	Ofer 1993: #332
29	Horvat G'rish	1616 1241 c. 3 dunams	P. many R?	Farmstead	Kochavi 1972: 38, #14
30	Khirbet Shahah	1399 1240 35 dunams	I IIB gap P H R	Farmstead(s)? Hamlet? Village?	Dagan 2000 : #68
31	Ras el-Kabir	1674 1237 ??	P B?	Farmstead	Kochavi 1972: 41, #27
32	Rujm el-Hedar	1647 1235 1 dunam	P.37% H.2% R.61%	Farmstead	Kochavi 1972: 40, #24 Ofer 1993: #326
33	Tel Safit	1356 1233 200 dunams	I IIB gap P H R	Village? Town? On tell	Dagan 2000: #84

34	Nemar	1665 1229 3 dunams	Iron IIC.12% gap P.88%	Farmstead	Ofer 1993: #325
35	Nahal Safitah	1345 1227 2 dunams	I IIB gap P gap R	Farmstead	Dagan 2000: #102
36	Khirbet Batan	1380 1226 30 dunams	I IIB gap P H R	Farmstead(s)? Hamlet? Village?	Dagan 2000: #110
37	Khirbet Alia	1654 1224 5 dunams	P.37% H.10% R.53%	Farmstead	Ofer 1993: #324
38	Khirbet Jizmia	1642 1217 5 dunams	I IIC.6% gap P.18% H.6% R.52%	Farmstead	Ofer 1993: #321
39	Khirbet Gharib	1647 1212 4 dunams	I IIC.3% gap P.42% H.6% R.44%	Farmstead	Kochavi 1972: 42, #34 Ofer 1993: #320
40	Barqoseh	1333 1208 45 dunams	I IIB gap P H R	Farmstead(s)? Hamlet?	Dagan 2000: #139
41	Rujm Artas	1677 1208 0.4 dunams	I IIC.56% gap P.44%	Farmstead? Watchtower?	Kochavi 1972: 43, #40 Ofer 1993: #317
42	Khirbet el-Tujeirah	1413 1205 30 dunams	I IIB gap P H R	Farmstead(s); Hamlet? Villages?	Dagan 2000: #146
43	el-Jab'a	1573 1203 ??	P? H R B	Village? On tell	Kochavi 1972: 42, #36
44	Khirbet 'Aqaba	1431 1201 25 dunams	I IIB gap P H R	Farmstead(s)? Hamlet? Village?	Dagan 2000: #153
45	Zakariah (north)	1615 1198 0.4 dunams	P.33% H.34%	Farmstead	Ofer 1993: #305
46	Khirbet el-Humeidiyye	1641 1197 12 dunams	I IIC.39% gap P.7% R.29%	Farmstead(s)? Village? Hamlet?	Kochavi 1972: 45, #45 Ofer 1993: #308
47	'En Faghur	1640 1195 3 dunams	I IIC.48% gap P.20% H.16%	Farmstead	Ofer 1993: #310
48	Khirbet Zakandah/Khirbet Faghur South	1641 1193 15 dunams	I IIC.4% gap P.37% H.15 RI.11%	Hamlet? Village?	Kochavi 1972: 44, #46 Ofer 1993: #309
49	Marsiyye (east)	1661 1187 1 dunam	P.37%	Farmstead	Ofer 1993: #299
50	Khirbet Madras	1440 1183 120 dunams	P H R	Hamlet? Village?	Dagan 2000: #164
51	Shamah	1665 1181 1.5 dunams	P.29%	Farmstead	Ofer 1993: #300

52	Khirbet Yarhaʿ	1450 1180 25 dunams	I IIB gap P H R	Farmstead(s)? Hamlet?	Dagan 2000: #166
53	Rujm es-Sabit	1636 1178 5 dunams	I I.68% gap I IID/P.3%	Farmstead	Kochavi 1972: 45, #54 Ofer 1993: #286
54	Khirbet Rujm e-Dharbi	1326 1176 15 dunams	I IIB gap P	Farmstead(s)? Hamlet?	Dagan 2000: #168
55	Khirbet Shushan	1433 1172 10 dunams	I IIB gap P H	Farmstead(s)? Hamlet?	Dagan 2000: #171
56	Salmuneh (north)	1655 1172 1 dunam	I IIC.20% gap P.65% R II:15%	Farmstead	Ofer 1993: #288
57	KhirbetMesad Kaklil (S)	1448 1171 12 dunams	I IIB gap P R	Farmstead(s)? Hamlet?	Dagan 2000: #172
58	Khirbet Berekot	1637 1168 25 dunams	P.25% R I.25%	Farmsteads? Hamlet?	Ofer 1993: #281
59	Selah (west)	1625 1162 0.4 dunams	P.55%	Farmstead	Ofer 1993: #279
60	Khirbet Umm et-Tala	1630 1160 6 dunams	I I.60% gap P.39%	Farmstead	Kochavi 1972: 45, #56 Ofer 1993: #280
61	Khirbet Ahali	1431 1159 15 dunams	P H R	Farmstead(s)? Hamlet?	Dagan 2000: #177
62	Selaʿ (east)	1636 1157 0.4 dunams	P.71%	Farmstead	Ofer 1993: #274
63	Fajjar (north)	1646 1156 0.4 dunams	I IIB.50% gap P.50%	Farmstead	Ofer 1993: #275
64	Fajjar (east)	1671 1146 0.4 dunams	P.100%	Farmstead	Ofer 1993: #266
65	Khirbet Shanah	1642 1144 2 dunams	P.74% H.21%	Farmstead	Ofer 1993: #263
66	Khirbet Khufrin	1609 1143 6 dunams	P.40% H.3% R.27%	Farmstead	Kochavi 1972: 47, #66 Ofer 1993:#258
67	Beit Ummar	1598 1143 15 dunams	P.20% H.25% R.5%	Farmstead(s)? Hamlet?	Kochavi 1972: 47, #65 Ofer 1993:#257
68	Khirbet el-Qarn	1620 1140 8 dunams	P.27% H.38% R.7%	Farmstead(s)	Kochavi 1972: 49, #73; Ofer 1993: #261
69	Tel ʿAttar	1385 1137 22 dunams	I IIB gap P H R	Farmsteads? Hamlet? On tell	Dagan 2000: #186
70	Khirbet Shelah	1324 1131 20 dunams	I IIB gap P	Farmsteads? Hamlet?	Dagan 2000: #189

71	Beit Guvrin	1403 1127 500 dunams	P H R	Farmsteads? Hamlet? Village?	Dagan 2000: #191
72	Khirbet Umm el-Daraj	1608 1124 2 dunams	P.71%	Farmstead	Kochavi 1972: 50, #80 Ofer 1993: #235
73	Halhul (east)	1621 1101 0.4 dunams	P.33% H.33%	Farmstead	Ofer 1993: #217
74	Khirbet el-Jebu	1381 1099 25 dunams	I IIB gap P gap R	Farmstead(s)? Hamlet? Village?	Dagan 1992: #45 Dagan 2000: #204
75	Nahal Guvrin	1479 1093 3 dunams	I IA B gap P	Farmstead	Dagan 2000: #241
76	Rujm el-Qasr	1664 1092 1 dunam	I IIC.42% gap P.22% H.9%	Farmstead? Watchtower?	Kochavi 1972: 55, #104 Ofer 1993: #211
77	Zohar Wadi Aziz	1462 1088 3 dunams	I IIB gap P	Farmstead	Dagan 2000: #234
78	Khirbet el-Simak	1664 1080 6 dunams	P.20%	Farmstead	Ofer 1993: #207
79	Khirbet Beit 'Anun	1621 1078 6 dunams	I IIB.16% gap P.13% R I.9%	Farmstead(s)	Kochavi 1972: 57, #118 Ofer 1993: #199
80	Khirbet Shem Tov	1439 1075 100 dunams	P H R	Hamlet?	Dagan 2000: #258
81	Khirbet Dahdah	1590 1074 4 dunams	P.30% H.30%	Farmstead	Ofer 1993: #194
82	Nahal Lakish	1391 1073 5 dunams	P (few) R	Farmstead	Dagan 1992: #183
83	Nahal Lakish	1393 1071 2 dunams	P	Farmstead	Dagan 1992: #176 Dagan 2000: #263
84	Khirbet er-Ras	1458 1071 5 dunams	I IIB gap P	Farmstead	Dagan 2000: #262
85	Khirbet Rasm Shu'liya	1393 1069 7 dunams	P H	Hamlet outside of fort	Dagan 1992: #217
86	Nahal Lakish	1387 1067 25 dunams	I II gap P	Farmstead(s)	Dagan 1992: #211
87	Wadi Idna	1442 1059 5 dunams	P H	Farmstead	Dagan 2000: #277
88	Tel Dumah	1418 1050 300 dunams	I IIB gap P H R	Hamlet? Village? On tel	Dagan 2000: #283
89	Jebel Nimra	1598 1048 3 dunams	P.100%	Farmstead	Ofer 1993: #181
90	Khirbet Arabiyye	1658 1042 4 dunams	P.9% H.54%	Farmstead	Ofer 1993: #182

91	Shuweib Riyyan	1411 1031 7 dunams	I IIB gap P gap R	Farmstead	Dagan 2000: #310
92	Mishlat Ma'ahaz/Kh. Makhas	1312 1022 2 dunams	I II gap P	Farmstead? Hamlet? Village?	Dagan 1992: #301
93	Khirbet Raya'	1425 1018 35 dunams	I IIB gap P H R	Farmstead(s)	Dagan 2000: #342
94	Khirbet Beit Awwa	1452 1018 3 dunams	P H R	Farmstead	Kochavi 1972: 62, #152 Dagan 2000: #344
95	Jebel Duweimar	1456 1008 15 dunams	I IIB gap P H	Farmstead(s)? Hamlet?	Dagan 2000: #362
96	Rasm el-Qa'aqir	1429 1004 30 dunams	I IIB gap P gap R	Farmstead(s)? Hamlet? Village?	Dagan 2000: #372
97	Wadi Harase	1454 1001 12 dunams	I IIB gap P gap R	Farmstead(s)? Hamlet?	Dagan 2000: #376
98	Tarame	1532 0986 6 dunams	P.4% H.32% R.56%	Farmstead	Kochavi 1972: 67, #175 Ofer 1993: #140
99	Hadab (South)	1550 0977 0.4 dunams	P.77%	Farmstead	Ofer 1993: #129
100	Jebel Basheh Suweir	1523 0976 1 dunam	P.88%	Farmstead	Ofer 1993: #126
101	Rujm el-Fahjeh	1628 0975 1 dunam	I IIB.22% gap P.9% gap RII.11%	Farmsteads	Kochavi 1972: 70, #189 Ofer 1993: #135
102	Ma'arav Bism	1531 0971 3 dunams	I IIC.1% gap P.4% H.64% R I.25%	No building remains visible; Farmstead?	Ofer 1993: #T21
103	Tel Goren	1870 0965	I IIC gap P gap H	Village?Town? Birah? On tell	Mazar 1993: 402-403
104	el-Aleika	1505 0936 5 dunams	P.100%	Farmstead	Ofer 1993: #101
105	Rabud (south)	1514 0922 8 dunams	I IIC.5% gap P.3% H.3%	No specific evidence of buildings visible; Farmsteads?	Ofer 1993: #T11
106	Nahal Yattir	1467 0774	I IIC gap P R	Villa	Govrin 1991: #87 Alon 1983: 80
107	Nahal Yattir	1402 0725	I I gap P	Hamlet beside fort	Govrin1991: #205
108[2]	Tel 'Ira/Kh. el-Gharra Stratum V	1486 0713	I II gap P	Hamlet or village on tell	Govrin1991: #240 Beit Arieh1999: 177

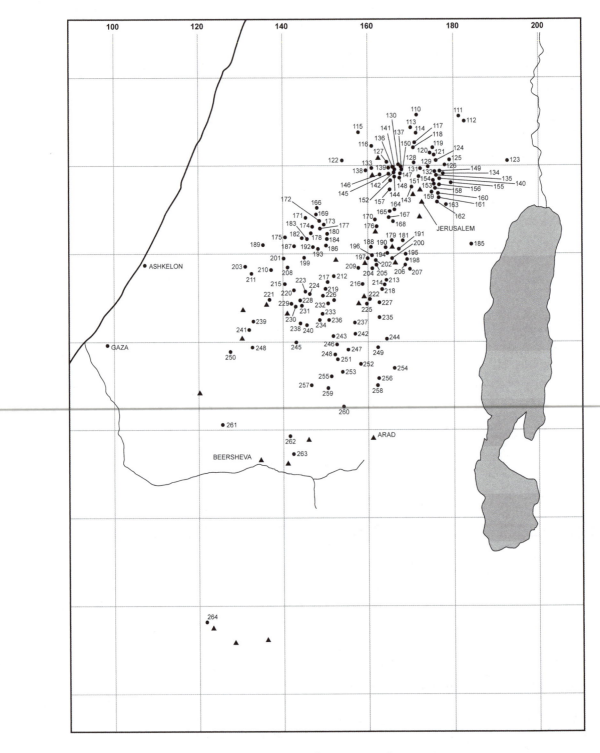

Figure 50. *Sites in Yehud with Iron IIC and Persian period occupation*

Sites That Had Previous Occupation in the Iron II Period

110	Beitin	1728 1481	I II H P H	Village	Kelso 1993 Finkelstein and Magen 1993: #82
111	------	1819 1481 0.5 dunams	I II/P	Farmstead	Finkelstein and Magen 1993: #355
112	------	1828 1473 ??	I II, P, H P	Farmstead?	Kochavi 1972: 111, #40
113	Ras et-Tahuna (south)	1702 1462 5 dun ams	I II.67% P.?? H.10%	Farmstead? Hamlet? Village? on tell	Kochavi 1972: 178, #94 Finkelstein and Magen 1993: #73
114	Khirbet Nisieh	1717 1449 15 dunams	I II.6% P.1% H.19% R 35%	Farmstead? Hamlet? Village?	Bimson and Livingston 1987 Finkelstein and Magen 1993: #184
115	Beit 'Ur et-Tahta	1582 1446 28 Dunams	I II.27% P.3% H.27% R.17%	Hamlet? Village? On tell	Finkelstein and Magen 1993: #22 Finkelstein, Lederman and Bunimovitz 1997: 161
116	Beit 'Ur el-Fauqa	1608 1436 6 dunams	I II.66% P.4% H.12%	Farmsteads or hamlet on tell	Finkelstein and Magen 1993: #28; Finkelstein, Lederman and Bunimovitz 1997: 303
117	------	1718 1434 3 dunams	I II.17% P.few P/H.few R.27%	Farmstead	Finkelstein and Magen 1993: #183
118	Tell en-Nasbeh	1706 1433 25 dunams	I II P H	Village? Town? Birah? On tell	Finkelstein and Magen 1993: #175
119	Khirbet Tell el- 'Askar	1767 1430 12 dunams	I II.few P.2 sherds R.5%	Farmstead? Hamlet?	Finkelstein and Magen 1993: #227
120	Khirbet el-Hara el- Fauqa and Mukhmas	1763 1424 40 dunams	I II.14% P.10% H.19% R.12%	Hamlet? Village? Town? On tell	Finkelstein and Magen 1993: #223
121	------	1767 1422 ??	I II.11% P.2 sherds R.23%	Farmstead?	Finkelstein and Magen 1993: #222
122	Khirbet Dhanab el- Kalb	1540 1420 8 dunams	I II.4% P.56%	Farmstead(s)	Finkelstein and Magen 1993: #125
123	Jericho/Tell es- Sultan	192 142	I II P	Hamlet? Village? Birah? On tell	Kenyon 1993: 680-81
124	------	1666 1416 18 dunams	I II. few P.few	Farmsteads? Hamlet??	Finkelstein and Magen 1993: #158

125	Judeira	1688 1406 ?? Arab village	I II.few P.few H.many R/B.many	Farmsteads	Finkelstein and Magen 1993: #163
126	Jab'a	1749 1405 20 dunams	I II.23% P.?? H.22% R.10%	Farmstead? Hamlet? Village? On tell	Kochavi 1972: 183, #125 Finkelstein and Magen 1993: #206
127	Khirbet Badd Abu Mu'ammar	1645 1403 2.4 dunams	I II.13% P.2% H.24% R.24%	Farmstead	Finkelstein and Magen 1993: #150
128	er-Ram	1721 1402 30 dunams	I II.20% P.2% H.13% R.8%	Farmsteads? Hamlet? Village?	Finkelstein and Magen 1993: #188
129	Jurat es-Saqqawi	1756 1398 ??	I II, P	Farmstead	Finkelstein and Magen 1993: #482
130	el-Jib	1676 1394 60 dunams	I II P gap H R B	Village or town on tell	Finkelstein and Magen 1993: #315
131	Khirbet Irha	1724 1394 10 dunams	I II.30% P.?? H.30%	Farmstead(s)	Finkelstein and Magen 1993: #430
132	------	1750 1389 ??	I II.most P	Farmstead	Finkelstein and Magen 1993: #481
133	Khirbet Ras el-Mughar	1619 1387 24 dunams	I II/P.few H-most R?	Farmsteads? Hamlet? Village?	Finkelstein and Magen 1993: #268
134	Khirbet el-Kharaba	1769 1386 3 dunams	I II. many P? H R	Farmstead	Finkelstein and Magen 1993: #497
135	Hizma	1754 1382 ?? Arab village	I II P R	Farmstead? Hamlet? Village?	Finkelstein and Magen 1993: #480
136	------	1657 1378 4 dunams	I II.8% P.20% H.65%	Farmstead	Finkelstein and Magen 1993: #298
137	en-Nebi Samwil	1672 1378 40 dunams	I II.36% P? H.15% R.8%	Farmstead?	Finkelstein and Magen 1993: #313
138	Khirbet el-Kafira	1602 1375 15 dunams	I II.81% P.few H/R.13%	Farmstead	Finkelstein and Magen 1993: #263
139	Khirbet Ein el-Keniseh	1646 1369 5.5 dunams	I II; I II/P.few H.few; R.few	Farmstead	Finkelstein and Magen 1993: #286
140	Khirbet 'Almit	1760 1369 70 dunams	I II P H/R most	Hamlet? Village?	Finkelstein and Magen 1993: #496; Har Even 2003
141	------	1667 1368 4 dunams	I II.7% I II/P.7% P/H.38%	Farmstead	Finkelstein and Magen 1993: #304
142	Khirbet el-Burj	1678 1367 30 dunams	I II.74% P.few P/H.9% H.8%, R.7%	Farmstead? Hamlet? On tell	Kochavi 1972: 186-87, #150 Finkelstein and Magen 1993: #311

143	Tell el-Ful	1719 1367	I II P check final report	Hamlet	Kloner 2000: [102]#79
144	Horvat Zimri, Deir Ghazali	1739 1363	I II P	Farmsteads or village	Kloner 2001: [102]#92
145	------	1667 1361 4 dunams	I II.7% I II/P.7% P/H.38%	Farmstead	Finkelstein and Magen 1993: #304
146	Khirbet el-Murran	1629 1359 20 dunams	I II/P.12% H.40% R.30%	Farmsteads? Hamlet?	Finkelstein and Magen 1993: #272
147	Khirbet el-'Alawina	1675 1354 7 dunams	I II.few P H.14% R.13%	Farmstead	Finkelstein and Magen 1993: #309 Milevski 1996/97: 15-18
148	------	1666 1353 35 dunams	I II.20% P.1 sherd, H.25% R.25%	Farmstead	Finkelstein and Magen 1993: #303
149	Khirbet Deir es-Sidd	1762 1353 30 dunams	I II.70% P H R	Farmstead(s)? Hamlet? Village?	Finkelstein and Magen 1993: #493
150	------	1677 1350 30 dunams	I II.1 sherd P.few	Farmstead(s)	Finkelstein and Magen 1993: #310
151	Ras el-Kharrubeh	1746 1350 10 dunams	I II P H R	Watchtower and farmstead	Biran 1983; Finkelstein and Magen 1993: #450
152	Khirbet Beit Mizza	1652 1349 10 dunams	I II.5% P.3% P/H.5% H.16%, R.10%	Farmstead(s)	Finkelstein and Magen 1993: #293
153	------	1758 1347 5.2 dunams	I II.1 sherd P.1 sherd	Farmstead	Finkelstein and Magen 1993: #469
154	Wadi Salim	1743 1344	I II P	2 farmsteads	Pomerantz 1982 Kloner 2001.[102] #205
155	------	1780 1344 ??	I II P	Farmstead	Finkelstein and Magen 1993: #524
156	el-Muntar	1770 1343 ??	I II/P.1 sherd R.many	Farmstead?	Finkelstein and Magen 1993: #506
157	------	1650 1341 23 dunams	I II.59% I II/P.2% P/H. 17% R.5%	Farmstead	Finkelstein and Magen 1993: #294
158	Khirbet Harabat 'Audeh	1749 1340 10 dunams	I II.most P.few	Farmstead(s)? Hamlet?	Finkelstein and Magen 1993: #448
159	Har ha-Zofim	1741 1330	I II P	Farmstead?	Kloner 2001:[102] #311

160	Ez-Zu'aiyim	1754 1329 ?? Arab village	I II.few P?.few H/R.few	Farmstead	Finkelstein and Magen 1993: #462
161	Ras Abu Subeitan	1748 1321 10 dunams	I II/P.7%	Farmstead	Finkelstein and Magen 1993: #444
162	el-'Eizariya	1744 1309 ?? Arab village	I II P H	Farmstead? Hamlet?	Saller 1957: 222, 237 Finkelstein and Magen 1993: #436
163	el-Khirbe	1774 1302 15 dunams	I II P? R	Farmstead(s) or Hamlet? Village?	Finkelstein and Magen 1993: #500
164	Qiryat Menahem/ Rujm et-Tarud	1658 1292	I II P	Farmstead?	Kloner 2000:[105] #4
165	'Ir Gannim	1657 1291	I II P	Farmstead(s)	Greenburg and Cinamon 2002
166	Khirbet Wadi Alein	1496 1282 45 dunams	I IIB I IIC P H R	Village? Town?	Dagan 2000: #19
167	Khirbet er-Ras West	1671 1282	I II P	Farmstead;	Onn and Rapuano 1995 Kloner 2000: [105] #39
168	Khirbet er-Ras East	1672 1281	I II P R	Storehouse? Farmstead?	Zehavi 1993
169	Nahal Yeshai	1493 1264 2 dunams	I IIB C P H R	Farmstead	Dagan 2000: #29
170	Khirbet el-Yahudi	1628 1264 ??	I II P H R	Farmstead? Hamlet? Village? On tell	Kochavi 1972: 36, #4
171	Khirbet Hisham	1456 1262 50 dunams	I IIB C P gap R	Village? Town?	Dagan 2000: #31
172	Khirbet Zanoah (north)	1504 1254 8 dunams	I IIA B C P H R	Farmstead(s)	Dagan 2000: #38
173	Khirbet Zanoah	1503 1253 62 dunams	I IIA B C P H R	Hamlet? Village? Town? On tell	Dagan 2000: #41
174	Khirbet el-'Aliyah/ Horvat 'Ali	1486 1248 48 dunams	I IIA B C P H R	Hamlet? Village? On tell	Dagan 2000: #51
175	Khirbet 'Amar	1411 1244 40 dunams	I IIB C P H R	Farmstead(s)? Hamlet? Village?	Dagan 2000: #59
176	Husan	1627 1244 ??	I IIC? P H R	Farmstead? Hamlet?	Kochavi 1972: 39, #17
177	Khirbet el-Keikh	1497 1243 22 dunams	I IIB C P H R	Farmstead(s)? Hamlet?	Dagan 2000: #60
178	Tel Yarmut	1477 1240 400 dunams	I IIB C P H R	Village? Town? On tell	Dagan 2000: #70

179	Ras el-Kabir	1674 1237 5 dunams	I IID. 15% P.40% H.2%	Farmstead	Kochavi 1972: 42, #27 Ofer 1993: #329
180	Nahal Hanativ	1510 1235 2 dunams	I IIB C P	Farmstead	Dagan 2000: #79
181	Bethlehem	1698 1235 12 dunams	I IIC. 51% I IID. 11% P.1% H.1% R.2%	Farmstead or Hamlet on tell	Ofer 1993: #330
182	Tel Azekah	1440 1231 40 dunams	I IIA, B C P H R	Hamlet? Village? On tell	Dagan 2000: #86
183	Khirbet Qeiyyafah	1460 1226 37 dunams	I IIA B C P gap R	Hamlet? Village? On tell	Dagan 2000: #107
184	Khirbet Umm el-Jaj	1514 1224 15 dunams	I IIB, C, P H R	Farmstead(s)?H amlet?	Dagan 2000: #117
185	Wadi el-Makari (Hyrcania Valley)	1861 1224	I II B-C P H	Farmstead	Patrich 1994: #112
186	Nahal Ha-'Elah	1504 1220 3 dunams	I IIA B C P H R	Farmstead	Dagan 2000: #122
187	Khirbet el-Rasam	1435 1219 2 dunams	I IIB C P H R	Farmstead	Dagan 2000: #126
188	Khirbet el-Kabirah	1607 1215 ??	I IIC P.many	Hamlet? Village?	Kochavi 1972: 42, #32
189	Tel Zafit	1357 1214	?? P	Village? on tel	Dagan 2002: 84*
190	Khirbet Jizmia south	1641 1214 2 dunams	I IIC. 48% I IID. 39% P.11%	Farmstead	Ofer 1993: #322
191	Khirbet el-Khwakh	1671 1214 ??	I II P H R	Farmstead? Hamlet? Village?	Kochavi 1972: 42, #35 Ofer 1993: #323
192	Khirbet Shakah	1476 1211 60 dunams	I IIB C P	Hanlet? Village? On tell	Dagan 2000: #136
193	Khirbet Sokoh	1480 1207 20 dunams	I IIC P	Farmstead(s)	Dagan 2000: #141
194	Khirbet Umm el- Qita'	1653 1202 6 dunams	I IID. 89% P.7% R.2%	Farmstead	Kochavi 1972: 43, #39 Ofer 1993: #315
195	Bideh (east)	1683 1194 3 dunams	I IID.50% P.50%	Farmstead	Ofer 1993: #312
196	Khirbet Beit Zakariah	1617 1189 10 dunams	I IIC/D.5% P.48% H.9% R.25%	Farmstead(s)	Kochavi 1972: 44, #50; Ofer 1993: #293
197	Khirbet Khubeilah	1602 1187 20 dunams	I IIC.35% I IID.40% P.6% H.4%	Farmstead? Hamlet?	Ofer 1993: #292

198	Khirbet Tab'a	1695 1185 12 dunams	I IIA-D.43% P.6% H.6% R.14%	Hamlet? Village?	Ofer 1993: #303
199	Horvat Yarha'/ Khirbet Subei'	1450 1180	I II P	Farmstead? Hamlet? Village?	Dagan 2000
200	Halil Ismail	1674 1175 5 dunams	I IID.20% P.20%	Farmstead	Ofer 1993: #290
201	Tel Kidonah/ el Siha Abu Rabia'	1400 1174 15 dunams	I IIB C P gap R	Farmstead(s)?; Hamlet?	Dagan 2000: #170
202	Tuweyyir	1625 1172 1 dunam	I IIC/D.15%, P.41% H.34%	Farmstead	Ofer 1993: #285
203	Khirbet 'Adamah	1313 1165 10 dunams	I II P H R	Farmstead(s)	Dagan 2000: #174
204	Seir (south)	1615 1165 7 dunams	I IIC.22% I IID.18% P.11%	Farmstead	Ofer 1993: #277
205	Deir Seir	1619 1165 10 dunams	I IIC.36% I IID.19% P.21% H.9%	Farmstead	Ofer 1993: #284
206	el-Beq'ah	1695 1165 3 dunams	I IIA.18% I IID.15% P.15% H.12%	Farmstead	Ofer 1993: #283
207	Khirbet et-Tuqu'	1700 1157 1701 1156 35 dunams	I II B.12% I IIC.40% I IID. 18% P H.5% R.19%	Farmstead(s) Hamlet	Kochavi 1972: 47, #62 Hirschfeld 1985: #37 Ofer 1993: #276
208	Tel Goded	1415 1156 47 dunams	I IIA B C P H R	Hamlet? Village on tell	Dagan 2000: #178
209	Khirbet Judur	1588 1156 24 dunams	I IIC-D.47% P.10% H.2% R.10%	Hamlet? Village? On tell	Kochavi 1972: 46, #60 Ofer 1993: #270
210	Tel Burna	1380 1153 35 dunams	I IIA B C P gap R	Village? On tel	Dagan 2000: #180
211	Tel Zayit	1339 1152 25 dunams	I IIB C P H R	Hamlet? Village? On tell	Dagan 2000: #181
212	Khirbet Qeilah	1504 1135 55 dunams	IIA B C P gap R	Village? Town? Birah? On tell	Kochavi 1972: 48, #70 Dagan 2000: #188
213	'Arub	1661 1132 1 dunam	I IID.78% P.18% H.2%	Farmstead	Ofer 1993: #252
214	Khirbet ez-Zawiyye	1651 1121 1 dunam	I IIC.34% I IID.33% P.5%	Farmstead	Kochavi 1972: 51, #85 Ofer 1993: #238

215	Tel Maresha	1405 1112 40 dunams	I IIB C P H R	Hamlet? Village? On tell	Dagan 2000: #196
216	Khirbet et-Tubeiqah	1590 1108 12 dunams	I IIC.21% I IID.19% P.3% H.19%	Farmstead	Ofer 1993: #216
217	Khirbet Beit Nasib esh Sharqiyye	1511 1104 25 dunams	I IIB C P H R	Farmsteads? Hamlet?	Kochavi 1972: 53-53, #96; Dagan 2000: #200
218	Si'ir	1637 1102 14 dunams	I IIC.33% I IID.10% P.3% H.3%	Farmstead	Kochavi 1972: 54, #100; Ofer 1993: #219
219	Khirbet Beit 'Elam	1491 1098 10 dunams	I IIA B C P H	Farmstead	Dagan 2000: #206
220	Nahal Maresha	1424 1097 5 dunams	I IIB C P	Farmstead	Dagan 2000: #209
221	Horvat Sheqofa/ Khirbet Sukeiyifeh	1376 1094 20 dunams	I IIB C P H R	Farmsteads? Hamlet?	Dagan 1992: #34 Dagan 2000: #219
222	Halhul	1603 1095 18 dunams	I IIA-B.32% I IIC.9% I IID.9% P.8% H.3%	Village? Town?	Kochavi 1972: 55, #103 Ofer 1993: #209
223	Nahal Guvrin	1469 1094 5 dunams	I IIB C P	Farmstead	Dagan 2000: #220
224	Tel Guvrin	1485 1093 12 dunams	I II P	Farmstead(s)? Hamlet?	Dagan 2000: #223
225	Mezadot Yehuda B	1598 1085	I II P	Watchtower and Farmstead	Batz 2003
226	Idna	1478 1083 1 dunam	I IIC P	Farmstead	Dagan 2000: #243
227	Khirbet Ras et-Tawil; Tor Abu 'Ali	1636 1083 40 dunams	I I.7% I IIA-B.31% I IIC.24% I IID.25% P.9% H.2%	Village? Town? On tell	Kochavi 1972: 56, #111 Ofer 1993: #205
228	Idna	1462 1082 35 dunams	I IIB C P gap R	Farmsteads? Hamlet? Village?	Dagan 2000: #247
229	Khirbet Beit Lei	1432 1080 40 dunams	I IIC P H R	Hamlet? Village?	Dagan 2000: #251
230	Idna	1477 1076 55 dunams	I IIB C P H (many) R (many)	Village? Town? On tell	Kochavi 1972: 56-57, #113 Dagan 2000: #260
231	Khirbet er-Ras	1459 1074 50 dunams	I IIB C P H R	Hamlet? Village? On tell	Dagan 2000: #259

232	Khirbet et-Taiyyibe	1531 1072 20 dunams	I IIA-B.20% I IIC.25% I IID.6% P.12% H.5% R.10%	Village	Kochavi 1972: 57, #115 Ofer 1993: #191
233	Taiyyibe (east)	1553 1072 20 dunams	I IIB.2% P.2%	Farmstead	Ofer 1993: #192
234	Halat el-Ful	1482 1066 3 dunams	I IIB C P	Farmstead	Dagan 2000: #271
235	Khirbet el-'Udeise	1632 1064 25 dunams	I IIA-B.13% I IIC.42% I IID.16% P.11% H.3% R.10%	Hamlet? Village? Town? On tell	Kochavi 1972: 58, #123 Ofer 1993: #190
236	Khirbet el-Fir'a	1513 1057 ??	I P H R	Farmstead? Hamlet? Village?	Kochavi 1972: 59, #132
237	Tafuh	1545 1052 20 dunams	I IIA-B.16% I IIC.27% I IID.17% P.10% H.8% R.8%	Hamlet? Village? On tell	Kochavi 1972: 59-60, #133 Ofer 1993: #184
238	Khirbet Ashbor	1445 1045 16 dunams	I IIB C P H R	Farmstead(s)? Hamlet?	Dagan 2000: #287
239	Khirbet Umm el Baqar	1300 1042 20 dunams	I IIB C P H R	Village on tell	Dagan 1992: #249 Dagan 2000: #292
240	Khirbet Farajit	1454 1042 35 dunams	I IIB C P H R	Hamlet? Village?	Dagan 2000: #293
241	Tel Haraqim/Tell Kharakah	1336 1036 15 dunams	I II B C P H	Village? On tell	Dagan 1992: #280 Dagan 2000: #306
242	Khirbet Kan'an	1572 1022 5 dunams	I IIB.5% I IIC.26% I IID.6% P.10% H.26% R.27%	Farmsteads? Hamlet? Village?	Kochavi 1972: 62, #149 Ofer 1993: #175
243	Dura	1526 1016 30 dunams	I IIA-B.13% I IIC.33% I IID.3% P.3% H.31% R I.1%	Farmsteads? Hamlet?	Kochavi 1972: 62, #154 Ofer 1993: #173
244	Khirbet Bani Dar; Khirbet Yukin	1645 1005 35 dunams	I IIA-B.21% I IIC.33% I IID.18% P.4% H.3% R.3%	Hamlet? Village? On tell	Kochavi 1972, 64, #162 Ofer 1993: #171
245	Khirbet Eitun e-Tahta	1424 1000 15 dunams	I IIA B C P H R	Farmstead(s)? Hamlet?	Dagan 2000: #380

246	Khirbet el-Marajim	1523 0996 25 dunams	I IIA-B.17% I IIC.33% I IID.30% P.14% H.5%	Hamlet? Village? On tell	Kochavi 1972: 66, #168 Ofer 1993: #155
247	el-Hadab	1551 0985 20 dunams	I IIA-B.25% I IIC.28% I IID.19% P.7% H.12% R.4%	Hamlet? Village? On tell	Kochavi 1972: 68, #176 Ofer 1993: #143
248	Tel Keleikh	1337 0984 30 dunams	I IIB C P H R	Hamlet? Village? On tell	Dagan 2000: #384
249	Tel Zif	1628 0982 18 dunams	I IIA-B.19% I IIC.20% I IID.4% P.3% H.17% R.22%	Hamlet? Village? On tell	Kochavi 1972: 68, #178 Ofer 1993: #147
250	Tel Milh	1287 0968 20 dunams	I IIB C P H R	Hamlet? On tell	Dagan 2000: #386
251	Khirbet Bism	1532 0967 8 dunams	I IIA-B.20% I IIC.26% I IID.26% P.6% H.3% R.2%	Hamlet? Village?	Kochavi 1972: 71, #193 Ofer 1993: #112
252	Yatta Ghuwein (east)	1584 0949 30 dunams	I IIB.8% I IIC.20% I IID.15% P.2% H.3% R.11%	Hamlet?	Magen and Baruch 2002 Ofer 1993: #93
253	Khirbet Umm el-'Amad	1543 0944 9 dunams	I IIB.1% I IIC.47% I IID.21% P.6% H.6% R.3%	Hamlet? Village? On tell	Kochavi 1972: 73, #173 Ofer 1993: #89
254	Khirbet Umm Lispa	1648 0940 5 dunams	I IIA-B.27% I IIC.25% I IID.22% P.6%	Hamlet? Village?	Ofer 1993: #96
255	Khirbet Rabud	1515 0934 60 dunams	I IIA-B.13% I IIC.43% I IID.16% P.1% H.1%	Hamlet? Village? On tell	Kochavi 1972, 74, #215 Ofer 1993: #78
256	Khirbet el-Karmil	1631 0923 12 dunams	I IIA-B.16% I IIC.20% I IID.16% P.2% H.3% R.13%	Hamlet? Village?	Kochavi 1972: 76, #222 Ofer 1993: #73

257	Khirbet 'Unnab es Saghir	1458 0912 14 dunams	I IIC.24% I IID.40% P.3% H.3%	Farmstead(s)? Hamlet?	Kochavi 1972: 76, #225 Ofer 1993: #54
258	Khirbet Ma'in	1628 0908 18 dunams	I IIA-B.22% I IIC.38% I IID.27% P.4% H.2% R.4%	Hamlet? Village? On tell	Kochavi 1972: 77, #231 Ofer1993: #49
259	Khirbet Shuweike	1508 0903 8 dunams	I IIA-B.17% I IIC.53% I IID.12% P.1% H.10% R.5%	Hamlet? On tell	Kochavi 1972: 77, #229 Ofer 1993: #31
260	Khirbet 'Anim; Ghuweim et-Tahta (south)	1560 0845 20 dunams	I IIC&D.36% P.10% H.27%	Hamlet? Village?	Kochavi 1972: 82, #250 Ofer 1993: #2
261	Duda'im Site	1262 0821	I P	Farmstead	Negev 2001: 113*
262	Tel Shoqet	1413 0798	I II P H	Village? On tell	Govrin 1991: #3
263	Horvat Yattin/ Khirbet el-Wutn	1425 0740	I II P	Hamlet? Village? On tell	Govrin 1991: #162
264	Nahal Besor	1224 0365	I P	Farmstead	Cohen 1985: #44

Military Sites

265	Rujm Abu Hashabe	1632 1419	P R: 12 × 12 m (prob later period)	Kochavi 1972: 181, #110
266	Khirbet Nijam/ Har Adar	1623 1372	P: 21.8 × 25.8 m	Dadon 1994
267	Horvat Zimri	1739 1363	P: 60 × 70 m	Nadelman 1993; Kloner 2001: [102] #92
268	Giv'at Shappira	1725 1343	I II P: 17 × 21 m	Negbi 1969; Kloner 2001: [102] #196
269	Ramat Rahel	1706 1274	I II P	Kloner 2000: [106] #95
270	Khirbet Umm el-Qal'a	1617 1243	I P: 35 × 55 m (expanded from earlier core?)	Kochavi 1972: 37-8, #13
271	Khirbet Kabbar	1665 1232	P: uncertain but at least 20 × 20 m	Kochavi 1972: 40, #26 Baruch and Srukh 2001
272	Khirbet Abu et-Twain	1585 1193	I IIC P: 31.5 × 29 m	Mazar 1982: 104-105
273	Khirbet er-Rasm	1502 1158	P: 27 × 29 m	Kochavi 1972: 46, #58
274	Khirbet el-Qatt	1602 1127 1 dunam	I IIB gap P.56%, H.29%, R.5%: 30 × 30 m	Kochavi 1972: 50, #79 Ofer 1993: #234 Dagan 2000: #112

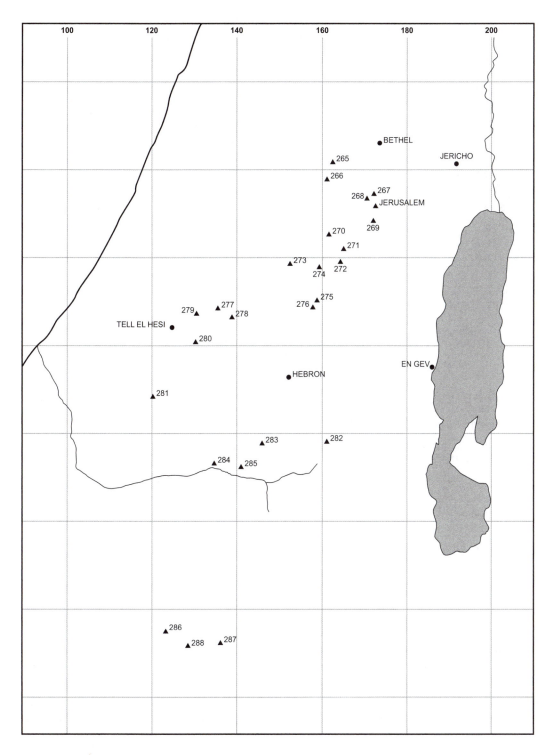

Figure 51. *Military sites in Persian-era Yehud*

275	Khirbet ez-Zawiyye	1651 1121	I IIC.6% gap P.88% H.2%: 40-50 × 80-100 m	Kochavi 1972: 52, #85 Ofer 1993: #240
276	Khirbet et-Tubeiqeh/ Bet-Zur	1590 1108	P H 33 × 41 m	Reich 1992a
277	Tell Lakish Level II	1357 1082 120 dunams	I IIB C gap P Residency: 36 × 45.5 m	Dagan 1992: #92 Dagan 2000: #246 Fantalkin and Tal 2005
278	Khirbet Rasm Shu'liya	1393 1069	P H: 25 × 25 m	Dagan 1992: #217
279	Khirbet Umm el-Baqar	1300 1042	I II P H: 15 × 15 m (later?)	Dagan 1992: #249
280	Tel Haraqim/ Tell Kharakah	1336 1036	I II gap P H: 18 × 24 m	Dagan 1992: #280
281	Tel Sera'/Tell esh-Shari'a Stratum III	119 088 16-20 dunams	Iron IIC gap P gap H/R Citadel in Area D: granary Area A	Oren 1993b: 1334
282	Tel Arad, Stratum V (mid fifth)	162 075	I IIC gap P H: c. 45 × 45 m	M Aharoni 1993: 82-85
283	Harei 'Anim	1464 0745	P? R-B: 31 × 34 m	Govrin 1991: #174
284	Tel Beersheva Tell es-Saba' Stratum H3	135 073	I II gap P ??: segment of casemate 40m long exposed	Aharoni 1973: pl 85 Herzog 1993: 172-73
285	Nahal Yattir	1402 0725	P: 23.5 × 23.5 m	Govrin 1991: #205
286	Horvat Mesora	1221 0365	P: 21 × 21m	Cohen 1985: #43 Cohen 1986b
287	Mesad Nahal Haro'a	1363 0354	P: 21.5 × 21.5 m	Cohen 1981: #65 Cohen 1986a
288	Horvat Ritma Stratum II	1283 0347	I I P: 21 × 21 m	Meshel 1977 Cohen 1985: #73

Analysis of Site Use and Settlement Patterns

There are no readily identifiable military sites guarding the northern border region with Samerina, which indicates that, in the eyes of the Persian administration, there was no sense of threat between these two provinces. Rujm Abu Hashabe (#265), a small facility measuring 12 × 12 meters, may have been built in the Persian period, but probably is late Persian or Hellenistic and not part of Yehud during the reign of Artaxerxes I. It was at most a relay station used to supply fresh horses and provisions for those travelling through the central hill-country from Samerina to Yehud.

At the southern end of the territory under investigation, we find four administrative facilities in the Beersheva Valley at Beersheva (#284) (40 × ? meters), Nahal Yattir (#285) (23.5 × 23.5 meters), Harei 'Anim (#283) (31 × 34 meters) and Arad (#282) (45 × 45 meters). Beersheva and Arad had housed forts at the end of the Iron Age, but is appears that new facilities were built at one or both. The other two sites were newly founded in the Persian period. Nahal Yattir has its own settlement immediately outside of the fortress walls (#107) and a reused site that may have served as a villa for the fort commander or local administrator/scribe (#106). Tel Shoqet (#262) and Horvat Yattin (#263) housed settlements on nearby tells that may have continued to be occupied from the Iron IIC into the Persian period. There was renewed settlement at Tel 'Ira (#108), which had housed a garrison and associated population at the end of the monarchy. Now, it seems to have become a civilian settlement.

The finding of Aramaic ostraca at Beersheva, Arad and Tel 'Ira during excavations can allow us to conclude that these facilities were all in existence in the mid-fourth century BCE. How much before that they had been built is not clear, but we need to consider the strong possibility that they were built after 400 BCE, when Egypt broke away from Persia and the valley became the effective southern frontier of the Persian empire. Whether Yattir fits the same profile is difficult to assess. If the border of Yehud extended as far south as the Beersheva Valley at any point during the fifth century, it is the most likely of the four to have been established prior to 400 BCE, only because no ostraca were found in the limited excavations conducted there. It sits back from the main valley road further than the others as well, which might suggest that a different rationale led to its occupation.

Much further south, in the Negev highlands, is another cluster of three facilities at Horvat Mesora (#286) (21 × 21 meters), Mesad Nahal Haro'a (#287) (21.5 × 21.5 meters), and Horvat Ritma (#288) (21 × 21 meters). Of these, the first two were newly built, while the last seems to have reused an earlier fort already in place from the Iron I period, which had been abandoned for a long time. A single farmstead or settlement lay near these three sites: #265, Nahal Besor.

Settlement Trends

In general, there is a trend toward small settlements consisting of unwalled farmsteads or hamlets, with very few possible village and town sites. This is the case in the territory of Benjamin as well as the territory of the Judean hills and the Shephelah. Thus, it is logical to conclude that the mainstay of the economy was agricultural production, probably combined with the raising of sheep and goats, as had been traditional in the region for millennia. Many of the farmsteads have evidence of oil presses and vats for processing grapes into wine, so it is likely that they produced primarily wine and olive oil alongside grains (wheat and barley). The settlement pattern overlaps in large part with what had been in place at the end of the monarchy, although there appear to have been more walled settlements interspersed among the farmsteads in the late Iron II period, as well as more military sites.

The pattern of farmsteads appears to have been well established in the Judean hills by the seventh century. 2 Chronicles 26.10 claims that King Uzziah (769–733 BCE) had placed farmers and vinedressers in the hills and in the fertile lands, so the process may have begun as early as the mid-eighth century, with increases over time as subsequent generations built new farmsteads in the region to accommodate their families. Alternatively, or in addition, there may have been a new influx of settlement in the region under Manasseh (698–642 BCE), after this land was regained from having been given by Sennacherib to the Philistines in 701 BCE. It is uncertain if the forty-six strong cities and walled forts, together with countless villages in their vicinity, which he claims to have separated from Judah, were only located in the Shephelah adjoining Philistine territory in the coastal plain or in both the Shephelah and the Judean highlands (for the relevant segment of text from his Annals, see Oppenheim 1969: 287-88).

The pattern of farmsteads in the region of Benjamin was probably put in place by the Neo-Babylonian administration, if it had not already existed to some degree under the Judahite monarchy. 2 Kings 25.11/Jer. 52.15 reports that after the destruction of Jerusalem and the exile of a large segment of its population, the captain of the guard in charge of local affairs named Nebuzaradan left some of the poorest of the land to be vinedressers and plowmen and appointed Gedaliah, from a prominent Jerusalemite family, to be in charge. Jeremiah 39.10 expands this statement to make it clear that those who remained were given land to own for the first time; during the monarchy, they had only been laborers without the means to own land.

The text does not specify where these farmsteads were located. It has been presumed that they would have been centered in the region of Benjamin because the new provincial seat was at Mizpah, there appears to have been continuous settlement at Bethel, Mizpah, and Gibeon, and the spread of the *m(w)ṣh*-stamped jars tends to fall within the region of Benjamin (so, e.g., Miller and Hayes 1986: 416-17; Ahlström 1993: 795; Zorn, Yellin and Hayes 1994: 183; Barstad 1996: 1996: 47-48; Milevski 1996/97: 21; Lipschits 1999: 179-85; Stern 2001: 321-23). However, the policy of land distribution would have been province-wide, and logically, it would have been in regions that had not recovered from the deportations carried out by Sennacherib in 701 BCE or in regions from which the population was deported to Babylonia in 586 BCE, where the existing farms would have been assigned to new owners, their former owners now gone. If there is little evidence of destruction and disruption in the Benjaminite region at the end of the monarchy, it might be best to locate these farmsteads elsewhere, in the northern Shephelah or central Judean highlands, for example.

The Shephelah had been heavily depopulated after 701 BCE, when Sennacherib had turned it over to the control of the Philistines. Shlomo Bunimovtiz and Zvi Lederman have argued that the Philistines carried out a policy of forcefully evicting Judahite settlers who had not been deported from their villages in this region, based on the short-lived attempt of resettlement at Bet-Shemesh many decades after the site's destruction in 701 BCE. In their view, the situation presumes that the Philistines prevented settlers from returning to the area while it was under their jurisdiction, and it was only after the land once again came under Judahite control that they were able to try to return (2003: 19-23). They believe this took place during the third quarter of the seventh century BCE, based on the pottery found in the water cistern, but was quickly ended by Philistine neighbors and Assyrian masters, who tore down their temporary houses and filled in the water cistern system to prevent any further attempts to reoccupy the site. However, their proposed reconstruction of events suggests that the Philistines may still have laid claim to the land during the reign of Josiah, especially if they were the ones who filled in the water cistern in order to prevent any subsequent attempts at resettlement after c. 650–625 BCE.

In contrast to the situation in the southern and central Judean highlands, the Shephelah does not appear to have recovered much, if at all, before the end of the monarchy. Resettlement in this foothill area in the Persian period took place after a much larger gap in time than at sites in Benjamin or the Judean hills that had been abandoned in 586 BCE and not reoccupied under the Neo-Babylonians.

Of the 109 sites that are able from survey results to be classified under the heading of newly settled or resettled in the Persian period, sixty were pristine establishments on new land while forty-nine were reoccupations of older facilities. The vast majority of the 109 sites cluster in five regions: (1) west of Bethel, Mizpah and Geva, in the territory of Benjamin (#1-22); (2) in the central Judean hill-country between latitudes 1263 and 1042, around the string of fortresses at Khirbet Umm el-Qala', Khirbet Kabbar, Khirbet Abu Twain, Khirbet el-Qatt, Khirbet Zawiyye, and Bet-Zur (#28, 29, 31, 32, 34, 37-39, 41, 45-51, 53, 56, 58-60, 62-68, 73, 78-79, 81, 89, 90); (3) in the Shephelah west of the fort at Khirbet er-Rasm between latitudes 1240 and 1159 (#30, 33, 35, 36, 40, 42-44, 52, 54, 55, 57, 61); (4) southeast of the facilities at Lakish and Khirbet Rasm Shu'liya, with a few to the north (#69-72, 74-77, 80, 82-88, 91-97); and (5) south of cluster 3 and southeast of cluster 4 in the southern Judean highlands (#98-102, 104-106).

Group 1, centered in the traditional territory of Benjamin, were all pristine foundations in the Persian period (#1-22). The remaining new foundations within the territory of Benjamin, which either lay east of the sites named above or west, but significantly south of the cluster of other sites, included two that were reoccupied after a previous founding in the Iron IIB period (#24, 26); both of these sites lay west of Jerusalem but south of the cluster of new foundations. One site, #23, which lay southeast of Geva, had been founded sometime earlier in the Iron II period and then abandoned, while two sites were pristine foundations in the Persian period (#25, 27). One lay northeast of Jerusalem and the other southwest of the *birah*.

These twenty-seven sites that were newly settled in the Benjaminite region in the Persian period were added to an area that already was rather densely settled. There were fifty-three settlements that appear to have continued from the Neo-Babylonian period into the Persian period (#110-22; 124-65).[3] The surveys did not beak down the Iron II period into sub-phases, so we cannot observe when within the Iron II period these sites would have been initially occupied. Notwithstanding, this area experienced fifty percent growth in the Persian period, most of which represented new farmsteads established for the first time on virgin soil. It appears that there would have been dozens of abandoned farmsteads available from the Iron IIC for people to occupy; according to O. Lipschits, there had been 146 sites occupied in the Iron II period (2003: 349). Two questions result from this information. First, why weren't more of the abandoned farmsteads occupied, which would have meant less work for the new occupants? Second, how many of these new foundations were due to the arrival of new settlers and how many were the result of natural population growth in the area, where new generations spread out into adjoining lands to set up house? One thing is certain: in the Persian period, Benjamin experienced a growth in occupied sites in comparison to the Neo-Babylonian period (so also Finkelstein and Magen 1993: 27) and not a continuing decline, as proposed by O. Lipschits (2003: 349).

Groupings 3 and 4 described above that lay in the Shephelah have a large number of sites that were newly reoccupied or newly founded in the Persian period. At first glance, this intense activity in the Persian period is consistent with this area's suggested extensive depopulation after 701 BCE during the monarchy, which presumably lasted through the Neo-Babylonian period, with a very limited recovery under King Josiah (e.g. Na'aman 1993: 113-15; Finkelstein 1994: 180-81; Bunimovitz and Lederman 2003: 20-23). The total number of occupied sites throughout the Shephelah dropped from 276 before 701 BCE to thirty-eight in the late-seventh/early-sixth century, indicating that the recovery was only beginning toward the end of the monarchy, if the sites are this early, and was comparatively limited (Dagan 1992; Finkelstein 1994: 173).

Nevertheless, according to the survey results of Y. Dagan, the northern (cluster 3) area appears to have had a significant number of sites that were occupied at some point after 701 BCE in the Iron IIC period. He does not use the designation Iron III or Iron IID to distinguish the Neo-Babylonian period from the late-monarchic era. For him, Iron IIC covers the seventh–sixth centuries BCE, including the Neo-Babylonian period from 586–538 BCE.

Yehuda Dagan's survey results can be understood in two ways. They could indicate that this northern portion of the Shephelah was partially repopulated in the late-monarchic period after a Judahite king regained control of it from the Philistines. The king in question might have been Manasseh (698–642 BCE), who became a loyal Assyrian vassal (so, e.g., Alt 1953: 248; Herrmann 1975: 259; Evans 1980: 168; Ahlström 1993: 734-35; Rainey 1983: 16; Halpern 1991: 60-65), but more likely would have been Josiah (639–609 BCE), during whose reign the Assyrian empire was on its last legs and under which many think that the settlement list in Joshua 15 was probably compiled (so, e.g., Rainey 1983: 16; Na'aman 1993: 114; Finkelstein 1994: 181; Bunimovitz and Lederman 2003: 23). Or, they could indicate that the northern region in grouping 3 was one of the areas where the Neo-Babylonians settled vinedressers into abandoned farmsteads, so that the bulk of resettlement took place after the end of the monarchy and gradually increased naturally over time in the Persian period, spreading out to reclaim other abandoned farmsteads in the region. In this case, the common assumption that there had been recovery before the end of the monarchy would need to be abandoned. Since there is little agreement about what changes, if any, took place in the pottery during the sixth century BCE under Neo-Babylonian rule, it is my opinion that the survey results are, by nature, too imprecise to be used to argue in favor of one alternative over the other.

In group 3 in the northern Shephelah, thirteen sites with new occupation in the Persian period were at farmsteads, hamlets, or villages abandoned in Iron IIB, presumably after 701 BCE (#30, 33, 35, 36, 40, 42-44, 52, 54, 55, 57, 61); only two were pristine foundations (#43, 61). By contrast, however, twenty of twenty-four sites settled in this area already in Iron IIC were at farmsteads, hamlets or villages abandoned in Iron IIB (#166, 169 171-175, 177-78, 180, 182-84 186-87, 192, 201, 208, 210-11). Only one was a pristine Iron IIC foundation (#193). Of the remaining three sites with possible continuous occupation from the Iron IIC into the Persian period, two had Iron II sherds that were not diagnostic enough to allow a distinction to be made between phases B and C (#199, 203), while one had questionable Iron II remains and so might have been a pristine Persian foundation as well (#189). There was a thirty-two percent increase in occupied sites in the Persian period.

Group 4 in the southern Shephelah had similar reoccupation in Iron IIC, but also experienced heavy expansion in the Persian period. Eighteen settlements were re-established in the region in Iron IIC and possibly occupied continuously into the Persian period (#215, 217, 219-21, 223-224, 226, 228-31, 238-41, 245, 248 and 250). Of these, thirteen were at sites that had been founded and probably abandoned in the Iron IIB, presumably after 701 BCE (#215, 217, 220, 221, 223, 228, 230, 231, 239, 240, 241, 248, 250) two were at sites occupied previously in the Iron II A and IIB (#219, 245); two were at sites that had been settled as pristine foundations in the Iron IIC (#226, 229), and one was at a site previously settled sometime in the Iron II period (#224). During the Persian period, when new settlement took place, twelve Iron IIB farmsteads were reoccupied (#69, 70, 74, 75, 77, 84, 88, 91, 93, 95, 96, 97), one Iron IIc (#76), and two others that had been occupied previously in the Iron II at some phase (#86, 92). Nine settlements were pristine Persian foundations, including the fort and adjoining settlement at settlements were pristine Persian foundations, including the fort and adjoining settlement at Khirbet Rasm Shuʻliyeh, just east of Lakish (#71, 72, 80, 82, 83, 85, 87, 94, 278). This reflects a fifty-five percent increase in newly occupied sites in the Persian Period.

The concentration of Persian-era settlement in group 4 in the southern Shephelah is probably to be linked to the building of the Residency at Lakish. If the building is dated to 450 BCE, then this cluster of settlements can be associated with new settlement initiatives in the province of Yehud at the time of Nehemiah during the reign of Artaxerxes I. If instead, it is dated to 400 BCE as A. Fantalkin and O. Tal have suggested, then the majority of the resettlement could be dated at this time and connected with the development of an economic base in Idumea.[4]

Persian-era settlement in the central Judean hills had a different history. There were twenty-two pristine settlements (# 28, 29, 31, 32, 37, 45, 49-51, 58, 59, 62, 64-68, 73, 78, 81, 89, 90) and only fourteen that were newly reoccupied after a gap of time (# 34, 38, 39, 41, 46, 47, 48, 53, 56, 60, 63, 76, 77, 79). Of the latter group, two had not been used since the Iron I period, (#53, 60), three had not been settled since Iron IIB, presumably since Sennacherib's campaigns in 701 BCE (#63, 77, 79) and the remaining nine were theoretically destroyed or abandoned in 586 BCE (#34, 38-40, 46-48, 56, 76). By contrast, there were thirty-seven settlements that were occupied at the end of the monarchy that may have continued to be occupied through the Neo-Babylonian period and into the Persian period within these same parameters (#164-65, 167-68, 170, 176, 179-80, 188, 190-91, 194-98, 200, 202, 204-207, 209, 212-214, 218, 222, 225, 227, 232-237). So the number of settlements increased by almost fifty percent in the Persian period. While some of this might have been due to natural growth, it is likely that a good proportion was the result of an influx of new settlers in conjunction with the building of the string of six forts and relay stations along the north–south trunk road that ran through the region (#270-72, 274-76).

It also seems likely that some or all of the thirty-seven sites that had continuous occupation in this region had been included among the farmsteads assigned by the new Neo-Babylonian provincial officials to those who had remained in the land after 586 BCE. The fort at Khirbet Abu Twain (#272) appears to have been occupied throughout the Neo-Babylonian period. It has a number of farmsteads with ongoing settlement in its immediate vicinity (#179-81, 186, 194-97, 200, 202, 204-206). Thus, the Persian expansion in this area appears to have reinforced a policy that already had been put in place under the Neo-Babylonians.[5]

The southern Judean hills also received a proportionately significant influx of new settlers in the Persian period. There were seventeen settlements that were potentially settled continuously from the end of the monarchy, through the Neo-Babylonian period, and into the Persian period

(#242-44, 246-49, 251-60). Of these, twelve had been established already in the Iron IIA period and have evidence of occupation in each subsequent sub-phase of the Iron II period. Three had been first established in Iron IIB (# 242, 252-53), while just two had been founded in Iron IIC, either at the end of the monarchy or during the Neo-Babylonian period (#257, 260). To this base of farmsteads, hamlets, and villages, seven new farmsteads were established in the Persian period, four of which were pristine foundations (#98-100, 105). Of the remaining three reoccupied farmsteads, one had been abandoned since the Iron IIB period, after 701 BCE (#101), and the other two had theoretically been abandoned after 586 BCE (#102, 106). This marked almost a thirty percent increase in the Persian-era population. Careful thought needs to be given to whether this increase was the result of a natural growth in the local population over time, an influx of new settlers, or both.[6]

The numbers just cited tend to indicate that the central and southern Judean hills recovered from whatever destruction of smaller sites took place in 701 BCE much more quickly and extensively than did the Shephelah. Without excavation, it is hard to tell if there was any sort of occupational gap following any destruction levels that might be found. On the surface, however, the results seem to suggest that there was a long-term, steady population in this region that remained or returned to their homes in spite of changes in the administrative control of the region. Whether under Philistine, Judahite, Neo-Babylonian, Edomite, or Persian control, they continued their traditional way of life, growing cereal crops, producing olives and wine, and raising sheep and goats.

The central and southern Judean hills may or may not have been ceded to Philistine control in 701 BCE by Sennacherib, along with the Shephelah. But either way, it has been suggested that the central and southern hill-country was once more under Judahite control by the reign of Manasseh or Josiah, and that there was a concerted effort to repopulate it rather than the Shephelah (e.g. Halpern 1991: 60; Finkelstein 1994: 176-81; Bunimovitz and Lederman 2003: 20-23). The impetus to resettle the highlands may have come from a need to provide olives as tribute payment to Assyria, for processing at Ekron (Finkelstein 1994: 180).

The current lack of excavated sites in the region, especially farmsteads, precludes a firm decision about whether or not there had been a region-wide occupational gap. The destruction of forts in the area at the end of the monarchy may not reflect the policy towards farmsteads; if the Neo-Babylonians were intending to make Judah a province, they may well have left some of the local farmers in place to continue to produce taxable income. There is no particular reason to assume a regional occupational gap, in which case, it is misleading to conclude that there would have been a deliberate Persian imperial policy of 'redevelopment'. It is clear that the area was under Judahite control in the closing years of the monarchy because it lay north of the string of forts in the Beersheva Valley and Negev Highlands that clearly belonged to the administrative system of Judah. Whether it had ever been under Philistine control, and if it had, how much before the closing decades of the monarchy it might have been returned, remain open questions.

None of the percentages for new settlements just cited in the preceding discussion for any sub-region within Yehud can be relied upon to reflect the actual settlement trends accurately. None should be cited in arguments concerning the changes in settled sites or demographics between the Neo-Babylonian and Persian periods. They reflect the information contained in survey and excavation reports, but since diagnostic pottery for the Neo-Babylonian period has not been firmly defined and may not exist, it is not possible to know with any degree of certainty which sites that are listed as having Iron IIC occupation and Persian occupation were continuously settled after 586 through the Neo-Babylonian period and into the Persian period, and which would have been abandoned in 586 BCE and resettled in the Persian period.

Forts and Relay Stations

Facilities Located along Internal Provincial Roads. Of the six sites in the eastern central Judean hills, only Khirbet Kabbar (#271) was a totally new foundation. Khirbet el-Qatt (#274) was reoccupied for the first time since the Iron IIB period, while Khirbet Umm el-Qal‘a (#270), whose founding date in the Iron II is uncertain, was probably expanded from its original Iron Age core. Khirbet Abu et-Twain (#272) appears to have remained in use through the Neo-Babylonian period and into the fifth century, but may have ceased to be used about the time of Artaxerxes' redevelopment of the area (Mazar 1982). Khirbet ez-Zawiyye (#275) was reused after a likely destruction in 586 BCE, and Bet-Zur (#276), which had housed a citadel for most of the Iron Age, became the site of a newly built fort/administrative complex in the Persian period. It is unclear if the rebuilding took place in the mid-fifth century or only in the fourth century, however (Reich 1992a).

This string of facilities traces the long-standing north–south trunk road through the central hills from the Beersheva Valley to Jerusalem. The road left the valley opposite Beersheva and went north, past Tel Shoqet (#262). It then mounted up past Khirbet Rabud (#255) via Khirbet Bism (#251), el-Hadab (#247) and Khirbet Kan‘an (#242). It skirted Hevron and headed north, past Halhul (#222), the fort at Bet-Zur/Khirbet et-Tubeiqeh (#276), the one at Khirbet ez-Zawiyye (#275), the fort at Khirbet el-Qatt (#274), and onwards past Khirbet Umm et-Tala‘ (#60), Rujm es-Sabit (#53), Khirbet Zakandah/Khirbet Faghur (#48) Khirbet Umm el-Qita‘ (#194) and Khirbet el-Kwakh (#191). Then passing by the forts of Khirbet Kabbar (#271) and Ramat Rahel (#269), it arrived at Jerusalem (Dorsey 1991: 119-23).

In light of the apparent importance of this route, it is likely that Beersheva was occupied prior to the creation of Idumea c. 400 BCE. As noted in the previous chapter (p. 268) excavations have revealed that the site was reoccupied by the fourth century. A small segment of wall belonging to a structure whose orientation was different from the later Hellenistic fort built over it, was built inside the old city walls, but most of the Persian-era finds were retrieved from pits that had been dug around the fort, but also within the city walls. The pits contained ash mixed with soil, animal bones, pottery sherds, and the fifty-eight Aramaic ostraca, dates on which ranged from 359–338 BCE. Thus, it is clear that the site was part of the administration of Idumea, but this does not rule out its reoccupation already in the second half of the fifth century.

This settlement appears to have served double-duty as an administrative and possibly military post and as a caravanserai. Having an efficient water cistern system inside the town walls,[7] the site was a logical place for caravans crossing the Beersheva Valley to stop and replenish their water supplies. Tolls could be collected by local administrators for access to the water. At the same time, it lay at the terminus of the north–south trunk road that entered the Judean hills and so would also have been a logical place to station a small post or relay station, where couriers could rest and collect food and water for the day's journey to the provincial seat.

Another route appears to have gone from the provincial seat at Jerusalem on a diagonal running southwest through the Shephelah to the coastal plain. The forts at Khirbet Umm el-Qal'a (#270) and Khirbet er-Rasm (#273) marked this route, which passed through the Shephelah at Khirbet Rasm Shu'liya (#278), and went on past Tel Lakish, with its governor's residency (#277), exiting the foothills at Khirbet Umm el-Baqar (#279). The specific route that was taken through the central hill-country is unclear; many options are possible (Dorsey 1991: 152).

It is clear in both instances that we have not yet identified all the government-related facilities along either of these routes. There are stretches where there should logically have been additional facilities, so it is likely that other posts were located at some of the tells along both of these routes. The self-standing posts have been readily identified through surface survey, but it will take excavations at the more complex sites to uncover such facilities.

The function of these forts needs consideration. Along the royal road systems in the empire, the Persians established postal relay stations a day's ride apart, where couriers could be relieved by a new rider and fresh team of horses (Briant 2002: 369-70). In addition, these roads had guard-posts spaced regularly, and stations that served as stopping places, with hostels (Briant 2002: 357). But it is highly unlikely that either route identified in Yehud qualified as a royal road. The north–south royal routes would have run through the coastal plain and perhaps in the Jordan Rift, while east–west royal routes would logically have cut through the Jezreel Valley and the Beersheva Valley. These had been the main roads for millennia.

That being said, there would have been designated routes by which couriers would have traveled to inland provincial capitals, like Jerusalem and Samaria. The two routes outlined above seem to have functioned in this secondary capacity. Relay stations and hostels would not have been required on either route since it would have been possible to reach Jerusalem within a day of traveling from the coastal plain, the Jordan Rift, or the Beersheva Valley.

Two alternative proposals have been made for the function of the Persian-era military sites in Yehud. The first is that they protected the western and southern borders. According to E. Stern, Yarmut, Azekah, and Adullam in the Shephelah contained forts that guarded against incursions from the province of Ashdod in the coastal plain, while forts at Bet-Zur, Khirbet el-Qatt, Khirbet ez-Zawiyye and 'En-Gedi guarded the southern border against Edomite raids (1984: 86). This suggestion has found little support, although G.W. Ahlström appears to have adopted the latter idea, but not the former (1993: 831). Of the Shephelah sites, only Azekah has been excavated and was dug before the introduction of modern methods, so there is no firm proof of forts at any of the sites. This proposal has probably found little acceptance because there was little threat of invasion in the Persian period; all the adjoining areas lay within the Persian empire.

The second purpose envisioned for the buildings has been the protection of trade routes that were vital for increased commercial activity while also providing a first line of defence for western territories of the empire against invasion by Egypt or Greece (Hoglund 1992: 202-205). The former purpose has been endorsed by P. Davies (1992: 80) while the latter has been adopted by C. Carter (1999: 293) and J. Berquist (1995: 108).

While there would have been a need to monitor trade routes crossing through the Negev highlands in unpopulated areas that were prone to raids launched by Arab tribes, there was not an equivalent issue along either internal road within the province of Yehud. It is also likely that all caravans had armed escorts, so that additional personnel would not have been needed for protection. As noted above, since Jerusalem was a single day's journey from the coastal plain or the Beersheva Valley, there would not have been any need for such rest or supply facilities, let alone so many closely spaced forts. Thus, the proposal that the forts protected trade routes within Yehud seems unlikely. The function of these forts to provide additional soldiers in case of invasion by Greece or Egypt after the rebellion of Inaros holds more merit, but still does not seem to have been the primary motivation for their creation. Had such an aim been in mind, it would have been more logical to increase the troops assigned to the string of fortresses running down the coast from Gaza to the Nile Delta or to have built more fortresses along the Mediterranean to prevent approach by sea.

The string of forts that are tightly spaced along the route from Beersheva to Jerusalem need another explanation. It seems more plausible to associate them with the practice of using fires to send important news to the provincial seat at Jerusalem from the main royal roads to the west and south (Briant 2002: 371). Such a system had already been used within the kingdom of Judah, as evidenced by Lakish ostracon 26, which mentions that the guards at that fort have been looking for the fire signals from Azekah but have not seen them (Pardee 1982: 89-95). Thus, in this case, it would have been a continuation of an established local practice, but now in the service of the larger Persian empire.

A Facility Serving as a Satellite Supply Depot for the Royal Road. The stratum 3 facility at Tel es-Sera' (#281) served as a huge grain storage facility that could provide rations for large nubers of troops moving through the region as well as authorized government personnel in transit. Its location at the edge of the Shephelah, facing the coastal plain, suggests that the supplies stored in the five-meter wide, brick-lined silo were used primarily by those passing along the main coastal route to Egypt. The grain must have been collected from a large region, in the form of taxes-in-kind, and sent there for storage and eventual distribution.

The Assyrians had set up a number of similar facilities in the same region in the seventh century, which had been maintained by the Neo-Babylonians. In the coastal plain near Tel es-Sera' were three Persian-era sites that had large grain-storing facilities: Tel Halif, Tell el-Hesi, and Tel Haror. The latter three were likely supplied from taxes paid in kind that had been produced in the agricultural hinterland under the administration of Gaza.

Tel Halif stratum V contained pits, grain bins, a large building, possibly a storehouse or barracks or military building, and at least two bread ovens (Jacobs and Borowski 1993: 69). Ceramic finds from the foundation trenches of the structure whose foundation walls measured 0.80 meter wide allowed it to be dated to the late-sixth–fifth centuries BCE (Seger 1980: 224). In addition, a large, ash-filled pit that covered all of Area F6/22, to the north, was uncovered. It contained several almost complete Persian lamps (Seger 1979: 247-48). This may have been some sort of grain storage facility, similar to the one at Tel es-Sera', but in use earlier.

Tel Jemme stratum AB housed a fort and another large structure in the fifth–fourth centuries BCE; their date has been established by Greek imports both within the buildings and underneath them. A large red-figured lekythos dating to c. 450 BCE, two smaller lekythoi, and substantial fragments of amphorae (large storage jars) were among these finds. The fort measured 38 × 29 meters. In addition, a number of small limestone incense burners were found in the two buildings, and camel bones found on site are thought to date to this period (Van Beek 1993: 672).

The eastern and western sectors of the site housed large silos that range in size from the smallest, with a diameter of 4.5–5 meters, to a medium range measuring 5.5–6 meters, to the largest, measuring 8–9 meters. So far, eleven have been excavated in the west, while one was found immediately beneath the surface in the east (Van Beek 1993: 673). One contained a large quantity of carbonized grain (Petrie 1928: 8). They are built out of bricks, including the floors, some of which had been repaved, and average about 1.8 meters deep. The pottery found within them dates to the late fourth–third centuries BCE (from the end of the Persian period and into the Hellenistic period), but it would reflect the final stages of use rather than the period of construction (Van Beek 1993: 673). It is likely that one or more of these silos was in use in conjunction with the buildings of stratum AB, although seven were thought by the original excavator, Sir Flinders Petrie, to have been cut into the fort building and other larger structure and so would have dated from a subsequent period (1928: pl. XIII). The three excavated in Area W could have been contemporaneous, however. The grain may have been sold in part to caravans heading home from Gaza (Van Beek 1993: 673) but may also have been intended to be readily available for troops that might have been sent through the region to Egypt.

At Tell el-Hesi, a small citadel was constructed atop a large platform in the early-fifth century BCE (stratum Vd). Its layout consisted of rooms surrounding a central courtyard, which had been standard for such facilities for a long period of time. There were significant quantities of imported Attic pottery that allowed a date to be assigned to this occupational level of 500–460 BCE. The citadel was then replaced by a simpler facility in Vc, which is likely to correspond to the early reign of Artaxerxes I, c. 460–440 BCE. The ceramics were indistinguishable from the preceding phase, although there was a high proportion of transport jars, probably containing wine and oil, that had not appeared earlier (Bennett and Blakely 1989: 221-23; Fargo 1993: 633-34). The succeeding phase, Vb, has been dated c. 440–404 BCE on the basis of Attic pottery found in its remains, and so would also fall partially within the reign of Artaxerxes. At this time the main building was subdivided and expanded, and a single grain silo pit appears to have been introduced (Bennett and Blakely 1989: 349, 352). In the earlier periods, any surplus grain produced at the site would have been stored in jars within the main building complex.

The land adjoining Tell el-Hesi is well suited for growing barley and wheat and a cemetery thought to be contemporaneous with phases Vb and c, located on the southern slope of the Iron Age acropolis, contained simple graves of men, women, and children (Bennett and Blakely 1989: 222, 347). Thus, it is likely that the facility was not strictly military in function at the time of Artaxerxes, but had a resident population whose primary task was to produce grain to be stored inside and used as needed by government personnel in transit. The settlers may have been given land to farm in exchange for serving military rotation at the central facility or being ready for call-up as needed. It is likely that this settlement would have been under the jurisdiction of Gaza.

Tel Haror similarly had a large building in Area G dating from the fifth–fourth centuries BCE with cobbled floor and grain and refuse pits. One pit measured 4 meters wide by 3 meters deep (Oren *et al.* 1985: 32). In Area D another large building was uncovered. It had stone foundations and adjoined a courtyard paved with stone slabs, indicating it served some sort of official rather than private purpose. Attic bowls, Greek amphorae and Cypriote imports have been used to establish the date (Oren *et al.;* 1985: 32; Oren 1993a: 584). A single Aramaic ostracon was found on site (Oren 1993a: 584).

In light of the successful campaign mounted by Cambyses in 525 BCE to conquer Egypt, in which troops were sent overland into the Delta, and the string of subsequent rebellions that required quashing by Xerxes, Artaxerxes I and his successors, it is likely that this massing of grain supplies at the edge of the desert between Cisjordan and Egypt was intended primarily for use in feeding troops being sent overland into Egypt and only secondarily for selling to caravans. Yehud was being relied upon to contribute grain annually for any such Persian enterprises.

Facilities in the Negev Highlands
Three Persian-era forts were established during the Persian period in the Negev Highlands: Horvat Mesora (#286), Mesad Nahal Haro'a (#287), and Horvat Ritma (#288). Their dates of establishment and function need careful consideration.

Horvat Mesora, which is located on a hill adjacent to the Nahal Besor, guards a segment of the road system in the central Negev. The site was surveyed in 1958 but a salvage dig was conducted at the eastern structure in 1985 that uncovered a building measuring 21 meters by 21 meters. It had a courtyard measuring 11 × 11 meters, in which was located a cistern 3 meters across × 4 meters deep. Nine rooms surrounded the courtyard. The gateway was in the eastern wall. The site had only one level of occupational debris, which was dated to the fifth–fourth centuries BCE on the basis of the ceramic finds. No Greek imports were found. Other small finds included a copper pin, a buckle, a spatula, grinding stones, and loom weights (Cohen 1986b).

Mesad Nahal Haro'a is located on a hill to the south of Mesad Mesora. It was surveyed in 1953 and again in 1965 before salvage excavations were conducted in 1985. Remains of a 21.5-meter square fortress were uncovered. Nine casemate rooms were arranged around a 12-meter square courtyard. One room contained a bread oven. A cistern had been hewn below the fortress, to the south. Remains from the beaten earth floors in the rooms included bowls, cooking pots, oil lamps and storage jars that dated to the fifth–fourth century BCE. In addition, a number of grinding stones, a bronze pin, ceramic loom weights and a stone incense-burner were recovered in the rubble. No Greek imports were found (Cohen 1986a).

Horvat Ritma is situated the furthest south of the cluster of sites. During excavations, a fort measuring 21 × 21 meters was uncovered, with a central courtyard measuring 9 × 8 meters surrounded by eight or nine rooms. This structure appears to have been built in the tenth century BCE; pottery from the earliest phase dates to this period. Only one and a half rooms of the structure were excavated. The water system that included three cisterns or water reservoirs that had been dug into the marl and partially faced with stone and some conduits and channels would have been built at the time of the first settlement (Meshel 1977: 112). The fort and cisterns were reused in the Persian period and again in the Roman era. Pottery from the final occupation was found inside the fort, but none from the Persian period, However, deposits of Persian pottery as deep as sixty centimeters were found inside subsidiary buildings A, C and E beside the fort. None was connected with a floor or occupational level; all appear to have been deliberately dumped inside these buildings as rubbish (Meshel 1977: 126, 128). Nevertheless, the diagnostic forms in this collection can be dated to the fifth–fourth centuries BCE, and the type of clay used is characteristic of the pottery of the hill-country, not the coastal region (Meshel 1977: 129).

The most likely explanation for the dumped Persian remains is that the Roman settlers cleared it out of the interior of the fort to make it habitable for themselves. Not wanting to use the subsidiary buildings, they considered them a logical place to dump the Persian refuse. Unfortunately, in the process, they severed these remains from their contexts, preventing us from learning anything about room use within the fort. Even so, they indicate that the fort was not newly built in the Persian period like the previous two had been: rather, the settlers at this site reoccupied an existing building.

The date and function of these three facilities which otherwise were fairly isolated, need consideration. The diagnostic pottery, all local forms with no Greek imports, would allow a date in the second half of the fifth century, under Artaxerxes I or his successor Darius II, to be proposed plausibly (c. 450–400 BCE) or one slightly later, in the early part of the fourth century BCE. Thus, it cannot help us determine if these facilities were built as part of a larger master plan authorized by Artaxerxes I, or in the wake of the creation of Idumea as a separate province c. 400 BCE. It can be noted that the clay used in the Persian-era pottery found on site is characteristic of the Judean hill-country versus the coastal region (Meshel 1977: 129), which would be consistent with its being administered by either Yehud or Idumea.

If the forts were under Idumean control, they might have served a primarily military function, patrolling the region against marauders and escorting caravans that would have needed more protection now that this region was a frontier adjoining an independent Egypt. Had they initially been established as part of Yehud's administrative remit, they probably would have served a similar function; even though Egypt was part of the empire, the open stretches of desert with little water were home to Arab tribes who knew them well and could prey upon those who strayed off course or did not pay enough *bakshish*. The Persians had a vital monetary interest in ensuring that caravans were able to pass through the region safely and pay the appropriate tolls in money and goods due to the imperial crown.

The clustering of three facilities relatively close together may have been a deliberate strategy to ward off attack. Through the use of fire signals, one fort could warn the others of approaching danger and receive back-up reinforcements in case of an actual attack. In this way, a surprise attack that might easily wipe out a single facility could be averted.

It can be noted that there is physical evidence for the renewed attempt to use Tell el-Kheleife as a port of trade in the Persian period and for the use of Qadesh Barnea as a caravanserai. These forts could have been designed to monitor the movement of caravans from Kheleife to Gaza in the coastal plain, as well as to the Nile Delta, via Qadesh Barnea.

At Qadesh Barnea, the casemate rooms on the eastern side of the upper Judahite fortress, which had been burned extensively, were reused as temporary dwellings in the fifth–fourth centuries BCE. There was no attempt, however, to refurbish the entire fort, nor to invest time and energy in building a new facility. This strongly suggests that the site was not rebuilt as a garrison, but rather served as a caravanserai. The springs on site made it a logical stopping place where water supplies could be replenished. Most of the remains dating to the Persian period were found in pits that contained storage jars, amphorae, bowls, and imported Greek ware. One *yhd* seal impression was found, as was an ostracon from an ash-filled pit that read 'offering/merchandise of Tob...' or 'good merchandise/offering' (Cohen 1993: 847).

All these finds are consistent with the site being a way-station for traders and also possibly used from time to time by couriers on official business. The single *yhd*-impression would have been from a jar that most likely contained food rations that had been allotted to a messenger. Normally, however, one would have expected such couriers to have taken the main royal road that ran close to the coast to access the Nile Delta by land from the southern Levant.

Tel el-Kheleife was resettled in the Persian period by a new group (stratum V). It appears as though many of the existing buildings were reused; only a few mud-brick walls were constructed on a different alignment than before. A few Phoenician and Aramaic ostraca, together with a handful of fifth-century black-glazed Greek body sherds and some sixth–fifth century bowls, jars, and storage vessels were found (Glueck 1993: 869; Pratico 1993b: 870). Contrary to the claims of E. Stern (2001: 458), no Phoenician coins were uncovered, which could have helped establish date parameters. Nevertheless, it may have been a Phoenician venture; the names on ostraca 2070 and 2071 are predominantly Phoenician (Divito 1993: 59-61). If the demise of stratum IV had been designed to eliminate Edomite use of this port of entry and western branch of Arabian trade, this route was apparently re-opened by a Phoenician city after the Persians became masters of the region. The three forts in the Negev highlands may then have been built in part to help safeguard this new venture. It was abandoned after an unknown length of time.

Unconfirmed Administrative and Military Facilities

Even though I have argued against the view that the towns or sites of Keilah, Bet-Zur, Bet-Hakkerem, Mizpah, and Jerusalem were official sub-district capitals, it is natural to assume that the province would have been subdivided into smaller administrative units, with certain towns serving as sub-district seats. Without the excavation of a number of the larger sites in the central and southern Judean hills and the Shephelah, it is not possible to identify these centers. Perhaps Mizpah continued to serve as the administrative seat for the Benjaminite region after provincial capital was transferred to Jerusalem. In light of the earlier analysis of the terms *sar* and *pelek*, it seems likely that Keilah, Bet-Zur and Bet-Hakkerem primarily served a military function, even if one or more of them also served double duty as a local storage facility for taxes-in-kind or housed administrative personnel as well as military personnel.

The sites said to have had 'daughters' in Neh. 11.25-35 may have served an administrative function at some point during the Persian period. The daughters would have been farmsteads located in the vicinity of the 'mother' site that were considered dependent on the larger settlement, perhaps supplying it with food in the form of taxes paid in kind. They include Kiryat-Arba, Divon, Yekavzeel, Beersheva, Mekonah, Adullam, Azekah and Bethel. In addition, Lakish is identified as having 'fields' rather than 'daughters'. As already seen in the previous chapter, this list does not reflect the reality of the time of Artaxerxes I; nevertheless, it needs to be considered whether it provides evidence of an administrative system that may have been in place already, or introduced when Yehud was 'reinvigorated' with new settlers. The practice of 'mother' towns with dependent 'daughters' was already underway during the monarchy (Joshua

15; 18.21-28; 19), although the location of towns with dependent farmsteads may have changed over time, according to the administrative needs of each new power system.

All the sites except Bethel lie within the territory that became Idumea after 400 BCE. Thus, it is possible that the list reflects specific administrative units that only were established within Idumea, after 400 BCE. However, I have argued that all of these sites would have lain within the borders of Yehud during the time of Artaxerxes as well. In this case, then, it is possible that the administrative arrangement it reflects had already been put in place and was carried on even after Idumea became a separate province. Until some of the tell sites in the central and southern Judean hills are excavated to determine the extent and nature of Persian-era settlement on them, nothing definitive can be said about whether the farmsteads in Yehud were assigned to the jurisdiction of a local fort or administrative town, whether they were administered from sub-provincial district seats, or whether they were all administered directly from the provincial seat in Jerusalem. It is clear from the Idumean ostraca discussed in Chapter 4 that after 400 BCE, those in the newly established province were administered locally, with farmsteads paying taxes-in-kind to locally designated facilities, either a fort (e.g. Arad) or a storage center (Makkedah/Idna).

We cannot safely extrapolate from the situation in Idumea, however, that the same practice would have been used in the adjoining province of Yehud. We do not know enough about Persian administration to know how much the overarching Achaemenid system forced the long-standing local systems to be changed or adapted. It is likely that an additional level of Persian bureaucracy was superimposed over existing systems and that there was variation in these lower-level systems. The range of land-ownership systems in the empire, for example, illustrates this tolerance for working within existing administrative systems where possible, while not hesitating to introduce additional systems for newly designated crown lands (Tuplin 1987: 111-12; Briant 1981, 2002: 415-63).

Pierre Briant has emphasized how the 'high economic command' of the Persian empire tended to use local techniques, while at the same time placing formerly local works under the aegis of a powerful state machine that could coordinate and motivate local knowledge for the profit of the assembled unity (1981: 19, 22). It succeeded in a coordinated use of existing technical and human resources that led to greater yields. For this reason, he says that it would be reductionist to classify the mechanisms of the Persian state as 'superstructures' that could be schematically distinguished from 'infrastructures' (1981: 22). We should therefore be cautious about seeing the Persians as having categorically imposed a new, upper tier of administration over existing systems; there was a more organic working within existing systems to improve the productivity of provinces, which inevitably introduced some changes, but which was not a single, imperial-wide solution imposed over the existing range of local forms of technology, production, and administration.

A Critique of the Hypothesis that Artaxerxes I Introduced a Unique Form of Fort in the Southern Levant

Kenneth Hoglund has identified a number of sites within Yehud as military installations that he thinks should be dated to the mid-fifth century and the reign of Artaxerxes I. Not all these sites have been excavated, but he has proposed a typology based on three that have been excavated, though only one lies within Yehud. He has then identified the others from reported surface finds in surveys that fit his criteria.

The single excavated site within Yehud is Horvat Mesora, which, as discussed above (p. 321), guarded a segment of the road system in the central Negev. Using his architectural typology of more or less square buildings with rooms arranged around a central courtyard space in a proportion that runs normally between twenty-five to thirty-three percent, Hoglund has identified the following sites within the territory of Yehud as military installations built under Artaxerxes I: Nahal Yattir south of Beersheva, Tel es-Sera' at the edge of the Shephelah adjoining the coastal plain, Horvat Ritma, level II, on top of a ridge slightly north and west of the modern settlement of Sede Boqer, Mesad Nahal Haro'a, Arad V, and Khirbet Abu et-Twain, on a height opposite the Ela Valley(1992: 175-76; 187-94).

Tel es-Sera' has Attic pottery that allows a date to be established in the mid-fifth–fourth century BCE (Oren 1982: 158). The Attic lamps and bowls with high ring-bases found in stratum V at Arad V, on the other hand, indicate a date in the mid-fourth century BCE (Herzog *et al.* 1984: 29). The biggest problem at this site is the lack of evidence of a Persian-era structure, although the Aramaic ostraca that probably date from the mid-fourth century refer to the presence of a *degel* or large military unit either on site or operative within the area. Rebuilding in the Hellenistic period may have effectively removed the Persian-era fort in use in the fourth century.[8] Although the founding date cannot be determined by the date of finds from what might be the last period of occupation, in this case, the imported ware does not tend to indicate that the site was occupied during the reign of Artxerxes I. Rather, it suggests that the site's reoccupation took place after the creation of Idumea c. 400 BCE and the decision to station a *degel* there. Hoglund thinks the fortress in phase I at Bet-Zur is probably post-Persian (1992: 184).

There is no reason to assume that the Persians would have used a standard template for constructing forts. The dimensions of the main building and location of subsidiary facilities would have been influenced by the specific features and contours of a given site as well as its intended function, staff size, and the local building materials available. At most, we might expect a general similarity in the organization of the interior space of a fort, although that might have varied depending on function. Those serving as fire signal stations may well have had different needs than others that doubled as a caravanserai, a postal relay station, or a supply depot. Hoglund's proposed use of the criterion of the ratio of courtyard size to surrounding rooms to define a Persian-era fort is misguided; it is not a valid means of establishing when a fort was built, and since Horvat Ritma was actually built in the Iron I period, he has not used a valid data pool to establish his ratio figures.

The fort at Khirbet Abu et-Twain (#272) had been used throughout the Neo-Babylonian period and so was not a new foundation. It may have gone out of use under Artaxerxes I, as the province was redeveloped. The pristine Persian-era forts at Khirbet Kabbar (#271) and Khirbet er-Rasm (#273) along the main north–south trunk road may have been more appropriately spaced for the Persian signal system or may have been located where adjoining land was available to assign to new settlers who were to help staff these facilities.

Nahal Yattir (#285) was a pristine Persian foundation. The question has to be asked, however, whether this facility was built as part of the redevelopment of Yehud under Artaxerxes I or as part of the subsequent fortification of the border area of the empire after the loss of Egypt in 403 BCE. It may have been built when Idumea was created as an independent province. Perhaps excavation of the site could clarify the date of founding. The Persian-era fort at Nahal Haro'a (#287) appears to have been a pristine Persian foundation, like the facility at Horvat Mesora (#286). Like Nahal Yattir, however, we need to be cautious about the founding date of these other two forts that were located further south, in the Negev highlands. All three may have been built after 400 BCE.

Finally, it is important not to overlook forts that were built on the site of former forts and so were not brand new foundations under Artaxerxes I. To understand Artaxerxes' plan for the redevelopment of Yehud, we need to take into consideration all forts and facilities that he may have made functional, whether they were built from scratch or reused existing facilities. To focus only on new foundations, as K. Hoglund has, misses the larger picture of government facilities that were put in place and what their locations can reveal about imperial concerns within the province.

Chapter Summary

The current information available from excavations and surveys is too imprecise to allow us to ascertain with any degree of certainty what the settlement patterns were in Yehud in the second half of the fifth century BCE. Not only is the pottery chronology too undifferentiated for this purpose, but almost none of the smaller farmsteads and hamlets that dotted the central and southern Judean hills, the Shephelah, and the hill-country of Benjamin have been excavated. As a result, it is possible to argue that a site that has evidence of occupation in Iron IIC and the Persian period was settled continuously throughout the Neo-Babylonian period, even if forts and larger towns in the vicinity may have been destroyed, or that it, too, was destroyed or abandoned in 586 BCE and only resettled again in the Persian period.[9]

Even when some of these small sites are excavated in the future, it will not be possible to distinguish between an abandonment and resettlement, on the one hand, and continuous occupation, on the other. Only evidence of destruction will provide a clear indication that a site experienced an occupational gap, and even then, it is possible that the site may have been resettled quickly, in the Neo-Babylonian period, by members of the family who escaped death or exile, or by a new family assigned the land by the Neo-Babylonian authorities.

Some of these many farmsteads would have formed the economic basis of the Neo-Babylonian province of Yehud, continuing to produce wine, oil, and woollen cloth as tribute in kind for the imperial court. These had been the main products exported from the region in trade or as tribute for centuries. Jeremiah 39.10 and 2 Kgs 25.12 state that the person who oversaw military operations against Jerusalem in 586 BCE, Nebuzaradan, left some of the poorest of the land to be vinedressers and plowmen. The Jeremiah passage is more explicit, claiming that these people had been landless at the end of the monarchy and were now being legally invested with their own fields and vineyards.

Both passages confirm the intention of the authorities to establish the region as a viable province and indicate that, for the new imperial power, the area was most valuable for its wine and agricultural produce. While wine was a long-time specialty, the emphasis on grain suggests a new policy in the region. The authorities may have wanted to stockpile food supplies to be used by troops in transit to Egypt, in anticipation of campaigns to conquer this rival power and include it within the empires borders. If so, their plans were cut short by the rise of Cyrus, which forced Nabonidus to enter a treaty with Egypt and with Lydia in a vain attempt to stem the expansion of his rival into the Babylonian empire.

Without knowing which sites remained occupied in the Neo-Babylonian period, we are unable to use the archaeological data to determine the extent of the newly created province of Yehud. As a result, we cannot use artifactual remains to argue whether the borders changed at a subsequent point when the Persians became the imperial rulers over this region. We can, however, have an overview of where the settlements lay, and then use this material to reconsider whether the borders deduced from the textual material are logical in terms of actual settlement patterns. We can see that, whether or not we conclude that some portions of the central and southern Judeans hills and the southern Shephelah were settled in the Neo-Babylonian period or not, there was substantial settlement in these areas in the Persian period.

However, until we can establish with more certainty when the province of Idumea was established, whether it originally was a sub-district within Yehud or not, and have a means of distinguishing pottery dating to the late-fifth century and from that in use in the early-fourth century (assuming Idumea was made a province c. 400 BCE), we cannot know in which province these settlements lay. They might have been part of Yehud, or part of Idumea, or originally part of Yehud that secondarily became Idumea. Thus, the administrative affiliation of these settlements is not determinable from the artefacts alone. With further excavation, it might be possible to use the geographical spread of *Yeh*(u)d and *Yah*-stamped jars to refine our thoughts on this subject, but even there, we must be cautious since we are uncertain what the functions of these jars were and so whether they would correlate well with the provincial boundaries of Yehud.

We also are unable to provide reliable figures indicating the percentage of decrease in population or settlements between the territory of the kingdom of Judah and the territory of the Neo-Babylonian province of Yehud, on the one hand, or between the Neo-Babylonian province of Yehud and the Persian province of Yehud, on the other (contra Lipschits 2003). Neither can we determine figures for either category within the Persian period itself (contra Carter 1999: 210; 214-48). The figures I have given in the preceding section based on published survey results should not be relied upon; we cannot determine with any degree of certainty how many of the sites were abandoned in 586 BCE and resettled at some point in the Persian period or were (re)occupied in the Neo-Babylonian period and into the Persian period (contra Milevski 1996/97: 16, 19). Finally, without much more extensive excavation, we cannot know the extent of Persian-era occupation at tells or medium-sized settlements that had been occupied extensively in the past. As a result, we cannot talk about site hierarchy (contra Milevsky 1996/97: 19, 21), or use Central-Place Theory (contra Hoglund 1989; Carter 1999: 92-93) to try to understand how settlements were organized in a larger administrative framework within Yehud in the Persian period.

That being said, however, the survey results clearly indicate that there were a number of newly established farmsteads or hamlets in the region of Benjamin, in the Shephelah, and in the central and southern Judean hills during the Persian period. If we count those sites that had occupation in the Iron IIB period and earlier, where we can establish definitively that there was an occupational gap that probably began with Sennacherib's devastation of the Judahite countryside in 701 BCE and only ended when the site was resettled in the Persian period, we have the following figures: twenty-six in Benjamin, fifteen in the northern Shephelah, twenty-one sites in the southern Shephelah, twenty-seven in the central Judean hills, and five in the southern Judean hills. We cannot be certain if these new farmsteads and hamlets were all established at the same time or gradually, or whether they represent an influx of new settlers, the spreading out of the indigenous population over time, or some of both. Nevertheless, they provide evidence for new settlement activity in the Persian period.

Since there were other pre-existing farmsteads that remained abandoned in the Persian period, we are left with the need to explain why some were reoccupied and others left idle, with new ones established on pristine land instead. Are we dealing with a distinction between new settlers who were of Judahite ancestry who reclaimed ancestral lands when they could establish their rights and when such lands were not already occupied and others of non-Judahite ancestry who simply were assigned unworked land over which there could be no prior claims? Is it a case of personal choice – a newly arrived settler could either opt to take over an abandoned farmstead and so avoid a lot of extra labor in cutting cisterns and clearing the land or start on a fresh piece of land, if he so chose? Or is it a combination of these factors, which we need to complicate further by allowing for the reoccupation of abandoned farmsteads and the creation of new ones from scratch as a result in the natural growth of the local population over time in addition to the possibility of new settlers? Here, the artifactual evidence has raised a new question that needs to be examined. Without textual evidence of how land registry worked within the Persian empire, however, we will be forced to lay out the possible options only and argue for greater and lesser degrees of probability.

The fact that so many of the Persian-era settlements were either farmsteads, hamlets or possibly villages, with no clear indication of walled towns that did not serve some sort of military capacity, suggests that the Persian policy for the economic exploitation of the province did not differ in principle from that already established by the Neo-Babylonians. The primary interest was in producing foodstuffs that would be paid as taxes-in-kind to the central authorities and put at their disposal for use locally or shipped elsewhere.

The huge grain silo measuring five meters wide at Tel es-Sera' stratum V, located in the southern Shephelah on the border of the coastal plain, indicates that a substantial portion of grain was being amassed locally at the southern limits of Cisjordan. This is in the same region where the Assyrians had also set up a number of similar facilities in the seventh century BCE. Tel es-Sera' was one of a cluster of such sites in the Persian period but appears to have been the only one that may have supplied grain produced in Yehud. Others were situated in the coastal plain at Tel Halif, Tell el-Hesi, and Tel Haror and presumably were supplied from taxes-in-kind produced within the agricultural hinterland assigned to the administration of Gaza.

The government facilities that can be readily identified through excavation or surface survey as free-standing forts or forts within walled complexes show a different orientation than those in place the end of the monarchy. The latter were regularly spaced in the Shephelah to guard the western edge of the kingdom and along the internal main road systems in the kingdom. Those in the Beersheva Valley seemed to have served double duty; they protected this important trade route and served as a line of defence against penetration into the Judean hill-country from the south. Even though there were Judahite forts in the Negev highlands and even one at Qadesh Barnea in the Sinai peninsula, indicating that Judah lay claim to control over this territory, this same region was largely unpopulated, lying south of the minimal isobar for raising crops by relying on rainfall, and was essentially an extension of the traditional, core territory of the kingdom.

The set-up of administrative facilities during the Neo-Babylonian period is largely unknown. The provincial seat was at Mizpah; otherwise, the location of forts and other government-sponsored caravanserai within the province of Yehud is largely unknown, outside of the fort at Khirbet Abu et-Twain. Until more excavations are conducted at sites that housed forts in the Iron IIC period or tells that may have become forts sites in the Neo-Babylonian period, we can say nothing about their orientation and purpose.

The Persian-era free-standing forts and *birot*, which have been more readily identified than those of the Neo-Babylonian period, on the other hand, can be seen to have had a different orientation than those in the late monarchy. Only a few have been excavated, and at those sites that have been dug, there often is limited exposure of the Persian-era occupation and remains. Nevertheless, it is immediately apparent that it was deemed unnecessary to defend the borders of the province. This comes as no surprise, since all the adjoining lands were either Persian provinces or vassal states. There should have been no need to worry on a regular basis about enemy invasion, given Yehud's location within the southern Levantine lands of the satrapy of Across-the-River.

The function of these free-standing forts along the main road from Jerusalem to Beersheva, from Jerusalem to the coastal plain via Lakish, north of Jerusalem, and along the main road from Jerusalem to Samerina seems to have been to facilitate the sending of fire-signals from the coastal plain and Beersheva Valley inland to the provincial capital of Yehud. Notwithstanding, we are unable to determine which of the forts or facilities were settled simultaneously and which were in use during reign of Artaxerxes I (465–432 BCE) or even the second half of the fifth century BCE (450–400 BCE).

We need to consider the logical course of Persian imperial policy for establishing such facilities within a province. I find it likely that the Neo-Babylonian arrangement would have been left intact until one of the Persian kings took an interest in this distant part of the empire, which was not as wealthy was many other areas, and ordered a review of its organization and potential use to the imperial court. At that point, a master plan would have been developed and implemented, probably by the satrap of Across-the-River in conjunction with officials at the Persian court, to integrate the province fully into the road and postal systems of the empire, to recruit potential soldiers from the region to further imperial expansion, and to make it as profitable as possible to the Persian court. Once the administrative, postal, and military facilities were in place in the province, they would not have changed unless new political, military, or economic developments arose that required some sort of modification or expansion. Practically speaking, this means that single forts or facilities would not have been built from reign to reign, added incrementally in small doses, but rather that a working system that included all the necessary facilities would have been introduced as part of a single master plan within a short span of time. There would not have been a problem with running over budget and having to postpone the construction of certain facilities until more resources were available, as in contemporary society. Corvée labor was available, and the personnel who would man these facilities could be used to construct them as well, if need be.

Bearing in mind the above suppositions, we need to allow for alterations in governmental facilities in this region once the province of Idumea was created. We cannot determine if the forts at Arad, Harei Anim and Nahal Yattir, Horvat Mesora, Nahal Haro'a, and Horvat Ritma, for example, would have been built in the second half of the fifth century by Artaxerxes I or Darius II, or the first half of the fourth century BCE. It makes a certain amount of sense, however, to suspect that they were built when Idumea became a province and the southern border of the Persian empire became the Negev highlands. This would have required new security for the Beersheva Valley, which became more vulnerable now that it was the edge of the settled limit of the empire. The three forts in the Negev highlands, on the other hand, would have served as caravanserai and offered protection, if necessary, against marauders to traders moving goods from Tell el-Kheleife to Gaza and to Egypt via Qadesh Barnea when this port was reopened.

Endnotes

1. In preparing the indexes I discovered I had failed to include the site of Khirbet Umm el 'Umdan in my list of sites, site maps, or calculations of site increases in the Persian period (Onn, Wexler-Bdolah, Rapuano and Kanlas 2002).

2. The omission of 109 is debiberate on my part due to an inadvertant duplication of material.

3. My data does not square with that of O. Lipschits, who claims that there were only a total of fifty-nine sites occupied in Benjamin in the Persian period (2003: 349); I have counted eighty; we may be using different boundaries.

4. I find no evidence to support the suggestion of O. Lipschits that these settlements were established by Arabs and Edomites during the Neo-Babylonian and early Persian periods, who gradually penetrated the region from the south. He proposes further that this incursion was only halted by the re-establishment of Yehudite settlements in the Persian period (2003: 344-45). It is not clear how he could prove the ethnic affiliation of the new settlers, but more importantly, these farmsteads would have been included within the taxation system of the local authority once established, and it is likely that they were included within the boundaries of Yehud in both periods.

5. For a different assessment of the settlement trends in the central hills between Bethlehem and Bet-Zur, see Lipschits 2003: 352-55. We agree that this area was not depopulated in the Neo-Babylonian period, contrary to common opinion.

6. It is unclear to me if O. Lipschits has included these settlements within Yehud or not. On the one hand, he says that sites between Hevron and the Beersheva Valley lay outside of Yehud while all sites north of Hevron lay within it (2003: 338, 352). On the other hand, he only discusses sites lying between Bethlehem and Bet-Zur in the Judean hill-country, so he seems to exclude this cluster of sites in the southern Judean hills from lying within Yehud.

7. The date of this well is commonly believed to be in the Iron I period, in the mid-twelfth–mid-eleventh centuries BCE. It is thought to have been dug by the founders of the unwalled settlement of stratum 9, even though it is acknowledged that it is difficult to determine the period of its digging (Herzog 1993: 169). However, Rupert Chapman has challenged this understanding. He believes that the well could not have been cut until after stratum 7, because the layer of sticky clay on the upper level of this ground had been deposited by drain 2165 from building 2309 of stratum 7 (Herzog 1984: 6). Had the well existed, it would have been filled by the drain outflow. Thus, it seems that building 1305, inside of which the well was located, was built in a later

stratum and that its foundations were cut into the layer of deposited clay from the earlier drain. Until the drain went out of use, or until the placement of building 1305 to divert the flow, the well could not have been dug, and it may not have been built at the same time that building 1305 was in operation. He also notes that wells of this type were extremely rare before the Roman period; there is one at Lakish (oral communication). Thus, it may not have existed in the Persian period, but even if this is the case, there was plenty of water available from the cistern system, which was built in the Iron Age.

8. It might be worth considering whether the site was used as a caravanserai in the mid-fifth century, in the earliest phase of stratum V, rather than as a military installation. The local pottery could be dated to the mid-fifth century BCE.

9. Avi Ofer is the only surveyor who has used the designation Iron IID and he has not indicated what pottery is diagnostic for this period. Currently, there is no recognized pottery repertoire for the sixth century. As a result, I am sceptical about the reliability of his distinction between Iron IIC and Iron IID, which means that in practice, I would not rely on sites #46, 47, 48, 56, 76, 102, 105 being new foundations in the Persian period after a gap in occupation because they have no Iron IID pottery. This also means that all the sites he lists as having Iron IID pottery need not have been settled in the Neo-Babylonian period; some may have been 'new' Persian-era settlements.

Chapter 6

PIETY OR PRAGMATISM? THE POLICY OF ARTAXERXES I
FOR THE DEVELOPMENT OF YEHUD

Introduction

Our analysis of the potentially relevant textual and artifactual source material concerning when and why the temple was rebuilt in the Persian period is now complete. We have concluded that the account in Ezra 1–6 is not historically reliable and does not reflect the use of any underlying sources that stem directly from this event in its composition. Haggai and Zechariah 1–8, on the other hand, seem to reflect prophecies made in connection with the temple's reconstruction. They have been secondarily arranged at a later time using the temple-building template, and in addition, an even later editor has assigned historically unreliable dates under Darius I and created an artificial gap in the construction process of two years in order to weave together the parallel accounts into a single narrative. The historical prophecies themselves are framed according to standard ancient Near Eastern thought about the temple-building process, leaving us without any reliable information about why the temple would have been rebuilt.

The artifactual evidence reveals an increase in the Persian period of new farmsteads and small hamlets in the regions of Benjamin, the Shephelah, and the central and southern Judean hill-country. A number of forts and relay stations were also constructed within the territory, along the main road from Beersheva to Jerusalem and from Jerusalem to the coastal plain via Lakish. None can be dated specifically to the reign of Artaxerxes I, so this increase in settlement may or may not be the result of policies instituted during his reign.

The genealogical information in the book of Nehemiah indicates that Zerubbabel and Nehemiah were probably a generation apart in age and either served contemporaneously in office as Persian-appointed officials or succeeded to the same office. As a result, we either need to move the temple-building, which Haggai and Zechariah set under the leadership of Zerubbabel, back in time to the early reign of Artaxerxes I (465–425 BCE) or possibly even at the end of the reign of Xerxes (486–465 BCE), or move the rebuilding of Jerusalem to be the provincial seat forward in time to the reign of Darius. Of these two options, the first is preferable. The editor of Haggai–Zechariah 8 has assigned a date for the rebuilding of the temple to Darius to show that Jeremiah's prediction that the land of Judah would lay desolate seventy years was accomplished in real time. His dates are not accurate. In addition, Elephantine papyrus *AP 30* confirms that Sanballat/Sinuballit, who was active as governor of Yehud during the time that Nehemiah was overseeing the rebuilding of Jerusalem, was either still alive in 410 BCE or was dead, but had two grown sons at this time. This information is consistent with his serving as governor during the 450s, when Jerusalem was being rebuilt. He cannot be moved back in time to the reign of Darius I.

In addition to this material, we have the claim in the secondary source of 2 Macc. 1.18 that Nehemiah built the temple and the altar that Josephus repeats (*Ant.* 11.165). He apparently considered the passage in 2 Maccabees to have contained reliable information. As discussed in the conclusion to Chapter 2, an ideological rejection of the right of the Davidic dynasty to return to power in the post-exilic community might have led the author of 2 Maccabees or of the letter in 1.10–2.18 to attribute the dedication secondarily to Nehemiah, to deprive Zerubbabel of any credit in the temple's restoration. On the other hand, this tradition might equally preserve the actual course of events, which was still known in priestly or in scribal circles over 300 years after the temple's rebuilding. In spite of literary attempts to alter this history to have prophetic predictions be fulfilled in real time through the production of Haggai–Zechariah 8 and Ezra 1–6, some details of the actual situation may have been handed down, either orally, or in records dating from this period.

Our evaluation of the written sources has pointed to the reign of Artaxerxes I as the time when the temple was rebuilt. This is also the time when the city walls were rebuilt and the site effectively was re-inhabited. It is logical to associate the two processes and to see the temple's reconstruction to be part of the larger refurbishment of Jerusalem. Why did Artaxerxes decide to rebuild Jerusalem, when Mizpah had been serving adequately as the provincial seat since 586 BCE?

Jerusalem was rebuilt as a *birah*. In this case, the term means more than a free-standing fort, although it appears it can be used to designate such a structure. The same term was used in Wadi Daliyeh papyri #1.1 and 4.1 to describe Samaria, the provincial seat of Samerina (Gropp 2001: 34-35, 65-66).[1] It also was used in the Elephantine papyri to describe the settlements at Yeb (e.g. *BMP* 3.4; 4.2; 5.2; 7.1, 2; 9.2; 10.2; 12.2, 3; 14.2; Kraeling 1953) and at Syene, on the bank of the Nile opposite the island (e.g. *BMP* 8.1; 11.13; Kraeling 1953). The common denominator seems to be the presence of a garrison within protective walls. There could be space for the families of the soldiers who were assigned to the fort on site, but this was optional. In the case of Samaria and Jerusalem, there would have been administrative buildings, including storehouses, registry offices, and the governor's complex as well within the walled complex, where official provincial business was recorded and transacted. It is likely that housing for scribes and other administrators were also present in these cases. As at Elephantine, it is probable that the *birot* of Samaria and Jerusalem contained a temple dedicated to the native deity for use by the local residents. Hanan Eshel has argued that Wadi Daliyeh papyrus 14 records the sale of a room within the temple in Samaria (1996).

Such a layout for provincial seats indicates that within the Persian imperial administration, such complexes were intended to be military and administrative in function. Soldiers were maintained on site to be used as needed for local patrols and could be called up for duty farther afield if necessary. Administrators managed the flow of taxes paid in kind and in money, probably storing a great many within the walled settlement itself but also making sure that adequate supplies were available at other facilities throughout the province, as needed. They also made sure that tolls and taxes owed by traders were dutifully paid to the crown.

Why was it deemed necessary to transfer the provincial seat from Mizpah to Jerusalem? Mizpah lay along the main internal north–south trunk road through the hill-country and relied on cisterns that collected rainfall as its source of on-site water; the closest perennial source of water was half a kilometer away. Jerusalem, by contrast, sat at a major juncture where one of the main roads that ran east to west through the hill-country intersected the main north–south trunk road. It also had a spring that produced a reliable water supply, and a long-standing protective tunnel system that gave access to it from inside the city walls. While Mizpah had served as the provincial seat for 121 years at the time Artaxerxes I ascended the throne, it was not as strategically located as Jerusalem was. Thus, it seems likely that the change in location of the provincial seat was predicated on pragmatic concerns: more direct access and an on-site perennial water supply.

The Early Reign of Artaxerxes I

The rebuilding of the temple and of Jerusalem itself needs to be situated within the imperial policy of Artaxerxes I, who was the authorizing agent for this work. We need to review what is known about the early reign of this king in order to try to understand why he would have ordered the moving of the provincial seat from Mizpah back to Jerusalem, the former capital of the kingdom of Judah.

Artaxerxes I spent the early years of his reign trying to quash a rebellion in Egypt led by Inaros and to break up an alliance that had been set up between this Egyptian leader and Athens. Details of this drawn-out process have been given by Herodotus (*Hist.* 3.11, 14, 160; 7.7), Thucydides (*Hist.* 1.104, 109-110, 112), Ctesias (*Persika* 16-17; see Auberger 1991: 77-81; König 1972: 13-15, §§32-40), and Diodorus Siculus (*Bibliotheca historica* 11. 71, 74, 75, 77; 12.3; see Skelton 1956/57). Of these authors, Herodotus probably wrote his history c. 430 BCE and so could have spoken with veterans of this war in addition to using oral tradition about it. His limited remarks are closest to the actual events and the least embellished and should be given priority over the longer, connected narratives of Ctesias and Diodorus Siculus, who have relied on secondary accounts for their understandings. Thucydides, who died c. 400 BCE while writing a history of the Peloponnesian War, might have had access to veterans who were still alive but probably relied on oral traditions.

Egypt had been added to the Persian empire by Cambyses in 525 BCE. It was an important satrapy that generated great revenues but which also did not take to the Persian yoke quietly. It revolted at Darius' accession in 522 BCE, but this revolt was quickly suppressed. It revolted again in 486 BCE, early in the reign of Xerxes, Artaxerxes' predecessor. After regaining control Xerxes had appointed his brother Achaemenes as satrap (Herodotus *Hist.* 7.5, 6). He was still in charge when Artaxerxes ascended the throne, and a new revolt broke out, headed by a Libyan chief named Inaros. According to Herodotus, Inaros' men managed to kill Achaemenes during a battle that was waged at a site called Papremis. At some point Amyrtaeus, another local chieftain in the Nile Delta region, joined forces with Inaros. The Delian League, consisting of Athens and its allies, were also brought in to support the Egyptian rebel cause. Eventually, a Persian army was sent to deal with the revolt, headed by Megabyzos. After the suppression of the revolt, the sons of the two rebel leaders were confirmed in office as successors to their rebel fathers, who presumably were captured and killed.

Thucidydes adds a few more details to the sketchy comments of Herodotus. Apparently after the battle at Papremis, the defeated Persian forces withdrew to the safety of the *birah* at Memphis, which also was known as 'The White Fortress' and which had served as the satrapal seat for Egypt. A fleet of Athenian ships arrived from the Mediterranean and sailed up the Nile toward Memphis, taking control of this stretch of the river, but were unable to take the *birah*. Eventually, the reinforcement troops arrived under Megabyses 'by land', defeated the Egyptians and Athenians, and blockaded the Athenian ships and their forces on the island of Prosopitus, in the western Nile Delta, for eighteen months. Finally, the Persians diverted the flow of one of the channels beside the island and were able to ground the Athenian boats and cross over the riverbed and take the fort.

Though not explicitly mentioned, the blockade against the Athenians meant that the Persians had received naval reinforcements in addition to the army that had arrived 'by land'. Ctesias is the first to mention explicitly the participation of naval forces in quashing the revolt. Diodorus Siculus provides even more details about the navy, claiming it was composed of Cypriote, Phoenician and Cilician ships. These were the usual contributors of boats for the Persian navy, so whether he had any independent knowledge or not is hard to ascertain. His account of the battle seems to confuse details derived from the initial battle at Papremis, however, which resulted in the Persian retreat to Memphis. Thus, while his account is probably not reliable, it is likely that the Persians had been aware of the secondary involvement of the Athenian fleet and had sent a navy to attack them directly in the water in addition to an army to attack the Egyptian land forces besieging Memphis.[2]

In addition to quashing this revolt, Artaxerxes I had to deal once again with the Delian League, which had conquered Kition and Marium on Cyprus after the Inaros affair. It is claimed that he decided to resolve this subsequent belligerent act diplomatically, through negotiations that have come to be known as 'The Peace of Callias', after the Athenian representative who allegedly spoke on behalf of the Greeks. Diodorus Siculus gives details of this agreement; he claims that a compromise was struck whereby Greek cities in Asia Minor were to be allowed to live under their own laws and that Persian satraps were banned from approaching the coast of Asia Minor and from deploying Persian naval units beyond a certain point in the Aegean. The Greeks, for their part, would not send armies into regions under imperial control. This accord was allegedly struck in 449 BCE (12.4), though internal inconsistencies call into question the reliability of the date (Hoglund 1992: 134). The historicity of this agreement has also been heavily debated (Meiggs 1972: 487-95). If it is historical, it essentially restricted Greek ships to Asia Minor and Aegean waters, which in turn, gave the Phoenicians a monopoly over maritime trade in the Persian empire.

Past Hypotheses Concerning the Rebuilding of Jerusalem under Nehemiah

It has been widely asserted that Nehemiah's mission to Jerusalem to rebuild the walls was the direct result of the experience of Inaros' revolt. The imperial court suddenly developed concern over the security of the western Levant, which served as a land bridge from the Fertile Crescent to Egypt, and took steps to assure loyalty among subject peoples living there. So, for example, K. Galling has seen the revolt, along with the subsequent revolt of Megabyzos in Cilicia, to have prompted the formation of Yehud as an independent province and not merely a sub-province of Samerina, which it had been since the Neo-Babylonian period. Its first governor was Nehemiah (Galling1937: 33-34; 44-47). He fails, however, to explain how this alleged creation of a new independent province would have created greater security or loyalty (Hoglund 1992: 86); there is no indication of any attempted revolt in this region in connection with the events in Egypt or Cilicia. In addition, it is unclear why Jerusalem, located in the hill-country away from the main roads, would have been rebuilt in the process. The view that Yehud fell under the official jurisdiction of Samerina after the assassination of Gedaliah in 552 BCE and was not an independent province until the time of Nehemiah is no longer held by most historians.

Martin Noth focused on the rebellion of Megabyzos in the wake of the quashing of Inaros' revolt as a wake-up call to the Persians that they needed to create calm in the Levant. Since Yehud was near the military route to Egypt, he argued that the crown was open to suggestions that would have appeased the locals there and in Palestine in general. Claiming that the Persians had always promoted the restoration of local traditions, he assumed that the same consideration would have been operative here. Nehemiah's appointment has been understood in this wider context (Noth 1960: 318, 321).

Sometime in the early years of Artaxerxes, part of the *golah* community in Yehud, which was under the jurisdiction of Samaria, had attempted to rebuild Jerusalem and its walls without permission from the local governor. The king had ordered the work to be stopped when he learned about it (Ezra 4.7-22). Now, Artaxerxes reversed his earlier order. He made Yehud an autonomous province and sent Nehemiah as governor with an official remit to rebuild Jerusalem as the provincial seat and to order life in the new province (Noth 1960: 321, 323).

Noth's reconstruction rests on some shaky assumptions. As noted already, it is likely that Yehud was an independent province already during the Neo-Babylonian period. In addition, his belief that the Persians promoted the restoration of local traditions is based in large part upon the claims of Cyrus and Darius to have restored gods to their local cults and their exiled peoples to their homes. He has failed to appreciate that these claims were standard topoi derived from narratives used on foundation deposits in temples. Darius' scribes probably emulated the claims that had been made by Cyrus in connection with actual temple restoration, placing them in the uncharacteristic setting of the autobiographical account of how Darius had secured the throne. Nevertheless, a legitimate function of the king was that of temple-builder, so their brief mention was not inappropriate as a way to portray the king to have restored order and begun his normal functions.

Morton Smith has added a continuing threat of Arab or Idumean raids into Yehud to the usual list of concerns over the security in the wake of the revolts of Inaros and Megabyzos as a motivating factor in the decision to rebuild Jerusalem to serve as a fortified, loyal center. He has argued that Ezra had begun to rebuild the city walls sometime after year 7 of Artaxerxes' reign during his posting as governor, but had been stopped by royal edict due to concern over a possible revolt (Ezra 4.21-22). The king subsequently reversed his decision as a personal favor to Nehemiah, his Cup-Bearer, who had requested that he do so, and sent him to Yehud as the new governor to oversee the work. In his opinion, the decision was a matter of personal whimsy rather than political expediency, though Smith admits that the memoir may not give all the facts here (1971: 114, 127-28).

In his view, after arriving in Jerusalem, Nehemiah immediately completed the city's outer fortifications and then set about winning popular support by cancelling interest and debts and reversing all confiscations of land and property as collateral for debt default. He may subsequently have completed building the temple. 2 Maccabees 1.18 and 2.13 credits him with this task, and according to Ezra 6.14, the temple was only completed during the reign of Artaxerxes. In support of this idea, Smith also cites Neh. 2.8, where the governor-to-be requests a letter to secure large timbers to use in the temple, and Sir. 48.13d, which refers to the other building that Nehemiah completed. He had at his disposal the commander of the citadel, soldiers of the garrison, and several brothers he had placed in positions of power (Neh. 1.2, 5.14; 7.2) (1971: 132-44, 153). Finally, Smith compares Nehemiah to a typical Greek tyrant in his actions: his public-work projects that gainfully employed a large section of the populace, the use of threats from outside powers to create community solidarity, the remitting of debts to prove his interest in public welfare, his forced resettlement of Jerusalem from local villages as a way to create a new urban center, and his hosting of lavish banquets for citizens and foreign guests (1971: 129, 142).

As already discussed in Chapter 5, it was not likely than an appeal to Arab or Edomite/ Idumean incursions as the basis for the need to create border forts would have underlain the creation of the string of free-standing forts within Yehud and, for the same reasons, is unlikely to have influenced the decision to rebuild the city wall of Jerusalem. Its status as the new provincial seat entitled it to have walls, unlike ordinary settlements. The historicity of Nehemiah's enforcement of religious reforms is not universally accepted, especially since Ezra is said to have enacted the same reforms and since ch. 13 is loosely connected to the preceding narrative and deals with events after an alleged return to visit the province. The fact that a number of Nehemiah's actions correspond to various deeds of individual tyrants should not be surprising; as governor, he was dealing with issues arising from the creation of a new provincial seat and would have used time-honored tactics to gain a positive solution.

On a more positive note, Smith's openness to the possibility that the temple was completed by Nehemiah is noteworthy, even though some of the evidence he cites does not support his position. Sirach 49.13d does not refer to the temple but to the houses of ordinary people that Nehemiah built inside Jerusalem. Zerubbabel and Yeshua are specifically named as the builders of the temple in 49.11-12. Also, Ezra 6.14 refers back to the halting of the work on the city walls by the command of Artaxerxes in 4.8-22 and, as argued in Chapter 3, the ordering of the kings as Cyrus, Artaxerxes and then Darius reflects a Seleucid historical perspective. The alleged letter and the response in 4.8-22 deals only with the city walls and not with the rebuilding of the temple. While the summary in 4.24 claims that work stopped on the temple until the second year of Darius, the implication in the narrative flow of events is that no work was done on the temple during the reign of Artaxerxes I.

Siegfried Herrmann has argued that the initial rebuilding of the city walls of Jerusalem at the beginning of the reign of Artaxerxes (Ezra 4.7-22) was stopped by royal edict in the wake of the revolt of Megabyzos and concern over internal security. He did not discuss the circumstances that had led to this initial effort. Nehemiah was subsequently given a royal remit to rebuild the walls as a special envoy but not as governor. Once in place, however, he was drawn into the whole complex of local problems confronting Jerusalem and the province. Although his original commission had not included the creation of a new administrative structure for the province, he took on more and more responsibility, divided Yehud into *pelek* sub-districts, and eventually was made governor. In his opinion, the opposition Nehemiah experienced from neighbors, especially Sanballat, would not have arisen had Nehemiah been a governor of equal status from the beginning (1975: 308, 313, 315).

This reconstruction is dependent upon the genuineness of the letter of Artaxerxes I in Ezra 4.7-22, which I have rejected as a secondary scribal composition in Chapter 3. In addition, it assumes that the five sites listed in Nehemiah 3 as *pelek*s were sub-district capitals. I have argued against this understanding and proposed instead that the labor forces from these five sites were performing corvée labor (pp. 213-16). Thus, I have not found Herrmann's arguments convincing.

Old ideas are not easily overturned, even if dressed up in new garb. Writing fifty-eight years after K. Galling, J. Berquist asserts that at the beginning of his reign, Artaxerxes I tried to place additional resources on his western border to support his campaign against Egypt and Greece. In his view, Persia needed to strengthen its loyal colonies along the Mediterranean to stabilize the area until it could quash the revolt and bring Egypt and Greece back under imperial control. To this end, Artaxerxes I appointed strong governors to rule Yehud, rebuild its walls and to minimize the economic distortions in the small colony. He increased the level of staffing for Persian outposts in places like Jerusalem with the aim of strengthening the border against further military incursions by Egypt and Greece. He also reinstated funding for religious services in the colonies so he could use religious authorities to sway populaces and to regain control of local administration, including what transpired through temples (1995: 108). According to Berquist, in the first half of the reign of Artaxerxes I, Yehud appeared to be a front-line of defense against the encroachment by rebellious Egypt and the Delian league. 'Fortifications, higher allowances for local spending, and greater authority exercised by local administrators all depict a coordinated attempt to maintain the loyalty and safety of this border community' (1995: 108).

Nehemiah was sent in 445 BCE to ensure the loyalty of Yehud and specifically, its non-involvement in the revolt underway in Cilicia to the north, led by the general who had put down the revolt in Egypt, Megabyzus. His hasty rebuild of the walls of Jerusalem had as a goal the prevention of surrounding nations from attacking the city in any attempt at rebellion (1995: 113). Berquist has associated the rebuilding of Jerusalem with two different situations in the early reign of Artaxerxes I: the quashing of the revolt of Egypt from 458–450 BCE, on the one hand, and the subsequent revolt of Cilicia in 445 BCE on the other. In both instances, he has identified the driving concern as a need for the Persian court to maintain the loyalty and safety of Yehud. Yet, in neither case is there evidence that the invasion of Yehud by Egypt or Greece was an actual threat; Egypt had thrown off Persian rule but had made no moves to expand its territorial holdings beyond their existing limits into the southwestern Levant. Athens and other members of the Delian League were undoubtedly interested in expanding their trade networks and markets, but there is nothing that indicates that they wanted to create new colonies inland in the southwestern Levant.

The placing of additional soldiers in garrisons in the southwestern Levant is unlikely; most of the units assigned to existing garrisons would have been called up to join the invasion force of

Megabyzus, leaving these garrisons almost deserted until the revolt was put down. It is possible that, as a precautionary measure, the strength of local garrisons in the Levant may have been temporarily increased after the termination of the revolt, in case of another attempt at uprising in the immediate future. But there is no evidence that such increased military power was introduced in anticipation of the overland campaign, or that there was a need for additional forces because of a threat of invasion by Egypt or the Delian League. Finally, Berquist has not specified the logic behind his proposed use of clergy and support of the temple to win the loyalty of the locals. He sees this as a policy that was introduced throughout the eastern Mediterranean, not just in Yehud; but it is not clear why Artaxerxes I would be able to count on the support of the priesthoods to convince the locals not to rebel. There seems to be an underlying assumption here that priests stood for peace, which is a modern view, not an ancient one.

Gösta Ahlström has diverged from the status quo on a number of points. He assumes that the rebuilding of Jerusalem was a long process and that once completed, alterations or repairs would have been required on a routine basis. This accounts for the reference to Nehemiah having (re)built the temple and dedicated the altar in 2 Macc. 1.18 (1993: 850). Assuming the historical reliability of the letter assigned to Artaxerxes I in Ezra 4.17-23, he thinks that work had begun on the walls at some point prior to the reign of this king, perhaps in conjunction with the building of the temple under Darius. Artaxerxes I then specifically forbade any further work on the walls at some point in the early part of his reign in response to the letter sent to him by Rehum (Ezra 4.6-16), but then reversed his decision and sent Nehemiah to complete the construction. Admitting that the reason for his reversal of policy can only be guessed, Ahlström suggests that 'the little society in and around Jerusalem was very insignificant politically and militarily so that a wall around the little city would not create [a] military problem that would shake the empire' (1993: 861). He thinks that the king may have found the existence of a 'bastion' in the south, close to the Egyptian sphere of influence a good idea and also suggests that he may have wanted to see a more stable situation in Yehud (1993: 862).

In Ahlström's opinion, however, Nehemiah overstepped his authority, rebuilt the walls, and effectively undercut the authority of Mizpah, the existing provincial seat, by constructing his new residence in Jerusalem and repopulating it (1993: 865). In his view, the transfer of the provincial seat from Mizpah to Jerusalem was not part of Artaxerxes' plan for Yehud, but the personal agenda of Nehemiah, who was able to carry out his plan without imperial intervention or explicit authorization for the move because he had been vested by the Persian court with local authority to act in the best interest of the crown.

The proposed reconstruction is not internally consistent; either Artaxerxes I authorized the rebuilding of the walls because it was politically expedient, or he did not, but Nehemiah did it anyway without repercussions, and the king subsequently accepted the transfer of the provincial seat that had been orchestrated without his knowledge. It must be one or the other, but not both. It is highly unlikely that the transfer of the provincial seat could have been accomplished without explicit imperial authorization. Corvée labor was used to rebuild the walls, indicating the project was considered official business. The king's 'eyes and ears' (spies) would have reported any unauthorized activity that would have taken place, which Ahlström has readily recognized in his discussion of how earlier work had been stopped in response to such a report.

It is likely, then, that Nehemiah's commission had included the transfer of the provincial seat from Mizpah to Jerusalem.

An important insight of this larger argument is the implicit recognition that the rebuilding of the city wall would have gone hand in hand with the rebuilding of the temple. Ahlström has not tied the initial efforts to refortify Jerusalem to the reign of Artaxerxes but seems to have associated it with the reign of Darius and the completion of the temple. While he has not developed this point, he has recognized that there is an underlying logic that would expect the temple to have been placed within a rebuilt, re-inhabited town and not built amongst ruins as a pilgrimage site.

Kenneth Hoglund has undertaken the most detailed and sustained investigation of the rebuilding of Jerusalem. He argues on the basis of the alliance struck between Inaros and the Delian League during the revolt of Egypt at the time of Artaxerxes' accession that the monarch implemented a new policy throughout the western Levant to reinforce Persian control in the eastern Mediterranean after quashing the revolt. He had a number of free-standing fortresses built throughout the region, including Yehud. Nehemiah was commissioned to rebuild Jerusalem's walls in order to provide an inland defensive center, but also was authorized to institute economic and social reforms in order to transform the relationship between an imperial center and an outlying territory in order to integrate Yehud into the Achaemenid imperial system. He specifically rejects the common assertion that the rebuilding was a reward to the *golah*-community in Yehud for its loyalty in the face of regional revolts. Rather than being a reward, he sees the missions of Ezra and Nehemiah to have been efforts to compel Yehudite loyalty to the imperial system by tying the community's self-interest to the goals of the empire (1992: 242-44).

As seen in Chapter 5, Hoglund's attempt to define a distinctive form of fortress that was unique to the mid-fifth century is seriously flawed and must be rejected as a viable criterion. He also has not fully explained why such a garrison would have been established within Jerusalem, so far removed from the main royal roads and any likely attack from enemies of the empire. This is especially the case since one would have expected the provincial seat at Mizpah to have had some sort of garrison. A more logical purpose would have been to keep an eye on the local population to provide psychological pressure for them to adhere to Persian imperial policies. In addition, it is unclear whether the legal reforms associated with Nehemiah or Ezra have an historical grounding; they may well have been set back in time from a subsequent period when intermarriage and ethnic identity became a bigger issue to the reconstitution of the post-exilic community, in order to set a precedent that had been put in place 'at the beginning'.

I agree with K. Hoglund that the changes made within Yehud during the reign of Artaxerxes I were designed to integrate the province more fully and efficiently into the Achaemenid imperial system, and not to try to win loyalty, but I differ from him about the nature of these changes and their underlying motivation.

A New Proposal for Understanding the Decision to Rebuild Jerusalem

The need to send an army overland via the coastal plain and down into the Delta region to lift the siege against Memphis in the early reign of Artaxerxes I served as an opportunity to assess the productivity and efficiency of the provincial set-up in Yehud, which adjoined the main route. Its governor would have been asked to supply food and drink and probably a contingent of troops as well for the army in transit. An extended drought in the region (Hag. 1.6, 11; 2.15-19; echoed in Neh. 5.1-5?) may have forced the Persian military strategists to seek food supplies for the army that would travel overland via the coast plain to Egypt from the inland provinces of Samerina and Yehud in addition to the costal provinces of Ashdod and Gaza. Past campaigns seem to have been able to have relied upon the huge supplies stockpiled at Tel Jemme and Tel el-Hesi in the coastal plain, without having to requisition additional supplies from the adjoining inland provinces. It is possible, of course, that some of the grain had been grown inland and sent to the central facilities in the coastal plain by royal request in these earlier periods. It is also possible that Samerina and Yehud would have supplied wine and oil for the soldiers on all these campaigns.

In the course of making arrangements to have these things in place as needed, royal couriers and possibly even army personnel would have been dispatched to Mizpah with orders and on missions to determine the amount of surplus available in the region from taxes paid in kind that could be requisitioned, as well as the available manpower and animal transport to be pressed into army service. The five-meter wide grain silo at Tel es-Sera' may have been built at this time to hold the grain supplies that were being transferred from throughout the province to a facility close to the main road, for easy transfer to the troops in transit. In this context of preparing for the invasion of Egypt, it would have been discovered that, up to that point, the province had not been well integrated into the imperial military, economic, and postal systems.

It appears that few, if any, changes had been introduced since Persia had become the new imperial lords. The Neo-Babylonian system of farmsteads producing agricultural surpluses was functioning, as was the provincial seat at Mizpah, and perhaps a few forts, particularly Khirbet Abu Twain in the central hills. But there was a lot of room for additional farmsteads, which would have yielded more food surpluses in taxes paid in kind while also putting at the crown's disposal more men who could be pressed into military service, as needed. In addition, the provincial seat did not have its own secure water supply but had to rely on cisterns gathering rainwater, and may or may not have had a local garrison stationed in it. There was no efficient signal method in place to send word on certain matters to the provincial seat from the major road systems in the lowlands; a messenger had to be dispatched, which took more time. In addition, it may have been discovered that the crown was losing valuable revenue from the spice trade that ran though the Beersheva Valley because it was not being carefully supervised and caravans could evade the existing custom post(s) near Gaza.

On the basis of reports that were sent back to the royal court, Artaxerxes I appears to have decided it was time to remedy the long-overdue integration of Yehud more fully and productively into the imperial systems. To this end, he devised himself or ordered court officials to design a master plan for the redevelopment of Yehud. It included the sending of a group of new settlers to increase the agricultural productivity of the land, the installation of a new governor who had ancestral ties to the region to oversee the smooth implementation of the plan, the moving of the provincial seat to Jerusalem, the building of a new series of structures to serve as fire-relay stations, and possibly, the transfer of jurisdiction over the Beersheva Valley to the governor of Yehud.

New Settlers

The Persians are known to have practiced deportation and resettlement, so such a move would not have been inconsistent with imperial policy (Lewis 1977: 6-7; Davies 1992: 78; Briant 1981: 14, 20; van der Spek 1982: 281; Kuhrt 1983: 94; Hoglund 1992: 237-38; Briant 2002: 505-506). An effort was made to include amongst the new settlers some who were descendants of Juda-hites who had been exiled to Babylonia in 586 BCE. This would have been a relatively easy task since many settlements in Babylonia had been named after the place of origin of their inhabi-tants. The archive of the Murashu family notes the following ethnically labeled towns in the vicinity of Nippur during the years 454–404 BCE: settlement of the people from Arum, of the people from Assa, of Carians, of Cimmerians, of suburbanites from Nippur, of people from Der, of people from Melitene, of people from Sharrabanu, of people from Shumutkuni, of Urartians, of Arabs, of Tyrians, of Indians, of Phrygians, of Sardinians and of people from Hamqadua (Stolper 1985: 23, 73-79). In a recently discovered set of ninety-three texts from the region of Borsippa, thirty were composed in a village or town outside of Nippur named 'town of the Judahites' (*âl-Jahûdu*) and another four, written elsewhere, mention the town (private commu-nication, Dr Laurie Pearce; for preliminary details, see Pearce 2005). Prior to the discovery of this cache of texts, one mention of this settlement was known (Joannès and Lemaire 1999: 24-27). The existence of this town or village outside of Nippur, taken in conjunction with the widespread practice of naming settlements in Babylonia after the homelands of the deportees who occupied them, indicates that such Judahite/Jewish settlements would have been readily identifiable. Anyone who was interested in identifying people of Judahite background in order to 'repatriate' them could have done so with little problem.

The new settlers also included those of non-Judahite descent, however, as indicated by the list in Nehemiah 7, which is not a census list from the time of Artaxerxes but which nev-ertheless indirectly reflects the results of his policy a few generations later: Elamites, (Neh. 7.12, 34), Persians associated with Bigvai (Neh. 7.19), and a group associated with Azgad (Neh. 7.13). Those registered under 'Bigvai' may have been Persian authorities and soldiers temporarily posted to the province: fort commanders, cavalry, couriers, and high-level administrators. The Elamites would have been resettled from their homeland in the region of modern-day Fars, in Iran. Due to pressure from Indo-Europeans, Medes and Persians to the north, by the Persian period, the native population had become more narrowly concentrated in Susiana, which was known as the province of Huja or Huvja in Achaemenid inscriptions (Vallat 1992: 424). The ethnic origin of the name Azgad is uncertain but it is not considered to be Semitic, so those included under this heading would also have been of foreign origin.[3]

The new settlers were assigned farmsteads and expected to increase the provincial agricultural yields; at the same time, having become landowners, they would have been liable to corvée and military service and so would have bolstered the numbers of men available for conscription as foot soldiers.[4] The increase of agricultural cultivation would have been con-sistent with Persian ideology, which stressed the importance of this enterprise as one of three forms of human productivity (work, production, reproduction) (Briant 1981: 13-23). Polybius claims that it was Persian policy to implant new agricultural communities on lands that for-merly, had never rendered any tribute (Briant 1981: 20). The founding in the Persian period of ninety-four new farmsteads on land that had never been worked before in Yehud would be con-sistent with this ideology.

We need to consider whether some of the new settlers were placed in Yehud because they had more specialized military training, perhaps as horse-handlers, cavalry, archers, or charioteers, and accordingly, were assigned farmsteads or 'bow estates' in the vicinity of one of the new fire signal facilities. It can be noted that the four facilities clustered in the western Shephelah: Lakish (#277), Rasm Shu'liya (#278), Khirbet Umm el Baqar (#279) and Tel Haraqim (#280), near the coastal plain, have a significant cluster of farmsteads in their hinterland that were newly established in the Persian period (#69-72, 75-77, 79-80, 82-88, 91-97). These would have supplied food and possibly rotating manpower for the four military sites nearby, to reinforce the few officers and personnel stationed there permanently.

It was Persian practice to distribute troops widely and in small units through the countryside in addition to stationing a complement of full-time soldiers inside the relatively few walled garrison cities that were allowed to exist within a satrapy (Tuplin 1987: 132). Yehud was a sub-province of Across-the-River, so responsibility for its military personnel would have rested ultimately with the satrap rather than with the local governor. The satrap was responsible for the safety of his entire territory, but may have delegated the oversight of the housing, maintenance, and drawing up of duty rosters to local governors in more outlying areas. In any event, he would have needed to post both types of personnel within the province of Yehud, and the proposed overhaul of Yehud's administrative system may well have included the settlement of soldiers in addition to farmers in the region, especially in the vicinity of the newly-built, free-standing forts.

A New Governor

A decision was made to install a new governor, of native ancestry, at the same time that the new settlers were transferred into the area. Zerubbabel, a descendant of the royal Davidic house, was selected to head the group of settlers being transferred from Babylonia to Yehud. Why would this have been deemed a wise move?

It can be noted that Artaxerxes I seems to have preferred to follow a policy of using local royal and chiefly lines to serve as provincial leaders. In the aftermath of the revolt of Inaros in Egypt, Herodotus reports that he confirmed the sons of the two rebel leaders, Inaros and Amyrtaeus, in power in districts in Egypt (*Hist.* 3.15). Artaxerxes seems to have been astute enough to realize that the removal of local leadership from power and the imposition of foreign administrators in their stead tended to breed resentment that could easily result in further rebellion. By showing mercy, he could gain the loyalty and cooperation of these troublesome tribes, while also putting in place Persian officials to oversee their movements and to intervene immediately at any hint of further rebellion.

The situation in Yehud, was different, however. There, the native dynasty had been removed from power by the Neo-Babylonians and, presumably, had not been re-instated in the intervening period. There is no evidence of an attempted local revolt in Yehud at the beginning of Artaxerxes' reign either, that would have led to the thought that the return of the native dynasty to power might help ease tension or discontent.

In this case, then, it seems that the choice of Zerubbabel as new governor was tied in some way to the resettlement of descendants of Judahite exiles. Perhaps it was thought that they would respect his leadership and cooperate with him in executing the larger plan for the redevelopment of Yehud. In this case, it would seem that Artaxerxes I must have been informed about the strong ideological ties that the diaspora community had to their former royal Davidic house, which could be put to the crown's advantage in implementing a major rebuilding and resettlement programme. He was not made aware, however, that not all those in Yehud shared such strong Davidic ties, and many in the region of Benjamin favored instead the royal line of Saul, David's predecessor (Edelman 2001: 2003a: 164-65).[5]

Jerusalem as the New Provincial Seat

The master plan also called for the moving of the provincial seat from Mizpah, where it had been located since 586 BCE, back to the site of the former capital of the defunct kingdom of Judah. As noted above, pragmatic concerns would have been foremost in this decision. Specifically, Jerusalem had the benefit of a perennial water source, unlike Mizpah, which was dependent on cisterns. In addition, Jerusalem was located at a major crossroads, making it directly accessible from all directions, while Mizpah was located only along the main road in the hill-country that ran north to south. Thus, it was less directly accessible. There is no indication that the decision to rebuild Jerusalem was tied in any way to the site being the former seat of power of the Davidic dynasty. Nothing suggests that the Persians would have decided to reinstate the royal Davidic line in its old capital in a gesture to gain local loyalty; such a move would have ignited nationalist aspirations to become a vassal kingdom rather than a province.

According to Neh. 2.8, Artaxerxes I gave official authorization not only for the repair of the protective walls, but also for the establishment inside of them of a *birah* or garrison, the governor's house/palace, and the temple. Nehemiah is said to have asked for an official letter from the king addressed to Asaph, the keeper of the king's private preserve (*pardes*) so that he might receive from him wood in order to construct the framework for 'the gates of the *birah*, which (will be) 'to' the 'house' and 'to' the city wall and 'to' the 'house' that I will enter for myself'. Most English translations have not captured the sense that the syntax of the Hebrew sentence requires. The expression, 'which (is) to' that follows 'for the gates of the *birah*', can have two meanings in Hebrew. It can express possession, as discussed in chapter 4 in the phrase in Neh. 3.7 concerning Mizpah, 'which was to the seat of the governor of Across-the-River' (p. 212); or, it can express physical proximity, in the sense of lying adjacent to another object or place, or being positioned beside it. The first meaning is ruled out in this case, because there are three objects governed by the preposition 'to' and the *birah* cannot be said to belong to all three. It is not wood for the gates of the *birah* of the 'house', of the city wall, and of the governor's house. Thus, the intended meaning is wood for the gates of the *birah*, which (will be) adjacent to the 'house', to the city wall, and to the governor's house that Nehemiah will build. The future tense is implied by the future verb describing the governor's palace; the entire rebuilding program is to be a future event.

Two Greek manuscripts omit either the Hebrew term *birah* or 'house'. On this basis, C. Torrey proposed that the original Hebrew text read either 'the gates of the *birah*, which is the temple', where the two nouns were used as synonyms, leading the Greek translator to omit one term, or to read 'the gates that (will belong to) the house', to which the term *birah* was added secondarily as a gloss (1896: 36). This argument seems to underlie many of the current English translations, which speak of 'the gates of the temple-fortress'. However, it is equally possible that the Greek translator chose to omit one of the two terms because he found the entire sentence a bit awkward and decided these two terms were perhaps synonymous or one was a gloss; whether he was right in his decision is another matter.

With its current word order, v. 8 has Nehemiah only seek wood from the royal estate to build the framework of the doors of the fort; it implies that the frameworks that will be used for doors in the temple, in the city wall, and in the palace will either be made of stone or will come from another source. The Greek reading does not eliminate this problem; it has the wood only for the gates of the temple-fortress and not for the remaining city walls or governor's palace. This seems an unlikely scenario since all of these projects would have been part of the same public works project whose materials and supplies would have been secured using provincial funds that were at the disposal of the crown.[6] Thus, the possibility should be considered that the original word order has been tampered with and that the sentence originally read, 'And a letter to Asaph, keeper of the royal estate, who will give me wood in order to construct the frames of the gates that will belong to the fort, to the temple, to the city wall, and to the palace into which I will enter…' This change could have been the result of inadvertent scribal error in which the relative clause 'which (will be to)' was relocated, or could have been deliberate.

The second item needing clarification in Neh. 2.8 is the meaning of 'the house'. As noted, there are two different 'houses' mentioned that will border on the garrison. The second is the house that Nehemiah will occupy, which would designate the governor's residency or palace complex. Normally, such a building would have had a wing for his private residential use but also would have contained the official audience room and chambers for archives and administrators. The first must be a different structure. The remaining logical referent is the temple, which regularly is described in the Hebrew Bible by the noun 'house' since it was conceived of as the earthly dwelling of the deity.

The author of the book of Nehemiah has named four major building projects that he thinks were overseen by Nehemiah: the building of a garrison, the repair of the city walls and the placement of new gates in it, the building of a new temple, and the building of a governor's residency. In his view, all of these projects received royal endorsement and so were funded from imperial coffers. In practical terms, this would mean that corvée labor would have been used for the construction but that any non-local materials or specialist artisans would have been paid for from tax monies levied locally that would be spent on provincial improvements instead of being sent on to the royal court. The new provincial seat had four distinguishing features that set it apart from ordinary settlements and towns: it was walled, it housed a garrison, it was the location of the governor's residency and provincial offices, and it housed a temple. These components should logically be found in all provincial seats throughout the empire.

The excavations at Mizpah (Tell en-Nasbeh) were conducted before current recording and stratigraphic methods were developed; the Neo-Babylonian occupational level has only recently been isolated in some sectors because of overlapping building lines on the report plans (Zorn 2003). Though much of the site was excavated, little can be deduced about its layout during the time that it served as the provincial seat. No clear remains of a garrison are indicated on the plans, but under the circumstances, little weight should be given to this situation (see illustration 31, Chapter 4).

Nevertheless, it allows the possibility to be raised that a garrison was not maintained on site by the Neo-Babylonians, and that none had been added subsequently when the province had passed to Persian control. Being a more insignificant province in the empire, it may have been largely overlooked until the reign of Artaxerxes, with existing systems left in place. I suggest this only as a possibility but do not want to place much emphasis on it since it is an argument primarily from silence. However, if it is correct, it would add another important reason for the relocation of the provincial seat: the desire to include a garrison among the governmental buildings on site and adequate housing for the soldiers assigned to it within the walls of the settlement.

If we accept the present form of the Hebrew text in Neh. 2.8, we are told that the *birah* would have backed onto the city wall and would have had the governor's residency and the temple on either side, leaving the front entrance free, or would have had one of the two 'houses' on one side and one opposite the entrance, across the street. If we reject it as a secondary corruption, then we have no information where the fort was located in relation to the temple or to the governor's residency.

The author of Nehemiah has military staff for the future garrison accompany Nehemiah. Nehemiah 2.9 mentions that the king had sent officers (*sare ḥayil*) and cavalry (*parashim*) with the former Cup-Bearer. This reference is commonly assumed to refer to a military escort that would have ensured Nehemiah's safe arrival (e.g. Myers 1965: 98; Smith 1971: 128; Herrmann 1975: 311; Blenkinsopp 1988: 216; Graf 1994: 169; Briant 2002: 368). However, this interpretation is unlikely. An emissary sent on imperial business would have had a military escort for his trip, so there would not have been a need to mention what was a routine procedure. In addition, the placement of this information in the narrative does not suggest that the primary function of these military personnel was to protect Nehemiah en route. Had that been the case, they should logically have been mentioned immediately before or after the reference to how the gracious hand of God had been upon Nehemiah at the end of v. 8, before mentioning the safe passage through the various governors' courts en route to Jerusalem. The official letters, which had been requested in 2.7, are what guaranteed safe passage (2.9a).

The mention of the army officers and cavalry begins a new segment that is developed in vv. 9b-10 in which Sanballat and Tobiah consider it a great evil when they learn that the king has sent the officers and cavalry; it signals that someone has arrived to seek 'good' on behalf of the children of Israel. It is unclear if these two individuals are supposed to be seen to be two of the governors of Across-the-River mentioned in v. 9a or are being introduced for the first time as the antagonists for ensuing plot developments. Notwithstanding, in the context, the presence of the military personnel sends a clear message to them that changes are about to be made that will introduce a stronger Persian presence into Yehud that will work to the benefit of the local population, and they are very displeased.

The military personnel accompanying Nehemiah for posting in Yehud are not described as ordinary soldiers, but officers, who presumably will head up regiments to be recruited from the locals. In addition, cavalry, a specialist division of the military whose members required extensive training, are sent to be stationed within the province. In the narrative world, Nehemiah is to build a garrison in Jerusalem (2.8) as part of his imperial commission, so it is logical to assume that the military personnel are intended to be stationed in the completed garrison.

Thus, this story detail indirectly addresses one of the four parts of Nehemiah's commission. The body of the narrative goes on to focus on how Nehemiah successfully completed only one of the four tasks, the rebuilding of the city walls, but the opening framework acknowledges that his commission covered a wider range of activities. The author of the 'autobiographical' narrative has used the literary principle of moving from the general to the specific to structure his story; by doing so, he has implied that Nehemiah was associated with all four tasks in tradition and probably accomplished all of them.

It appears as though the temple was an integral part of the master plan for the rebuilding of Jerusalem. This is indicated primarily by the inclusion of priestly personnel and Yeshua, who was to serve as the head priest, amongst the new settlers being relocated from Babylonia. Had the temple not been included as one of the public buildings that would be located within the provincial seat, there would not have been a need for priestly personnel; good farming and military skills would have been the criteria used to select settlers, unless whole settlements were targeted and forced to emigrate, regardless of occupation or age.

Yeshua could not have been a member of the non-*golah* community already resident in Yehud, officiating at a local sanctuary and who was then transferred to service in Jerusalem after the temple was rebuilt. The cult that was practiced in the restored temple differed in its conception and theology from the cult that would have continued to be practiced in Yehud under the Neo-Babylonians and which was practiced in Elephantine by the soldiers of Judahite descent. The latter was a form of Yahwism that still had room for Yahweh to have a female partner and which still conceived of the deity as physically occupying his earthly temple and being fed by sacrifices. The cult that was instituted in the temple in Jerusalem, by contrast, honored the new deity Yahweh Elohim, who had no partners or rivals in heaven, eliminated the Ark as a legitimate cult symbol of this new deity, and converted sacrifices into a pleasing odor that no longer fed the deity. The god's name dwelt in the temple, but not the god himself.

Had Yeshua been a non-*golah* priest officiating in the ongoing cult of Yahweh Sebaot, perhaps at Bethel or at Mizpah or at Gibeon, he would not have shared the new religious developments concerning Yahweh Elohim that evolved amongst the priestly and scribal elites who had been resettled in Babylonia. They had felt a need to evolve their conception of Yahweh from a local god tied to the territory of Cisjordan into a universal god who needed no earthly home and who had revealed his will to his people in words that had been recorded and were to be studied by the faithful in place of sacrifices. It is safe to conclude, therefore, that Yeshua accompanied Zerubbabel and the other new settlers from Babylonia to Yehud, and that there were other priests and temple personnel included in the group being relocated, who shared the new vision of Yahweh Elohim that had developed in certain Jewish circles in Babylonia.

Why was a temple included in the master plan for the new provincial seat? Two pragmatic considerations would have been at work. Jewish soldiers serving at the *birah* and Jewish administrators working in the provincial seat would have needed a place to worship the local god of the land. It was standard for provincial centers to have at least one temple within their midst; most had been the seats of independent kingdoms in the past and so had temples to the former national gods within the acropolis area. It is likely that there had been a Yahwistic temple functioning in Mizpah, the former provincial seat.

Jeremiah 41.4-8 talks of a group of men from Shechem, Shiloh, and Samaria who arrived at Mizpah the day after the murder of Gedaliah, in order to present incense and grain at the temple of Yahweh. The verb *bw'* in v. 4 can have the meaning of either 'to arrive' or 'to enter', but in light of the claim in v. 5 that Ishmael went out to meet them, or perhaps, more specifically, provided an escort into the city as an act of courtesy (*yaṣa' liqra't*) (Blenkinsopp 1994: 26), the first meaning is suggested by the context. The group 'arrived' outside the city gate and were met outside the gate and walls by Ishmael, who then diverted them from their intended destination, the temple inside of Mizpah, to the palace complex, where they were murdered instead. The fragmentary remains that have been identified as having belonged to the Neo-Babylonian and early-Persian periods on the site include a long segment of wall south of the gate in the southeast quadrant that conceivably could have been the outer wall of a temple complex (see illustration 31, Chapter 4).

Secondly, a temple traditionally doubled as a treasury where precious metals and valuable objects could be stored in safety. While major treasuries were located in royal and satrapal capitals, it is likely that it was standard also to have a treasury in a provincial capital (Tuplin 1978: 128). Some of the annual taxes and taxes assessed on caravans that were collected on behalf of the imperial court were paid in precious metal or in coin. A secure place was needed to store this gold, silver, copper, iron and tin before it was shipped to one of the royal courts or used locally. Silver and gold would have been used to pay for capital investments that had been authorized within the province that required the purchase of raw materials not otherwise available or the hiring of skilled craftsmen.

The Elephantine papyri indicate that soldiers stationed in that *birah* received a wage paid in metal, so money or silver would have been needed within Yehud to pay salaries. When coins eventually were minted in Yehud, it is likely that the foundry was located within the temple precincts, close to the place where the silver and new coins into which it had been converted were safeguarded (Torrey 1936; Schaper 1995). Copper, tin and iron, on the other hand, would have been needed to make weapons for the garrisons and for soldiers assigned to duty at the new series of fire-relay stations established in the province, as well as for equestrian gear (especially bridle bits) and chariots.

New Fire-Relay Stations

Another element in the master plan seems to have been an overhaul of the communications system within the province, which led to the building of a series of free-standing fire signal stations that were perched roughly along two internal roads that gave access from the coastal plan and the Beersheva Valley to the new provincial seat at Jerusalem. Some of these forts were pristine foundations and others were placed in former forts, whose structures would have been refurbished. These structures are fairly closely spaced and so would not have served in a primary capacity as postal relay stations or hostels for travellers en route to Jerusalem. The distances to the provincial seat along either road were not big enough to have required such facilities. It also seems unlikely that these routes would have been so prone to attacks by robbers and bandits that the primary purpose of the forts would have been to guard the roads they were perched above. Nevertheless, the constant presence of a small contingent of men on duty at each facility could have been an added deterrent to robbers, since they could have sounded an alarm quickly and dispatched men in hot pursuit.[7]

These relay stations may have had a core of full-time professional military personnel assigned to them, which was supplemented by local men who were fulfilling their obligatory corvée duty. In this way, the imperial court would have been able to have a greater number of trained militia physically present in Yehud and ready for call-up, as necessary.

Extended Jurisdiction?

A final possible element in the larger master plan might have been the assignment of control over the Beersheva Valley to Yehud. As discussed in Chapter 4, it appears that under the Neo-Babylonians, the monitoring of the valley had been assigned to Edom, and that toward the end of the Neo-Babylonian period or possibly in the early Achaemenid period, control might have been ceded to the Arabs. If the fort of Beersheva was rebuilt as part of the redevelopment plan, lying at the terminus of the road that left the Valley and cut up to Jerusalem, then part of its purpose may have been to elicit payment for access to the water supplies at Beersheva from caravans that regularly stopped there. In addition, it is possible that the three forts in the Negev highlands, Horvat Mesora, Mesad Nahal Haro'a and Horvat Ritma, were made operative at this time, to oversee the newly reinstated trade route that the Phoenicians were running from Tell el-Kheleife to the coast. The venture at Tell el-Kheleife may have been a reward from the Persian crown to the king of Sidon, of Tyre, or to a Phoenician cooperative for having turned the tide in the revolt in Egypt headed by Inaros. For the same reason, Tyre may have been granted a trading monopoly in Yehud as part of the larger plan for the latter's incorporation into the economic network of the empire (Edelman 2005b). We must remain cautious on the entire issue of extended jurisdiction, however, since an equally strong case could be made that the re-opening of the Red Sea trade route as well as reassignment of its control as well as that over the Beersheva Valley took place after the formation of Idumea c. 400 BCE.

Piety or Pragmatism?

Was the rebuilding of the temple by Artaxerxes I motivated by piety, as commonly suggested, or by pragmatism? Situated within the larger context of the rebuilding of Jerusalem and the redevelopment of Yehud, I have made the case that pragmatic concerns undergirded all aspects of a carefully developed plan to integrate Yehud more fully into the economic and military imperial system. The rebuilding of the temple was an integral part of a multi-pronged plan and not an isolated move to gain the favor of locals by reinstating their god.

It is interesting that although no modern scholar seems to have previously linked the temple-rebuilding to the rebuilding of Jerusalem, the same rationale has been widely used to justify the building of the temple and the rebuilding of the city walls. If we return to the hypotheses summarized in the introduction for why the temple was rebuilt, the idea of a Persian desire to preserve or restore ancient religious traditions as a way of winning the support of the subject people living on the border of the as-yet unconquered Egypt figures prominently (Noth 1960: 306-15; Myers 1965: xxix [the second part represented by the phrase 'political reasons']; Ackroyd 1968: 140-52; Herrmann 1975: 300-305; Miller and Hayes 1986: 440-60; Meyers and Meyers 1987: xxxi-xl, 37-38, 390). Interestingly, almost the same motivation is suggested to underlie the rebuilding of the city walls: an imperial desire to win the support of a subject people living on the border of a restless Egypt by honoring local history/ custom (assuming that Jerusalem's status as the former capital of the kingdom of Judah and ancestral seat of power of the Davidic dynasty remained an important concern in the psyche of Jews) (Galling 1937: 33-34; 44-47; Noth 1960: 318, 321; Berquist 1995: 108). Yet the first is theoretically rooted in the specifics of the reign of Cyrus, who allegedly announced an empire-wide policy of cult restoration, while the latter is rooted in the circumstances of the reign of Artaxerxes I. It seems that piety is viewed as a general trait of Persian monarchs and so can be operative in a wide range of historical situations, which is not helpful if we are trying to understand why the temple was specifically rebuilt in a single period.

By contrast, those who have identified more pragmatic concerns as having motivated the rebuilding of the temple by either Cyrus (Ahlström 1993: 841-48; Bedford 2001: 301-10) or Darius (Bickerman 1981: 23-28; Berquist 1995: 57-63) have rooted their understandings more firmly in the events that transpired within the reigns of these kings so that in most instances, they would not be able to be transferred to the reign of a different king, who was faced with a different set of circumstances. As a result, however, their proposals concerning the motivation behind the rebuilding of the temple cannot be accepted because they are rooted in the specifics of the reign of the wrong king.

A final point needs to be addressed in light of the likelihood that the temple was rebuilt at the same time that the city of Jerusalem was rebuilt. Historically, these two events took place at the same time and so, logically, would have been overseen by a single governor. Yet, they have been deliberately separated in time by almost seventy years, to show how God's word is accomplished in history, and as a result, have had to be placed under the governorship of two different individuals: Zerubbabel and Nehemiah.

The books of Haggai and Zechariah name Zerubbabel as being actively involved in the rebuilding of the temple (Hag. 2.23; Zech. 3.8; 4.7, 9-10; 6.9-13) but are silent on his involvement in the rebuilding of the city walls. It can be noted, however, that visions 2 (1.16) and 3 (2.5-10 [English 2.1-5]) refer to the rebuilding of the city alongside the rebuilding of the temple and so could be taken to imply that Zerubbabel was to oversee this work as well. The book of Ezra fails to mention his participation in the dedication of the temple, though it does claim that he and Yeshua built and dedicated the altar (3.1-4). The book of Nehemiah names Nehemiah as the rebuilder of the city walls but also may have him receive a royal mandate to seek timber to be used in the construction of door frames for a garrison (*birah*) inside the walls, as well as the doorways of temple and of the governor's residency where he will reside.[8] The book only gives details of his work on the walls, however.

Ben Sirah, who wrote his book c. 190 BCE, knows the tradition of Zerubbabel and Yeshua as the builders of the temple and of Nehemiah as the builder of the temple walls and gates and houses of citizens inside the walls (49.12-13). 1 Esdras, on the other hand, written perhaps in the late-second century BCE, has Zerubbabel, a member of Darius' bodyguard, remind the king of a vow he made on the day of his royal accession to rebuild Jerusalem and rebuild the temple, which the king upholds by sending Zerubbabel back with a group of Jews to rebuild the city (4.43-49). He is given letters both for safe passage and to secure timber to rebuild the city (4.47-48). In this narrative, Zerubbabel is credited with rebuilding the city as well as with rebuilding the temple. 2 Maccabees 1.18, written probably between 104–63 BCE, claims that Nehemiah built the temple and dedicated its altar and has no mention of Zerubbabel or Yeshua in this role. It mentions instead an individual named Jonathan who led the prayer at the dedication of the altar, to which the priests, Nehemiah, and all those present with the priests responded (2 Macc. 1.23-24).

It is possible that these two individuals succeeded each other in office as governor in Yehud, with the temple being started under Zerubbabel but completed under Nehemiah, who turned his attention to the rebuilding of the city walls only after the temple was completed. Yet, would the walls have been the final task undertaken in the rebuilding of Jerusalem, or one of the first projects? The other option that is raised by the circumstantial evidence is that Zerubbabel and Nehemiah represent the same historical person who has been split into two different people in the literature as a result of the decision to place the rebuilding of the temple almost seventy years earlier than the rebuilding of Jerusalem, for ideological reasons (Edelman 2005c). Which of these options is the more cogent explanation of the literature remains an open question that merits further investigation.

Endnotes

1.   Both papyri use the standard formula, 'in Samaria, the *birah*, in Samerina, the province' to describe the place where the document was written after giving the date, but neither has the full form of the formula intact. Papyrus 1, line 1 has *bšmry[n]*, 'in Samaria', which is only missing the final letter N of the name of the city, but lacks the rest of the formula. Papyrus 4 lacks the opening name but has *[b]yrt' bšmryn mdynt'*, 'the *birah* in Samerina, the province'.

2.   For a thorough evaluation of the sources and likely sequence of events, see Hoglund 1992: 97-164.

3.   The existence of non-ethnic 'Jews' amongst the returnees has received little attention in the past. An exception has been P. Davies, who has cautioned that the returnees were not necessarily 'exiles' going home (1992: 78).

4.   My proposal is consistent with the evidence from surface surveys, but since it is impossible to date any site to the reign of a specific king on the basis of diagnostic pottery, the same evidence could be consistent with other hypothetical historical scenarios.

5.   In light of the research contained in this book, my dating of the conflict between the non-*golah* and *golah* factions and the re-surfacing of Saulide-Davidic rivalry that led to editing of the Saul and David stories needs to be moved to the mid-fifth century and the reign of Artaxerxes from the traditional date under Darius I c. 520–515 BCE.

6.   The suggestion by L. Batten that Asaph was keeper of the royal mules (*prdym*) rather than the royal preserve (*prds*) on the basis of a double reading in the Greek text is unlikely (1913: 197). He sees the request for the mules to relate to the caravan to travel to Yehud from Babylonia, which would require the entire reference to the wood to build the frames of the gates of the four structures to be a secondary expansion.

7.   My proposal is consistent with the archaeological evidence, but is not the only reconstruction possible of the archaeological material, which cannot be dated to the reign of a specific king.

8.   It should also be noted that his request to be sent 'to Yehud, to the city of my ancestors' graves, so that I may rebuild it' (Neh. 2.5) is appropriate to a person of royal lineage, since city-building was a normal prerogative of kingship, but is out of character for a person of lesser rank or ancestry.

A List of Persian Kings and their Dates

Cyrus	553–525 BCE
Cambyses	525–522 BCE
Darius I	522–486 BCE
Xerxes	486–465 BCE
Artaxerxes I	465–425 BCE
Darius II Nothus	425–405 BCE
Cyrus the Younger	405–401 BCE
Artaxerxes II Mnemon	405/404–359/358 BCE
Artaxerxes III Ochus	359/358–338 BCE
Arses (Artaxerxes IV)	338–337 BCE
Darius III Codomon	337–330 BCE

Appendix I

THE OLD PERSIAN TEXT OF THE BEHISTUN INSCRIPTION

A slight adaptation of the English translation made by Roland Kent in *Old Persian Grammar, Texts, Lexicon* (1953): 116-34.

Copyright permission granted by the American Oriental Society

Column 1

§1. 1.1-3. I am Darius the Great King, King of Kings, King in Persia, King of countries, son of Hystaspes, grandson of Arsames, an Achaemenian.

§2. 1.3-6. Says Darius the King: My father was Hystaspes; Hystaspes' father was Arsames; Arsames' father was Ariaramnes; Ariaramnes' father was Teispes; Teispes' father was Achaemenes.

§3. 1.6-8. Says Darius the King: For this reason we are called Achaemenians. From long ago we have been noble. From long ago our family has been kings.

§4. 1.8-11. Says Darius the king: VIII of our family (there are) who were kings before; I am the ninth; IX in succession we have been kings.

§5. 1.11-12. Says Darius the king: By the favor of Ahuramazda I am king; Ahuramazda bestowed the kingdom upon me.

§6. 1.12-17. Says Darius the King: These are the countries that came to me; by the favor of Ahuramazda I was king of them: Persia, Elam, Babylonia, Assyria, Arabia, Egypt, (those) who are beside the sea, Sardis, Ionia, Media, Armenia, Cappadocia, Parthia, Drangiana, Aria, Chorasmia, Bactria, Sogdiana, Gandara, Scythia, Sattagydia, Arachosia, Maka: in all, XXIII provinces.

§7. 1.17-20. Says Darius the King: These are the countries that came to me; by the favor of Ahuramazda they were my subjects; they bore tribute to me; what was said to them by me either by night or by day, that was done.

§8. 1.20-24. Says Darius the King: Within these countries, the man who was loyal, him I rewarded well; (him) who was evil, him I punished well; by the favor of Ahuramazda these countries showed respect toward my law; as was said to them by me, thus was it done.

§9. 1.24-26. Says Darius the King: Ahuramazda bestowed the kingdom upon me; Ahuramazda bore me aid until I got possession of this kingdom; by the favor of Ahurmazda I hold this kingdom.

§10. 1.26-35. Says Darius the King: This is what was done by me after I became king. A son of Cyrus, Cambyses by name, of our family – he was king here. Of that Cambyses there was a brother, Smerdis by name, having the same mother and the same father as Cambyses. Afterwards, Cambyses slew that Smerdis. When Cambyses slew Smerdis, it did not become known to the people that Smerdis had been slain. Afterwards, Cambyses went to Egypt. When Cambyses had gone off to Egypt, after that the people became evil. After that the lie waxed great in the country, both in Persia and in Media and in the other provinces.

§11. 1.35-43. Says Darius the King: Afterwards, there was one man, a Magian, Gaumata by name; he rose up from Paishiyauvada. A mountain by the name Arakadri – from there XIV days of the month Viyakhu were past when he rose up. He lied to the people thus: 'I am Smerdis, the son of Cyrus, brother of Cambyses'. After that, all the people became rebellious from Cambyses (and) went over to him, both Persia and Media and the other provinces. He seized the kingdom; of the month Garmapada IX days were past, then he seized the kingdom. After that, Cambyses died by his own hand.

§12. 1.43-48. Says Darius the King: This kingdom that Gaumata the Magian took away from Cambyses, this kingdom from long ago had belonged to our family. After that, Gaumata the Magian took (it) from Cambyses; he took to himself both Persia and Media and the other provinces, he made (them) his own possession, he became king.

§13. 1.48-61. Says Darius the king: There was not a man, neither a Persian or a Mede nor anyone of our family, who might make that Gaumata the Magian deprived of the kingdom. The people feared him greatly, (thinking that) he would slay in numbers the people who previously had known Smerdis. For this reason he would slay the people: 'lest they know me, that I am not Smerdis the son of Cyrus'. Not anyone dared say anything about Gaumata the Magian, until I came. After that I besought help of Ahuramazda; Ahurmazda bore me aid; of the month Bagayadi X days were past, then I with a few men slew that Gaumata the Magian and those who were his foremost followers. A fortress by name Sikayauvati, a district by name Nisaya, in Media – there I slew him. I took the kingdom from him. By the favor of Ahuramazda I became king; Ahuramazda bestowed the kingdom upon me.

§14. 1.61-71. Says Darius the King: The kingdom that had been taken away from our family, that I put in its place; I reestablished it on its foundation. As before, so I made the sanctuaries that Gaumata the Magian destroyed. I restored to the people the pastures and the herds, the household slaves and the houses that Gaumata the Magian took away from them. I reestablished the people on its foundation, both Persia and Media and the other provinces. As before, so I brought back what had been taken away. By the favor of Ahuramazda this I did: I strove until I reestablished our royal house on its foundations as (it was) before. So I strove, by the favor of Ahuramazda, so that Gaumata the Magian did not remove our royal house.

§15. 1.71-72. Says Darius the King: This is what I did after that I became king.

§16. 1.72-81. Says Darius the king: When I had slain Gaumata the Magian, afterwards, one man, by name Açina, son of Apardama – he rose up in Elam. To the people thus he said: 'I am king in Elam'. Afterwards the Elamites became rebellious (and) went over to that Açina; he became king in Elam. And one man, a Babylonian, by name Nidintu-Bel, son of Ainaira – he rose up in Babylon. Thus he deceived the people: 'I am Nebuchadrezzar the son of Nabonidus'. Afterwards the Babylonian people all went over to that Nidintu-Bel; Babylonia became rebellious; he seized the kingdom of Babylon.

§17. 1.81-83. Says Darius the King: After that I sent (a message) to Elam. This Açina was led to me bound; I slew him.

§18. 1.83-90. Says Darius the King: After that I went off to Babylon, against that Nidintu-Bel who called himself Nebuchadrezzar. The army of Nidintu-Bel held the Tigris; there it took its stand, and on account of the waters (the Tigris) was unfordable. Thereupon (some of) my army I supported on (inflated) skins, others I made camel-borne, for others I brought horses. Ahuramazda bore me aid; by the favor of Ahuramazda we got across the Tigris. There I smote that army of Nidintu-Bel exceedingly; of the month Açiyadiya XXVI days were past, then we fought the battle.

§19. 1.90-96. Says Darius the King: After that I went off to Babylon. When I had not arrived at Babylon, a town by name Zazana, beside the Euphrates – there this Nidintu-Bel who called himself Nebuchadrezzar came with an army against me to deliver battle. Thereupon we joined battle; Ahuramazda bore me aid. By the favor of Ahuramazda I smote that army of Nidintu-Bel exceedingly. The rest was thrown into the water (and) the water carried it away. Of the month Anamaka II days were past, then we fought the battle.

Column II

§20. 2.1-5. Says Darius the King: After that, Nidintu-Bel with a few horsemen fled; he went off to Babylon. Thereupon I went to Babylon. By the favor of Ahurmazda I both seized Babylon and I took that Nidintu-Bel prisoner. After that, I slew that Nidintu-Bel at Babylon.

§21. 2.5-8. Says Darius the king: While I was in Babylon, these are the provinces that became rebellious from me: Persia, Elam, Media, Assyria, Egypt, Parthia, Margiana, Sattagydia, Scythia.

§22. 2.8-11. Says Darius the King: One man, by name Martiya, son of Cincikhri – a town by name Kuganaka, in Persia – there he abode. He rose up in Elam. To the people thus he said: 'I am Imanish, king in Elam'.

§23. 2.11-13. Says Darius the King: At that time I was near Elam. Thereupon the Elamites were afraid of me; they seized that Martiya who was their chief and slew him.

§24. 2.13-17. Says Darius the King: One man, by name Phraortes, a Median, – he rose up in Media. To the people thus he said: 'I am Khshathrita, of the family of Cyaxerxes'. Thereafter the Median army that (was) in the palace became rebellious from me (and) went over to that Phraortes. He became king in Media.

§25. 2.18-29. Says Darius the King: The Persian and Median army that was with me, this was a small (force). Thereupon I sent forth an army. A Persian by name Hydarnes, my subject – him I made chief of them. Thus I said to them: 'Go forth, smite that Median army that does not call itself mine!' Thereupon this Hydarnes with the army marched off. When he arrived in Media, a town by name Maru, in Media – there he joined battle with the Medes. He who was chief among the Medes, he at that time was not there. Ahuramazda bore me aid; by the favor of Ahuramazda my army smote that rebellious army exceedingly. Of the month Anamaka XXVII days were past, then the battle was fought by them. Thereafter this army of mine a district by name Kampanda in Media – there it waited for me until I arrived in Media.

§26. 2.29-37 Says Darius the King: An Armenian by name Dadarshi, my subject – him I sent forth to Armenia. Thus I said to him: 'Go forth, that rebellious army that does not call itself mine, that (one) shall you smite'. Thereupon, Dadarshi marched off. When he arrived in Armenia, thereafter the rebels assembled (and) came out against Dadarshi to join battle. A place by name Zuzahya, in Armenia – there they joined battle. Ahuramazda bore me aid; by the favor of Ahuramazda my army smote that rebellious army exceedingly; of the month Thuravahara VIII days were past, then the battle was fought by them.

§27. 2.37-42. Says Darius the King: Again a second time the rebels assembled (and) came out against Dadarshi to join battle. A stronghold by name Tigra in Armenia – there they joined battle. Ahuramazda bore me aid; by the favor of Ahuramazda my army smote that rebellious army exceedingly; of the month Thuravahara XVIII days were past, then the battle was fought by them.

§28. 2.42-49. Says Darius the King: Again a third time the rebels assembled (and) came out against Dadarshi to join battle. A fortress by name Uyama in Armenia – there they joined battle. Ahuramazda bore me aid; by the favor of Ahuramazda my army smote that rebellious army exceedingly; of the month Thaigarci IX days were past, then the battle was fought by them. Thereafter Dadarshi waited for me until I arrived in Media.

§29. 2.49-57. Says Darius the King: Thereafter a Persian by name Vaumisa, my subject – him I sent forth to Armenia. Thus I said to him: 'Go forth; the rebellious army that does not call itself mine – that shall you smite!' Thereupon Vaumisa marched off. When he arrived in Armenia, then the rebels assembled (and) came out against Vaumisa to join battle. A district by name Izala, in Assyria – there they joined battle. Ahuramazda bore me aid; by the favor of Ahuramazda my army smote that rebellious army exceedingly; of the month Anamaka XV days were past, then the battle was fought against them.

§30. 2.57-63. Says Darius the King: Again a second time the rebels assembled (and) came out against Vaumisa to join battle. A district by name Autiyara, in Armenia – there they joined battle. Ahuramazda bore me aid; by the favor of Ahuramazda my army smote that rebellious army exceedingly; on the last day of the month Thuravahara – then the battle was fought by them. After that, Vaumisa waited for me in Armenia until I arrived in Media.

§31. 2.64-70. Says Darius the King: Thereafter I went away from Babylon (and) arrived in Media. When I arrived in Media, a town by name Kunduru in Media – there this Phraortes who called himself king in Media came with an army against me to join battle. Thereafter we joined battle. Ahurmazda bore me aid; by the favor of Ahurmazda that army of Phraortes I smote exceedingly; of the month Adukanaisha XXV days were past, then we fought the battle.

§32. 2.70-78. Says Darius the King: Thereafter Phraortes with a few horsemen fled. A district by name Raga in Media – along there he went off. Thereafter I sent an army in pursuit. Phraortes, seized, was led to me. I cut off his nose and ears and tongue and put out one eye; he was kept bound at my palace entrance. All the people saw him. Afterward I impaled him at Ecbatana, and the men who were his foremost followers, those at Ecbatana within the fortress I (flayed and) hung out (their hides, stuffed with straw).

§33. 2.78-91. Says Darius the King: One man by name Ciçantakhma, a Sagartian – he became rebellious to me. Thus he said to the people: 'I am king in Sagartia, of the family of Cyaxerxes'. Thereupon I sent off a Persian and Median army; a Mede by name Takhmaspada, my subject – him I made chief of them. Thus I said to them: 'Go forth; the hostile army that shall not call itself mine, that shall you smite!' Thereupon Takhmaspada with the army went off; he joined battle with Ciçantakhma. Ahuramazda bore me aid; by the favor of Ahurmazda my army smote that rebellious army and took Ciçantakhma prisoner (and) led him to me. Afterwards I cut off both his nose and ears and put out one eye. He was kept bound at my palace entrance. All the people saw him. Afterwards I impaled him at Arbela.

§34. 2.91-92. Says Darius the King: This is what was done by me in Media.

§35. 2.92-98. Says Darius the King: Parthia and Hyrcania became rebellious from me, called themselves (adherents) of Phraortes. Hystaspes my father – he was in Parthia. Him the people abandoned, became rebellious. Thereupon Hystaspes went forth with the army that was faithful to him. A town by name Vishpauzati in Parthia – there he joined battle with the Parthians. Ahuramazda bore me aid; by the favor of Ahuramazda Hystaspes smote that rebellious army exceedingly; of the month Viyakhna XXII days were past – then the battle was fought by them.

Column 3
§36. 3.1-9. Says Darius the King: After that I sent forth a Persian army to Hystaspes from Raga. When this army came to Hystaspes, thereupon Hystaspes took that army (and) marched out. A town by name Patrigrabana in Parthia – there he joined battle with the rebels. Ahuramazda bore me aid; by the favor of Ahuramazda Hystaspes smote that rebellious army exceedingly; of the month Garmapada I day was past – then the battle was fought by them.

§37. 3.9-10. Says Darius the King: After that the province became mine. This is what was done by me in Parthia.

§38. 3.10-19. Says Darius the King: A province by name Margiana – it became rebellious to me. One man by name Frada, a Margian – him they made chief. Thereupon I sent forth against him a Persian by name Dadarshi, my subject, satrap in Bactria. This I said to him: 'Go forth, smite that army that does not call itself mine!' After that, Dadarshi marched out with the army; he joined battle with the Margians. Ahuramazda bore me aid; by the favor of Ahuramazda my army smote that rebellious army exceedingly; of the month Açiyadiya XXIII days were past – then the battle was fought by them.

§39. 3.19-21. Says Darius the King: After that the province became mine. This is what was done by me in Bactria.

§40. 3.21-28. Says Darius the King: One man by name Vahyazdata – a town by name Tarava, a district by name Yautiya in Persia – there he abode. He made the second uprising in Persia. To the people thus he said: 'I am Smerdis, the son of Cyrus'. Thereupon the Persian army that (was) in the palace, (having come) from Anshan previously – it became rebellious from me, went over to that Vahyazdata. He became king in Persia.

§41. 3.28-40. Says Darius the King: Thereupon I sent forth the Persian and Median army that was by me. A Persian by name Artavardiya, my subject – him I made chief of them. The rest of the Persian army went forth behind me to Media. Thereupon Artavardiya with his army went forth to Persia. When he arrived in Persia, a town by name Rakha in Persia – there this Vahyazdata who called himself Smerdis came with his army against Artavardiya to join battle. Thereupon they joined battle. Ahuramazda bore me aid; by the favor of Ahuramazda my army smote that army of Vahyazdata exceedingly; of the month Thuravahara XII days were past – then the battle was fought by them.

§42. 3.40-49. Says Darius the King: After that, this Vahyazdata with a few horsemen fled; he went off to Paishiyauvada. From there he got an army. Later he came against Artaverdiya to join battle. A mountain by name Parga – there he joined battle. Ahuramazda bore me aid; by the favor of Ahuramazda my army smote that army of Vahyazdata exceedingly; of the month Garmapada V days were past – then the battle was fought by them and that Vahyazdata they took prisoner and those who were his foremost followers they captured.

§43. 3.49-52. Says Darius the king: After that I and Vahyazdata and those who were his foremost followers – a town by name Uvadaicaya in Persia – there I impaled them.

§44. 3.52-53. Says Darius the King: This is what was done by me in Persia.

§45. 3.54-64. Says Darius the King: This Vahyazdata who called himself Smerdis had sent an army to Arachosia – a Persian by name Vivana, my subject, satrap in Arachosia – against him; and he had made one man their chief. Thus he said to them: 'Go forth, smite Vivana and that army which calls itself King Darius'!' Thereupon this army marched off, which Vahyazdata had sent forth against Vivana to join battle. A fortress by name Kapishakani – there they joined battle. Ahuramazda bore me aid; by the favor of Ahuramazda my army smote that rebellious army exceedingly; of the month Anamaka XIII days were past – then the battle was fought by them.

§46. 3.64-69. Says Darius the King: Again later the rebels assembled (and) came out against Vivana to join battle. A district by name Gandtava – there they joined battle. Ahuramazda bore me aid; by the favor of Ahuramazda my army smote that rebellious army exceedingly; of the month Viyakhna VII days were past – then the battle was fought by them.

§47. 3.69-75. Says Darius the king: After that, this man who was the chief of that army that Vahyazdata had sent forth against Vivana – he fled with a few horsemen (and) got away. A fortress by name Arshada in Arachosia – past that he went. Afterwards Vivana with his army went off in pursuit of them; there he took him prisoner and the men who were his foremost followers (and) slew (them).

§48. 3.75-76. Says Darius the King: after that the province became mine. This is what was done by me in Arachosia.

§49. 3.76-83. Says Darius the King: While I was in Persia and Media, again a second time the Babylonians became rebellious from me. One man by name Arkha, an Armenian, son of Haldita – he rose up in Babylon. A district by name Dubala – from there he thus lied to the people: 'I am Nebuchadrezzar the son of Nabonidus'. Thereupon the Babylonian people became rebellious from me (and) went over to that Arkha. He seized Babylon; he became king in Babylon.

§50. 3.83-92. Says Darius the King: Thereupon I sent forth an army to Babylon. A Persian by name Intaphernes, my subject – him I made their chief. Thus I said to them: 'Go forth, that Babylonian army smite that will not call itself mine!' Thereupon Intaphernes with the army marched off to Babylon. Ahuramazda bore me aid; by the favor of Ahuramazda Intaphernes smote the Babylonians and led them in bonds; of the month Varkazana XXII days were past – then that Arkha who falsely called himself Nebuchadrezzar and the men who were his foremost followers he took prisoner. I issued an order: this Arkha and the men who were his foremost followers were impaled in Babylon.

Column 4

§51. 4.1-2. Says Darius the King: This is what was done by me in Babylon.

§52. 4.2-31. Says Darius the King: This is what I did by the favor of Ahuramazda in one and the same year after that I became king. XIX battles I fought; by the favor of Ahuramazda I smote them and took prisoner IX kings. One was Gaumata by name, a Magian; he lied. Thus he said: 'I am Smerdis, the son of Cyrus'. He made Persia rebellious. One, Açina by name, an Elamite; he lied. Thus he said: 'I am king in Elam'. He made Elam rebellious to me. One, Nidintu-Bel by name, a Babylonian; he lied. Thus he said: 'I am Nebuchadrezzar, the son of Nabonidus'. He made Babylon rebellious. One, Martiya by name, a Persian; he lied. Thus he said: 'I am Imanish, king in Elam'. He made Elam rebellious. One, Phraortes by name, a Mede; he lied. Thus he said: 'I am Khshathrita, of the family of Cyaxerxes'. He made Media rebellious. One Ciçantakhma by name, a Sagartian; he lied. Thus he said: 'I am king in Sagartia, of the family of Cyaxerxes'. He made Sagartia rebellious. One, Frada by name, a Margian; he lied. Thus he said: 'I am king in Margiana'. He made Margiana rebellious. One, Vahyazdata by name, a Persian; he lied. Thus he said: 'I am Smerdis, the son of Cyrus'. He made Persia rebellious. One, Arkha by name, an Armenian; he lied. Thus he said: 'I am Nebuchadrezzar, the son of Nabonidus'. He made Babylon rebellious.

§53. 4.31-32. Says Darius the King: these IX kings I took prisoner within these battles.

§54. 4.33-36. Says Darius the King: These are the provinces that became rebellious. The Lie made them rebellious, so that these (men) deceived the people. Afterwards Ahuramazda put them into my hand; as was my desire, so I did to them.

§55. 4.36-40 Says Darius the King: You who shall be king hereafter, protect yourself vigorously from the Lie. The man who shall be a Lie-follower, him punish well if thus you shall think: 'May my country be secure!'

§56. 4.40-43. Says Darius the King: This is what I did; by the favor of Ahuramazda, I one and the same year I did (it). You who shall hereafter read this inscription, let that which has been done by me convince you; do not think it a lie.

§57. 4.43-45. Says Darius the King: I turn myself quickly to Ahuramazda, that this (is) true, not false, (which) I did in one and the same year.

§58. 4.45-50. Says Darius the King: By the favor of Ahuramazda and of me much else was done that has not been inscribed on this inscription. For this reason it has not been inscribed: lest whoever shall hereafter read this inscription, to him what has been done by me seem excessive (and) it not convince him, (but) he think it false.

§59. 4.50-52. Says Darius the King: Those who were the former kings, as long as they lived, by them was not done thus as by the favor of Ahuramazda was done by me in one and the same year.

§60. 4.52-56. Says Darius the King: Now let that which has been done by me convince you. Thus to the people impart, do not conceal it: if this record you shall not conceal (but) tell it to the people, may Ahuramazda be your friend and may you have family in abundance and may you live long!

§61. 4.57-59. Says Darius the King: If this record you shall conceal (and) not tell it to the people, may Ahuramazda be a smiter to you and may you not have family!

§62. 4.59-61. Says Darius the King: This which I did in one and the same year, by the favor of Ahuramazda I did. Ahuramazda bore me aid and the other gods who are.

§63. 4.61-67. Says Darius the King: For this reason Ahuramazda bore aid, and the other gods who are: because I was not hostile; I was not a Lie-follower. I was not a doer of wrong – neither I nor my family. According to righteousness I conducted myself. Neither to the weak nor to the powerful did I do wrong. The man who cooperated with my house, him I rewarded well. Whoever did injury, him I punished well.

§64. 4.67-69. Says Darius the King: You who shall be king hereafter; the man who shall be a Lie-follower or who shall be a doer of wrong – do not be their friend (but) punish them well.

§65. 4.69-72. Says Darius the King: You who shall hereafter look upon this inscription that I have inscribed or these sculptures; do not destroy them (but) henceforward protect them as long as you shall be in good strength!

§66. 4.72-76. Says Darius the King: If you shall look upon this inscription or these sculptures (and) shall not destroy them and shall protect them as long as you have strength, may Ahuramazda be your friend and may you have family in abundance and may you live long and what you shall do, may Ahuramazda make (it) successful for you!

§67. 4.76-80. Says Darius the King: If you shall look upon this inscription or these sculptures (and) shall destroy them and shall not protect them as long as you have strength, may Ahuramazda be your smiter and may you not have family and what you shall do, that may Ahuramazda utterly destroy for you!

§68. 4.80-86. Says Darius the King: These are the men who were there at the time when I slew Gaumata the Magian who called himself Smerdis. At that time these men cooperated as my followers: Intaphernes by name, son of Vayaspara, a Persian; Otanes by name, son of Thukhra, a Persian; Gobryas by name, son of Mardonius, a Persian; Hydarnes by name, son of Bagabigna, a Persian; Megabyzus by name, son of Datuvahya, a Persian; Ardumanish by name, son of Vahauka, a Persian.

§69. 4.86-88. Says Darius the King: You who shall be king hereafter, protect well the family of these men.

§70. 4.88-92. Says Darius the king: By the favor of Ahuramazda this is the inscription that I made. In addition, it was in Aryan and on clay tablets and on parchment it was composed. In addition, a sculptured figure of myself I made. In addition, I made my lineage. And it was inscribed and read off before me. Afterwards this inscription I sent off everywhere among the provinces. The people worked on it as one.

Column 5

§71. 5.1-14. Says Darius the King: This is what I did in both the second and third year after I became king. A province by name Elam – this became rebellious. One man by name Atamaita, an Elamite – him they made chief. Thereupon I sent forth an army. One man by name Gobryas, a Persian, my subject – him I made chief of them. After that, Gobryas with the army marched off to Elam; he joined battle with the Elamites. Thereupon, Gobryas smote and crushed the Elamites and captured their chief. He led him to me and I killed him. After that the province became mine.

§72. 5.14-17. Says Darius the King: Those Elamites were faithless and by them Ahuramazda was not worshipped. I worshipped Ahuramazda; by the favor of Ahuramazda, as was my desire, thus I did to them.

§73. 5.18-20. Says Darius the King: Whoever shall worship Ahuramazda, divine blessing will be upon him, both (while) living and (when) dead.

§74. 5.20-30. Says Darius the King: Afterwards with an army I went off to Scythia, after the Scythians who wear a pointed cap. These Scythians went from me. When I arrived at the sea, beyond it then with all my army I crossed. Afterwards, I smote the Scythians exceedingly. Another (leader) I took captive. This one was led bound to me and I slew him. Their chief, by name Skunkha – him they seized and led to me. Then I made another their chief, as was my desire. After that, the province became mine.

§75. 5.30-33 Says Darius the King: Those Scythians were faithless and by them Ahuramazda was not worshipped. I worshipped Ahuramazda; by the favor of Ahuramazda, as was my desire, thus I did to them.

§76. 5.33-36. Says Darius the King: Whoever shall worship Ahuramazda, divine blessing will be upon him, both (while) living and (when) dead.

Appendix II

The Cyrus Cylinder

Translation by Leo Oppenheim. Taken from *Ancient Near Eastern Texts Relating to the Old Testament* (2nd edn, 1955): 315-16. Copyright permission granted by Princeton University Press.

One line destroyed
...[r]ims (of the world)...a weakling had been installed as the *enu* of his country; [the correct images of the gods he removed from their thrones, imi]tations he ordered to place upon them. A replica of the temple Esagila he had...for Ur and the other sacred cities inappropriate rituals...daily he blabbered [incorrect prayers]. He (furthermore) interrupted in a fiendish was the regular offerings, he...he established with the sacred cities. The worship of Marduk, king of the gods, he [chang]ed into abomination; daily he used to do evil against his (i.e. Marduk's) city... He [tormented] its [inhabitant]s with corvée-work (literally, a yoke) without relief; he ruined them all.

Upon their complaints the lord of all the gods became terribly angry and [he departed from] their region; (also) the (other) gods living among them left their mansions, angry that he had brought (them) into Babylon. (But) Marduk [who cares for]...on account of (the fact that) the sanctuaries of all their settlements were in ruins and the inhabitants of Sumer and Akkad had become like (living dead), turned back (his face); [his] an[ger] [abated] and he had mercy (upon them). He scanned and looked (through) all the countries, searching for a righteous ruler willing to lead him (i.e. Marduk) (in the annual procession). (Then) he pronounced the name of Cyrus, king of Anshan, pronounced [his] name to be(come) the ruler of all the world. He made the Guti country and all the Manda-hordes bow in submission to his (i.e. Cyrus') feet.

And he (Cyrus) has always endeavored to treat the black-headed (people) whom he (Marduk) made him conquer according to justice. Marduk, the great lord, a protector of his people/worshippers, beheld with pleasure his (i.e. Cyrius') good deeds and his upright mind (lit. heart) (and therefore) ordered him to march against his city Babylon. He made him set out on the road to Babylon, going at his side like a real friend. His widespread troops – their number like that of the water of a river could not be established – strolled along, their weapons packed away. Without any battle, he made them enter his town Babylon, sparing Babylon any calamity. He delivered into his (i.e. Cyrus') hands Nabonidus, the king who did not worship him (i.e. Marduk). All the inhabitants of Babylon as well as the entire country of Sumer and Akkad, princes and governors (included), bowed to him (Cyrus) and kissed his feet, jubilant that he (had received) the kingship, and with shining faces. Happily they greeted him as a master through whose help they had come (again) to life from death (and) had all been spared damage and disaster, and they worshipped his (very) name.

I am Cyrus, king of the world, great king, legitimate king, king of Babylon, king of Sumer and Akkad, king of the four rims (of the earth), son of Cambyses, son of Cyrus, great king, King of Anshan, descendant of Teispes, great king, king of Anshan, of a family (that) always (exercised) kingship; whose rule Bel and Nabu love, whom they want as king to please their hearts.

When I entered Babylon as a friend and (when) I established the seat of the government in the palace of the ruler under jubilation and rejoicing, Marduk, the great lord, [induced] the magnanimous inhabitants of Babylon [to love me], and I was daily endeavoring to worship him. My numerous troops walked around in Babylon in peace; I did not allow anyone to terrorize (any place) of the [country of Sumer] and Akkad. I strove for peace in Babylon and in all his (other) sacred cities. As to the inhabitants of Babylon, [who] against the will of the gods [had/ were…, I abolished] the corvée (lit. yoke) that was against their (social) standing. I brought relief to their dilapidated housing, (thus) putting an end to their complaints. Marduk, the great lord, was well pleased with my deeds and sent friendly blessings to me, Cyrus, the king who worshipped him, to Cambyses, my son, the offspring of [my] loins, as well as to all my troops, and we [praised] his great [godhead] joyously, standing before him in peace.

All the kings of the entire world from the Upper to the Lower Sea, those who are seated in throne rooms, (those who) live in other [types of buildings as well as] all the kings of the West land living in tents, brought their heavy tributes and kissed my feet in Babylon. (As to the region) from…as far as Asshur and Susa, Agade, Eshnunna, the towns Zamban, Me-Turnu, Der as well as the region of the Gutians, I returned to (the) sacred cities on the other side of the Tigris, whose settlements had been established of old (or abandoned previously)[1] for a long time, the images that (used) to live therein and established for them permanent sanctuaries. I (also) gathered their (former) inhabitants and returned (to them) their habitations. Furthermore, I resettled upon the command of Marduk, the great lord, all the gods of Sumer and Akkad whom Nabonidus had brought into Babylon to the anger of the lord of the gods, unharmed in their (former) chapels/sanctuaries, the places that make them happy.

May all the gods whom I have resettled in their sacred cities ask daily Bel and Nabu for a long life for me and may they recommend me (to him); to Marduk, my lord, may they thus say this: 'Cyrus, the king who worships you, and Cambyses his son…' …all of them I settled in a peaceful place…ducks and doves,… I endeavored to fortify/repair their dwelling places…

Six lines destroyed.

Endnote

1. Oppenheim rendered this phrase, 'I returned to the sacred cities on (the) other side of the Tigris, the sanctuaries of which had been in ruins for a long time…' I am adopting the alternative readings that have been proposed by J.N. Postgate in private correspondence to H.G.M. Williamson.

GLOSSARY

accession: the formal act of being crowned and assuming the responsibility of governing the kingdom.

Achaemenid: of or belonging to the clan of Achaemenes, from which the early Persian kings claimed membership and descent. It belonged to the Pasargadae tribe, which was the most distinguished of the three main tribes that Cyrus I had assembled and persuaded to revolt against their Median rulers in the late 550s BCE The other two were the Maraphii and Maspii. Each tribe and clan had a territory of its own.

acropolis: in an ancient city, the highest point, which usually housed a citadel, temple, and/or palace complex that was separated from the lower part of the city by an encircling inner wall. It was also known as the 'upper city'.

almanac: a manual detailing the correct months within the year in which to tend to various agricultural activities necessary to produce good yearly crops.

amphora: a large, two-handled jar of varying proportions with a prominent neck. The handles can run vertically between the neck and the body of the jar or sit horizontally on the body alone. It was usually used to transport grain or liquids.

annalistic: relating to materials recorded in annals. In the ancient Near East, annals tended to chronicle military and religious accomplishments and building activities of a king year by year during his reign.

anointing: the act of pouring or smearing oil over or on the head of an individual to invest him in office. In ancient Judah, the act was done when kings were installed in office; in the later periods, the high priest appears to have been anointed instead. The practice was probably borrowed from Egypt, where anointing was a means of transferring some of the power and spirit of pharaoh into his lesser officials who were acting on his behalf. In Judah, an extra portion of God's spirit was transferred to his earthly vice-regent, the king and later, to the high priest.

apposition: in grammar, the placing of a word or expression beside another so that the second explains and has the same grammatical construction as the first.

Aquila: a translator who worked c. 100-125 CE and produced a version of the Hebrew Bible/Old Testament in Greek. According to tradition, he was born a pagan, converted to Christianity, and then to Judaism. It is thought that his version was merely a revision of an earlier Greek translation known as the *kaige*, which rendered the Hebrew term *gam*, 'also', with *kaige*. It had been created at some point after the first translation had been made into Greek, which is known as the Old Greek text. His text, though written in Greek, followed Hebrew word order as closely as possible, producing a text that was not idiomatic in Greek.

aryballos: a small flask with a round or pear-shaped body and a narrow neck with a wide, flat lip and a handle running from the lip to the body of the vessel. It may have contained perfume.

archaizing: the use of language and ideas that are old-fashioned, in an attempt to make the literature written in an archaizing style appear to be older than it is.

ashlar masonry: blocks of stone that have been carefully shaped with a chisel, usually into a rectangle, that were used in the construction of monumental buildings.

Attic ware: pottery that was made in the region of Attica in Greece.

bakshish: bribe money.

balk: a narrow strip of soil, usually 0.5–1 meter wide, left untouched between two squares being excavated in order to allow the removal of soil from each efficiently and to provide a visual record of loci that have removed but whose remains were still present in the resulting untouched 'wall'.

balsam: an aromatic, resinous sap collected from certain trees and shrubs that was used in medicines and perfumes.

BCE: Before the Common Era – the equivalent of BC but religiously neutral. It refers to dates before the year 0.

Behistun inscription: an autobiographical inscription of Darius I carved into the face of a cliff near the modern town of Behistun/Bisitun in three languages: Old Persian, Elamite, and Aramaic. It details how he had come to power by killing the imposter who had assumed the identity of the brother of Cambyses and had unlawfully assumed the throne after the latter's death. Darius was then crowned in his stead, claiming to be entitled because of his status as grandson of Arsames, an Achemenid. However, he had to suppress rebellions in ten countries in years 1 and 3 of his reign order to gain control of the throne. For an English translation of the text, see Appendix I.

birah: an Aramaic word, feminine, singular, and indefinite in form, which designates either a free-standing military installation like a fort, or a walled settlement that contains a fort manned by military personnel within it.

birot: the plural form of *birah*.

Book of the Twelve: The collection of the Minor Prophets (Hosea, Joel, Amos, Obadiah, Jonah, Micah, Nahum, Habakkuk, Zephaniah, Haggai, Zechariah, and Malachi) in the Hebrew Bible/Old Testament that came to be written together on a single scroll, with editorial links added to relate the originally distinct compositions into a larger, single unit.

bow estate: a type of land grant made by the Persian king in exchange for mandatory military service in which the person had to supply his own horse, weapons, and rations.

brazier: a portable metal container used to hold burning coals. It often was used to heat interior spaces in cold weather.

bulla: a lump of clay used to hold closed a document written on leather or papyrus, in which a seal is impressed, leaving its image. Often the documents rot away over time but the seals remain intact and are found in excavations or in illicit digging.

Byzantine period: in archaeology, the period from 324–638 CE.

c.: abbreviation for *circa*, meaning 'about' or 'approximately'.

canonical: relating to a canon, a body of literature that is deemed authoritative and binding by a given community. Different communities have different canons. The Bible is a canon; however, its contents are defined differently by Jews and Christians on the one hand, and by the Catholic Church, Protestants denominations and eastern orthodoxy, on the other.

caravanserai: stopping places along routes travelled by caravans, where animals and humans alike can eat, drink water, and rest in relative safety. They are usually a walled complex with buildings around the perimeter and a large open, central courtyard.

Carian: of or relating to the ancient kingdom of Caria, located in the region of southwestern Asia Minor.

cartouche: in Egyptian hieroglyphs, an oval in which the name and titles of a pharaoh were written.

casemate room: a space that was created when a settlement was defended by a casemate wall system, consisting of two parallel defensive walls, built a few meters apart. The air space in between could then be partitioned into rooms by inserting short perpendicular walls that ran between the two parallel walls, which could be used for storage or dwelling. This defensive system afforded good protection while requiring less building material and less hours of labor to erect than a single solid wall thick enough to withstand a battering ram.

CE: Common Era, the equivalent of AD but religiously neutral. It refers to dates after the year 0.

censer: a container, often ornamental, in which incense is burned.

Central-Place theory: the hypothesis that socio-economic relationships within a given geographical region between larger central sites and smaller satellite sites of varying size is best represented graphically through a series of interconnected hexagons. The largest site will be in the center, with smaller towns and even smaller villages and farmsteads , its dependencies, surrounding it.

chiasm/chiastic: a literary compositional principle or technique in which similar elements are used to frame a central core: ABCB´A´.

Chronicler's history: a phrase used to describe the books of 1 and 2 Chronicles, which give a parallel but separate version of the history of the kingdoms of Israel and Judah to that found within 1 and 2 Kings. Some scholars include Ezra and Nehemiah within the history, believing that they were composed by the same person who created 1 and 2 Chronicles. Others reject this linkage, seeing Ezra and Nehemiah to have been appended as a update to the history, recounting the rebuilding of the temple, which plays a central role in 1 Chronicles.

Cisjordan: the geographical region on the western side of the Jordan River, comprising modern Israel today.

cistern: a hole in the ground hewn out of rock or soil, often lined with plaster to make it waterproof, that was used to catch and hold rainwater.

citadel: a fortress on a commanding height for the defense of a city; a fortified place or stronghold.

client king: a king who is in a subordinate position to another, greater king, usually within the context of an empire, where the former is allowed to rule over his ancestral territory that otherwise is the equivalent of a province ruled directly by an appointed governor within the larger empire.

corpus: a 'body' or a collection of similar artifacts, like seals or bullae.

corvée: mandatory annual labor service owed by citizens to the king.

cowrie shell: a small oval shell, often speckled on the top, with a slit on the underside.

crucible: a vessel or pot made of a material that has been tempered to resist extreme heat, used for melting ores and metals.

cultic center: a place where religion was practised, usually by offering sacrifices.

cultic vessels: ceramic and metal containers used to perform rituals associated with the worship of one or more gods. Miniatures of regular jugs, bowls and plates are common as well as stands to hold bowls and ewers, incense altars, animal-formed spouted vessels for pouring out liquid, and special rings with multiple spouts.

cuneiform: a system of writing in which a pen made from a cut reed is impressed into wet clay forming clusters of wedge-shaped groupings, each of which represents a consonant and vowel together. This form of writing was developed in Mesopotamia in the fourth millennium BCE and was used to write the Sumerian, Akkadian, Hittite, Hurrian, Urartian, Elamite, and Ugaritic languages.

Cup-Bearer: an important office at the Persian court whose holder sampled wine before it was served to the king in case it was poisoned.

Cyrus cylinder: an octagonal clay inscription found in Babylon in 1879 that probably was buried as a foundation deposit. It is a typical Mesopotamian building text that focuses on various civil projects that Cyrus undertook after capturing the city, including the repair of the main temples, city wall, moats, and private houses. Its purpose in part was to portray this Persian king as the legitimate successor to the Neo-Babylonian kings, to gain him support in the former capital of the the the Neo-Babylonian empire.

Davidic/Davidide: of or relating to David, king of Israel and Judah, and/or his descendants, who formed the official dynasty of the kingdom of Judah.

Dedan: an ancient, sixth-century BCE settlement located at one of the major oases in northwest Arabia. It has been identified with the ruins at Khuraybah, just north of the modern village of al-'Ula in the Hijaz. That central town was the administrative center for a series of agriculturally based villages that extended along a thirteen-kilometer stretch of valley.

degel: a military division, consisting of 1,000 men at full force, which contained sub-units of 100 men.

Demotic: a form of Egyptian writing in cursive style, not hieroglyphs.

Deuteronomistic: of or relating to the ideas contained in the book of Deuteronomy or imitating its style of phraseology. The 'Deuteronomistic History' is thought to be a self-contained narrative that included the books of Deuteronomy, Joshua, Judges, 1 and 2 Samuel, and 1 and 2 Kings, which presented a history of Israel in five periods.

diaspora: a technical term used to describe Jews living outside of the territory of ancient Israel and Judah.

dolomite: a rock consisting mainly of magnesium carbonate and calcium carbonate. Its base can be limestone or marble if it contains much magnesium carbonate.

doublet: a variant form of a tradition that is similar to another, yet differing on certain details enough to make it distinguishable as an independent version from the other.

dunam: a metric land measurement, constituting a tenth of a hectare or 1,000 square meters or .2471 acre.

Edomite: of or relating to the ancient kingdom of Edom, whose capital was at Bozrah, i.e. Buseirah in modern-day Jordan, and which constituted Judah's southeastern neighbor. It lay south of the kingdom of Moab.

Elephantine: an island in the Nile River, just south of modern Aswan, which housed a military colony that contained Jewish soldiers. Some thirty-five papyri, not all intact, were found by chance and during excavation. They document various aspects of the lives of some of the Jewish families living there in the fifth century BCE.

emendation: a proposed change to a received text in order to make it better by correcting a perceived fault or error.

epagonal: relating to the period of approximately eleven days by which the solar year exceeds the lunar year, or the period within a given month by which the solar calendar exceeds the lunar calendar.

ephod: (1) a priestly garment made of linen; (2) an image of a deity.

epigraphy: inscriptions, collectively.

eponym: a real or fictional person from whose name the name of a nation, group, or institution is derived; an ancestor.

eschatological: relating to the end of the world and the final judgment that will take at that time in Judaeo-Christian tradition.

exilic period: a designation derived from the Hebrew Bible and applied to the period from the Neo-Babylonian destruction of Jerusalem and the conversion of the former kingdom of Judah into the province named Yehud in 586 BCE to the Persian conquest of Babylon and assumption of control over the empire that controlled the ancient Near East in its stead, in 539 BCE. The book of Ezra claims that Cyrus, the first king of the Persian empire, authorized the return of exiled Jews to Yehud in the first year of his reign, effectively ending the period of the exile in 538 BCE.

extra-biblical: occurring or found outside the Bible.

extramural: located outside of city walls.

favissa: a pit dug in order to bury objects that once had been used ritually.

flax: a plant that grows beside and in shallow standing water whose stem is used to make linen and whose seeds are edible.

flourit: main or peak period of use.

foundry: a place used to melt and mold metal.

gentilic: a surname or designation that indicates a person's extended family, clan, or place of origin.

golah: a Hebrew word meaning 'emigration, exile(s)', it is used in the Bible to describe the descendants of those who were forcibly resettled in Babylonia after Jerusalem was destroyed in 586 BCE, who were forced to return to their homeland by one or more Persian kings.

graffito: the singular of graffiti; an inscription or drawing found on rocks, on the walls of ancient ruins, or on whole or broken pieces of stone or ceramic vessels.

Hasmonean: relating to a family of high priests and kings who descended from Mattathias, the father of Judah Maccabee, who captured the city of Jerusalem from Seleucid forces and rededicated the temple for Jewish worship. This family was prominent in Judea from 175–37 BCE and controlled it as rulers from 142–63 BCE. Mattathias rebelled against the anti-Jewish decrees of the ruler of the time, Antiochus IV Epiphanes, and his sons were able to reoccupy and rededicate the temple in Jerusalem. His fifth son, Yonatan, was made provincial governor and his successor, his brother Simon, the third son of Mattathias, declared himself ruler of an independent Hellenistic state.

hattirsata: an Iranian word meaning 'the prince'.

Hellenistic period: the era when Alexander and his successors ruled the ancient Near East, from 332–37 BCE. Yehud was a province during most of the period but became a client kingdom ruled by the Hasmoneans from 142–37 BCE.

hemerology: an accounting of the lucky or unlucky nature of certain days in a month and activities that are allowed or forbidden on individual days.

Herodotus: a famous historian, born in 484 BCE in Halicarnassus, who is known as 'the father of history' because he was the first important prose writer of classical Greece. He wrote his *History of the Persian Wars* in Athens c. 445 BCE. He is our chief source for Median and Persian history. After completing the work, he settled as a colonist in Thurii in southern Italy, where he died and was buried.

hiphil: a Hebrew verbal conjugation that expresses causation.

historicity: the authenticity or historical nature of reported events.

humus: decomposed organic matter.

iconography: the representation of objects by means of images, drawings, paintings, sculpture, mosaics, or other techniques.

Idumea: a province established perhaps c. 400 BCE in the southern territory of the hill-country of Judah, carved out from territory that had formerly belonged to the province of Yehud. After Egypt gained its independence from Persia c. 400 BCE, the imperial court may have decided to strengthen its control over the trade routes passing through the Beersheva Valley, which now lay within a border region and so established a separate administrative unit there, whose farmsteads could supply food and supplies to local patrols.

intercalation: the addition of a day, month, or year to the calendar or more generally, the interpolation or insertion of something into a given context or document.

Iron Age: an archaeological period that spans the period from 1200–538 BCE. It is subdivided into Iron IA (1200–1150 BCE), Iron IB (1150–1000 BCE), Iron IIA (1000–900 BCE), Iron IIB (900–700 BCE), and IIC (700–586 or 538 BCE if not using IID/III), and Iron IID/Iron III (586–538 BCE).

isobar: a line drawn on a map to connect those places around the globe that experience the same barometric pressure over time and thus experience the same amount of annual rainfall.

Josephus: a Jewish politician, soldier and historian, born in 37 CE, who was captured while serving as a general of Jewish forces in Galilee in the revolt against Rome in 67 CE. Subsequently, he became a Roman citizen and lived in an apartment in the house of the emperors Vespasian, Titus, and Domitian, where he devoted his time to writing. His work, *Jewish Antiquities*, recounts Jewish history from creation to the Jewish War (67–70 CE), which he wrote to justify Jewish culture and religion to a Roman audience.

Judah: the name of a kingdom that existed from c. 975 BCE to 586 BCE, whose capital was Jerusalem.

Judahite: of or related to the kingdom of Judah, which existed from c. 975–586 BCE. The adjective is usually used to designate a citizen of this political entity.

Judean: of or related to the province of Yehud, which was established in 586 BCE by the Neo-Babylonians in the former territory of the kingdom of Judah, and which remained in place under the Persians, even after being split in two c. 400 BCE with the creation of Idumea, under the Greeks, and after a brief period as a client kingdom ruled by the Hasmoneans from 142–37 BCE, became a Roman province whose Aramaic name was replaced by its Greek equivalent, Judea. The term is frequently used to designate a citizen of the province in the Neo-Babylonian, Persian, and Greek periods (586–142 BCE).

krater: a large bowl with a foot, two handles, and a rim that curves inward that was usually used to mix wine and water.

Late Bronze Age: in archaeology, the period from 1550–1200 BCE. It is subdivided into LB I (1550–1400 BCE) and LB IIA (1400–1300 BCE) and LB IIB (1300–1200 BCE).

Latin Vulgate: the translation of the Hebrew Bible and New Testament into Latin.

lekythos: an elongated flask with a narrow opening and usually only one handle, which contained oil to be used for personal grooming.

Levant: the regions of the eastern Mediterranean including Lebanon, Syria, Jordan, and Israel.

Levite: a term designating a person who worked within the bureaucracy of ancient Judah.

locus: in archaeology, any three-dimensional feature that is uncovered in the process of excavation, such as a floor, a wall, fill, or destruction debris.

loess soil: a fine-grained, yellowish-brown, extremely fertile loam deposited by the wind.

logogram: a sign that represents a word or a syllable consisting of at least one consonant and a vowel. Sumerian and Akkadian were written using logograms rather than alphabets, whose letters represented individual sounds.

Maccabean period: the era in which the family of high priests who led a successful revolt against the Seleucid rulers of Yehud came to prominence, overthrew them, and eventually ruled as client kings over the province of Yehud. This would include the years roughly between 175 BCE, when Antiochus IV ascended the throne of the Seleucid empire, to 37 BCE, when the reign of last Hasmonean king, Matthias Antigonus, ended and the area became a Roman province As such, it is a synonym for the Hasmonean period. More narrowly, however, it could be used to represent the period from 175–152 BCE, when Judas Maccabee and his sons freed the country from Seleucid rule, before their family became client kings.

magnate: a very important or influential person in any field of activity, but especially in a large business.

magus: a priest who officiated in ancient Persian religion. According to the Greek historian Herodotus, the magi had been a Median tribe who functioned as diviners, interpreters of dreams, as well as priests who served before fire altars and poured out libations.

marl: a crumbly soil consisting mainly of clay, sand, and calcium carbonate, used as a fertilizer and in making cement or bricks.

medinah: an administrative unit used within the Persian empire, apparently to describe a province. It was a term that had been used in the Assyrian and Neo-Babylonian empires and taken over by the Persian administration for use in its western land holdings.

melek: a Hebrew term meaning 'king'.

menology: a calendar of the months, with their events.

metonym/metonymically: in literature, the use of the name of one thing in substitution for another.

Middle Bronze Age: an archaeological period dating from 2200–550 BCE, which is subdivided into MB I, also known as the Intermediate Early Bronze-Middle Bronze Age (2200–2000 BCE), MB IIA (2000–1750 BCE) and MB IIB (1750–1550 BCE).

Minean: of or relating to an ancient tribal group inhabiting Arabia.

monarchic period: the time during which Judah existed as an independent kingdom ruled by its own king, from ca 975 BCE to 586 BCE.

mortaria: a stone vessel thought to have contained oils and lotions that typically was deposited as a grave good in burials.

MT: abbreviation of 'Masoretic text', which is the traditional text of the Hebrew Bible that has been handed down within Jewish tradition. A group of scribes known as the Masoretes devised a system of points that represented vowels, which they added to the received consonantal text in order to preserve the pronunciation intact for future generations. They were active from the sixth to ninth century CE, and also wrote critical notes, counted the letters and words of the text, and discussed grammatical rules, vowels, and accents in order to guard the text against error.

Nabateans: an Arab tribal group who set up a kingdom with its capital at Petra, in modern Jordan, as early as the second century BCE; the first known Nabatean king, Aretas, was active from 170–160 BCE. They flourished in the late Hellenistic and early Roman periods (to c. 100 CE) and their territory included parts of southern

Syria, Jordan, the Negev, Sinai, the eastern desert region of Egypt and the northwest of Saudi Arabia. They ran the caravan routes that transported frankincense and myrrh from south Arabia to coastal markets.

nasi': a Hebrew word meaning 'one lifted up', used to describe various officials in the Hebrew Bible/Old Testament like a prince, a tribal chief, a ruler of the congregation, or a leader of a group.

Natufian: a culture that existed c. 10,000–8,300 BCE within the later part of Epipaleolithic or Mesolithic period (c. 18,000–8,000 BCE). It was characterized by agricultural settlements marking sedentarization, in which people used sickle blades to harvest crops, ground stone objects, and artistic objects, and buried their dead in cemeteries.

Negev: a geographical term meaning 'dry, parched' used to designate the region beginning in the Beersheva Valley and extending south, through the central highlands, to the southern desert as far as the gulf of Aqaba. The north receives 200 centimeters of rainfall annually, which is the threshold for farming dependent on rain, while the highlands receive between 75–150 centimeters and the south less than 50 centimeters of rainfall annually, making permanent habitation difficult in most of the region if there is no local spring.

Neo-Babylonian: of or relating to the Babylonian empire that rose to power at the end of the seventh century BCE after defeating the Assyrians, c. 625 BCE, and became the rulers of the ancient Near east until they were conquered by the Persians in 539 BCE.

non-*golah*: the citizens of Judah who were not forced into exile by the Neo-Babylonians in 586 BCE, who remained in the land as citizens of the province of Yehud under the Neo-Babylonians and then the Persians.

obol: a small unit of weight and denomination of silver coin equivalent to a sixth of a drachma.

ordinal: the adjectival form of numbers that designate their sequential order: first, second, third etc.

ostracon: a piece of broken pottery that has been used as a writing surface to record information. The message is written in pen and ink. The plural form is ostraca.

papponymy: the principle of naming a male child after his grandfather.

papyrus: a form of paper created by pounding together cross-layers of fibres from the stem of the papyrus plant, which grows in shallow water.

Passover: an ancient festival commemorating Israel's divine deliverance from slavery in Egypt. It was celebrated in the spring, for a week, at the time of the barley harvest.

patronymic: a phrase designating someone's origin by referring to his or her father: e.g. David son of Jesse.

pehah: an Aramaic term that was used within Persian administration to designate a range of officials, from lesser inspectors to the governor.

pelek: a Hebrew word meaning either an administrative sub-district or a mandatory tax to be fulfilled through the annual performance of physical labor on behalf of the crown.

Persian period: the time period when the kings of Persian ruled over the territory that had once been the kingdom of Judah, which became known as the province of Yehud within the Persian empire. It covers the period from 538 BCE to 332 BCE.

phase: in archaeology, a layer of occupation discerned in a given area of excavation. In final reports, the phases uncovered in various areas are collated and joined together, where possible, to create stratigraphic levels that hold across a large segment of the site.

Phoenician: of or relating to the land of Phoenicia, which was located on the coast of modern-day Lebanon. It main cities were Sidon, Tyre, Arwad, Tripoli, and Byblos. The Phoenicians were renowned ship-builders and maritime traders.

piel: in Hebrew, a verbal conjugation that intensifies the meaning of a basic verb or makes an intransitive basic verb transitive.

post-exilic period: a term that is derived from the biblical account of the history of Israel and Judah. It is used to refer to the period after which some Jews returned to Yehud, their ancestral homeland, their families having been forceably removed in 598 BCE and 586 BCE and resettled in various towns and cities in Babylonia. According to Ezra 1–6, this took place in 537 BCE. The period lasts until the destruction of the Second Temple in 70 CE by the Romans.

primogeniture: in law, the right of the eldest son to inherit his father's estate. More generally, the first-born child of two specific parents.

pristine: untouched; never used, worked, or occupied.

proleptic: anticipatory; relating to something that looks forward to later developments in the plot or the story line.

province: within an empire, a large administrative subdivision, often which had once been a independent kingdom, headed by a governor and directly regulated by the imperial court.

pseudepigraphical: written under a false name, usually the name of a well-known figure in the distant past.

qab: a unit of dry measure.

Qedar: the most powerful of group of tribes in north Arabia that is mentioned in texts from 738 to the 200s BCE.

rebellion of Inaros: a revolt in Egypt against Persian control that lasted six years, between 460–455 BCE. It was led by Inaros, son of Psammetichus, a Libyan prince, and was limited to the Delta region. Athens provided naval support, which allowed the first attempt by the Persians to quash it in 459 to be repelled at Papremis. It eventually was suppressed by the Persian general Megabyzos.

redaction: an editing process in which later generations rewrite parts of inherited texts to fit better with their contemporary circumstances or philosophies.

redactor: a person who engages in redaction.

regnal year: a year in which a king (or queen) sits on the throne and rules his (or her) realm. A king might rule twenty-two years; each of those twenty-two years is a distinct regnal year.

relay station: a small outpost that is used to transmit a fire signal received from one post on to another in a chain of such facilities.

remit: assignment, responsibility.

returnee: a term designating someone whose ancestors were exiled from Judah to Babylonia in 586 BCE and who was sent back to the province of Yehud under the Achaemenids to farm and possibly do military duty. The book of Ezra claims that there were multiple returns under Cyrus and Artaxerxes I, while the books of Haggai and Zechariah imply a return under Darius I. I argue for a single return under Artaxerxes I.

Rhodian: of or relating to the island of Rhodes or its main political entities.

ring-base: a method of forming the base of a ceramic pot by applying a ring of clay as a stabilizer.

Roman period: the era in which Yehud/Judea was a province of the Roman empire, including the years from 37 BCE–324 CE.

rosette: a stylized floral design.

2 Isaiah: chapters 40–53 of the book of Isaiah, which were written by an individual who lived in the Neo-Babylonian and early Persian periods, and whose prophecies were written soon after Cyrus conquered the Neo-Babylonian empire in 539 and made the Persians the rulers of the ancient Near East.

sar: a Hebrew term designating a range of civil and military leaders.

satrap: a governor of a Persian province.

satrapy: a Persian province.

seah: a unit of dry measure.

Septuagint: the translation of the Hebrew Bible into Greek, which tradition claims took place in Egypt during the reign of Ptolemy II Philadelphus (285–246 BCE).

Shephelah: the western foothills of Judah that lead down from the Judean highlands or hill-country to the coastal plain bordering the Mediterranean Sea.

scribal gloss: a textual addition that was deliberately introduced by a later scribe copying a manuscript to clarify, modify, or cross-reference a point.

Seleucid: relating to the portion of Alexander's empire that was ruled by Seleucus upon Alexander's death and which passed down in his family line for generations thereafter. The heart of this territory was Syria, and Yehud fell within it for a time.

sherd: a broken piece of pottery.

signet ring: a ring in which a personal seal was surrounded by a band, allowing it to be worn on a finger or strung on a cord and worn as a necklace. It could be removed and used to seal a document by being pressed into a lump of clay to form a bulla.

socle: a plain block or face of stone at the base of a wall.

square script: the style in which Hebrew came to be written that superceded the older Paleco-Hebrew letters, which is found today in scrolls used in Jewish temples.

stele: a upright stone slab or pillar engraved with an inscription or design and used as a monument or grave marker.

stratigraphic: of or relating to an occupational layer at an ancient, inhabited site, usually a tel.

stratum: an occupational layer at a ancient inhabited site, usually a tel.

Symmachus: a Jewish translator who worked either c. 150–175 CE or 225–250 CE, after both Aquila and Theodotion. His translation of the underlying Hebrew text was freer than that of Aquila, producing more flowing, idiomatic Greek. He knew and used material from the *kaige* Greek translation, like Aquila, but tended to offer translations of uncertain words, based on his best guesses, rather than simply leaving those words in Hebrew, as was done in the *kaige* version (in which the Hebrew word *gam*, 'also', was translated as *kaige*).

Syriac version: the Bible translated from its original languages of Hebrew, Aramaic and Greek into the Semitic language of Syriac for use in the Syrian orthodox church.

targum: a loose translation of the Hebrew Bible into Aramaic that was used in synagogues so that Jews, who no longer spoke Hebrew, could understand the daily portion of text. They were in use in Roman times, but may have been introduced in the Hasmonean period, when many territories were forcibly converted to Judaism whose populations could not understand Hebrew.

taxes-in-kind: taxes that are paid in agricultural and animal products rather than in money.

tel: a mound that contains within it thousands of years of occupation held in place by the encircling city walls.

telescoping: foreshortening or the collapsing down of distinctive segments or events into a single frame, often combining what were separate events into a jumbled, single event that never took place.

tendentious: biased, espousing a particular point of view over against others.

tetradrachm: an ancient Greek silver coin worth four drachms. The drachm(a) was a standard weight unit and denomination of coin whose value varied over time and region.

theocracy: a form of governance in which god is the ultimate authoriy and 'head of state'.

Theodotion: a Jewish translator from Ephesus, in Asia Minor, who worked in the mid-second century CE. He produced a Greek translation of the Hebrew Bible/Old Testament that revised the original translation into Greek, known as the Old Greek version, to reflect more closely the Hebrew form of the text that was preserved eventually by the Masoretes. It belongs to the *kaige* translation tradition, in which the Hebrew word *gam* ('also') is rendered in Greek as *kaige*. This Hebrew text differed from the one that had been known in Egypt at the time the first translation into Greek had been made. He also standardized the renderings of key Hebrew words and phrases that had been translated in more than one way in the Old Greek, and transliterated Hebrew words whose meanings were obscure or uncertain rather than speculate about possible meanings.

theophanic: relating to or describing ways in which a deity reveals or makes itself known in this world.

theophoric: having a god's name as an element. This term is usually used to describe proper names in Hebrew and other ancient Semitic languages, which often contain a verbal element and a god's name, or a god's name and an adjective.

topoi: in literature or rhetoric, stock themes, topics, or expressions. The singular form of this word is topos.

Torah: a term that means 'that which is pointed out, shown', which can refer to a single legal decision, but which frequently is used to designate the first five books in the Hebrew Bible/Old Testament (Genesis, Exodus, Leviticus, Numbers, Deuteronomy).

tuyeres: pipes through which air is forced into a blast furnace or pottery kiln to feed the flame and raise the temperature.

typology: a classification system. A pottery typology groups vessels under subheadings that represent major forms that move from being open in their interior to closed: cup, bowl, chalice, krater, cooking pot, pithos, jar, jug, juglet, decanter, pilgrim flask, pyxis, lamp. Witin these groups, styles of rims, handles, decoration, bases, and body forms change slowly over time and can be used to date the contexts in which they are found within a time frame of about 100–150 years.

Urim and Thummim: two stones carried inside a pouch worn over the chest of the main priest of Judah that he used to determine the divine will. A question was posed to the deity that had only two possible responses, often 'yes' or 'no', The priest then reached into a central pouch and pulled out one of the two stones. Whichever option it represented provided the decision of the deity on the issue under examination.

vassalship: a condition of political dependency in which two parties are of unequal power. The lesser party, the vassal, is obligated to supply the stronger party, the overlord, with tribute, gifts, and troops as needed in exchange for 'protection'. This was an arrangement that was used when one ruler or kingdom conquered another but did not want to annex the land; instead, he left the native political system intact, often even with the same dynasty in place. He was able to drain the area of its resources on a regular basis without having to assume full responsibility for its economy, mode of production, or internal regulation.

vetch: a crop plant used as animal fodder, although it is thought that its seeds could were also eaten by humans if other sources of food were not readily available.

vice-regent: a person who shares the rulership or governance of a kingdom with another.

vinedressers: people specializing in the growing of grapes to produce wine, who know how to trim the grape vines after the annual harvest to prevent disease and promote new growth in the next year.

vitrified clay: clay with a glass glaze applied to its surface.

Yahweh: the name of the Hebrew god, with vowels added. It is never written with vowels in the ancient manuscripts, only with the four consonants YHWH. Thus, this is a scholarly attempt to reproduce what is thought to be a verb form in Hebrew. In orthodox Judaism, the formal name of god is never pronounced; it is considered blasphemy.

Yahweh Sebaot: the title used of the national god of the kingdom of Judah, which was closely associated with the cultic item known as the Ark. The title usually is translated 'Lord of Hosts' in English. 'Hosts' refers to the army. The Ark was a box that probably was taken into war during the time that Judah was an independent kingdom. This title seems then to be used of the Hebrew god when his role as a war god is being emphasized.

Yahwistic: of or relating to Yahweh. When used of personal names, it would indicate that one of the elements making up the name reflected a form of the name of this god, like *yo* or *yahu*.

Yehud: the name of the province that had formerly been the kingdom of Judah until 586 BCE, when the Neo-Babylonians annexed the territory into their empire, reducing it to a province. The name is the Aramaic version of the Hebrew name, Judah; Aramaic was the official language of correspondence in the western portion of the empire. When the Persians conquered the Neo-Babylonians and became the new empire controlling the ancient Near East, they inherited Yehud and left the name intact. Under the Greeks, the name was changed to Judea, reflecting the adoption of Greek as the new official language. This is how they rendered the foreign name into Greek.

Zenon papyri: a collection of letters written on papyri that were discovered at the ancient site of Philadelphia in Egypt, at the edge of the Feinan oasis. They belonged to the archive of a treasury official named Xenon, who served under Ptolemy II Philadelphus (285–246 BCE). Their contents give us insight into conditions in Palestine at the time and commerce between that region and Egypt.

BIBLIOGRAPHY

Abel, Felix-Marie
  1967   *Géographie de la Palestine*. II. *Géographie politique: Les villes* (Etudes bibliques; Paris: J. Gabalda et Cie, 3rd edn).
Achtemeier, Elizabeth
  1986   *Nahum – Malachi* (Interpretation; Atlanta: John Knox Press).
Ackroyd, Peter R.
  1951   'Studies in the Book of Haggai', *Journal of Jewish Studies* 2: 163-76.
  1952a   'Studies in the Book of Haggai', *Journal of Jewish Studies* 3: 1-13.
  1952b   'The Book of Haggai and Zechariah I-VIII', *Journal of Jewish Studies* 3: 151-56.
  1958   'Two Old Testament Historical Problems of the Early Persian Period', *Journal of Near Eastern Studies* 17: 13-27.
  1968   *Exile and Restoration: A Study of Hebrew Thought of the Sixth Century B.C.* (London: SCM Press).
  1970   *Judah under Babylon and Persia* (Oxford: Oxford University Press).
Adler, Elkan Nathan, *et al.*
  1939   *The Adler Papyri* (London: Oxford University Press).
Aharoni, Miriam
  1993   'Arad, Tel: The Israelite Citadels', in Ephraim Stern (ed.), *The New Encyclopedia of Archaeological Excavations in the Holy Land* (Jerusalem: The Israel Exploration Society): I, 82-87.
Aharoni, Yohanan
  1964   *Excavations at Ramat Raḥel II: Seasons 1961 and 1962* (Universita di Roma – Centro di Studi Semitici; Serie Archeologica, 6; Rome: Centro di Studi Semitici).
  1973   *Beer-Sheba I, Excavations at Tel Beer-sheba, 1969–1971 Seasons* (Publications of the Institute of Archaeology 2; Tel Aviv: Tel Aviv University Institute of Archaeology).
  1979   *The Land of the Bible: A Historical Geography* (rev. and enlarged edn; trans. from Hebrew by A. Rainey; Philadelphia: Westminster Press).
  1981   *Arad Inscriptions* (ed. and rev. A. Rainey; trans. from the Hebrew by J. Ben-Or; Judean Desert Studies; Jerusalem: Israel Exploration Society).
  1993   'Ramat Rahel', in Ephraim Stern (ed.), *The New Encyclopedia of Archaeological Excavations in the Holy Land* (Jerusalem: The Israel Exploration Society): IV, 1261-67.
Ahlström, Gösta W.
  1993   *The History of Palestine from the Palaeolithic Period to Alexander's Conquest* (*Journal for the Study of the Old Testament*, Supplement Series, 146; Sheffield: Sheffield Academic Press).
Albright, William Foxwell
  1925   'The Conquests of Nabonidus in Arabia', *Journal of the Royal Asiatic Society* 61: 293-95.
  1941   'Ostracon No. 6043 from Ezion-Geber', *Bulletin of the American Schools of Oriental Research* 82: 11-15.
Allen, Leslie C.
  1976   *The Books of Joel, Obadiah, Jonah and Micah* (New International Commentary on the Old Testament; London: Hodder & Stoughton).
Allrik, H.L.
  1954   'The Lists of Zerubbabel (Nehemiah 7 and Ezra 2) and the Hebrew Numerical Notation', *Bulletin of the American Schools of Oriental Research* 136: 21-27.
Alon, David
  1983   'Nahal Yattir', *Excavations and Surveys in Israel* 2: 79-81.

Alt, Albrecht

1925   'Judas Gaue unter Josiah', *Palästinajahrbuch* 21: 100-17.

1953a   'Die territorialgeschichtliche Bedeutung von Sanheribs Eingriff in Palästina', in *Kleine Schriften zur Geschichte des Volkes Israel* (Munich: Beck): II, 242-49.

1953b   'Judas Nachbarn zur Zeit Nehemia', in *Kleine Schriften zur Geschichte des Volkes Israel* (Munich: Beck): II, 338-45.

Amusin, Joseph D., and Michael L. Heltzer

1964   'The Inscription from Meṣad Ḥashavyahu: Complaint of a Reaper of the Seventh Century B.C.', *Israel Exploration Journal* 14: 148-57.

Auberger, Janick

1991   *Ctésias: Histoires de l'Orient* (La roue à livres; Paris: Les belles lettres).

Auerbauch, Elias

1952   'Die babylonische Datierung im Pentateuch und das Alter des Priesterkodex', *Vetus Testamentum* 2: 334-42.

Avalos, Hector

1992   'Sepharad', in David Noel Freedman (ed.), *The Anchor Bible Dictionary* (New York: Doubleday): V, 1089-90.

Avigad, Nahman

1958   'New Light on the MṢH Seal Impressions', *Israel Exploration Journal* 8: 113-19.

1976   *Bullae and Seals from a Post-Exilic Judean Archive* (Qedem, 4; Jerusalem: Institute of Archaeology, Hebrew University of Jerusalem).

1997   *Corpus of West Semitic Stamp Seals* (rev. and completed by B. Sass; Jerusalem: Israel Academy of Sciences and Humanities, Israel Exploration Society, and Institute of Archaeology, University of Jerusalem).

Avi-Yonah, Michael

1966   *The Holy Land: From the Persian to the Arab Conquests (536 B.C. to A.D. 640)* (Grand Rapids, MI: Baker Book House).

Babelon, Ernest

1910a   *Traité des monnaies grecques et romaines. Deuxième partie; description historique. Tome deuxième* (Paris: Ernest Leroux).

1910b   *Traité des monnaies grecques et romaine. Troisième partie, album des planches. Planches LXXXVI à CLXXXV* (Paris: Ernest Leroux).

Baldwin, Joyce E.

1974   *Haggai, Zechariah, Malachi: An Introduction and Commentary* (Tyndale Old Testament Commentaries; London: Tyndale Press).

Banning, Edward B.

2002   *Archaeological Survey* (Manuals in Archaeological Method, Theory, and Technique; London: Kluwer Academic/Plenum Publishers).

Barag, Dan P.

1966   'The Effects of the Tennes Rebellion on Palestine', *Bulletin of the American Schools of Oriental Research* 183: 6-12.

1985   'Some Notes on Silver Coins of Johanan the High Priest', *Biblical Archaeologist* 48: 166-68.

Barstad, Hans

1996   *The Myth of the Empty Land: A Study in the History and Archaeology of Judah during the 'Exilic' Period* (Symbolae Osloenses fasc. Supplet, 28; Oslo: Scandinavian Press).

Barthélemy, Dominique

1992   *Critique textuelle de l'Ancien Testament. III. Ézéchiel, Daniel et les 12 Prophètes* (Orbis biblicus et orientalis, 50.3; Fribourg: Editions Universitaires).

Bartlett, John R.

1982   'Edom and the Fall of Jerusalem, 587 BCE', *Palestine Exploration Quarterly* 114: 13-24.

1989   *Edom and the Edomites* (Journal for the Study of the Old Testament, Supplement Series, 77; Sheffield: Sheffield Academic Press).

Baruch, Yuval, and Ibrahim Srukh
2001   'Khirbet Kabbar', *Excavations and Surveys in Israel* 113: 97*-98*.

Batten, Loring W.
1913   *A Critical and Exegetical Commentary on the Books of Ezra and Nehemiah* (International Critical Commentary; Edinburgh: T. & T. Clark).

Batz, Shahar
2003   'Meẓadot Yehuda B', *Excavations and Surveys in Israel* 115: 62*.

Beaulieu, Paul-Alain
1989   *The Reign of Nabonidus King of Babylon 556–539 B.C.* (Yale Near Eastern Researches, 10; New Haven: Yale University Press).

Beck, Pirhiya
1995   'Catalogue of Cult Objects and Study of the Iconography', in Itzhaq Beit-Arieh (ed.), *Horvat Qitmit: An Edomite Shrine in the Biblical Negev* (Sonia and Marco Nadler Institute of Archaeology Monograph Series, 11; Tel Aviv: Tel Aviv University): 27-197.
1996   'Horvat Qitmit Revisited via 'En Ḥaṣeva', *Tel Aviv* 23: 102-114.

Bedford, Peter R.
2001   *Temple Restoration in Early Achaemenid Judah* (Supplements to the *Journal for the Study of Judaism*, 65; Leiden: E.J. Brill).

Beit Arieh, Itzhaq
1993a   'Radum, Horvat', in Ephraim Stern (ed.), *The New Encyclopedia of Archaeological Excavations in the Holy Land* (Jerusalem: The Israel Exploration Society): IV, 1254-255.
1993b   ''Uza, Horvat', in Ephraim Stern (ed.), *The New Encyclopedia of Archaeological Excavations in the Holy Land* (Jerusalem: The Israel Exploration Society): IV, 1495-97.
1995a   'The Edomites in Cisjordan', in Diana V. Edelman (ed.), *You Shall not Abhor an Edomite for He is your Brother: Edom and Seir in History and Tradition* (Archaeology and Biblical Studies, 3; Atlanta: Scholars Press): 33-40.
1995b   *Horvat Qitmit: An Edomite Shrine in the Biblical Negev* (Sonia and Marco Nadler Institute of Archaeology Monograph Series, 11; Tel Aviv: Tel Aviv University).
1999   'Stratigraphy and Historical Background', in Itzhaq Beit Arieh (ed.), *Tel 'Ira: A Stronghold in the Biblical Negev* (Sonia and Marco Nadler Institute of Archaeology Monograph Series, 15; Tel Aviv: Emery and Claire Yass Publications in Archaeology of the Institute of Archaeology, Tel Aviv University): 170-80.

Beit Arieh, Itzhaq, and Bruce Cresson
1985   'An Edomite Ostracon from Horvat 'Uza', *Tel Aviv* 12: 96-101.
1991   'Horvat 'Uza: A Fortified Outpost on the Eastern Negev Border', *Biblical Archaeologist* 54: 126-35.

Bennett, Crystal M.
1983   'Excavations at Buseirah (Biblical Bozrah)', in John F.A. Sawyer and David J.A. Clines (eds.), *Midian, Moab and Edom: The History and Archaeology of Late Bronze and Iron Ages Jordan and North-West Arabia* (*Journal for the Study of the Old Testament*, Supplement Series, 24; Sheffield: JSOT Press): 9-17.

Bennett, W.J., and Jeffrey A. Blakely
1989   *Tell el-Hesi: The Persian Period (Stratum V)* (American Schools of Oriental Research Excavation Reports; The Joint Archaeological Expedition to Tell el-Hesi, 3; Winona Lake, IN: Eisenbrauns).

Bentzen, Aage
1930   'Quelques remarques sur le mouvement messianique parmis les Juifs aux environs de l'an 520 avant Jésus-Christ', *Revue de l'histoire et de philosophie religieuse* 10: 493-503.

Ben Zvi, Ehud
1996   *A Historical-Critical Study of the Book of Obadiah* (Beihefte zur Zeitschrift für die alttestamentliche Wissenschaft, 242; Berlin: W. de Gruyter).

Berlin, Adele
1983   *The Poetics and Interpretation of Biblical Narrative* (Bible and Literature Series, 9; Sheffield: Almond Press).

Berquist, Jon L.
    1995   *Judaism in Persia's Shadow: A Social and Historical Approach* (Minneapolis: Fortress Press).

Betlyon, John Wilson
    1982   *The Coinage and Mints of Phoenicia: The Pre-Alexandrine Period* (Harvard Semitic Monographs, 26; Chico, CA: Scholars Press).
    1986   'The Provincial Government of Persian Period Judea and the Yehud Coins', *Journal of Biblical Literature* 105: 633-42.

Beuken, Wim A.M.
    1967   *Haggai-Sacharja 1–8: Studien zur Überlieferungsgeschichte der Frühnach-exilischen Prophetie* (Studia Semitica Neerlandica, 10; Assen: Van Gorcum).

Bewer, Julius A.
    1911   *A Critical and Exegetical Commentary on Micah, Zephaniah, Nahum, Habakkuk, Obadiah and Joel* (International Critical Commentary; Edinburgh: T. &. T. Clark).
    1919   'Ancient Babylonian Parallels to the Prophecies of Haggai', *The American Journal of Semitic Languages and Literatures* 35: 128-33.
    1922   *Der Text des Buches Ezra: Beiträge zu seiner Wiederherstellung* (Forschungen zur Religion und Literatur des Alten und Neuen Testaments Neue Folge, 14; Göttingen: Vandenhoeck & Ruprecht).

Bickerman, Elias J.
    1946   'The Edict of Cyrus in Ezra 1', *Journal of Biblical Literature* 65: 247-57.
    1968   *Chronology of the Ancient World* (Aspects of Greek and Roman Life; London: Thames & Hudson).
    1981   'En marge de l'écriture', *Revue biblique* 88: 19-41.

Bienkowski, Piotr
    1995   'The Edomites: The Archaeological Evidence from Transjordan', in Diana V. Edelman (ed.), *You Shall not Abhor an Edomite for He is your Brother: Edom and Seir in History and Tradition* (Archaeology and Biblical Studies, 3; Atlanta: Scholars Press): 41-92.
    2001   'The Persian Period', in Burton MacDonald, Russell Adams and Piotr Bienkowski (eds.), *The Archaeology of Jordan* (Levantine Archaeology, 1; Sheffield: Sheffield Academic Press): 347-65.
    2002   *Busayra Excavations by Crystal M. Bennett 1971–1980* (British Academy Monographs in Archaeology, 13; Oxford: Oxford University Press for the Council for British Research in the Levant).

Bienkowski, Piotr, and Eveline van der Steen
    2001   'Tribes, Trade, and Towns: A New Framework for the Late Iron Age in Southern Jordan and the Negev', *Bulletin of the American Schools of Oriental Research* 323: 21-47.

Bimson, John J., and D. Livingston
    1987   'Redating the Exodus', *Biblical Archaeology Review* 13.5: 40-53.

Biran, Avraham
    1983   'Ras el-Kharrube (Anathoth)', *Excavations and Surveys of Israel* 2: 89.
    1993   'Aroer (in Judea)', in Ephraim Stern (ed.), *The New Encyclopedia of Archaeological Excavations in the Holy Land* (Jerusalem: The Israel Exploration Society): I, 89-92.

Biran, Avraham, and Rudolph Cohen
    1979   'Notes and News. Tel 'Ira', *Israel Exploration Journal* 29: 124-25.

Blenkinsopp, Joseph
    1988   *Ezra-Nehemiah: A Commentary* (Old Testament Library; Philadelphia: Westminster Press).
    1994   'Judaean Priesthood during the Neo-Babylonian and Achaemenid Periods: A Hypothetical Reconstruction', *Catholic Biblical Quarterly* 60: 25-43.

Bloomhardt, Paul F.
    1928   'The Poems of Haggai', *Hebrew Union College Annual* 5: 153-95.

Bodi, Daniel
    2001   'Le prophète critique la monarchie: le terme nasi' chez Ezéchiel', in André Lemaire (ed.), *Prophètes et rois: Bible et Proche-Orient* (Lectio divina hors série; Paris: Editions du Cerf): 249-57.

Borger, Riekele
    1956   *Die Inschriften Asarhaddons Königs von Assyrien* (Archiv für Orientforschung Beiheft, 9; Osnabrück: Biblio-Verlag).

Borowski, Oded
    2002   *Agriculture in Iron Age Israel* (Boston: American Schools of Oriental Research).
Bresciani, Edda
    1960   'Papiri aramaInternational Critical Commentaryi egiziani di epoca persiana presso il Museo Civico di
               Padova', *Rivista degli studi orientali* 35: 11-24.
Briant, Pierre
    1978/79 'Contrainte militaire, dependence rurale et exploitation des territoires en Asie achéménide', *Index* 8:
               175-225.
    1981   'Appareils d'état et developpement des forces productives au Moyen-Orient ancien: le cas de l'empire
               achéménide', *La pensée* 217/218 (Janvier-Fevrier): 9-23.
    2002   *From Cyrus to Alexander: A History of the Persian Empire* (trans. from French by P. Daniels; Winona
               Lake, IN: Eisenbrauns).
Brockelmann, Carl
    1908   *Grundriss der vergleichenden Grammatik der semitischen Sprache. I. Laut-und Formenlehre* (Berlin:
               Reuther & Reichard).
Brockington, Leonard H.
    1969   *Ezra, Nehemiah and Esther* (New Century Bible; London: Thomas Nelson).
Browne, Laurence E.
    1916   'A Jewish Sanctuary in Babylonia', *Journal of Theological Studies* 17: 400-401.
    1952   *Ezekiel and Alexander* (London: SPCK).
Bunimovtiz, Shlomo, and Zvi Lederman
    2003   'The Final Destruction of Beth Shemesh and the *Pax Assyriaca* in the Judean Shephelah', *Tel Aviv* 30:
               3-26.
Burrows, Milton
    1933–34 'Nehemiah 3:1-32 as a Source for the Topography of Ancient Jerusalem', *Annual of the American
               Schools of Oriental Research* 14: 115-40.
Busink, Th.A.
    1980   *Der Tempel von Jerusalem von Salomo bis Herodotus: eine archäologisch-historische Studie unter
               Berücksichtigung des westsemitischen Tempelbaus. II. Von Ezechiel bis Middot* (Studia Francisci Schol-
               ten memoriae dicata, 3; Leiden: E.J. Brill).
Byrne, Ryan
    2003   'Early Assyrian Contacts with Arabs and the Impact on Levantine Vassal Trade', *Bulletin of the Ameri-
               can Schools of Oriental Research* 331: 11-25.
Cahill, Jane M.
    1999   'Rosette Stamp Seal Impressions', in Itzhaq Beit Arieh (eds.), *Tel 'Ira: A Stronghold in the Biblical
               Negev* (Sonia and Marco Nadler Institute of Archaeology Monograph Series, 15; Tel Aviv: Emery and
               Claire Yass Publications in Archaeology of the Institute of Archaeology, Tel Aviv University): 360-73.
Callaway, Joseph A.
    1993   'Ai', in Ephraim Stern (ed.), *The New Encyclopedia of Archaeological Excavations in the Holy Land*
               (Jerusalem: The Israel Exploration Society): I, 39-45.
Cameron, George C.
    1941   'Darius and Xerxes in Babylonia', *The American Journal of Semitic Languages and Literatures* 58: 314-
               25.
Caquot, André
    1964   'Le Messianisme d'Ezéchiel', *Semitica* 14: 5-23.
Carradice, Ian
    1987   'The "Regal" Coinage of the Persian Empire', in *idem* (ed.), *Coinage and Administration in the
               Athenian and Persian Empires: The Ninth Oxford Symposium on Coinage and Monetary History* (BAR
               International Series, 343; Oxford: B.A.R.): 73-93.
Carroll, Robert P.
    1994   'So What Do We *Know* about the Temple? The Temple in the Prophets', in Tamara C. Eskenazi and
               Kent H. Richards (eds.), *Second Temple Studies 2: Temple Community in the Persian Period* (*Journal
               for the Study of the Old Testament*, Supplement Series, 175; Sheffield: Sheffield Academic Press): 34-51.

Carter, Charles E.
  1999   *The Emergence of Yehud in the Persian Period: A Social and Demographic Study* (*Journal for the Study of the Old Testament*, Supplement Series, 297; Sheffield: Sheffield Academic Press).

Caskel, Werner
  1954   *Lihyan und Lihyanisch* (Arbeitsgemeinschaft für Forschung des Landes Nordrhein – Westfalen; Geisteswissenschaften, 4; Köln: Westdeutscher Verlag).

Charles, Michael P.
  1985   'An Introduction to the Legumes and Oil Plants of Mesopotamia', *Bulletin on Sumerian Agriculture* 2: 39-61.

Chary, Theophane
  1969   *Aggée-Zacharie Malachie* (Source bibliques; Paris: J. Gabalda).

Christaller, Walter
  1966   *Central Places in Southern Germany* (trans. from German by Carlisle W. Baskin; Englewood Cliffs, NJ: Prentice-Hall).

Clark, David
  1983   'Problems in Haggai 2.15-19', *Bible Translator* 34: 432-39.

Clines, David J.A.
  1974   'The Evidence for an Autumnal New Year in Pre-exilic Israel', *Journal of Biblical Literature* 73: 22-40.
  1984   *Ezra, Nehemiah, Esther* (New Century Bible Commentary; London: Marshall, Morgan & Scott).
  1994   'Haggai's Temple Constructed, Deconstructed and Reconstructed', in Tamara C. Eskenazi and Kent H. Richards (eds.), *Second Temple Studies 2: Temple Community in the Persian Period* (*Journal for the Study of the Old Testament*, Supplement Series, 175; Sheffield: Sheffield Academic Press): 60-87.

Coacci Polselli, Gianna
  1984   'Nouvo luce sulla datazione dei re Sidoni?', *Rivista di Studi Fenici* 12: 169-73.

Coggins, Richard James
  1976   *The Books of Ezra and Nehemiah* (Cambridge Bible Commentary; Cambridge: Cambridge University Press).

Cohen, Abraham
  1948   *The Twelve Prophets: Hebrew Text, English Translation and Commentary* (Soncino Books of the Bible; Bournemouth: Soncino Press).

Cohen, Rudolph
  1981   *Archaeological Survey of Israel Map of Sede-Boqer-East (168) 13-03* (Jerusalem: The Archaeological Survey of Israel).
  1983   'Excavations at Kadesh-Barnea', *Qadmoniot* 16.1: 2-14.
  1985   *Archaeological Survey of Israel Map of Sede-Boqer-West (167) 12-03* (Jerusalem: Department of Antiquities and Museums, Archaeological Survey of Israel).
  1986a   'Notes and News: Meṣad Naḥal Haro'a', *Israel Exploration Journal* 36: 112-13.
  1986b   'Notes and News: Horvat Mesora', *Israel Exploration Journal* 36: 113.
  1993   'Kadesh Barnea. The Israelite Fortress', in Ephraim Stern (ed.), *The New Encyclopedia of Archaeological Excavations in the Holy Land* (Jerusalem: Israel Exploration Society): III, 843-47.
  1994   'The Fortresses at 'En Haseva', *Biblical Archaeologist* 57: 203-14.

Cohen, Rudolph, and Yigal Yisrael
  1995   'The Iron Age Fortresses at 'En Haseva', *Biblical Archaeologist* 58: 223-35.

Collins, James M., and Brian Leigh Molyneaux
  2003   *Archaeological Survey* (Archaeologist's Toolkit, 2; Oxford: Altamira Press).

Conrad, Edward T.
  1999   *Zechariah* (Readings; Sheffield: Sheffield Academic Press).

Cowley, Arthur E.
  1917   'The Meaning of Mqwm in Hebrew', *Journal of Theological Studies* 17: 174-76.
  1923   *Aramaic Papyri of the Fifth Century B.C.* (Oxford: Clarendon Press).

Craigie, Peter
  1982   'Amos the *noqed* in the Light of Ugaritic', *Studies in Religion* 11: 29-35.

Cross, Frank Moore, Jr

1962   'Epigraphic Notes on Hebrew Documents of the Eighth-Sixth Centuries B.C.: II. The Murabba'ât Papyrus and the Letter Found near Yabneh-Yam', *Bulletin of the American Schools of Oriental Research* 165: 34-46.

1963   'The Discovery of the Samaria Papyri', *The Biblical Archaeologist* 26.4: 111-21.

1966   'An Aramaic Inscription from Daskyleion', *Bulletin of the American Schools of Oriental Research* 184: 7-10.

1969   'Judean Stamps', *Eretz Israel* 9 (1969): 19-27.

1974   'The Papyri and their Historical Implications', in P.W. Lapp and N.L. Lapp (eds.), *Discoveries in the Wâdi ed-Dâliyeh* (Annual of the American Schools of Oriental Research, 41; Cambridge, MA: ASOR): 17-29.

1975   'A Reconstruction of the Judean Restoration', *Journal of Biblical Literature* 94: 4-18.

2003   'Inscriptions from Tel Sera', in *Leaves from an Epigrapher's Notebook: Collected Papers in Hebrew and West Semitic Paleography and Epigraphy* (Harvard Semitic Studies, 51; Winona Lake, IN: Eisenbrauns): 155-63.

Dadon, Michael

1994   'Har Adar', *Excavations and Surveys in Israel* 14: 87-88.

Dagan, Yehuda

1992   *Israel Antiquities Authority Archaeological Survey of Israel Map of Lakhish (98)* (Jerusalem: Israel Antiquities Authority).

2000   'The Settlement in the Judean Shephela in the Second and First Millennium B.C.: A Test-Case of Settlement Processes in a Geographic Region' (PhD thesis, Tel Aviv University).

2002   'Survey of the Tel Zafit Region', *Excavations and Surveys of Israel* 114: 83*-85*.

Dalley, Stephanie

2003   'The Transition from Neo-Assyrians to Neo-Babylonians: Break or Continuity?', *Eretz Israel* 27: 25*-28*.

Dalley, Stephanie and Anne Goguel

1997   'The Sela' Sculpture: A Neo-Babylonian Rock Relief in Southern Jordan', *Annual of the Department of Antiquities of Jordan* 41: 169-76.

Dalley, Stephanie, and J. Nicholas Postgate

1984   *Tablets from Fort Shalmaneser* (Cuneiform Texts from Nimrud, 3; Oxford: British School of Archaeology in Iraq).

Dandamaev, Muhammad A.

1994   'Achaemenid Mesopotamia', in Heleen Sancisi-Weerdenburg, Amélie Kuhrt and Margaret Cool Root (eds.), *Achaemenid History VIII: Continuity and Change: Proceedings of the Last Achaemenid History Workshop April 6–8, 1990 (Ann Arbor, Michigan)* (Leiden: Nederlands Instituut voor het Nabije Oosten), pp. 229-34.

Dandamaev, Muhammad A., and V.L. Lukonin

1989   *The Culture and Social Institutions of Ancient Iran* (trans. from Russian by Philip L. Kohl and D.J. Dadson; Cambridge: Cambridge University Press).

Davies, Graham I.

1991   *Ancient Hebrew Inscriptions: Corpus and Concordance* (Cambridge: Cambridge University).

Davies, Philip R.

1992   *In Search of 'Ancient Israel'* (*Journal for the Study of the Old Testament*, Supplement Series, 148; Sheffield: Sheffield Academic Press).

Davison, John Armstrong

1947   'The First Greek Triremes', *Classical Quarterly* 41: 18-24.

Deissler, Alfons

1984   *Zwölf Propheten II: Obadja, Jona, Micha, Nahum, Habakuk* (Die neue Echter Bibel, Altes Testament; Würzburg: Echter).

Delitzsch, Friedrich

1907   *Vorderasiatische Schriftdenkmäler der königlichen Museen zu Berlin, Heft III* (Leipzig: J.C. Hinrichs).

Demsky, Aaron
    1983   'Pelekh in Nehemiah 3', *Israel Exploration Journal* 33: 242-44.

Depuydt, Leo
    1995   'Evidence for Accession Dating under the Achaemenids', *Journal of the American Oriental Society* 115: 193-204.

Dequeker, Luc
    1993   'Darius the Persian and the Reconstruction of the Jewish Temple in Jerusalem (Ezra 4,24)', in J. Quaegebeur (ed.), *Ritual and Sacrifice in the Ancient Near East* (Orientalia Lovaniensia Analecta, 55; Leuven: Peeters): 67-92.

Deutsch, Robert
    1999   *Messages from the Past: Hebrew Bullae from the Time of Isaiah through the Destruction of the First Temple* (Tel Aviv: Archaeological Center Publication).
    2003   *Biblical Period Hebrew Bullae: The Joseph Chaim Kaufman Collection* (Tel Aviv: Archaeological Center Publication).

Deutsch, Robert, and Michael Heltzer
    1994   *Forty New Ancient West Semitic Inscriptions* (Tel Aviv: Archaeological Center Publication).

Dicou, Bert
    1994   *Edom, Israel's Brother and Antagonist: The Role of Edom in Biblical Prophecy and Story* (*Journal for the Study of the Old Testament*, Supplement Series, 169; Sheffield. Sheffield Academic Press).

Diebner, Bernd, and Hermann Schult
    1975   'Edom in alttestamentlichen Texten der Makkabäerzeit. Otto Plöger in Dankbarkeit gewidmet', *Dielheimer Blätter zum Alten Testament* 8: 11-17.

Dinur, Uri
    1987/88 'Jerusalem Region, Survey of Map 102', *Excavations and Surveys in Israel* 6: 62-65.

Divito, Robert A.
    1993   'The Tell el-Kehleifeh Inscriptions', in Gary D. Pratico (ed.), *Nelson Glueck's 1938–1940 Excavations at Tell el-Kheleifeh: A Reappraisal* (American Schools of Oriental Research Archaeological Reports, 3; Atlanta: Scholars Press): 51-63.

Dorsey, David A.
    1991   *The Roads and Highways of Ancient Israel* (London: The Johns Hopkins University Press).

Dozeman, Thomas B.
    2003   'Geography and History in Herodotus and in Ezra-Nehemiah', *Journal of Biblical Literature* 122: 449-66.

Dressel, Heinrich
    1904   'Erwebungen des Königlichen Münzcabinets in den Jahren 1898–1900 (Antike Münzen) (Tafel I-IV)', *Zeitschrift für Numismatik* 24: 17-104.

Driver, Godfrey Rolles
    1931   'Studies in the Vocabulary of the Old Testament, III', *Journal of Theological Studies* 32: 361-66.

Driver, Samuel Rolles
    1906   *The Minor Prophets. II. Nahum, Habakkuk, Zephaniah, Haggai, Zechariah, Malachi* (The New Century Bible; Edinburgh: T.C. & E.C. Jack).

Duhm, Bernhard
    1911   'Anmerkungen zu den Zwölf Propheten. VIII Buch Obadja', *Zeitschrift für die alttestamentliche Wissenschaft* 31: 175-78.

Dumbrell, William J.
    1971   'The Tell el-Mashkuta Bowls and the "Kingdom" of Qedar in the Persian Period', *Bulletin of the American Schools of Oriental Research* 203: 33-44.

Dunand, Maurice
    1975-1976 'Les rois de Sidon au temps des Perses', *Mélanges de l'université Saint- Joseph* 49: 491-99.

Dupont-Sommer, André
    1944   ' "Bêl et Nabû, Samas et Nergal" sur un ostracon araméen inédit d'Eléphantine', *Revue de l'histoire des religions* 128: 28-39.

1966   'Une inscription araméene inédite d'époque perse trouvée à Daskyléion (Turquie)', *Comptes Rendus de l'Académie des Inscriptions et Belles Lettres*: 44-57.

Eames, Samantha
2003   'Between "The Desert and the Sown": The Hauran as a Frontier Zone in the Middle Bronze Age', *Palestine Exploration Quarterly* 135: 88-107.

Ebeling, Erich
1920   *Keilschrifttexte aus Assur religiösen Inhalts. Fünftes Heft (zweiter Band, 1. Heft)* (Wissenschaftliche Veröffentlichung der Deutschen Orient-Gesellschaft, 34.1; Leipzig: J.C. Hinrichs).

Edelman, Diana
1995a   'Introduction', in Diana V. Edelman (ed.), *The Triumph of Elohim: From Yahwisms to Judaisms* (Contributions to Biblical Exegesis & Theology, 13; Kampen: Kok Pharos): 14-25.
1995b   'Tracking Observance of the Aniconic Tradition through Numismatics', in Diana V. Edelman (ed.), *The Triumph of Elohim: From Yahwisms to Judaisms* (Contributions to Biblical Exegesis & Theology, 13; Kampen: Kok Pharos): 185-225.
2001   'Did Saulide-Davidic Rivalry Resurface in the Early Persian Period?', in J. Andrew Dearman and M. Patrick Arnold (eds.), *The Land That I Will Show You: Essays on the History and Archaeology of the Ancient Near East in Honor of J. Maxwell Miller* (Journal for the Study of the Old Testament, Supplement Series, 343; Sheffield: Sheffield Academic Press): 69-91.
2003a   'Gibeon and the Gibeonites Revisited', in Oded Lipschits and Joseph Blenkinsopp (eds.), *Judah and Judeans in the Neo-Babylonian Period* (Winona Lake, IN: Eisenbrauns): 153-67.
2003b   'Proving Yahweh Killed his Wife', *Biblical Interpretation* 11: 335-44.
2004   'The Meaning and Function of the *m(w)sh*-Stamped Jar Handles', in Aren M. Meir and Pierre de Miroschedji (eds.), *'I Will Speak the Riddles of Ancient Times' (Ps 78:2b): Archaeological and Historical Studies in Honor of Amihai Mazar on the Occasion of his Sixtieth Birthday* (Winona Lake, IN: Eisenbrauns).
2005a   'Tyrian Trade in Yehud under Artaxerxes I: Real or Fictional? Independent or Crown-Endorsed?', in Oded Lipschits and Manfred Oeming (eds.), *Judah and the Judeans in the Persian Period* (Winona Lake, IN: Esienbrauns).
2005b   'The "Empty Land" as a Lamentations Motif', in George Brooke and T. Römer (eds.), *Ancient and Modern Scriptural Historiography* (Bibliotheca ephemeridum theologicarum lovaniensium; Leuven: Peeters).
2005c   'Were Zerubbabel and Nehemiah the Same Person?', in Duncan Burns (ed.), *Festschrift for Philip Davies* (Journal for the Study of the Old Testament, Supplement Series; London: T&T Clark).

Edgar, Campbell C.
1919a   'Selected Papyri from the Archives of Zenon (Nos. 1-10)', *Annales du Service des antiquités de l'Egypte* 18: 159-82.
1919b   'Selected Papyri from the Archives of Zenon (Nos. 11-21)', *Annales du Service des antiquités de l'Egypte* 18: 225-44.
1931   *Zenon Papyri in the University of Michigan Collection* (University of Michigan Studies, Humanistic Series, 24; Ann Arbor: University of Michigan Press).

Eilers, Wilhelm
1940   *Iranische Beamtennamen in der keilschriftlichen Überlieferung* (Abhandlungen für die Kunde des Morgenlandes, 25.5; Leipzig: Deutsche Morgenländische Gegesellschaft).

Elayi, Josette
1990   *Sidon, cité autonome de l'empire perse* (Paris: editions Idéaphane, 2nd edn).
1992   'Le phénomène monétaire dans les cités phéniciennes à l'époque perse', in Tony Hackens and Ghislaine Moucharte (eds.), *Studia Phoenicia IX: Numismatique et histoire économique phéniciennes et puniques* (Publications d'histoire et de l'art et d'archéologie de l'Université Catholique de Louvain, 58; Louvain-la-neuve: Séminaire de numismatique Marcel Hoc; Université Catholique de Louvain): 21-31.
1994   'Recensions. H.T. Wallinga, *Ships and Sea Power before the Great Persian War: The Ancestry of the Ancient Trireme*'. *Transeuphratène* 8: 177-80.

Elayi, Josette, and A.G. Elayi
1993   *Trésors de monnaies phéniciennes et circulation monetaire (Ve-IVe siècles avant J.-C.)* (Supplements à *Transeuphratène*, 1; Paris: Gabalda).

Ellis, Richard S.
1968   *Foundation Deposits in Ancient Mesopotamia* (Yale Near Eastern Researches, 2; New Haven: Yale University Press).

Eph'al, Israel
1982   *The Ancient Arabs: Nomads on the Borders of the Fertile Crescent, 9th-5th Centuries B.C.* (Jerusalem: Magnes Press).
1998   'Changes in Palestine during the Persian Period in Light of Epigraphic Sources', *Israel Exploration Journal* 48: 106-19.

Eph'al, Israel, and Joseph Naveh
1996   *Aramaic Ostraca of the Fourth Century BC from Idumaea* (Jerusalem: Israel Exploration Society).

Eshel, Hanan
1996   'Document 14 of Wadi Daliyeh and the Temple in the City of Samaria', *Sion* 61: 359-65 (Hebrew).

Eskenazi, Tamara Cohn
1988   *In an Age of Prose: A Literary Approach to Ezra-Nehemiah* (Society of Biblical Literature Monograph Series, 36; Atlanta: Scholars Press).
1992   'Tobiah', in D.N. Freedman (ed.), *The Anchor Bible Dictionary* (New York: Doubelday): VI, 584-85.

Evans, Carl D.
1980   'Judah's Foreign Policy from Hezekiah to Josiah', in Carl D. Evans, William W. Hallo and John B. White (eds.), *Scripture in Context: Essays on the Comparative Method* (Pittsburgh Theological Monograph Series, 34; Pittsburgh: The Pickwick Press): 157-78.

Eybers, Ian H.
1975   'The Rebuilding of the Temple according to Haggai and Zechariah', in W.C. van Wyk (ed.), *Studies in Old Testament Prophecy. Papers Read at the Thirteenth and Fourteenth Meetings of die Ou-Testamentiese Werkgemeenskap in Suid-Afrika 1970–1971* (Potchefstroom: Potchefstroom Herald): 15-26.

Fantalkin, Alexander, and Oren Tal
2005   'Re-Dating Lakhish Level I: Identifying Achaemenid Imperial Policy at the Southern Frontier of the Fifth Satrapy', in Oded Lipschits and Manfred Oeming (eds.), *Judah and Judeans in the Early Persian Period* (Winona Lake, IN: Eisenbrauns), forthcoming.

Fargo, Valerie M.
1993   'Hesi, Tell el-', in Ephraim Stern (eds.), *The New Encyclopedia of Archaeological Excavations in the Holy Land* (Jerusalem: The Israel Exploration Society): II, 630-34.

Feigin, Samuel
1926   'Etymological Notes', *American Journal of Semitic Languages* 43: 53-60.

Fensham, F. Charles
1982   *The Books of Ezra and Nehemiah* (New International Commentary on the Old Testament; Grand Rapids, MI: Eerdmans).

Finkelstein, Israel
1992   'Horvat Qitmit and the Southern Trade in the Late Iron Age II', *Zeitschrift des Deutschen Palästina Vereins* 108: 156-70.
1994   'The Archaeology of the Days of Manasseh', in Michael D. Coogan, J. Cheryl Exum and Lawrence E Stager (eds.), *Scripture and Other Artifacts: Essays on the Bible and Archaeology in Honor of Philip J. King* (Louisville: Westminster John Knox Press): 169-187.
1995   *Living on the Fringe: The Archaeology and History of the Negev, Sinai and Neighboring Regions in the Bronze and Iron Ages* (Monographs in Mediterranean Archaeology, 6; Sheffield: Sheffield Academic Press).
1997   'Pots and People Revisited: Ethnic Boundaries in the Iron Age I', in N.A. Silberman and D.B. Small (eds.), *The Archaeology of Israel: Constructing the Past, Interpreting the Present* (*Journal for the Study of the Old Testament*, Supplement Series, 237; Sheffield: Sheffield Academic Press): 216-37.

Finkelstein, Israel, and Yitzhak Magen
1993   *Archaeological Survey of the Hill Country of Benjamin* (Jerusalem: Israel Antiquities Authority).

Finkelstein, Israel, Zvi Lederman and Shlomo Bunimovitz
1997   *Highlands of Many Cultures: The Southern Samaria Survey. The Sites,* I (Sonia and Marco Nadelman

Institute of Archaeology Monograph Series, 14; Tel Aviv: Monograph Series of the Institute of Archaeology).

Fishbane, Michael
1980 'Revelation and Tradition: Aspects of Inner-biblical Exegesis', *Journal of Biblical Literature* 99: 355-58.

Foerster, Gideon
1993 'Jericho, Hellenistic to early Arab Periods, History', in Ephraim Stern (ed.), *The New Encyclopedia of Archaeological Excavations in the Holy Land* (Jerusalem: The Israel Exploration Society): II, 681-82.

Freedman, David Noel
1956 'The Babylonian Chronicle', *Biblical Archaeologist* 19: 50-60.

Freedy, K.S., and Donald B. Redford
1976 'The Dates in Ezekiel in Relation to Biblical, Babylonian and Egyptian Sources', *Journal of the American Oriental Society* 90: 462-85.

Freud, Liora
1999 'Part Two: Finds. Pottery. The Iron Age', in Itzhaq Beit Arieh (ed.), *Tel 'Ira: A Stronghold in the Biblical Negev* (Sonia and Marco Nadler Institute of Archaeology Monograph Series, 15; Tel Aviv: Emery and Claire Yass Publications in Archaeology of the Institute of Archaeology, Tel Aviv University): 189-289.

Fritz, Volkmar
1983 '3.4 Die Ostraka', in Volkmar Fritz and Aharon Kempinski (eds.), *Ergebnisse der Ausgrabungen auf der Hirbet el-MŠAŠ (Tel Masos) (1972–1975)*. I. *Textband* (Abhandlungen des Deutschen Palästinavereins; Wiesbaden: Otto Harrrassowitz): 133-37.

Galil, Gershon
1991 'The Babylonian Calendar and the Chronology of the Last Kings of Judah', *Biblica* 72: 367-78.

Galling, Kurt
1935 'Assyrische und persische Präfekten in Geser', *Palästina-Jahrbuch* 31: 75-93.
1937 *Syrien in der Politik der Achemeniden bis zum Aufstand des Megabyzos 448 v. Chr.* (Der Alter Orient 36.3/4; Leipzig: J.C. Hinrichs).
1951a 'Kronzeugen des Artaxerxes?', *Zeitschrift für die alttestamentliche Wissenschaft* 63: 66-74.
1951b 'The "Gola-List" According to Ezra 2/Neh. 7', *Journal of Biblical Literature* 70: 149-58.
1964 *Studien zur Geschichte Israels im persischen Zeitalter* (Tübingen: J.C.B. Mohr).

Gamberoni, Johann
1997 'maqôm', in G. Johannes Botterweck and Helmer Ringgren (eds.), *Theological Dictionary of the Old Testament* (trans. from German by J.T. Willis; Grand Rapids: Eerdmans): VIII, 532-44.

Gazit, Dan
1996 *Israel Antiquities Authority Archaeological Survey of Israel Map of Urim (125)* (Jerusalem: Israel Antiquities Authority).

Gelin, Albert
1960 *Le livre de Esdras et Néhémie* (La Sainte Bible; Paris: Les Éditions de Cerf, 2nd edn).

Gelston, Anthony
1966 'The Foundations of the Second Temple', *Vetus Testamentum* 16: 232-35.

Geus, C.H.J. de
1979–80 'Idumaea', *Jaarbericht Vooraziatisch-Egyptisch Gezelschap 'Ex Oriente Lux'* 26: 53-74.

Gibson, John C.L.
1982 *Textbook of Syrian Semitic Inscriptions*. III. *Phoenician Inscriptions including Inscriptions in the Mixed Dialect of Arslan Tash* (Oxford: Clarendon Press).

Glueck, Nelson
1993 'Kheleife, Tel el-', in Ephraim Stern (ed.), *The New Encyclopedia of Archaeological Excavations in the Holy Land* (Jerusalem: the Israel Explorarion Society): III, 867-69.

Goldstein, Jonathan A.
1983 *II Maccabees: A New Translation with Introduction and Commentary* (Anchor Bible, 41A; Garden City, NY: Doubleday).

Gophna, Ram, and Itzhaq Beit-Arieh
1997 *Israel Antiquities Authority Archaeological Survey of Israel Map of Lod (80)* (Jerusalem: Israel Antiquities Authority).

Govrin, Yehuda
1991 *Israel Antiquities Authority Archaeological Survey of Israel Map of Nahal Yattir (139)* (Jerusalem: Israel Antiquities Authority).

Grabbe, Lester L.
1987 'Josephus and the Judean Restoration', *Journal of Biblical Literature* 106: 231-46.
1998 *Ezra-Nehemiah* (Old Testament Readings; London: Routledge).

Graetz, Heinrich H.
1876 *Geschichte der Israeliten bis zum Tode des Königs Salomo bis zum Tode des Juda Makkabi* (Geschichte der Jüdens, 2; Leipzig: Oskar Leinar).

Graf, David F.
1990 'Arabia during Achaemenid Times', in Heleen Sancisi-Weerdenburg and Amélie Kuhrt (eds.), *Centre and Periphery: Proceedings of the Groningen 1986 Achaemenid History Workshop* (Leiden: Nederlands Instituut voor het Nabije Oosten): 131-48.
1992 'Dedan', in David Noel Freedman (ed.), *Anchor Bible Dictionary* (New York: Doubleday): II, 121-23.
1993 'The Persian Royal Road System in Syria-Palestine', *Transeuphratène* 6: 149-66.
1994 'The Persian Royal Road System', in Heleen Sancisi-Weerdenburrg, Amélie Kuhrt and Margaret Cool Root (eds.), *Achaemenid History VIII: Continuity and Change. Proceedings of the Last Achaemenid History Workshop April 6-8, 1990 (AnnArbor, Michigan)* (Leiden: Nederlands Instituut voor het Nabije Oosten): 167-89.

Gray, John
1953 'The Diaspora of Israel and Judah in Obadiah 20', *Zeitschrift für die alttestamentliche Wissenschaft* 65: 53-59.

Greenburg, Raphael, and Gilad Cinamon
2002 'Jerusalem, 'Ir Gannim', *Excavations and Surveys in Israel* 114: 80*-81*.

Greenfield, Jonas C., and Bezalel Porten
1982 *The Bisitun Inscription of Darius the Great: Aramaic Version* (Corpus Inscriptionum Iranicum; London: Lund Humphries).

Gropp, Douglas Marvin
2001 '*Wadi Daliyeh II, XVIII*. II. *The Samarian Papyri from Wadi Daliyeh* (Discoveries in the Judean Desert, 28; Oxford: Clarendon Press).

Güterbock, Hans
1934 'Die historische Tradition und ihre literarische Gestaltung bei Babylonien und Hethitern bis 1200', *Zeitschrift für Assyriologie* 2: 1-91.
1938 'Die historische Tradition und ihre literarische Gestaltung bei Babylonien und Hethitern bis 1200', *Zeitschrift für Assyriologie* 4: 45-149.

Haiman, Mordechai
1991 *Israel Antiquities Authority Archaeological Survey of Israel: Mizpé Ramon Southwest (200)* (Jerusalem: Israel Antiquities Authority).
1993 *Israel Antiquities Authority Archaeological Survey of Israel Map of Har Hamran Southeast (199)* (Jerusalem: Israel Antiquities Authority).
1999 *Israel Antiquities Authority Archaeological Survey of Israel Amp of Har Ramon (203)* (Jerusalem: Israel Antiquities Authority).

Halévy, Joseph
1907 'Recherches bibliques. Le livre d'Obadia', *Revue sémitique* 15: 165-83.

Hallock, Richard T.
1960 'The "One Year" of Darius I', *Journal of Near Eastern Studies* 19: 36-39.
1969 *Persepolis Fortification Tablets* (University of Chicago Oriental Institute Publications, 92; Chicago: University of Chicago Press).

Halpern, Baruch
1978 'The Ritual Background of Zechariah's Temple Song', *Catholic Biblical Quarterly* 40: 167-90.
1990 'A Historiographic Commentary on Ezra 1-6: A Chronological Narrative and Dual Chronology in Israelite Historiography', in William Henry Propp, Baruch Halpern and D.N. Freedman (eds.), *The*

Hebrew Bible and its Interpreters (Biblical and Judaic Studies for the University of California, San Diego, 1; Winona Lake, IN: Eisenbrauns): 81-142.

1991 'Jerusalem and the Lineages in the Seventh Century BCE: Kinship and the Rise of Individual Moral Responsibility', in Baruch Halpern and Deborah W. Hobson (eds.), *Law and Ideology in Monarchic Israel (Journal for the Study of the Old Testament, Supplement Series, 124; Sheffield: Sheffield Academic Press*): 11-107.

Har-El, Menashe
1977 'The Valley of the Craftsmen (Ge' Haharašim)', *Palestine Exploration Quarterly* 109: 75-86.

Har-Even, Benjamin
2003 'Khirbet 'Almit', *Excavations and Surveys in Israel* 115: 48*-49*.

Haupt, Paul
1913 'The Visions of Zechariah', *Journal of Biblical Literature* 32: 107-22.

Havet, Ernest
1889 'La modernité des prophètes', *Revue des deux mondes (troisième partie)* 94: 799-830.

Hayes, John H.
1988 *Amos: The Eighth Century Prophet. His Times and his Preaching* (Nashville: Abingdon Press).

Heltzer, Michael
2000 'Some Questions about Royal Property in the Vth Satrapy and Profits of the Royal Treasury', *Transeuphratène* 19: 127-29.

Herrmann, Siegfried
1975 *A History of Israel in Old Testament Times* (trans. from German by J. Bowden; Philadelphia: Fortress Press, 1975).

Herzog, Ze'ev
1984 *Beer-sheba II: The Early Iron Age Settlements* (Publications of the Institute of Archaeology, 7; Tel Aviv: Institute of Archaeology, Tel Aviv University).
1993 'Tel Beersheva', in Ephraim Stern (ed.), *The New Encyclopedia of Archaeological Excavations in the Holy Land* (Jerusalem: The Israel Exploration Society): I, 167-73.

Herzog, Ze'ev, *et al.*
1984 'The Israelite Fortress at Arad', *Bulletin of the American Schools of Oriental Research* 254: 1-34.

Hill, George Francis
1922 *Catalogue of the Greek Coins of Arabia, Mesopotamia and Persia (Nabataea, Arabia Provincia, S. Arabia, Mesopotamia, Babylonia, Assyria, Persia, Alexandrine Empire of the East, Persis, Elymais,Characene)* (London: Longman).
1965 *Catalogue of the Greek Coins of Phoenicia: A Catalogue of the Greek Coins in the British Museum* (Bologna: Arnaldo Forni-Editore).

Hinz, Walther
1970 'Die elamischen Buchungstäfelchen der Darius-Zeit', *Orientalia* 39: 421-40.

Hirschfeld, Yizhar
1985 *Archaeological Survey of Israel Map of Herodium (108/2) 17-11* (Jerusalem: The Department of Antiquities and Museums, The Archaeological Survey of Israel).

Hoffman, Yair
2003 'The Fasts in the Book of Zechariah and the Fashioning of National Remembrance', in Oded Lipschits and Joseph Blenkinsopp (eds.), *Judah and the Judeans in the Neo-Babylonian Period* (Winona Lake, IN: Eisenbrauns): 169-218.

Hoglund, Kenneth G.
1989 'The Establishment of a Rural Economy in the Judean Hill Country during the Late Sixth Century BCE', Paper presented at the Southeastern Regional Meeting of the Society of Biblical Literature, American Academy of Religion, and American Schools of Oriental Research, Charlotte, NC, 16–18 March.
1992 *Achaemenid Imperial Administration in Syria-Palestine and the Missions of Ezra and Nehemiah* (Sociey of Biblical Literature Dissertations Series, 125; Atlanta, GA: Scholars Press).

Hölscher, Gustav
1923 'Die Bücher Esra und Nehemia', in Emil Kautzsch and Alfred Bertholet (eds.), *Die Heilige Schrift des Alten Testaments Zweiter Band: Hosea bis Chronik* (Tübingen: J.C.B. Mohr): 491-562.

1926   'Les origins de la communauté juive à l'époque perse', *Revue d'histoire et de philosophie religieuses* 6: 105-26.

Hoonacker, Albin van
1908   *Les douze petits prophètes traduits et commentés* (Etudes bibliques; Paris: J. Gabalda).

Horst, Friedrich
1964   *Die Zwölf kleinen Propheten. Hosea bis Micha* (Handbuch zum Alten Testament, 1.14; Tübingen: J.C.B. Mohr, 3rd edn).

Howorth, Henry H.
1893   'A Criticism of the Sources and the Relative Importance and Value of the Canonical Book of Ezra and the Apocryphal Book Known as Esdras I', in E. Delmer Morgan (ed.), *Transactions of the Ninth International Congress of Orientalists (held in London, 5th–12th September 1892)* (London: The Committee of the Congress): II, 68-85.

Hübner, Ulrich
1992   'Idumea', in D.N. Freedman (ed.), *The Anchor Bible Dictionary* (New York: Doubleday): III, 382-83.

Hurowitz, Victor (Avigdor)
1992   *I Have Built You an Exalted House: Temple Building in the Bible in Light of Mesopotamian and Northwest Semitic Writings* (Journal for the Study of the Old Testament, Supplement Series, 115; American Schools of Oriental Research Monograph Series, 5; Sheffield: Sheffield Academic Press).

Hyatt, J. Philip
1937   'A Babylonian Parallel to Bethel-Šareser, Zech 7:2', *Journal of Biblical Literature* 56: 387-94.

Jacobs, Paul F. and Oded Borowski
1993   'Notes and News. Tell Halif, 1992', *Israel Exploration Journal* 43: 66-70.

Jacobsen, Thorkild
1987   *The Harps That Once... Sumerian Poetry in Translation* (London: Yale University Press).

Jahn, Gustav
1909   *Die Bücher Esra (A und B) und Nehemja, text-critisch und historisch-kritisch Untersucht mit Erklärung der einschlägigen Prophetenstellen und einem Anhang über hebräische Eigennamen* (Leiden: E.J. Brill).

Japhet, Sarah
1965   'The Supposed Common Authorship of Chronicles and Ezra-Nehemiah Investigated Anew', *Vetus Testamentum* 18: 330-71.
1982   'Sheshbazzar and Zerubbabel', *Zeitschrift für die alttestamentliche Wissenschaft* 94: 66-98; 95 (1983): 218-29.
1991   ' "History" and "Literature" in the Persian Period: The Restoration of the Temple', in Mordechai Cogan and Hayim Tadmor (eds.), *Ah, Assyria... Studies in Assyrian History and Ancient Near Eastern Historiography Presented to Hayim Tadmor* (Scripta Hierosolymitana, 33; Jerusalem: Magnes Press): 174-88.

Joannès, Francis
1982   *Textes économiques de la Babylonie Récente (Etude des textes de TBER-Cahier n° 6)* (Etudes assyriologiques, 5; Paris: Editions Recherche sur les civilisations).

Joannès, Francis, and André Lemaire
1999   'Trois tablettes cunéiformes à onomastique ouest-sémitique', *Transeuphratène* 17: 17-34.

Johns, Claude Hermann Walter
1905   'The New Cuneiform Tablet from Gezer', *Palestine Exploration Fund Quarterly Statement* 37: 206-210.

Johnson, Marshall D.
1969   *The Purpose of the Biblical Genealogies: With Special Reference to the Setting of the Genealogies of Jesus* (Cambridge: Cambridge University Press).

Jones, Douglas Rawlinson
1962   *Haggai, Zechariah and Malachi: Introduction and Commentary* (Torch Bible Commentaries; London: SCM Press).

Joüon, Paul
1947   *Grammaire de l'Hebreu biblique* (Rome: Institut biblique pontifical, 10th edn).

Kallai, Zecharia
1986   *Historical Geography of the Bible: The Tribal Territories of Israel* (Jerusalem: Magnes Press; Leiden: E.J. Brill).

Kapelrud, Arvid S.
    1956   *Central Ideas in Amos* (Oslo: Aschehoug).
    1963   'Temple Building, a Task for Gods and Kings', *Orientalia* 32: 56-62.
Kataja, Laura, and Robert Whiting
    1995   *Grants, Decrees and Gifts of the Neo-Assyrian Period* (State Archives of Assyria, 12; Helsinki: Helsinki University Press).
Katzenstein, H. Jacob
    1994   'Gaza in the Neo-Babylonian period (629–539 B.C.E.)', *Transeuphratène* 7: 35-49.
Kaufman, Yehezkiel
    1954   'Das Kalendar und das Alter des Priesterkodex', *Vetus Testamentum* 4: 307-13.
Kautsch, Ernest and Cowley, Arthur E.
    1982   *Gesenius' Hebrew Grammar* (Oxford: Clarendon Press, 2nd English edn, imprint 16).
Keller, Carl A.
    1965   *Abdias*, in Edmond Jacob, Carl A. Keller and Samuel Amsler (eds.), *Osée, Joel, Amos, Abdias, Jona, Amos* (Commentaire de l'Ancien Testament, 11a; Neuchâtel: Delachaux & Niestlé).
Kellermann, Ulrich
    1966   'Die Listen in Nehemia 11 eine Dokumentation aus den letzten Jahren des Reiches Juda?', *Zeitschrift des Deutschen Palästina-Vereins* 82: 209-27.
    1967   *Nehemia: Quellen, Überlieferung und Geschichte* (Beihefte zur Zeitschrfit für die alttestamentliche Wissenschaft, 102; Berlin: Alfred Töpelmann).
Kelso, James Leon
    1993   'Bethel', in Ephraim Stern (ed.), *The New Encyclopedia of Archaeological Excavations in the Holy Land* (Jerusalem: The Israel Exploration Society): I, 192-94.
Kent, Roland G.
    1953   *Old Persian, Grammar, Texts, Lexicon* (American Oriental Series, 33; New Haven, CT: American Oriental Society).
Kenyon, Kathleen M.
    1993   'Jericho, Tell es-Sultan', in Ephraim Stern (eds.), *The New Encyclopedia of Archaeological Excavations in the Holy Land* (Jerusalem: The Israel Exploration Society): II, 674-81.
Kessler, John
    2002   *The Book of Haggai: Prophecy and Society in Early Persian Yehud* (Vetus Testamentum Supplements, 91; Leiden: E.J. Brill).
Klein, Ralph L.
    1984   *Micah-Malachi* (Word Biblical Commentary, 32; Waco, TX: Word Books).
Kloner, Amos
    2000   *Israel Antiquities Authority Archaeological Survey of Israel Survey of Jerusalem. The Southern Sector* (Jerusalem: Israel Antiquities Authority).
    2001   *Israel Antiquities Authority Archaeological Survey of Israel Survey of Jerusalem. The Northeastern Sector* (Jerusalem: The Israel Antiquities Authority).
    2003   *Israel Antiquities Authority Archaeological Survey of Israel Survey of Jerusalem. The Northwestern Sector Introduction and Indices* (Jerusalem: Israel Antiquities Authority).
Knauf-Belleri, Axel
    1995   'Edom: the Social and Economic History', in Diana V. Edelman (ed.), *You Shall Not Abhor an Edomite for He is your Brother: Edom and Seir in History and Tradition* (Archaeology and Biblical Studies, 3; Atlanta, GA: Scholars Press): 93-117.
Kochavi, Moshe
    1972   *Judaea Samaria and the Golan: Archaeological Survey 1967–1968* (Jerusalem: The Archaeological Survey of Israel).
    1993   'Malḥata, Tel', in Ephraim Stern (ed.), *The New Encyclopedia of Archaeological Excavations in the Holy Land* (Jerusalem: The Israel Exploration Society): III, 934-36.
Koehler, Ludwig, and Walter Baumgartner
    1996   *The Hebrew and Aramaic Lexicon of the Old Testament III Sh-P* (trans. and ed. under the supervision of M.E.J. Richardson; Leiden: E.J. Brill).

König, Friedrich Wilhelm
    1972   *Die Persika des Ktesias von Knidos* (Archiv für Orientforschung Beiheft, 18; Graz: Ferdinand Berger & Söhne).

Kosters, Willem Hendrik
    1895   *Die Wiederhersterlung Israels in der persischen Periode* (trans. from Dutch by A. Basedow; Heidelberg: n.p.).

Kraeling, Emil G.
    1953   *The Brooklyn Museum Aramaic Papyri: New Documents of the Fifth Century B.C. from the Jewish Colony at Elephantine* (New Haven: Yale University Press).

Kuhrt, Amélie
    1982   'Assyrian and Babylonian Traditions in Classical Authors: A Critical Synthesis', in Hans-Jörg Nissen and Johannes Renger (eds.), *Mesopotamien und seine Nachbarn: politische und kulturelle Wechselbeziehungen v. Chr. XXV. Rencontre assyriologique internationale Berlin, 3. bis 7. Juli 1978* (Berliner Beiträge zum Vorderen Orient, 1; Berlin: Dietrich Reimer): II, 539-53.
    1983   'The Cyrus Cylinder and Achaemenid Imperial Policy', *Journal for the Study of the Old Testament* 25: 83-97.

Laato, Antti
    1994   'Zachariah 4,6b-10a and the Akkadian Royal Building Inscriptions', *Zeitschrift für die alttestamentliche Wissenschaft* 106: 53-69.

Labat, René
    1939   *Hémérologies et ménologies d'Assur* (Etudes d'assyriologie, 1; Paris: Adrien-Maisonneuve).
    1965   *Un calendrier babylonien des travaux des signes et des mois (séries iqqur îpush)* (Bibliothèque de l'école des hautes études, Ive section [sciences historiques et philologiques], 321. Paris: Librairie Honoré Champion).

Langdon, Stephen
    1935   *Babylonian Menologies and the Semitic Calendars* (The Schweich Lectures of the British Academy 1933; London: Oxford University Press for the British Academy).

Laperoussaz, Ernest-Marie
    1989   'Jérusalem à l'époque perse (étendue et statut)', *Transeuphratène* 1: 55-65.

Lapp, Paul W.
    1974   'An Account of the Discovery', in Paul W. Lapp and Nancy L. Lapp (eds.), *Discoveries in the Wadi ed-Daliyeh* (Annual of the American Schools of Oriental Research, 41; Cambridge, MA: ASOR): 1-6.
    1977   'The Importance of Dating', *Biblical Archaeological Review* 3.1: 13-22.

Larsson, Gerhard
    1967   'When did the Babylonian Captivity Begin?', *Journal of Theological Studies* 18: 417-23.

Lasine, Stuart
    2001   *Knowing Kings: Knowledge, Power, and Narcissism in the Hebrew Bible* (Semeia Studies, 40; Atlanta: Society of Biblical Literature).

Le Bas, Edwin E.
    1950   'Zechariah's Enigmatical Contribution to the Corner-Stone', *Palestine Exploration Quarterly* 82: 102-22.
    1951   'Zechariah's Climax to the Career of the Cornerstone', *Palestine Exploration Quarterly* 83: 139-55.

Lee, Thomas S.
    1994   'Propaganda and the Verse Account of Nabonidus' Reign', *Bulletin of the Canadian Society for Mesopotamian Studies* 28: 31-36.

Leith, Mary Joan Winn
    1997   *Wadi Daliyeh I, The Wadi Daliyeh Seal Impressions* (Discoveries in the Judean Desert, 24; Oxford: Clarendon Press).

Lemaire, André
    1977   'Review of *Bullae and Seals from a Post-Exilic Judean Archive* by N. Avigad', *Syria* 54: 129-31.
    1988   'Recherches actuelles sur les sceaux nord-ouest semitiques', *Vetus Testamentum* 38: 220-30.
    1989   'Remarques à propos du monnayage cilicien d'époque perse et de ses legendes araméenes', *Revue des études anciennes* 91: 141-56.

1990 'Populations et territoires de la Palestine à l'époque perse', *Transeuphratène* 3: 31-74.

1996 'Zorobabel et la Judée à la lumière de l'épigraphie (fin du Vie S. Av. J.-C.)', *Revue biblique* 103: 48-57.

1998 'Les formules de datation en Palestine au premier millénaire avant J.-C', in Françoise Briquel-Chatonnet and Hélène Lozachmeur (eds.), *Proche-Orient ancien. Temps vécu, temps pensé. Actes de la Table-Ronde du 15 novembre 1997 organisée par l'URA 1062 'Etudes Sémitiques'* (Antiquités Sémitiques, 3; Paris: Jean Maisonneuve; Librairie d'Amérique et d'Orient): 53-82.

2000 'L'économie de l'Idumée d'après les nouveaux ostraca araméens', *Transeuphratène* 19: 131-43.

2001a 'Épigraphie et religion en Palestine à l'époque achéménide', *Transeuphratène* 22: 97-113.

2001b 'Les religions de Sud de la Palestine au IVe siècle av. J.-C.-d'après les ostraca araméens d'Idumée', in *Académie des inscriptions et belles lettres comptes rendus des séances de l'année 2001 avril-juin* (Paris: Diffusion de Boccard): 1141-58.

2002 *Nouvelles inscriptions araméennes d'Idumée*, II (Supplement à *Transeuphratène*, 9; Paris: Gabalda).

2003 'Nabonidus in Arabia and Judah in the Neo-Babylonian Period', in Oded Lipschits and Joseph Blenkinsopp (eds.), *Judah and the Judeans in the Neo-Babylonian Period* (Winona Lake, IN: Eisenbrauns): 285-98.

Lemaire, André, and Hélène Lozachmeur
1987 *'Birah/Birta'* en araméen', *Syria* 64: 261-66.

Lemche, Niels Peter
1995 'Kings and Clients: On Loyalty between the Ruler and the Ruled in Ancient Israel', *Semeia* 66: 119-32.

Lender, Yesha'yahu
1990 *Israel Antiquities Authority. The Archaeological Survey of Israel Map of Har Nafḥa (196) 12-01* (Jerusalem: Israel Antiquities Authority).

Leuze, Oscar
1935 *Die Satrapieneinleitung im Syrien und im Zweistromlande von 520–320* (Königsberger gelehrten Gesellschaft Schriften, geisteswissenschaftliche Klasse, 4; Halle: Niemeyer).

Levant, Edoardo
1986 *Sylloge Nummerum Gracorum Swtizerland I. Levante-Cilicia* (Bern: Staempfli [for the British Academy, Union Académique Internationale and the International Numismatic Commission]).

Lewis, David M.
1977 *Sparta and Persia: Lectures Delivered at the University of Cincinnati, Autumn, 1976* (Cincinnati Classical Studies, New Series, 1; Leiden: E.J. Brill).

Limet, Henri
2000 'Les exploitations agricoles en Transeuphratène au Ier millénaire à la lumière des pratiques assyriennes', *Transeuphratène* 19: 35-50.

Lindsay, John
1976 'The Babylonian Kings and Edom', *Palestine Exploration Quarterly* 108: 23-39.

Lipiński, Eduard
1970 'Recherches sur le livre de Zacharie', *Vetus Testamentum* 20: 25-55.

1973 'Obadiah 20', *Vetus Testamentum* 23: 368-70.

1989 "Celleriers' de la province de Juda', *Transeuphratène* 1: 107-109.

Lipschits, Oded
1997 'The Origin of the Jewish Population of Mod'in and its Vicinity', *Cathedra* 85: 7-32 (Hebrew).

1998 'Nebuchadrezzar's Policy in "Hattu-Land" and the Fate of the Kingdom of Judah', *Ugarit Forschungen* 30: 467-87.

1999 'The History of the Benjaminite Region under Babylonian Rule', *Tel Aviv* 26.2: 155-90.

2002 'Literary and Ideological Aspects of Nehemiah 11', *Journal of Biblical Literature* 121: 423-40.

2003 'Demographic Changes in Judah between the Seventh and the Fifth Centuries B.C.E.', in Oded Lipschits and Joseph Blenkinsopp (eds.), *Judah and the Judeans in the Neo-Babylonian Period* (Winona Lake, IN: Eisenbrauns): 323-76.

Longman, Tremper, III
1991 *Fictional Akkadian Autobiography: A Generic and Comparative Study* (Winona Lake, IN: Eisenbrauns).

Love, Mark Cameron
    1999   *The Evasive Text: Zechariah 1–8 and the Frustrated Reader* (*Journal for the Study of the Old Testament*, Supplement Series, 296; Sheffield: Sheffield Academic Press).

Luckenbill, Daniel David
    1924/25 'The Black Stone of Esarhaddon', *American Journal of Semitic Language* 41: 166-67.
    1975   *Ancient Records of Assyria and Babylonia*. II. *Historical Records of Assyria from Sargon to the End* (New York: Greenwood Press [Chicago: University of Chicago Press, 1927]).

Lundquist, John M.
    1984   'The Common Temple Ideology of the Ancient Near East', in T.G. Madsen (ed.), *The Temple in Antiquity* (Religious Monograph Series, 9; Provo, UT: Brigham Young University): 53-76.

McCowan, Chester Charlton
    1957   'The 'Araq el-Emir and the Tobiads', *Biblical Archeologist* 20: 63-76.

Magen, Yitzhak, and Yuval Baruch
    2002   'Yatta', *Excavations and Surveys of Israel* 114: 95*-96*.

Magen, Yitzhaq, and Ephraim Stern
    2000   'The First Phase of the Samaritan Temple on Mt. Gerizim – New Archaeological Evidence', *Qadmoniot* 33.2: 119-24.

Malamat, Abraham
    1953   'The Historical Background of the Assassination of Amon, King of Judah', *Israel Exploration Journal* 3: 26-29.
    1968   'The Last Kings of Judah and the Fall of Jerusalem', *Israel Exploration Journal* 18: 137-55.

Marcus, Ralph
    1937   *Josephus V. I Jewish Antiquities, Books IX-XI* (The Loeb Classical Library; London: Heinemann).

Marinkovic, Peter
    1994   'What Does Zechariah 1–8 Tell us about the Second Temple?', in Tamara C. Eskenazi and Kent H. Richards (eds.), *Second Temple Studies 2. Temple Community in the Persian Period* (*Journal for the Study of the Old Testament*, Supplement Series, 175; Sheffield: Sheffield Academic Press): 88-103.

Markoe, Glenn E.
    2000   *Phoenicians* (People of the Bible; London: British Museum).

Marquart, Josef
    1896   *Fundamente israelitischer und jüdischer Geschichte* (Göttingen: Dieterich).

Mason, Rex
    1977   *Haggai, Zechariah, and Malachi* (Cambridge Bible Commentary; Cambridge: Cambridge University Press).

May, Herbert G.
    1938   'A Key to the Interpretation of Zechariah's Visions', *Journal of Biblical Literature* 57: 173-85.
    1974   *Oxford Bible Atlas* (Oxford: Oxford University Press).

Mazar, Amihai
    1982   'Iron Age Fortresses in the Judean Hills', *Palestine Exploration Quarterly* 114: 86-109.

Mazar, Benjamin
    1957   'The Tobiads', *Israel Exploration Journal* 7: 137-45, 229-38.
    1993   'En-Gedi', in Ephraim Stern (ed.), *The New Encyclopedia of Archaeological Excavations in the Holy Land* (Jerusalem: The Israel Exploration Society): II, 399-405.

Mazar, Benjamin, Trude Dothan and Immanuel Dunayevsky
    1966   *En-Gedi: The First and Second Seasons of Excavations 1961–1962* ('Atiqot, 5; Jerusalem: Jerusalem Academic Press).

Meiggs, Russell
    1972   *The Athenian Empire* (Oxford: Clarendon Press).

Mendelsohn, Isaac
    1962   'On Corvée Labor in Ancient Canaan and Israel', *Bulletin of the American Schools of Oriental Research* 167: 31-35.

Meshel, Ze'ev
    1977   'Horvat Ritma – An Iron Age Fortress in the Negev Highlands', *Tel Aviv* 4: 110-35.

Meshorer, Yaakov
    1990/91 'Ancient Jewish Coins. Addendum I', *Israel Numismatic Journal* 11.
Meshorer, Yaakov, and Shraga Qedar
    1999   *Samarian Coinage* (Numismatic Studies and Researches, 9; Jerusalem: Israel Numismatic Society).
Mettinger, Tryggve N.D.
    1982   *The Dethronement of Sebaot: Studies in the Shem and Kabod Theologies* (Coniectanea Biblica Old Testament Series, 18; Lund: C.W.K. Gleerup).
Meyer, Eduard
    1896   *Die Entstehung des Judentums: eine historische Untersuchung* (Halle: Max Niemeyer).
Meyers, Carol L., and Eric M. Meyers
    1987   *Haggai, Zechariah 1–8: A New Translation with Introduction and Commentary* (Anchor Bible, 25B; Garden City, NY: Doubleday).
Meyers, Eric M.
    1985   'The Shelomit Seal and the Judean Restoration: Some Additional Considerations', *Eretz Israel* 18: 33*-38*.
Michaeli, Frank
    1967   *Les livres des Chroniques, d'Esdras et de Néhémie* (Commentaire de l'Ancien Testament, 16; Neuchâtel: Delachaux & Niestlé).
Mildenberg, Leo
    1990–91 'Notes on Coin Issues of Mazday', *Israel Numismatic Journal* 11: 9-23.
Milevski, Ianur
    1996/97 'Settlement Patterns in Northern Judah during the Achaemenid Period, According to the Hill Country of Benjamin and Jerusalem Surveys', *Bulletin of the Anglo-Israel Archaeological Society* 15: 7-29.
Millard, Alan
    1976   'Assyrian Royal Names in Biblical Hebrew', *Journal of Semitic Studies* 21: 1-14.
    1995   'Nabu', in Karel Van der Toorn, Bob Becking and Pieter W. van der Horst (eds.), *Dictionary of Deities and Demons in the Bible* (Leiden: E.J. Brill): cols. 1141-47.
    1997   'King Solomon in his Ancient Context', in Lowell Handy (ed.), *The Age of Solomon: Scholarship at the Turn of the Millennium* (Studies in the History and Culture of the Ancient Near East, 11; Leiden: E.J. Brill): 30-53.
Miller, J. Maxwell, and John H. Hayes
    1986   *History of Ancient Israel and Judah* (Philadelphia: Westminster Press).
Mitchell, Hinkley G., John M.P. Smith and Julius A. Bewer
    1912   *A Critical and Exegetical Commentary on Haggai, Zechariah, Malachi, and Jonah* (International Critical Commentary; Edinburgh: T. & T. Clark).
Monson, James
    1979   *Student Map Manual: Historical Geography of the Bible Lands* (Israel: Pictorial Archives [Near Eastern History]).
Morgenstern, Julius
    1924   'The Three Calendars of Ancient Israel', *Hebrew Union College Annual* 1: 13-78.
    1929   'Beena Marriage (Matriarchate) in Ancient Israel and its Historical Implications', *Zeitschrift für die alttestamentliche Wissenschaft* 47: 91-110.
    1938   'A Chapter in the History of the High-Priesthood', *The American Journal of Semitic Languages and Literatures* 55: 1-24; 183-97; 360-77.
Mowinckel, Sigmund
    1964a   *Studien zu dem Buche Ezra-Nehemia. I. Die nachchronische Redaktion des Buches. Die Listen* (Skrifter utgitt av det Norske videnskaps-akademie i Oslo.II. Hist.-filos. Klasse ny serie, 3; Oslo: Universitetsforlaget).
    1964b   *Studien zu dem Buche Ezra-Nehemia. II. Die Nehemiah-Denkschrift* (Skrifter utgitt av det Norske videnskaps-akademie i Oslo.II. Hist.-filos. Klasse ny serie, 5; Oslo: Universitetsforlaget).
Murtonen, Aimo
    1952   'The Prophet Amos – A Hepatoscoper?', *Vetus Testamentum* 2: 170-71.

Mussell, Marie-Louise
    1999   'Tel Kheleife', *ACOR Newsletter* 11/1: 5-6.
Myers, Jacob M.
    1960   *Hosea to Jonah* (The Layman's Bible Commentary, 14; London: SCM Press).
    1965   *Ezra, Nehemiah: Introduction, Translation and Notes* (Anchor Bible, 14; Garden City, NY: Doubleday).
Na'aman, Nadav
    1991   'The Kingdom of Josiah', *Tel Aviv* 18: 3-71.
    1993   'Population Changes in Palestine following Assyrian Deportations', *Tel Aviv* 20: 104-24.
    1995   'Province System and Settlement Pattern in Southern Syria and Palestine in the Neo-Assyrian Period', in Mario Liverani (ed.), *Neo-Assyrian Geography* (Università di Roma 'La Sapienza' Dipartimento do Scienze storiche, archeologiche e antropologiche dell'Antichità Quaderni di Geografia Storica, 5; Rome: University of Rome): 103-115.
    2001   'An Assyrian Residence at Ramat Rahel?', *Tel Aviv* 28: 260-80.
Nadelman, Yonatan
    1993   'Jerusalem, Pisgat Ze'ev D (H. Zimri)', *Excavations and Surveys of Israel* 12: 54-56.
Naveh, Joseph
    1960   'A Hebrew Letter from the Seventh Century, B.C', *Israel Exploration Journal* 10: 130-36.
    1962a   'More Hebrew Inscriptions from Meṣad Ḥashavyahu', *Israel Exploration Journal* 12: 27-32.
    1962b   'The Excavations at Meṣad Ḥashavyahu: Preliminary Report', *Israel Exploration Journal* 12: 89-99.
    1973   'The Aramaic Ostraca', in *Beer-Sheba I. Excavations at Tel Beer-Sheba 1969–1971 Seasons* (Tel Aviv University Institute of Archaeology Publications, 2; Tel Aviv: Tel Aviv University Institute of Archaeology): 79-82.
    1979   'The Aramaic Ostraca from Tel Beer-sheba', *Tel Aviv* 6: 182-98.
    1981   'The Aramaic Ostraca from Arad', in Yohanan Aharoni (ed.), *Arad Inscriptions* (Judean Desert Studies; Jerusalem: The Israel Exploration Society): 153-76.
    1996   'Gleanings of Some Pottery Inscriptions', *Israel Exploration Journal* 46: 44-51.
    1999   'Aramaic Ostraca', in Itzhaq Beit Arieh (ed.), *Tel 'Ira: A Stronghold in the Biblical Negev* (Sonia and Marco Nadler Institute of Archaeology Monograph Series, 15; Tel Aviv: Emery and Claire Yass Publications in Archaeology of the institute of Archaeology, Tel Aviv University): 412-13.
Negbi, Ora
    1969   'Remains of a Fortress next to French Hill', *Hadashot Arkheologiyot* 31-32: 18 (Hebrew).
Negev, Nimrod
    2001   'Dudaim Site, Survey (G-125/99*)', *Excavations and Surveys in Israel* 113: 113*-14*.
Niehr, Herbert
    2004   'Sar', in G. Johannes Botterweck, Helmer Ringgren and Heinz-Josef Fabry (eds.), *Theological Dictionary of the Old Testament* (trans. from German by Douglas W. Stott; Grand Rapids, MI: Eerdmans): XIV, 191-215.
Nikel, Johannes
    1900   *Die Wiederherstellung des jüdischen Gemeinwesens nach dem babylonischen Exil* (Bibische Studien, 5/2 and 3; Freiburg im Breisgau: Herder).
Nogalski, James
    1993a   *Literary Precursors to the Book of the Twelve* (Beihefte zur *Zeitschrift für die alttestamentliche Wissenschaft*, 217; Berlin: W. de Gruyter).
    1993b   *Redactional Processes in the Book of the Twelve* (Beihefte zur *Zeitschrift für die alttestamentliche Wissenschaft*, 218; Berlin: W. de Gruyter).
Noth, Martin
    1960   *The History of Israel* (New York: Harper & Row, 3rd English translation).
    1967   *Überlieferungsgeschichtliche Studien* (Tübingen: Niemeyer [1947]).
Oded, Bustanay
    1979   *Mass Deportations and Deportees in the Neo-Assyrian Empire* (Wiesbaden: Reichert).
Ofer, Avi
    1993   'The Highland of Judah during the Biblical Period' (2 vols.; Unpublished PhD thesis, Tel Aviv University).

Olmstead, Albert Ten Eyck
    1938   'Darius and his Behistun Inscription', *The American Journal of Semitic Languages and Literatures* 55: 392-416.
    1944   'Tattenai, Governor of "Across the River"', *Journal of Near Eastern Studies* 3: 46.
Onn, Alexander, and Rapuano, Yehuda
    1995   'Jerusalem, Kh. er-Ras', *Excavations and Surveys in Israel* 14: 71.
Onn, Alexander, Shlomit Wexler-Bdolah, Yehuda Rapuano and Tzah Kanias
    2002   'Khirbet Umm el-'Umdan', *Excavations and Surveys in Israel* 114: 64*-68*.
Oppenheim, Leo
    1969   'Babylonian and Assyrian Historical Texts', in James B. Pritchard (ed.), *Ancient Near Eastern Texts Relating to the Old Testament* (Princeton, NJ: Princeton University Press, 3rd edn with supplement): 265-317.
Oren, Eliezer
    1972   'News and Notes. Tel Sera' (Tell esh-Shari'a)', *Israel Exploration Journal* 22: 167-69.
    1973   'News and Notes. Tel Sera' (Tell esh-Shari'a)', *Israel Exploration Journal* 23: 251-54.
    1974   'News and Notes. Tel Sera' (Tell esh-Shari'a)', *Israel Exploration Journal* 24: 265-66.
    1982   'Ziklag-A Biblical City on the Edge of the Negev', *Biblical Archaeologist* 45: 155-66.
    1993a   'Haror, Tel', in Ephraim Stern (ed.), *The New Encyclopedia of Archaeological Excavations in the Holy Land* (Jerusalem: The Israel Exploration Society):II, 580-84.
    1993b   'Sera', Tel', in Ephraim Stern (ed.), *The New Encyclopedia of Archaeological Excavations in the Holy Land* (Jerusalem: The Israel Exploration Society):IV, 1329-35.
Oren, Eliezer, *et al.*
    1985   ' "Gerar" – 1985', *Excavations and Surveys in Israel* 4: 30-33.
Orr, Avigdor
    1956   'The Seventy Years of Babylon', *Vetus Testamentum* 6: 304-306.
Pardee, Dennis, *et al.*
    1982   *Handbook of Ancient Hebrew Letters* (SBL Sources for Bibical Study, 15; Chico, CA: Scholars Press).
Parker, Richard A.
    1941   'Persian and Egyptian Chronology', *The American Journal of Semitic Languages and Literatures* 58: 285-301.
Parker, Richard A., and Waldo H. Dubberstein
    1956   *Babylonian Chronology 626 B.C.–A.D. 75* (Brown University Studies, 19; Providence: Brown University Press).
Patrich, Joseph
    1994   *Israel Antiquities Authority Archaeological Survey in Judea and Samaria Map of Deir Mar Saba (109/7)* (Jerusalem: Israel Antiquities Authority).
Paul, Shalom M.
    1991   *Amos: A Commentary on the Book of Amos* (Minneapolis: Fortress Press).
Pearce, Laurie
  Forthcoming 'New Evidence for Judeans in Babylonia', in Oded Lipschits and Manfred Oeming (eds.), *Judah and the Judeans in the Persian Period* (Winona Lake, IN: Eisenbrauns).
Peckham, J. Brian
    1968   *The Development of the Late Phoenician Scripts* (Harvard Semitic Monographs, 20; Cambridge, MA: Harvard University).
Petersen, David L.
    1974   'Zerubbabel and Jerusalem Temple Reconstruction', *Catholic Biblical Quarterly* 36: 366-72.
    1984   *Haggai & Zechariah 1–8: A Commentary* (Old Testament Library; London: SCM Press).
Petit, Thierry
    1988   'L'evolution sémantique des termes hébreux et araméens *phh* et *sgn* et accadiens *pahatu* et *saknu*', *Journal of Biblical Literature* 107: 53-67.
Petitjean, Albert
    1966   'La mission de Zorobbabel et la reconstruction du temple', *Ephemerides Theologicae Lovanienses* 42: 40-71.

1969   *Les oracles du Proto-Zacharie: Un programme de restauration pour la communauté juive après l'exil* (Etudes bibliques; Paris: J. Gabalda).

Petrie, Sir Flinders
1928   *Gerar* (London: British School of Archaeology in Egypt, University College, and Bernard Quaritch).

Pfeiffer, Robert H.
1941   *Introduction to the Old Testament* (New York: Harper, 4th edn).

Poebel, Arno
1938   'Chronology of Darius' First Year of Reign', DETAILS?: 142-65, 285-314.

Pomerantz, Inna
1982   'Jerusalem. 'Isawiye – Survey of New Road', *Excavations and Surveys in Israel* 1: 54-55.

Porten, Bezalel
1968   *Archives from Elephantine: The Life of an Ancient Jewish Military Colony* (Los Angeles: University of California Press).
1992   'Elephantine Papyri', in David N. Freedman (ed.), *The Anchor Bible Dictionary* (New York: Doubleday): 2, 445-55.

Postgate, J. Nicholas
1974   *Taxation and Conscription in the Assyrian Empire* (Studia Pohl; Series Maior, 3; Rome: Biblical Institute Press).
1992   *Early Mesopotamia: Society and Economy at the Dawn of History* (London: Routledge).

Pratico, Gary D.
1993a   *Nelson Glueck's 1938–1940 Excavations at Tell el-Kheleifeh: A Reappraisal* (American Schools of Oriental Research Archaeological Reports, 3; Atlanta: Scholars Press).
1993b   'Kheleife, Tell el-', in Ephraim Stern (ed.), *The New Encyclopedia of Archaeological Excavations in the Holy Land* (Jerusalem: The Israel Exploration Society): III, 869-70.

Quintus Curtius
1946   *History of Alexander I. Books I–IV* (ed. John C. Rolfe; Loeb Classical Library; London: Heinemann).

Raabe, Paul R.
1996   *Obadiah: A New Translation with Introduction and Commentary* (Anchor Bible, 24D; New York: Doubleday).

Rabinowitz, Isaac
1956   'Aramaic Inscriptions of the Fifth Century B.C.E. from a North-Arab Shrine in Egypt', *Journal of Near Eastern Studies* 15: 1-9.

Rad, Gerhard von
1930   *Das Geschichtsbild des chronistischen Werk* (Beiträge zur Wissenschaft vom Alten und Neuen Testament, 54; Stuttgart: W. Kohlhammer).

Rainey, Anson F.
1983   'The Biblical Shephelah of Judah', *Bulletin of the American Schools of Oriental Research* 251: 1-22.

Rainier, Chris
2003   'In Sahara, Salt-Hauling Camel Trains Struggle On', *National Geographic News* (May 28).

Reade, Julian E.
2001   'Ninive', in Erich Ebeling, Bruno Meissner *et al.* (eds.), *Reallexicon der Assyriologie* (Berlin: W. de Gruyter): IX, 388-433.

Redditt, Paul L.
1992   'Zerubbabel, Joshua, and the Night Visions of Zechariah', *Catholic Biblical Quarterly* 54: 249-59.
1995   *The New Century Bible Commentary: Haggai, Zechariah, Malachi* (London: Marshall Pickering).

Reich, Ronny
1992a   'The Bet-Zur Citadel II-A Persian Residency?', *Tel Aviv* 19: 113-23.
1992b   'Palaces and Residencies in the Iron Age', in Aharon Kempinski and Ronny Reich (eds.), *The Architecture of Ancient Israel from the Prehistoric to the Persian Period* (Jerusalem: Israel Exploration Society): 202-22.

Roth, Martha Tobi
1987   'Age at Marriage and the Household: A Study of Neo-Assyrian and Neo-Babylonian Forms', *Comparative Studies in Society and History* 29/4: 717-47.

1995 *Law Collections from Mesopotamia and Asia Minor* (SBL Writings from the Ancient World Series, 6; Atlanta: Scholars Press).

Rothstein, Johann Wilhelm
1908 *Juden und Samaritaner: die grundlegende Scheidung von Judentum und Heidentum: eine kritische Studie zum Buche Haggai und zur jüdischen Geschichte im ersten nachexilishcen Jahrhundert* (Beiträge zur Wissenschaft vom Alten Testament, 3; Leipzig: J.C. Hinrichs).

Rowley, Harold H.
1955/56 'Sanballat and the Samaritan Temple', *Bulletin of the John Rylands Library* 38: 166-98.
1963 *Men of God: Studies in Old Testament History and Prophecy* (London: Nelson).

Rudolph, Wilhelm
1931 'Obadja', *Zeitschrift für die alttestamentliche Wissenschaft* 49: 222-31.
1949 *Esra und Nehemiah samt 3. Esra* (Handbuch zum Alten Testament, I, 20; Tübingen: J.C.B. Mohr).
1976 *Haggai-Sacharja 1–8, 9–14, Maleachi* (Kommentar zum Alten Testament, 13.4; Gutersloh: Mohn).

Ryle, Herbert Edward
1893 *The Books of Ezra and Nehemiah with Introduction, Notes and Maps* (The Cambridge Bible for Schools and Colleges; London: Cambridge University Press, 5th repr., 1923).

Saley, Richard J.
1978 'The Date of Nehemiah Reconsidered', in G.A. Tuttle (ed.), *Biblical and Near Eastern Studies: Essays in Honor of William Sanford LaSor* (Grand Rapids, MI: Eerdmans): 151-65.

Saller, Sylvester J.
1957 *Excavations at Bethany (1949–1953)* (Publications of the Studium Biblicum Franciscanum, 12; Jerusalem: Franciscan Press).

Samuel, Alan E.
1962 *Ptolemaic Chronology* (Münchener Beiträge zur Papyrusforschung und antiken Rechtsgeschichte, 43; München: C.H. Beck'sche Verlagsbuchhandlung).

San Nicolò, Mariano
1948 'Materialen zur Viehwirtschaft in den neubabylonischen Tempeln', *Orientalia* 17: 273-93.

Sapin, Jean
2004 'La frontière judéo-iduméene au IVe s. avant J.-C', *Transeuphraténe* 27: 109-54.

Schaeder, Hans H.
1930 *Esra der Schreiber* (Beiträge zur historischen Theologie, 5; Tübingen: J.C.B. Mohr).

Schaper, Joachim
1995 'The Jerusalem Temple as an Instrument of the Achaemenid Fiscal Administration', *Vetus Testamentum* 44: 528-39.

Scheftelowitz, Isidor
1901 *Arisches im alten Testament* (Berlin).

Schneider, Heinrich
1959 *Die Bücher Esra und Nehemia übersetzt und erklärt* (Die heilige Schrift des Alten Testaments IV, 2; Bonn: Peter Hanstein Verlag).

Schrader, Eberhard
1888 *The Cuneiform Inscriptions and the Old Testament*, II (trans. from second enlarged German edn by O.C. Whitehouse; London: Williams and Norgate).

Schwartz, Daniel R.
1990 'On Some Papyri and Josephus' Sources and Chronology for the Persian Period', *Journal for the Study of Judaism* 21: 175-99.

Schwenzner, Walther
1923 'Gobryas', *Klio* 18: 226-52.

Segal, Judah Benzion
1957 'Intercalation and the Hebrew Calendar', *Vetus Testamentum* 7: 250-307.

Seger, Joseph
1970 'Notes and News. Tel Halif (Lahav), 1979', *Israel Exploration Journal* 29: 247-49.
1971 'Notes and News. Tel Halif, 1980', *Israel Exploration Journal* 30: 223-26.

Sérandour, Arnaud
    2001   'Zacharie et les autorités de son temps', in André Lemaire (ed.), *Prophèts et rois: Bible et Proche-Orient* (Lectio divina hors série; Paris: Éditions du Cerf): 259-98.

Seybold, Klaus
    1980   חָלָה *chālāh*; חֳלִי *chᵒlî*; חָלָה פָנִים *chillāh phānîm*', in G. Johannes Botterweck and Helmer Ringren (eds.), *Theological Dictionary of the Old Testament* (translated from German by David E. Green; Grand Rapids: Eerdmans): IV, 399-409.

Shennan, Stephen
    1985   *Experiments in the Collection and analysis of Archaeological Survey Data: the East Hampshire Survey* (Sheffield: Department of Archaeology and Prehistory).

Siebeneck, Robert T.
    1957   'The Messianism of Aggeus and Proto-Zacharias', *Catholic Biblical Quarterly* 19: 312-28.

Singer-Avitz, Lilly
    1999   'Beer-Sheba – A Gateway Community in Southern Arabian Long-Distance Trade in the Eighth Century B.C.E', *Tel Aviv* 26: 3-75.

Skelton, John
    1956/57 *Diodorus Siculus: The Bibliotheca Historica* (Early English Text Society, Series 233, 239; London: Oxford University Press for the Early English Text Society).

Smith, George Adam
    1896   *The Historical Geography of the Holy Land, Especially in Relation to the History of Israel and of the Early Church* (London: Hodder & Stoughton, 4th edn).
    1908   *The Book of the Twelve Prophets Commonly Called the Minor* (2 vols.; London: Hodder & Stoughton, 10th edn).

Smith, Morton
    1971   *Palestinian Parties and Politics That Shaped the Old Testament* (Lectures on the History of Religion Sponsored by the American Council of Learned Societies, New Series, 9; London: Columbia University Press).

Smith, Ralph L.
    1984   *Micah–Malachi* (Word Biblical Commentary, 32; Waco, TX: Word Books).

Smith, Sidney
    1944   *Isaiah Chapters XL–LV: Literary Criticism and History* (The Schweich Lectures of the British Academy, 1940; London: The British Academy).
    1945   'Foundations: Ezra iv, 12; v, 16; vi, 3', in I. Epstein, E. Levine and C. Roth (eds.), *Essays in Honour of the Very Rev. Dr. J.H. Hertz, Chief Rabbi of the United Hebrew Congregations of the British Empire on the Occasion of his Seventieth Birthday, September 25, 1942 (5703)* (London: Edward Goldston): 385-96.

Snaith, Norman Henry
    1934   *Studies in the Psalter* (London: Epworth Press).

Soden, Wolfram von
    1972   'pilku(m) I, pilku II', in *Akkadisches Handwörterbuch* (Wiesbaden: Otto Harrassowitz): II, 863.

Spaer, Arnold
    1986/87 'Jaddua the High Priest?', *Israel Numismatic Journal* 9: 1-3.

Spak, Isaac
    1911   *Der Bericht des Josephus über Alexander den Grossen* (Königsberg: Hartungsche Buchdruckerei).

Spek, R.J. van der
    1982   'Did Cyrus the Great Introduce a New Policy towards Subdued Nations? Cyrus in Assyrian Perspective', *Persika* 10: 278-83.

Stern, Ephraim
    1982   *Material Culture of the Land of the Bible in the Persian Period 538–332 B.C.* (Warminster: Aris & Phillips).
    1984   'The Persian Empire and the Political and Social History of Palestine in the Persian period', in William David Davies and Louis Finkelstein (eds.), *The Cambridge History of Judaism in the Persian Period*. I. *Introduction: The Persian Period* (Cambridge: Cambridge University Press): 70-87.
    1990   'New Evidence on the Administrative Division of Palestine in the Persian Period', in Heleen Sancisi-

Werdenburg and Amélie Kuhrt (eds.), *Achaemenid History IV: Centre and Periphery* (Leiden: Nederlands Instituut voor het Nabije Oosten): 221-26.

2001   *Archaeology of the Land of the Bible, Volume II: The Assyrian, Babylonian, and Persian Periods, 732–332 BCE* (The Anchor Bible Reference Library; New York: Doubleday).

Stol, Marten
1985   'Remarks on the Cultivation of Sesame and the Extraction of its Oil', *Bulletin on Sumerian Agriculture* 2: 119-26.

Stolper, Matthew W.
1985   *Entrepreneurs and Empire: The Murašu Archive, the Murašu Firm, and Persian Rule in Babylonia* (Uitgaven van het Nederlands Historisch-Archaeologisch Instituut te Istanbul, 54; Istanbul: Nederlands Historisch-Archaeologisch Instituut te Istanbul).
1989   'The Governor of Babylon and Across-the-River in 486 B.C.', *Journal of Near Eastern Studies* 48: 283-305.

Stuart, Douglas
1987   *Hosea-Jonah* (Word Biblical Commentary, 31; Waco, TX: Word Books).

Sweeny, Marvin A.
2000   *The Twelve Prophets*, II (Berit Olam; Collegeville, MN: The Liturgical Press/Michael Glazier).

Tadmor, Hayim
1965   'The Inscriptions of Nabunaid: Historical Arrangement', in Hans G. Güterbock and Thorkild Jacobsen (eds.), *Studies in Honor of Benno Landsberger on his Seventy-Fifth Birthday, April 21, 1965* (Assyriological Studies, 16; Chicago: University of Chicago Press): 351-63.
1981   'History and Ideology in the Assyrian Royal Inscriptions', in F.M. Fales Orientis (ed.), *Assyrian Royal Inscriptions: New Horizons in Literary, Ideological, and Historical Analysis. Papers of a Symposium Held in Cetona (Siena) June 26–28, 1980* (Antiqui collectio, 17; Rome: Istituto per l'Oriente, Centro per le Antichità e la Storia dell'Arte del Vicion Oriente): 13-33.
1999   ' "The Appointed Time Has Not Yet Arrived": The Historical Background of Haggai 1:2', in R. Chazan, W.W. Hallo and L.H. Schiffman (eds.), *Ki Baruch Hu: Ancient Near Eastern, Biblical, and Judaic Studies in Honor of Baruch A. Levine* (Winona Lake, IN: Eisenbrauns): 401-408.

Tallqvist, Knut L.
1914   *Assyrian Personal Names* (Acta Societatis scientiarum fennicae, 43.1; Helsingfors: s.n.).

Talmon, Shemaryahu
1976   'Ezra and Nehemiah', in Keith Crim (ed.), *Interpreter's Dictionary of the Bible Supplementary Volume* (Nashville: Abingdon Press): 317-28.

Talshir, Zipora
1999   *I Esdras: From Origin to Translation* (Society of Biblical Literature Septuagint and Cognate Studies Series, 47; Atlanta: Society of Biblical Literature).

Teixidor, Javier
1978   'The Aramaic Text in the Trilingual Stele from Xanthus', *Journal of Near Eastern Studies* 37: 180-85.

Thiele, Edwin R.
1965   *The Mysterious Numbers of the Hebrew Kings: A Reconstruction of the Chronology of the Kingdoms of Israel and Judah* (Exeter: Paternoster Press, 2nd edn).

Thompson, John Arthur
1956   'The Book of Obadiah: Introduction and Exegesis', in George A. Buttrick, *et al.* (eds.), *The Interpreter's Bible* (Nashville: Abingdon Press): IV, 857-68.

Thomson, Andrew
1932   'An Inquiry Concerning the Books of Ezra and Nehemiah', *The American Journal of Semitic Languages and Literatures* 48: 99-132.

Thureau-Dangin, François
1921   *Rituels accadiens* (Paris: Ernest Léroux).

Tollington, Janet A.
1993   *Tradition and Innovation in Haggai and Zechariah 1–8* (Journal for the Study of the Old Testament, Supplement Series, 150; Sheffield: Sheffield Academic Press).

Torrey, Charles C.

1896   *The Composition and Historical Value of Ezra-Nehemiah* (Beihefte zur *Zeitschrift für die alttestamentliche Wissenschaft*, 2; Giessen: Ricker).

1928   'Sanballat "the Horonite"', *Journal of Biblical Literature* 47: 380-89.

1936   'The Foundry of the Second Temple', *Journal of Biblical Literature* 55: 247-60.

1969   *Ezra Studies* (Reprint, with prolegomenon by W.F. Stinespring; The Library of Biblical Studies; New York: Ktav [1910]).

Trotter, James M.

2001   'Was the Second Jerusalem Temple a Primarily Persian Project?', *Scandinavian Journal of the Old Testament* 15: 276-94.

Tufnell, Olga

1953   *Lakhish III (Tell ed. Duweir): The Iron Age* (The Wellcome-Marston Archaeological Research Expedition to the Near East, 3; London: The Trustees of the late Sir Henry Wellcome by Oxford University Press).

Tuland, Carl G.

1958   ''uššayyā' and 'uššarnâ: A Clarification of Terms, Date and Text', *Journal of Near Eastern Studies* 17: 269-75.

1966   'Josephus, *Antiquities*, Book 11', *Andrews University Seminary Studies* 4: 176-92.

1968   'Hanani-Hananiah', *Journal of Biblical Literature* 77: 157-61.

Tuplin, Christopher

1987   'The Administration of the Achaemenid Empire', in Ian Carradice (ed.), *Coinage and Administration in the Athenian and Persian Empires: The Ninth Oxford Symposium on Coinage and Monetary History* (BAR International Series, 343; Oxford: B.A.R.): 109-66.

1998   'The Seasonal Migration of Achaemenid Kings: A Report on Old and New Evidence', in Maria Brosius and Amélie Kuhrt (eds.), *Studies in Persian History: Essays in Memory of David M. Lewis* (Achaemenid History, 11; Leiden: Nederlands Instituut voor het Nabije Oosten): 63-114.

Ungnad, Arthur

1940/41 'Keilinschriftliche Beiträge zum Buch Esra und Ester', *Zeitschrift für die alttestamentliche Wissenschaft* 58: 240-43.

Ussishkin, David

1978   'Excavations at Tel Lakhish – 1973–1977. Preliminary Report', *Tel Aviv* 5: 1-97.

Vallat, François

1992   'Elam', in D.N. Freedman (ed.), *The Anchor Bible Dictionary* (London: Doubleday): II, 424-29.

Van Beek, Gus W.

1993   'Jemmeh, Tell', in *The New Encyclopedia of Archaeological Excavations in the Holy Land* (Tel Aviv: The Israel Exploration Society): II, 67-74.

Vanderkam, James C.

2000   *From Revelation to Canon: Studies in the Hebrew Bible and Second Temple Literature* (Journal for the Study of Judaism Supplements, 62; Leiden: E.J. Brill).

Van der Ploeg, Jan

1950   'Les chefs du peuple d'Israël et leurs titres', *Revue biblique* 57: 50-61.

Vattioni, Francesco

1973   'L'inscription 177 de Beth She'arim', *Revue biblique* 80: 261-63.

Vaux, Roland de

1961   *Ancient Israel: Its Life and Institutions* (trans. from the French by John McHugh; London: Darton, Longman & Todd).

1972   'The Decrees of Cyrus and Darius on the Rebuilding of the Temple', in *The Bible and the Ancient Near East* (trans. from French by Damian McHugh; London: Darton, Longman & Todd): 63-96.

Verhoef, Pieter A.

1987   *The Books of Haggai and Malachi* (The New International Commentary on the Old Testament; Grand Rapids, MI: Eerdmans).

Voigtlander, Elizabeth N. von

    1978   *The Bisitun Inscription of Darius the Great Babylonian Version* (Corpus Inscriptionum Iranicum; London: Lund Humphries).

Wallinga, Herman T.

    1987   'The Ancient Persian Navy and its Predecessors', in Heleen Sancisi-Weerdenburg (ed.), *Achaemenid History I: Sources, Structures and Synthesis. Proceedings of the Groningen 1983 Achaemenid History Workshop* (Leiden: Nederlands Instituut voor het Nabije Oosten): 47-77.

    1993   *Ships and Sea-Power before the Great Persian War: The Ancestry of the Ancient Trireme* (Mnemosyne; Bibliotheca Calssica Batavia Supplements, 121; Leiden: E.J. Brill).

Waterman, Leroy

    1954   'The Camouflaged Purge of the Three Messianic Conspirators', *Journal of Near Eastern Studies* 13: 73-78.

Watts, John D.W.

    1969   *Obadiah: A Critical Exegetical Commentary* (Grand Rapids, MI: Eerdmans).

Weinberg, Joel

    1992   *The Citizen-Temple Community* (trans. from German by D.L. Smith-Christopher; *Journal for the Study of the Old Testament*, Supplement Series, 151; Sheffield: Sheffield Academic Press).

Weinfeld, Moshe

    2000   'Pelekh in Nehemiah 3', in Gershon Galil and Moshe Weinfeld (eds.), *Studies in Historical Geography & Biblical Historiography Presented to Zecharia Kallai* (Vetus Testamentum Supplements, 81; Leiden: E.J. Brill): 249-50.

Weissbach, Franz Heinrich

    1903   *Babylonische Miscellen* (Wissenschaftliche Veröffenlichungen der Deutschen Orient-Geschellschaft, 4; Leipzig: J.C. Hinrichs).

Wellhausen, Julius

    1893   *Die Kleinen Propheten übersetzt, mit Noten* (Skizzen und Vorarbeiten, 5; Berlin: G. Reimer).

Wexler, Lior

    2002   *Surveys and Excavations of Caves in the Northern Judean Desert (CNJD)–1993*, (Atiqot 41.2; Jerusalem: Israel Antiquitues Authority).

Whitley, Charles F.

    1954   'The Term Seventy Years Captivity', *Vetus Testamentum* 4: 60-72.

Widengren, Geo

    1977   'The Persian Period', in John H. Hayes and J. Maxwell Miller (eds.), *Israelite and Judean History* (Philadelphia: Westminster Press): 489-538.

Will, Ernest

    1987   'Qu'est ce qu'une *Baris*?', *Syria* 49: 253-59.

Williamson, Hugh G.M.

    1977   'The Historical Value of Josephus' *Jewish Antiquities* XI.297-301', *Journal of Theological Studies* 28: 49-66.

    1982   *1 and 2 Chronicles* (New Century Bible Commentary; London: Marshall, Morgan & Scott).

    1983   'The Composition of Ezra i-vi', *Journal of Theological Studies* 34: 1-30.

    1985   *Ezra, Nehemiah* (Word Biblical Commentary, 16; Waco, TX: Word Books).

    1987   *Ezra and Nehemiah* (Old Testament Guides; Sheffield: Sheffield Academic Press).

    1988   'The Governors of Judah under the Persians', *Tyndale Bulletin* 39: 59-82.

Wilson, Robert Dick

    1915   'Titles of the Persian Kings', in Gotthold Weil (ed.), *Festschrift Eduard Sachau zum siebzigsten Geburtstage gewidmet von Freunden und Schülern* (Berlin: G. Reimer): 179-207.

Wilson, Robert R.

    1977   *Prophecy and Society in Ancient Israel* (Philadelphia: Fortress Press).

Winckler, Hugo

    1892   *alttestamentliche Untersuchungen* (Leipzig: Eduard Pfeiffer).

Winnett, Frederick Victor, and William LaForest Reed
    1970   *Ancient Records from North Arabia* (Near and Middle East Series; Toronto: University of Toronto Press).

Wiseman, Donald John
    1956   *Chronicles of Chaldean kings (626–556 B.C.) in the British Museum* (London: Trustees of the British Museum).

Wolfe, Rolland E.
    1935   'The Editing of the Book of the Twelve', *Zeitschrift für die alttestamentliche Wissenschaft* 12: 90-120.

Wolff, Hans Walter
    1986   *Obadiah and Jonah: A Commentary* (trans. from the German by M. Kohl; Minneapolis: Augsburg).
    1988   *Haggai: A Commentary* (trans. from the German by M. Kohl; Minneapolis: Augsburg).

Wright, Charles Henry Hamilton
    1879   *Zechariah and his Prophecies, Considered in Relation to Modern Criticism: With a Critical and Grammatical Commentary and New Translation* (Bampton Lectures; London: Hodder & Stoughton).

Wright, George Ernest
    1962   *Biblical Archaeology* (London: Gerald Duckworth, rev. edn).

Yamashita, Tadanori
    1975   'Noqed', in Loren R. Fisher (ed.), *Ras Shamra Parallels: The Texts from Ugarit and the Hebrew Bible* (Analecta Orientalia, 50; Rome: Pontifical Biblical Institute), II, 63-64.

Yeivin, Shemuel
    1962   'The Judicial Petition from Meṣad Ḥashavyahu', *Bibliotheca Orientalis* 29: 3-10.

Zadok, Ran
    1988   *The Pre-Hellenistic Israelite Anthroponymy and Prosopography* (Orientalia Lovaniensia Analecta, 28; Leuven: Peeters).

Zehavi, Alon
    1993   'Jerusalem, Manahat', *Excavations and Surveys of Israel* 12: 66-67.

Zimhoni, Orna
    1983   '3.2 The Pottery', in Fritz Volkmar and Aharon Kempinski (eds.), *Ergebnisse der Ausgrabungen auf der Hirbet el-MŠAŠ (Tel Masos) (1972–1975). I. Textband* (Abhandlungen des Deutschen Palästinavereins; Wiesbaden: Otto Harrrassowitz): 127-30.

Zohary, Michael
    1982   *Plants of the Bible: A Complete Handbook to All the Plants with 200 Full-Color Plates Taken in the Natural Habitat* (Cambridge: Cambridge University Press).

Zorn, Jeffrey R.
    2003   'Tell en-Naṣbeh and the Problem of the Material Culture of the Sixth Century', in Oded Lipschits and Joseph Blenkinsopp (eds.), *Judah and Judeans in the Neo-Babylonian Period* (Winona Lake, IN: Eisenbrauns): 413-47.

Zorn, Jeffrey R., Joseph Yellin and John Hayes
    1994   'The *m(w)ṣh* Stamp Impressions and the Neo-Babylonian Period', *Israel Exploration Journal* 44: 161-83.

Zuckerman, Bruce, and Lynn Swartz Dodd
    2003   'Pots and Alphabets: Refractions of Reflections on Typological Method', *Maarav* 10: 89-133.

INDEXES

INDEX OF AUTHORS AND INDIVIDUALS CITED

BIBLICAL

INDEX OF PERSONAL NAMES

Index of Subjects